WRITERSMARKET.COM

Instant access
to thousands of editors and agents

Sure, you already know *Guide to Literary Agents* is the essential tool for selling your writing. Now, to complement your trusty "writing bible," you can subscribe to WritersMarket.com! **It's $10 off the regular price!**

As a purchaser of *2005 Guide to Literary Agents*, get a $10 discount off the regular $29.99 subscription price for WritersMarket.com. Simply enter coupon code **WM5MB** on the subscription page at www.WritersMarket.com.

www.WritersMarket.com
The Ultimate Research Tool for Writers

Tear out your handy bookmark
for fast reference to symbols and abbreviations used in this book

---

TEAR ALONG PERFORATION

2005 GUIDE TO LITERARY AGENTS
KEYS TO SYMBOLS

 market new to this edition

 Canadian agency

 agency located outside of the U.S. and Canada

 newer agency actively seeking clients

 agency seeks both new and established writers

 agency prefers to work with established writers, mostly obtains new clients through referrals

 agency handling only certain types of work or work by writers under certain circumstances

 agency not currently seeking new clients

• comment from the editor of *Guide to Literary Agents*

 agency's specializations

ms, mss manuscript(s)

SASE self-addressed, stamped envelope

SAE self-addressed envelope

IRC International Reply Coupon, for use in countries other than your own

(For definitions of words and expressions used throughout the book, see the Glossary. For translations of acronyms of organizations connected with agenting or writing, refer to the Table of Acronyms.)

2005 GUIDE TO LITERARY AGENTS KEYS TO SYMBOLS

 market new to this edition

 Canadian agency

 agency located outside of the U.S. and Canada

 newer agency actively seeking clients

 agency seeks both new and established writers

 agency prefers to work with established writers, mostly obtains new clients through referrals

 agency handling only certain types of work or work by writers under certain circumstances

 agency not currently seeking new clients

• comment from the editor of *Guide to Literary Agents*

 agency's specializations

ms, mss manuscript(s)

SASE self-addressed, stamped envelope

SAE self-addressed envelope

IRC International Reply Coupon, for use in countries other than your own

(For definitions of words and expressions used throughout the book, see the Glossary. For translations of acronyms of organizations connected with agenting or writing, refer to the Table of Acronyms.)

TEAR ALONG PERFORATION

Tear out your handy bookmark
for fast reference to symbols and abbreviations used in this book

2005 Guide to Literary Agents

Kathryn S. Brogan, Editor

WRITER'S DIGEST BOOKS
CINCINNATI, OH

Editorial Director, Writer's Digest Books: Barbara Kuroff
Managing Editor, Writer's Digest Books: Alice Pope

Writer's Market website: www.writersmarket.com

Writer's Digest website: www.writersdigest.com

International Standard Serial Number 1078-6945
International Standard Book Number 1-58297-328-8

Cover design by Nick and Diane Gliebe, Design Matters

Interior design by Clare Finney

Attention Booksellers: This is an annual directory of F + W Publications.
Return deadline for this edition is December 31, 2005.

Contents

SCRIPT CONTESTS

INDEPENDENT PUBLICISTS

WRITERS' CONFERENCES

RESOURCES

INDEXES

From the Editor

I t seems that every time I open an e-mail from a writer or attend a writers' conference, the most commonly asked questions are: Do I need an agent? And, how do I find one?

The reality of the situation is that more book publishers (including the "big five" publishing houses in New York) are closing their doors to unagented writers and are no longer accepting unsolicited submissions.

Right now, you're probably asking yourself, "Is there any hope?" And, my answer to you is a resounding, "Yes!" It is easier than ever before to find and get an agent to represent your book or script! You may not realize it, but you've already completed (or are at least close to completing) one of the most important steps to finding an agent: You've finished writing your book or script (or if you're writing a nonfiction book, you've at least written your book proposal).

And, interestingly enough, you've already taken the second most important step to finding an agent—you've purchased this book. Here in *Guide to Literary Agents*, you'll find everything you need to know about **finding** an agent, **contacting** an agent, **submitting to** an agent, and **working with** an agent. More importantly, though, you have access to contact information for **more than 400 agents**—all of whom are nonfee-charging agents and who are respected members of the publishing community. Plus, you will find additional articles and contact information for **production companies**, **publicists**, **script contests**, and **writers' conferences**—all important resources to help you find an agent and secure representation.

Now all you have to do is use this information to find the agent best suited for you and your work! You knew there would be a catch, didn't you? Really, all joking aside, we've made it easier for you to find, contact, and work with an agent. In addition to a number of new features that make it easier for you to locate the information you need (including **reference icons** within the articles, **tabs** for each section of information, and an **easy-to-read** design), we've also carefully chosen and screened the agents who appear in this book.

While there's a wealth of useful information within these pages, I encourage you to keep in mind that good agents know the marketplace well. When you find an agent to represent your work, you'll be in some of the most capable hands in the industry.

Kathryn Struckel Brogan

Kathryn Struckel Brogan
Editor, *Guide to Literary Agents*
literaryagents@fwpubs.com

Getting Started

How to Use Guide to Literary Agents

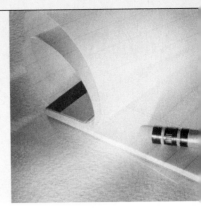

tarting a search for a literary agent can seem overwhelming, whether you've just finished your first book or you have several publishing credits on your résumé. You are more than likely eager to start pursuing agents—anxious to see your name on the spine of a book. But before you go directly to the listings of agencies in this book, take a few minutes to familiarize yourself with the way agents work and how you should approach them. By doing so, you will be more prepared for your search and ultimately save yourself time and unnecessary grief.

Read the articles

Important

This book begins with feature articles that give advice on the best strategies for contacting agents and provide perspectives on the author/agent relationship. The articles are organized into four sections appropriate for each stage of the search process: **Before You Start**, **Finding the Right Agent**, **Contacting Agents**, and **Before You Sign**. You may want to start by reading through each article, and then refer back to relevant articles during each stage of your search for an agent.

Because there are many ways to make that initial contact with an agent, we've provided Insider Reports throughout the book. These personalized interviews with agents and published authors offer both information and inspiration for any writer hoping to find representation.

Decide what you're looking for

An independent publicist can promote your work—before or after an agent or publisher has taken an interest in it. If you're looking for a publicist, we offer a section of **Independent Publicists.** Often publicists can drum up media time for their clients and help them get the exposure they need to make a sale or increase the number of copies sold.

A literary or script agent will actually present your work directly to editors or producers. It's his job to get his client's work published or sold and to negotiate a fair contract. In the **Literary Agents** and **Script Agents** sections, we list each agent's contact information and explain what type of work the agency represents and how to submit your work for consideration.

For face-to-face contact, many writers prefer to meet agents at conferences. In this way, writers can assess an agent's personality, attend workshops, and usually have a chance to get more feedback on their work than they can by submitting their work through the mail and waiting for a response. The section for **Writers' Conferences** is divided into regions and lists only those conferences where agents will be in attendance. In many cases, private

Frequently asked questions

1 **Why do you include agents who are not seeking new clients?** We provide contact information for agents who are members of the Association of Authors' Representatives who have not answered our request for information. Because of these agents' reputations, we feel the book would be incomplete without an acknowledgement of their companies. Some agents even ask that their listings indicate they are currently closed to new clients.

2 **Why do you exclude fee-charging agents?** There is a great debate in the publishing industry about whether literary agents should charge writers a reading or critiquing fee. There are fee-charging agents who make sales to prominent publishers. However, we have received a number of complaints in the past regarding fees, and therefore we've chosen to list only those agents who do not charge fees to writers.

3 **Why are some agents not listed in *Guide to Literary Agents*?** Some agents may not have returned our request for information. We have taken others out of the book because we received very serious complaints about their agencies. Refer to the Listings Index in the back of the book to see why an agency isn't listed in this edition.

4 **Do I need more than one agent if I write in different genres?** More than likely, no. If you have written in one genre and want to switch to a new style of writing, ask your agent if he is willing to represent you in your new endeavor. Most agents will continue to represent clients no matter what genre they choose to write. Occasionally, an agent may feel he has no knowledge of a certain genre and will recommend an appropriate agent to his client. Regardless, you should always talk to your agent about any potential career move.

5 **Why don't you list foreign agents?** Most U.S. agents have relationships with "foreign co-agents" in other countries. It is more common for a U.S. agent to work with a co-agent to sell a client's book abroad than for a writer to work directly with a foreign agent. We do, however, list agents in England and Canada who sell to both U.S. and foreign publishers.

6 **Do agents ever contact a writer who is self-published?** Occasionally. If a self-published author attracts the attention of the media, or if her book sells extremely well, an agent might approach the author in hopes of representing her.

7 **Why won't the agent I queried return my material?** An agent may not answer your query or return your manuscript for several reasons. Perhaps you did not include a self-addressed, stamped envelope (SASE). Many agents will throw away a submission without a SASE. Or the agent may have moved. To avoid using expired addresses, use the most current edition of *Guide to Literary Agents*, or access the information online at www.writersmarket.com. Another possibility is that the agent is swamped with submissions. Agents can be overwhelmed with queries, especially if the agent has recently spoken at a conference or has been featured in an article or book.

consultations can be arranged, and agents attend with the hope of finding new clients to represent.

For script writers, we have sections of **Script Contests** and **Independent Production Companies**. Winning a contest can help you gain recognition in the film industry, land an internship, or impress an agent. Or, you can use the producers section to market your work directly to independent production companies. Once you have some experience in the industry, you'll make important connections, find additional work, and have the credentials to impress an agent who will help you with your long-term career goals.

Do I Need an Agent?

I f you have a book ready to be published, you may be wondering if you need a literary agent. If you're not sure whether you want to work with an agent, consider the following factors.

WHAT CAN AN AGENT DO FOR YOU?

An agent will believe in your writing and know an audience interested in what you write. As the representative for your work, your agent will tell editors your manuscript is the best thing to land on her desk this year. But beyond being enthusiastic about your manuscript, there are a lot of benefits to using an agent.

For starters, today's competitive marketplace can be difficult to break into, especially for previously unpublished writers. Many larger publishing houses will only look at manuscripts from agents. In fact, approximately 80 percent of books published by the major houses are sold to them by agents.

But an agent's job isn't just getting your book through a publisher's door. That's only a small part of what an agent can do for you. The following describes the various jobs agents do for their clients, many of which would be difficult for a writer to do without outside help.

Agents know editors' tastes and needs

An agent possesses information on a complex web of publishing houses and a multitude of editors to make sure her clients' manuscripts are placed in the right hands. This knowledge is gathered through relationships she cultivates with acquisition editors—the people who decide which books to present to their publisher for possible publication. Through her industry connections, an agent becomes aware of the specializations of publishing houses and their imprints, knowing that one publisher only wants contemporary romances while another is interested solely in nonfiction books about the military. By networking with editors over lunch, an agent also learns more specialized information—which editor is looking for a crafty Agatha Christie-style mystery for the fall catalog, for example.

Agents track changes in publishing

Being attentive to constant market changes and vacillating trends is also a major requirement of an agent's job. An agent understands what it may mean for clients when publisher A merges with publisher B and when an editor from house C moves to house D. Or what it means when readers—and therefore editors—are no longer interested in westerns, but instead can't get their hands on enough Stephen King-style suspense novels.

Agents get your manuscript read faster

Although it may seem like an extra step to send your manuscript to an agent instead of directly to a publishing house, the truth is an agent can prevent writers from wasting months sending manuscripts to the wrong places or being buried in someone's slush pile. Editors rely on agents to save them time as well. With little time to sift through the hundreds of unsolicited submissions arriving weekly in the mail, an editor is naturally going to prefer a work that has already been approved by a qualified reader (i.e., the agent) and from a reader who knows the editors preferences. For this reason, many of the larger publishers only accept agented submissions.

Agents understand contracts

When publishers write contracts, they are primarily interested in their own bottom line rather than the best interests of the author. Writers unfamiliar with contractual language may find themselves bound to a publisher with whom they no longer want to work or bound to a publisher who prevented them from getting royalties on their first book until they have written several more books. An agent uses her experience to negotiate a contract that benefits the writer while still respecting the publisher's needs.

Agents negotiate—and exploit—subsidiary rights

Beyond publication, a savvy agent keeps in mind other opportunities for your manuscript. If your agent believes your book will also be successful as an audio book, a Book-of-the-Month Club selection, or even a blockbuster movie, these options will be considered when the agent shops your manuscript. These additional opportunities for your writing are called "subsidiary rights." Part of an agent's job is to keep track of the strengths and weaknesses of different publishers' subsidiary rights offices to determine the deposition of these rights to your work. After the contract is negotiated, an agent will seek additional money-making opportunities for the rights he kept for his client.

Agents get escalators

An escalator is a bonus that an agent can negotiate as part of the book contract. It is commonly given when a book appears on a best-seller list or if a client appears on a popular television show. For example, a publisher might give a writer a $50,000 bonus if she is picked for a book club. Both the agent and the editor know such media attention will sell more books, and the agent negotiates an escalator to ensure the writer benefits from this increase in sales.

Agents track payments

Because an agent only receives payment when the publisher pays the writer, it is in the agent's best interests to make sure the writer is paid on schedule. Some publishing houses are notorious for late payments. Having an agent distances you from any conflict over payment and allows you to spend your time writing instead of making phone calls.

Agents are strong advocates

Besides standing up for your right to be paid on time, agents can ensure your book gets more attention from the publisher's marketing department, a better cover design, or other benefits you may not know to ask for during the publishing process. An agent can also provide advice during each step of this process, as well as guidance about your long-term writing career.

WHEN YOU MIGHT NOT NEED AN AGENT

Although there are many reasons to work with an agent, an author can benefit from submitting his own work. For example, if your writing focuses on a very specific area, you may want to work with a small or specialized publisher. These houses are usually open to receiving material directly from writers. Smaller houses can often give more attention to a writer than a large house can, providing editorial help, marketing expertise, and other advice directly to the writer.

Some writers use a lawyer or entertainment attorney instead of an agent. If a lawyer specializes in intellectual property, he can help a writer with contract negotiations. Instead of giving the lawyer a commission, the lawyer is paid for his time only.

And, of course, some people prefer working independently instead of relying on others to do their work. If you are one of these people, it is probably better to shop your own work instead of constantly butting heads with an agent. And despite the benefits of working with an agent, it is possible to sell your work directly to a publisher—people do it all the time!

FAQs About Agents

Compiled by Robert Lee Brewer

Many questions emerge at writers' conferences and workshops, particularly when the subject of agents is announced. These are often the basic questions to which no one except for agents know the answers. Here five respected agents share their inside knowledge and answer the most frequently asked questions about agents and agenting. You can find these questions and answers, and other frequently asked questions on Writers Market.com under the Agent Q&A section.

Richard Curtis, president of Richard Curtis Associates, Inc., was a past president of the Association of Authors' Representatives (AAR), and the first president of the Independent Literary Agents Association. Curtis is a leading New York literary agent, a well-known author advocate, and the author of numerous works of fiction and nonfiction, including several books about the publishing industry.

Noah Lukeman is president of Lukeman Literary Management, Ltd., a New York-based literary agency, which he founded in 1996. Lukeman is the author of the best-selling book, *The First Five Pages* (Simon & Schuster), and *The Plot Thickens* (St. Martin's Press).

Photo by Leslie Curtis

Richard Curtis

Jane Dystel is the founder and president of Jane Dystel Literary Management. Dystel has been an agent since 1986, with editorial experience at Bantam Books, Grosset & Dunlap, and World Almanac Publications, where she created her own imprint.

Michelle Tessler is a member agent at Carlisle & Co. Tessler represents literary fiction and nonfiction, including narrative, biography, cultural and social history, memoir, popular science, travel, and spirituality.

Michael Congdon is an agent with Don Congdon Associates, Inc. Congdon is also a longtime member and currently a vice president of AAR.

Photo by Kevin Flatow

Noah Lukeman

ROBERT LEE BREWER is co-editor of WritersMarket.com and its biweekly e-mail newsletter, Market Update. Brewer also assists with the production of *Writer's Market*, *Writer's Market Deluxe Edition*, *Novel & Short Story Writer's Market*, and *Guide to Literary Agents*. He can be contacted via e-mail at robert.brewer@fwpubs.com.

What do agents do?

Lukeman: The primary duties of the literary agent are to get an author a book deal, to negotiate the advance (and other terms of publication), and to negotiate the contract. Indeed, many books are shopped around by agents and never sold at all. So, if an agent can get you a deal and a good advance and contract, he has done a good job for you.

The agent also, in general, acts as the liaison between you and the publisher. There are other things an agent can do, such as helping you brainstorm or develop ideas for a book, helping you edit the proposal or book, helping you with publicity or promotion—although these are not the main tasks of the agent.

What fees should I expect to spend on agents? When should I expect to pay them?

Dystel: Reputable agents (those who are members of the AAR or are recognized by the Authors' Guild) do not charge any reading or editing fees of any sort. They should only charge a commission once the book project is sold and that commission is taken from what the publisher pays for the project. The only other expenses you might be likely to incur (and this varies from agency to agency) are photocopying costs or mailing/shipping costs for the copies of the manuscript that will be used on submission to publishers. However, if an agent is telling you that he needs $500 up front in order to read and evaluate your manuscript, you should not do business with him.

Jane Dystel

Photo by Tess Steinkolk

I've noticed that many agents are members of organizations like AAR and the Writers Guild of America (WGA). How important is it for an agent to be a member of such an organization?

Congdon: While not being a member of such an organization doesn't mean an agent isn't responsible or knowledgeable, there are advantages for agents, and their clients, if they are members.

For instance, the AAR requires its members to meet certain professional standards and adhere to a Canon of Ethics (found online at www.aar-online.org), which prohibits members from charging authors reading fees. In addition, there are many national organizations of agents, literary and dramatic, which provide information about current trends in publishing and arranges programs to educate its members, and coordinates with other groups, such as the Authors' Guild, to influence issues important to writers, like copyright or the clarity of royalty statements.

Michael Congdon

Photo by Greg Martin

If I were an author looking for an agent, I would consider membership in one or more of these organizations an important part of an agent's résumé.

Do agents have to come from New York to be legitimate?

Lukeman: Agents do not have to come from New York to be legitimate. There are many good agents outside of New York who represent excellent clients and make amazing deals. That said, the vast majority of effective, legitimate agents are in New York, just like the vast majority of the movie business is in Los Angeles. Part of the reason for this is that the majority of major publishers are located in New York, and agents could not have lunch or attend other social engagements every day with them if they were not also located in New York.

Publishing is a social business, and many deals are made over lunch (or other personal meetings). So, in that regard, it can make a difference. Then again, just because an agent is located in New York does not mean he is legitimate or effective either.

In general, if you're trying to decide whether to sign with an agent, the most important thing will be to examine his track record, see what books he's sold and to which publishers.

When researching agents, how does a writer find the agent of a particular author or book?

Curtis: The best way is to find out who published the book (the publisher), then contact either the contracts or the publicity department of that publisher. Most of them will give that information out, as there's no reason to keep it a secret.

Is it okay to pitch more than one idea in a query?

Tessler: There may be different opinions here, but I prefer to see only one idea. Somehow seeing ten is overwhelming, and suggests to me that the author is prolific when it comes to generating ideas, but less successful at placing these ideas or knowing which one is strongest. Agents definitely like to sign writers with careers in front of them and tend not to take clients on for only a "one-off" project. But nonetheless, I think agents are sold in part on the basis of how passionate writers are about what they're working on. It's harder to believe that a writer has the right level of enthusiasm for his or her project, when there are 99 others he or she is also willing to pursue.

How do you know if a book subject and theme are salable?

Lukeman: Assuming nonfiction, let me begin by saying there is no way to offer a blanket, general answer for what is salable. That's the whole art of being an agent: determining, on a case-by-case basis, what is salable and what isn't. (Even several agents can disagree over any given proposal.) When we begin to dissect a proposal, we think of the genre, the current competition, what's currently in the pipeline in the publishing world, the size of the audience, the author's credentials, the author's platform, the author's past publications, the author's track record, the originality of the idea, and the quality of the writing—to name just a few factors.

A good idea is not enough. Expertise is not enough. It has to be a convergence of many factors—and all at exactly the right time in the market. What is salable in September may not be in October. That's the agent's job [to know this kind of information]. All you can do is thoroughly research the competition, make sure there is nothing like your proposal, make sure the market is huge and there is a need, build up your own credentials and platform, polish your writing, and find the appropriate agent.

If an agent suggests editorial changes, do I have to make them? Will I lose my agent if I don't?

Dystel: Agents are publishing professionals and most are pretty savvy about what will sell, or they wouldn't be in business. Assuming you've snagged a good agent, you should be open to any editorial suggestions she has. Most likely she will make the book stronger or more salable. Having said that, your conscience and your own critical faculties should be your guides regarding changes anyone requests. If you can make a good argument for why you don't want to make the suggested changes, a good agent should respect your decision and go forward. The work is first and foremost yours, and you must feel good about what goes out with your name on it. But, it's always the finest writers, in my opinion, who are willing to take criticism and use it to make their work better.

Author-Agent Etiquette

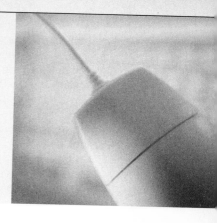

by Barbara Doyen

Yesterday two opposite things occurred: I got a scathing e-mail response to the personal advice I generously (and unnecessarily) offered in a rejection letter; and I got a beautiful thank-you card as a result of my handwritten comment added to the bottom of another rejection letter. Who do you think I'm more inclined to consider working with in the future?

There are so many similar examples. Yesterday I also got an e-mail complaint saying I rejected a project too quickly and therefore hadn't read it (I had!) and a phone complaint because I hadn't read the author's 800-page unsolicited manuscript within 24 hours of receiving it. The e-mail was unnecessary and inappropriate, and the phone call interfered with an incoming book offer. Neither author endeared himself or herself as future clients.

Occasionally I get phone calls from wanna-be writers who demand my complete client list, including the books I've placed and the amount paid for each. Often they expect this information before they will share any details about their project. They never consider how they'd feel to have their financial information freely revealed to anyone who called their agent.

Some writers get mad if we respond too quickly, and mad if we take too long to reply. Others expect a few words of feedback to help them improve their submissions, yet resent even the most tactful suggestions. Some writers feel entitled to confidential business information. Understandably, this sort of thing results in many agents issuing the blandest of form rejection letters, and it causes some to close their doors to new authors or unpublished writers.

What should an author who wants representation do (and not do!)?

First of all, get an agent directory—this one will do nicely!—and actually read the listings. Select those agents who sound most compatible with your project. Then, approach them exactly the way the listing indicates.

If the listing states, ''Queries only,'' this means to write a one-page, typed letter, telling the agent something about your book and something about you as the author of this book. Send it via snail mail along with a self-addressed, stamped envelope (SASE) that you fold and include with the query letter. Does this sound like I'm being terribly specific? Consider some of the mistakes commonly made by would-be clients—even after they tell the agent they got her name from this directory:

BARBARA DOYEN is President of Doyen Literary Services, Inc., an agency representing more than 100 authors. Her writing credits include articles and five published books, both fiction and nonfiction, and an audiocassette instructional series that was endorsed by James Michener. Her Write To $ell® seminars have assisted thousands of attendees in furthering their writing careers.

- **Mailing the whole manuscript or the proposal** when the agent indicated she wants the query letter only, and then will advise you if she wishes to read more.
- **Failing to send along the required SASE** or neglecting the postage.
- **Calling to ask if the agent accepts poetry,** or children's books, or action/adventure novels, or whatever. Since the caller has already said they got our number from this directory, where this information is given in detail, this call is unnecessary.
- **Calling to tell the agent about the book.** Since you are trying to sell the agent on your writing ability, you should contact her in writing. There are only a few exceptions to this, which I hesitate to mention, because doing so in the past has only caused more authors to violate protocol.

Tip

- **Having your spouse, best friend, co-worker, mother, or secretary call** to tell the agent about your book. (This happens more often than you might think!) Or having your spouse, best friend, co-worker, mother, or secretary write to get the agent to request your wonderful material, usually using the "too busy" excuse for the writer not doing it himself. Would you send a substitute to fill in for you at a job interview? That's really what this amounts to.
- **Sending a manuscript reeking of cigarette smoke,** or spraying the mailer with perfume can be a big turn-off. So is bad-mouthing your previous publisher or agent. Or outright lying, like saying a celebrity has endorsed your book when they haven't, or that one of our clients has recommended you when they don't even know you.

Any of these mistakes can end any agent relationship before it has even begun.

The agent asks to see your work, but what next?

That's easy—do exactly as the agent's letter (or e-mail or sometimes even phone call) says. If you have written a novel and the agent requests the first three chapters as a sample, send the first three chapters. Do not send chapters 3, 8, and 25 because you think they are your best. Do not neglect the SASE if you wish the material returned. Do not "forget" to send the requested synopsis just because you don't know how to write one.

It's a good idea to include a copy of your query letter with your package because the agent probably won't take the time to find your initial letter and may not remember just why they were interested in you in the first place. This copy of the query letter should be placed right under your new cover letter for the whole package. The cover letter should not repeat what was in the query letter, but should include additional information about your work. State up front that the agent requested the material—and no, you should never say it was requested if it wasn't.

When sending the package to the agent, do not send your materials piecemeal—the sample chapters in one package, the synopsis in another. Some people realize they forgot to include their return mailer after the fact, and it arrives in yet another package a few days later. Why should this matter? Just imagine receiving dozens and dozens of author submissions. Would you like to sort through the pile to find several packages that should have been sent together?

And don't call the agent to see how she liked your work. The agent will respond. Remember, existing clients get top priority. If several weeks have gone by, snail mail a polite letter asking about the status of your submission.

The agent is considering representing you, now what?

You've followed submission etiquette, and now the agent loves your work and is thinking of offering representation. Often the next step will be a phone call from the agent, to get to know you, and to tell you something about the agency and how it operates. Things to keep in mind:

- **Don't take over the conversation.** The agent has a specific agenda, and if you don't allow her to cover her agenda, she may decide not to represent you after all. The agent believes your writing has potential, now she needs to determine if you are the kind of person with whom she wants to work. You will probably have a chance to ask questions, but initially let the discussion unfold her way.

- **Don't demand information.** At this point you are entitled to know more about the agency, but ask questions politely. And use discretion. For instance, even if you know the names of some of the agent's clients, don't ask about their income or current projects. Client information is confidential and most agents consider it unethical to reveal these details.

- **Do speak freely.** My previous advice is not an indication that you should hold back, or give only short answers to questions. This is a conversation and it should have give and take so that both you and the agent feel comfortable with each other.

- **Be a good communicator.** You should feel welcome to contact your agent, but don't abuse the privilege. This means you do not call or e-mail your agent over trivial things, making a pest of yourself. Do contact your agent whenever needed, and you can reasonably expect the agent to get back to you in a day or two, especially if you use e-mail, which makes it so easy to keep in touch.

Frequent phone calls are a breach of etiquette, particularly during business hours when the agent should be calling editors about your great work, or getting phone calls from editors about your great work. This can't happen when clients monopolize the agent's time. If a call is warranted, it's best to request a phone date via e-mail, and let the agent call you when her schedule permits. When planning a phone conversation, it is helpful to give your agent a range of convenient times to call.

Reminder

Understand that it can be quite difficult to make and keep a phone appointment, because just as the agent is preparing to dial your number, an incoming call might announce a big offer from a publisher. Naturally, the agent is going to give this conversation a high priority. For this reason, some agents are willing to speak with the client during nonbusiness hours.

- **Have appropriate expectations.** Many agents provide the client with the submission history for their book once marketing is complete—if this is your agent's practice, don't ask for premature reports. If your agent periodically updates her authors with a list of publishers contacted, and it has been a while since you've been filled in, do e-mail your request for an update. Then, give the agent time to respond, knowing how busy she is, and understanding that she'd prefer to be spending the time calling new editors on your behalf.

We e-mail the author each time a rejection comes in, sharing any particulars, saving us the need to do periodic updates. The author is not automatically entitled to photocopies of rejection letters because they may contain confidential information, perhaps pertaining to other clients. Understand that there may not even be a rejection letter, as editors often call or e-mail a response to an agent.

- **Maintain a positive outlook.** A great attitude goes a long way toward ensuring a long-lasting author-agent relationship, which is in both the author's and the agent's best interest. Although it is common in some circles to believe the author ''hires'' an agent, you do not. You are partnering with the agent, who becomes your guide through the publishing process. Understand that if you are an unknown, the agent is doing you a big favor by taking you on, demonstrating a lot of faith in your future. Be thoughtful and courteous every time you contact your agent, and your attitude will motivate her to work even harder for you.

Writers need to know that it's a buyer's market and there is a seemingly unlimited supply of talented authors available in a declining market. Successful agents—and that's the kind you want to get—are extremely busy people. Most of us already have a great list of clients. Yet many agents remain approachable if you follow our established protocol. Dreams of finding a fabulous new writer keep us motivated to tackle the submissions pile, which agents must do beyond office hours and without pay. Simple etiquette and common sense will indicate professionalism and distinguish a promising writer from the crowd—and get you the representation you seek.

Agents Share Their Secrets

by Robert Lee Brewer

Agents are busy people. They're constantly pushing to get their clients' books sold to the right publisher for the right price with the best rights reserved for future subsidiary sales (i.e., movie options and foreign editions) in other markets. Agents also keep track of royalties earned to ensure that they and their clients are paid appropriately and on time.

Despite the busy life of agents, they nearly all harbor the same goal: Discovering the next breakout writer. That's why most agents devote several unpaid hours a week to reading scores of unsolicited queries and proposals, hoping to find a future client with whom to build a successful career in publishing. There's plenty of competition as far as the number of submissions, but most agents will say that a truly professional submission is rare.

Below, four very experienced and successful literary agents discuss what writers can do to command more attention to their submissions. While specific needs may change

Peter Rubie

from agent to agent, this roundtable helps show that a basic level of professionalism will move a writer several steps closer to becoming a successfully published author.

Peter Rubie is the president of The Peter Rubie Literary Agency in New York. Rubie is the author of two novels and several books of nonfiction, including *Writer's Market FAQs* (Writer's Digest Books).

Harvey Klinger founded Harvey Klinger, Inc., in 1977, after beginning his publishing career at Doubleday and working for 18 months for a literary agent. He personally loves great fiction and nonfiction books that teach or enlighten the reader.

James C. Vines entered the publishing business in 1989 with Raines & Raines, where he worked for three years before moving to the Virginia Barber Literary Agency. In 1995 he started The Vines Agency, Inc., which represents many best-selling and award-winning authors, including Joe R. Lansdale, Snoop Dogg, and Michael Stipe.

Rita Rosenkranz founded the Rita Rosenkranz Literary Agency in 1990. The agency focuses on adult nonfiction and represents various authors, including Pat Solley and Jason Blume.

ROBERT LEE BREWER is co-editor of WritersMarket.com and its biweekly e-mail newsletter, Market Update. Brewer also assists with the production of *Writer's Market, Writer's Market Deluxe Edition, Novel & Short Story Writer's Market,* and *Guide to Literary Agents.* He can be contacted via e-mail at robert.brewer@fwpubs.com.

What do you look for in new/potential clients?

Rubie: I'm still moved most by great writing. And it's so hard to find. Frankly, I'd try to sell the telephone book if the author was a great writer. I really look for a strong voice in the writing because that in turn leads to an intriguing mind. That's what catches us when we read and keeps us reading when we really should turn out the light and go to sleep.

Harvey Klinger

I also want to work collaboratively, as one of my strengths is editorial input—not everyone is comfortable with that. After all, it is, in part, my reputation that's on the line when I send out something. So I want to make sure the manuscript or proposal is the best I think it can be. Of course, it's the writer's book and he or she has the last word, but I'm not really into this idea of an agent as some sort of used-car salesman.

Klinger: More than anything, I look for terrific writing and a voice that sounds fresh and inviting. I'm moved by a manuscript that just about leaps off the page, but can never quantify exactly what that's going to be or when that's going to happen. It's a visceral response, much like meeting someone to whom you're instantly attracted.

Vines: If the author is writing nonfiction, I want the author to already have a strong platform, such as a syndicated newspaper column, 40-plus paid speaking engagements per year, and solid credentials. If the author is a novelist, I'm looking for a strong, assured narrative voice and character development that happens by way of plot. It's amazing to me how many first-time novelists haven't read deeply in the field in which they're trying to write. Before a novelist attempts to write and market her novel, she should steep herself in her genre by reading literally hundreds of her competitors' books.

Rosenkranz: I look for clients who are stellar advocates for their work—clients who are able to defend their work passionately and promote it tirelessly.

How do you prefer to be contacted by a writer?

Rubie: They can send me an e-mail query letter, or a hard copy proposal, but don't send me an e-mail attachment unbidden.

Klinger: Via e-mail.

Vines: A one-page query letter with a #10 self-addressed, stamped envelope (SASE) is the preferred method, although we also read one-paragraph queries by e-mail if they don't have attachments.

Rosenkranz: I prefer an author contact me with a query letter via regular mail, including a SASE for my response.

What is the biggest mistake a writer makes when contacting you?

Rubie: Not knowing the publishing industry and being unprofessional. Authors send manuscripts I haven't asked for in hardcopy or by e-mail and then don't give me a clue what the book is about or who the author is. Recently, I've been getting more and more e-mailed attachments labeled something inane like: mybook.doc, with no author telephone number or contact info included. My agency gets something like 200-plus e-mail queries and maybe 500 or more hardcopy proposals and queries per month. We have over 100 active clients we need to give priority. Make my life easier and more pleasant, not harder, by giving me a challenge I haven't asked for or sought.

Klinger: Trying to be a salesman never works for me; the material has to speak for itself. A writer who tells me everything he or she is going to do to promote a book doesn't work either. Tell me what you've already done, not what you want to do. Other than Jonathan Franzen, I've never known an author who said, "I do not want to be on *Oprah*!"

Vines: Any author who thinks he can "sell" me on his book is mistaken. Sales jazz in a query letter is just noise. After 15 years in this business, I can spot a good project a mile away, and nobody needs to do anything spectacular to grab my attention. Let the book speak for itself by shaping a concise and appealing one-page query letter.

Rosenkranz: One of the biggest mistakes authors might make is to not describe their work well in a query letter. Since this is the first contact with an agent, on which the relationship will either progress or not, it's critical that the letter be professional, both in its content and format.

How can a writer convince you that you should represent him?

Rubie: You can't convince me, in that regard. It's like asking, "How can I make so-and-so fall in love with me?" Certainly, I want a strong writer, a professional, ideally someone who has a track record in some regard, and is an expert or has access to experts, and who is an intriguing mind. It's not just about selling a book, but ideally helping shape and develop a writer's career.

Klinger: He simply cannot convince me to represent him. Either I respond to the material in hand, or I don't. Publishing is a completely subjective business and choosing a new client is no different. Either you connect with someone or you don't.

Vines: Just by writing a book that I think will reach millions (or at least hundreds of thousands) of readers, and by presenting it to me as I mentioned earlier.

Rosenkranz: Key elements in convincing me that I am a good match [to the writer] are the author's clear description of the benefits of the work, how the work differs from, if not surpasses, those on the market, and the author's strong relationship to the subject.

What is the one thing a writer should know as he goes on his quest to find an agent?

Rubie: Try and find someone who loves your work and can talk to you intelligently about it, and who is able to call the right editors at a particular house and pitch your project.

Klinger: Usually, a grateful author acknowledges one's agent. Go to a bookstore and look for books in the same genre as yours. I'm always impressed when a potential client has done that and says, "I think my book is similar to your client . . . and that's why I'm contacting you." It demonstrates a certain amount of initiative on the part of the writer, and that appeals to me.

Rita Rosenkranz

Vines: Every writer should understand that all of us in the publishing business are trying to find books that will appeal to a large segment of the reading public. I have always believed that authors who want to attain a measure of commercial success with their writing should read books from the *New York Times* Bestseller List, from time to time, to keep current with what the reading public is responding to. How many aspiring authors can even name three books on the *New York Times* Bestseller List right now? It boggles the mind when I hear authors say they want to get on the list, yet they don't know much about the list.

Rosenkranz: The author should do due diligence when seeking an agent. There are several things I consider extremely important: Make sure the agent is reputable, has good experience—preferably with a track record in that author's category—and strong contacts with publishers.

What's easier to sell—fiction or nonfiction? Why?

Rubie: Frankly, nothing is easy to sell at the moment. Fiction is splashier and often gets more immediate attention, but nonfiction tends to endure longer on the shelves and can be sold on a proposal; whereas fiction really has to be sold on a finished manuscript.

Klinger: Nonfiction is easier to sell, as long as the author has a strong platform, i.e., the person is already known in one's respective field and has had national exposure as an expert on the subject. First novels are tough to sell because most bookstores just want "brand names" these days, but I sure do love finding a great first novel and busting my butt to sell it! And when you do, it's indescribably wonderful.

Vines: Nonfiction is easier to sell, if you have an author with real credentials and a platform. It's easier because the news media will interview the nonfiction author because they have information of value to the general public. Novelists, on the other hand, can only talk about the craft of writing much of the time, and the news media has found that the general public doesn't want to hear about that.

Rosenkranz: Since I represent nonfiction almost exclusively, I'm afraid I have a clear preference. But it all depends on where an agent's strength resides.

When is the best time for a writer to get an agent?

Rubie: When they have an offer on a book. But that's a glib response. We read all the time, searching for that golden nugget among the reams of paper we get sent all the time, so in that regard it doesn't really matter when you send it in. If it's good, we'll respond quickly and positively.

Klinger: Any time is the best time, but submitting when the writer thinks his or her material is in the best possible shape is much better than submitting a work-in-progress. Once your manuscript is truly ready, the right agent will be waiting for it.

Vines: The best time for a novelist to find an agent is after he or she has a complete manuscript ready to show. The best time for a nonfiction writer to find an agent is after he has developed his career as a speaker and educator to the point where he has something truly valuable to offer.

Rosenkranz: When the author considers his or her project ready to be made public, so if an agent requests to see the proposal, the author is ready to submit it.

How to Find the Right Agent

writer's job is to write. A literary agent's job is to find publishers for her clients' books. Any writer who has endeavored to attract the attention of a publishing house knows this is no easy task. But beyond selling manuscripts, an agent must keep track of the ever-changing industry, writers' royalty statements, and fluctuating reading habits. And the list continues.

Because publishing houses receive more unsolicited manuscripts each year, securing an agent is becoming more of a necessity. Nevertheless, finding an eager *and* reputable agent is a difficult task. Even the most patient of writers can become frustrated, even disillusioned. Therefore, as a writer seeking agent representation, you should prepare yourself before starting your search. By learning effective strategies for approaching agents, as well as what to expect from an author/agent relationship, you will save yourself time—and quite possibly, heartache. This article provides the basic information on literary agents and how to find one who will best benefit your writing career.

Make sure you are ready for an agent

See Also

With an agent's job in mind, you should ask yourself if you and your work are at a stage where you need an agent. Look at A Ten-Step Checklist (provided both for nonfiction and fiction writers) on pages 21 and 22, and judge how prepared you are for contacting an agent. Have you spent enough time researching or polishing your manuscript? Sending an agent an incomplete project not only wastes your time but also may turn the agent off in the process. Literary agents are not magicians. An agent cannot sell an unsalable property or solve your personal problems. An agent will not be your banker, CPA, social secretary, or therapist. Instead, an agent will endeavor to sell your book because that is how he earns his living.

Moreover, your material may not be appropriate for an agent. Most agents do not represent poetry, magazine articles, short stories, or material suitable for academic or small presses; the agents' commission earned does not justify spending time submitting these types of works. Those agents who do take on such material generally represent authors on larger projects first, and then represent these smaller items only as a favor for their clients.

If you strongly believe your work is ready to be placed with an agent, make sure you are personally ready to be represented. In other words, before you contact an agent, consider the direction in which your writing career is headed. Besides skillful writers, agencies want clients with the ability to produce more than one book. Most agents will say they represent careers, not books. So as you compose your query letter—your initial contact with an agent— briefly mention your potential. Let an agent know if you've already started drafting your second novel—let him know that your writing is more than a half-hearted hobby.

The importance of research

Most people would not buy a used car without at least checking the odometer, and the savvy shopper would consult the blue books, take a test drive, and even ask for a mechanic's opinion. Much like the savvy car shopper, you want to obtain the best possible agent for your writing, so you should do some research on the business of agents before sending out query letters. Understanding how agents operate will help you find an agent appropriate for your work, as well as alert you to the types of agents to avoid.

We often receive complaints from writers regarding agents *after* they have already lost money or their work is tied into a contract with an ineffective agent. If they'd put the same amount of effort into researching agents as they did writing their manuscripts, the writers would have saved themselves unnecessary grief.

The best way to educate yourself is to read all you can about agents and other authors. The articles in this book will give you insight not only on how to contact an agent but also how the author/agent relationship works. Organizations such as the Association of Authors' Representatives (AAR), the National Writers Union (NWU), American Society of Journalists and Authors (ASJA), and Poets & Writers, Inc., all have informational material on finding and working with an agent. (These, along with other helpful organizations, are listed in the back of this book beginning on page 263.) *Publishers Weekly* (www. publishersweekly.com) covers publishing news affecting agents and others in the publishing industry in general; discusses specific events in the ''Hot Deals'' and ''Behind the Bestsellers'' columns; and occasionally lists individual author's agents in the ''Forecasts'' section.

Useful
Websites

Even the Internet has a wide range of sites devoted to agents. Through the different forums provided on the Web, you can learn basic information about preparing for your initial contact or more specific material about individual agents. Keep in mind, however, that not everything printed on the Web is a solid fact; you may come across the site of a writer who is bitter because an agent rejected his manuscript. Your best bet is to use the Internet to supplement your other research. For particularly useful sites, refer to Websites of Interest on page 265.

See Also

Through your research, you will discover the need to be wary of some agents. Anybody can go to the neighborhood copy center and order business cards that say she is a literary agent, but that title does not mean she can sell your book. She may ask for a large sum of money, then disappear from society. Becoming knowledgeable about the different types of fees agents may charge is a *crucial* step to take before contacting any agent. Before paying any type of fee, read Understanding Agents' Fees—What Writers Need to Know on page 28.

An agent also may not have any connections with others in the publishing industry. An agent's reputation with editors can be a major strength or weakness. While it's true that even top agents are not able to sell every book they represent, an inexperienced agent who submits too many inappropriate submissions will quickly lose her standing with any editor. It is acceptable to ask an agent for recent sales before he agrees to represent you, but keep in mind that some agents consider this information confidential. If an agent does give you a list of recent sales, you can call the publishers' contracts departments to ensure the sale was actually made by that agent.

The importance of location

For years, the major editors and agents were located in New York City. If a writer wanted to be published with a big-name house, he had to contact a New York agency. But this has changed over time for many reasons. For starters, publishing companies are appearing all over the country—San Francisco, Seattle, Chicago, Minneapolis. And naturally, agents are locating closer to these smaller publishing hubs.

Advances in technology have also had an impact on the importance of location. Thanks to fax machines, the Internet, e-mail, express mail, and inexpensive long-distance telephone rates, an agent no longer needs to work (or be) in New York to work closely with a New York publisher. Besides, if a manuscript is truly excellent, a smart editor will not care where the agent is located.

Nevertheless, there are simply more opportunities for agents located in New York to network with editors. They are able to meet face-to-face over lunch. The editor can share his specific needs, and the agent can promote her newest talent. As long as New York remains the publishing capital of the world, the majority of agents will be found there, too.

Contacting agents

Once your manuscript is prepared and you have a solid understanding of how literary agents work, the time is right to contact an agent. Your initial contact is the first impression you make on an agent; therefore, you want to be professional and brief.

See Also

Because approaching agents is an important topic, we've included several articles on contacting agents in this book: How Do I Contact Agents? on page 30; Script Agents— What They Want and How to Contact Them on page 32; How to Write a Query Letter on page 41; The Perfect Pitch on page 44; The Art of the Synopsis on page 46; and Professional Proposals—Creating a Nonfiction Proposal on page 51.

Again, research plays an important role in getting an agent's attention. You'll want to show the agent you've done your homework. Read the listings in this book to learn agents' areas of interest, check agents' websites to learn more about how they operate their businesses, and find out the names of some of their clients. If there is an author whose book is similar to yours, call the author's publisher. Someone in the contracts department can tell you the name of the agent who sold the title, provided an agent was used. Contact that agent, and impress her with your knowledge of her agency.

Evaluate any offer

Once you've received an offer of representation, you must determine if the agent is right for you. As flattering as any offer may be, you need to be confident that you are going to work well with this agent and that this agent is going to work hard to sell your manuscript.

You need to know what to expect once you enter into a business relationship. You should know how much editorial input to expect from your agent; how often your agent gives updates about where your manuscript has been and who has seen it; and what subsidiary rights the agent represents.

More importantly, you should know when you will be paid. The publisher will send your advance and any subsequent royalty checks directly to the agent. After deducting his commission—usually 10 to 15 percent—your agent will send you the remaining balance. Most agents charge a higher commission of 20 to 25 percent when using a co-agent for foreign, dramatic, or other specialized rights. As you enter into a relationship with an agent, have the agent explain his specific commission rates and payment policy.

As your potential partner, you have the right to ask an agent for information that convinces you she knows what she's doing. Be reasonable about what you ask, however. Asking for recent sales is okay; asking for the average size of clients' advances is not. Remember, agents are very busy. Often asking a general question like, "How do you work?," or requesting a sample contract can quickly answer your concerns. If you are polite and the agent responds with anger or contempt, that tells you something you need to know about this potential working relationship.

Evaluate the agent's level of experience. Agents who have been in the business awhile have a larger number of contacts, but new agents may be hungrier, as well as more open to

A ten-step checklist for nonfiction writers

1 **Formulate a concrete idea** for your book. Sketch a brief outline making sure you have enough material for an entire book-length manuscript.

2 **Research** works on similar topics to understand the competition and determine how yours is unique.

3 **Compose sample chapters.** This step should indicate how much time you will need to finish and if your writing needs editorial help.

4 **Publish** completed chapters in journals. This validates your work to agents and provides writing samples for later in the process.

5 **Polish your outline** so you can refer to it while drafting a query letter and so you can avoid wasting time when agents contact you.

6 **Brainstorm** three to four subject categories that best describe your material.

7 **Use the indexes in the back of this book** to find agents who are interested in at least two of your subject areas and who are looking for new clients.

8 **Rank your list.** Narrow your list further by reading the listings of agencies you found in the indexes, and organize the list according to your preferences.

9 **Write your query.** Professionally and succinctly describe your premise and your experience to give an agent an excellent first impression.

10 **Read about the business** of agents so you are knowledgeable and prepared to act on any offer.

Narrowing Your List

previously unpublished writers. Talk to other writers about their interactions with specific agents. Writers' organizations, such as the National Writers Association (NWA), the American Society of Journalists and Authors (ASJA), and the National Writers Union (NWU), maintain files on agents with whom their members have dealt, and can share this information by written request or through their membership newsletters.

Understand any contract before you sign

Some agents offer written contracts; some do not. If your prospective agent does not, at least ask for a "memorandum of understanding" that details the basic relationship of expenses and commissions. If your agent does offer a contract, be sure to read it carefully, and keep a copy for yourself. Because contracts can be confusing, you may want to have a lawyer or knowledgeable writer friend check it out before you sign anything.

The National Writers Union (NWU) has drafted a Preferred Literary Agent Agreement and a pamphlet, *Understand the Author-Agent Relationship*, which is available to members. (Membership is based on your annual writing income and open to all writers actively pursuing a writing career. See Professional Organizations on page 263 in the back of the book for the NWU's address.) The NWU suggests clauses that delineate such issues as:

See Also

A ten-step checklist for fiction writers

1. **Finish your novel** or short story collection. An agent can do nothing for fiction without a finished product.

2. **Revise your novel.** Have other writers offer criticism to ensure your manuscript is as polished as you believe possible.

3. **Proofread.** Don't ruin a potential relationship with an agent by submitting work that contains typos or poor grammar.

4. **Publish** short stories or novel excerpts in literary journals, proving to potential agents that editors see quality in your writing.

5. **Research** to find the agents of writers you admire or whose work is similar to your own.

6. **Use the indexes in the back of this book** to construct a list of agents who are open to new writers and who are looking for your type of fiction (i.e., literary, romance, mystery).

7. **Rank your list.** Use the listings in this book to determine the agents most suitable for you and your work and to eliminate inappropriate agencies.

8. **Write your synopsis.** Completing this step early will help you write your query letter and save you time later when agents contact you.

9. **Compose your query letter.** As an agent's first impression of you, this brief letter should be polished and to the point.

10. **Read about the business** of agents so you are knowledgeable and prepared to act on any offer.

- the scope of representation (One work? One work with the right of refusal on the next? All work completed in the coming year? All work completed until the agreement is terminated?)
- the extension of authority to the agent to negotiate on behalf of the author
- compensation for the agent, and any co-agent, if used
- manner and time frame for forwarding monies received by the agent on behalf of the client
- termination clause, allowing client to give about 30 days to terminate the agreement
- the effect of termination on concluded agreements as well as ongoing negotiations
- arbitration in the event of a dispute between agent and client.

If things don't work out

Because this is a business relationship, a time may come when it is beneficial for you and your agent to part ways. Unlike a marriage, you don't need to go through counseling to keep the relationship together. Instead, you end it professionally on terms upon which you both agree.

First, check to see if your written agreement spells out any specific procedures. If not, write a brief, businesslike letter, stating that you no longer think the relationship is advantageous and you wish to terminate it. Instruct the agent not to make any new submissions and give her a 30- to 60-day limit to continue as representative on submissions already under consideration. You can ask for a list of all publishers who have rejected your unsold work, as well as a list of those who are currently considering it. If your agent charges for office expenses, you will have to reimburse your agent upon terminating the contract. For this reason, you may want to ask for a cap on expenses when you originally enter into an agency agreement. If your agent has made sales for you, he will continue to receive those monies from the publisher, deduct his commission and remit the balance to you. A statement and your share of the money should be sent to you within 30 days. You can also ask that all manuscripts in your agent's possession be returned to you.

Narrowing Your List

How I Found My Agent

by Will Allison

Research the market. "Send your manuscript and/or query to agents." "Sit back and pray." That's the standard advice for finding an agent, but often as not, it doesn't happen like that. In fact, there is no "normal" way writers and agents come together. Sometimes they're introduced by a mutual friend; sometimes they meet at a writers' conference; other times, it's just plain, dumb luck. In the following interview, six fiction writers share very different stories about how they found their agents.

Michael Crummey

Michael Crummey was born in Buchans, Newfoundland, and grew up there and in Wabush, Labrador. He is the award-winning author of three books of poetry, a collection of short stories, *Flesh & Blood*, and a novel, *River Thieves* (Houghton Mifflin, 2002).

Michael Crummey

Photo by Julie van der Meulen

"I found my agent through a friend of mine in Kingston, Ontario. He had published a couple of story collections with a small Canadian publisher that won rave reviews and a number of awards. The agent had recently moved to Toronto from England, where she had been a literary agent for years. She was looking to build a 'stable' of authors in Canada and called him up out of the blue, asking if she could represent him.

"He suggested I call her on a number of occasions. I had published only poetry and a slender volume of stories up to that point and had never considered trying for an agent. Fifteen percent of nothing is nothing, after all. My friend wrote the agent's phone number on a scrap of paper at a bar one night, and I carried it around in my wallet for six months. Finally, I screwed up the courage to call and almost hung up when she answered the phone. My side of the conversation went something like this: 'Hi. You don't know me. I'm a friend of X. I don't really have anything you could sell. Want to be my agent?'

"For reasons that remain a mystery to me, she didn't hang up the phone. She asked what I was planning on working on and then to see my collection of stories—she sold one of them to a top literary magazine. She also lit a fire under my arse to work on the novel I had a vague notion of at the time—and, when I finished it, she sold the rights in five countries."

WILL ALLISON's short stories have appeared in *Zoetrope: All-Story, Kenyon Review, Shenandoah, American Short Fiction*, and other magazines.

Patrick Downes (Agent: Kit Ward of Christina Ward Literary Agency)

Patrick Downes

Patrick Downes lives in Vermont, and is working on his second novel.

"Experience has me convinced the rewards of writing come as much by chance and sudden discovery as by planning. This seems true for both business and art. I wasn't looking for Kit when we found each other at the Bread Loaf Writers' Conference. I had little more than a handful of stories and 20-some pages of a novel, and I was unprepared to talk about my prospects. We got along right off, though, talking easily about the present if not the future. Kit offered her encouragement and phone number, and we parted warmly, even friends. Then, I put it all out of my head.

"The following Spring, an excerpt from my novel appeared in a respected literary magazine, and I began receiving calls from interested editors and agents. I hadn't any idea how to handle the attention. Remembering my few minutes with Kit at Bread Loaf, I searched out her number and called. I hoped for her indulgence. 'Can I tell an editor I'm not ready?' I said, the chitchat behind us. 'Can I ask an agent to call back?' She answered, 'Yes' and 'Yes.' If she found me tactless or naïve, she didn't say. She was generous, I was grateful, and we hung up.

"I arrived for my second year at Bread Loaf with one goal: to ask Kit if she would represent me. She agreed. Miraculously, she sold my novel two weeks later.

"Kit is, in a word, my ally. She will sell my fiction when she gets it; provide counsel when necessary; and remind me from time to time that our work is linked. I'm not alone in this hard business."

George Harrar (Agent: Esmond Harmsworth of Zachary Schuster Harmsworth)

George Harrar

George Harrar is the author of several novels, including *The Spinning Man* (Putnam, 2003, paperback 2004), a literary suspense novel. He lives in Wayland, Massachusetts.

"After years of wondering how to land an agent, I hit on the surefire method: win a major fiction contest. In the fall of 1998, my story titled 'The 5:22' won the Carson McCullers Prize for the Short Story from *Story* magazine. With that recognition in hand, I sent off queries to a half-dozen agencies and finally decided to go with Zachary Shuster Harmsworth in Boston, near where I live. I write fiction for adults through teenagers and down to middle-grade readers, so it was important for me to find an agent who was comfortable marketing my split writing personality.

"A few months after I signed on with Esmond Harmsworth, 'The 5:22' was chosen for *The Best American Short Stories 1999*, and suddenly agents were soliciting me—an odd turn of events, and a little too late. Even though I had a number of publishing credits in short stories, everyone I talked to during the agent-hunting process wanted to know if I had an idea for a novel. A successful short story is great bait for an agent, but to land one, a writer probably needs a solid novel in progress to offer.

"I know many writers don't submit to contests, believing the odds too long and the entry fees too expensive. But I think spending $100 a year to enter a half-dozen contests is a worthwhile investment with a potentially great payoff."

Narrowing Your List

Dylan Landis (Agent: Joy Harris of The Joy Harris Literary Agency, Inc.)

Dylan Landis is writing a novel, *Floorwork*, and a collection of linked stories, *Rana Fegrina*. Her fiction appears in *Best American Nonrequired Reading 2003* and *Bestial Noise: The Tin House Fiction Reader*.

Dylan Landis

Photo by Don Coscarelli

"After six years, I was finishing a novel—endlessly polishing its sentences, while sending out short stories, which is where the first door opened: Rob Spillman, editor of *Tin House* magazine, called to say he wanted two stories—and what else was I working on?

"I described the novel, *Floorwork*. (Vaguely recall stammering. Lesson One: Learn to swiftly, enticingly, describe your book.)

"*Tin House*, as it happened, had a new book imprint under Bloomsbury USA. Would I send the novel? Yes and no: I wanted an agent to send the whole manuscript. I sent four chapters, though, and Rob called again: Would I like his help finding an agent?

"And here is where doors started flying open like in a Poltergeist movie.

"Rob chose, and phoned, six agents. (Lesson Two: A connection can be someone who likes your work—and who is generous. It is not necessarily about having contacts.) 'Send each agent four chapters,' he said. (Lesson Three: Open a FedEx account; they deliver supplies and pre-printed labels, free.) Within days, all six agents called: Send the rest. I swooned. Then sent it. (Lesson Four: Upload your manuscript to kinkos.com and have them drive the printouts back.) Ultimately, four agents wanted *Floorwork*. I flew to New York, met them, admired their client lists and their passion, basked in the courtship, and finally asked how to choose wisely. (Lessons Five and Six, courtesy of Mr. Spillman: Pick an agent who reads your work correctly—and pick the one you'd want to call if things go wrong.)

Susan Perabo (Agent: Elyse Cheney of Sanford J. Greenburger Associates)

Susan Perabo is the author of a collection of short stories, *Who I Was Supposed to Be*, and a novel, *The Broken Places*. She is Writer in Residence and Associate Professor of English at Dickinson College.

Susan Perabo

Photo by Susan Perabo

"I started trying to get an agent after I finished my first novel. I had had some success placing stories and had even been contacted by some agents who liked my work, so I was encouraged by my prospects. Some teachers and friends were generous enough to give me solid leads, to say a kind word about me to their own agents, but none of these leads panned out. Thing was, no one liked my novel very much. Even those agents who had previously written me expressing interest wrote back pleasant rejection letters to the tune of 'Anything else? I really did like that story I read in—!' It was an excruciating and dispiriting experience, and it took up time—and especially energy—that would have been much better spent writing.

"After almost two years of shopping this novel around—and revising it based on the comments of agents who had thought it was good (but not good enough)—I came to the painful conclusion that the novel I had so suffered and so loved might never be published. And indeed, it was not.

"I returned to stories, finished enough for a collection, and a year or so after dropping out of the agent hunt, reentered it, for a blessedly brief time. I sent the stories to the agent who had written me the most letters; not only had she written to ask for work and then given me a thoughtful and lengthy response to the novel, but she had written again, in the interim, to say that my work was still on her mind. I appreciated that third letter so much that I wanted to send her the stories first. She accepted me as a client immediately and sold my book in two weeks.

"So, I guess my lesson is that perseverance doesn't always pay off in the way we think it will. I could still be shopping around that first novel, feeling cheated and misunderstood. Putting it away—then removing myself from the hunt and putting the focus back where it belonged, on the work itself—was one of the smartest things I ever did."

Lisa Tucker (Agent: Marly Rusoff of Marly Rusoff & Associates, Inc.)

Photo by Bob Godwin

Lisa Tucker

Lisa Tucker is the author of two novels, *The Song Reader* (Downtown Press, 2003) and *Shout Down the Moon* (Downtown Press, 2004). Her fiction has appeared in *Seventeen*, *Pages*, and the music-inspired anthology *Lit Riffs*. She lives in New Mexico.

"I found my first agent at a writers' conference in 1997. I hadn't been writing long, and I almost didn't apply for the conference; I'd never done a workshop and the idea was a little terrifying. When a very well-regarded agent offered to sign my novel, I could not have been more surprised. She told me her plans for the book and they sounded fabulous. She was sending it to top editors in New York; she even hinted there might be an auction.

"I wonder now what would have happened if that auction had come to pass. I still think the novel was good, but I know it wouldn't have been the best book to start a publishing career because it had a relatively small potential audience. Of course, at the time I was very unhappy that it didn't sell, yet I started working on another novel. When the second novel didn't sell either, my agent and I finally parted company.

"It was a tough time in my career. Leaving your agent has been compared to getting a divorce, and there's definitely truth to that. I did keep writing—writers write, that's what we do—and eventually, I finished a third novel. Then, I had to find a way to try and sell it. Since I knew all too well that having an agent didn't guarantee finding a publisher, I decided to go straight to editors this time. I started with Nan Talese at Doubleday because I knew she had published some of my favorite writers.

"I sent Nan the first chapter of *The Song Reader*, along with a query letter telling her how much I admired her taste, and why I thought she might like the novel. A few days later, I got an e-mail, but not from Nan, from an agent! She explained that she rarely took on new clients, but she and Nan were friends, and Nan had passed along my sample chapter. She said she liked what she'd read so far—would I send along the rest?

"I did, and less than a week later, she called to say she loved the book, and she'd like to represent me. Honestly, I didn't have a lot of faith that anything would come of this relationship, but I didn't know Marly Rusoff yet. She started sending out *The Song Reader* in January 2002 and already had two offers a month later. I felt very lucky and of course grateful to Nan Talese. Normally editors don't read unagented queries; I still don't know why she ended up reading mine.

"My story has a happy ending. I now have an agent who is both a publishing legend and an accessible, brilliant, hard working, funny, down-to-earth gal—everything an author could want. I've just published another book with Simon & Schuster and, thanks to Marly, we have a great contract for two more. I feel like I finally won the agent lottery."

Narrowing Your List

Understanding Agents' Fees

What Writers Need to Know

Before starting your search for an agent, it is extremely important to have an understanding of the various fees some agencies charge. Most agents make their living from the commissions they receive after selling their clients' books, and these are the agents we've listed. Charging writers for office expenses incurred on their behalf is standard, though there are agents who do not charge for this service. Agents also typically make 15% commission on sales. The editors of *Guide to Literary Agents* discourage the payment of any other fees to agents.

Office expenses

Many agents—both those who do and do not charge additional fees—ask the author to pay for photocopying, postage, and long-distance phone calls. An agent should only ask for office expenses after agreeing to represent the writer. These expenses should be discussed up front, and the writer should receive a statement accounting for them. This money is sometimes returned to the author upon sale of the manuscript. Be wary if there is an up-front fee amounting to hundreds of dollars, which is excessive.

Reading fees

Agents who do not charge reading fees earn their money from commissions. Agencies that do charge reading fees often do so to cover the cost of additional readers or the time spent reading that could have been spent selling. This practice can save the agent time, open the agency to a larger number of submissions, and may allow the agent time to consider each manuscript more extensively. Whether such promises are kept depends upon the honesty of the agency. You may pay a fee and never receive a response from the agent, or you may pay someone who will not submit your manuscript to publishers. In this book, we have not included those literary agents who charge reading fees.

Important

Reading fees vary from $25 to $500 or more. The fee is usually nonrefundable, but sometimes agents agree to refund the money if they take a writer on as a client, or if they sell the writer's manuscript. Keep in mind, however, that payment of a reading fee does not ensure representation. If you find that a literary agent listed in this book charges a reading fee, please contact the editor.

Officially, the Association of Authors' Representatives (AAR) in their Canon of Ethics prohibits members from directly or indirectly charging a reading fee, and the Writers Guild of America (WGA) does not allow WGA signatory agencies to charge a reading fee to WGA members, as stated in the WGA's Artists' Manager Basic Agreement. A signatory may charge you a fee if you are not a member, but most signatory agencies do not charge a reading fee as an across-the-board policy.

Critique fees

Sometimes a manuscript will interest an agent, but the agent will point out areas still needing development. Some agencies offer criticism services for an additional fee. Like reading fees, payment of a critique fee does not ensure representation. When deciding if you will benefit from having someone critique your manuscript, keep in mind that the quality and quantity of comments vary widely. The critique's usefulness will depend on the agent's knowledge of the market. Also be aware that an agent who spends a significant portion of his time commenting on manuscripts will have less time to actively market work he currently represents. We strongly advise writers not to use critiquing services offered through an agency. Instead, we recommend hiring a freelance editor or joining a writer's group until your work is ready to be submitted to agents who do not charge fees.

Narrowing Your List

How Do I Contact Agents?

Once you and your manuscript are thoroughly prepared, the time is right to contact an agent. Finding an agent can often be as difficult as finding a publisher. Nevertheless, there are four ways to maximize your chances of finding the right agent: Obtain a referral from someone who knows the agent; meet the agent in person at a writers' conference; submit a query letter or proposal; or attract the agent's attention with your own published writing.

Referrals

The best way to get your foot in an agent's door is to be referred by one of his clients or by an editor or another agent he has worked with in the past. Because an agent trusts his clients, he will usually read referred work before over-the-transom submissions. If you are friends with anyone in the publishing business who has connections with agents, ask politely for a referral. However, don't be offended if another writer will not share the name of his agent.

If you don't have a wide network of publishing professionals, use the resources you do have to get an agent's attention.

Conferences

Going to a conference is your best bet for meeting an agent in person. Many conferences invite agents to give a speech or simply be available for meetings with authors, and agents view conferences as a way to find writers. Agents often set aside time for one-on-one discussions with writers, and occasionally they may even look at material writers bring to the conference. If an agent is impressed with you and your work, the agent may ask for writing samples after the conference. When you send your query, be sure to mention the specific conference where you met the agent and that she asked to see your work.

See Also

Because this is an effective way to connect with agents, we've asked agents to indicate in their listings which conferences they regularly attend. We've also included a section of **Writers' Conferences**, starting on page 235, where you can find more information about a particular conference.

Submissions

The most common way to contact an agent is through a query letter or a proposal package. Most agents will accept unsolicited queries. Some will also look at outlines and sample chapters. Almost none want unsolicited complete manuscripts. Check the **How to Contact** subhead in each listing to learn exactly how an agent prefers to be solicited. Never call; let the writing in your query letter speak for itself.

Because a query letter is your first impression on an agent, it should be professional and to the point. As a brief introduction to your manuscript, a query letter should only be one page in length.

- The first paragraph should quickly state your purpose: You want representation.
- In the second paragraph, mention why you have chosen to query that specific agent. Perhaps the agent specializes in your areas of interest or represents authors you admire. Show the agent you have done your homework.
- In the next paragraph or two, describe the project, the proposed audience, why your book will sell, etc. Be sure to mention the approximate length and any special features of your book.
- Then discuss why you are the perfect person to write this book, listing your professional credentials or relative experience.
- Close your query with an offer to send an outline, sample chapters, or the complete manuscript—depending on your type of book.

Step By Step

Agents agree to be listed in directories such as *Guide to Literary Agents* to indicate to writers what they want to see and how they wish to receive submissions. As you start to query agents, make sure you follow their individual submission directions. This, too, shows an agent you've done your research.

Like publishers, agencies have specialties. Some are only interested in novel-length works. Others are open to a wide variety of subjects and may actually have member agents within the agency who specialize in only a handful of the topics covered by the entire agency.

Before querying any agent, first consult the **Agent Specialties Indexes** in the back of this book for your manuscript's subject and identify those agents who handle what you write. Then, read the agents' listings to see which are appropriate for you and for your work.

Publishing credits

Some agents read magazines or journals to find writers to represent. If you have had an outstanding piece published in a periodical, you may be contacted by an agent wishing to represent you. In such cases, make sure the agent has read your work. Some agents send form letters to writers, and such agents often make their living entirely from charging reading fees, not from commissions on sales.

However, many reputable and respected agents do contact potential clients in this way. For them, you already possess attributes of a good client: You have publishing credits, and an editor has validated your work. To receive a letter from a reputable agent who has read your material and wants to represent you is an honor.

Occasionally, writers who have self-published or who have had their work published electronically may attract an agent's attention, especially if the self-published book has sold well or received a lot of positive reviews.

Recently, writers have been posting their work on the Internet in hope of attracting an agent's eye. With all the submissions most agents receive, they likely have little time to peruse writers' websites. Nevertheless, there are agents who do consider the Internet a resource for finding fresh voices.

Contacting Agents

Script Agents

*What They Want and How
to Contact Them*

by Mark Sevi

t's only natural. The next question a writer asks after, "What should I write," is "How do I sell it?" To do that, you need to find representation—a Herculean task all on its own. I interviewed agents and managers and asked them the same questions: What does a writer have to do to get your attention? What do you look for? How should that material be presented?

It really goes without saying with these professionals so I'll say it here for them: Don't even think about contacting an agent or manager until you've actually finished something. No one can do anything with a property that is only three-quarters finished. And forget selling a pitch unless you have a track record of proven success.

Following are the questions and the answers from six agents who represent the gamut of the industry; they are managers and agents in all shapes, sizes, and flavors—the people who will be deciding your scriptwriting fate. Take them at their word, no matter what else you might have heard. They represent an aggregate of hundreds of years of experience. They are the real deal.

Marc Hernandez is a literary manager and managing partner of Crescendo Entertainment Group, a literary management and production company, founded in 2002. Prior to forming Crescendo Entertainment Group, Mr. Hernandez was a literary manager with Zide/Perry Entertainment; vice president of development for ShowBIZ Data; and before that, worked in the literary department of United Talent Agency where he serviced and interfaced with over 40 high-profile screenwriters and directors.

Debora Koslowsky is the founder of Working Artists Agency, started in 1994. She has worked for 11 years as an agent, with five of those years as a literary agent. The Working Artists Agency represents most genres except science fiction.

Rima Bauer Greer is the president and founder of Above The Line Agency. Her clients are credited writers on *Constantine* (filming), *Backdraft*, *Jumanji*, *Bill & Ted's Excellent Adventure*, *Charlie's Angels*, and *Memphis Belle*, among others. She has over 15 years of experience.

Bruce Bartlett is a literary agent at Above The Line Agency specializing in feature film writers and directors. He has eight years of industry experience, prior to which he attended USC's graduate film school and managed a brokerage firm.

David Saunders is a partner at the Agency for the Performing Arts (APA) and co-head of

MARK SEVI is a professional screenwriter and screenwriting teacher. He has 16 produced films to his credit, and his 17th, *Pterodactyl*, is in pre-production at the SciFi Channel. He can be reached at fadeout@comcast.net.

the literary department. He represents such clients as Rod Lurie (*Line of Fire*), Bruce Feirstein (the James Bond writer), and Tony Gayton (*Salton Sea*).

Paul Canterna is a literary manager and producer for Seven Summits Pictures and Management. Before enrolling in the famed Peter Stark Producing Program at the University of Southern California, he was an attorney for a number of years in Pittsburgh, Pennsylvania.

What does it take to break in?

Hernandez: Talent, and a strong, unwavering will to succeed.

Koslowsky: It takes incredible perseverance—a maniacal refusal to fail.

Bauer Greer: Talent, perseverance, material, and dumb luck.

Bartlett: You have to be "good in a room." Established writers—or even new writers—who are up for a writing assignment are all going to be about the same level of skill and talent based on a writing sample, a produced film, etc. You need to be able to convince a producer of your vision of how *The Last Samurai III* should go. If you can't infuse the people in the meeting with your enthusiasm and vision for that particular project, then you are not going to get the job.

Saunders: The business has never been easy. It's always been tough to sell a script to anyone, and that will never change. A new writer has to continue to write and believe in himself in order to break through that wall.

What is the most common mistake new writers make?

Hernandez: First impressions in this business are everything. I am shocked at the numbers of writers who don't do their homework and don't even understand proper formatting—binding, proper brads, and fonts. If someone submits material to Crescendo and it's in the wrong font, bound in a three-ring notebook, has cast lists, pictures, etc., it screams "uninformed novice," and we will pass on it immediately. Why? Because chances are good that the script is not going to sell to anyone anyway. We focus on the ones where the writer has done the right things.

Bartlett: New writers just don't understand that less is more when it comes to telling a film story. Visually brief, in other words.

Saunders: The reason I didn't become a writer is because great writers sit and rework material until it's perfect. It's difficult and tedious and absolutely necessary if you want your material to be recognized above the rest.

Canterna: A sloppy, half-written script says to me that you're not ready to break in.

What's the most serious misconception new writers have?

Hernandez: Most think this is easy to do because they see a movie or take a class and say, "I can do that." Wrong on many levels. Sure, maybe it's not that hard to write a script, but producing something that any of us want to represent is quite another thing. That takes a lot of hard work.

Bauer Greer: The biggest misconception is that we need new writers. We don't. We don't make any money discovering new writers.

Bartlett: We really need to focus on our current client list. Adding a new writer isn't a priority. Selling our current clients is. We're really not dying to sign new writers, so you have to be exceptional for us to even consider you.

What, if anything, has changed about the business in the last five to ten years?

Saunders: A lot of independent companies have gone out of business. Those left have consolidated in order to better compete. During the dot-com boom, there were a lot of

Contacting Agents

Dos and don'ts from the pros

For More Info

- **DO** Ceaselessly write scripts, watch movies, and read scripts.
- **DO** Be professional in all aspects. If this is a hobby to you, go home now.
- **DO** Study the art and history of screenwriting, including contemporary structure.
- **DO** Understand your market by reading the trades or following the industry on the Internet.
- **DO** Learn how to take criticism.
- **DO** Focus on commercial, marketable ideas.
- **DO** Make as many contacts in the industry as you can, and use them to promote your material when it's ready.
- **DO** Always look for ways to make your script fresh.
- **DO** Know the agency you're submitting to, spell the names right, etc.
- **DO** Understand the business you're trying to work in—do your homework.

- **DON'T** Release material before it's ready.
- **DON'T** Ever say your work is good, unique—don't use value judgments in describing your work—your opinion doesn't matter. Let the pros judge the value of your work.
- **DON'T** Have only one script to sell.
- **DON'T** Take it for granted that this is an easy business to break into.
- **DON'T** Follow trends.
- **DON'T** Make excuses.
- **DON'T** Write clichés.
- **DON'T** Give up.

mini-buyers willing to plunk down a lot of money for spec scripts. Now we're more limited to the studios who say, "Gee, we really like it, but we have something similar in development." But I do see an upward trend lately with some small companies like SpyGlass coming back.

Canterna: Agreed, but at the same time there are more and more avenues to get your script noticed. There are more contests, and the Internet has really opened that up so you can upload scripts directly to managers and production companies (like www.zide.com and www.triggerstreet.com). But most also agree the competition for writing jobs has increased dramatically.

You all seem to preach quality and consistency. Why are movies so bad these days? Is it the writing? And isn't it true that special effects sell tickets and not necessarily a good story?

Koslowsky: The huge-budget films have difficulty telling good stories because there are so many people involved in the vision of the film, i.e., a story by committee. That doesn't mean a writer shouldn't turn in his or her best material, even if that material gets changed later on down the line. Only your best is going to get you noticed by any of us.

Bauer Greer: I think movies in a lot of ways have actually gotten better, but I also think there's a trend to the lowest common denominator to sell the most tickets these days. That has had a deleterious effect on story versus special effects. But again, write the best script you can first. You don't have any control over any other aspect of the film anyway.

What qualities do you look for in a writer you'd like to represent?

Hernandez: Smart, innovative, distinctive storytelling ability.

Koslowsky: Passion, creativity, flexibility, humor, and a body armor that is thick enough to repel the cannon shots of rejection and criticism.

Saunders: Someone who strives to be original, someone who tells the whole story. I represent Bruce Feirstein, the writer of the last few Pierce Brosnan James Bond films. For *Tomorrow Never Dies*, he had to sit for three weeks and try to envision a scene that had never appeared in any Bond film before. His solution was the remote controlled BMW—that's what it takes to deliver on something original.

How aggressive should a writer be in getting representation?

Tip

Saunders: A writer should be very aggressive in promoting his material, but he also needs the goods. If you're going to shout at me how great you are, you'd better be that great.

Canterna: You are a business like Starbucks. You have to promote yourself in all the same ways. I'm not looking for the Don King Effect here—in other words, hype and no substance. When I order that coffee it better be the best coffee I ever had, or I'm not going to consider buying it again because there's too much competition. And you have to be on every street corner in this town.

Should a writer try to capitalize on trends for you to consider them?

Hernandez: You should create the market rather than let the market create you.

Bauer Greer: By the time a writer gets material to market, that market has passed him or her by.

Bartlett: What everyone is really looking for is the other side of the horizon—what they can't see now.

Saunders: Films aren't timely. It just takes too long for the studios to bring something to the screen.

What's more important to you when you're considering a writer's work—a solid, well-constructed story or a good concept?

Bartlett: What's it like to be a firefighter, an angel, a mutant? Which racehorse had the most heart? How painful is it to live inside a mind that's brilliant but diseased? I can only (initially) go to the movies to get those questions answered. If you want melodrama, you can get that on TV. If you want unexplored worlds on a grand scale, you typically have to come to the movies to do that. I only want to represent a script that takes me and whoever is reading it into those unexplored worlds.

Saunders: I really hate to say this, but concept is key. I can sell a concept a lot easier than I can sell a well-told story that doesn't have a strong conceptual basis.

From Script to Screen

Formatting and Submitting Your Script

by Jerry Jackson, Jr.

The days of the screenwriter struggling over a manual typewriter trying to set margins and line spaces are long over. With computers and spell check, there is no excuse for typos or improper formatting. The mark of a serious writer is attention to detail, and agents and production companies will often discard manuscripts that show incorrect formatting or numerous spelling errors.

FORMATTING YOUR SCRIPT

A properly formatted script allows a trained reader to quickly and accurately gauge its running time, while also making it easy to identify key requirements such as talent, locations, and props. One of the best ways to get an understanding of proper script structure is to read as many formatted scripts as you can. In general, margins are set in pica type and the industry standard font for text is Courier; word processing manuals can help you set up your page.

Character names, props, and sounds

When writing a script, it's important to CAPITALIZE THE NAME OF EVERY CHARACTER. No matter how minor the character may be, everyone from ADAM to ZOE to A WAITER, must be indicated in capital letters in your script.

Likewise, it is essential that you CAPITALIZE ANY IMPORTANT PROPS OR SOUNDS. If it's important that the audience hears a gunshot in the background, make it stand out on the page in capital letters. The same goes for props. If we need to see the murder weapon in the main character's desk drawer, CAPITALIZE IT—THE BLOODY KNIFE WAS IN THE TOP RIGHT-HAND CORNER OF THE DESK DRAWER.

Slug lines

Slug lines indicate a location/camera change. A sample slug line would be ''INT. JOHN'S BEDROOM'' which means the action is taking place in John's bedroom, which is an interior location. If your characters move into the bathroom, even if it's attached to John's bedroom, then you need a new slug line.

Paragraph structure

Paragraphs should never exceed five lines. In most cases, paragraphs should be somewhere between one and three sentences long. Sometimes you may need to break up some of the

JERRY JACKSON, JR. is a writer/editor in Cincinnati, Ohio. He was an editor for *Writer's Digest* magazine and executive editor of *Scriptwriting Secrets* magazine between 2000 and 2003.

longer paragraphs in your script; other times, you'll need to rewrite the longer paragraphs so you can condense them into one or two lines. The reason paragraphs should not exceed five lines is because the action and dialogue are the most important elements of your script. Obviously, no one in the theater is going to read your long, descriptive paragraphs of the scenes. More to the point, a director is likely to ignore your descriptive paragraphs completely unless they are essential to the script.

Formatting resources

Two of the most commonly read books on script formatting are *The Complete Guide to Standard Script Formats* (CMC Publishing), by Hillis Cole & Judith Haag, and *Elements of Style for Screenwriters* (Lone Eagle Publishing Co.), by Paul Argentini. Depending on your level of computer savvy, you may or may not have trouble transferring the formatting instructions in these books into actual settings on your computer.

For those who don't want to study the industry-standard format of scripts, you can invest in a software program like Final Draft (www.finaldraft.com) or Movie Magic Screenwriter (www.screenplay.com) that automatically formats your script according to the appropriate genre.

Useful
Websites

SUBMITTING YOUR SCRIPT

As obvious as it may seem, the first step to submitting your script to an agent or production company is writing it. It's a myth that screenwriters make fortunes in Hollywood simply by selling "ideas." The reality is: There is no such thing as a screenwriter who doesn't write scripts.

Your script is what opens doors for you as a screenwriter. You can have the most impressive résumé in the business with a list of film and television credits as long as your arm, but if you don't have a good script (or the ability to write a good script in a very short period of time) no one is going to hire you as a screenwriter. Furthermore, no one is going to pay you for an "idea." Ideas, no matter how wonderful they might sound, are a dime a dozen. If you give the same idea to a dozen writers, you'll get a dozen completely different scripts. What matters in this business is the execution of that idea, the specific character traits, dialogue, and plot turns that make a good script. Here's an example: "A sports team made up of players without a shred of athletic talent struggle to overcome far superior opponents. Through perseverance and blind luck, the team transforms from an underdog into a playoff contender." Is this the idea behind *The Bad News Bears*, *Major League*, or *Necessary Roughness*? The answer: All three.

Every year, hundreds of amateur screenwriters attempt to sue production companies, studios, and networks claiming that someone stole their "idea" for a film or television show. What most people don't know is that about 99.9 percent of these cases are thrown out of court before trial because these claims just aren't true. There are about 9,000 professional screenwriters and tens of thousands of aspiring writers throwing out ideas every year. With those kinds of numbers, similarity of ideas is inevitable. In Hollywood legal terms, it's called "simultaneous creation." We all watch the same TV shows, movies, news broadcasts, and plays. We all read the same books, magazines, and newspapers. When multiple people are exposed to the same stimuli, they can develop very similar ideas. Your friends and family might think you have an original idea, but there are tens of thousands of other creative souls out there, and at least one of them has had the same idea.

Copyright issues

Copyright does not protect ideas or concepts. Copyright protects you from someone stealing your story, but you need to be able to prove three things in court: 1) you created the story before the other person; 2) the other person had access to your story before they created their version of the story; and 3) there are unique elements to your story that have been used in the other person's story.

New scriptwriters worry about having their ideas stolen all the time. Since you cannot copyright your idea and can only copyright the way in which you tell the story, it is highly recommended that you write a complete script before you hand over the idea. Again, your script is your key to the front door of Hollywood.

Spec scripts

Your script should not simply be a good idea sewn together with the same kind of dialogue you've seen on the big and small screen; it should be better. Hollywood is flooded with scripts sent in on speculation (on spec) by would-be writers and from professional writers whose shows have been cancelled and are looking for work. A highly rated television show, for example, may receive as many as 4,000 such scripts every year, excluding several thousand more from agents.

So, your spec script must stand out from the rest. It must be polished until each line of dialogue shines, and each scene progresses both the characters and the plot. Why do you have to work so hard on your script? Because one of the few things people in Hollywood agree on is that a good script will find its way to an agent or producer. Your spec script proves to the Hollywood establishment that you know how to tell a story through dialogue, how to format your script properly, how to write for existing characters or invent entertaining ones of your own, how to make your audience feel an emotion, and how to craft a compelling plot—in short, how to write.

THE TOOLS YOU NEED

In the world of film and television, there are four tools you may need if you want to convince an agent or producer you have a great script: a logline, a synopsis, a treatment, and a pitch.

Logline

In short, a logline is one or two enticing sentences (about 25-35 words total) used to convince an agent or a producer to request a script. A logline can be a great selling tool and is usually used in query letters. If someone is interested in your logline, he may ask to see your script or a synopsis. The bottom line: If you can't summarize your script in one or two brief sentences, you either don't know what your script is about or your script is poorly written—which is precisely why agents and producers want writers to include loglines in queries.

Synopsis

A synopsis is a one- to three-page summary of the situation (plot), main characters, and the important action in your script. The trick to a good synopsis is not to get bogged down in description. The only details you need in a synopsis are those that are essential to helping an agent or producer understand your script and spark their interest.

Treatment

A treatment is a longer and more detailed synopsis usually written at the request of a studio, producer, or agent. The purpose of a treatment is to identify and solve any problems in your script's core elements. A treatment is essentially a written outline of your script.

Experienced writers know a strong treatment may entice a producer into paying the writer to write a fresh script. That said, a treatment is not a shortcut to success for new writers who haven't established themselves. Few producers are interested in developing a script if they are unfamiliar with your work. The lesson here: Your finished script is still your most salable commodity.

A treatment needs to be as polished as your finished script and packed with information. It is written in paragraph form, using quotation marks for dialogue, and can run anywhere from 5 to 30 pages depending on the script. A treatment should always be written in the present tense, single-spaced, with paragraphs separated by a line of space rather than indented. A general guideline is to summarize the beginning of your script in one page, the middle in two or three pages, and the end in one page. Keep the focus on the main characters, their relationships, and the emotional undercurrent of the story, the key plot points, and your theme. Remember that a treatment should be written at the request of a producer or agent. In a standard Writers Guild of America (WGA) contract, the writer is due almost a third of his salary for the treatment part of the assignment. This should drive home the point that producers and agents expect a detailed story and character development in a treatment.

Tip

Pitch

Even if an agent or producer rejects your script, he or she still may like your writing style and invite you to ''pitch'' more ideas in person or over the phone. It may seem antithetical that a writer should be asked to explain his ideas orally, but pitches serve a purpose: The WGA won't allow writers to be asked to write something without being paid, so you have to tell people your ideas before getting a contract to write them.

Your ''pitch'' is essentially an extended logline: A short (one to three sentences) description of your script, which you can expand upon to add detailed information as you generate interest from an agent or producer. For example, the pitch for *Life as a House* might have started something like this: ''A middle-aged man with a failed marriage and a failed career suddenly discovers he has only months to live. He begins a monumental project that draws in his son and ex-wife, and reestablishes ties of love.'' From that starting point the writer can provide more information about the story, characters, and plot twists, focusing on whatever elements seem to spark the interest of the agent or producer.

Think of the way you describe an interesting movie you've seen to a friend. You're enthusiastic, you summarize the big picture, you answer questions about details, and you get to the point. This is exactly what you do when you pitch. You're essentially telling an agent or producer about a wonderful film they haven't seen, but that you've seen in your head. Remember to keep it brief.

A pitch can last from a few seconds to as much as 15 minutes if the agent or producer is interested and keeps asking for more information. Be sure to go to a pitch meeting armed with several ideas. If the first one sinks, you'll have something to say if the agent asks, ''So what else are you working on?''

FINDING AN AGENT

Once you've polished your script to perfection, your next step is finding someone in the business to read it. Enter the agent. Unfortunately, getting an agent to represent you might be harder than getting your first film produced.

Here's the paradox: Agents need to read what you've written to decide if they'll represent you. And even though agents are always looking for the next hot property, many say they won't read unsolicited scripts. They might, however, read a query letter.

Your first step is to find an agent who's willing to read your script. One of the best methods of accomplishing this is to have a friend who is already represented recommend you and your script to his agent. If a current client recommends you, the agent is already more interested in you than any of the other unsolicited scripts in his slush pile. The biggest agencies (Creative Artists Agency, International Creative Management, and William Morris) won't accept unsolicited scripts unless you're recommended by one of their current clients. You don't need to be related to one of the agent's current clients—just find someone who has an agent, get him to read your script or listen to your pitch, and convince him to put in a good word for you.

Useful Websites

Another common way to find an agent is to ''cold call'' or to submit query letters to agents listed here in *Guide to Literary Agents* or the list of agents published by the WGA West (www.wga.org). Not all agents are open to new writers, and some agents are very specific about the kind of writers they work with (only TV drama writers, only feature film comedy writers, only sitcom writers, etc.), so pay attention to the specific information contained in the listings, and don't call or send queries to agents that don't handle your kind of material. If an agent likes your query, he will call and either ask for the complete script or ask for a more detailed pitch.

Contacting Agents

How to Write a Query Letter

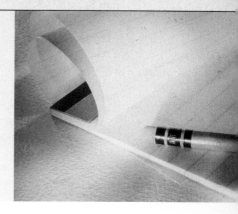

by Kathryn S. Brogan

The query letter is the catalyst in the chemical reaction of publishing. Overall, writing a query letter is a fairly simple process that serves one purpose—getting an agent or editor to read your manuscript. A query letter is the tool that sells you and your book using brief, attention-getting text.

Generally speaking, a query letter has basic elements that are shared when pitching both novels and nonfiction books, but there are some differences you should consider depending on whether you have written fiction or nonfiction.

Query letters for novels

A general rule of thumb when querying an agent for a fiction manuscript: Do not query the agent about your novel until the entire manuscript is written and ready to be sent.

A query letter for a work of fiction generally follows a short, six-paragraph structure that contains the following elements.

- **The hook.** Usually, your first paragraph should be written to "hook" the agent, and get him to request a few chapters or the whole manuscript. The hook usually is a special plot detail or a unique element that's going to grab the agent's attention.
- **About the book.** It is important you provide the agent with the "technical" statistics about your book: title, genre, and word count. Evan Marshall, an agent and the author of *The Marshall Plan for Getting Your Novel Published* (Writer's Digest Books), says that an easy way to estimate your manuscript's word count is to multiply the number of manuscript pages by 250 and then round that number to the nearest 10,000.

Step By Step

- **The story.** This is the part of your letter where you provide a summary of your plot, introduce your main characters, and hint at the main conflict that drives the story. Be careful not to go overboard here (both in content and length): Only provide the agent with the basic elements needed to make a decision about your manuscript.
- **The audience.** You need to be able to tell the agent who the intended audience is for your novel. Many writers find it helpful to tell the agent the theme of their novel, which then, in turn, signifies the intended audience and to whom the novel will appeal.
- **About you.** Tell the agent who you are and how you came to write your novel. In this paragraph, you should only provide those qualifications that are relevant to your novel. List any special qualities you have for writing a book in your genre. Also, list any writing

---

KATHRYN S. BROGAN is the editor of *Writer's Market*, *Writer's Market Deluxe Edition*, and *Guide to Literary Agents*.

groups to which you belong, publishing credentials, awards won, etc. Remember, though, if you don't have any of the above credits, don't stress your inexperience or dwell on what you haven't done.

- **The closing.** Make sure you end your query on a positive and optimistic note. That means you should thank the agent for his time and offer to send more information (a synopsis, sample chapters, or the complete manuscript), upon the agent's request. Be sure to mention you've enclosed a self-addressed, stamped envelope (SASE) for the agent's convenience.

Query letters for nonfiction books

Unlike fiction manuscripts, it is okay to query an agent about a nonfiction book before the manuscript is complete.

Generally, a query letter for a nonfiction book contains many of the same elements found in a query for a novel.

- **The referral.** Why are you contacting this particular agent? On a recommendation from an author he currently represents? Due to an acknowledgement in a book he has represented? Because the agent has a strong track record of selling books on the subject about which you're writing? No matter the answer, knowing what type of work the agent represents shows him you're a professional.
- **The hook.** The hook is usually a special detail or a unique element that's going to grab the agent's attention and pull him in. Often, nonfiction writers use statistics or survey results, especially if the results are astoundingly unique, to reel in the agent.
- **About the book.** It's important to provide the agent with the ''technical'' statistics about your book, including the title and ''sales handle.'' The ''handle'' is a short, one-line statement that explains the primary goal of your book. Agent Michael Larsen, in his book *How to Write a Book Proposal, 3rd Edition* (Writer's Digest Books), says that a book's handle ''may be its thematic or stylistic resemblance to one or two successful books or authors,'' for example ''*Fast Food Nation* meets fashion.'' Essentially, the handle helps the agent decide whether your book is a project he can sell.
- **Markets.** Tell the agent who will buy your book (i.e., the audience) and where people will buy it. Research potential markets according to various demographics (including age, gender, income, profession, etc.), and then use the information to find solid, concrete figures that verify your book's audience is significant enough to convince the agent that your book should be published—and he should represent it! The more you know about the potential markets for your book (usually the top three or four markets), the more professional you appear.
- **About you.** Tell the agent who you are, and why you are the best person to write this book. In this paragraph, you should only provide qualifications that are relevant to your book, including your profession, academic background, publication credentials (as they relate to the subject of your book), etc.
- **The closing.** Make sure you end your query on a positive and optimistic note. That means you should thank the agent for his time, and tell him what items you have ready to submit (mini-proposal, proposal, sample chapters, complete manuscript, etc.), upon his request. Also mention that you've enclosed a SASE or postcard for the agent's convenience.

Formatting a query letter

There are no hard-and-fast rules when it comes to formatting your query letter, but there are some general, widely accepted guidelines like those listed below which are adapted from

Step By Step

Formatting & Submitting Your Manuscript, by Jack and Glenda Neff, and Don Prues (Writer's Digest Books), that cross industry lines. (Editor's Note: See *Formatting & Submitting Your Manuscript Edition 2*, by Cynthia Laufenberg and the Editors of Writer's Digest Books for more information.)

- Use a standard font or typeface (avoid bold, script, or italics, except for publication titles), like 12-point Times New Roman.
- Your name, address, and phone number (plus e-mail address and fax, if possible) should appear in the top right corner or on your letterhead. If you would like, you can create your own letterhead so you appear professional. Simply type the same information listed above (name, address, etc.), center it at the top of the page, and print or photocopy it on quality paper.
- Use a 1-inch margin on all sides.
- Address the query to a specific agent. Note: The listings in *Guide to Literary Agents* provide a contact name for all submissions.
- Keep the letter to one page.
- Include a SASE or postcard for reply, and state in the letter you have done so, preferably in your closing paragraph.
- Use block format (no indentations, extra space between paragraphs).
- Single-space the body of the letter and double-space between paragraphs.
- Thank the agent for considering your query letter.

Reminder

Query letter mistakes to avoid

For More Info

- **DON'T** use any "cute," attention-getting devices like colored stationery or odd fonts.
- **DON'T** send any unnecessary enclosures, such as a picture of you or your family pet.
- **DON'T** waste time telling the agent you're writing to him in the hopes that he will represent your book. Get immediately to the heart of the matter—your book.
- **DON'T** try to "sell" the agent by telling him how great your book is or comparing it to those written by best-selling authors.
- **DON'T** mention that your family, friends, or "readers" loved it.
- **DON'T** send sample chapters that are not consecutive chapters.

Contacting Agents

The Perfect Pitch

by Donald Maass

Y ou have done it. Your breakout novel is complete. Your critique group raves; you have taken a leap in your writing, they say. You think so, too. This one was more work, a lot more. You are proud. You are also nervous. Will the folks in New York publishing recognize what you have accomplished?

Are you even sure yourself?

Whether or not you have written your breakout novel is a major question. Riding on the answer is years of work, lots of hope, perhaps the only shot you feel that you will ever have at the top of your publisher's list. You probably believe that this is *it*: the make-or-break book. If this doesn't work, you certainly are not going to go to this much trouble ever again!

So, who or what decides whether this is indeed your breakout novel? Your agent? Your editor? His editorial board? An auction? Catalog position? The media in 20 cities? The sales force? The bookstore chains? I have some good news and some bad news, and they are the same: The jury that will decide whether or not you have written your breakout novel is the public.

That is bad news because publication is a year or more away; plus, there are so many other factors that influence a book's success in the retail marketplace: cover, promo, season, timing, competition.

The good news is that if you have indeed written your breakout novel, chances are some people along the road to publication are going to think so, too.

THE PITCH

Query letter, fax, phone call, e-mail? The guidebooks (like *Guide to Literary Agents*) will tell you what each agent prefers. Generally speaking, skip fax and e-mail. The first feels arrogant (I don't know why but it does), and the second is too casual. If you have an offer from a publisher in hand, a phone call is appropriate, if a little nerve-wracking.

With no offer in hand, a query letter with SASE (that is, a self-addressed stamped envelope with sufficient postage to return to you the agent's reply and/or your material) is a business-like way to make your first approach.

Do not be intimidated by the legendary volume of agents' query mail, the so-called "slush pile." A well-written letter and a solid premise always stand out.

DONALD MAASS is president of the Donald Maass Literary Agency in New York, which he founded in 1980. Excerpted from *Writing the Breakout Novel* copyright © 2002 by Donald Maass. Used with permission of Writer's Digest Books, an imprint of F + W Publications, Inc. Visit your local bookseller or call 1-800-754-2912 to obtain your copy.

Now, the pitch: Why are novelists so bad at selling their own stories? Never mind, I know why. This is the crucial moment, though, when it pays to practice the art of the pitch. A good query letter has four components: introduction, summary, credentials, closing. The first and last should be, and usually are, short. It is the middle two that give people problems.

The summary

How to sum up your long, layered breakout novel in 100 to 200 words? It is a challenge, but there are guidelines. First, remember the purpose of your query letter is not to tell the whole plot or to convince me you are the hottest new writer since last week. Rather, the purpose of your query is simply to get me to read your manuscript. With that in mind, a summary gets easier.

The setting, protagonist, and problem

There are only three things you need to get me, or anybody, hooked on a story: setting, protagonist, problem. Deliver those briefly and with punch, and you have a basic pitch. Conveying some of your story's layers is a tougher challenge. My advice is to be brief and to focus on the elements that lend your story plausibility (its real-world inspiration, briefly stated, can help), inherent conflict, originality, and gut emotional appeal.

Things to avoid in your pitch

No-no's to avoid are adjectives, superlatives, and anything more than a word or two on your theme.

Also, skip all that junk about the size of the audience for your novel. Your ambition, years of effort, professional attitude, willingness to promote, etc., are also unnecessary. You are ahead of yourself. What matters at this stage is your story.

Items you may want to include in your pitch

Publishing credentials can be helpful to include. Prior novel publications always make me sit up and take notice, although self-publication has the opposite effect—unless it resulted in an Edgar Award nomination, or similar. Short story sales to recognized magazines are also good. Journalistic experience, professional articles, ad writing and the like are nice but do not imply skill as a novelist.

What if you have never been published? What if this is your first piece of writing? No doubt about it, you may have a tough time persuading any top agent that your book is worth a look. The novel is a vastly complicated art form that takes years to master. For that reason, I am happier to hear that the offered manuscript is the author's third or fourth. That said, the right first novel pitched well can be a big winner.

There are other things that get my attention, too. A M.F.A. in writing or study with a reputable teacher are pluses. So are referrals from published novelists. The best recommendation of all, needless to say, is a novel that sounds dynamite. Work on your pitch. Mention your models. If your premise is good, your approach professional, and your skill evident, it is entirely possible to interest even a top New York agent.

CONTACTING AGENTS

The Art of the Synopsis

by Evan Marshall

Many new writers think that when their manuscripts are finished, their work is done. Wrong! Nowadays agents and editors are likely to ask to see a synopsis as well as your manuscript. As a marketing tool, the synopsis is even more important than the query letter—though if your query letter isn't just right, you won't reach the synopsis stage at all.

Too often at my agency I hear something to the effect of, "Why should I have to write a synopsis of my novel? I've already written the novel!" Or, "By the time I finish the synopsis, I could have half the novel written!"

Unfortunately, the synopsis is a necessary tool you're going to have to learn to master if you want to make it as a novelist. It's something agents need; very often, in response to a query letter, they will ask to see a synopsis and the first three chapters of your novel, or they may ask to see the synopsis alone. Everyone works differently.

Editors, too, need a synopsis. They often request that a writer or agent include one with the manuscript. Why? Editors are extremely overworked and must plow through mountains of material. A simple way to find out whether a novel is worth spending a lot of time on is to read the sample chapters, and if the writing is appealing, read the synopsis to see if the writer also knows how to plot a good story. Those are the two factors agents and editors look for in their hunt for new talent: good writing and good storytelling.

SYNOPSIS BASICS

So what, exactly, *is* a synopsis? It's a summary of your novel, written in a way that conveys the excitement of the novel itself.

The synopsis is always written in the present tense. In the synopsis, you tell your *whole* story. You do not—even in the case of a mystery—leave out the solution in an attempt to induce an agent or editor to request the manuscript. Nor do you pick up where your sample chapters leave off. As mentioned above, your synopsis is your novel—your entire novel—in miniature.

See Also

There's no hard-and-fast rule about how long a synopsis should be, but most agents and editors agree that a too-long synopsis defeats its own purpose. Some agents and editors request extremely short synopses (see The Short Synopsis on page 49), which aren't really

EVAN MARSHALL is a successful literary agent and author with nearly 30 years of publishing experience. Excerpted from *The Marshall Plan for Getting Your Novel Published* copyright © 2003 by Evan Marshall. Used with permission of Writer's Digest Books, an imprint of F+W Publications, Inc. Visit your local bookseller or call 1-800-754-2912 to obtain your copy.

synopses at all, but more like jacket or cover copy, or what Hollywood calls "coverage." As a rule, I like to aim for a page of synopsis for every 25 pages of manuscript. This would mean a 400-page manuscript gets a synopsis of about 16 pages. But this rule is often broken, depending on the novel itself. A mystery, for example, may require a longer synopsis because of the level of detail that must be presented. Eventually, you'll find yourself allowing your synopses to seek their own length, and that they'll almost always come out about right.

To achieve such conciseness, you must write as clean and tight as you know how. Don't do what many writers do and try to keep boiling down your actual novel until it's short enough. Instead, learn to write in a synoptic style—read a section or chapter of your novel and simply retell it, as you might describe a great book or movie to a friend.

Leaving out unnecessary adverbs and adjectives, focus on your story's essential points. Much must be left out, such as inconsequential specifics of a particular incident.

Actual dialogue from your novel is rarely needed, though a few chosen lines can be effective. Remember, overall, that whereas in a novel you should *show* rather than *tell*, in a synopsis you *should* tell. Here, it's okay simply to write: *Yvette is furious*, though you would not write that in your novel, you would show us how Yvette's anger manifests itself.

Write your synopsis as one unified narrative. Don't divide it into sections or chapters. Use paragraphing and short transitions to signify these breaks.

Professional novelists know how to put together a synopsis that makes agents and editors sit up and take notice—and ask for the manuscript.

SYNOPSIS SPECIFICS
The hook

To create an arresting hook for your synopsis, start with your story's lead character and the crisis that has befallen him—the crisis that begins the story. Then explain what your lead must do in order to remedy the crisis; in other words, what is his story goal? For example:

> RHONDA STERN has always considered herself immune to the danger and unpleasantness of the outside world, quietly creating tapestries in the house she occupies alone on lush, secluded Bainbridge Island, Washington. But the world intrudes in a horrible way when one morning a desperate criminal breaks into Rhonda's home and takes her hostage, threatening to kill her if she doesn't help him get off the island. Now Rhonda must fight to save her life while at the same time trying not to help a man she knows is guilty of murder.

The back-up

Right after your hook paragraph, back up a little to give some further background that makes the situation clearer. This is where you should also make sure you've covered the basics: your lead's age, occupation, marital status (if you haven't already given us this information in the hook); the time (past—if so, when?—present, or future); and the place.

The meat

Now move on to the action of your story. Give us not only the things that happen to make up your plot, but also how your lead character feels about them or is affected by them.

So many synopses are dull because the author has left out the emotional component. Remember that people read novels primarily to be moved emotionally; they want to live the story through the lead. The only way they can do that is to know how the lead feels. In other words, emotions and feelings are plot; they are as important as the things that happen.

Words are precious in the synopsis, so pick the best ones you can! Use strong action words, and keep the action crisp, clean, and clear.

Formatting your synopsis

Type your real name (not a pseudonym if you are using one).

Your novel's genre.

Double space twice.

Type your name (or pseudonym if you are using one).

Indent first paragraph and start text of synopsis.

Use sluglines as shown.

Your name   Mystery
Your street address
City, State ZIP code
Day and evening phone numbers
E-mail address

TOASTING TINA

by

Evan Marshall

    RHONDA STERN has always considered herself immune to the danger and unpleasantness of the outside world, quietly creating tapestries in the house she occupies alone on lush, secluded Bainbridge Island, Washington. But the world intrudes in a horrible way when one morning a desperate criminal breaks into Rhonda's home and takes her hostage, threatening to kill her if she doesn't help him get off the island. Now Rhonda must fight to save her life while at the same time trying not to help a man she knows is guilty of murder.

    Rhonda, a blonde, ethereally beautiful 24-year-old, has heard about

Marshall/TOASTING TINA/Synopsis2

a string of murders on the island, but the authorities believe the killer has already escaped to the mainland. But he's here, in her house, and now Rhonda finds herself wishing she hadn't asked her husband to move out only two weeks ago.

    The intruder, who introduces himself as RYDER CANNON, barricades himself and Rhonda in her workroom, allowing her to leave only to get him some food. He is limping and she soon discovers why: He has an ugly gash in his upper thigh—the work, he says, of a neighbor's vicious dog. He's bleeding profusely. He tells Rhonda to bring him some rags to wrap around the wound, and as she watches him her heart goes out to him, in spite of what she believes he's done, for under his

Think miniature

Very often in a novel, there are secrets and other information that must at some point be revealed. For some reason, many writers believe that in a synopsis they must reveal all of this information right up front. Not so. In your synopsis, reveal secrets and other surprising information in exactly the same spots where you have done so (or intend to do so) in the novel itself.

Stay out of it

Don't let your scaffolding show. By this I mean don't use devices that suggest the mechanical aspects of your story. This is another reason you shouldn't run character sketches at the beginning of the synopsis, or use headings within the synopsis such as *Background* or *Setting*. Work these elements smoothly into the synopsis; give us background when it's necessary for the reader to understand something.

Pace it right

As you near the end of your story, indicate its quickened pace by using shorter paragraphs that give a speeded-up, staccato effect. For example:

> Rhonda stands at the edge of the bridge, her gaze locked on Ryder as he slips deeper into the water. At the other end of the bridge, Denis cries out to her, begging her to believe he's not the killer.

The short synopsis

Tip

Here are some tips for writing a short synopsis:

- Use the present tense.

- Lead off with a strong hook sentence—anything that will grab the attention of your reader.

- Paragraph only for broad transitions in your story.

- Use no dialogue.

- Quickly introduce your lead, the opposition, the romantic interest, and any other important characters, while setting up the story in terms of place and time.

- Quickly state the conflict between your lead and the opposition; then state the lead's story goal.

- Stick to the high points of your lead's main story line.

- Do not include any subplots.

- Move smoothly from one event to another; avoid the choppiness often seen in beginners' short synopses—a result of having whittled down a longer synopsis without regard for smoothness of reading.

- Use powerful verbs and few, if any, adverbs and adjectives.

- Tell the entire story.

Maximum drama

This is your novel in miniature, and you want to leave the reader of your synopsis with the same great feeling he'll have after reading your book. The way to do that is to slow down a little at the novel's end, after the story has resolved itself, and really bear down on the emotional elements. These are what produce that goose-bumps-at-the-back-of-the-neck feeling when we finish a wonderful novel. Go into more detail here; give us a line of dialogue if that's appropriate.

Polish it

The editing of your synopsis is, in a way, more important than the editing of your book—though I would never tell you it's okay to do less than your best work on either.

Because a synopsis is more brief than a novel, errors stand out more clearly. Make yours as close to perfect as you can, even if that means several rounds of editing. Check for misspelled words, awkward sentence structure, confusing writing, grammatical errors, and typographical errors. Be consistent in referring to your characters: don't write *Ryder* in one place and *Gannon* in another. Stick with one name for each character to avoid confusion.

Make it your business to master the synopsis. Don't be one of those writers who says, "I just can't write a synopsis." They're usually the writers who get the poorer deals or no deal at all.

The synopsis is a necessary tool for a novelist, as, say, the preliminary study is for many painters. Once you get the technique down, you'll probably even find synopsis writing fun.

Professional Proposals

Creating a Nonfiction Proposal

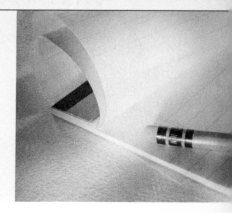

by Michael Larsen

Some writers find it easier to write a book than a proposal. For others, writing the proposal is the most creative part of producing a book. Why? Because you have the freedom to plan the book in the way that excites you most without bearing the responsibility for writing it, changing your vision to suit your publisher's needs, or being pressured by the deadline that comes with a contract.

Even one of the following 10 hot buttons can excite editors enough to buy your book:

1. Your idea
2. Your title
3. Your writing
4. Your credentials
5. Your book's timing
6. Your ability to promote your book
7. The size of the markets for your book
8. Your book's subsidiary-rights potential
9. Your book's potential for bulk sales to businesses
10. Your book's potential as a series of books that sell each other

Your job: Push as many hot buttons as you can.

As competitive books prove, there is not just one way to write a proposal any more than there is just one way to write a book. My approach has evolved over the last three decades, and it continues to evolve as editors' needs change.

Most proposals range from 30 to 50 pages. Your proposal will have three parts (the introduction, the outline, and the sample chapter) in a logical sequence, each of which has a goal. Your goal is to impress agents and editors enough with each part of your proposal to convince them to go on to the next.

THE INTRODUCTION

Your introduction should prove that you have a marketable, practical idea and that you are the right person to write about it and promote it. The introduction has three parts: the

MICHAEL LARSEN is a literary agent in San Francisco. In 1972, Larsen and his wife Elizabeth started Michael Larsen/ Elizabeth Pomada Literary Agents. Excerpted from *How to Write a Book Proposal, 3rd ed.* copyright © 2003 by Michael Larsen. Used with permission of Writer's Digest Books, an imprint of F + W Publications, Inc. Visit your local bookseller or call 1-800-754-2912 to obtain your copy.

Preparing your proposal

DO type on one side of 8 1/2 x 11, 20-pound bond paper.

DO number pages consecutively, not by section or chapter.

DO use a standard 12-point typeface (like Times New Roman).

DO type 25, 10-word, 60-character lines, about 250 words on a page.

DON'T leave "widows"— a sub-head at the bottom of a page, or the last line of a chapter at the top.

DO use running headers as shown.

DON'T justify the right margin.

DON'T add extra spaces between paragraphs.

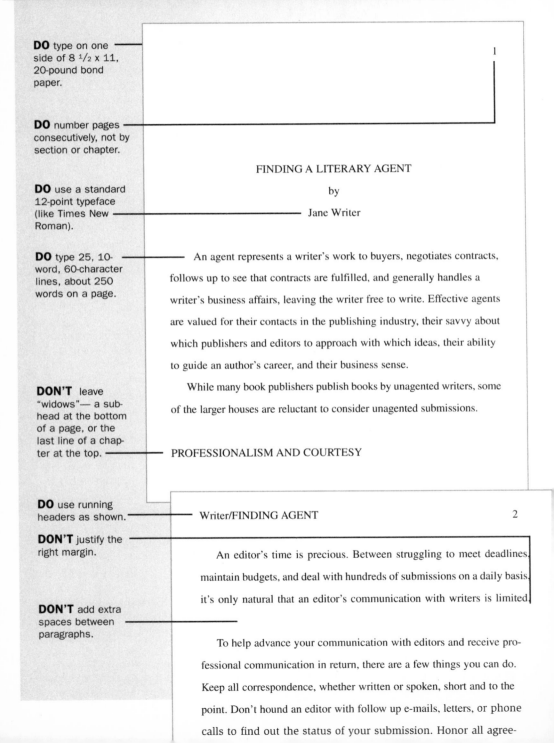

1

FINDING A LITERARY AGENT

by

Jane Writer

An agent represents a writer's work to buyers, negotiates contracts, follows up to see that contracts are fulfilled, and generally handles a writer's business affairs, leaving the writer free to write. Effective agents are valued for their contacts in the publishing industry, their savvy about which publishers and editors to approach with which ideas, their ability to guide an author's career, and their business sense.

While many book publishers publish books by unagented writers, some of the larger houses are reluctant to consider unagented submissions.

PROFESSIONALISM AND COURTESY

Writer/FINDING AGENT   2

An editor's time is precious. Between struggling to meet deadlines, maintain budgets, and deal with hundreds of submissions on a daily basis, it's only natural that an editor's communication with writers is limited.

To help advance your communication with editors and receive professional communication in return, there are a few things you can do. Keep all correspondence, whether written or spoken, short and to the point. Don't hound an editor with follow up e-mails, letters, or phone calls to find out the status of your submission. Honor all agree-

"overview," "resources needed to complete the book," and "about the author." They give you the opportunity to provide as much ammunition about you and your book as you can muster.

The Overview

The overview consists of 12 parts, 9 of which are optional:

Your subject hook: This is the most exciting, compelling thing that you can write in as few words as possible that justifies the existence of your book. Use a quote, event, fact, trend, anecdote, statistic, idea, or joke. For example, your subject hook could be an anecdote about someone using your advice to solve a problem followed by a statistic about the number of people with the problem.

Your book hook: This includes your title, your selling handle, and the length of your book:

- **Your title:** The titles for most books have to tell and sell. Make sure yours says what your book is and gives browsers an irresistible reason to buy it.
- **Your selling handle:** This is a sentence that ideally says, "[*Your book's title*] will be the first book to . . ." You can also use Hollywood shorthand by comparing your book to one or two successful books: "[*Your book's title*] is *Seabiscuit* meets *What to Expect When You're Expecting*."
- **The length of your book (and number of illustrations, if it will have them):** Provide a page or word count for your manuscript that you determine by outlining your book and estimating the length of your chapters and back matter.

Markets for your book: List the groups of people who will buy your book and the channels through which it can be sold, starting with the largest ones.

Your book's special features (Optional): This includes humor, structure, anecdotes, checklists, exercises, sidebars, the tone and style of your book, and anything you will do to give the text visual appeal. Use competitive books as models.

A foreword by a well-known authority (Optional): Find someone who will give your book credibility and salability in 50 states 2 years from now to write a foreword. If getting a foreword isn't possible, write: "The author will contact [names of three potential authorities] for a foreword."

Answers to technical or legal questions (Optional): If your book's on a specialized subject, name the expert who has reviewed it. If your book may present legal problems, name the intellectual-property attorney who has reviewed it.

Your back matter (Optional): Check competitive books to see if your book needs an appendix, a glossary, a resource directory, a bibliography, or footnotes.

Your book's subsidiary-rights possibilities (Optional): Start with the most commercial category, whether it's movie rights, foreign rights, book club rights, or even merchandising rights (for products like T-shirts), which usually require a book to be a bestseller before manufacturers will be interested.

Spin-offs (Optional): If your book can be a series or lend itself to sequels, mention up to five of them in descending order of their commercial appeal.

A mission statement (Optional): If you feel a sense of mission about writing and promoting your book, describe it in one, first-person paragraph.

Your platform (Optional): In descending order of impressiveness, list what you have done and are doing to promote your work and yourself.

Your promotion plan (Optional): List in descending order of importance what you will do to promote your book when and after it's published. If you're writing a reference book or a gift book, you may not need a promotion plan. Also, small and medium-sized houses

A professional presentation

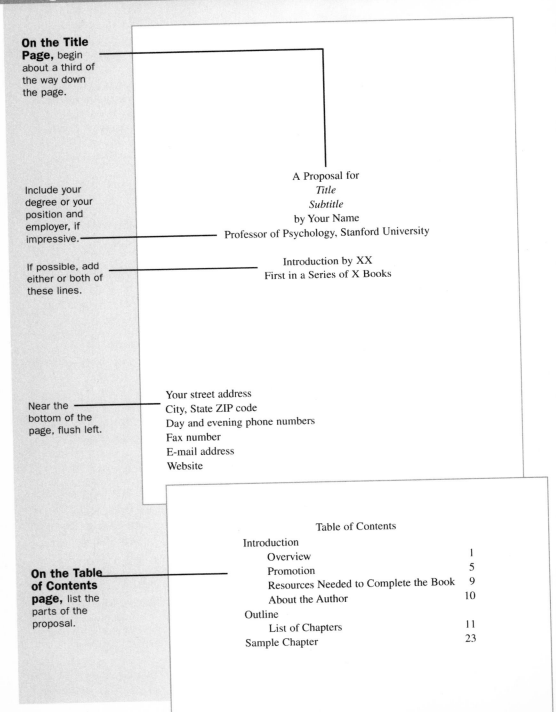

On the Title Page, begin about a third of the way down the page.

Include your degree or your position and employer, if impressive.

If possible, add either or both of these lines.

Near the bottom of the page, flush left.

A Proposal for
Title
Subtitle
by Your Name
Professor of Psychology, Stanford University

Introduction by XX
First in a Series of X Books

Your street address
City, State ZIP code
Day and evening phone numbers
Fax number
E-mail address
Website

On the Table of Contents page, list the parts of the proposal.

Table of Contents

Contacting Agents

outside of New York don't need the promotional ammunition big publishers do. At the beginning of your career, or if your idea or your ability to promote your book isn't as strong as it needs to be to excite Big Apple publishers, you may find small and medium-sized publishers more receptive to your work.

Also list books that will compete with and complement yours. Provide basic information on the half-dozen most important titles.

Resources needed to complete the book

Starting with the largest expense, list out-of-pocket expenses of $500 or more for a foreword, permissions, travel, or illustrations (not for office expenses). Use a round figure for how much each will cost and give the total. (You may decide not to include the dollar amounts when submitting your proposal, but you do have to know what they are because they affect the money you need to write your book as well as the negotiation of your contract.)

About the author

Include everything that you want editors to know about you in descending order of relevance and importance that is not in your platform.

THE OUTLINE

Your outline is a paragraph to a page of prose outlining your chapters to prove that there's a book's worth of information in your idea and that you have devised the best structure for organizing it. Aim for about one line of outline for every page of text you guesstimate; for example, 19 lines of outline for a 19-page chapter. To help make your outlines enjoyable to read, start each one with the strongest anecdote or slice of copy from each chapter, then outline it.

SAMPLE CHAPTER

Include the one sample chapter that best shows how you will make your book as enjoyable to read as it is informative.

Tips for proofreading and submitting

Tip

- **Read aloud,** and follow along with your index finger under each word.
- **Proofread back to front,** so you can concentrate on the words and not be seduced into reading the proposal.
- **Submit without staples.** Always submit your work without any form of binding. Paper clips are acceptable, but they leave indentations.
- **Use paper portfolios.** Insert your proposal in the right-side of a double-pocket portfolio. You can use the left pocket for writing samples, illustrations, supporting documents, and your business card if the left flap is scored. Put a self-adhesive label on the front of the folder with your book's title and your name.
- **Make everything 8 $1/2$ × **11.** This makes it easy to reproduce and submit via mail or e-mail.

Scam Alert!

If you were going into business with another person, you'd make sure you knew him, felt comfortable with him, had the same vision as he did—and that he'd never had trouble with the law or a history of bankruptcy, wouldn't you? As obvious as this sounds, many writers take for granted that any agent who expresses interest in their work is trustworthy. They'll sign a contract before asking any questions, cross their fingers for luck, and simply hope everything will turn out okay.

But don't fall into this trap. Doing a little research ahead of time can save you a lot of frustration later. So how do you check up on an agent? How do you spot a scam before you're already taken in by it?

BEFORE YOU SUBMIT

First, research the agency itself. What kind of reputation does it have? If it's a well-established literary agency and all the agents are members of the Association of Authors' Representatives (AAR), you should be safe from scams.

Useful Websites

All AAR members are required to abide by a certain code of ethics, and they are not permitted to charge any fees to writers. An agent's salary should be earned exclusively with commissions. If you feel an AAR member may be violating the code of ethics, you can contact the AAR at www.aar-online.org or by writing to: The Association of Authors' Representatives, Inc., P.O. Box 237201, Ansonia Station, New York, NY 10003.

A writer should never pay any fees to an agent, including reading fees, retainers, marketing fees, or submission fees. And rather than paying an agent for a critique service, join a writer's group. Invest your time instead of your money. Give feedback to others in exchange for their feedback to you.

BEFORE YOU SIGN

If you have any concerns about the agency's practices, ask the agent about them before you sign. Once an agent is interested in representing you, he should be willing to answer any questions or concerns that you have. If the agent is rude or unresponsive or tries to tell you that information is confidential or classified, the agent is uncommunicative at best and, at worst, is already trying to hide something from you.

An agent should be willing to discuss his recent sales with you: how many, what type of books, and to what publishers. If it's a new agent without a track record, be aware that you're taking more of a risk signing with that agent than with a more established agent. However, even a new agent should not be new to publishing. Many agents were editors before they were agents, or they worked at an agency as an assistant. This experience in publishing is crucial for making contacts in the publishing industry and learning about rights and contracts. So, ask the agent how long he's been an agent and what he did before becoming an agent. Ask the agent to name a few editors off the top of his head who he thinks may be interested in your work and why they sprang to mind. Has he sold to them before? Do they publish books in your genre?

If an agent has no contacts in the business, he has no more clout than you do yourself. Without publishing prowess, the agent's just an expensive mailing service. Anyone can make photocopies, slide them into an envelope, and address them to "Editor." Unfortunately, without a contact name and a familiar return address on the envelope or a phone call from a trusted colleague letting an editor know a wonderful submission is on its way, your work will land in the slush pile with all the other submissions that don't have representation. And you can do your own mailings with higher priority than such an agent could.

Occasionally, an agent will charge for the cost of photocopies, postage, and long-distance phone calls made on your behalf. This is acceptable, so long as he keeps an itemized account of the expenses, and you've agreed on a ceiling cost. Be sure to talk over any expenses, you don't understand until you have a clear grasp of what you're paying for.

Other times, an agent will recognize the value of the content of your work but will recommend hiring an editor to revise it before he is comfortable submitting it to publishers. In this case, the agent may suggest an editor (someone with references you'll check) who understands your subject matter or genre and has some experience getting manuscripts into shape. Occasionally, if your story is exceptional or your ideas and credentials are marketable but your writing needs help, you will work with a ghostwriter or co-author who will share a percentage of your commission or work with you at an agreed upon cost per hour.

An agent may refer you to editors he knows, or you may choose an editor in your area yourself. Many editors do freelance work and would be happy to help you with your writing project. Of course, before entering into an agreement, make sure you know what you'll be getting for your money. Ask the editor for writing samples, references, or critiques he's done in the past. Make sure you feel comfortable working with him before you give him your business.

Important

An honest agent will not make any money for referring you to an editor.

Some agents claim that charging a reading fee cuts down on the number of submissions they receive, and while that is a very real possibility, we recommend writers work with nonfee-charging agents if at all possible. Nonfee-charging agents have a stronger incentive to sell your work. After all, until they make a sale, they don't make a dime.

Agencies who charge fees don't have the same urgency to sell your work. If you do the math, you can see how much money they're bringing in without selling anything: If an agency has 300 clients, each sending in quarterly marketing fees of $100, the agent is making $400 a year from each client. That's $120,000 a year—and that doesn't include the reading fees or any other fees they collect.

AFTER YOU'VE SIGNED

Periodically, you should ask your agent for a full report of where your manuscript has been sent, including the names of the publishing houses and editors. Then, contact a few of the editors/publishers on the list to see if they know your agent and have a strong working relationship with him.

If the agent has ever successfully sold anything to the editor before (or at least sent the editor some promising work before), the editor should remember his name. It's a small world in publishing, and news of an agent's reputation spreads very fast.

But this industry is all about contacts, and if you can't find a worthy agent to make contacts for you, it's entirely possible to do it yourself. Think about it: The agent was once an unknown too. He or she made first contact by knocking on doors or schmoozing at conferences. You can do this too. The doors aren't locked to outsiders; they're just harder to find.

It might seem like making toast before baking the bread, but if you can find an interested editor, publisher, or producer at a conference or by referral, she can probably recommend an agent to you. If you mention a credible person interested in your work, many agents would be delighted to take over the contract negotiations for you. And letting a legitimate agent haggle over your contract instead of going at it yourself will help you keep your rights and negotiate the best advance.

Not everyone has this gift for making contacts, so many writers must rely on agents for the agents' pre-existing contacts. The trouble is, unless you know an agent's track record, you're taking the agent's word for it that he indeed has these contacts. If he doesn't, even if he lives right there in New York, he's no more able to sell your work for you than you are, even if you're living in Massachusetts. So check out the agent's references and make sure he's made recent sales with legitimate publishers or production companies.

As a side note, agents should return clients' phone calls or e-mails quickly and keep the clients informed about prospects. An agent should also consult clients about any offers before accepting or rejecting them.

IF YOU'VE BEEN SCAMMED

If you have trouble with your agent and you've already tried to resolve it yourself to no avail, it may be time to call for help. Please alert the writing community to protect others. If you find agents online, in directories, or in this book who aren't living up to their promises or

If you've been scammed . . .

For More Info

. . . or if you're trying to prevent a scam, the following resources should be of help. You can contact:

- **The Federal Trade Commission, Bureau of Consumer Protection** (CRC-240, Washington DC 20580, 1-877-382-4357). While they won't resolve individual consumer problems, the FTC depends on your complaints to help them investigate fraud, and your speaking up may even lead to law enforcement action. Contact them by mail or phone, or visit their website at www.ftc.gov.

- **Volunteer Lawyers for the Arts** (1 E. 53rd St., New York NY 10022) is a group of volunteers from the legal profession who assist with questions of law pertaining to the arts. You can phone their hotline at (212)319-2787, ext. 1, and have your questions answered for the price of the phone call. For further information you can also visit their website at www.vlany.org.

- **The Better Business Bureau** (check local listings or visit www.bbb.org)—is the organization to contact if you have a complaint or if you want to investigate a publisher, literary agent, or other business related to writing and writers.

- **Your State's Attorney General.** Don't know your attorney general's name? Go to www.attorneygeneral.gov/ags. Here you'll find a wealth of contact information, including a complete list of links to the attorney general's website for each state.

are charging you money when they're listed as nonfee-charging agents, please let the web-master or editor of the publication know. Sometimes they can intervene for an author, and if no solution can be found, they can at the very least remove a listing from their directory so no other authors will be scammed in the future. All efforts are made to keep scam artists out, but in a world where agencies are bought and sold, a reputation can change overnight.

If you have complaints about any business, you can call the Better Business Bureau (BBB) to report them. The BBB will at least file your complaint, and that way, if anyone contacts the BBB before dealing with the business, the BBB will inform them of any unresolved complaints against the business. Their website is www.bbb.org, or you may send a written complaint to: The Council of Better Business Bureaus, 4200 Wilson Blvd., Suite 800, Arlington, VA 22203-1838.

Finally, legal action may seem like a drastic step, but sometimes people do it. You can file a suit with the Attorney General and try to find other writers who want to sue for fraud with you. The Science Fiction Writers of America's website, www.sfwa.org, offers sound advice on recourse you can take in these situations. For further details see: www.sfwa.org/beware/overview.html.)

Useful Websites

If you live in the same state as your agent, it may be possible to settle the case in small claims court. This is a viable option for collecting smaller damages and a way to avoid lawyer fees. The jurisdiction of the small claims court includes cases in which the claim is $5,000

Warning signs! Beware of:

Important

- **Excessive typos or poor grammar** in an agent's correspondence.

- **A form letter accepting you as a client,** praising generic things about your book that could apply to any book. An agent should call or send a personalized letter. A good agent doesn't take on a new client very often, so when she does, it's a special occasion that warrants a personal note or phone call.

- **Unprofessional contracts** that ask you for money up front, contain clauses you haven't discussed, or are covered with amateur clip-art or silly borders.

- **Rudeness** when you inquire about any points you're unsure of. Don't employ any business partner who doesn't treat you with respect.

- **Pressure,** by way of threats, bullying, or bribes. A good agent is not desperate to represent more clients. He invites worthy authors but leaves the final decision up to them.

- **Promises of publication.** No agent can guarantee you a sale. Not even the top agents sell everything they choose to represent. They can only send your work to the most appropriate places, have it read with priority, and negotiate you a better contract if a sale does happen.

- **A print-on-demand book contract** or any contract offering you no advance. You can sell your own book to an e-publisher any time you wish without an agent's help. An agent should pursue traditional publishing routes with respectable advances.

or less. (This varies from state to state but should still cover the amount for which you're suing.) Keep in mind suing takes a lot of effort and time. You'll have to research all the necessary legal steps. If you have lawyers in your family, that could be a huge benefit if they'll agree to help you organize your case, but legal assistance is not necessary.

MOVING ON AND STARTING AGAIN

Above all, if you've been scammed, don't waste time blaming yourself. It's not your fault if someone lies to you. People who scam, cheat, lie, and steal—they'll get what's coming to them. Respect in the literary world is built on reputation, and word about bad agents gets around. Editors ignore their submissions. Writers begin to avoid them. Without clients or buyers, a swindling agent will find his business collapsing.

Meanwhile you'll keep writing and believing in yourself. One day, you'll see your work in print, and you'll tell everyone what a rough road it was to get there but how you wouldn't trade it for anything in the world.

BEFORE YOU SIGN

What Should I Ask?

13 Questions to Ask an Agent

by The Association of Authors' Representatives

The following is a suggested list of topics for authors to discuss with literary agents who have offered to represent them. Please bear in mind that most agents are *not* going to be willing to spend the time answering these questions unless they have already read your material and wish to represent you.

1. Are you a member of the Association of Authors' Representatives?
2. How long have you been in business as an agent?
3. Do you have specialists at your agency who handle movie and television rights? Foreign rights?
4. Do you have subagents or corresponding agents in Hollywood and overseas?
5. Who in your agency will actually be handling my work? Will the other staff members be familiar with my work and the status of my business at your agency?
6. Will you oversee or at least keep me apprised of the work that your agency is doing on my behalf?
7. Do you issue an agent-author agreement? May I review the language of the agency clause that appears in contracts you negotiate for your clients?
8. How do you keep your clients informed of your activities on their behalf?
9. Do you consult with your clients on any and all offers?
10. What are your commission rates? What are your procedures and time-frames for processing and disbursing client funds? Do you keep different bank accounts separating author funds from agency revenue? What are your policies about charging clients for expenses incurred by your agency?
11. When you issue 1099 tax forms at the end of each year, do you also furnish clients, upon request, with a detailed account of their financial activity, such as gross income, commissions and other deductions, and net income, for the past year?
12. In the event of your death or disability, what provisions exist for my continued representation?
13. If we should part company, what is your policy about handling any unsold subsidiary rights in my work?

Know Your Rights

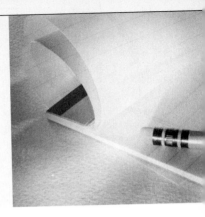

Most writers who want to be published envision their book in store fronts and on their friends' coffee tables. They imagine book signings and maybe even an interview on *Oprah*. Usually the dream ends there; having a book published seems exciting enough. In actuality, a whole world of opportunities exists for published writers beyond seeing their books in print. These opportunities are called "subsidiary rights."

Subsidiary rights, or sub-rights, are the additional ways that a book can be presented. Any time a book is made into a movie or excerpted in a magazine, a subsidiary right has been sold. If these additional rights to your book are properly "exploited," you'll not only see your book in a variety of forms, but you'll also make a lot more money than you would have on book sales alone.

Unfortunately, the terminology of subsidiary rights can be confusing. Phrases like "secondary rights," "traditional splits," or "advance against royalty" could perplex any writer. And the thought of negotiating the terms of these rights with a publisher can be daunting.

Although there are many advantages to working with agents, the ability to negotiate sub-rights is one of their most beneficial attributes. Through experience, an agent knows which publishing houses have great sub-rights departments. If the agent knows a house can make money with a right, the agent will grant that right to the publisher when the contract is negotiated. Otherwise, the agent will keep, or "retain," certain rights for her clients, which she will try to exploit by selling them to her own connections. In an interview in a previous *Guide to Literary Agents*, writer Octavia Butler said that working with an agent, "is certainly a good thing if you don't know the business. It's a good way to hang onto your foreign and subsidiary rights and have somebody actively peddling those rights because there were years when I lived off subsidiary rights."

Important

If you want to work with an agent, you should have a basic understanding of sub-rights for two reasons. First, you'll want to be able to discuss these rights with your agent intelligently. (Although, you should feel comfortable asking your agent any question you have about sub-rights.) Secondly, different agents have more expertise in some sub-right areas than others. If you think your book would make a great movie, you should research the agents who have strong film connections. A knowledge of sub-rights can help you find the agent best suited to help you achieve your dreams.

An agent negotiates sub-rights with the publishing house at the same time a book is sold. In fact, the sale of certain sub-rights can even determine how much money the publisher offers for the book. But the author doesn't get paid immediately for these rights. Instead, the author is paid an "advance against royalties." An advance is a loan to the author that is paid back when the book starts earning money. Once the advance is paid, the author starts earning royalties, which are a pre-determined percentage of the book's profit.

The agent always keeps certain rights, the publisher always buys certain rights, and the others are negotiated. When an agent keeps a right, she is then free to sell it at will. If she does sell it, the money she receives from the purchasing company goes immediately to the author, minus the agent's commission. Usually the companies who purchase rights pay royalties instead of a one-time payment.

If the publisher keeps the right, any money that is made from it goes toward paying off the advance. Because the publisher kept the right, they will keep part of the money it makes. For most rights, half the money goes to the publisher and half goes to the writer, although for some rights the percentages are different. This separation of payment is called a "traditional split" because it has become standard over the years. And, of course, the agent takes her commission from the author's half.

Most agents have dealt with certain publishers so many times that they have pre-set, or "boilerplate," contracts, which means they've already agreed to the terms of certain rights, leaving only a few rights to negotiate. The following describes the main sub-rights and discusses what factors an agent takes into account when deciding whether or not to keep a right. As you read through this piece, carefully consider the many opportunities for your book, and encourage your agent and publisher to exploit these rights every chance they get.

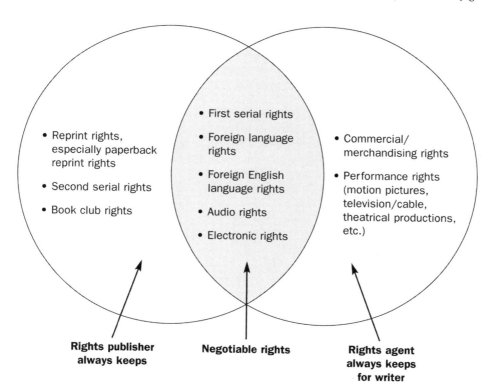

- Reprint rights, especially paperback reprint rights

- Second serial rights

- Book club rights

- First serial rights

- Foreign language rights

- Foreign English language rights

- Audio rights

- Electronic rights

- Commercial/ merchandising rights

- Performance rights (motion pictures, television/cable, theatrical productions, etc.)

Rights publisher always keeps   **Negotiable rights**   **Rights agent always keeps for writer**

RIGHTS THE PUBLISHER ALWAYS KEEPS

The following sub-rights are always kept by the publisher and are often called "nonnegotiable rights." Money earned from these rights is split between the publisher and the author, and the author's share goes toward paying back the advance. Selling these rights helps repay the advance faster, which hopefully means the writer will receive royalty checks sooner.

Reprint rights

In publishing, a "reprint right" refers to the paperback edition of the book. When a hardcover book is reprinted in paperback, the reprint right has been used. According to Donald Maass of the Donald Maass Literary Agency, "In deals with major trade publishers, it's a long-standing practice to grant them control of reprint rights. However, in some cases, a small-press deal, for instance, we withhold these rights." Traditionally, if a hardcover book sold really well, paperback houses bought the rights to reprint the book in a more affordable version. Any money earned from the paperback was then split 50/50 between the publisher and writer. Paperback houses often paid substantial amounts of money for these reprint rights.

But the recent consolidation of publishing houses has changed the value of reprint rights. "In the old days, most books were hardcover, and paperbacks were cheap versions of the book," explains Maass. "Today so many paperback publishers have either merged with a hardcover publisher or begun their own hardcover publisher that the business of selling reprint rights has diminished." Now many publishers make what is called a "hard/soft deal," meaning the house will first print the book in hardcover and, if the book sells well, they reprint the book in paperback. This type of deal can still benefit writers because they no longer have to split the money earned from reprint with the publisher. Instead, the writer earns royalties from both the hardcover and paperback versions.

Book club rights

These days it seems that a book club exists for every possible interest. There are the traditional book clubs, like Book-of-the-Month and its paperback counterpart, the Quality Paperback Book Club. But there are also mystery book clubs, New Age book clubs, book clubs for writers and artists, and even online book clubs. Most book clubs are very selective, and you should be flattered if your book is chosen for a book club. Like reprint rights, any money made from book club rights is split 50/50 between the publisher and the writer. If an agent believes a book will appeal to a certain book club's audience, the agent will target the manu-script to publishers who have good relationships with—or who own—that book club.

Serial rights

A serial is an excerpt of the book that appears in a magazine or in another book. To have your book serialized is wonderful because excerpts not only make additional money for you but they also provide wonderful publicity for your book. There are actually two types of serial rights: first serial and second serial. First serial means the excerpt of the book is avail-able before the book is printed. A second serial is an excerpt that appears after the book is already in bookstores. First serial rights are actually negotiable; sometimes the right to use them is kept by the agent. Usually an agent's decision is based upon her knowledge of the publications available in the book's subject. If she doesn't know the various magazines, she will let the publisher have this right. Second serial rights, however, are almost always granted to the publisher.

Nonfiction books are more commonly excerpted than fiction. Nonfiction excerpts usually stands alone well, and magazines are eager to use these excerpts because they usually cost less than hiring a freelancer to write original material. Recently, though, serialized fiction has regained popularity. A few years ago, John Grisham's *A Painted House* (Doubleday, 2001) made a giant splash by appearing in six installments in *The Oxford American*.

RIGHTS NEGOTIATED BETWEEN THE AGENT AND PUBLISHER

The owner of these sub-rights is always determined when the book is sold. Often an agent and editor must compromise for these rights. In other words, an agent may agree to sell foreign rights if she can keep electronic rights. Or an editor will offer more money if he can obtain the audio rights to a book.

Foreign language rights

If your book might appeal to audiences in a non-English-speaking country, then you'll want an agent who has good connections with foreign co-agents. According to James Vines of The Vines Agency, Inc., a "foreign co-agent is someone who specializes in the sales of foreign publishing rights and who has good relationships with the heads of publishing houses throughout the world. These agents work on behalf of a New York City agency and approach the foreign publishers with manuscripts and proposals. They will typically have appointments booked at big trade shows like Frankfurt Book Fair, London Book Fair, and BookExpo America. That's where a lot of the big foreign deals happen." Usually an agent charges a 20 percent commission when a foreign co-agent is used, and the two split the earnings.

"All of my clients have benefited from the sale of foreign rights," continues Vines. "For example, *Kokology* (Fireside, 2003), by Tadahiko Nagao and Isamu Saito started as a big phenomenon in Japan, selling over 4 million copies. A game you play about psychology, it's one of those ideas that crosses all languages and cultural boundaries because it's uniquely human. We all want to know more about ourselves." Vines sold the book to Simon & Schuster, and then worked with a co-agent to sell it all over the world.

When agents are considering how a book will do abroad, they must be aware of trends in other countries. "Most agents try to stay on top of the foreign markets as much as possible and listen to what foreign co-agents have to say," says Vines. "Trends vary from territory to territory, and I try to keep those trends in mind." Vines also points out that writers can benefit from different sub-rights over a period of time depending on how well a sub-right is selling.

Many publishing houses have foreign counterparts, and often an agent will grant the publisher these rights if she knows the book can be printed by one of these foreign houses. If the publisher has foreign language rights, the author receives an average of 75 percent of any money made when the book is sold to a foreign publisher.

British rights

Like foreign language rights, the owner of a book's British rights can sell the book to publishers in England. Australia was once included in these rights, but Australian publishers are becoming more independent. If an agent keeps these rights, she will use a co-agent in England and the two will likely split a 20 percent commission. If a publisher has these rights, the traditional split is 80/20 with the author receiving the larger share.

Electronic rights

A few years ago, Stephen King caused a big commotion in the publishing world first by using an electronic publisher for his book, *Riding the Bullet*, and then by self-publishing his serialized novel, *The Plant*. Many publishing professionals worried that King would start a trend drawing writers away from publishers, while others claimed only high-profile writers like King could ever compete successfully against the vast amounts of information on the Web. Regardless, King's achievement showed that readers are paying attention to the Internet.

Basically, electronic rights refer to the hand-held electronic, Internet, and print-on-demand versions of a book. This right is currently one of the hottest points of contention between agents and publishers because the potential for these rights is unknown—it is quite possible that electronic versions of a book will make a lot of money one day.

This area of publishing is changing so rapidly that both agents and editors struggle with how to handle electronic rights. Many publishers believe any version of a book is the same material as the printed book, and, therefore, they should own the rights. Agents worry, however, that if the publisher lets the book go out of print, the rights to the book will never be returned to the author.

Audio rights

Before people feared that the Internet would cause the end of traditional book publishing, people worried that audio versions of books would erase the need to have printed books. In actuality, audio books have complimented their printed counterparts and have proved to be a fantastic source of additional income for the person who owns the rights to produce the book in audio form—whether through cassette tape or compact disc.

Many publishers own audio imprints and even audio book clubs, and if they are successful with these ventures, an agent will likely grant the audio rights to the publisher. The traditional split is 50/50. Otherwise, the agent will try to save this right and sell it to a company that can turn it into a profit.

RIGHTS THE WRITER ALWAYS KEEPS

When a book is sold, an agent always reserves two rights for his authors: performance and merchandising. Some books are naturally more conducive to being made into films or products. And when they do, there is usually a lot of money to be made. And a smart agent can quickly identify when a book will be successful in these areas.

Important

Performance rights

Many writers fantasize about seeing their book on the big screen. And a lot of times, agents share this dream—especially for best-selling titles. If your agent feels your book will work well as a movie, or even as a television show or video game, she will sell these rights to someone in the entertainment industry. This industry works fairly differently than the publishing industry. Usually a producer "options" the right to make your book into a movie. An option means the producer can only make the movie during a specific amount of time, like a year. If the movie isn't made during that time period, the rights revert back to you. You can actually option these rights over and over—making money for every option—without the book ever being made into a movie.

As with foreign rights, agents usually work with another agent to sell performance rights. Usually these agents live in Los Angeles and have the connections to producers that agents outside California just don't have. Agents normally take a 20 percent commission from any money made from performance rights. That 20 percent will be split if two agents partner to sell the rights.

Merchandising rights

Merchandising rights create products—like calendars, cards, action figures, stickers, dolls, and so on—that are based on characters or other elements of your book. Few books transfer well into such products, but they can be successful when they do. Keep in mind that if a producer options the performance rights to your book, the merchandising rights are usually included in the deal.

For example, a few years ago agent Steven Malk, of Writers House, made wonderful use of these two rights for his client Elise Primavera and her book, *Auntie Claus* (Silver Whistle/Harcourt, 1999). According to Malk, "When I first read the manuscript of *Auntie Claus* and saw a couple of Primavera's sample illustrations, I immediately knew the book had a lot of possibilities in the sub-rights realm. First of all, the character of Auntie Claus is extremely memorable and unique, and from a visual standpoint, she's stunning. Also, the basic concept

Listing policy and complaint procedure

For More Info

Listings in *Guide to Literary Agents* are compiled from detailed question-naires, phone interviews, and information provided by agents. The industry is volatile, and agencies change frequently. We rely on our readers for informa-tion on their dealings with agents and changes in policies or fees that differ from what has been reported to the editor of this book. Write to us (*Guide to Literary Agents*, 4700 E. Galbraith Rd., Cincinnati, OH 45236) or e-mail us (literaryagents@fwpubs.com) if you have new information, questions, or prob-lems dealing with the agencies listed.

Listings are published free of charge and are not advertisements. Although the information is as accurate as possible, the listings are not endorsed or guaranteed by the editor or publisher of *Guide to Literary Agents*. If you feel you have not been treated fairly by an agent or representative listed in *Guide to Literary Agents*, we advise you to take the following steps:

- Try to contact the agency. Sometimes one phone call or a letter can clear up the matter.

- Document all your correspondence with the agency. When you write to us with a complaint, provide the name of your manuscript, the date of your first contact with the agency, and the nature of your subsequent correspondence.

We will enter your letter into our files and attempt to contact the agency. The number, frequency, and severity of complaints will be considered in our decision whether or not to delete the listing from the next edition. *Guide to Literary Agents* reserves the right to exclude any agency for any reason.

of the book is completely fresh and original, which is very hard to accomplish with a Christ-mas book.

"The first thing I did was to approach Saks Fifth Avenue with the idea of featuring *Auntie Claus* in their Christmas windows. In addition to using the book as the theme for their window displays, they created some merchandise that was sold through Saks. It's a perfect project for them; the character of Auntie Claus is so sophisticated and refined, and it seemed ideal for their windows. Shortly after that, the movie rights were optioned by Nickelodeon."

Like Malk did for Primavera, many agents successfully exploit subsidiary rights every day. If you want the most for your book, look for an agent who has the know-how and connections to take your publishing dream to its fullest potential. Use the information in this article to help your agent make the most of your subsidiary rights.

Literary Agents

Agents listed in this section generate 98 to 100 percent of their income from commission on sales. They do not charge for reading, critiquing, or editing your manuscript or book proposal. It's the goal of an agent to find salable manuscripts: Her income depends on finding the best publisher for your manuscript.

Because an agent's time is better spent meeting with editors, she will have little or no time to critique your writing. Agents who don't charge fees must be selective and often prefer to work with established authors, celebrities, or those with professional credentials in a particular field.

Some agents in this section may charge clients for office expenses such as photocopying, foreign postage, long-distance phone calls, or Express Mail services. Make sure you have a clear understanding of what these expenses are before signing any agency agreement. While most agents deduct expenses from the advance or royalties a book earns, a few agents included in this section charge their clients a one-time up-front, "marketing" or "handling" fee.

Canadian and international agents are included in this section. Canadian agents have a ◆ icon preceding their listing, and international agents have a ⊕ icon preceding their listing. Remember to include an International Reply Coupon (IRC) with your self-addressed envelope when contacting Canadian and international agents.

SUBHEADS

Each agent/agency listing is broken down into specific subheads to make locating information within the listing easier. In the first section, you'll find contact information for each agency. You'll also learn if the agents within the agency belong to any professional organizations; membership in these organizations can tell you a lot about an agency. For example, members of the Association of Authors' Representatives (AAR) are prohibited from charging reading or evaluating fees. This book contains contact information for all agents who are currently registered with the AAR (www.aar-online.org). Additional information in this section includes the size of each agency, its willingness to work with new or previously unpublished writers, and its general areas of interest.

Useful Websites

Member Agents: Agencies comprised of more than one agent list member agents and their individual specialties. This information will help you determine the appropriate person to whom you should send your query letter.

Represents: This section allows agencies to specify what nonfiction and fiction subjects they represent. Make sure you query only those agents who represent the type of material you write. To help narrow your search, check the **Literary Agents Specialties Index** in the back of the book.

☞ Look for the key icon to quickly learn an agent's areas of specialization. In this portion of the listing, agents mention the specific subject areas they're currently seeking, as well as those areas they do not want to receive.

How to Contact: Most agents open to submissions initially prefer to receive a query letter briefly describing your work (see How to Write a Query Letter on page 41). While some agents may ask for an outline and a specific number of sample chapters, most don't. You should send these items only if the agent requests them. In this section, agents also mention if they accept queries by fax or e-mail; if they consider simultaneous submissions; and how they prefer to solicit new clients.

Recent Sales: To give you a sense of the types of material they represent, the agents list specific titles they've sold, as well as a sampling of clients' names. However, it is important to note that some agents consider their client list confidential and may only share client names once they agree to represent you.

Terms: Provided here are details of an agent's commission; whether a contract is offered and for how long; and what additional office expenses you might have to pay if the agent agrees to represent you. Standard commissions range from 10 to 15 percent for domestic sales, and 15 to 20 percent for foreign or dramatic sales (with the difference going to the co-agent who places the work).

Writers' Conferences: A great way to meet an agent is at a writers' conference. Here agents list the conferences they usually attend. For more information about a specific conference, check the **Writers' Conferences** section starting on page 235.

Tips: In this section, agents offer advice and additional instructions for writers.

See Also

| LEVEL OF OPENNESS | AGENCY'S SPECIALIZATIONS | WHO DO I SEND TO? | AGENT'S PROFESSIONAL BACKGROUND | AREAS OF EXPERTISE |

☑ **ANDREA BROWN LITERARY AGENCY, INC.**
1076 Eagle Dr., Salinas CA 93905. (831)422-5925.Fax: (831)422-5915. E-mail: iwablit@redshift.com.
Contact: Andrea Brown, president. Estab. 1981. 10% of clients are new/unpublished writers. Currently handles: 95% juvenile nonfiction nonfiction books; 5% adult nonfiction and fiction.
  • Prior to opening her agency, Ms. Brown served as an editorial assistant at Random House and Dell Publishing and as an editor with Alfred A. Knopf.
Member Agents: Andrea Brown; Laura Rennert; Caryn Wiseman.
Represents: Nonfiction books (juvenile). **Considers these nonfiction areas:** Animals; anthropology/archaeology; art/architecture/design; biography/autobiography; current affairs; ethnic/cultural interests; history; how-to; juvenile nonfiction; nature/environment; photography; popular culture; science/technology; sociology; sports; All nonfiction subjects for juveniles and adults.
  ☞ This agency specializes in "all kinds of children's books—illustrators and authors." Considers all juvenile fiction areas; all genres of nonfiction.
How to Contact: Query with SASE. Accepts e-mail queries. No fax queries. Considers simultaneous queries. Obtains most new clients through recommendations from others, referrals from editors, clients, and agents.
Terms: Agent receives 15% commission on domestic sales; 20% commission on foreign sales. Offers written contract. Charges clients for shipping costs.
Writers' Conferences: Austin Writers League; SCBWI, Orange County Conferences; Mills College Childrens Literature Conference (Oakland CA); Asilomar (Pacific Grove CA); Maui Writers Conference.

| ADDITIONAL EXPENSES | AGENT'S COMMISSION | WHAT DO I SEND? | CONFERENCES AGENT ATTENDS |

Literary Agents

2005 GUIDE TO LITERARY AGENTS KEYS TO SYMBOLS

ICONS FOR EASY REFERENCE

[N] market new to this edition

Canadian agency

agency located outside of the U.S. and Canada

newer agency actively seeking clients

INDICATES LEVEL OF OPENNESS

agency seeks both new and established writers

agency prefers to work with established writers, mostly obtains new clients through referrals

agency handling only certain types of work or work by writers under certain circumstances

EDITOR'S COMMENT

agency not currently seeking new clients

• comment from the editor of *Guide to Literary Agents*

O━ agency's specializations

ms, mss manuscript(s)

COMMON ABBREVIATIONS

SASE self-addressed, stamped envelope

SAE self-addressed envelope

IRC International Reply Coupon, for use in countries other than your own

(For definitions of words and expressions used throughout the book, see the Glossary. For translations of acronyms of organizations connected with agenting or writing, refer to the Table of Acronyms.)

SPECIAL INDEXES TO REFINE YOUR SEARCH

Literary Agents Specialties Index: In the back of the book on page 274 is an index which organizes agencies according to the subjects they are interested in receiving. This index should help you compose a list of agents specializing in your areas. Cross-referencing categories and concentrating on agents interested in two or more aspects of your manuscript might increase your chances of success.

Agencies Indexed by Openness to Submissions: This index lists agencies according to how receptive they are to new clients.

Geographic Index: For writers looking for an agent close to home, this index lists agents according to the state in which they are located.

Agents Index: Often you will read about an agent who is an employee of a larger agency, and you may not be able to locate her contact information. Starting on page 345 is a list of agents' names in alphabetical order along with the name of the agency for which they work. Find the name of the person you would like to contact, and then check the agency listing.

General Index: This index lists all agencies, independent publicists, production companies, script contests, and writers' conferences appearing in the book.

Ⓝ DOMINICK ABEL LITERARY AGENCY, INC.

146 W. 82nd St., #1B, New York NY 10024. Fax: (212)595-4622. E-mail: agency@dalainc.com. Estab. 1975. Member of AAR. Represents 100 clients. Currently handles: adult nonfiction books; adult novels.
How to Contact: Query with SASE by mail.
Terms: Agent receives 15% commission on domestic sales; 20% commission on foreign sales.

Ⓝ ◪ CAROLE ABEL LITERARY AGENT

160 W. 87th St., New York NY 10024. Fax: (212)724-1384. E-mail: caroleabel@aol.com. Member of AAR. 50% of clients are new/unpublished writers. Currently handles: nonfiction books.
Represents: Nonfiction books.
How to Contact: Query with SASE by mail only. No e-mail or fax queries.
Recent Sales: *Instant Self Hypnosis*, by Forbes Blair (Sourcebooks); *Word Play*, by L. Myers/L. Goodman (McGraw Hill).

⬙ ◪ ACACIA HOUSE PUBLISHING SERVICES, LTD.

51 Acacia Rd., Toronto ON M4S 2K6, Canada. (416)484-8356. Fax: (416)484-8356. E-mail: fhanna.acacia@rogers.com. **Contact:** (Ms.) Frances Hanna. Estab. 1985. Represents 100 clients. Works with a small number of new/unpublished writers. Currently handles: 30% nonfiction books; 70% novels.

- Ms. Hanna has been in the publishing business for 30 years, first in London (UK) as a fiction editor with Barrie & Jenkins and Pan Books, and as a senior editor with a packager of mainly illustrated books. She was condensed books editor for 6 years for *Reader's Digest* in Montreal, senior editor and foreign rights manager for (the then) William Collins & Sons (now HarperCollins) in Toronto. Her husband, vice president Bill Hanna, has over 40 years experience in the publishing business.

Member Agents: Bill Hanna, vice president (business, self-help, modern history).
Represents: Nonfiction books, novels. **Considers these nonfiction areas:** Animals; biography/autobiography; language/literature/criticism; memoirs; military/war; music/dance; nature/environment; theater/film; travel. **Considers these fiction areas:** Action/adventure; detective/police/crime; literary; mainstream/contemporary; mystery/suspense; thriller.

- ○━ This agency specializes in contemporary fiction: literary or commercial. Actively seeking "outstanding first novels with literary merit." Does not want to receive horror, occult, science fiction.

How to Contact: Query with outline and SASE. *No unsolicited mss.* No e-mail or fax queries. Responds in 6 weeks to queries. Returns materials only with SASE.
Recent Sales: Sold over 75 titles in the last year. Also made numerous international rights sales. This agency prefers not to share information on specific sales or clients.
Terms: Agent receives 15% commission on English language sales, 20% on dramatic sales, 25% commission on foreign sales. Charges clients for photocopying, postage, and courier, as necessary.
Tips: "We prefer that writers be previously published, with at least a few short stories or articles to their credit. Strongest consideration will be given to those with, say, 3 or more published books. However, we would take on an unpublished writer of outstanding talent."

Ⓝ ◪ BRET ADAMS LTD. AGENCY

448 W. 44th St., New York NY 10036. (212)765-5630. **Contact:** Bruce Ostler. Member of AAR.

- Query before submitting.

◪ AGENTS, INC., FOR MEDICAL AND MENTAL HEALTH PROFESSIONALS

P.O. Box 4956, Fresno CA 93744. (559)438-8289. **Contact:** Sydney H. Harriet, Ph.D., Psy. D., director. Estab. 1987. Member of APA. Represents 49 clients. 70% of clients are new/unpublished writers. Currently handles: 80% nonfiction books; 20% novels; multimedia.

- Prior to opening his agency, Dr. Harriet was a professor of English, psychologist, and radio and television reporter.

Member Agents: Sydney Harriet, Ph.D., director.
Represents: Nonfiction books, novels. **Considers these nonfiction areas:** Cooking/foods/nutrition; health/medicine (mind-body healing); psychology; science/technology; self-help/personal improvement; sociology; sports (medicine, psychology); law. **Considers these fiction areas:** *Currently representing previously published novelists only.*

- ○━ This agency specializes in writers who have education and experience in the business, legal, and health professions. It is helpful if the writer is licensed but not necessary. Prior nonfiction book publication not necessary. For fiction, previously published fiction is prerequisite for representation. Does not want memoirs, autobiographies, stories about overcoming an illness, science fiction, fantasy, religious materials, and children's books.

How to Contact: Query with SASE. Considers simultaneous queries. Responds in 1 month to queries; 1 month to mss.

Recent Sales: Sold 5 titles in the last year. *Infantry Soldier*, by George Neil (University of Oklahoma Press); *SAMe, The European Arthritis and Depression Breakthrough*, by Sol Grazi, M.D. and Maria Costa (Prima); *What to Eat if You Have Diabetes*, by Danielle Chase M.S. (Contemporary); *How to Turn Your Fat Husband Into a Lean Lover*, by Maureen Keane (Random House).

Terms: Agent receives 15% commission on domestic sales; 20% commission on foreign sales. Offers written contract, binding for 6-12 months (negotiable). Writers reimbursed for office fees after the sale of ms.

Writers' Conferences: "Scheduled as a speaker at a number of conferences across the country in 2005. Contact agency to book authors and agents for conferences."

Tips: "Remember, query first. Do not call to pitch an idea. The only way we can judge the quality of your idea is to see how you write. Please, unsolicited manuscripts will not be read if they arrive without a SASE. Currently, we are receiving more than 200 query letters and proposals each month. Send complete proposal/manuscript only if requested. Please, ask yourself why someone would be compelled to buy your book. If you think the idea is unique, spend the time to create a query and then a proposal where every word counts. Fiction writers need to understand that the craft is just as important as the idea. 99% of the fiction is rejected because of sloppy, overwritten dialogue, wooden characters, predictable plotting, and lifeless narrative. Once you finish your novel, put it away and let it percolate, then take it out and work on fine-tuning it some more. A novel is never finished until you stop working on it. Would love to represent more fiction writers and probably will when we read a manuscript that has gone through a dozen or more drafts. Because of rising costs, we no longer can respond to queries, proposals, and/or complete manuscripts without receiving a return envelope and sufficient postage."

☑ THE AHEARN AGENCY, INC.

2021 Pine St., New Orleans LA 70118-5456. (504)861-8395. Fax: (504)866-6434. E-mail: pahearn@aol.com. **Contact:** Pamela G. Ahearn. Estab. 1992. Member of RWA. Represents 25 clients. 20% of clients are new/unpublished writers. Currently handles: 10% nonfiction books; 90% novels.

● Prior to opening her agency, Ms. Ahearn was an agent for 8 years and an editor with Bantam Books.

Represents: Nonfiction books, novels, short story collections (if stories previously published). **Considers these nonfiction areas:** Animals; child guidance/parenting; current affairs; ethnic/cultural interests; gay/lesbian issues; health/medicine; history; music/dance; popular culture; self-help/personal improvement; theater/film; true crime/investigative; women's issues/studies. **Considers these fiction areas:** Action/adventure; contemporary issues; detective/police/crime; ethnic; family saga; feminist; gay/lesbian; glitz; historical; humor/satire; literary; mainstream/contemporary; mystery/suspense; psychic/supernatural; regional; romance; thriller.

O╼ This agency specializes in historical romance; also very interested in mysteries and suspense fiction. Does not want to receive category romance, science fiction, or fantasy.

How to Contact: Query with SASE. Accepts e-mail queries, no attachments. Considers simultaneous queries. Responds in 8 weeks to queries; 10 weeks to mss. Obtains most new clients through recommendations from others, solicitations, conferences.

Recent Sales: *The Amber Room*, by Steve Berry (Balantine); *The Dragon King's Palace*, by Laura Joh Rowland (St. Martin's); *Dance of Seduction*, by Sabrina Jeffries (Avon).

Terms: Agent receives 15% commission on domestic sales; 20% commission on foreign sales. Offers written contract, binding for 1 year; renewable by mutual consent.

Writers' Conferences: Moonlight & Magnolias; RWA National Conference (Orlando); Virginia Romance Writers (Williamsburg VA); Florida Romance Writers (Ft. Lauderdale FL); Golden Triangle Writers Conference; Bouchercon (Monterey, November); Malice Domestic (DC, May).

Tips: "Be professional! Always send in exactly what an agent/editor asks for, no more, no less. Keep query letters brief and to the point, giving your writing credentials and a very brief summary of your book. If one agent rejects you, keep trying—there are a lot of us out there!"

☑ ALIVE COMMUNICATIONS, INC.

7680 Goddard St., Suite 200, Colorado Springs CO 80920. (719)260-7080. Fax: (719)260-8223. Website: www.ali vecom.com. Estab. 1989. Member of CBA. Represents 200+ clients. 5% of clients are new/unpublished writers. Currently handles: 50% nonfiction books; 30% novels; 4% story collections; 5% novellas; 10% juvenile books; 1% syndicated material.

Member Agents: Rick Christian, president (blockbusters, bestsellers); Jerry "Chip" MacGregor (popular/commercial nonfiction and fiction, new authors with breakout potential); Andrea Christian (gift, women's fiction/

nonfiction, Christian living); Lee Hough (popular/commercial nonfiction and fiction, thoughtful spirituality, children's).

Represents: Nonfiction books, novels, short story collections, novellas. **Considers these nonfiction areas:** Biography/autobiography; business/economics; child guidance/parenting; how-to; memoirs; religious/inspirational; self-help/personal improvement; sports; women's issues/studies. **Considers these fiction areas:** Action/adventure; contemporary issues; detective/police/crime; family saga; historical; humor/satire; literary; mainstream/contemporary; mystery/suspense; religious/inspirational; thriller; westerns/frontier; young adult.

O— This agency specializes in fiction, Christian living, how-to, and commercial nonfiction. Actively seeking inspirational/literary/mainstream fiction and work from authors with established track record and platforms. Does not want poetry, young adult paperback, scripts, dark themes.

How to Contact: Works primarily with well-established, bestselling, and career authors. Returns materials only with SASE. Obtains most new clients through obtains most new clients through recommendations from others. "On rare occasions accepts new clients through referrals."

Recent Sales: Sold 300 titles in the last year. Left Behind Series, by Tim LaHaye and Jerry B. Jenkins (Tyndale); *Let's Roll*, by Lisa Beamer (Tyndale); *The Message*, by Eugene Peterson (NavPress); *Every Man Series*, by Stephen Arterburn (Waterbrook); *Cape Refuge*, by Terri Blackstock (Zondervan).

Terms: Agent receives 15% commission on domestic sales; 10% commission on foreign sales. Offers written contract; 2-month written notice notice must be given to terminate contract.

Tips: "Rewrite and polish until the words on the page shine. Endorsements and great connections may help, provided you can write with power and passion. Network with publishing professionals by making contacts, joining critique groups, and attending writers' conferences in order to make personal connections in publishing and to get feedback. Alive Communications, Inc., has established itself as a premiere literary agency. Based in Colorado Springs, we serve an elite group of authors who are critically acclaimed and commercially successful in both Christian and general markets."

◙ LINDA ALLEN LITERARY AGENCY

1949 Green St., Suite 5, San Francisco CA 94123-4829. (415)921-6437. **Contact:** Linda Allen. Estab. 1982. Member of AAR. Represents 35-40 clients.

Represents: Novels (adult). **Considers these fiction areas:** Literary; mainstream/contemporary.

How to Contact: Query with SASE. Considers simultaneous queries. Responds in 3 weeks to queries. Returns materials only with SASE. Obtains most new clients through recommendations from others.

Recent Sales: This agency prefers not to share information on specific sales.

Terms: Agent receives 15% commission on domestic sales. Charges for photocopying.

◙ ALTAIR LITERARY AGENCY, LLC

P.O. Box 11656, Washington DC 20008. (202)237-8282. Website: www.altairliteraryagency.com. Estab. 1996. Member of AAR. Represents 60 clients. 50% of clients are new/unpublished writers. Currently handles: 80% nonfiction books; 5% novels; 15% children's novelty/activity only.

Member Agents: Andrea Pedolsky, partner; Nicholas Smith, partner.

Represents: Nonfiction books. **Considers these nonfiction areas:** History; money/finance (published journalists only); popular culture; science/technology (history of); sports; illustrated; current events/contemporary issues, museum, organization, and corporate-brand books. **Considers these fiction areas:** Historical (pre-20th century mysteries only).

O— This agency specializes in nonfiction with an emphasis on authors who have credentials and professional recognition for their topic, and a high level of public exposure. Actively seeking solid, well-informed authors who have a public platform for the subject specialty.

How to Contact: Query with SASE or see website for more specific query information. Considers simultaneous queries. Responds in 2-4 weeks to queries; 1 month to mss. Obtains most new clients through recommendations from others, solicitations, author queries.

Recent Sales: *Stillpoint Dhammapada*, by Geri Larkin (Harper SF); *Cutting Edge Runner*, by Matt Fitzgerald (Rodale); *Rules for a Pretty Woman*, by Suzette Francis (Avon); *Genealogy 101*, by Barbara Renick, NGS Series (Rutledge Hill Press); *Solar System*, by Christine Corning Malloy with the American Museum of Natural History (Chronicle Children's Books); *The Introvert Advantage*, by Marti Laney (Workman).

Terms: Agent receives 15% commission on domestic sales; 20% commission on foreign sales. Offers written contract, binding for 1 year; 2-month notice must be given to terminate contract. Charges clients for postage, copying, messengers and Fedex and UPS.

◙ MIRIAM ALTSHULER LITERARY AGENCY

53 Old Post Rd. N., Red Hook NY 12571. (845)758-9408. Fax: (845)758-3118. **Contact:** Miriam Altshuler. Estab.

1994. Member of AAR. Represents 40 clients. Currently handles: 45% nonfiction books; 45% novels; 5% story collections; 5% juvenile books.

• Ms. Altshuler has been an agent since 1982.

Represents: Nonfiction books, novels, short story collections, juvenile books. **Considers these nonfiction areas:** Biography/autobiography; ethnic/cultural interests; history; language/literature/criticism; memoirs; multicultural; music/dance; nature/environment; popular culture; psychology; sociology; theater/film; women's issues/studies. **Considers these fiction areas:** Literary; mainstream/contemporary; multicultural; thriller.

O→ Does not want self-help. mystery, how-to, romance, horror, spiritual, or screenplays.

How to Contact: Query with SASE. Prefers to read materials exclusively. No e-mail or fax queries. Considers simultaneous queries. Responds in 2 weeks to queries; 3 weeks to mss. Returns materials only with SASE. Obtains most new clients through recommendations from others.

Terms: Agent receives 15% commission on domestic sales; 20% commission on foreign sales. No written contract. Charges clients for overseas mailing, photocopies, overnight mail when requested by author.

Writers' Conferences: Bread Loaf Writers' Conference (Middlebury VT, August); Washington Independent Writers Conference (Washington DC, June).

☑ BETSY AMSTER LITERARY ENTERPRISES

P.O. Box 27788, Los Angeles CA 90027-0788. **Contact:** Betsy Amster. Estab. 1992. Member of AAR. Represents over 65 clients. 35% of clients are new/unpublished writers. Currently handles: 65% nonfiction books; 35% novels.

• Prior to opening her agency, Ms. Amster was an editor at Pantheon and Vintage for 10 years, and served as editorial director for the Globe Pequot Press for 2 years. "This experience gives me a wider perspective on the business and the ability to give focused editorial feedback to my clients."

Represents: Nonfiction books, novels. **Considers these nonfiction areas:** Biography/autobiography; child guidance/parenting; ethnic/cultural interests; gardening; health/medicine; history; money/finance; psychology; sociology; women's issues/studies; career. **Considers these fiction areas:** Ethnic; literary; mystery/suspense (quirky); thriller (quirky); women's (high quality).

O→ Actively seeking "strong narrative nonfiction, particularly by journalists; outstanding literary fiction (the next Michael Chabon or Jhumpa Lahiri); witty, intelligent, commercial women's fiction (the next Elinor Lipman or Jennifer Weiner); and high-profile, self-help and psychology, preferably research based." Does not want to receive poetry, children's books, romances, westerns, science fiction.

How to Contact: For fiction, send query, first 3 pages, and SASE. For nonfiction, send query or proposal with SASE. No e-mail or fax queries. Considers simultaneous queries. Responds in 1 month to queries; 2 months to mss. Obtains most new clients through recommendations from others, solicitations, conferences.

Recent Sales: *Rejuvenile: How a New Species of Reluctant Adults is Redefining Maturity*, by Christopher Noxon (Crown); *My Therapist's Dog*, by Diana Wells (Algonquin); *The Reluctant Tuscan*, by Phil Doran (Gotham); *Pen on Fire*, by Barbara DeMarco-Barrett (Harcourt). Other clients include Dwight Allen, Dr. Elaine N. Aron, Dr. Helen Brenner, Robin Chotzinoff, Frank Clifford, Rob Cohen & David Wollock, Jan DeBlieu, María Amparo Escandón, Margaret Lobenstine, Paul Mandelbaum, Wendy Mogel, Sharon Montrose, Joy Nicholson, Katie Singer, Louise Steinman.

Terms: Agent receives 15% commission on domestic sales; 20% commission on foreign sales. Offers written contract, binding for 1-2 years; 3-month notice must be given to terminate contract. Charges for photocopying, postage, long distance phone calls, messengers, and galleys and books used in submissions to foreign and film agents and to magazines for first serial rights.

Writers' Conferences: Squaw Valley; San Diego Writers Conference; UCLA Extension Writer's Program; The Loft Literary Center (Minneapolis).

☑ MARCIA AMSTERDAM AGENCY

41 W. 82nd St., New York NY 10024-5613. (212)873-4945. **Contact:** Marcia Amsterdam. Estab. 1970. Signatory of WGA. Currently handles: 15% nonfiction books; 70% novels; 5% movie scripts; 10% TV scripts.

• Prior to opening her agency, Ms. Amsterdam was an editor.

Represents: Nonfiction books, novels, feature film, TV movie of the week, sitcom. **Considers these nonfiction areas:** Child guidance/parenting; popular culture; self-help/personal improvement. **Considers these fiction areas:** Action/adventure; detective/police/crime; horror; mainstream/contemporary; mystery/suspense; romance (contemporary, historical); science fiction; thriller; westerns/frontier; young adult. **Considers these script subject areas:** Comedy; mainstream; mystery/suspense; romantic comedy; romantic drama.

How to Contact: Submit outline, 3 sample chapter(s), SASE. Responds in 1 month to queries.

Recent Sales: *Rosey in the Present Tense*, by Louise Hawes (Walker); *Flash Factor*, by William H. Lovejoy (Kensington); *Lucky Leonardo*, by Jonathan Canter (Landmark); *Hidden Child*, by Isaac Millman (Frances Foster Books, FSG).

Terms: Agent receives 15% commission on domestic sales; 20% commission on foreign sales; 10% commission on dramatic rights sales. Offers written contract, binding for 1 year. Charges clients for extra office expenses, foreign postage, copying, legal fees (when agreed upon).
Tips: "We are always looking for interesting literary voices."

◙ BART ANDREWS & ASSOCIATES

7510 Sunset Blvd., Suite 100, Los Angeles CA 90046. (310)271-9916. **Contact:** Bart Andrews. Estab. 1982. Represents 25 clients. 25% of clients are new/unpublished writers. Currently handles: 100% nonfiction books.
Represents: Nonfiction books. **Considers these nonfiction areas:** Biography/autobiography; music/dance; theater/film; TV.
    O➜ This agency specializes in nonfiction only, and in the general category of entertainment (movies, TV, biographies, autobiographies).
How to Contact: Query with SASE. Considers simultaneous queries. Responds in 1 week to queries; 1 month to mss.
Recent Sales: Sold 25 titles in the last year. *Roseanne*, by J. Randy Taraborrelli (G.P. Putnam's Sons); *Out of the Madness*, by Rose Books packaging firm (HarperCollins).
Terms: Agent receives 15% commission on domestic sales; 15% (after subagent takes his 10%) commission on foreign sales. Offers written contract. Charges clients for all photocopying, mailing, phone calls, postage, etc; Writers reimbursed for office fees after the sale of ms.
Writers' Conferences: Frequently lectures at UCLA in Los Angeles.
Tips: "Recommendations from existing clients or professionals are best, although I find a lot of new clients by seeking them out myself. I rarely find a new client through the mail. Spend time writing a query letter. Sell yourself like a product. The bottom line is writing ability, and then the idea itself. It takes a lot to convince me. I've seen it all! I hear from too many first-time authors who don't do their homework. They're trying to get a book published, and they haven't the faintest idea what is required of them. There are plenty of good books on the subject and, in my opinion, it's their responsibility—not mine—to educate themselves before they try to find an agent to represent their work. When I ask an author to see a manuscript or even a partial manuscript, I really must be convinced I want to read it—based on a strong query letter—because of wasting my time reading just for the fun of it."

ℕ ⊕ ◙ ANUBIS LITERARY AGENCY

6 Birdhaven Close Lighthorne Heath, Banbury Rd., Warwick, Warwickshire CV35 0BE, Great Britain. 01926 642588. Fax: 01926 642588. E-mail: anubis278@hotmail.com. **Contact:** Steve Calcutt. Estab. 1994. Represents 25 clients. 50% of clients are new/unpublished writers. Currently handles: 100% novels.
    • Prior to becoming an agent, Mr. Calcutt taught creative writing for Warwick University, plus American history—US Civil War.
Member Agents: Steve Calcutt (horror/science fiction).
Represents: Novels. **Considers these fiction areas:** Horror; science fiction; dark fantasy.
    O➜ "We are very keen on developing talented new writers. We give support, encouragement, and editorial guidance." Actively seeking horror fiction. Does not want to receive children's, nonfiction, journalism, or TV/film scripts.
How to Contact: Query with SASE, submit proposal package, outline, IRCs. Returns materials only with SASE or IRCs. No e-mail or fax queries. Responds in 6 weeks to queries; 3 months to mss. Obtains most new clients through solicitations.
Recent Sales: *Odd Folks*, by Tim Lebbon (Dorchester). Other clients include Richard Irvine, Steve Savile, Lesley Asquith, Zoe Sharp, Anthea Ingham, Adam Roberts, Sarah Pinborough, Brett A. Savory, Tim Lebbon.
Terms: Agent receives 15% commission on domestic sales; 20% commission on foreign sales. No written contract.

◙ APPLESEEDS MANAGEMENT

200 E. 30th St., Suite 302, San Bernardino CA 92404. (909)882-1667. **Contact:** S. James Foiles. Estab. 1988. 40% of clients are new/unpublished writers. Currently handles: 15% nonfiction books; 85% novels.
Represents: Nonfiction books, novels. **Considers these nonfiction areas:** True crime/investigative. **Considers these fiction areas:** Detective/police/crime; mystery/suspense.
How to Contact: Query with SASE. Responds in 2 weeks to queries; 2 months to mss.
Recent Sales: This agency prefers not to share information on specific sales.
Terms: Agent receives 10-15% commission on domestic sales; 20% commission on foreign sales. Offers written contract, binding for 1-7 years.
Tips: "Appleseeds specializes in mysteries with a detective who could be in a continuing series because readership of mysteries is expanding."

N 🔲 ARCADIA

31 Lake Place North, Danbury CT 06810. E-mail: arcadialit@att.net. **Contact:** Victoria Gould Pryor. Member of AAR.
Represents: Nonfiction books (readable, serious), novels. **Considers these nonfiction areas:** Biography/autobiography; business/economics; current affairs; history; memoirs; psychology; science/technology; self-help/personal improvement; true crime/investigative; women's issues/studies; medicine; investigative journalism; culture; classical music; life transforming. **Considers these fiction areas:** "I'm drawn to character-driven, well-plotted, imaginative, and unusual fiction, both literary and commercial."

    O—⊓ "I'm a very hands-on agent, necessary in this competitive marketplace. I work with authors on revisions until whatever we present to publishers is as perfect as it can be. I represent talented, dedicated, intelligent, and ambitious writers who are looking for a long-term relationship based on professional success and mutual respect."

How to Contact: Query with SASE. E-mail queries accepted without attachments.
Recent Sales: This agency prefers not to share information on specific sales.

🔲 AUTHENTIC CREATIONS LITERARY AGENCY

875 Lawrenceville-Suwanee Rd., Suite 310-306, Lawrenceville GA 30043. (770)339-3774. Fax: (770)339-7126. E-mail: ron@authenticcreations.com. Website: www.authenticcreations.com. **Contact:** Mary Lee Laitsch. Estab. 1993. Member of AAR, Authors Guild. Represents 70 clients. 30% of clients are new/unpublished writers. Currently handles: 60% nonfiction books; 40% novels.

    • Prior to becoming agents, Ms. Laitsch was a librarian and elementary school teacher; Mr. Laitsch was an attorney and a writer.

Member Agents: Mary Lee Laitsch; Ronald Laitsch; Jason Laitsch.
Represents: Nonfiction books, novels, scholarly books. **Considers these nonfiction areas:** Anthropology/archaeology; biography/autobiography; child guidance/parenting; crafts/hobbies; current affairs; history; how-to; science/technology; self-help/personal improvement; sports; true crime/investigative; women's issues/studies. **Considers these fiction areas:** Action/adventure; contemporary issues; detective/police/crime; family saga; literary; mainstream/contemporary; mystery/suspense; romance; sports; thriller.
How to Contact: Query with SASE. No e-mail or fax queries. Considers simultaneous queries. Responds in 2 weeks to queries; 2 months to mss.
Recent Sales: Sold 20 titles in the last year. *Secret Agent*, by Robyn Spizman and Mark Johnston (Simon & Schuster); *Beauchamp Beseiged*, by Elaine Knighton (Harlequin); *Visible Differences*, by Dominic Pulera (Continuum).
Terms: Agent receives 15% commission on domestic sales; 15% commission on foreign sales. Charges clients for photocopying.
Tips: "We thoroughly enjoy what we do. What makes being an agent so satisfying for us is having the opportunity to work with authors who are as excited about the works they write as we are about representing them."

🔲 AUTHORS & ARTISTS GROUP, INC.

41 E. 11th St., 11th Floor, New York NY 10003. (212)944-9898. Fax: (212)944-6484. **Contact:** Al Lowman, president. Estab. 1984. Represents 50 clients. 25% of clients are new/unpublished writers. Currently handles: 95% nonfiction books; 5% novels.

    • Prior to becoming an agent, Mr. Lowman was an advertising executive.

Member Agents: B.G. Dilworth (nonfiction); Al Lowman (president nonfiction).
Represents: Nonfiction books, novels. **Considers these nonfiction areas:** Biography/autobiography; business/economics; child guidance/parenting; cooking/foods/nutrition; current affairs; education; ethnic/cultural interests; gay/lesbian issues; health/medicine; history; how-to; humor/satire; interior design/decorating; memoirs; money/finance; music/dance; nature/environment; New Age/metaphysics; photography; popular culture; psychology; religious/inspirational; science/technology; self-help/personal improvement; sociology; sports; true crime/investigative; women's issues/studies. **Considers these fiction areas:** Contemporary issues; ethnic; gay/lesbian; humor/satire; mainstream/contemporary; religious/inspirational.

    O—⊓ This agency specializes in celebrity-based autobiographies and self-help books; and any books that bring its readers to "higher ground." Actively seeking fresh, full-length, adult nonfiction ideas and established novelists. Does not want to receive film and TV scripts, children's stories, poetry, or short stories.

How to Contact: Fax 1 page query. Considers simultaneous queries. Responds in 3 weeks to queries. Obtains most new clients through recommendations from others.
Recent Sales: Sold 20 titles in the last year. *Labelle Cuisine*, by Patti Labelle (Broadway); *The Sexy Years*, by Suzanne Somers (Crown); *Chaka!*, by Chaka Khan (Rodale); *Death & Justice*, by Mark Fuhrman (William Morrow); *Superfoods*, by Steven Pratt, M.D., and Kathy Matthews (William Morrow); *Sanity and Grace*, by

Judy Collins (Tarcher). Other clients include Sarah, Duchess of York, Diana Ross, Mary Lou Retton.
Terms: Agent receives 15% commission on domestic sales; 20% commission on foreign sales. Charges clients for office expenses such as postage and photocopying (not to exceed $1,000 without permission of author).

☻ THE AXELROD AGENCY

55 Main St., P.O. Box 357, Chatham NY 12037. (518)392-2100. Fax: (518)392-2944. E-mail: steve@axelrodagency.com. **Contact:** Steven Axelrod. Estab. 1983. Member of AAR. Represents 20-30 clients. 1% of clients are new/unpublished writers. Currently handles: 5% nonfiction books; 95% novels.
  • Prior to becoming an agent, Mr. Axelrod was a book club editor.
Represents: Nonfiction books, novels. **Considers these fiction areas:** Mystery/suspense; romance; women's.
How to Contact: Query with SASE. Considers simultaneous queries. Responds in 3 weeks to queries; 6 weeks to mss. Returns materials only with SASE. Obtains most new clients through recommendations from others.
Recent Sales: This agency prefers not to share information on specific sales.
Terms: Agent receives 15% commission on domestic sales; 20% commission on foreign sales. No written contract.
Writers' Conferences: Romance Writers of America (July).

Ⓝ ☻ JULIAN BACH LITERARY AGENCY

22 E. 71st St., New York NY 10021. Member of AAR.
  • This agency did not respond to our request for information. Query before submitting.

☻ BALKIN AGENCY, INC.

P.O. Box 222, Amherst MA 01004. (413)548-9835. Fax: (413)548-9836. **Contact:** Rick Balkin, president. Estab. 1972. Member of AAR. Represents 50 clients. 10% of clients are new/unpublished writers. Currently handles: 85% nonfiction books; 5% scholarly books; 5% textbooks; 5% reference books.
  • Prior to opening his agency, Mr. Balkin served as executive editor with Bobbs-Merrill Company.
Represents: Nonfiction books, scholarly books, textbooks. **Considers these nonfiction areas:** Animals; anthropology/archaeology; biography/autobiography; current affairs; health/medicine; history; how-to; language/literature/criticism; music/dance; nature/environment; popular culture; science/technology; sociology; translation; travel; true crime/investigative.
  ⌐ This agency specializes in adult nonfiction. Does not want to receive fiction, poetry, screenplays, computer books.
How to Contact: Query with SASE, proposal package, outline. No e-mail or fax queries. Responds in 1 week to queries; 2 weeks to mss. Returns materials only with SASE. Obtains most new clients through recommendations from others.
Recent Sales: Sold 30 titles in the last year. *The Liar's Tale*, (W.W. Norton Co.); *Adolescent Depression*, (Henry Holt); *Eliz. Van Lew: A Union Spy in the Heart of the Confederacy*, (biography, Oxford U.P.).
Terms: Agent receives 15% commission on domestic sales; 20% commission on foreign sales. Offers written contract, binding for 1 year. Charges clients for photocopying and express or foreign mail.
Tips: "I do not take on books described as bestsellers or potential bestsellers. Any nonfiction work that is either unique, paradigmatic, a contribution, truly witty, or a labor of love is grist for my mill."

☻ LORETTA BARRETT BOOKS, INC.

101 Fifth Ave., New York NY 10003. (212)242-3420. Fax: (212)807-9579. E-mail: mail orettabarrettbooks.com. **Contact:** Loretta A. Barrett or Nick Mullendore. Estab. 1990. Member of AAR. Represents 90 clients. Currently handles: 60% nonfiction books; 40% novels.
  • Prior to opening her agency, Ms. Barrett was vice president and executive editor at Doubleday for 25 years.
Represents: Nonfiction books, novels. **Considers these nonfiction areas:** Americana; animals; anthropology/archaeology; biography/autobiography; business/economics; child guidance/parenting; computers/electronic; cooking/foods/nutrition; crafts/hobbies; creative nonfiction; current affairs; education; ethnic/cultural interests; gay/lesbian issues; government/politics/law; health/medicine; history; how-to; language/literature/criticism; memoirs; money/finance; multicultural; music/dance; nature/environment; New Age/metaphysics; philosophy; popular culture; psychology; religious/inspirational; science/technology; self-help/personal improvement; sociology; spirituality; sports; women's issues/studies. **Considers these fiction areas:** Action/adventure; confession; contemporary issues; detective/police/crime; ethnic; family saga; feminist; gay/lesbian; glitz; historical; literary; mainstream/contemporary; mystery/suspense; psychic/supernatural; thriller.
  ⌐ This agency specializes in general interest books. No children's or juvenile.
How to Contact: Query with SASE. No e-mail or fax queries. Considers simultaneous queries. Responds in 6 weeks to queries. Returns materials only with SASE.

Recent Sales: *A Lady First*, by Letitia Baldrige (Viking); *The Singularity is Near*, by Ray Kurzweil (Viking); *Flesh Tones*, by MJ Rose (Ballantine Books); *The Lake of Dead Languages*, by Carol Goodman (Ballantine Books); *The Bad Witness*, by Laura Van Wormer (Mira Books).

Terms: Agent receives 15% commission on domestic sales; 20% commission on foreign sales. Offers written contract. Charges clients for shipping and photocopying.

Writers' Conferences: San Diego State University Writer's Conference; Maui Writer's Conference.

Ⓝ Ⓩ BEACON ARTISTS AGENCY

208 W. 30th St., Suite 401, New York NY 10001. (212)736-6630. Fax: (212)868-1052. **Contact:** Patricia McLaughlin. Member of AAR.

• Query before submitting.

Ⓝ Ⓩ BERMAN, BOALS, & FLYNN, INC.

208 W. 30th St., Room 401, New York NY 10001. (212)868-1068. Fax: (212)868-1052. **Contact:** Judy Boals. Member of AAR.

• Query before submitting.

Ⓩ MEREDITH BERNSTEIN LITERARY AGENCY

2112 Broadway, Suite 503A, New York NY 10023. (212)799-1007. Fax: (212)799-1145. Estab. 1981. Member of AAR. Represents 85 clients. 20% of clients are new/unpublished writers. Currently handles: 50% nonfiction books; 50% fiction.

• Prior to opening her agency, Ms. Bernstein served in another agency for 5 years.

Member Agents: Meredith Bernstein; Elizabeth Cavanaugh.

Represents: Nonfiction books, fiction of all kinds. **Considers these nonfiction areas:** Any area of nonfiction in which the author has an established. **Considers these fiction areas:** Literary; mystery/suspense; romance; thriller; women's.

○┓ This agency does not specialize, "very eclectic."

How to Contact: Query with SASE. No e-mail or fax queries. Considers simultaneous queries. Obtains most new clients through recommendations from others, conferences, also develops and packages own ideas.

Recent Sales: Nancy Pickard, 3-book (women's fiction) deal with Ballantine; *Secret of O Milagre*, by Catherine Mulvaney (Pocket Books); Elizabeth Pantley, untitled book on sleep solutions for kids 2-6 (McGraw Hill).

Terms: Agent receives 15% commission on domestic sales; 20% commission on foreign sales. Charges clients $75 disbursement fee/year.

Writers' Conferences: SouthWest Writers Conference (Albuquereque, August); Rocky Moutnain Writers' Conference (Denver, September); Golden Triangle (Beaumont TX, October); Pacific Northwest Writers Conference; Austin League Writers Conference; Willamette Writers Conference (Portland, OR); Lafayette Writers Conference (Lafayette, LA); Surrey Writers Conference (Surrey, BC.); San Diego State University Writers Conference (San Diego, CA).

Ⓩ DANIEL BIAL AGENCY

41 W. 83rd St., Suite 5-C, New York NY 10024-5246. (212)721-1786. Fax: (309)213-0230. E-mail: dbialagency@juno.com. **Contact:** Daniel Bial. Estab. 1992. Represents under 50 clients. 15% of clients are new/unpublished writers. Currently handles: 95% nonfiction books; 5% novels.

• Prior to opening his agency, Mr. Bial was an editor for 15 years.

Represents: Nonfiction books, novels. **Considers these nonfiction areas:** Animals; anthropology/archaeology; biography/autobiography; business/economics; child guidance/parenting; cooking/foods/nutrition; current affairs; ethnic/cultural interests; gay/lesbian issues; government/politics/law; history; how-to; humor/satire; language/literature/criticism; memoirs; military/war; money/finance; music/dance; nature/environment; New Age/metaphysics; popular culture; psychology; religious/inspirational; science/technology; self-help/personal improvement; sociology; spirituality; sports; theater/film; travel; true crime/investigative; women's issues/ studies. **Considers these fiction areas:** Action/adventure; contemporary issues; detective/police/crime; erotica; ethnic; feminist; gay/lesbian; humor/satire; literary.

How to Contact: Submit proposal package, outline. Responds in 2 weeks to queries. Returns materials only with SASE. Obtains most new clients through recommendations from others, solicitations, "good rolodex"

Recent Sales: This agency recently had a No. 1 *New York Times* bestseller with *Osama Bin Ladin: The Man Who Delcared War on America*, by Yossef Bodansky.

Terms: Agent receives 15% commission on domestic sales; 25% commission on foreign sales. Offers written contract, binding for 1 year with cancellation clause. Charges clients for overseas calls, overnight mailing, photocopying, messenger expenses.

Literary Agents

Tips: "Publishers are looking for authors with platforms—that is, people who already have positioned themselves in order to get their books heard and sold."

BIGSCORE PRODUCTIONS, INC.

P.O. Box 4575, Lancaster PA 17604. (717)293-0247. Fax: (717)293-1945. E-mail: bigscore@bigscoreproductions. com. Website: www.bigscoreproductions.com. **Contact:** David A. Robie, agent; Sharon Hanby-Robie, agent. Estab. 1995. Represents 50-75 clients. 25% of clients are new/unpublished writers.

Represents: Nonfiction and fiction (see website for categories of interest).

O┓ This agency specializes in inspirational and self-help nonfiction and fiction and has over 30 years in the publishing and agenting business.

How to Contact: See website for submission guidelines. Query by e-mail or mail. No fax queries. Considers simultaneous queries. Responds in 2 months to proposals.

Terms: Agent receives 15% commission on domestic sales. Offers written contract, binding for 6 months. Charges clients for expedited shipping, ms photocopying and preparation, and books for subsidiary rights submissions.

Tips: "Very open to taking on new clients. Submit a well-prepared proposal that will take minimal fine-tuning for presentation to publishers. Nonfiction writers must be highly marketable and media savvy—the more established in speaking or in your profession, the better. Bigscore Productions works with all major general and Christian publishers"

N ⊘ VICKY BIJUR LITERARY AGENCY

333 West End Ave., Apt. 5B, New York NY 10023. Member of AAR.

• This agency did not respond to our request for information. Query before submitting.

DAVID BLACK LITERARY AGENCY

156 Fifth Ave., New York NY 10010. (212)242-5080. Fax: (212)924-6609. **Contact:** David Black, owner. Estab. 1990. Member of AAR. Represents 150 clients. Currently handles: 90% nonfiction books; 10% novels.

Member Agents: Susan Raihofer (general nonfiction to literary fiction); Gary Morris (commercial fiction to psychology); Joy E. Tutela (general nonfiction to literary fiction); Linda Loewenthal (nonfiction).

Represents: Nonfiction books, novels. **Considers these nonfiction areas:** Biography/autobiography; business/ economics; government/politics/law; history; memoirs; military/war; money/finance; multicultural; sports. **Considers these fiction areas:** Literary; mainstream/contemporary; commercial.

O┓ This agency specializes in business, sports, politics, and novels.

How to Contact: Query with SASE, outline. No e-mail or fax queries. Considers simultaneous queries. Responds in 2 months to queries. Returns materials only with SASE.

Recent Sales: *Body for Life*, by Bill Phillips with Mike D'Orso (HarperCollins); *Walking with the Wind*, by John Lewis with Micke D'Orso (Simon & Schuster).

Terms: Agent receives 15% commission on domestic sales. Charges clients for photocopying and books purchased for sale of foreign rights.

BLEECKER STREET ASSOCIATES, INC.

532 LaGuardia Place, #617, New York NY 10012. (212)677-4492. Fax: (212)388-0001. **Contact:** Agnes Birnbaum. Estab. 1984. Member of AAR, RWA, MWA. Represents 60 clients. 20% of clients are new/unpublished writers. Currently handles: 75% nonfiction books; 25% novels.

• Prior to becoming an agent, Ms. Birnbaum was a senior editor at Simon & Schuster, Dutton/Signet, and other publishing houses.

Represents: Nonfiction books, novels. **Considers these nonfiction areas:** Animals; biography/autobiography; business/economics; child guidance/parenting; computers/electronic; cooking/foods/nutrition; current affairs; ethnic/cultural interests; government/politics/law; health/medicine; history; how-to; memoirs; military/war; money/finance; nature/environment; New Age/metaphysics; popular culture; psychology; religious/inspirational; science/technology; self-help/personal improvement; sociology; sports; true crime/investigative; women's issues/studies. **Considers these fiction areas:** Ethnic; historical; literary; mystery/suspense; romance; thriller; women's interest.

O┓ "We're very hands-on and accessible. We try to be truly creative in our submission approaches. We've had especially good luck with first-time authors." Does not want to receive science fiction, westerns, poetry, children's books, academic/scholarly/professional books, plays, scripts, short stories.

How to Contact: Query with SASE. No email, phone, or fax queries. Considers simultaneous queries. Responds in 2 weeks to queries; 1 month to mss. Returns materials only with SASE. Obtains most new clients through recommendations from others, solicitations, conferences, "plus, I will approach someone with a letter if his/ her work impresses me."

Literary Agents

Recent Sales: Sold 30 titles in the last year. *The Art of War*, by Bevin Alexander (Crown); *The Dim Sum of All Things*, by Kim Wong Keltner (Morrow/Avon); *Impresario*, by James Maguire (Billboard Books).

Terms: Agent receives 15% commission on domestic sales; 25% commission on foreign sales. Offers written contract; 1-month notice must be given to terminate contract. Charges for postage, long distance, fax, messengers, photocopies, not to exceed $200.

Tips: "Keep query letters short and to the point; include only information pertaining to book or background as writer. Try to avoid superlatives in description. Work needs to stand on its own, so how much editing it may have received has no place in a query letter."

THE BLUMER LITERARY AGENCY, INC.

P.O. Box 20754, Park West Station, New York NY 10025-1516. (212)749-8853. Fax: (212)749-1603. **Contact:** Ms. Olivia B. Blumer. Estab. 2002; Board member of AAR. Represents 34 clients. 60% of clients are new/unpublished writers. Currently handles: 67% nonfiction books; 33% novels.

● Prior to becoming an agent, Ms. Blumer spent 25 years in publishing-subsidiary rights, publicity, editorial.

Represents: Nonfiction and fiction. **Considers these nonfiction areas:** Agriculture/horticulture; animals; anthropology/archaeology; art/architecture/design; biography/autobiography; business/economics; cooking/foods/nutrition; ethnic/cultural interests; health/medicine; how-to; humor/satire; language/literature/criticism; memoirs; money/finance; nature/environment; photography; popular culture; psychology; religious/inspirational; self-help/personal improvement; true crime/investigative; women's issues/studies; crafts/hobbies; interior design/decorating, new age/metaphysics. **Considers these fiction areas:** Detective/police/crime; ethnic; family saga; feminist; historical; humor/satire; literary; mainstream/contemporary; mystery/suspense; regional; thriller.

○→ Actively seeking quality fiction, practical nonfiction, memoir with a larger purpose.

How to Contact: Query with SASE. No e-mail or fax queries. Responds in 2 weeks to queries; 4-6 weeks to mss. Returns materials only with SASE. Obtains most new clients through recommendations from others, but significant exceptions have come from slush pile.

Recent Sales: Sold 14 titles in the last year. *Almost French*, by Sarah Turnbull (Gotham/Penguin); *What Happened to Henry*, by Sharon Pywell (Putnam) Other clients include Joan Anderson, Marialisa Calta, Ellen Rolfes, Mark Forstater, Laura Karr, Liz McGregor, Constance Snow, Lauri Ward, Michelle Curry Wright, Susann Cokal, Dennis L. Smith.

Terms: Agent receives 15% commission on domestic sales; 20% commission on foreign sales. Charges for photocopying, overseas shipping, and Fed Ex/UPS.

REID BOATES LITERARY AGENCY

69 Cooks Crossroad, Pittstown NJ 08867. (908)730-8523. Fax: (908)730-8931. E-mail: boatesliterary@att.net. **Contact:** Reid Boates. Estab. 1985. Represents 45 clients. 5% of clients are new/unpublished writers. Currently handles: 85% nonfiction books; 15% novels; very rarely story collections.

How to Contact: No unsolicited queries of any kind. Obtains most new clients through recommendations from others, new clients by personal referral only.

Recent Sales: Sold 20 titles in the last year. This agency prefers not to share information on specific sales.

Terms: Agent receives 15% commission on domestic sales; 20% commission on foreign sales.

BOOK DEALS, INC.

244 Fifth Ave., Suite 2164, New York NY 10001-7604. (212)252-2701. Fax: (212)591-6211. **Contact:** Caroline Francis Carney. Estab. 1996. Member of AAR. Represents 40 clients. 15% of clients are new/unpublished writers. Currently handles: 85% nonfiction books; 15% novels.

● Prior to opening her agency, Ms. Carney was editorial director for a consumer book imprint within Times Mirror and held senior editorial positions in McGraw-Hill and NYIF/Simon & Schuster.

Represents: Nonfiction books, novels (commercial and literary). **Considers these nonfiction areas:** Business/economics; child guidance/parenting; ethnic/cultural interests; health/medicine (nutrition); history; how-to; money/finance; multicultural; popular culture; psychology (popular); religious/inspirational; science/technology; self-help/personal improvement; spirituality. **Considers these fiction areas:** Ethnic; literary; mainstream/contemporary; women's (contemporary); urban literature.

○→ This agency specializes in highly commercial nonfiction and books for African-American readers and women. Actively seeking well-crafted fiction and nonfiction from authors with engaging voices and impeccable credentials.

How to Contact: Query with SASE. Considers simultaneous queries.

Recent Sales: Sold 25 titles in the last year. *Eat Right for Your Personality Type*, by Dr. Robert Kushner & Nancy Kushner (St. Martin's Press); *Self-Proclaimed*, by Rochelle Shapiro (Simon & Schuster); *Par for the Course*, by Alice Dye and Mark Shaw (HarperCollins).

Terms: Agent receives 15% commission on domestic sales; 20% commission on foreign sales. Offers written contract. Charges clients for photocopying and postage.

Ⓝ Ⓞ BOOK PEDDLERS

15245 Minnetonka Blvd., Minnetonka MN 55345-1510. (612)912-0036. Fax: (612)912-0105. **Contact:** Vicki Lansky. Member of AAR.
- Query before submitting.

BOOKENDS, LLC

136 Long Hill Rd., Gillette NJ 07933. (908)362-0090. E-mail: editor@bookends-inc.com. Website: www.bookends-inc.com. **Contact:** Jessica Faust or Jacky Sach. Estab. 1999. Represents 50 clients. 40% of clients are new/unpublished writers. Currently handles: 50% nonfiction books; 50% novels.
- Prior to opening their agency, Ms. Faust and Ms. Sach worked at such publishing houses as Berkley, Penguin Putnam, Macmillan, and IDG.

Member Agents: Jessica Faust (mysteries, romance [in all areas], chic lit, women's fiction, relationships, parenting, health, women's interest, business, finance, pets, general self-help); Jacky Sach (suspense thrillers, mysteries, romantic suspense, women's fiction, spirituality, pets, general self-help)

Represents: Nonfiction books, novels. **Considers these nonfiction areas:** Animals; biography/autobiography; business/economics; child guidance/parenting; cooking/foods/nutrition; crafts/hobbies; current affairs; ethnic/cultural interests; gay/lesbian issues; health/medicine; how-to; humor/satire; memoirs; money/finance; New Age/metaphysics; psychology; religious/inspirational; self-help/personal improvement; women's issues/studies. **Considers these fiction areas:** Contemporary issues; ethnic; family saga; feminist; glitz; historical; mainstream/contemporary; mystery/suspense; romance; thriller; detective/police/crime/cozies.
- ○┯ BookEnds specializes in genre fiction and personality-driven nonfiction. Actively seeking romance, mystery, women's fiction, literary fiction and suspense thrillers. For nonfiction, relationships, business, general self-help, women's interest, parenting, pets, spirituality, health, and psychology. Does not want to receive children's books, screenplays, science fiction, poetry, technical/military thrillers.

How to Contact: Submit outline, 3 sample chapter(s). Considers simultaneous queries. Responds in 4-6 weeks to queries. 8-10 weeks to samples and ms. Returns materials only with SASE. Obtains most new clients through recommendations from others, solicitations, conferences.

Recent Sales: Sold 70 titles in the last year. *Fabulous Foreplay*, by Dr. Patti Britton (Rodale); *Hoe Lot of Trouble*, by Heather Webber (Avon); *Restylane*, by Dr. Alan Engler and Sonia Weiss (Berkley); *The Night She Died*, by Jennifer Patrick (Soho Press); *Dr. Rachel's Guide to Surviving Multiple Pregnancy* (St. Martin's); *Althea's Chance*, by Barbara Gale (Harlequin); *Down from the Mountain*, by Barbara Gale (Harlequin).

Terms: Agent receives 15% commission on domestic sales; 20% commission on foreign sales. Offers written contract. Charges clients for photocopying, messenger, cables, overseas postage, long-distance phone calls, copies of the published book when purchases for subsidiary rights submissions. Expenses will not exceed $150.

Writers' Conferences: Silken Sands Romance Writers Conference (Pensacola Beach FL, April); OWFI (Oklahoma, April); First Coast Writer's Conference (Florida, May); RWA National; Central Florida Romance Writers Conference (Orlando FL, September); Emerald Coast Writer's Conference (Amarillo TX, June).

Tips: "When submitting material be sure to include any information that might be helpful to the agent. In your query letter you should include the title of the book, your name, your publishing history and a brief 1 or 2 sentence description of the book. Also be sure to let the agent know if you see this book as part of a series and if you've already begun work on other books. Once an agent has expressed interest in representing you it is crucial to let her know who has seen your book and even supply copies of any correspondence you've had with prospective editors."

Ⓞ BOOKS & SUCH

4788 Carissa Ave., Santa Rosa CA 95405. (707)538-4184. Fax: (707)538-3937. E-mail: janet@janetgrant.com. Website: janetgrant.com. **Contact:** Janet Kobobel Grant. Estab. 1996. Member of CBA (associate). Represents 40 clients. 10% of clients are new/unpublished writers. Currently handles: 42% nonfiction books; 46% novels; 2% juvenile books; 10% children's picture books.
- Prior to becoming an agent, Ms. Grant was an editor for Zondervan and managing editor for *Focus on the Family*.

Represents: Nonfiction books, novels, juvenile books. **Considers these nonfiction areas:** Child guidance/parenting; humor/satire; juvenile nonfiction; religious/inspirational; self-help/personal improvement; women's issues/studies. **Considers these fiction areas:** Contemporary issues; family saga; historical; juvenile; mainstream/contemporary; picture books; religious/inspirational; romance; young adult.
- ○┯ This agency specializes in "general and inspirational fiction, romance, and in the Christian booksellers market." Actively seeking "material appropriate to the Christian market."

How to Contact: Query with SASE. Considers simultaneous queries. Responds in 1 month to queries; 2 months to mss. Returns materials only with SASE. Obtains most new clients through recommendations from others, conferences.

Recent Sales: Sold 60 titles in the last year. *Boo Who*, by Renee Gutterridge; *The Weave*, by Nancy Moser; *Gardinia's for Breakfast*, by Robin Jones Gunn. Other clients include Janet McHenry, Jane Orcutt, Gayle Roper, Stephanie Grace Whitson.

Terms: Agent receives 15% commission on domestic sales; 15% commission on foreign sales. Offers written contract; 2-month notice must be given to terminate contract. Charges clients for postage, photocopying, telephone calls, fax, and express mail.

Writers' Conferences: Romance Writers of America; Mt. Hermon Writers Conference (Mt. Hermon CA, March 22-26); Sandy Cove (Maryland, November).

Tips: "The heart of my motivation is to develop relationships with the authors I serve, to do what I can to shine the light of success on them, and to help be a caretaker of their gifts and time."

🌑 GEORGES BORCHARDT, INC.

136 E. 57th St., New York NY 10022. (212)753-5785. Fax: (212)838-6518. Estab. 1967. Member of AAR. Represents 200 clients. 10% of clients are new/unpublished writers. Currently handles: 60% nonfiction books; 37% novels; 1% novellas; 1% juvenile books; 1% poetry.

Member Agents: Anne Borchardt; Georges Borchardt; DeAnna Heindel; Valerie Borchardt.

Represents: Nonfiction books, novels. **Considers these nonfiction areas:** Anthropology/archaeology; biography/autobiography; current affairs; history; memoirs; travel; women's issues/studies. **Considers these fiction areas:** Literary.

○➼ This agency specializes in literary fiction and outstanding nonfiction.

How to Contact: Responds in 1 week to queries; 1 month to mss. Obtains most new clients through recommendations from others.

Recent Sales: Sold 100 titles in the last year. *The Inner Circle*, by T. Coraghessan Boyle (Viking/Penguin); *Fascination*, by William Boyd (Knopf); *A Free World*, by Timothy Garton Ash (Random House).

Terms: Agent receives 15% commission on domestic sales; 20% commission on foreign sales. Offers written contract. "We charge clients cost of outside photocopying and shipping manuscripts or books overseas."

🌑 THE BARBARA BOVA LITERARY AGENCY

3951 Gulfshore Blvd. N., PH1-B, Naples FL 34103. (941)649-7237. Fax: (239)649-7263. Website: www.barbarabovaliteraryagency.com. **Contact:** Barbara Bova. Estab. 1974. Represents 30 clients. Currently handles: 20% nonfiction books; 80% novels.

Represents: Nonfiction books, novels. **Considers these nonfiction areas:** Biography/autobiography; science/technology; self-help/personal improvement; true crime/investigative; women's issues/studies; social sciences. **Considers these fiction areas:** Action/adventure; detective/police/crime; glitz; mystery/suspense; science fiction; thriller.

○➼ This agency specializes in fiction and nonfiction, hard and soft science.

How to Contact: Query with SASE. Obtains most new clients through recommendations from others.

Recent Sales: Sold 6 titles in the last year. *Saturn*, by Ben Bova; *Crystal City*, by Orson Scott Card; *Bone Cold*, by Rick Wilber.

Terms: Agent receives 15% commission on domestic sales; 20% commission on foreign sales.

Tips: This agency also handles foreign rights, movies, television, audio.

🌑 BRANDT & HOCHMAN LITERARY AGENTS, INC.

1501 Broadway, New York NY 10036. (212)840-5760. Fax: (212)840-5776. **Contact:** Carl Brandt; Gail Hochman; Marianne Merola; Charles Schlessiger; Bill Contardi. Estab. 1913. Member of AAR. Represents 200 clients.

Represents: Nonfiction books, novels, short story collections, juvenile books, journalism. **Considers these nonfiction areas:** Biography/autobiography; current affairs; ethnic/cultural interests; government/politics/law; history; women's issues/studies. **Considers these fiction areas:** Contemporary issues; ethnic; historical; literary; mainstream/contemporary; mystery/suspense; romance; thriller; young adult.

How to Contact: Query with SASE. No e-mail or fax queries. Considers simultaneous queries. Responds in 1 month to queries. Returns materials only with SASE. Obtains most new clients through recommendations from others.

Recent Sales: Sold 50 titles in the last year. This agency prefers not to share information on specific sales. Other clients include Scott Turow, Carlos Fuentes, Ursula Hegi, Michael Cunningham, Mary Pope Osborne, Julia Glass.

Terms: Agent receives 15% commission on domestic sales; 20% commission on foreign sales. Charges clients for "manuscript duplication or other special expenses agreed to in advance."

Tips: "Write a letter which will give the agent a sense of you as a professional writer, your long-term interests as well as a short description of the work at hand."

✪ THE JOAN BRANDT AGENCY

788 Wesley Dr., Atlanta GA 30305-3933. (404)351-8877. **Contact:** Joan Brandt. Estab. 1980. Represents 30 clients. 50% of clients are new/unpublished writers. Currently handles: 50% nonfiction books; 50% novels. **Represents:** Nonfiction books, novels, short story collections. **Considers these fiction areas:** Contemporary issues; detective/police/crime; family saga; literary; mainstream/contemporary; mystery/suspense; thriller.
How to Contact: Query with SASE. No e-mail or fax queries. Considers simultaneous queries. Returns materials only with SASE.
Recent Sales: This agency prefers not to share information on specific sales.
Terms: Agent receives 15% commission on domestic sales; 20% commission on foreign sales. No written contract.

N ✪ THE HELEN BRANN AGENCY, INC.

94 Curtis Rd., Bridgewater CT 06752. Member of AAR.
 • This agency did not respond to our request for information. Query before submitting.

N ✪ BARBARA BRAUN ASSOCIATES, INC.

115 W. 18th St., 5th floor, New York NY 10011. **Contact:** Barbara Braun. Member of AAR.
 • This agency did not respond to our request for information. Query before submitting.

N ✪ BROADWAY PLAY PUBLISHING

56 E. 81st St., New York NY 10028-0202. Member of AAR.
 • This agency did not respond to our request for information. Query before submitting.
Member Agents: Christopher Gould.

✪ MARIE BROWN ASSOCIATES, INC.

412 W. 154th St., New York NY 10032. (212)939-9725. Fax: (212)939-9728. E-mail: mbrownlit@aol.com. **Contact:** Marie Brown. Estab. 1984. Represents 60 clients. Currently handles: 75% nonfiction books; 10% juvenile books; 15% other.
Member Agents: Janell Walden Agyeman (Miami, Florida).
Represents: Nonfiction books, juvenile books. **Considers these nonfiction areas:** Art/architecture/design; biography/autobiography; business/economics; ethnic/cultural interests; history; juvenile nonfiction; music/dance; religious/inspirational; self-help/personal improvement; theater/film; women's issues/studies. **Considers these fiction areas:** Contemporary issues; ethnic; juvenile; literary; mainstream/contemporary.
 ⟳ This agency specializes in multicultural and African-American writers.
How to Contact: Query with SASE. Prefers to read materials exclusively. Responds in 6-10 to queries. Obtains most new clients through recommendations from others.
Recent Sales: *Would I Lie to You?*, by Trisha R. Thomas; *The Coyote Kings*, by Malcolm Azania; *Dad Interrupted*, by Van Whitfield.
Terms: Agent receives 15% commission on domestic sales; 20% commission on foreign sales. Offers written contract.

✪ ANDREA BROWN LITERARY AGENCY, INC.

1076 Eagle Dr., Salinas CA 93905. (831)422-5925. Fax: (831)422-5915. E-mail: ablit@redshift.com. **Contact:** Andrea Brown, president. Estab. 1981. 10% of clients are new/unpublished writers. Currently handles: 95% juvenile nonfiction nonfiction books; 5% adult nonfiction and fiction.
 • Prior to opening her agency, Ms. Brown served as an editorial assistant at Random House and Dell Publishing and as an editor with Alfred A. Knopf.
Member Agents: Andrea Brown, Laura Rennert, Caryn Wiseman.
Represents: Nonfiction books (juvenile). **Considers these nonfiction areas:** Animals; anthropology/archaeology; art/architecture/design; biography/autobiography; current affairs; ethnic/cultural interests; history; how-to; juvenile nonfiction; nature/environment; photography; popular culture; science/technology; sociology; sports; all nonfiction subjects for juveniles and adults. **Considers these fiction areas:** Juvenile; young adult; All fiction genres for juveniles.
 ⟳ This agency specializes in "all kinds of children's books—illustrators and authors." Considers all juvenile fiction areas; all genres of nonfiction.
How to Contact: Query with SASE. Accepts e-mail queries. No fax queries. Considers simultaneous queries. Obtains most new clients through recommendations from others, referrals from editors, clients, and agents.

Recent Sales: *Not So Scary Monster Handbook*, by Dave Ross (HarperCollins); *Sasha Lohen Autobiography* (HarperCollins); *The Five Ancestors*, by Jeff Stone (Random House).

Terms: Agent receives 15% commission on domestic sales; 20% commission on foreign sales. Offers written contract. Charges clients for shipping costs.

Writers' Conferences: Austin Writers League; SCBWI, Orange County Conferences; Mills College Childrens Literature Conference (Oakland CA); Asilomar (Pacific Grove CA); Maui Writers Conference; Southwest Writers Conference; San Diego State University Writer's Conference; Big Sur Children's Writing Workshop (Director); William Saroyan Conference; Columbus Writers Conference; Willamette Writers Conference.

Tips: "Query first—so many submissions come in it takes 3-4 months to get a response. Taking on very few picture books. Must be unique—no rhyme, no anthropomorphism. Handling some adult historical fiction."

◘ CURTIS BROWN, LTD.

10 Astor Place, New York NY 10003-6935. (212)473-5400. Also: 1750 Montgomery St., San Fancisco CA 94111. (415)954-8566. **Contact:** Perry Knowlton, chairman; Timothy Knowlton, CEO; Peter L. Ginsberg, president. Member of AAR; signatory of WGA.

Member Agents: Laura Blake Peterson; Ellen Geiger; Emilie Jacobson, vice president; Maureen Walters, vice president; Virginia Knowlton (literary, adult, children's); Timothy Knowlton (film, screenplays, plays; Ed Wintle (film, screenplays, plays); Mitchell Waters; Elizabeth Harding; Kristen Manges; Dave Barber (translation rights).

Represents: Nonfiction books, novels, short story collections, novellas, juvenile books, poetry books, movie scripts, feature film, TV scripts, TV movie of the week, stage plays. **Considers these nonfiction areas:** Agriculture/horticulture; Americana; animals; anthropology/archaeology; art/architecture/design; biography/autobiography; business/economics; child guidance/parenting; computers/electronic; cooking/foods/nutrition; crafts/hobbies; creative nonfiction; current affairs; education; ethnic/cultural interests; gardening; gay/lesbian issues; government/politics/law; health/medicine; history; how-to; humor/satire; interior design/decorating; juvenile nonfiction; language/literature/criticism; memoirs; military/war; money/finance; multicultural; music/dance; nature/environment; New Age/metaphysics; philosophy; photography; popular culture; psychology; recreation; regional; religious/inspirational; science/technology; self-help/personal improvement; sex; sociology; software; spirituality; sports; theater/film; translation; travel; true crime/investigative; women's issues/studies; young adult. **Considers these fiction areas:** Action/adventure; comic books/cartoon; confession; contemporary issues; detective/police/crime; erotica; ethnic; experimental; family saga; fantasy; feminist; gay/lesbian; glitz; gothic; hi-lo; historical; horror; humor/satire; juvenile; literary; mainstream/contemporary; military/war; multicultural; multimedia; mystery/suspense; New Age; occult; picture books; plays; poetry; poetry in translation; psychic/supernatural; regional; religious/inspirational; romance; science fiction; short story collections; spiritual; sports; thriller; translation; westerns/frontier; young adult; women's. **Considers these script subject areas:** Action/adventure; comedy; detective/police/crime; ethnic; feminist; gay/lesbian; historical; horror; mainstream; mystery/suspense; psychic/supernatural; romantic comedy; romantic drama; thriller; western/frontier.

How to Contact: Query with SASE. Prefers to read materials exclusively. *No unsolicited mss.* No e-mail or fax queries. Responds in 3 weeks to queries; 5 weeks to mss. Obtains most new clients through recommendations from others, solicitations, conferences.

Recent Sales: This agency prefers not to share information on specific sales.

Terms: Offers written contract. Charges for photocopying, some postage.

◙ BROWNE & MILLER LITERARY ASSOCIATES

(formerly Multimedia Product Development, Inc.), 410 S. Michigan Ave., Suite 460, Chicago IL 60605-1465. (312)922-3063. E-mail: mail@browneandmiller.com. **Contact:** Danielle Egan-Miller. Estab. 1971. Member of AAR, RWA, MWA, SCBWI. Represents 150 clients. 2% of clients are new/unpublished writers. Currently handles: 60% nonfiction books; 40% novels.

Member Agents: Danielle Egan-Miller.

Represents: Nonfiction books, novels. **Considers these nonfiction areas:** Agriculture/horticulture; animals; anthropology/archaeology; biography/autobiography; business/economics; child guidance/parenting; cooking/foods/nutrition; crafts/hobbies; creative nonfiction; current affairs; ethnic/cultural interests; health/medicine; how-to; humor/satire; juvenile nonfiction; memoirs; money/finance; nature/environment; popular culture; psychology; religious/inspirational; science/technology; self-help/personal improvement; sociology; sports; travel; true crime/investigative; women's issues/studies. **Considers these fiction areas:** Contemporary issues; detective/police/crime; ethnic; family saga; glitz; historical; juvenile; literary; mainstream/contemporary; mystery/suspense; picture books; religious/inspirational; romance (contemporary, gothic, historical, regency, western); sports; thriller.

    o—ᴙ "We are generalists looking for professional writers with finely honed skills in writing. We are partial to authors with promotion savvy. We work closely with our authors through the entire publishing process, from proposal to after publication.'' Actively seeking highly commercial mainstream fiction and nonfiction. Does not want to receive poetry, short stories, plays, screenplays, articles, children's books.

How to Contact: Query by mail, SASE required. *No unsolicited mss.* Prefers to read material exclusively. Responds in 1 month to queries. Returns materials only with SASE. Obtains most new clients through ''referrals, queries by professional, marketable authors.''

Terms: Agent receives 15% commission on domestic sales; 20% commission on foreign sales. Offers written contract, binding for 2 years. Charges clients for photocopying, overseas postage, faxes, phone calls.

Writers' Conferences: BEA (June); Frankfurt Book Fair (October); RWA (July); CBA (July); London International Book Fair (March); Boucheron (October).

Tips: ''If interested in agency representation, be well informed.''

N ✉ JOANNE BROWNSTEIN

502 Bloomfield Ave., #1, Hoboken NJ 07030. **Contact:** Joanne Brownstein. Member of AAR.
• Query before submitting.

N ✉ KNOX BURGER ASSOCIATES, LTD.

10 W. 15th St., Suite 1914, New York NY 10011. Member of AAR.
• This agency did not respond to our request for information. Query before submitting.

✉ SHEREE BYKOFSKY ASSOCIATES, INC.

577 2nd Ave., PMB 109, New York NY 10016. Website: www.shereebee.com. **Contact:** Sheree Bykofsky. Estab. 1984, incorporated 1991. Member of AAR, ASJA, WNBA. Currently handles: 80% nonfiction books; 20% novels.
• Prior to opening her agency, Ms. Bykofsky served as executive editor of The Stonesong Press and managing editor of Chiron Press. She is also the author or co-author of more than 17 books, including *The Complete Idiot's Guide to Getting Published*. Ms. Bykofsky teaches publishing at NYU and The 92nd St. Y.

Member Agents: Janet Rosen, associate; Megan Buckley, associate.

Represents: Nonfiction books, novels. **Considers these nonfiction areas:** Americana; animals; art/architecture/design; biography/autobiography; business/economics; child guidance/parenting; cooking/foods/nutrition; crafts/hobbies; creative nonfiction; current affairs; education; ethnic/cultural interests; gardening; gay/lesbian issues; government/politics/law; health/medicine; history; how-to; humor/satire; interior design/decorating; language/literature/criticism; memoirs; military/war; money/finance (personal finance); multicultural; music/dance; nature/environment; New Age/metaphysics; philosophy; photography; popular culture; psychology; recreation; regional; religious/inspirational; science/technology; self-help/personal improvement; sex; sociology; spirituality; sports; theater/film; translation; travel; true crime/investigative; women's issues/studies; anthropolgy. **Considers these fiction areas:** Literary; mainstream/contemporary; mystery/suspense.
○→ This agency specializes in popular reference nonfiction, commercial fiction with a literary quality, and mysteries. ''I have wide-ranging interests, but it really depends on quality of writing, originality, and how a particular project appeals to me (or not). I take on fiction when I completely love it—it doesn't matter what area or genre.'' Does not want to receive poetry, material for children, screenplays, westerns, horror, science fiction, or fantasy.

How to Contact: Query with SASE. No unsolicited mss or phone calls. Considers simultaneous queries. Responds in 1 week to queries with SASE. Responds in 1 month to requested mss. Returns materials only with SASE. Obtains most new clients through recommendations from others.

Recent Sales: Sold 100 titles in the last year. *10 Sure Signs a Movie Character Is Doomed and Other Surprising Movie Lists*, by Richard Roeper (Hyperion); *What Is Love?*, by Taro Gold (Andrews & McMeel); *How to Make Someone Love You in 90 Minutes or Less—And Make it Last Forever*, by Nick Boothman.

Terms: Agent receives 15% commission on domestic sales; 20% commission on foreign sales. Offers written contract, binding for 1 year. Charges for postage, photocopying and fax.

Writers' Conferences: ASJA (New York City); Asilomar (Pacific Grove CA); St. Petersburg; Whidbey Island; Jacksonville; Albuquerque; Austin; Columbus; Southwestern Writers; Willamette (Portland); Dorothy Canfield Fisher (San Diego); Writers Union (Maui); Pacific NW; IWWG; and many others.

Tips: ''Read the agent listing carefully, and comply with guidelines.''

N ✉ THE JOHN CAMBELL AGENCY

160 Fifth Ave., Suite 624, New York NY 10010-7003. (212)989-2550. E-mail: litraryagt@aol.com. **Contact:** John Campbell. Estab. 1985. Currently handles: 90% nonfiction books; 10% novels.

Represents: Nonfiction books, novels. **Considers these nonfiction areas:** Art/architecture/design; biography/autobiography; ethnic/cultural interests; health/medicine; history; how-to; interior design/decorating; lan-

guage/literature/criticism; photography; popular culture; psychology; self-help/personal improvement. **Considers these fiction areas:** Action/adventure; literary; thriller.
  O—*This agency specializes in high-quality nonfiction, illustrated, reference, how-to and entertainment books. Does not want to receive poetry, memoir, children's fiction, category fiction, romance, science fiction, or horror.*
How to Contact: Submit proposal package, outline, SASE. Prefers to read materials exclusively. Accepts e-mail queries. No fax queries. Responds in 5 days to queries; 2 weeks to mss. Obtains most new clients through recommendations from others, solicitations.
Recent Sales: Sold 38 titles in the last year. *In Character*, by Howard Schatz (Bulfinch); *The Essential Dale Chihuly* (Abrams); *Faces*, by Angela Carol/Fisher Beckwith (National Geographic).
Terms: Agent receives 15% commission on domestic sales. Offers written contract; 1- to 2-month notice must be given to terminate contract. Offers criticism service, included in 15% commission. Charges clients for photocopying, long-distance telephone, overnight express-mail, messengering.
Tips: "We welcome submissions from new authors, but proposals must be unique, of high commercial interest, and well written. Follow your talent. Write with passion. Know your market. Submit polished work instead of apologizing for its mistakes, typos, incompleteness, etc. We want to see your best work."

N ☑ CANTON SMITH AGENCY
194 Broadway, Amityville NY 11701. (631)842-9476 or (701)483-0153. E-mail: bookhold2@yahoo.com. **Contact:** Eric Smith, senior partner; Chamein Canton, partner; M. Kessler, administrative assistant. Estab. 2001. Represents 10 clients. 100% of clients are new/unpublished writers. Currently handles: 40% nonfiction books; 20% novels; 5% story collections; 15% juvenile books; 5% scholarly books; 5% textbooks; 5% poetry; 5% movie scripts.
  • Prior to becoming agents, Mr. Smith was in advertising and bookstore retail; Ms. Canton was a writer and a paralegal.
Member Agents: Eric Smith (science fiction, fantasy, sports, literature); Chamein Canton (how-to, reference, literary, women's, multicultural, ethnic, crafts, cooking, health.
Represents: Nonfiction books, novels, short story collections, juvenile books, scholarly books, textbooks, poetry books, movie scripts. **Considers these nonfiction areas:** Art/architecture/design; business/economics; child guidance/parenting; cooking/foods/nutrition; education; ethnic/cultural interests; health/medicine; history; how-to; humor/satire; language/literature/criticism; military/war; music/dance; photography; psychology; sports; translation; women's issues/studies. **Considers these fiction areas:** Action/adventure; comic books/cartoon (cartoons); ethnic; fantasy; feminist; historical; humor/satire; juvenile; literary; mainstream/contemporary; picture books; romance; science fiction; sports; young adult. **Considers these script subject areas:** Action/adventure; comedy; romantic comedy; romantic drama; science fiction.
  O—*"We specialize in helping new and established writers expand their marketing potential for prospective publishers." Actively seeking well-written and researched nonfiction (all genres)—cooking, business, craft, how-to, home, reference, translations. Does not want New Age, metaphysics, erotica, agriculture, experimental, westerns, regional.*
How to Contact: Query with SASE or e-mail query with synopsis (preferred). Considers simultaneous queries. Responds in 3 weeks to queries; 6 weeks to mss. Obtains most new clients through recommendations from others.
Recent Sales: Sold 2 titles in the last year. Other clients include Robert Koger, Sheila Smestad, Maureen Einfeldt; Robert Beers, Diana Smith, Deb Mohr, Melissa Graf, Robert Zavala, Seth Ahonen.
Terms: Agent receives 15% commission on domestic sales; 20% commission on foreign sales. Offers written contract; 2-months notice must be given to terminate contract.
Tips: "Know your market. Agents, as well as publishers, are keenly interested in writers with their finger on the pulse of their said market."

CARLISLE & CO.
6 W. 18th St., New York NY 10011. (212)813-1881. Fax: (212)813-9567. E-mail: mtessler@carlisleco.com. Website: www.carlisleco.com. **Contact:** Michelle Tessler. Estab. 1998. Member of AAR. Represents 200 clients. Currently handles: 70% nonfiction books; 30% novels.
  • Prior to opening his agency, Mr. Carlisle was the Vice President of William Morris for 18 years.
Member Agents: Michael Carlisle, Michelle Tessler, Joe Veltre, George Lucas. Affiliates: Donald S. Lamm, Robert Bernstein, Paul Bresnick, Diane Gedymin, Kathy Green.
Represents: Nonfiction books, fiction. **Considers these nonfiction areas:** Biography/autobiography; business/economics; cooking/foods/nutrition; health/medicine; history; memoirs; popular culture; psychology; science/technology; lifestyle; military history. **Considers these fiction areas:** Action/adventure; literary; mainstream/contemporary; mystery/suspense; thriller.

O— This agency has "expertise in nonfiction and literary fiction. We have a strong focus on editorial input before submission." Does not want to receive science fiction, fantasy, or romance.

How to Contact: Query with SASE. Responds in 10 days to queries; 3 weeks to mss. Obtains most new clients through recommendations from others.

Recent Sales: Sold 100 titles in the last year. This agency prefers not to share information about specific sales.

Terms: Agent receives 15% commission on domestic sales; 20% commission on foreign sales. Offers written contract, binding for 1 book only.

Writers' Conferences: Squaw Valley Community Conference (California).

Tips: "Be sure to write as original a story as possible. Remember, you're asking the public to pay $25 for your book."

MARIA CARVAINIS AGENCY, INC.

1350 Avenue of the Americas, Suite 2905, New York NY 10019. (212)245-6365. Fax: (212)245-7196. E-mail: mca@mariacarvainisagency.com. **Contact:** Maria Carvainis, president. Estab. 1977. Member of AAR, Authors Guild, Women's Media Group, ABA, MWA, RWA; signatory of WGA. Represents 60 clients. 10% of clients are new/unpublished writers. Currently handles: 34% nonfiction books; 65% novels; 1% poetry.

● Prior to opening her agency, Ms. Carvainis spent more than 10 years in the publishing industry as a senior editor with Macmillan Publishing, Basic Books, Avon Books, and Crown Publishers. Ms. Carvainis has served as a member of the AAR Board of Directors and AAR Treasurer, as well as serving as chair of the AAR Contracts Committee. She presently serves on the AAR Royalty Committee.

Member Agents: Moira Sullivan (literary assistant); David Harvey (literary assistant); Anna Del Vecchio (contracts manager).

Represents: Nonfiction books, novels. **Considers these nonfiction areas:** Biography/autobiography; business/economics; history; memoirs; science/technology (pop science); women's issues/studies. **Considers these fiction areas:** Historical; literary; mainstream/contemporary; mystery/suspense; thriller; middle grade and young adult, women's fiction.

O— Does not want to receive science fiction or children's picture books.

How to Contact: Query with SASE. Responds in 1 week to queries; 3 months to mss. Obtains most new clients through recommendations from others, conferences, 60% from conferences/referrals; 40% from query letters.

Recent Sales: *Slightly Dangerous*, by Mary Balogh (Delacorte); *White Hot*, by Sandra Brown (Simon & Schuster); *Winterset*, by Candace Camp (MIRA); *Collara Killer*, by Lee Charles Kelley (Morrow/Avon); *Love and Madness*, by Martin Levy (William Morrow); *Island of Bones*, by P.J. Parrish (Kensington); *Women of America*, by Charlie Smith (W.W. Norton); *Some Danger Involved*, by Will Thomas (Touchstone Fireside). Other clients include Sue Erikson Bloland, Pam Conrad, S.V. Date, Michael G. Downs, Phillip DePoy, Carlos Dews, Tyler Dilts, Keith Dunlap, Cindy Gerard, Ellen Newmark, Kristine Rolofson, Janet Mansfield Soares, Christine Sneed, Ernest Suarez.

Terms: Agent receives 15% commission on domestic sales; 20% commission on foreign sales. Offers written contract, binding for 2 years on a book-by-book basis. Charges clients for foreign postage, bulk copying.

Writers' Conferences: BEA; Frankfurt Book Fair; London Book Fair.

CASTIGLIA LITERARY AGENCY

1155 Camino Del Mar, Suite 510, Del Mar CA 92014. (858)755-8761. Fax: (858)755-7063. **Contact:** Julie Castiglia. Estab. 1993. Member of AAR, PEN. Represents 50 clients. Currently handles: 55% nonfiction books; 45% novels.

Member Agents: Winifred Golden; Julie Castiglia.

Represents: Nonfiction books, novels. **Considers these nonfiction areas:** Animals; anthropology/archaeology; biography/autobiography; business/economics; child guidance/parenting; cooking/foods/nutrition; current affairs; ethnic/cultural interests; health/medicine; history; language/literature/criticism; money/finance; nature/environment; New Age/metaphysics; psychology; religious/inspirational; science/technology; self-help/personal improvement; sociology; women's issues/studies. **Considers these fiction areas:** Contemporary issues; ethnic; literary; mainstream/contemporary; mystery/suspense; women's (especially).

O— Does not want to receive horror, screenplays, or academic nonfiction.

How to Contact: Query with SASE. No fax queries. Responds in 2 months to mss. Returns materials only with SASE. Obtains most new clients through recommendations from others, solicitations, conferences.

Recent Sales: Sold 22 titles in the last year. 3 untitle novels by Susan Squires (St. Martin's); *Maya Running*, by Anjali Banerjee (Random House).

Terms: Agent receives 15% commission on domestic sales; 25% commission on foreign sales. Offers written contract; 6-week notice must be given to terminate contract. Charges clients for Fed Ex or Messenger.

Writers' Conferences: Southwestern Writers Conference (Albuquerque NM, August); National Writers Conference; Willamette Writers Conference (OR); San Diego State University (CA); Writers at Work (Utah); Austin Conference (TX).

Tips: "Be professional with submissions. Attend workshops and conferences before you approach an agent."

📧 💿 ◉ CHARISMA COMMUNICATIONS, LTD., (Specialized: organization)

787 7th Ave., 9th Floor, New York NY 10019. (212)832-3020. Fax: (212)786-6017. E-mail: chariscomm@aol.com. **Contact:** James W. Grau. Estab. 1972. Represents 10 clients. 20% of clients are new/unpublished writers. Currently handles: 50% nonfiction books; 20% movie scripts; 20% TV scripts; 10%.

Member Agents: Phil Howart; Rena Delduca (reader).

Represents: Nonfiction books, novels, feature film, TV movie of the week, documentary, miniseries. **Considers these nonfiction areas:** Biography/autobiography; current affairs; government/politics/law; military/war; true crime/investigative. **Considers these fiction areas:** Detective/police/crime; mystery/suspense; religious/inspirational; sports; cult issues.

> 🔑 This agency specializes in organized crime, Indian casinos, FBI, CIA, secret service, NSA, corporate and private security, casino gaming, KGB.

How to Contact: Submit proposal package, outline. Responds in 1 month to queries; 2 months to mss.

Recent Sales: Untitled documentary (Scripps Howard).

Terms: Agent receives 10% commission on domestic sales; variable commission on foreign sales. Offers written contract; 100% of business is derived from commissions on ms sales.

📧 ⊘ JANE CHELIUS LITERARY AGENCY

548 Second St., Brooklyn NY 11215. Member of AAR.

> ● This agency did not respond to our request for information. Query before submitting.

📧 ⊘ LINDA CHESTER AND ASSOCIATES

630 Fifth Ave., New York NY 10111. Member of AAR.

> ● This agency did not respond to our request for information. Query before submitting.

📧 ⊘ CINE/LIT REPRESENTATION

P.O. Box 802918, Santa Clarita CA 91380-2918. **Contact:** Mary Alice Kier. Member of AAR.

> ● This agency did not respond to our request for information. Query before submitting.

💿 WM CLARK ASSOCIATES

355 W. 22nd St., New York NY 10011. (212)675-2784. Fax: (646)349-1658. E-mail: query@wmclark.com. Website: www.wmclark.com. Estab. 1997. Member of AAR. 50% of clients are new/unpublished writers. Currently handles: 50% nonfiction books; 50% novels.

> ● Prior to opening WCA, Mr. Clark was an agent at the William Morris Agency.

Represents: Nonfiction books, novels. **Considers these nonfiction areas:** Art/architecture/design; biography/autobiography; current affairs; ethnic/cultural interests; history; memoirs; music/dance; popular culture; religious/inspirational (Eastern philosophy only); science/technology; sociology; theater/film; translation. **Considers these fiction areas:** Contemporary issues; ethnic; historical; literary; mainstream/contemporary; Southern fiction.

> 🔑 "Building on a reputation for moving quickly and strategically on behalf of his clients, and offering individual focus and a global presence, William Clark practices an agressive, innovative, and broad-ranged approach to the representation of content and the talent that creates it, ranging from authors of first fiction and award-winning bestselling narrative nonfiction, to international authors in translation, musicians, and artists."

How to Contact: E-mail queries only. Prefers to read requested materials exclusively. Responds in 1-2 months to queries.

Recent Sales: Sold 25 titles in the last year. *Fallingwater Rising: E.J. Kaufman and Frank Lloyd Wright Create the Most Exciting House in the World*, by Franklin Toker (Alfred A. Knopf); *The Balthazar Cookbook*, by Riad Nasr, Lee Hanson, and Keith McNally (Clarkson Potter); *The Book of 'Exodus': The Making and Meaning of Bob Marley's Album of the Century*, by Vivien Goldman (Crown/Three Rivers Press); *Hungry Ghost*, by Keith Kachtick (HarperCollins). Other clients include Russell Martin, Daye Haddon, Bjork, Mian Mian, Jonathan Stone, Jocko Weyland, Peter Hessler, Rev. Billy (aka BillY Talen).

Terms: Agent receives 15% commission on domestic sales; 20% commission on foreign sales. Offers written contract.

Tips: "WCA works on a reciprocal basis with Ed Victor Ltd. (UK) in representing select properties to the U.S. market and vice versa. Translation rights are sold directly in the German, Italian, Spanish, Portuguese, Latin American, French, Dutch, and Scandinavian territories in association with Andrew Nurnberg Associates Ltd.

(UK); through offices in China, Bulgaria, Czech Republic, Latvia, Poland, Hungary, and Russia; and through corresponding agents in Japan, Greece, Israel, Turkey, Korea, Taiwan, and Thailand.''

☑ CLAUSEN, MAYS & TAHAN, LLC

P.O. Box 1015, New York NY 10276. (212)714-8181. **Contact:** Stedman Mays, Mary M. Tahan. Estab. 1976. 10% of clients are new/unpublished writers. Currently handles: nonfiction books; novels.
Member Agents: Stedman Mays; Mary M. Tahan; Jena Anderson.
Represents: Nonfiction books, novels. **Considers these nonfiction areas:** Biography/autobiography; cooking/foods/nutrition; health/medicine; history; how-to; humor/satire; memoirs; money/finance; psychology; religious/inspirational; spirituality; women's issues/studies; fashion/beauty/style; relationships; also rights for books optioned for TV movies and feature films.
How to Contact: Query with SASE, proposal package, outline. No e-mail or fax queries. Considers simultaneous queries. Responds in 3 weeks to queries; 1 month to mss. Returns materials only with SASE.
Recent Sales: *And If I Perish*, by Evelyn Monahan and Rosemary Neidle-Greenlee (Knopf); *The Rules for Online Dating*, by Ellen Fein and Sherrie Schneider (Pocket Books); *The Anti-Inflammation Diet*, by Richard Fleming, M.D. with Tom Monte (Putnam).
Terms: Agent receives 15% commission on domestic sales; 20% commission on foreign sales. Charges clients for postage, shipping, and photocopying.
Tips: ''Research proposal writing and the publishing process. Always study your book's competition. Send a proposal and outline instead of a complete manuscript for faster response. Always pitch books in writing, not over the phone.''

☑ RUTH COHEN, INC., LITERARY AGENCY

P.O. Box 2244, La Jolla CA 92038-2244. (858)456-5805. **Contact:** Ruth Cohen. Estab. 1982. Member of AAR, Authors Guild, Sisters in Crime, RWA, SCBWI. Represents 39 clients. 15% of clients are new/unpublished writers. Currently handles: 60% novels; 40% juvenile books.
 • Prior to becoming an agent, Ms. Cohen served as directing editor at Scott Foresman & Co. (now Pearson).
Represents: Novels (adult), juvenile books. **Considers these fiction areas:** Ethnic; historical; juvenile; literary; mainstream/contemporary; mystery/suspense; young adult.
 O→ This agency specializes in ''quality writing in contemporary fiction, women's fiction, mysteries, thrillers and juvenile fiction.'' Does not want to receive poetry, westerns, film scripts, or how-to books.
How to Contact: Submit outline, 1 sample chapter(s). Responds in 3 weeks to queries. Returns materials only with SASE. Obtains most new clients through recommendations from others, solicitations.
Recent Sales: This agency prefers not to share information on specific sales.
Terms: Agent receives 15% commission on domestic sales; 25% commission on foreign sales. Offers written contract, binding for 1 year. Charges for foreign postage, phone calls, photocopying submissions, and overnight delivery of mss when appropriate.
Tips: ''As the publishing world merges and changes, there seem to be fewer opportunities for new writers to succeed in the work that they love. We urge you to develop the patience, persistence, and preseverance that have made this agency so successful. Prepare a well-written and well-crafted manuscript, and our combined best efforts can help advance both our careers.''

ⓝ ☑ JOANNA LEWIS COLE, LITERARY AGENT

404 Riverside Dr., New York NY 10025. Member of AAR.
 • This agency did not respond to our request for information. Query before submitting.

☑ FRANCES COLLIN, LITERARY AGENT

P.O. Box 33, Wayne PA 19087-0033. Website: www.francescollin.com. **Contact:** Frances Collin. Estab. 1948. Member of AAR. Represents 90 clients. 1% of clients are new/unpublished writers. Currently handles: 50% nonfiction books; 48% novels; 1% textbooks; 1% poetry.
Represents: Nonfiction books, fiction.
 O→ Almost no new clients, unless recommended by publishing professionals or clients. Does not want cookbooks, crafts, children's books, software, or original screenplays.
How to Contact: Query with SASE and brief proposal. No electronic submissions or telephone inquiries. Enclose sufficient IRCs if outside the US. Considers simultaneous queries.
Terms: Agent receives 15% commission on domestic sales; 20% commission on foreign sales. Offers written contract. Charges clients for overseas postage for books mailed to foreign agents; photocopying of mss, books, proposals; copyright registration fees; registered mail fees; passes along cost of any books purchased.

ⓝ COLLINS MCCORMICK LITERARY AGENCY

10 Leonard St., New York NY 10013. (212)219-2894. Fax: (212)219-2895. E-mail: info@collinsmccormick.com.

Website: www.collinsmccormick.com. **Contact:** David McCormick or Nina Collins. Estab. 2002. Member of AAR. Represents 150 clients. 60% of clients are new/unpublished writers. Currently handles: 60% nonfiction books; 30% novels; 5% story collections; 5% poetry.

- Prior to becoming an agent, Mr. McCormick was an editor at *The New Yorker* and *Texas Monthly*; Ms. McCormick was a book scout for foreign publishers and film and TV companies.

Member Agents: Leslie Falk (literary fiction, narrative nonfiction); Brist Carlson (literary fiction, narrative nonfiction).

[N] [♥] DON CONGDON ASSOCIATES INC.

156 Fifth Ave., Suite 625, New York NY 10010-7002. (212)645-1229. Fax: (212)727-2688. E-mail: dca@doncongdon.com. **Contact:** Don Congdon, Michael Congdon, Susan Ramer, Cristina Concepcion. Estab. 1983. Member of AAR. Represents 100 clients. Currently handles: 60% nonfiction books; 40% fiction.

Represents: Nonfiction books, fiction. **Considers these nonfiction areas:** Anthropology/archaeology; biography/autobiography; child guidance/parenting; cooking/foods/nutrition; creative nonfiction; current affairs; ethnic/cultural interests; government/politics/law; health/medicine; history; humor/satire; language/literature/criticism; memoirs; military/war; multicultural; music/dance; nature/environment; popular culture; psychology; science/technology; sociology; theater/film; travel; true crime/investigative; women's issues/studies. **Considers these fiction areas:** Action/adventure; detective/police/crime; horror; humor/satire; literary (especially); mainstream/contemporary; multicultural; mystery/suspense; short story collections; thriller; women's.

How to Contact: Query with SASE or via e-mail (material should be copied and pasted into e-mail as "we don't download attachments for security reasons"). Responds in 1 week to queries; 1 month to mss. Obtains most new clients through recommendations from others.

Terms: Agent receives 15% commission on domestic sales; 19% commission on foreign sales. Charges client for extra shipping costs, photocopying, copyright fees, and book purchases.

Tips: "Writing a query letter with a self-addressed stamped envelope is a must. No phone calls. We never download attachments to e-mail queries for security reasons, so please copy and paste material into your e-mail."

[M] [✏] THE COOKE AGENCY

278 Bloor St. E., Suite 305, Toronto ON M4W 3M4, Canada. (416)406-3390. Fax: (416)406-3389. E-mail: agents@cookeagency.ca. **Contact:** Elizabeth Griffin. Estab. 1992. Represents 60 clients. 30% of clients are new/unpublished writers. Open to Canadian writers only. Currently handles: 50% nonfiction books; 50% novels.

- Prior to becoming an agent, Mr. Cooke was the publisher of Seal Bantam Books Canada.

Member Agents: Dean Cooke (literary fiction, nonfiction).

Represents: Nonfiction books, novels, juvenile books. **Considers these nonfiction areas:** Biography/autobiography; business/economics; child guidance/parenting; current affairs; gay/lesbian issues; health/medicine; popular culture; science/technology; young adult. **Considers these fiction areas:** Juvenile; literary; women's.

- The Cooke Agency represents some of the best Canadian writers in the world. "Through our contacts and sub-agents, we are building an international reputation for quality. Curtis Brown Canada is jointly owned by Dean Cooke and Curtis Brown New York. It represents Curtis Brown New York authors in Canada." Does not want to receive how-to, self-help, spirituality, genre fiction (science fiction, fantasy, mystery, thriller, horror).

How to Contact: Query with SASE. Accepts e-mail and fax queries. Considers simultaneous queries. Responds in 1 month to queries; 6 weeks to mss. Returns materials only with SASE. Obtains most new clients through recommendations from others.

Recent Sales: Sold 20 titles and sold 4 scripts in the last year. *Last Crossing*, by Guy Vanderhaeghe (Grove/Atlantic); *Clara Callan*, by Richard B. Wright (Harperflamingo Canada); *Stanley Park*, by Timothy Taylor (Knopf Canada); *Your Mouth is Lovely*, by Nancy Richler (Harper Collins); *A Keen Soldier*, by Andrew Clark (Knopf Canada); *Possesing Genius: The Bizarre Odyssey of Eintein's Brain*, by Caroline Abraham (Penguin Canada, St. Martin's Press, Icon Books UK). Other clients include Rui Umezawa, Lauren B. Davis, Doug Hunter, Andrew Podnieks, Tony Hillerman, Robertson Davies, Brian Moore.

Terms: Agent receives 15% commission on domestic sales; 20% commission on foreign sales. Offers written contract. Charges clients for postage, photocopying, courier.

[✏] THE DOE COOVER AGENCY

P.O. Box 668, Winchester MA 01890. (781)721-6000. Fax: (781)721-6727. **Contact:** Doe Coover, president. Estab. 1985. Represents over 100 clients. Currently handles: 80% nonfiction books; 20% novels.

- Prior to becoming agents, Ms. Coover and Ms. Mohyde were editors for over a decade.

Member Agents: Doe Coover (cooking, general nonfiction); Colleen Mohyde (literary and commercial fiction, general nonfiction and journalism); Frances Kennedy, assistant; Amanda Lewis, assistant.

Represents: Nonfiction books, novels. **Considers these nonfiction areas:** Anthropology/archaeology; biography/autobiography; business/economics; child guidance/parenting; cooking/foods/nutrition; ethnic/cultural interests; health/medicine; history; language/literature/criticism; memoirs; money/finance; nature/environment; psychology; sociology; travel; true crime/investigative; women's issues/studies. **Considers these fiction areas:** Literary; mainstream/contemporary (commercial).

O— This agency specializes in cookbooks, serious nonfiction—particularly books on social issues—as well as fiction (literary and commercial), journalism and general nonfiction. Does very few children's books.

How to Contact: Query with SASE, outline. No e-mail or fax queries. Considers simultaneous queries. Returns materials only with SASE. Obtains most new clients through recommendations from others, solicitations.

Recent Sales: Sold 25-30 titles in the last year. *The Gourmet Cookbook*, by Gourmet Magazine (Houghton Mifflin); *The Cradle of Flavor*, by James Oseland (W.W. Norton); *Seven Things Your Teenager Doesn't Want You to Know*, by Jennifer Lippincott and Robin Deutsch (Ballantine). *Movie/TV MOW script(s) optioned/sold: Drinking: A Love Story*, by Caroline Knapp. Other clients include WGBH, Peter Lynch, Jacques Pepin, Deborah Madison, Rick Bayless, Adria Bernardi, Suzanne Berne and Thrity Umrigar.

Terms: Agent receives 15% commission on domestic sales; 15% commission on foreign sales.

Writers' Conferences: BEA.

◪ CORNERSTONE LITERARY, INC.

4500 Wilshire Blvd., 3rd floor, Los Angeles CA 90010. (323)930-6039. Fax: (323)930-0407. Website: www.cornerstoneliterary.com. **Contact:** Helen Breitwieser. Estab. 1998. Member of AAR; Author's Guild; MWA; RWA. Represents 40 clients. 30% of clients are new/unpublished writers.

● Prior to founding her own boutique agency, Ms. Breitwieser was a literary agent at The William Morris Agency.

Represents: Novels. **Considers these fiction areas:** Detective/police/crime; erotica; ethnic; family saga; glitz; historical; literary; mainstream/contemporary; multicultural; mystery/suspense; romance; thriller.

O— Actively seeking first fiction, literary. Does not want to receive science fiction, westerns, children's books, poetry, screenplays, fantasy, gay/lesbian, horror, self-help, psychology, business.

How to Contact: Query with SASE. Responds in 6-8 weeks to queries; 2 months to mss. Returns materials only with SASE. Obtains most new clients through recommendations from others.

Recent Sales: Sold 38 titles in the last year. *The Earth Moved*, by Carmen Reid (Pocket); *The Delta Sisters*, by Kayla Perrin (St. Martin's Press); *The Sweetest Taboo*, by Carole Matthews (HarperCollins). Other clients include Stan Diehl, Elaine Coffman, Danielle Girard, R.J. Kaiser, Rachel Lee.

Terms: Agent receives 15% commission on domestic sales; 20% commission on foreign sales. Offers written contract, binding for 1 year; 2-month notice must be given to terminate contract.

Tips: ''Don't query about more than 1 manuscript. Do not e-mail queries/submissions.''

◪ CRAWFORD LITERARY AGENCY

94 Evans Rd., Barnstead NH 03218. (603)269-5851. Fax: (603)269-2533. E-mail: crawfordlit@att.net. Winter Office: 3920 Bayside Rd., Fort Myers Beach FL 33931. (239)463-4651. Fax: (239)463-0125. **Contact:** Susan Crawford. Estab. 1988. Represents 45 clients. 10% of clients are new/unpublished writers. Currently handles: 50% nonfiction books; 50% novels.

Member Agents: Susan Crawford; Lorne Crawford (commercial fiction and nonfiction); Scott Neister (scientific/techno thrillers).

Represents: Nonfiction books, novels. **Considers these nonfiction areas:** Psychology; religious/inspirational; self-help/personal improvement; women's issues/studies; celebrity/media. **Considers these fiction areas:** Action/adventure; mystery/suspense; thriller (medical).

O— This agency specializes in celebrity and/or media-based books and authors. Actively seeking action/adventure stories, medical thrillers, self-help, inspirational, how-to, and women's issues. Does not want to receive short stories, poetry.

How to Contact: Query with SASE. Considers simultaneous queries. Responds in 3 weeks to queries. Returns materials only with SASE. Obtains most new clients through recommendations from others, solicitations, conferences.

Recent Sales: Sold 42 titles in the last year. *Excelsior! The Amazing Life of Stan Lee*, by Stan Lee (Simon & Schuster); *Web Thinking*, by Dr. Linda Seger (Inner Ocean Publishing); *Gray Matter*, by Gary Braven; *The Soul of a Butterfly*, by Muhammad Ali with Hana Ali (Simon & Schuster); *I Shook Up the World!*, by Marxum Ali (Beyond Word Publishing). Other clients include John Travolta, Cal Morris,MD, Mimi Donaldson, Ruby Dee, Ossie Davis.

Terms: Agent receives 15% commission on domestic sales; 20% commission on foreign sales. Offers written contract, binding for 3-month; 100% of business is derived from commissions on ms sales.

Writers' Conferences: International Film & Television Workshops (Rockport ME); Maui Writers Conference.

Tips: "Keep learning to improve your craft. Attend conferences and network."

Ⓝ ⊘ THE CREATIVE CULTURE, INC.

72 Spring St., Suite 304, New York NY 10012. **Contact:** Debra Goldstein. Member of AAR.
- This agency did not respond to our request for information. Query before submitting.

◐ RICHARD CURTIS ASSOCIATES, INC.

171 E. 74th St., New York NY 10021. (212)772-7363. Fax: (212)772-7393. Website: www.curtisagency.com. Estab. 1979. Member of RWA; MWA; WWA; SFWA; signatory of WGA. Represents 100 clients. 1% of clients are new/unpublished writers. Currently handles: 75% nonfiction books; 25% novels.
- Prior to opening his agency, Mr. Curtis was an agent with the Scott Meredith Literary Agency for 7 years and has authored over 50 published books.

Member Agents: Richard Curtis; Pamela Valvera.
Represents: Commercial nonfiction, commercial and literary fiction. **Considers these nonfiction areas:** Popular culture; young adult. **Considers these fiction areas:** Fantasy; romance; science fiction; thriller; young adult.
How to Contact: One-page query letter, plus no more than a 1-page synopsis of proposed submission. No submission of ms unless specifically requested. If requested, submission must be accompanied by a SASE, or "we will assume you don't want your submission back." No e-mail or fax queries. Returns materials only with SASE.
Recent Sales: Sold 150 titles in the last year. *Olympos*, by Dan Simmons; *The Side-Effects Solution*, by Frederic Vagnini and Barry Fox; *Dead Lines*, by Greg Bear. Other clients include Janet Dailey, Jennifer Blake, Leonard Maltin, Earl Mindell, Barbara Parker.
Terms: Agent receives 15% commission on domestic sales; 25% commission on foreign sales. Offers written contract, binding for book-by-book basis. Charges for photocopying, express, international freight, book orders.
Writers' Conferences: Science Fiction Writers of America; Horror Writers of America; Romance Writers of America; World Fantasy Conference.

⊘ JAMES R. CYPHER, THE CYPHER AGENCY

816 Wolcott Ave., Beacon NY 12508-4261. Phone/fax: (845)831-5677. E-mail: jimcypher@prodigy.net. Website: pages.prodigy.net/jimcypher/. **Contact:** James R. Cypher. Estab. 1993. Member of AAR, Authors Guild. Represents 40 clients. 40% of clients are new/unpublished writers. Currently handles: 100% nonfiction books.
- Prior to opening his agency, Mr. Cypher worked as a corporate public relations manager for a Fortune 500 multi-national computer company for 28 years.

Represents: Nonfiction books. **Considers these nonfiction areas:** Biography/autobiography; current affairs; ethnic/cultural interests; gay/lesbian issues; government/politics/law; health/medicine; history; how-to; language/literature/criticism; memoirs (travel); money/finance; music/dance; nature/environment; popular culture; psychology; science/technology; self-help/personal improvement; sociology; sports; theater/film; travel (memoirs); true crime/investigative; women's issues/studies.
- ○━ Actively seeking a wide variety of topical nonfiction. Does not want to receive humor, pets, gardening, cooking books, crafts, spiritual, religious, or New Age topics.

How to Contact: Query with SASE, proposal package, outline, 2 sample chapter(s). Accepts e-mail and fax queries. Considers simultaneous queries. Responds in 2 weeks to queries; 6 weeks to mss. Obtains most new clients through recommendations from others, conferences, networking on online computer service.
Recent Sales: Sold 5 titles in the last year. *The Night the Defeos Died: Reinvestigating the Amityville Murders*, by Ric Osuna (Katco Literary & Media); *Revolution in Zanzibar: An American's Cold War Tale*, by Donald Petterson (Westview Press); *Once Upon a Word: True Tales of Word Origins*, by Rob Kyff (Tapestry Press).
Terms: Agent receives 15% commission on domestic sales; 20% commission on foreign sales. Offers written contract; 1-month notice must be given to terminate contract. 100% of business is derived from commissions on ms sales. Charges clients for postage, photocopying, overseas phone calls and faxes.

Ⓝ ⊘ LAURA DAIL LITERARY AGENCY, INC.

80 5th Ave., Suite 1503, New York NY, 10011. **Contact:** Laura Dail. Member of AAR.
- This agency did not respond to our request for information. Query before submitting.

⊘ DARHANSOFF, VERRILL, FELDMAN LITERARY AGENTS

236 W. 26th St., Suite 802, New York NY 10001. (917)305-1300. Fax: (917)305-1400. Estab. 1975. Member of AAR. Represents 120 clients. 10% of clients are new/unpublished writers. Currently handles: 25% nonfiction books; 60% novels; 15% story collections.
Member Agents: Liz Darhansoff; Charles Verrill; Leigh Feldman.
Represents: Novels, short story collections. **Considers these nonfiction areas:** Narrative nonfiction.

O—¬ Specializes in literary fiction.

How to Contact: Obtains most new clients through recommendations from others.

◙ LIZA DAWSON ASSOCIATES

240 W. 35th St., Suite 500, New York NY 10001. (212)465-9071. **Contact:** Liza Dawson, Caitlin Blasdell. Member of AAR, MWA, Women's Media Group. Represents 50 clients. 15% of clients are new/unpublished writers. Currently handles: 60% nonfiction books; 40% novels.

• Prior to becoming an agent, Ms. Dawson was an editor for 20 years, spending 11 years at William Morrow as vice president and 2 at Putnam as executive editor. Ms. Blasdell was a senior editor at HarperCollins and Avon.

Member Agents: Liza Dawson; Caitlin Blasdell.

Represents: Nonfiction books, novels, scholarly books. **Considers these nonfiction areas:** Biography/autobiography; business/economics; child guidance/parenting; health/medicine; history; memoirs; psychology; sociology; women's issues/studies. **Considers these fiction areas:** Ethnic; family saga; historical; literary; mystery/suspense; regional; science fiction (Blasdell only); thriller.

O—¬ This agency specializes in readable literary fiction, thrillers, mainstream historicals, and women's fiction, academics, historians, business, journalists, and psychology. Does not want to receive westerns, sports, computers, juvenile.

How to Contact: Query with SASE. Responds in 3 weeks to queries; 6 weeks to mss. Obtains most new clients through recommendations from others, conferences.

Recent Sales: Sold 40 titles in the last year. *IDA B.*, by Karen E. Quinones Miller (Simon and Schuster); *Mayada: Daughter of Iraq* by Jean Sasson (Dutton); *The Nanny Murders*, by Merry Jones (St. Martin's); *WORDCRAFT: How to Write Like a Professional*, by Jack Hart (Pantheon); *...And a Time to Die: How Hospitals Shape the End of Life Experience*, by Dr. Sharon Kaufman (Scribner).

Terms: Agent receives 15% commission on domestic sales; 20% commission on foreign sales. Offers written contract. Charges clients for photocopying and overseas postage.

◙ DEFIORE & CO.

72 Spring St., Suite 304, New York NY 10012. (212)925-7744. Fax: (212)925-9803. E-mail: info@defioreandco.com. Website: www.defioreandco.com. **Contact:** Brian DeFiore. Estab. 1999. Represents 55 clients. 50% of clients are new/unpublished writers. Currently handles: 70% nonfiction books; 30% novels.

• Prior to becoming an agent, Mr. DeFiore was Publisher of Villard Books 1997-1998; Editor-in-Chief of Hyperion 1992-1997; Editorial Director of Delacorte Press 1988-1992.

Member Agents: Brian DeFiore (popular nonfiction, business, pop culture, parenting, commercial fiction); Laurie Abkemeier (nonfiction only—memoir, health, parenting, business, how-to/self-help, cooking, spirituality, popular science); Kate Garrick (literary fiction, crime, pop culture, politics, history, psychology, narrative nonfiction).

Represents: Nonfiction books, novels. **Considers these nonfiction areas:** Biography/autobiography; business/economics; child guidance/parenting; cooking/foods/nutrition; health/medicine; money/finance; multicultural; popular culture; psychology; religious/inspirational; self-help/personal improvement; sports. **Considers these fiction areas:** Ethnic; literary; mainstream/contemporary; mystery/suspense; thriller.

How to Contact: Query with SASE. Considers simultaneous queries. Responds in 3 weeks to queries; 2 months to mss. Returns materials only with SASE. Obtains most new clients through recommendations from others.

Recent Sales: Sold 20 titles in the last year. *The Little Stuff Matters Most*, by Bernie Brillstein and David Resin (Gotham Books); *The Power of the Actor*, by Ivana Chubbuck (Gotham Books); *I Need a Beat: The Def Jam Records Story*, by Stacy Gueraseva (Ballantine); *Life is a Series of Presentations*, by Tony Jeary with Kim Dower and J.E. Fishman (Simon & Schuster); *How To Win At College*, by Cal Newport (Broadway); *What No One Tells the Mom*, by Marg Stark (Perigee); *The Ballecore Body Shaping Book*, by Molly Weeks (Ballantine); *Confessions of a Tax Collector*, by Rick Yancey (HarperCollins). Other clients include David Rensin, Loretta LaRoche, Jason Starr, Joel Engel, Christopher Keane, Robin McMillan, Jessica Teich, Ronna Lichtenberg, Fran Sorin, Christine Dimmick, Jimmy Lerner, Lou Manfredini, Dan Hays, Bally's Total Fitness, Federico Castelluccio, Hilary Devries, Norm Green, Lisa Kusel.

Terms: Agent receives 15% commission on domestic sales; 20% commission on foreign sales. Offers written contract; 10-day notice must be given to terminate contract. Charges clients for photocopying, overnight delivery (deducted only after a sale is made).

Writers' Conferences: Maui Writers Conference (Maui HI, September); Pacific Northwest Writers Association Conference; North Carolina Writer's Network Conference.

Ⓝ ◙ DH LITERARY, INC.

P.O. Box 990, Nyack NY 10960-0990. (212)753-7942. E-mail: dhendin@aol.com. **Contact:** David Hendin. Estab.

1993. Member of AAR. Represents 5 clients. Currently handles: 80% nonfiction books; 10% novels; 10% scholarly books.

- Prior to opening his agency, Mr. Hendin served as president and publisher for Pharos Books/World Almanac as well as senior VP and COO at sister company United Feature Syndicate.

○━ Not accepting new clients.

Recent Sales: *No Vulgar Hotel*, by Judith Martin (Norton); *Murder Between the Covers* (mystery series), by Elaine Viets (Penguin/Putnam); *Coined by God*, by Jeffrey McQuain and Stanley Malless (Norton).

Terms: Agent receives 15% commission on domestic sales; 20% commission on foreign sales. Offers written contract, binding for 1 year. Charges for out-of-pocket expenses for overseas postage specifically related to sale. No other fees.

◑ DHS LITERARY, INC.

2528 Elm St., Suite 350, Dallas TX 75226. (214)363-4422. Fax: (214)363-4423. E-mail: submissions@dhsliterary. com. Website: www.dhsliterary.com. **Contact:** David Hale Smith, president. Estab. 1994. Represents 35 clients. 15% of clients are new/unpublished writers. Currently handles: 60% nonfiction books; 40% novels.

- Prior to opening his agency, Mr. Smith was an editor at a newswire service.

Represents: Nonfiction books, novels. **Considers these nonfiction areas:** Biography/autobiography; business/economics; child guidance/parenting; cooking/foods/nutrition; current affairs; ethnic/cultural interests; popular culture; sports; true crime/investigative. **Considers these fiction areas:** Detective/police/crime; ethnic; literary; mainstream/contemporary; mystery/suspense; thriller; westerns/frontier.

○━ This agency specializes in commercial fiction and nonfiction for the adult trade market. Actively seeking thrillers, mysteries, suspense, etc., and narrative nonfiction. Does not want to receive poetry, short fiction, children's books.

How to Contact: Accepts new material by referral only. *No unsolicited mss.* Considers simultaneous queries. Responds in 1 month to queries. Obtains most new clients through recommendations from others.

Recent Sales: Sold 35 titles in the last year. *The Curve of the World*, by Marcus Stevens (Algonquin); *City on Fire*, by Bill Minutaglio (Morrow).

Terms: Agent receives 15% commission on domestic sales; 25% commission on foreign sales. Offers written contract; 10-day notice must be given to terminate contract. Charges for client expenses, i.e., postage, photocopying. 100% of business is derived from commissions on sales.

Tips: "Remember to be courteous and professional, and to treat marketing your work and approaching an agent as you would any formal business matter. When in doubt, always query first via e-mail. Visit our website for more information."

◙ SANDRA DIJKSTRA LITERARY AGENCY

1155 Camino del Mar, PMB 515, Del Mar CA 92014-2605. (858)755-3115. Fax: (858) 794-2822. E-mail: sdla@dijk straagency.com. **Contact:** Elise Capron. Estab. 1981. Member of AAR, Authors Guild, PEN West, Poets and Editors, MWA. Represents 200 clients. 30% of clients are new/unpublished writers. Currently handles: 50% nonfiction books; 45% novels; 5% juvenile books.

- We specialize in a number of fields.

Member Agents: Sandra Dijkstra.

Represents: Nonfiction books, novels. **Considers these nonfiction areas:** Anthropology/archaeology; business/economics; child guidance/parenting; cooking/foods/nutrition; ethnic/cultural interests; government/politics/law; health/medicine; history; language/literature/criticism; military/war; money/finance; nature/environment; psychology; science/technology; sociology; women's issues/studies. **Considers these fiction areas:** Ethnic; literary; mainstream/contemporary; mystery/suspense; thriller.

How to Contact: Submit proposal package, outline, sample chapter(s), author bio, SASE. No e-mail or fax queries. Responds in 1 month to queries; 6 weeks to mss. Obtains most new clients through recommendations from others, solicitations, conferences.

Recent Sales: Sold over 40 titles in the last year. *The Hottentot Venus*, by Barbara Chase-Riboud (Doubleday); *The Lady, The Chef and the Lover*, by Marisol Konczal (Harper Collins); *End of Adolescence*, by Robert Epstein (Harcourt).

Terms: Agent receives 15% commission on domestic sales; 20% commission on foreign sales. Offers written contract. Charges clients for expenses "to cover domestic costs so that we can spend time selling books instead of accounting expenses. We also charge for the photocopying of the full manuscript or nonfiction proposal and for foreign postage."

Writers' Conferences: "Have attended Squaw Valley, Santa Barbara, Asilomar, Southern California Writers Conference, Rocky Mountain Fiction Writers, to name a few. We also speak regularly for writers groups such as PEN West and the Independent Writers Association."

Tips: "Be professional and learn the standard procedures for submitting your work. Give full biographical information on yourself, especially for a nonfiction project. Send no more than 50 pages of your manuscript, a very brief synopsis, detailed author bio (awards, publications, accomplishments) and a SASE. We will not respond to submissions without a SASE. Nine-page letters telling us your life story, or your book's, are unprofessional and usually not read. Tell us about your book and write your query well. It's our first introduction to who you are and what you can do. Call if you don't hear within 6 weeks. Be a regular patron of bookstores, and study what kind of books are being published. Read. Check out your local library and bookstores—you'll find lots of books on writing and the publishing industry that will help you. At conferences, ask published writers about their agents. Don't believe the myth that an agent has to be in New York to be successful—we've already disproved it!''

[N] [○] THE JONATHAN DOLGER AGENCY

49 E. 96th St., Suite 9B, New York NY 10128. (212)427-1853. **Contact:** Herbert Erinmore; President: Jonathan Dolger. Estab. 1980. Member of AAR. Represents 70 clients. 25% of clients are new/unpublished writers.
• Query before submitting.
Represents: Nonfiction books, novels, illustrated books.
○━ This agency specializes in adult trade fiction and nonfiction, and illustrated books.
How to Contact: Query with SASE.
Recent Sales: Sold 15-20 titles in the last year. This agency prefers not to share information on specific sales.
Terms: Agent receives 15% commission on domestic sales; 25% commission on foreign sales. Charges clients for ''standard expenses.''
Tips: ''Writer must have been previously published if submitting fiction. Prefers to work with published/ established authors; works with a small number of new/previously unpublished writers.''

[N] [○] DONADIO & ASHWORTH, INC.

121 W. 27th St., Suite 704, New York NY, 10001. Member of AAR.
• Query before submitting.
Member Agents: Neil Olson, Ira Silverberg.

[○] JANIS A. DONNAUD & ASSOCIATES, INC.

525 Broadway, 2nd Floor, New York NY 10012. (212)431-2664. Fax: (212)431-2667. E-mail: jdonnaud@aol.com. **Contact:** Janis A. Donnaud. Member of AAR; signatory of WGA. Represents 40 clients. 5% of clients are new/unpublished writers. Currently handles: 100% nonfiction books.
• Prior to opening her agency, Ms. Donnaud was vice president, associate publisher of Random House Adult Trade Group.
Represents: Nonfiction books. **Considers these nonfiction areas:** Biography/autobiography; child guidance/ parenting; cooking/foods/nutrition; current affairs; health/medicine; humor/satire; psychology (pop); women's issues/studies; lifestyle.
○━ This agency specializes in health, medical, cooking, humor, pop psychology, narrative nonfiction, photography, biography, parenting, current affairs. ''We give a lot of service and attention to clients.'' Actively seeking serious narrative nonfiction; cookbooks; health and medical all written by experts with an already established platform in their area of specialty. Does not want to receive fiction, poetry, mysteries, juvenile books, romances, science fiction, young adult, religious, fantasy.
How to Contact: Query with SASE, description of book, and 2-3 pages of sample material. Prefers to read materials exclusively. Responds in 1 month to queries; 1 month to mss. Obtains most new clients through recommendations from others.
Recent Sales: Sold 25 titles in the last year. *Made for Each Other: Fashion and the Oscars*, by Bronwyn Cosgrave (Bloomsbury); *Sunday Suppers from Lucques*, by Suzanne Goin (Knopf).
Terms: Agent receives 15% commission on domestic sales; 20% commission on foreign sales; 20% commission on dramatic rights sales. Offers written contract; 1-month notice must be given to terminate contract. Charges clients for messengers, photocopying, purchase of books.

[○] JIM DONOVAN LITERARY

4515 Prentice St., Suite 109, Dallas TX 75206. **Contact:** Jim Donovan, president; Kathryn Lindsey. Estab. 1993. Represents 30 clients. 20% of clients are new/unpublished writers. Currently handles: 65% nonfiction books; 35% novels.
Member Agents: Jim Donovan (president); Kathryn Lindsey.
Represents: Nonfiction books, novels. **Considers these nonfiction areas:** Biography/autobiography; business/ economics; child guidance/parenting; current affairs; health/medicine; history; military/war; money/finance; music/dance; nature/environment; popular culture; sports; true crime/investigative. **Considers these fiction**

areas: Action/adventure; detective/police/crime; historical; horror; literary; mainstream/contemporary; mystery/suspense; sports; thriller; westerns/frontier.

⊶ This agency specializes in commercial fiction and nonfiction. Does not want to receive poetry, humor, short stories, juvenile, romance, or religious work.

How to Contact: Query with SASE. For nonfiction, send query letter. For fiction, send 2- to 5-page outline and 3 sample chapters. No e-mail or fax queries. Considers simultaneous queries. Responds in 1 month to queries; 1 month to mss. Obtains most new clients through recommendations from others, solicitations.

Recent Sales: Sold 24 titles in the last year. *The Killing Ground*, by Bill Sloan (Simon & Schuster); *Halfbreed*, by David Halaas and Andy Masich (Da Capo); *Given Up for Dead*, by Bill Sloan (Bantam); *Duel in the Sun*, by Curt Sampson (Pocket/Atria); *Streetcar: Blanche Dubois, Marlon Brando, and the Movie that Outraged America*, by Sam Staggs (St. Martin's).

Terms: Agent receives 15% commission on domestic sales; 20% commission on foreign sales. Offers written contract, binding for 1 year; written notice must be given to terminate contract.

Tips: ''The vast majority of material I receive, particularly fiction, is not ready for publication. Do everything you can to get your fiction work in top shape before you try to find an agent. I've been in the book business since 1981, in retail (as a chain buyer), as an editor, and as a published author. I'm open to working with new writers if they're serious about their writing and are prepared to put in the work necessary—the rewriting—to become publishable.''

◖ DOYEN LITERARY SERVICES, INC.

1931 660th St., Newell IA 50568-7613. (712)272-3300. Website: www.barbaradoyen.com. **Contact:** (Ms.) B.J. Doyen, president. Estab. 1988. Represents over 100 clients. 20% of clients are new/unpublished writers. Currently handles: 95% nonfiction books; 5% novels.

● Prior to opening her agency, Ms. Doyen worked as a published author, teacher, guest speaker, and wrote and appeared in her own weekly TV show airing in 7 states.

Represents: Nonfiction books, novels. **Considers these nonfiction areas:** Agriculture/horticulture; Americana; animals; anthropology/archaeology; art/architecture/design; biography/autobiography; business/economics; child guidance/parenting; computers/electronic; cooking/foods/nutrition; crafts/hobbies; creative nonfiction; current affairs; education; ethnic/cultural interests; gardening; government/politics/law; health/medicine; history; how-to; humor/satire; interior design/decorating; juvenile nonfiction; language/literature/criticism; memoirs; military/war; money/finance; multicultural; music/dance; nature/environment; New Age/metaphysics; philosophy; photography; popular culture; psychology; recreation; regional; religious/inspirational; science/technology; self-help/personal improvement; sex; sociology; software; spirituality; sports; theater/film; translation; travel; true crime/investigative; women's issues/studies; young adult. **Considers these fiction areas:** Contemporary issues; family saga; historical; literary; mainstream/contemporary; occult; psychic/supernatural.

⊶ This agency specializes in nonfiction and occasionally handles genre and mainstream fiction for adults. Actively seeking business, health, how-to, psychology; all kinds of adult nonfiction suitable for the major trade publishers. Does not want to receive pornography, children's, poetry.

How to Contact: Query with SASE. No e-mail or fax queries. Considers simultaneous queries. Responds in 3 weeks to mss. Responds immediately to queries. Returns materials only with SASE. *The Birth Order Effect for Couples*, by Isaacson/Schneider (Fairwinds); *An Egg On Three Sticks*, by Fischer (St. Martin's Griffin).

Terms: Agent receives 15% commission on domestic sales; 20% commission on foreign sales. Offers written contract, binding for 1 year.

Tips: ''Our authors receive personalized attention. We market aggressively, undeterred by rejection. We get the best possible publishing contracts. We are very interested in nonfiction book ideas at this time; will consider most topics. Many writers come to us from referrals, but we also get quite a few who initially approach us with query letters. Do not use phone queries unless you are successfully published or a celebrity. It is best if you do not collect editorial rejections prior to seeking an agent, but if you do, be up-front and honest about it. Do not submit your manuscript to more than 1 agent at a time—querying first can save you (and us) much time. We're open to established or beginning writers—just send us a terrific letter with SASE!''

Ⓝ ◖ ROBERT DUCAS

The Barn House, 244 Westside Rd., Norfolk CT 06058. (860)542-5733. Fax: (860)542-5469. E-mail: robertducas @aol.com. **Contact:** Robert Ducas. Estab. 1981. 15% of clients are new/unpublished writers. Currently handles: 70% nonfiction books; 28% novels; 2% scholarly books.

● Prior to opening his agency, Mr. Ducas ran the *London Times* and the *Sunday Times* in the US from 1966-1981.

Represents: Nonfiction books, novels. **Considers these nonfiction areas:** Animals; biography/autobiography; business/economics; current affairs; gay/lesbian issues; government/politics/law; health/medicine; history;

memoirs; military/war; money/finance; nature/environment; science/technology; sports; travel; true crime/investigative. **Considers these fiction areas:** Action/adventure; contemporary issues; detective/police/crime; family saga; literary; mainstream/contemporary; mystery/suspense; sports.

    ○━ This agency specializes in nonfiction, journalistic exposé, biography, history. Does not want to receive women's fiction.

How to Contact: Query with SASE. Responds in 2 weeks to queries; 2 months to mss. Obtains most new clients through recommendations from others.

Recent Sales: Sold 10 titles in the last year. This agency prefers not to share information on specific sales.

Terms: Agent receives 15% commission on domestic sales; 20% commission on foreign sales. Charges clients for photocopying, postage, messengers, overseas couriers to subagents.

☑ DUNHAM LITERARY, INC.

156 Fifth Ave., Suite 625, New York NY 10010-7002. (212)929-0994. Website: www.dunhamlit.com. **Contact:** Jennie Dunham. Estab. 2000. Member of AAR. Represents 50 clients. 15% of clients are new/unpublished writers. Currently handles: 25% nonfiction books; 25% novels; 50% juvenile books.

    • Prior to opening her agency, Ms. Dunham worked as a literary agent for Russell & Volkening. The Rhoda Weyr Agency is now a division of Dunham Literary, Inc.

Represents: Nonfiction books, novels, short story collections, juvenile books. **Considers these nonfiction areas:** Anthropology/archaeology; biography/autobiography; ethnic/cultural interests; government/politics/law; health/medicine; history; language/literature/criticism; nature/environment; popular culture; psychology; science/technology; women's issues/studies. **Considers these fiction areas:** Ethnic; juvenile; literary; mainstream/contemporary; picture books; young adult.

How to Contact: Query with SASE. No e-mail or fax queries. Responds in 1 week to queries; 2 months to mss. Obtains most new clients through recommendations from others, solicitations.

Recent Sales: *Alice in Wonderland*, by Robert Sabuda; *Dahlia*, by Barbara McClintock; *Living Dead Girl*, by Tod Goldberg; *In My Mother's House*, by Margaret McMulla; *Black Hawk Down*, by Mark Bowden; *Look Back All the Green Valley*, by Fred Chappell; *Even Now*, by Susan S. Kelly.

Terms: Agent receives 15% commission on domestic sales; 20% commission on foreign sales. Writers reimbursed for office fees after the sale of ms.

Ⓝ ☑ HENRY DUNOW LITERARY AGENCY

22 W. 23rd St., 5th Floor, New York NY 10010. Member of AAR.

    • This agency did not respond to our request for information. Query before submitting.

Member Agents: Jennifer Carlson (associate member).

Ⓝ ☑ DUPREE/MILLER AND ASSOCIATES INC. LITERARY

100 Highland Park Village, Suite 350, Dallas TX 75205. (214)559-BOOK. Fax: (214)559-PAGE. E-mail: dmabook @aol.com. **Contact:** Submissions Department. President: Jan Miller. Estab. 1984. Member of ABA. Represents 200 clients. 20% of clients are new/unpublished writers. Currently handles: 90% nonfiction books; 10% novels.

Member Agents: Jan Miller; Michael Broussard; Shannon Miser-Marven (business affairs); Kym Wilson.

Represents: Nonfiction books, novels, scholarly books, syndicated material. **Considers these nonfiction areas:** Agriculture/horticulture; Americana; animals; anthropology/archaeology; art/architecture/design; biography/autobiography; business/economics; child guidance/parenting; computers/electronic; cooking/foods/nutrition; crafts/hobbies; creative nonfiction; current affairs; education; ethnic/cultural interests; gardening; gay/lesbian issues; government/politics/law; health/medicine; history; how-to; humor/satire; interior design/decorating; juvenile nonfiction; language/literature/criticism; memoirs; military/war; money/finance; multicultural; music/dance; nature/environment; New Age/metaphysics; philosophy; photography; popular culture; psychology; recreation; regional; religious/inspirational; science/technology; self-help/personal improvement; sex; sociology; software; spirituality; sports; theater/film; translation; travel; true crime/investigative; women's issues/studies; young adult. **Considers these fiction areas:** Action/adventure; contemporary issues; detective/police/crime; ethnic; experimental; family saga; feminist; gay/lesbian; glitz; historical; humor/satire; literary; mainstream/contemporary; mystery/suspense; picture books; psychic/supernatural; religious/inspirational; sports; thriller.

    ○━ This agency specializes in commercial fiction, nonfiction.

How to Contact: Query with SASE, outline. Considers simultaneous queries. Responds in 3 months to mss. Obtains most new clients through recommendations from others, conferences, lectures and "very frequently through publisher's referrals."

Recent Sales: Sold 25 titles in the last year. *The Ultimate Weight Solution*, by Dr. Phil McGraw (Simon & Schuster); *The Ultimate Weight Solution for Teens*, by Jay McGraw (Simon & Schuster); *Home Rules*, by Nate Berkus (Hyperion); *The Automatic Millionaire*, by David Bach (Broadway).

Terms: Agent receives 15% commission on domestic sales. Offers written contract.

Writers' Conferences: Southwest Writers (Albuquerque NM); Brazos Writers (College Station TX).

Tips: If interested in agency representation, "it is vital to have the material in the proper working format. As agents' policies differ, it is important to follow their guidelines. The best advice I can give is to work on establishing a strong proposal that provides sample chapters, an overall synopsis (fairly detailed), and some bio information on yourself. Do not send your proposal in pieces; it should be complete upon submission. Remember you are trying to sell your work, and it should be in its best condition."

⊘ DWYER & O'GRADY, INC.

P.O. Box 790, Cedar Key FL 32625. (352)543-9307. Website: www.dwyerogrady.com. **Contact:** Elizabeth O'Grady. Estab. 1990. Member of SCBWI. Represents 20 clients. Currently handles: 100% juvenile books.

 • Prior to opening their agency, Mr. Dwyer and Ms. Grady were booksellers and publishers.

Member Agents: Elizabeth O'Grady (children's books); Jeff Dwyer (children's books).

Represents: Juvenile books. **Considers these nonfiction areas:** Juvenile nonfiction. **Considers these fiction areas:** Juvenile; picture books; young adult.

 ⊶ This agency represents only writers and illustrators of children's books. Does not want to receive submissions that are not for juvenile audiences.

How to Contact: Not accepting new clients. *No unsolicited mss.* Obtains most new clients through recommendations from others, direct approach by agent to writer whose work they've read.

Recent Sales: Sold 22 titles in the last year. Other clients include Kim Ablon Whitney, Mary Azarian, Tom Bodett, Odds Bodkin, Donna Clair, Leonard Jenkins, E.B. Lewis, Steve Schuch, Virginia Stroud, Natasha Tarpley, Zong-Zhou Wang, Rashida Watson, Rich Michelson, Barry Moser, Peter Syluada.

Terms: Agent receives 15% commission on domestic sales; 20% commission on foreign sales. Offers written contract; 1-month notice must be given to terminate contract. Charges clients for "photocopying of longer manuscripts or mutually agreed upon marketing expenses."

Writers' Conferences: Book Expo; American Library Association; Society of Children's Book Writers & Illustrators.

⊘ DYSTEL & GODERICH LITERARY MANAGEMENT

1 Union Square W., Suite 904, New York NY 10003. (212)627-9100. Fax: (212)627-9313. E-mail: miriam@dystel.com. Website: www.dystel.com. **Contact:** Miriam Goderich. Estab. 1994. Member of AAR. Represents 300 clients. 50% of clients are new/unpublished writers. Currently handles: 65% nonfiction books; 25% novels; 10% cookbooks.

 • Dystel & Goderich Literary Management recently acquired the client list of Bedford Book Works.

Member Agents: Stacey Glick; Jane Dystel; Miriam Goderich; Michael Bourret; Jessica Papin; Jim McCarthy.

Represents: Nonfiction books, novels, cookbooks. **Considers these nonfiction areas:** Animals; anthropology/archaeology; biography/autobiography; business/economics; child guidance/parenting; cooking/foods/nutrition; current affairs; education; ethnic/cultural interests; gay/lesbian issues; government/politics/law; health/medicine; history; humor/satire; military/war; money/finance; New Age/metaphysics; popular culture; psychology; religious/inspirational; science/technology; true crime/investigative; women's issues/studies. **Considers these fiction areas:** Action/adventure; contemporary issues; detective/police/crime; ethnic; family saga; gay/lesbian; literary; mainstream/contemporary; mystery/suspense; thriller (especially).

 ⊶ This agency specializes in commercial and literary fiction and nonfiction, plus cookbooks.

How to Contact: Query with SASE. Considers simultaneous queries. Responds in 1 month to queries; 6 weeks to mss. Obtains most new clients through recommendations from others, solicitations, conferences.

Recent Sales: *The Gift of Jazzy*, by Cindy Adams; *Whiskey Sour*, by J.A. Konrath; *Bittersweet*, by Alice Medrich; *Douglass' Women*, by Jewell Parker Rhodes; *Taste: Pure and Simple*, by Michel Nischan; *The Mapmaker's Wife*, by Robert Whitaker; *Kushiel's Avatar*, by Jacqueline Carey; *The Last Goodbye*, by Reed Arvin; *Boy Gets Grill*, by Bobby Flay.

Terms: Agent receives 15% commission on domestic sales; 19% commission on foreign sales. Offers written contract, binding for book-to-book basis. Charges for photocopying. Galley charges and book charges from the publisher are passed on to the author.

Writers' Conferences: West Coast Writers Conference (Whidbey Island WA, Columbus Day weekend); University of Iowa Writer's Conference; Pacific Northwest Writer's Conference; Pike's Peak Writer's Conference; Santa Barbara Writer's Conference; Harriette Austin's Writer's Conference; Sandhills Writers Conference; ASU Writers Conference.

Tips: "Work on sending professional, well-written queries that are concise and addressed to the specific agent the author is contacting. No dear Sirs/Madam."

Ⓝ ⊘ ANNE EDELSTEIN LITERARY AGENCY

404 Riverside Dr., New York NY 10025. Member of AAR.

• This agency did not respond to our request for information. Query before submitting.

⑬ ☑ ◎ EDUCATIONAL DESIGN SERVICES, INC., (Specialized: education)

P.O. Box 253, Wantagh NY 11793-0253. (718)539-4107 or (516)221-0995. **Contact:** Bertram L. Linder, president; Edwin Selzer, vice president. Estab. 1979. Represents 17 clients. 70% of clients are new/unpublished writers. Currently handles: 100% textbooks.

Represents: Scholarly books, textbooks. **Considers these nonfiction areas:** Anthropology/archaeology; business/economics; child guidance/parenting; current affairs; education; ethnic/cultural interests; government/politics/law; history; language/literature/criticism; military/war; money/finance; science/technology; sociology; women's issues/studies.

○┬ This agency specializes in textual material for the educational (K-12) market.

How to Contact: Query with SASE, proposal package, outline, 1-2 sample chapter(s). Considers simultaneous queries. Responds in 1 month to queries; 6 weeks to mss. Returns materials only with SASE. Obtains most new clients through recommendations from others, solicitations, conferences.

Recent Sales: Sold 4 titles in the last year. *Minority Report*, by H. Gunn & J. Singh (Scarecrow Press); *Spreadsheets for School Administrators & Supervisors* (Scarecrow Press); *How to Solve the Word Problems in Arithmetic Grades 6-8*, by P. Pullman (McGraw-Hill/Schaum); *How to Solve Math Word Problems on Standardized Tests*, by D. Wayne (McGraw-Hill/Schaum); *First Principles of Cosmology*, by E.V. Linder (Addison-Wesley Longman).

Terms: Agent receives 15% commission on domestic sales; 25% commission on foreign sales. Offers written contract. Charges clients for photocopying, actual postage/shipping costs.

☑ ETHAN ELLENBERG LITERARY AGENCY

548 Broadway, #5-E, New York NY 10012. (212)431-4554. Fax: (212)941-4652. E-mail: agent@ethanellenberg.com. Website: www.ethanellenberg.com. **Contact:** Ethan Ellenberg, Michael Psaltis. Estab. 1983. Represents 80 clients. 10% of clients are new/unpublished writers. Currently handles: 25% nonfiction books; 75% novels.

• Prior to opening his agency, Mr. Ellenberg was contracts manager of Berkley/Jove, and associate contracts manager for Bantam.

Member Agents: Michael Psaltis (serious and commercial nonfiction, including science, health, popular culture, cooking, current events, politics, business, memoir, and other unique projects; and commercial and literary fiction); Ethan Ellenberg.

Represents: Nonfiction books, novels. **Considers these nonfiction areas:** Biography/autobiography; health/medicine; history; military/war; New Age/metaphysics; religious/inspirational; science/technology. **Considers these fiction areas:** Fantasy; romance; science fiction; thriller; women's.

○┬ This agency specializes in commercial fiction, especially thrillers, romance/women's fiction, and specialized nonfiction. "We also do a lot of children's books." For children's books: Send introductory letter (with credits, if any), up to 3 picture book mss, outline, and first 3 chapters for longer projects, SASE. Actively seeking commercial and literary fiction, children's books, break-through nonfiction. Does not want to receive poetry, short stories, westerns, autobiographies.

How to Contact: For fiction, send introductory letter (with credits, if any), outline, first 3 chapters, and SASE. For nonfiction, send query letter and/or proposal, 1 sample chapter, if written, and SASE. No fax queries. Accepts e-mail queries, no attachments. Considers simultaneous queries. Responds in 2 weeks to queries; 4-6 weeks to mss. Returns materials only with SASE.

Recent Sales: Has sold over 100 titles in the last 3 years. *My Friend Robin*, by Eric Rohann; *Last Exit*, by Lori Broten.

Terms: Agent receives 15% commission on domestic sales; 10% commission on foreign sales. Offers written contract. Charges clients for "direct expenses only limited to photocopying, postage, by writer's consent only."

Writers' Conferences: RWA National; Novelists, Inc; and other regional conferences.

Tips: "We do consider new material from unsolicited authors. Write a good, clear letter with a succinct description of your book. We prefer the first 3 chapters when we consider fiction. For all submissions you must include a SASE for return or the material is discarded. It's always hard to break in, but talent will find a home. Check our website for complete submission guidelines. We continue to see natural storytellers and nonfiction writers with important books."

☑ NICHOLAS ELLISON, INC.

affiliated with Sanford J. Greenburger Associates, 55 Fifth Ave., 15th Floor, New York NY 10003. (212)206-6050. Fax: (212)463-8718. Website: www.greenburger.com. **Contact:** Jennifer Cayea. Estab. 1983. Represents 70 clients. Currently handles: 50% nonfiction books; 50% novels.

• Prior to becoming an agent, Mr. Ellison was an editor at Minerva Editions, Harper & Row, and editor-in-chief at Delacorte.

Member Agents: Jennifer Cayea.

Represents: Nonfiction books, novels. **Considers these nonfiction areas:** Considers most nonfiction areas. **Considers these fiction areas:** Literary; mainstream/contemporary.

How to Contact: Query with SASE. Responds in 6 weeks to queries.

Recent Sales: *Up Country*, by Nelson DeMille (Warner); *The Anniversary*, by Amy Gutman (Little, Brown); *The Big Love*, by Sarah Dunn (Little, Brown). Other clients include Olivia Goldsmith, P.T. Deutermann, Nancy Geary.

Terms: Agent receives 15% commission on domestic sales; 20% commission on foreign sales.

◑ ANN ELMO AGENCY, INC.

60 E. 42nd St., New York NY 10165. (212)661-2880, 2881. Fax: (212)661-2883. **Contact:** Lettie Lee. Estab. 1959. Member of AAR, MWA, Authors Guild.

Member Agents: Lettie Lee; Mari Cronin (plays); A.L. Abecassis (nonfiction).

Represents: Nonfiction books, novels. **Considers these nonfiction areas:** Biography/autobiography; current affairs; health/medicine; history; how-to; money/finance; music/dance; popular culture; psychology; science/technology; self-help/personal improvement; theater/film. **Considers these fiction areas:** Contemporary issues; ethnic; family saga; mainstream/contemporary; romance (contemporary, gothic, historical, regency); thriller; women's.

How to Contact: Letter queries only with SASE. No fax queries. Responds in 3 months to queries. Obtains most new clients through recommendations from others.

Recent Sales: This agency prefers not to share information on specific sales.

Terms: Agent receives 15% commission on domestic sales; 20% commission on foreign sales. Offers written contract. Charges clients for "special mailings or shipping considerations or multiple international calls. No charge for usual cost of doing business."

Tips: "Query first, and when asked only please send properly prepared manuscript. A double-spaced, readable manuscript is the best recommendation. Include SASE, of course."

◒ ELAINE P. ENGLISH

Graybill & English, LLC, 1875 Connecticut Ave. NW, Suite 712, Washington DC 20009. (202)588-9798, ext. 143. Fax: (202)457-0662. E-mail: elaineengl@aol.com. Website: www.graybillandenglish.com. **Contact:** Elaine English. Member of AAR. Represents 18 clients. 50% of clients are new/unpublished writers. Currently handles: 100% novels.

 • Ms. English is also an attorney specializing in media and publishing law.

Member Agents: Elaine English (women's fiction, including romance and mysteries).

Represents: Novels. **Considers these fiction areas:** Historical; mainstream/contemporary; multicultural; mystery/suspense; romance (including single titles); thriller; women's.

 ○➘ "While not as an agent, per se, I have been working in publishing for over 15 years. Also, I'm affiliated with other agents who represent a broad spectrum of projects." Actively seeking women's fiction, including single-title romances. Does not want to receive anything other than above.

How to Contact: Submit synopsis first, 3 chapters, SASE. Responds in 6 weeks to queries; 6 months to mss. Returns materials only with SASE. Obtains most new clients through solicitations.

Terms: Agent receives 15% commission on domestic sales; 20% commission on foreign sales. Offers written contract; 30-day notice must be given to terminate contract. Charges only for expenses directly related to sales of manuscript (long distance, postage, copying).

Writers' Conferences: Washington Romance Writers (Harpers Ferry VA, April); RWA Nationals (Dallas TX, July; SEAK Medical Fiction Writing for Physcians (Cape Cod, September); Emerald City (Seattle WA, October).

◓ FELICIA ETH LITERARY REPRESENTATION

555 Bryant St., Suite 350, Palo Alto CA 94301-1700. (650)375-1276. Fax: (650)401-8892. E-mail: feliciaeth@aol.com. **Contact:** Felicia Eth. Estab. 1988. Member of AAR. Represents 25-35 clients. Works with established and new writers. Currently handles: 85% nonfiction books; 15% adult novels.

Represents: Nonfiction books, novels. **Considers these nonfiction areas:** Animals; anthropology/archaeology; biography/autobiography; business/economics; child guidance/parenting; current affairs; ethnic/cultural interests; gay/lesbian issues; government/politics/law; health/medicine; history; nature/environment; popular culture; psychology; science/technology; sociology; true crime/investigative; women's issues/studies. **Considers these fiction areas:** Ethnic; feminist; gay/lesbian; literary; mainstream/contemporary; thriller.

 ○➘ This agency specializes in "provocative, intelligent, thoughtful nonfiction on a wide array of subjects which are commercial, and high-quality fiction—preferably mainstream and contemporary."

How to Contact: Query with SASE, outline. Considers simultaneous queries. Responds in 3 weeks to queries; 4-6 weeks to mss.

Recent Sales: Sold 7-10 titles in the last year. *Jane Austen in Boca*, by Paula Marantz Cohen (St. Martin's

Press); *Beyond Pink and Blue*, by Dr. Leonard Sax (Doubleday/Random House); *Lavendar Road to Success*, by Kirk Snyder (Ten Speed Press).

Terms: Agent receives 15% commission on domestic sales; 20% commission on foreign sales; 20% commission on dramatic rights sales. Charges clients for photocopying, express mail service—extraordinary expenses.

Writers' Conferences: Independent Writers of LA (Los Angeles); Conference of National Coalition of Independent Scholars (Berkley CA); Writers Guild.

Tips: "For nonfiction, established expertise is certainly a plus, as is magazine publication—though not a prerequisite. I am highly dedicated to those projects I represent, but highly selective in what I choose."

N Ø MARY EVANS, INC.

242 E. Fifth St., New York NY 10003. (212)979-0880. Member of AAR.
   • Query before submitting.
Member Agents: Mary Evans, Tanya McKinnon.

Ø FARBER LITERARY AGENCY, INC.

14 E. 75th St., #2E, New York NY 10021. (212)861-7075. Fax: (212)861-7076. E-mail: farberlit@aol.com. Website: www.donaldfarber.com. **Contact:** Ann Farber; Dr. Seth Farber. Estab. 1989. Represents 40 clients. 50% of clients are new/unpublished writers. Currently handles: 25% nonfiction books; 15% scholarly books; 25% stage plays; 35% fiction books.

Member Agents: Ann Farber (novels); Seth Farber (plays, scholarly books, novels); Donald C. Farber (attorney, all entertainment media).

Represents: Nonfiction books, novels, juvenile books, textbooks, stage plays. **Considers these nonfiction areas:** Child guidance/parenting; cooking/foods/nutrition; music/dance; psychology; theater/film. **Considers these fiction areas:** Action/adventure; contemporary issues; humor/satire; juvenile; literary; mainstream/contemporary; mystery/suspense; thriller; young adult.

How to Contact: Submit outline, 3 sample chapter(s), SASE. Prefers to read materials exclusively. Responds in 1 month to queries; 2 month to mss. Obtains most new clients through recommendations from others.

Recent Sales: Sold 5 titles in the last year. *The Eden Express*, by Mark Vonnegut (Seven Stories-Eden); *The Gardens of Frau Hess*, by Milton Marcus; *Hot Feat*, by Ed Bullins; *Bright Freedom Song*, by Gloria Houston (Harcourt Brace & Co.).

Terms: Agent receives 15% commission on domestic sales; 20% commission on foreign sales. Offers written contract, binding for 1 year. Client must furnish copies of ms, treatments, and any other items for submission.

Tips: "Our attorney, Donald C. Farber, is the author of many books. His services are available to the agency's clients as part of the agency service at no additional charge."

N Ø DIANA FINCH LITERARY AGENCY

116 W. 23rd St., Suite 500, New York NY 10011. (646)375-2081. Fax: (212)851-8405. E-mail: diana.finch@verizon.net. **Contact:** Diana Finch. Estab. 2003. Member of AAR. Represents 35 clients. 20% of clients are new/unpublished writers. Currently handles: 60% nonfiction books; 25% novels; 5% story collections; 5% juvenile books; 5% multimedia.
   • Prior to becoming an agent, Ms. Finch was an assistant editor at St. Martin's Press.

Represents: Nonfiction books, novels, scholarly books. **Considers these nonfiction areas:** Biography/autobiography; business/economics; child guidance/parenting; computers/electronic; current affairs; ethnic/cultural interests; government/politics/law; health/medicine; history; how-to; humor/satire; memoirs; military/war; money/finance; music/dance; nature/environment; photography; popular culture; psychology; science/technology; self-help/personal improvement; sports; theater/film; translation; true crime/investigative; women's issues/studies; juvenile. **Considers these fiction areas:** Action/adventure; detective/police/crime; ethnic; historical; literary; mainstream/contemporary; thriller; young adult.

   o— Actively seeking narrative nonfiction, popular science, and health topics. Does not want romance, mysteries, or children's picture books.

How to Contact: Query with SASE. Considers simultaneous queries. Returns materials only with SASE. Obtains most new clients through recommendations from others.

Recent Sales: Untitled nonfiction, by Greg Palast (Penguin US and UK); *Journey of the Magi*, by Tudor Parfitt (Farrar, Straus, & Giroux); *Sixth Grade*, by Susie Morgenstern (Viking Children's); *We Were There: African-American Vets*, by Yvonne Latty and Ron Tarver (HarperCollins). Other clients include Keith Devlin, Daniel Duane, Thomas Goltz, Hugh Pope, Sebastian Matthews, Joan Lambert, Dr. Robert Marion.

Terms: Agent receives 15% commission on domestic sales; 20% commission on foreign sales. Offers written contract. "I charge for photocopying, overseas postage, galleys, and books purchased, and try to recap these costs from earnings received for a client, rather than charging outright."

Tips: "Do as much research as you can on agents before you query. Have someone critique your query letter before you send it. It should be only 1 page and describe your book clearly—and why you are writing it—but also demonstrate creativity and a sense of your writing style."

FLAMING STAR LITERARY ENTERPRISES

320 Riverside Dr., New York NY 10025. **Contact:** Joseph B. Vallely or Janis C. Vallely. Estab. 1985. Represents 100 clients. 25% of clients are new/unpublished writers. Currently handles: 100% nonfiction books.

● Prior to opening the agency, Joseph Vallely served as national sales manager for Dell; Janis Vallely was vice president of Doubleday.

Represents: Nonfiction books. **Considers these nonfiction areas:** Current affairs; government/politics/law; health/medicine; nature/environment; New Age/metaphysics; science/technology; self-help/personal improvement; spirituality; sports.

O➜ This agency specializes in upscale commercial nonfiction.

How to Contact: Query with SASE. Obtains most new clients through recommendations from others, solicitations.

Terms: Agent receives 15% commission on domestic sales; 20% commission on foreign sales. Offers written contract. Charges clients for photocopying, postage only.

FLANNERY LITERARY

1140 Wickfield Court, Naperville IL 60563-3300. (630)428-2682. Fax: (630)428-2683. **Contact:** Jennifer Flannery. Estab. 1992. Represents 33 clients. 90% of clients are new/unpublished writers. Currently handles: 100% juvenile books.

● Prior to opening her agency, Ms. Flannery was an editorial assistant.

Represents: Juvenile books. **Considers these nonfiction areas:** Juvenile nonfiction; young adult. **Considers these fiction areas:** Juvenile; picture books; young adult.

O➜ This agency specializes in children's and young adult, juvenile fiction and nonfiction.

How to Contact: Query with SASE. No fax or e-mail queries, please. No e-mail or fax queries. Responds in 3 weeks to queries; 1 month to mss. Obtains most new clients through recommendations from others, submissions.

Recent Sales: Sold 20 titles in the last year. This agency prefers not to share information on specific sales.

Terms: Agent receives 15% commission on domestic sales; 20% commission on foreign sales. Offers written contract, binding for life of book in print; 1-month notice must be given to terminate contract. 100% of business is derived from commissions on ms sales.

Writers' Conferences: SCBWI Fall Conference.

Tips: "Write an engrossing, succinct query describing your work."

PETER FLEMING AGENCY

P.O. Box 458, Pacific Palisades CA 90272. (310)454-1373. **Contact:** Peter Fleming. Estab. 1962. Currently handles: 100% nonfiction books.

Represents: Nonfiction books.

O➜ This agency specializes in "nonfiction books that unearth innovative and uncomfortable truths with bestseller potential."

How to Contact: Query with SASE. Obtains most new clients through "through a different, one-of-a-kind idea for a book often backed by the writer's experience in that area of expertise."

Recent Sales: *Rulers of Evil*, by F. Tupper Saussy (HarperCollins); *Why Is It Always About You-Saving Yourself from the Narcissists in Your Life*, by Sandy Hotchkiss (Free Press).

Terms: Agent receives 15% commission on domestic sales; 25% commission on foreign sales. Offers written contract, binding for 1 year. Charges clients "only those fees agreed to in writing, i.e., NY-ABA expenses shared. We may ask for a TV contract, too."

Tips: "You can begin by self-publishing, test marketing with direct sales, and starting your own website."

B.R. FLEURY AGENCY

P.O. Box 149352, Orlando FL 32814-9352. (407)895-8494. Fax: (407)898-3923 or (888)310-8142. E-mail: brfleury agency@juno.com. **Contact:** Blanche or Margaret. Estab. 1994. Signatory of WGA. Currently handles: 30% nonfiction books; 60% novels; 10% movie scripts.

Represents: Nonfiction books, novels, feature film, TV movie of the week. **Considers these nonfiction areas:** Health/medicine; how-to; humor/satire; money/finance; New Age/metaphysics; self-help/personal improvement; spirituality; true crime/investigative. **Considers these fiction areas:** Fantasy; horror; humor/satire; literary; psychic/supernatural; thriller. **Considers these script subject areas:** Detective/police/crime; fantasy; horror; mystery/suspense; psychic/supernatural; thriller.

O─ Only accepts scripts "if adapted from manuscripts by writers whom we represent." Not accepting new submissions until after January 2005.

How to Contact: Prefers to read materials exclusively. Query with 1-page letter and SASE; or call for information. Accepts 1-page e-mail queries, no attachments and snail mail with no enclosures. Responds in 3 months to mss. Responds immediately to queries.

Recent Sales: Sold 5 manuscripts and 1 screenplay in the last year. This agency prefers not to share information on specific sales.

Terms: Agent receives 15% commission on domestic sales. Offers written contract, binding for as per contract. Receives screenplay commission according to WGA guidelines. Charges clients for business expenses directly related to work represented.

Tips: "Read your work aloud with someone who is not in love with you before you send it to us." E-mail queries should be 1 page maximum, no attachments. Queries with attachments or additional information will be returned unread.

⬛ THE FOGELMAN LITERARY AGENCY

7515 Greenville, Suite 712, Dallas TX 75231. (214)361-9956. Fax: (214)361-9553. E-mail: foglit@aol.com. Website: www.fogelman.com. Also: 599 Lexington Ave., Suite 2300; New York NY 10022; (212)836-4803. **Contact:** Evan Fogelman. Estab. 1990. Member of AAR. Represents 100 clients. 2% of clients are new/unpublished writers. Currently handles: 40% nonfiction books; 40% novels; 10% scholarly books; 10% TV scripts.

• Prior to opening his agency, Mr. Fogelman was an entertainment lawyer. He is still active in the field and serves as chairman of the Texas Entertainment and Sports Lawyers Association.

Member Agents: Evan Fogelman (nonfiction, women's fiction); Linda Kruger (women's fiction, nonfiction); Helen Brown (literary fiction/nonfiction).

Represents: Nonfiction books, novels. **Considers these nonfiction areas:** Biography/autobiography; business/economics; child guidance/parenting; current affairs; education; ethnic/cultural interests; government/politics/law; health/medicine; popular culture; psychology; sports; true crime/investigative; women's issues/studies. **Considers these fiction areas:** Historical; literary; mainstream/contemporary; romance (all sub-genres).

O─ This agency specializes in women's fiction and nonfiction. "Zealous advocacy" makes this agency stand apart from others. Actively seeking "nonfiction of all types; romance fiction." Does not want to receive children's/juvenile.

How to Contact: Query with SASE. Considers simultaneous queries. Responds in 3 months to mss. Responds "next business day" to queries. Returns materials only with SASE. Obtains most new clients through recommendations from others.

Recent Sales: Sold 60 titles in the last year. Other clients include Caroline Hunt, Katherine Sutcliffe, Crystal Stovall.

Terms: Agent receives 15% commission on domestic sales; 10% commission on foreign sales. Offers written contract, binding for project to project.

Writers' Conferences: Romance Writers of America; Novelists, Inc.

Tips: "Finish your manuscript, and see our website."

⬛ FORT ROSS, INC., RUSSIAN-AMERICAN PUBLISHING PROJECTS

26 Arthur Place, Yonkers NY 10701-1703. (914)375-6448. Fax: (914)375-6439. E-mail: fort.ross@verizon.net. Website: www.fortross.net. **Contact:** Dr. Vladimir P. Kartsev. Estab. 1992. Represents about 100 clients. 2% of clients are new/unpublished writers. Currently handles: 50% nonfiction books; 40% novels; 10% juvenile books.

Member Agents: Ms. Olga Borodyanskaya, St. Petersburg, Russia, phone: 7-812-1738607 (fiction, nonfiction); Mr. Konstantin Paltchikov, Moscow, Russia, phone: 7-095-2388272 (romance, science fiction, fantasy, thriller).

Represents: Nonfiction books, novels, juvenile books. **Considers these nonfiction areas:** Biography/autobiography; history; memoirs; psychology; self-help/personal improvement; true crime/investigative. **Considers these fiction areas:** Action/adventure; detective/police/crime; fantasy; horror; juvenile; mystery/suspense; romance (contemporary, gothic, historical, regency); science fiction; thriller; young adult.

O─ This agency specializes in selling rights for Russian books and illustrations (covers) to American publishers, and American books and illustrations for Europe; also Russian-English and English-Russian translations. Actively seeking adventure, fiction, mystery, romance, science fiction, thriller from established authors and illustrators for Russian and European markets.

How to Contact: Send published book or galleys. Accepts e-mail and fax queries. Considers simultaneous queries. Returns materials only with SASE.

Recent Sales: Sold 12 titles in the last year. *Mastering Judo with Vladimir Putin*, by Vladimir Putin et al (North Atlantic Books [USA]); *Max*, by Howard Fast (Baronet [Czech Republic]); *Kiss of Midas*, by George Vainer (Neri [Italy]); *Redemption*, by Howard Fast (Oram [Israel]); *A Suitcase*, by Sergey Doveatov (Amber [Poland]).

Literary Agents

Terms: Agent receives 10% commission on domestic sales; 20% commission on foreign sales. Offers written contract, binding for 2 years; 2-month notice must be given to terminate contract.

Tips: "Established authors and book illustrators (especially cover art) are welcome for the following genres: romance, fantasy, science fiction, mystery, and adventure."

 FOX CHASE AGENCY, INC.

Walnut Hill Plaza #140, 150 S. Warner Rd., King of Prussia PA 19406. (610)341-9840. Fax: (610)341-9842. Member of AAR.

   • This agency did not respond to our request for information. Query before submitting.

Member Agents: A. L. Hart, Jo C. Hart.

LYNN C. FRANKLIN ASSOCIATES, LTD.

1350 Broadway, Suite 2015, New York NY 10018. (212)868-6311. Fax: (212)868-6312. E-mail: agency@fsainc.com. **Contact:** Lynn Franklin and Claudia Nys. Estab. 1987. Member of PEN America. Represents 30-35 clients. 50% of clients are new/unpublished writers. Currently handles: 90% nonfiction books; 10% novels.

Represents: Nonfiction books, novels. **Considers these nonfiction areas:** Biography/autobiography; current affairs; health/medicine; history; memoirs; New Age/metaphysics; psychology; religious/inspirational (inspirational); self-help/personal improvement; spirituality. **Considers these fiction areas:** Literary; mainstream/contemporary (commercial).

   0⇝ This agency specializes in general nonfiction with a special interest in health, biography, international affairs, and spirituality.

How to Contact: Query with SASE. Accepts mail and e-mail queries. *No unsolicited mss.* Accepts e-mail and fax queries. Considers simultaneous queries. Responds in 2 weeks to queries; 6 weeks to mss. Obtains most new clients through recommendations from others, solicitations.

Recent Sales: *God Has a Dream*, by Desmond Tutu (Doubleday); *Sister North*, by Jim Kokoris (St. Martin's); *The Rich Part of Life*, by Jim Kokoris (St. Martin's Press/film rights secured by Columbia Pictures); *Total Renewal: 7 Key Steps to Resilience, Vitality, Long-Term Health*, by Frank Lipman, M.D. (Tarcher/Putnam); *After Breast Cancer Treatment: A Survivor's Guide to Renewed Health and Happiness*, by Hester Hill Schnipper (Bantam/Dell); *Meeting Faith: the Forest Journals of a Black Buddhist Nun in Thailand*, by Faith Adiele (W.W. Norton).

Terms: Agent receives 15% commission on domestic sales; 20% commission on foreign sales. Offers written contract; 2-month notice must be given to terminate contract. 100% of business is derived from commissions on ms sales. Charges clients for postage, photocopying, long distance telephone if significant.

FRANKLIN WEINRIB RUDDELL VASSALLO

488 Madison Ave., New York NY 10022. (212)935-5500. **Contact:** Elliot Brown, Esq. Member of AAR.

   • Query before submitting.

JEANNE FREDERICKS LITERARY AGENCY, INC.

221 Benedict Hill Rd., New Canaan CT 06840. (203)972-3011. Fax: (203)972-3011. E-mail: jfredrks@optonline.net. **Contact:** Jeanne Fredericks. Estab. 1997. Member of AAR, Authors Guild. Represents 90 clients. 10% of clients are new/unpublished writers. Currently handles: 100% nonfiction books.

   • Prior to opening her agency, Ms. Fredericks was an agent and acting director with the Susan P. Urstadt, Inc. Agency. In an earlier career she held editorial positions in trade publishing, most recently as editorial director of Ziff-Davis Books.

Represents: Nonfiction books. **Considers these nonfiction areas:** Animals; biography/autobiography; child guidance/parenting; cooking/foods/nutrition; gardening; health/medicine (and alternative health); history; how-to; interior design/decorating; money/finance; nature/environment; photography; psychology; self-help/personal improvement; sports (not spectator sports); women's issues/studies.

   0⇝ This agency specializes in quality adult nonfiction by authorities in their fields. Does not want to receive children's books or fiction.

How to Contact: Query first with SASE, then send outline/proposal, 1-2 sample chapters and SASE. No fax queries. Accepts e-mail queries if short; no attachments. Considers simultaneous queries. Responds in 3-5 weeks to queries; 2-4 months to mss. Returns materials only with SASE. Obtains most new clients through recommendations from others, solicitations, conferences.

Recent Sales: Sold 12 titles in the last year. *Lilias! Yoga Gets Better with Age*, by Lilias Folan (Rodale); *Outdoors, the Perfect Fit*, by Anne Halpin (Rodale); *Creating Optimism: The Uplift Program for Healing Past Trauma and Current Depression*, by Bob Murray, Ph.D., and Alice Fortinberry, M.S; *Yoga for Men*, by Tom Claire (Career Press); *Cowboys and Dragons: Achieving Successful American-Chinese Business Relations*, by Charles Lee (Dearborn).

Terms: Agent receives 15% commission on domestic sales; 25% commission on foreign sales with co-agent; without co-agent receives 20% commission on foreign sales. Offers written contract, binding for 9 months; 2 months notice must be given to terminate contract. Charges client for photocopying of whole proposals and mss, overseas postage, priority mail, and express mail services.

Writers' Conferences: PEN Women Conference (Williamsburg VA, February); Connecticut Press Club Biennial Writer's Conference (Stamford CT, April); ASJA Annual Writers' Conference East (New York NY, May); BEA (Chicago, June); Garden Writers of America Conference (New York, November).

Tips: ''Be sure to research the competition for your work and be able to justify why there's a need for it. I enjoy building an author's career, particularly if s(he) is professional, hardworking, and courteous. Aside from 10 years of agenting experience, I've had 10 years of editorial experience in adult trade book publishing that enables me to help an author polish a proposal so that it's more appealing to prospective editors. My MBA in marketing also distinguishes me from other agents.''

ROBERT A. FREEDMAN DRAMATIC AGENCY, INC.

1501 Broadway, Suite 2310, New York NY 10036. (212)840-5760. Fax: (212)840-5776. Member of AAR.
• Query before submitting.
Member Agents: Robert Freedman, Robin Kaver, Selma Luttinger, Marta Praeger.

SARAH JANE FREYMANN LITERARY AGENCY

59 W. 71st St., Suite 9B, New York NY 10023. (212)362-9277. Fax: (212)501-8240. E-mail: sjfs@aol.com. **Contact:** Sarah Jane Freymann. Represents 100 clients. 20% of clients are new/unpublished writers. Currently handles: 75% nonfiction books; 23% novels; 2% juvenile books.

Represents: Nonfiction books, novels, illustrated books. **Considers these nonfiction areas:** Animals; anthropology/archaeology; art/architecture/design; biography/autobiography; business/economics; child guidance/parenting; cooking/foods/nutrition; current affairs; ethnic/cultural interests; health/medicine; history; interior design/decorating; memoirs (narrative, non-fiction); nature/environment; psychology; religious/inspirational; self-help/personal improvement; women's issues/studies; lifestyle. **Considers these fiction areas:** Contemporary issues; ethnic; literary; mainstream/contemporary; mystery/suspense; thriller.

How to Contact: Query with SASE. Responds in 2 weeks to queries; 6 weeks to mss. Obtains most new clients through recommendations from others.

Recent Sales: *The Earth Knows My Name*, by Patricia Klindenst (Beacon); *Around the Bloc*, by Stephanie Elizondo Griest (Villard); *Cooking One-on-One*, by John Ash, with Amy Mintzer (Clarkson Potter); *I'm Almost Always Hungry*, by Lora Zarubin (Abrahms); *To Finish the Quest*, by Diana Durham (Tarcher); *Holding Fast*, by Gary Nebhan (Houghton Mifflin); *Crossing the Blvd.*, by Warren Lehrer and Judith Sloan.

Terms: Agent receives 15% commission on domestic sales; 20% commission on foreign sales. Offers written contract. Charges clients for long distance, overseas postage, photocopying. 100% of business is derived from commissions on ms sales.

Tips: ''I love fresh, new, passionate works by authors who love what they are doing and have both natural talent and carefully honed skill.''

CANDICE FUHRMAN LITERARY AGENCY

60 Greenwood Way, Mill Valley CA 94941. (415)383-6081. Fax: (415)383-9649. E-mail: candicef@pacbell.net. **Contact:** Candice Fuhrman. Estab. 1987. Member of AAR.
Member Agents: Elsa Hurley.
Represents: Nonfiction books (adult), novels (adult). **Considers these nonfiction areas:** Current affairs; health/medicine; popular culture; psychology; women's issues/studies; adventure, mind/body/spirit, lifestyle. **Considers these fiction areas:** Literary.
• No children's category, no genre.
How to Contact: *No unsolicited mss.* Please query first. Query with SASE and include e-mail address.
Terms: Agent receives 15% commission on domestic sales; 20-30% commission on foreign sales.

MAX GARTENBERG, LITERARY AGENT

12 Westminster Dr., Livingston NJ 07039-1414. (973)994-4457. Fax: (973)535-5033. E-mail: gartenbook@att.n et. **Contact:** Max Gartenberg, Anne Devlin and Will Devlin (912 N. Pennsylvania Ave., Yardley PA 19067). Estab. 1954. Represents 30 clients. 5% of clients are new/unpublished writers. Currently handles: 90% nonfiction books; 10% novels.

Represents: Nonfiction books, novels. **Considers these nonfiction areas:** Agriculture/horticulture; animals; art/architecture/design; biography/autobiography; child guidance/parenting; current affairs; health/medicine; history; military/war; money/finance; music/dance; nature/environment; psychology; science/technology; self-help/personal improvement; sports; theater/film; true crime/investigative; women's issues/studies.

How to Contact: Query with SASE. Considers simultaneous queries. Responds in 2 weeks to queries; 6 weeks to mss. Obtains most new clients through recommendations from others, occasionally by "following up on good query letters"

Recent Sales: *The Tao of War*, by Ralph D. Sawyer (Westview Press); *Passing Gas and Other Towns Along the American Highway*, by Gary Gladstone (Ten Speed Press); *Ogallala Blue*, by William Ashworth (W.W. Norton).

Terms: Agent receives 15% commission on first domestic sales; 10% subsequent commission on domestic sales; 15-20% commission on foreign sales.

Tips: "This agency has recently expanded, with more access for new writers to the associate agents named above."

☑ GELFMAN, SCHNEIDER, LITERARY AGENTS, INC.

250 W. 57th St., New York NY 10107. (212)245-1993. Fax: (212)245-8678. **Contact:** Jane Gelfman, Deborah Schneider. Estab. 1981. Member of AAR. Represents 300+ clients. 10% of clients are new/unpublished writers.

Represents: Nonfiction books, novels, "We represent adult, general, hardcover fiction and nonfiction, literary and commercial, and some mysteries." **Considers these fiction areas:** Literary; mainstream/contemporary; mystery/suspense.

   O━ Does not want to receive romances, science fiction, westerns, or children's books.

How to Contact: Query with SASE. No e-mail queries accepted. Responds in 1 month to queries; 2 months to mss. Obtains most new clients through recommendations from others.

Terms: Agent receives 15% commission on domestic sales; 20% commission on foreign sales. Offers written contract. Charges clients for photocopying, messengers and couriers.

ℕ ☑ THE GERSH AGENCY

130 W. 42nd St., New York NY 10036. (212)634-1818. Fax: (212)391-8459. Member of AAR.

   ● Query before submitting.

Member Agents: John Buzzetti, Peter Franklin, Peter Hagan.

GHOSTS & COLLABORATORS INTERNATIONAL

Division of James Peter Associates, Inc., P.O. Box 358, New Canaan CT 06840. (203)972-1070. E-mail: gene_brissie@msn.com. **Contact:** Gene Brissie. Estab. 1971. Represents 75 clients. Currently handles: 100% nonfiction books.

Represents: Nonfiction collaborations and ghost writing assignments.

   O━ This agency specializes in representing only published ghost writers and collaborators, nonfiction only.

How to Contact: Prefers to read materials exclusively.

Recent Sales: Sold 50 titles in the last year. Other clients include Clients include Alan Axelrod, Carol Turkington, Edward Purcell, George Mair, Brandon Toropov, Richard Marek, Susan Shelly, Carlo Devito.

Terms: Agent receives 15% commission on domestic sales; 20% commission on foreign sales. Offers written contract.

Tips: "We would like to hear from professional writers who are looking for ghosting and collaboration projects. We invite inquiries from book publishers who are seeking writers to develop house-generated ideas and to work with their authors who need professional assistance."

☑ THE GISLASON AGENCY

219 Main St. SE, Suite 506, Minneapolis MN 55414-2160. (612)331-8033. Fax: (612)331-8115. E-mail: gislasonbj@aol.com. Website: www.thegislasonagency.com. **Contact:** Barbara J. Gislason, literary agent. Estab. 1992. Member of Minnesota State Bar Association, Art & Entertainment Law Section (former chair), Animal Law Committee, Internet Committee, Minnesota Intellectual Property Law Association Copyright Committee (former chair); also a member of SFWA, MWA, Sisters in Crime, Oak Street Arts Board (former board member), Icelandic Association of Minnesota (president) and American Academy of Acupuncture and Oriental Medicine (advisory board member). 80% of clients are new/unpublished writers. Currently handles: 10% nonfiction books; 90% novels.

   ● Ms. Gislason became an attorney in 1980, and continues to practice Art & Entertainment Law. She has been nationally recognized as a Leading American Attorney and a Super Lawyer. She is also the owner of Blue Raven Press, which publishes fiction and nonfiction about animals.

Member Agents: Deborah Sweeney (fantasy, science fiction); Kellie Hultgren (fantasy, science fiction); Lisa Higgs (mystery, literary fiction); Kris Olson (mystery); Kevin Hedman (fantasy, science fiction, mystery, literary fiction).

Represents: Nonfiction books, novels. **Considers these nonfiction areas:** Animals (behavior/communications). **Considers these fiction areas:** Fantasy; literary; mystery/suspense; science fiction; thriller (legal).

○━ Do not send personal memoirs, poetry, short stories, screenplays, or children's books.

How to Contact: For fiction, query with synopsis, first 3 chapters, and SASE. For nonfiction, query with proposal and sample chapters; published authors may submit complete ms. No e-mail or fax queries. Responds in 2 months to queries; 3 months to mss. Obtains most new clients through recommendations from others, conferences, *Guide to Literary Agents, Literary Market Place*, and other reference books.

Recent Sales: *Historical Romance # 4*, by Linda Cook (Kensington); *Dancing Dead*, by Deborah Woodworth (HarperCollins); *Owen Keane's Lonely Journey*, by Terence Faherty (Harlequin).

Terms: Agent receives 15% commission on domestic sales; 20% commission on foreign sales. Offers written contract, binding for 1 year with option to renew. Charges clients for photocopying and postage.

Writers' Conferences: SouthWest Writers; Willamette Writers; Wrangling with Writing. Also attends other state and regional writers conferences.

Tips: "Cover letter should be well written and include a detailed synopsis (if fiction) or proposal (if nonfiction), the first 3 chapters, and author bio. Appropriate SASE required. We are looking for a great writer with a poetic, lyrical, or quirky writing style who can create intriguing ambiguities. We expect a well-researched, imaginative, and fresh plot that reflects a familiarity with the applicable genre. If submitting nonfiction work, explain how the submission differs from and adds to previously published works in the field. Scenes with sex and violence must be intrinsic to the plot. Remember to proofread. If the work was written with a specific publisher in mind, this should be communicated. In addition to owning an agency, Ms. Gislason practices law in the area of art and entertainment and has a broad spectrum of entertainment industry contacts."

☻ GOLDFARB & ASSOCIATES

721 Gibbon St., Alexandria VA 22314. (202)466-3030. Fax: (703)836-5644. E-mail: rglawlit@aol.com. **Contact:** Ronald Goldfarb. Estab. 1966. Currently handles: 75% nonfiction books; 25% novels; increasing TV and movie deals.

• Ron Goldfarb's book (his ninth), *Perfect Villains, Imperfect Heroes*, was published by Random House. His tenth, *TV or not TV: Courts, Television, and Justice* (NYU Press), 1998.

Member Agents: B. Farley Chase (New York office); Robbie Anna Hare; Louise Wheatley.

Represents: Nonfiction books, novels. **Considers these nonfiction areas:** Art/architecture/design; biography/autobiography; business/economics; cooking/foods/nutrition; current affairs; education; ethnic/cultural interests; government/politics/law; health/medicine; history; language/literature/criticism; memoirs; military/war; money/finance; multicultural; nature/environment; popular culture; sociology; sports; theater/film; travel; true crime/investigative; women's issues/studies. **Considers these fiction areas:** Action/adventure; contemporary issues; detective/police/crime; ethnic; literary; mainstream/contemporary; mystery/suspense; thriller.

○━ This agency specializes primarily in nonfiction but has a growing interest in well-written fiction. "Given our D.C. location, we represent many journalists, politicians, and former federal officials. We arrange collaborations. We also represent a broad range of nonfiction writers and novelists." Actively seeking "fiction with literary overtones; strong nonfiction ideas." Does very little children's fiction or poetry.

How to Contact: No fax queries. Responds in 1 month to queries; 2 months to mss. Obtains most new clients through recommendations from others.

Recent Sales: Sold 35 titles in the last year. *Imperfect Justice*, by Stuart Eizenstat; *Sargent Shriver*, by Scott Stossell. Other clients include former Congressman John Kasich, Diane Rehm, Susan Eisenhower, Dan Moldea, Roy Gutman, Leonard Garment, United States Holocaust Memorial Museum, Harlem Jazz Museum.

Terms: Charges clients for photocopying, long distance phone calls, postage.

Writers' Conferences: Washington Independent Writers Conference; Medical Writers Conference; VCCA; participates in many ad hoc writers' and publishers' groups and events each year.

Tips: "We are a law firm which can help writers with related legal problems, Freedom of Information Act requests, libel, copyright, contracts, etc. As published authors ourselves, we understand the creative process."

Ⓝ ☻ FRANCES GOLDIN LITERARY AGENCY, INC.

57 E. 11th St., Suite 5B, New York NY 10003. (212)777-0047. Fax: (212)228-1660. E-mail: agency@goldinlit.com. Estab. 1975. Member of AAR. 50% of clients are new/unpublished writers. Currently handles: nonfiction books; novels; story collections.

Member Agents: Francis Goldin; Sydelle Kramer; Matt McGowan; Sam Stoloff; David Csontos.

Represents: Nonfiction books, novels. **Considers these nonfiction areas:** Serious, progressive nonfiction. **Considers these fiction areas:** Adult literary.

○━ "We are hands-on, and we work intensively with clients on proposal and manuscript development." Does not want anything that is racist, sexist, agist, homophobic, or pornographic. No software.

How to Contact: Query with SASE. *No unsolicited mss*, or work previously submitted to publishers. *Skin Deep*, by Dalton Conley (Pantheon); Untitled Essay Collection, by Harriett McBryde Johnson (Henry Holt); *The School Among the Ruins*, by Adrienne Rich (Norton).

[N] [M] GOODMAN ASSOCIATES

500 West End Ave., New York NY 10024-4317. (212)873-4806. **Contact:** Elise Simon Goodman. Estab. 1976. Member of AAR. Represents 50 clients.

• Arnold Goodman is current chair of the AAR Ethics Committee.

Member Agents: Elise Simon Goodman; Arnold P. Goodman.

Represents: Nonfiction books, novels. **Considers these nonfiction areas:** Americana; animals; anthropology/archaeology; biography/autobiography; business/economics; child guidance/parenting; cooking/foods/nutrition; creative nonfiction; current affairs; education; ethnic/cultural interests; government/politics/law; health/medicine; history; language/literature/criticism; memoirs; military/war; money/finance; multicultural; music/dance; nature/environment; philosophy; popular culture; psychology; recreation; regional; science/technology; sex; sociology; sports; theater/film; translation; travel; true crime/investigative; women's issues/studies. **Considers these fiction areas:** Action/adventure; contemporary issues; detective/police/crime; erotica; ethnic; family saga; historical; literary; mainstream/contemporary; military/war; multicultural; multimedia; mystery/suspense; regional; sports; thriller; translation.

⚷ Accepting new clients by recommendation only. Does not want to receive poetry, articles, individual stories, children's, or YA material.

How to Contact: Query with SASE. Responds in 10 days to queries; 1 month to mss.

Terms: Agent receives 15% commission on domestic sales; 20% commission on foreign sales. Charges clients for certain expenses: faxes, toll calls, overseas postage, photocopying, book purchases.

[N] [M] THE THOMAS GRADY AGENCY

209 Bassett St., Petaluma CA 94952-2668. (707)765-6229. Fax: (707)765-6810. E-mail: tom@tgrady.com. Website: www.tgrady.com. **Contact:** Thomas Grady. Member of AAR. 10% of clients are new/unpublished writers.

How to Contact: E-mail queries preferred.

[N] [M] GRAYBILL & ENGLISH

1875 Connecticut Ave. NW, Suite 712, Washington DC 20009. (202)588-9798. Fax: (202)457-0662. Website: www.graybillandenglish.com. **Contact:** See website for agents' interests and submission guidelines. Estab. 1997. Member of AAR. Represents 100 clients. 25-75% of clients are new/unpublished writers. Currently handles: 70% nonfiction books; 30% novels.

Member Agents: Nina Graybill (serious and narrative nonfiction, literary fiction); Elaine English (commercial women's fiction, including romance and mystery); Jeff Kleinman (narrative and practical nonfiction, literary and commercial fiction, thrillers); Lynn Whittaker (narrative and serious nonfiction, sports, literary fiction, mystery/suspense); Kristen Auclair (practical and narrative nonfiction, literary fiction).

Represents: Nonfiction books, novels, short story collections. **Considers these nonfiction areas:** Animals; anthropology/archaeology; biography/autobiography; business/economics; child guidance/parenting; cooking/foods/nutrition; crafts/hobbies; current affairs; education; ethnic/cultural interests; government/politics/law; health/medicine; history; how-to; humor/satire; memoirs; military/war; nature/environment; popular culture; psychology; self-help/personal improvement; sociology; sports; true crime/investigative; women's issues/studies. **Considers these fiction areas:** Contemporary issues; detective/police/crime; ethnic; family saga; fantasy; feminist; glitz; historical; humor/satire; literary; mainstream/contemporary; mystery/suspense; romance; science fiction; sports; thriller.

⚷ Narrative and practical nonfiction; literary fiction, and well-written commercial women's fiction. Actively seeking narrative, serious and practical nonfiction, literary fiction, commercial women's fiction. Does not want novellas, poetry, children's, or young adult books.

How to Contact: Query with SASE, submit outline/proposal. Considers simultaneous queries. Responds in 2-12 to queries; 3-6 months to mss. Returns materials only with SASE. Obtains most new clients through recommendations from others, solicitations, conferences.

Recent Sales: *O Artful Death*, by Sarah Stewart Taylor (St. Martin's); *The Mind-Body Diabetes Revolution*, by Richard Surwit, Ph.D. (The Free Press); *The Memory of Running*, by Ron McLorty (Viking); *Open My Eyes, Open My Soul*, by Yolanda King and Elodia Tate (McGraw-Hill); *The People Next Door*, by Bettye Griffin (Dafina/Kensington).

Terms: Agent receives 15% commission on domestic sales; 20% commission on foreign sales. Offers written contract; 1-month notice must be given to terminate contract. Minimal office expenses (copying, postage, phone).

Writers' Conferences: Creative Nonfiction Conference (Baltimore MD); Words and Music Conference (New Orleans LA); Romance Writers of America (New York NY); Associated Writing Programs (Chicago IL); Boucheron (Toronto).

[M] ASHLEY GRAYSON LITERARY AGENCY

1342 18th St., San Pedro CA 90732. Fax: (310)514-1148. Member of AAR. Represents 100 clients. 5% of clients

are new/unpublished writers. Currently handles: 20% nonfiction books; 50% novels; 30% juvenile books.
Member Agents: Ashley Grayson (commercial and literary fiction, historical novels, mysteries, science fiction, thrillers, young adult); Carolyn Grayson (mainstream commercial fiction, mainstream women's fiction, romance, crime fiction, suspense, thrillers, horror, true crime, young adult, science, medical, health, self-help, how-to, pop culture, creative nonfiction); Dan Hooker (commercial fiction, mysteries, thrillers, suspense, hard science fiction, contemporary and dark fantasy, horror, young adult and middle grade, popular subjects and treatment with high commercial potential, New Age by published professionals).

○₋ "We prefer to work with published (traditional print publishing), established authors. We will give first consideration to authors who come recommended to us by our clients or other publishing professionals. We accept a very small number of new, previously unpublished authors."

How to Contact: Published authors: "We would prefer you send us a written letter with SASE to introduce yourself."

Recent Sales: Sold more than 100 titles in the last year. *Dreaming Pachinko*, by Isaac Adamson (HarperCollins); *The Sky So Big and Black*, by John Barnes (Tor); *Move Your Stuff, Change Your Life*, by Karen Rauch Carter (Simon & Schuster).

Terms: Agent receives 15% commission on domestic sales; 20% commission on foreign sales.

🔲 SANFORD J. GREENBURGER ASSOCIATES, INC.

55 Fifth Ave., New York NY 10003. (212)206-5600. Fax: (212)463-8718. Website: www.greenburger.com. **Contact:** Heide Lange. Estab. 1945. Member of AAR. Represents 500 clients.

Member Agents: Heide Lange, Faith Hamlin, Theresa Park, Elyse Cheney, Dan Mandel, Julie Barer, Matthew Bialer.

Represents: Nonfiction books, novels. **Considers these nonfiction areas:** Agriculture/horticulture; Americana; animals; anthropology/archaeology; art/architecture/design; biography/autobiography; business/economics; child guidance/parenting; computers/electronic; cooking/foods/nutrition; crafts/hobbies; current affairs; education; ethnic/cultural interests; gardening; gay/lesbian issues; government/politics/law; health/medicine; history; how-to; humor/satire; interior design/decorating; juvenile nonfiction; language/literature/criticism; memoirs; military/war; money/finance; multicultural; music/dance; nature/environment; New Age/metaphysics; philosophy; photography; popular culture; psychology; recreation; regional; religious/inspirational; science/technology; self-help/personal improvement; sex; sociology; software; sports; theater/film; translation; travel; true crime/investigative; women's issues/studies; young adult. **Considers these fiction areas:** Action/adventure; contemporary issues; detective/police/crime; ethnic; family saga; feminist; gay/lesbian; glitz; historical; humor/satire; literary; mainstream/contemporary; mystery/suspense; psychic/supernatural; regional; sports; thriller.

○₋ Does not want to receive romances or westerns.

How to Contact: Query with SASE. Considers simultaneous queries. Responds in 3 weeks to queries; 2 months to mss.

Recent Sales: Sold 200 titles in the last year. This agency prefers not to share information on specific sales. Other clients include Andrew Ross, Margaret Cuthbert, Nicholas Sparks, Mary Kurcinka, Linda Nichols, Edy Clarke, Brad Thor, Dan Brown, Sallie Bissell.

Terms: Agent receives 15% commission on domestic sales; 20% commission on foreign sales. Charges for photocopying, books for foreign and subsidiary rights submissions.

🌐 ☑ GREGORY & CO. AUTHORS' AGENTS

3 Barb Mews, London W6 7PA, England. 020-7610-4676. Fax: 020-7610-4686. E-mail: info@gregoryandcompany.co.uk. Website: www.gregoryandcompany.co.uk. **Contact:** Jane Gregory, sales; Broo Doherty, editorial; Claire Morris, rights. Estab. 1987. Member of Association of Authors' Agents. Represents 60 clients. Currently handles: 10% nonfiction books; 90% novels.

● Prior to becoming an agent, Ms. Gregory was Rights Director for Chatto & Windus.

Member Agents: Jane Gregory (sales); Broo Doherty (editorial); Claire Morris (rights).

Represents: Nonfiction books, and fiction books. **Considers these nonfiction areas:** Biography/autobiography; history. **Considers these fiction areas:** Detective/police/crime; historical; literary; mainstream/contemporary; thriller; contemporary women's fiction.

○₋ "Jane Gregory is successful at selling rights all over the world, including film and television rights. As a British agency we do not generally take on American authors." Actively seeking well-written, accessible modern novels. Does not want to receive horror, science fiction, fantasy, mind/body/spirit, children's books, screenplays and plays, short stories, poetry.

How to Contact: Query with SASE, or submit outline, 3 sample chapters, SASE. Considers simultaneous queries. Returns materials only with SASE. Obtains most new clients through recommendations from others, conferences.

Recent Sales: Sold 100 titles in the last year. *Tokyo*, by Mo Hayder (Bantam UK/Doubleday USA); *The Torment* *of Others*, by Val McDermid (HarperCollins UK/St. Martin's Press NY); *Disordered Minds*, by Minette Walters (MacMillan UK/Putnam USA); *The Lover*, by Laura Wilson (Orion UK/Bantam USA); *Keep Me Alive*, by Natasha Cooper (Simon & Schuster UK/St. Martin's Press USA).

Terms: Agent receives 15% commission on domestic sales; 20% commission on foreign sales. Offers written contract; 3-month notice must be given to terminate contract. Charges clients for photocopying of whole typescripts and copies of book for submissions.

Writers' Conferences: CWA Conference (United Kingdom, Spring); Dead on Deansgate (Manchester, Autumn); Harrogate Literary Festival (United Kingdom, Summer); Bouchercon (location varies, Autumn).

🅽 ⊘ BLANCHE C. GREGORY, INC.

2 Tudor City Place, New York NY 10017. (212)697-0828. Member of AAR.

● Query before submitting.

Member Agents: Gertrude Bregman, Merry Gregory Pantano.

🅽 ⊘ MAXINE GROFFSKY LITERARY AGENCY

853 Broadway, Suite 708, New York NY 10003. (212)979-1500. Fax: (212)979-1405. Member of AAR.

● This agency did not respond to our request for information. Query before submitting.

⊙ JILL GROSJEAN LITERARY AGENCY

1390 Millstone Rd., Sag Harbor NY 11963-2214. (631)725-7419. Fax: (631)725-8632. E-mail: jill6981@aol.com. Website: www.hometown.aol.com/jill6981/myhomepage/index.html. **Contact:** Jill Grosjean. Estab. 1999. Represents 27 clients. 100% of clients are new/unpublished writers. Currently handles: 100% novels.

● Prior to becoming an agent, Ms. Grosjean was manager of an independent bookstore. She also worked in publishing and advertising.

Represents: Novels (exclusively). **Considers these fiction areas:** Contemporary issues; historical; literary; mainstream/contemporary; mystery/suspense; regional; romance.

    O→ This agency offers some editorial assistance (i.e., line-by-line edits). Actively seeking literary novels and mysteries.

How to Contact: Query with SASE. No cold calls, please. Considers simultaneous queries. Responds in 1 week to queries; 1 month to mss. Returns materials only with SASE. Obtains most new clients through recommendations from others, solicitations.

Recent Sales: *I Love You Like a Tomato*, by Marie Giordano (Forge Books); *Nectar*, by David C. Fickett (Forge Books); *Cycling*, by Greg Garrett (Kensington); *Sanctuary*, by Greg Garrett (Kensington); *Spectres in the Smoke*, by Tony Broadbent (St. Martin's/Minotaur).

Terms: Agent receives 15% commission on domestic sales; 20% commission on foreign sales. No written contract. Charges clients for photocopying, mailing expenses; Writers reimbursed for office fees after the sale of ms.

Writers' Conferences: Book Passages Mystery Writer's Conference (Corte Madera CA, July); Writers' League of Texas Conference (Austin TX, July).

⊙ THE GROSVENOR LITERARY AGENCY

5510 Grosvenor Lane, Bethesda MD 20814. Fax: (301)581-9401. E-mail: dcgrosveno@aol.com. **Contact:** Deborah C. Grosvenor. Estab. 1996. Member of National Press Club. Represents 30 clients. 10% of clients are new/unpublished writers. Currently handles: 80% nonfiction books; 20% novels.

● Prior to opening her agency, Ms. Grosvenor was a book editor for 16 years.

Represents: Nonfiction books, novels. **Considers these nonfiction areas:** Animals; anthropology/archaeology; art/architecture/design; biography/autobiography; business/economics; child guidance/parenting; current affairs; government/politics/law; health/medicine; history; how-to; language/literature/criticism; military/war; money/finance; music/dance; nature/environment; photography; popular culture; psychology; religious/inspirational; science/technology; self-help/personal improvement; sociology; spirituality; theater/film; translation; true crime/investigative; women's issues/studies. **Considers these fiction areas:** Contemporary issues; detective/police/crime; family saga; historical; literary; mainstream/contemporary; mystery/suspense; romance (contemporary, gothic, historical); thriller.

How to Contact: Send outline/proposal for nonfiction; send query and 3 sample chapters for fiction. No fax queries. Responds in 1 month to queries; 2 months to mss. Returns materials only with SASE. Obtains most new clients through recommendations from others.

Terms: Agent receives 15% commission on domestic sales; 20% commission on foreign sales. Offers written contract; 10-day notice must be given to terminate contract.

⊙ REECE HALSEY NORTH

98 Main St., Tiburon CA 94920. Fax: (310)652-7595. E-mail: info@reecehalseynorth.com. Website: www.reeceh

alseynorth.com. **Contact:** Kimberley Cameron (all queries) at Reece Halsey North. Estab. 1957. Member of AAR. Represents 40 clients. 30% of clients are new/unpublished writers. Currently handles: 30% nonfiction books; 60% novels; 10% movie scripts.

- The Reece Halsey Agency has an illustrious client list largely of established writers, including the estate of Aldous Huxley and has represented Upton Sinclair, William Faulkner, and Henry Miller.

Member Agents: Dorris Halsey; Kimberley Cameron.

Represents: Nonfiction books, novels. **Considers these nonfiction areas:** Biography/autobiography; current affairs; history; language/literature/criticism; popular culture; true crime/investigative; women's issues/studies. **Considers these fiction areas:** Action/adventure; contemporary issues; detective/police/crime; ethnic; family saga; historical; literary; mainstream/contemporary; mystery/suspense; science fiction; thriller; women's.

O— This agency specializes mostly in books/excellent writing.

How to Contact: Query with SASE. Prefers to read materials exclusively. No e-mail or fax queries. Responds in 3 weeks to queries; 3 months to mss. Obtains most new clients through recommendations from others, solicitations.

Terms: Agent receives 15% commission on domestic sales; 10% commission on dramatic rights sales. Offers written contract, binding for 1 year. Requests 6 copies of ms if representing an author.

Writers' Conferences: Maui Writers Conference; ABA.

Tips: "Always send a well-written query and include a SASE with it."

⋈ ☑ THE MITCHELL J. HAMILBURG AGENCY

11718 Barrington Ct., #732, Los Angeles CA 90049-2930. (310) 471-4024. Fax: (310) 471-9588. **Contact:** Michael Hamilburg. Estab. 1937. Signatory of WGA. Represents 70 clients. Currently handles: 70% nonfiction books; 30% novels.

Represents: Nonfiction books, novels. **Considers these nonfiction areas:** Agriculture/horticulture; Americana; animals; anthropology/archaeology; art/architecture/design; biography/autobiography; business/economics; child guidance/parenting; computers/electronic; cooking/foods/nutrition; crafts/hobbies; creative nonfiction; current affairs; education; ethnic/cultural interests; gardening; gay/lesbian issues; government/politics/law; health/medicine; history; how-to; humor/satire; interior design/decorating; juvenile nonfiction; language/literature/criticism; memoirs; military/war; money/finance; multicultural; music/dance; nature/environment; New Age/metaphysics; philosophy; photography; popular culture; psychology; recreation; regional; religious/inspirational; science/technology; self-help/personal improvement; sex; sociology; software; spirituality; sports; theater/film; translation; travel; true crime/investigative; women's issues/studies; young adult; romance. **Considers these fiction areas:** Action/adventure; comic books/cartoon; confession; contemporary issues; detective/police/crime; erotica; ethnic; experimental; family saga; fantasy; feminist; gay/lesbian; glitz; gothic; hi-lo; historical; horror; humor/satire; juvenile; literary; mainstream/contemporary; military/war; multicultural; multimedia; mystery/suspense; New Age; occult; picture books; plays; poetry; poetry in translation; psychic/supernatural; regional; religious/inspirational; romance; science fiction; short story collections; spiritual; sports; thriller; translation; westerns/frontier; young adult.

How to Contact: Query with SASE, submit outline, 2 sample chapter(s). Responds in 1 month to mss. Obtains most new clients through recommendations from others, conferences, personal search.

Recent Sales: *Fatal North*, by Bruce Henderson (Dutton); *Wildlife Wars*, by Richard Leakey and Virginia Morell (St. Martin's Press); *The Siege of Shangri-La*, by Michael Macrae (Broadway Books).

Terms: Agent receives 10-15% commission on domestic sales.

☑ THE JOY HARRIS LITERARY AGENCY, INC.

156 Fifth Ave., Suite 617, New York NY 10010. (212)924-6269. Fax: (212)924-6609. E-mail: gen.office@jhlitagent.com. **Contact:** Joy Harris. Member of AAR. Represents over 100 clients. Currently handles: 50% nonfiction books; 50% novels.

Member Agents: Leslie Daniels; Stéphanie Abou; Alexia Paul.

Represents: Nonfiction books, novels. **Considers these fiction areas:** Contemporary issues; ethnic; experimental; family saga; feminist; gay/lesbian; glitz; hi-lo; historical; humor/satire; literary; mainstream/contemporary; multicultural; multimedia; mystery/suspense; picture books; regional; short story collections; spiritual; translation; women's.

O— Does not want to receive screenplays.

How to Contact: Query with sample chapter, outline/proposal, SASE. Considers simultaneous queries. Responds in 2 months to queries. Obtains most new clients through recommendations from clients and editors.

Recent Sales: Sold 15 titles in the last year. This agency prefers not to share information on specific sales.

Terms: Agent receives 15% commission on domestic sales; 20% commission on foreign sales. Charges clients for some office expenses.

◖ HARTLINE LITERARY AGENCY

123 Queenston Dr., Pittsburgh PA 15235-5429. (412)829-2495 or 2483. Fax: (412)829-2450. E-mail: joyce@hartli neliterary.com. Website: www.hartlineliterary.com. **Contact:** Joyce A. Hart. Estab. 1990. Represents 40 clients. 30% of clients are new/unpublished writers. Currently handles: 40% nonfiction books; 60% novels.
Member Agents: Joyce A. Hart, principal agent; Janet Benrey; Tamela Hancock Murray; Andrea Boeshaar.
Represents: Nonfiction books, novels. **Considers these nonfiction areas:** Business/economics; child guidance/ parenting; cooking/foods/nutrition; money/finance; religious/inspirational; self-help/personal improvement; women's issues/studies. **Considers these fiction areas:** Action/adventure; contemporary issues; family saga; historical; literary; mystery/suspense (amateur sleuth, cozy); regional; religious/inspirational; romance (contemporary, gothic, historical, regency); thriller.

    ☐ This agency specializes in the Christian bookseller market. Actively seeking adult fiction, self-help, nutritional books, devotional, business. Does not want to receive science fiction, erotica, gay/lesbian, fantasy, horror, etc.

How to Contact: Submit outline, 3 sample chapter(s). Accepts e-mail and fax queries. Considers simultaneous queries. Responds in 2 months to queries; 3 months to mss. Returns materials only with SASE. Obtains most new clients through recommendations from others.
Recent Sales: 3-book contract for Jane Kirkpatrick (Waterbrook); *Christmas Homecoming Novella*, by Pamela Griffin (Tyndale House); *Without Warning*, by Ward Tannenberg (Kregel Publishing); *Mysterious Ways*, by Terry Burns (RiverOak Publishing); Heirs of Anton Series, by Susan Downs and Susan May Warren (Barbour Publishing); *Mercy Me & Land Sakes*, by Margaret Graham (Revell Publishing).
Terms: Agent receives 15% commission on domestic sales. Offers written contract.

◖ JOHN HAWKINS & ASSOCIATES, INC.

71 W. 23rd St., Suite 1600, New York NY 10010. (212)807-7040. Fax: (212)807-9555. E-mail: jha@jhaliterary.c om. Website: jhaliterary.com. **Contact:** John Hawkins, William Reiss. Estab. 1893. Member of AAR. Represents over 100 clients. 5-10% of clients are new/unpublished writers. Currently handles: 40% nonfiction books; 40% novels; 20% juvenile books.
Member Agents: Moses Cardona; Warren Frazier; Anne Hawkins; John Hawkins; William Reiss.
Represents: Nonfiction books, novels, juvenile books. **Considers these nonfiction areas:** Agriculture/horticulture; Americana; anthropology/archaeology; art/architecture/design; biography/autobiography; business/economics; creative nonfiction; current affairs; education; ethnic/cultural interests; gardening; gay/lesbian issues; government/politics/law; health/medicine; history; how-to; interior design/decorating; language/literature/ criticism; memoirs; money/finance; multicultural; nature/environment; philosophy; popular culture; psychology; recreation; science/technology; self-help/personal improvement; sex; sociology; software; theater/film; travel; true crime/investigative; young adult; music. **Considers these fiction areas:** Action/adventure; contemporary issues; detective/police/crime; ethnic; experimental; family saga; feminist; gay/lesbian; glitz; gothic; hilo; historical; literary; mainstream/contemporary; military/war; multicultural; multimedia; mystery/suspense; psychic/supernatural; religious/inspirational; short story collections; sports; thriller; translation; westerns/frontier; young adult; women's.
How to Contact: Query with SASE, submit proposal package, outline. Considers simultaneous queries. Responds in 1 month to queries. Returns materials only with SASE. Obtains most new clients through recommendations from others.
Recent Sales: *Mad Man's Tale*, by John Katzenbach; *Ghost Heart*, by Cecilia Samartin.
Terms: Agent receives 15% commission on domestic sales; 20% commission on foreign sales. Charges clients for photocopying.

◖ RICHARD HENSHAW GROUP

127 W. 24th St., 4th Floor, New York NY 10011. (212)414-1172. Fax: (212)414-1172. E-mail: submissions@hens haw.com. Website: www.rich.henshaw.com. **Contact:** Rich Henshaw. Estab. 1995. Member of AAR, SinC, MWA, HWA, SFWA, RWA. Represents 35 clients. 20% of clients are new/unpublished writers. Currently handles: 30% nonfiction books; 70% novels.

    ● Prior to opening his agency, Mr. Henshaw served as an agent with Richard Curtis Associates, Inc.

Represents: Nonfiction books, novels. **Considers these nonfiction areas:** Animals; biography/autobiography; business/economics; child guidance/parenting; computers/electronic; cooking/foods/nutrition; current affairs; gay/lesbian issues; government/politics/law; health/medicine; how-to; humor/satire; military/war; money/ finance; music/dance; nature/environment; New Age/metaphysics; popular culture; psychology; science/technology; self-help/personal improvement; sociology; sports; true crime/investigative; women's issues/studies. **Considers these fiction areas:** Action/adventure; detective/police/crime; ethnic; family saga; fantasy; glitz; historical; horror; humor/satire; literary; mainstream/contemporary; mystery/suspense; psychic/supernatural; romance; science fiction; sports; thriller.

O— This agency specializes in thrillers, mysteries, science fiction, fantasy, and horror.

How to Contact: Query with SASE. Responds in 3 weeks to queries; 6 weeks to mss. Obtains most new clients through recommendations from others, solicitations, conferences.

Recent Sales: *A Grave Denied*, by Dana Stabenow (St. Martin's); *Killing Raven*, by Margaret Coel (Berkley); *The Well-Educated Mind*, by Susan Wise Bauer (Norton); *Dead Soul*, by James D. Doss (St. Martin's). Other clients include Jessie Wise, Peter van Dijk.

Terms: Agent receives 15% commission on domestic sales; 20% commission on foreign sales. No written contract. 100% of business is derived from commissions on ms sales. Charges clients for photocopying mss and book orders.

Tips: "While we do not have any reason to believe that our submission guidelines will change in the near future, writers can find up-to-date submission policy information on our website. Always include a SASE with correct return postage."

◲ THE JEFF HERMAN AGENCY, LLC

P.O. Box 1522, Stockbridge MA 01262. (413)298-0077. Fax: (413)298-8188. E-mail: jeff@jeffherman.com. Website: www.jeffherman.com. **Contact:** Jeffrey H. Herman. Estab. 1985. Represents 100 clients. 10% of clients are new/unpublished writers. Currently handles: 85% nonfiction books; 5% scholarly books; 5% textbooks.

• Prior to opening his agency, Mr. Herman served as a public relations executive.

Member Agents: Deborah Levine (vice president, nonfiction book doctor); Jeff Herman.

Represents: Nonfiction books. **Considers these nonfiction areas:** Business/economics; government/politics/law; health/medicine (and recovery issues); history; how-to; psychology (pop); self-help/personal improvement; spirituality; popular reference, technology.

O— This agency specializes in adult nonfiction.

How to Contact: Query with SASE. Accepts e-mail and fax queries. Considers simultaneous queries.

Recent Sales: Sold 35 titles in the last year. This agency prefers not to share information on specific sales.

Terms: Agent receives 15% commission on domestic sales. Offers written contract. Charges clients for copying, postage.

◲ SUSAN HERNER RIGHTS AGENCY

P.O. Box 57, Pounds Ridge NY 10576. (914)234-2864. Fax: (914)234-2866. E-mail: sherneragency@optonline.net. **Contact:** Susan Herner. Estab. 1987. Represents 100 clients. 30% of clients are new/unpublished writers. Currently handles: 60% nonfiction books; 40% novels.

Member Agents: Susan Herner, president (nonfiction, thriller, mystery, strong women's fiction).

Represents: Nonfiction books (adult), novels (adult). **Considers these nonfiction areas:** Anthropology/archaeology; business/economics; child guidance/parenting; current affairs; ethnic/cultural interests; gay/lesbian issues; government/politics/law; health/medicine; history; how-to; language/literature/criticism; nature/environment; New Age/metaphysics; popular culture; psychology; religious/inspirational; science/technology; self-help/personal improvement; sociology; spirituality; true crime/investigative; women's issues/studies; biography. **Considers these fiction areas:** Action/adventure; contemporary issues; detective/police/crime; ethnic; feminist; glitz; horror; literary; mainstream/contemporary; mystery/suspense; thriller.

O— "I'm particularly looking for strong women's fiction and thrillers. I'm particularly interested in women's issues, popular science, and feminist spirituality."

How to Contact: Query with SASE, outline, sample chapter(s), or query by e-mail (no attachments). Considers simultaneous queries. Responds in 1 month to queries. Returns materials only with SASE.

Recent Sales: *If Cooks Could Kill*, by Joanne Pence (Avon); *Our Improbable Universe*, by Michael Mallary (4 Walls 8 Windows); *Everything You Need to Know About Latino History*, by Himilce Novas (Plume).

Terms: Agent receives 15% commission on domestic sales; 20% commission on foreign sales; 20% commission on dramatic rights sales. Charges clients for extraordinary postage and photocopying. "Agency has 2 divisions: one represents writers on a commission-only basis; the other represents the rights for small publishers and packagers who do not have in-house subsidiary rights representation. Percentage of income derived from each division is currently 80-20."

◲ FREDERICK HILL BONNIE NADELL, INC.

1842 Union St., San Francisco CA 94123. (415)921-2910. Fax: (415)921-2802. **Contact:** Irene Moore. Estab. 1979. Represents 100 clients.

Member Agents: Fred Hill (president); Bonnie Nadell (vice president); Irene Moore (associate).

Represents: Nonfiction books, novels. **Considers these nonfiction areas:** Cooking/foods/nutrition (cookbooks); current affairs; language/literature/criticism; nature/environment; Biography; government/politics.

Considers these fiction areas: Literary; mainstream/contemporary.

How to Contact: Query with SASE. No e-mail or fax queries. Considers simultaneous queries. Returns materials only with SASE.

Recent Sales: *Hope in the Dark*, by Rebecca Solnit; *Balance of Power*, by Richard North Patterson; *Oblivion*, by David Foster Wallace.

Terms: Agent receives 15% commission on domestic sales; 20% commission on foreign sales; 15% commission on dramatic rights sales. Charges clients for photocopying.

JOHN L. HOCHMANN BOOKS

320 E. 58th St., New York NY 10022-2220. (212)319-0505. **Contact:** Theodora Eagle. Director: John L. Hochmann. Estab. 1976. Member of PEN. Represents 23 clients. Prefers to work with previously published/established authors. Currently handles: 100% nonfiction books.

Member Agents: Theodora Eagle (popular medical and nutrition books).

Represents: Nonfiction books, textbooks (college). **Considers these nonfiction areas:** Anthropology/archaeology; art/architecture/design; biography/autobiography; cooking/foods/nutrition; current affairs; gay/lesbian issues; government/politics/law; health/medicine; history; military/war; music/dance; sociology; theater/film.

> This agency specializes in nonfiction books. "Writers must have demonstrable eminence in field or previous publications."

How to Contact: Query first with detailed chapter outline, titles, and sample reviews of previously published books. Responds in 1 week to queries. Reports in 1 month to solicited mss. Obtains most new clients through recommendations from authors and editors.

Recent Sales: Sold 6 titles in the last year. *Granite and Rainbow: The Life of Virginia Woolf*, by Mitchell Leaska (Farrar, Straus & Giroux); *Manuel Puig and the Spider Woman*, by Suzanne Jill Levine (Farrar, Straus & Giroux); *Part-Time Vegetarian*, by Louise Lambert-Lagasse (Stoddart).

Terms: Agent receives 15% commission on domestic sales.

Tips: "Detailed outlines are read carefully; letters and proposals written like flap copy get chucked. We make multiple submissions to editors, but we do not accept multiple submissions from authors. Why? Editors are on salary, but we work for commission, and do not have time to read manuscripts on spec."

BARBARA HOGENSON AGENCY

165 West End Ave., Suite 19-C, New York NY 10023. (212)874-8084. Fax: (212)362-3011. **Contact:** Barbara Hogenson. Member of AAR.

● Query before submitting.

HOPKINS LITERARY ASSOCIATES

2117 Buffalo Rd., Suite 327, Rochester NY 14624-1507. (585)352-6268. **Contact:** Pam Hopkins. Estab. 1996. Member of AAR, RWA. Represents 30 clients. 5% of clients are new/unpublished writers. Currently handles: 100% novels.

Represents: Novels. **Considers these fiction areas:** Historical; mainstream/contemporary; romance; women's.

> This agency specializes in women's fiction, particularly historical, contemporary, and category romance as well as mainstream work.

How to Contact: Submit outline, 3 sample chapter(s). No e-mail or fax queries. Considers simultaneous queries. Responds in 2 weeks to queries; 1 month to mss. Returns materials only with SASE. Obtains most new clients through recommendations from others, solicitations, conferences.

Recent Sales: Sold 50 titles in the last year. *The First Mistake*, by Merline Lovelace (Mira); *The Romantic*, by Madeline Hunter (Bantam); *The Damsel in this Dress*, by Marianne Stillings (Avon).

Terms: Agent receives 15% commission on domestic sales; 20% commission on foreign sales. No written contract.

Writers' Conferences: Romance Writers of America.

HORNFISCHER LITERARY MANAGEMENT, INC.

P.O. Box 50544, Austin TX 78763. E-mail: jim@hornfischerlit.com. Website: www.hornfischerliterarymanagem ent.com. **Contact:** James D. Hornfischer, president. Estab. 2001. Represents 45 clients. 20% of clients are new/unpublished writers. Currently handles: 98% nonfiction books; 2% novels.

● Prior to opening his agency, Mr. Hornfischer was an agent with Literary Group International and held editorial positions at HarperCollins and McGraw-Hill. "I work hard to make an author's first trip to market a successful one. That means closely working with my clients prior to submission to produce the strongest possible book proposal or manuscript. My New York editorial background, at HarperCollins and McGraw-Hill, where I worked on books by a variety of best-selling authors such as Erma Bombeck, Jared Diamond, and Erica Jong among others, is useful in this regard. In 8 years as an agent I've handled 2 number 1 *New York Times* nonfiction bestsellers, and in 2001 one of my clients was a finalist for the Pulitzer Prize."

Represents: Nonfiction books, novels. **Considers these nonfiction areas:** Anthropology/archaeology; biography/autobiography; business/economics; child guidance/parenting; current affairs; government/politics/law; health/medicine; history; how-to; humor/satire; memoirs; military/war; money/finance; multicultural; nature/environment; popular culture; psychology; religious/inspirational; science/technology; self-help/personal improvement; sociology; sports; true crime/investigative. **Considers these fiction areas:** Historical; literary; mainstream/contemporary; thriller.

    ○━ Actively seeking the best work of terrific writers. Does not want poetry, genre mysteries, romance, or science fiction.

How to Contact: Submit proposal package, outline, 2 sample chapter(s). Considers simultaneous queries. Responds in 1 month to queries. Returns materials only with SASE. Obtains most new clients through referrals from clients; reading books and magazines; pursuing ideas with New York editors.

Recent Sales: *Lone Star Nation*, by H.W. Brands (Doubleday); *Grand Old Party*, by Lewis L. Gould (Random House); *My Life Had Stood a Loaded Gun*, by Theo Padnos (Miramax); *The Laughter of God's Creatures*, by Ron Powers (Free Press); *A Good Forest for Dying*, by Patrick Beach (Doubleday).

Terms: Agent receives 15% commission on domestic sales; 25% commission on foreign sales. Offers written contract. Reasonable expenses deducted from proceeds after book is sold.

Tips: "When you query agents and send out proposals, present yourself as someone who's in command of his material and comfortable in his own skin. Too many writers have a palpable sense of anxiety and insecurity. Take a deep breath and realize that—if you're good—someone in the publishing world will want you."

◨ INTERNATIONAL CREATIVE MANAGEMENT

40 W. 57th St., New York NY 10019. (212)556-5600. Fax: (212)556-5665. **Contact:** Literary Department. Member of AAR; signatory of WGA.

Member Agents: Esther Newberg and Amanda Urban, department heads; Richard Abate; Lisa Bankoff; Sam Cohn; Kristine Dahl; Mitch Douglas; Liz Farrell; Sloan Harris; Jennifer Joel.

How to Contact: Not currently accepting submissions. Obtains most new clients through recommendations from others.

Terms: Agent receives 15% commission on domestic sales; 20% commission on foreign sales.

◨ J DE S ASSOCIATES, INC.

9 Shagbark Rd., Wilson Point, South Norwalk CT 06854. (203)838-7571. **Contact:** Jacques de Spoelberch. Estab. 1975. Represents 50 clients. Currently handles: 50% nonfiction books; 50% novels.

    ● Prior to opening his agency, Mr. de Spoelberch was an editor with Houghton Mifflin.

Represents: Nonfiction books, novels. **Considers these nonfiction areas:** Biography/autobiography; business/economics; current affairs; ethnic/cultural interests; government/politics/law; health/medicine; history; military/war; New Age/metaphysics; self-help/personal improvement; sociology; sports; translation. **Considers these fiction areas:** Detective/police/crime; historical; juvenile; literary; mainstream/contemporary; mystery/suspense; New Age; westerns/frontier; young adult.

How to Contact: Query with SASE. Responds in 2 months to queries. Obtains most new clients through recommendations from authors and other clients.

Terms: Agent receives 15% commission on domestic sales; 20% commission on foreign sales. Charges clients for foreign postage and photocopying.

◨ JABBERWOCKY LITERARY AGENCY

P.O. Box 4558, Sunnyside NY 11104-0558. (718)392-5985. **Contact:** Joshua Bilmes. Estab. 1994. Member of SFWA. Represents 40 clients. 15% of clients are new/unpublished writers. Currently handles: 15% nonfiction books; 75% novels; 5% scholarly books; 5% other.

Represents: Nonfiction books, novels, scholarly books. **Considers these nonfiction areas:** Biography/autobiography; business/economics; cooking/foods/nutrition; current affairs; gay/lesbian issues; government/politics/law; health/medicine; history; humor/satire; language/literature/criticism; military/war; money/finance; nature/environment; popular culture; science/technology; sociology; sports; theater/film; true crime/investigative; women's issues/studies. **Considers these fiction areas:** Action/adventure; contemporary issues; detective/police/crime; ethnic; family saga; fantasy; gay/lesbian; glitz; historical; horror; humor/satire; literary; mainstream/contemporary; psychic/supernatural; regional; science fiction; sports; thriller.

    ○━ This agency represents quite a lot of genre fiction and is actively seeking to increase amount of nonfiction projects. It does not handle juvenile or young adult. Book-length material only; no poetry, articles, or short fiction.

How to Contact: Query with SASE. No mss unless requested. No e-mail or fax queries. Considers simultaneous queries. Responds in 2 weeks to queries. Returns materials only with SASE. Obtains most new clients through solicitations, recommendation by current clients.

Literary Agents

Recent Sales: Sold 20 titles in the last year. *Dead to the World*, by Charlaine Harris (ACE); *Trading in Danger*, by Elizabeth Moon (Ballantine); *Deathstalker Coda*, by Simon Green (ROC). Other clients include Tanya Huff, Kristine Smith, Edo Van Belkom.

Terms: Agent receives 15% commission on domestic sales; 20% commission on foreign sales. Offers written contract, binding for 1 year. Charges clients for book purchases, photocopying, international book/ms mailing.

Writers' Conferences: Malice Domestic (Washington DC, May); World SF Convention (Glasgow, August); Icon (Stony Brook NY, April).

Tips: "In approaching with a query, the most important things to me are your credits and your biographical background to the extent it's relevant to your work. I (and most agents) will ignore the adjectives you may choose to describe your own work."

JAMES PETER ASSOCIATES, INC.

P.O. Box 358, New Canaan CT 06840. (203)972-1070. E-mail: gene_brissie@msn.com. **Contact:** Gene Brissie. Estab. 1971. Represents 75 individual and 6 corporate clients. 15% of clients are new/unpublished writers. Currently handles: 100% nonfiction books.

Member Agents: Gene Brissie.

Represents: Nonfiction books. **Considers these nonfiction areas:** Anthropology/archaeology; art/architecture/design; biography/autobiography; business/economics; child guidance/parenting; current affairs; ethnic/cultural interests; gay/lesbian issues; government/politics/law; health/medicine; history; language/literature/criticism; memoirs (political or business); military/war; money/finance; music/dance; popular culture; psychology; self-help/personal improvement; theater/film; travel; women's issues/studies.

⌐ This agency specializes in all categories of nonfiction. "We are especially interested in general, trade, and reference." Actively seeking "good ideas in all areas of adult nonfiction." Does not want to receive "children's and young adult books, poetry, fiction."

How to Contact: Submit proposal package, outline, SASE. Prefers to read materials exclusively. No e-mail or fax queries. Responds in 1 month to queries. Returns materials only with SASE. Obtains most new clients through recommendations from others, solicitations, contact "with people who are doing interesting things."

Recent Sales: Sold 50 titles in the last year. *Nothing to Fear*, by Dr. Alan Axelrod (Prentice-Hall); *The Right Way*, by Mark Smith, Esq. (Regnery); *Churchill's Folly*, by Christopher Catherwood (Carroll & Graf); *The Encyclopedia of Cancer*, by Carol Turkington (Facts on File); *The Lazy Person's Guide to Investing*, by Paul Farrell (Warner Books); *The Subject Is Left-Handed*, by Barney Rosset (Algonquin Books); *It's OK to Be Neurotic*, by Dr. Frank Bruno (Adams Media).

Terms: Agent receives 15% commission on domestic sales; 20% commission on foreign sales. Offers written contract.

JANKLOW & NESBIT ASSOCIATES

445 Park Ave., New York NY 10022. (212)421-1700. Fax: (212)980-3671. **Contact:** Morton L. Janklow; Lynn Nesbit. Estab. 1989. Member of AAR.

Member Agents: Tina Bennett; Luke Janklow; Richard Morris; Eric Simonoff; Anne Sibbald.

Represents: Nonfiction books (commerical and literary), novels (commercial and literary).

JCA LITERARY AGENCY

27 W. 20th St., Suite 1103, New York NY 10011. (212)807-0888. Fax: (212)807-0461. Website: www.jcalit.com. **Contact:** Jeff Gerecke. Estab. 1978. Member of AAR. Represents 100 clients. 10% of clients are new/unpublished writers. Currently handles: 20% nonfiction books; 75% novels; 5% scholarly books.

Member Agents: Jeff Gerecke, Tom Cushman, Peter Steinberg.

Represents: Nonfiction books, novels. **Considers these nonfiction areas:** Biography/autobiography; business/economics; current affairs; government/politics/law; history; language/literature/criticism; memoirs; military/war; money/finance; nature/environment; popular culture; science/technology; sociology; sports; theater/film; translation; true crime/investigative. **Considers these fiction areas:** Action/adventure; contemporary issues; detective/police/crime; family saga; historical; literary; mainstream/contemporary; mystery/suspense; sports; thriller.

⌐ Does not want to receive screenplays, poetry, children's books, science fiction/fantasy, genre romance.

How to Contact: Query with SASE. No e-mail or fax queries. Considers simultaneous queries. Responds in 2 weeks to queries; 10 weeks to mss. Returns materials only with SASE. Obtains most new clients through recommendations from others, solicitations, conferences.

Recent Sales: *Jury of One*, by David Ellis (Putnam); *The Heaven of Mercury*, by Brad Watson (Norton); *The Rope Eater*, by Ben Jones; *The Circus in Winter*, by Cathy Dial. Other clients include Ernest J. Gaines, Gwen Hunter.

Terms: Agent receives 15% commission on domestic sales; 20% commission on foreign sales. No written contract. "We work with our clients on a handshake basis." Charges for postage on overseas submissions, photocopying, mss for submission, books purchased for subrights submission, and bank charges, where applicable. "We deduct the cost from payments received from publishers."

Tips: "We do not ourselves provide legal, accounting, or public relations services for our clients, although some of the advice we give falls somewhat into these realms. In cases where it seems necessary we will recommend obtaining outside advice or assistance in these areas from professionals who are not in any way connected to the agency."

LAWRENCE JORDAN LITERARY AGENCY

a Morning Star Communications, LLC Co., 345 W. 121st St., New York NY 10027. (212)662-7871. Fax: (212)662-8138. E-mail: ljlagency@aol.com. **Contact:** President: Lawrence Jordan. Estab. 1978. Represents 50 clients. 25% of clients are new/unpublished writers. Works with a small number of new/previously unpublished authors. Currently handles: 70% nonfiction books; 30% novels.

- Prior to opening his agency, Mr. Jordan served as an editor with Doubleday & Co.

Represents: Nonfiction books, novels. **Considers these nonfiction areas:** Biography/autobiography; business/economics; cooking/foods/nutrition (cookbooks); health/medicine; memoirs; religious/inspirational; science/technology; self-help/personal improvement; sports; travel.

- O—┐ This agency specializes in general adult fiction and nonfiction. Actively seeking spiritual and religious books, mystery novels, action suspense, thrillers, biographies, autobiographies, celebrity books. Does not want to receive poetry, movie scripts, stage plays, juvenile books, fantasy novels, science fiction.

How to Contact: Query with SASE, outline. Responds in 3 weeks to queries; 6 weeks to mss.

Recent Sales: *The Undiscovered Paul Robeson, Vol. II*, by Paul Robeson, Jr. (Wiley); *A View from the Wreckage: A Black Political Perspective*, by Paul Robeson, Jr. (Seven Stories Press).

Terms: Agent receives 15% commission on domestic sales; 20% commission on foreign sales; 20% commission on dramatic rights sales. 99% of business is derived from commissions on ms sales. Charges for long-distance calls, photocopying, foreign submission costs, postage, cables, and messengers.

☑ NATASHA KERN LITERARY AGENCY

P.O. Box 2908, Portland OR 97208-2908. (503)297-6190. Website: www.natashakern.com. **Contact:** Natasha Kern. Estab. 1986. Member of RWA, MWA, SinC.

- Prior to opening her agency, Ms. Kern worked as an editor and publicist for New York publishers (Simon & Schuster, Bantam, Ballantine). "This agency has sold over 500 books."

Member Agents: Natasha Kern; Ruth Widener.

Represents: Adult commercial nonfiction and fiction. **Considers these nonfiction areas:** Animals; anthropology/archaeology; business/economics; child guidance/parenting; current affairs; ethnic/cultural interests; gardening; health/medicine; nature/environment; New Age/metaphysics; popular culture; psychology; religious/inspirational; science/technology; self-help/personal improvement; spirituality; women's issues/studies; investigative journalism. **Considers these fiction areas:** Ethnic; feminist; historical; mainstream/contemporary; mystery/suspense; religious/inspirational; romance (contemporary, historical); thriller (medical, scientific, historical).

- O—┐ This agency specializes in commercial fiction and nonfiction for adults. "A full service agency." Does not represent sports, true crime, scholarly works, coffee table books, war memoirs, software, scripts, literary fiction, photography, poetry, short stories, children's, horror, fantasy, genre science fiction, stage plays, or traditional Westerns.

How to Contact: Query with SASE, include submission history, writing credits, length of ms. "Visit our website before querying." For fiction, send 2-3 page synopsis and 3-5 first pages. For nonfiction, send overview, describe market, and how ms is different/better than similar works, author bio, and ms length. No phone or fax queries. Considers simultaneous queries. Responds in 3 weeks to queries.

Recent Sales: Sold 53 titles in the last year. *Firstborn*, by Robin Lee Hatcher (Tyndale); *The Waiting Child*, by Cindy Champnella; *The Power of Losing Control*, by Joe Caruso (Penguin/Putnam).

Terms: Agent receives 15% commission on domestic sales; 20% commission on foreign sales; 15% commission on dramatic rights sales.

Writers' Conferences: RWA National Conference; MWA National Conference; and many regional conferences.

Tips: "Your chances of being accepted for representation will be greatly enhanced by going to our website first. Our idea of a dream client is someone who participates in a mutually respectful business relationship, is clear about needs and goals, and communicates about career planning. If we know what you need and want, we can help you achieve it. A dream client has a storytelling gift, a commitment to a writing career, a desire to learn and grow, and a passion for excellence. We want clients who are expressing their own unique voice and truly have something of their own to communicate. This client understands that many people have to work together for a book to succeed and that everything in publishing takes far longer than one imagines. Trust and communication are truly essential.''

⬛ LOUISE B. KETZ AGENCY

1485 First Ave., Suite 4B, New York NY 10021-1363. (212)535-9259. Fax: (212)249-3103. E-mail: ketzagency@a ol.com. **Contact:** Louise B. Ketz. Estab. 1983. Represents 25 clients. 15% of clients are new/unpublished writers. Currently handles: 100% nonfiction books.
Represents: Nonfiction books. **Considers these nonfiction areas:** Current affairs; history; military/war; science/technology; economics.

    O—¬ This agency specializes in science, history, and reference.
How to Contact: Submit outline, 2 sample chapter(s), author bio, with qualifications for authorship of work. Responds in 6 weeks to mss. Obtains most new clients through recommendations from others, idea development.
Terms: Agent receives 15% commission on domestic sales.

⬛ VIRGINIA KIDD AGENCY, INC.

538 E. Harford St., P.O. Box 278, Milford PA 18337-0278. (570)296-6205. Fax: (570)296-7266. E-mail: vkagency @ptd.net. **Contact:** Linn Prentis, Nanci McCloskey. Estab. 1965. Member of SFWA, SFRA. Represents 80 clients.
Member Agents: Nanci McCloskey; Linn Prentis; Christine Cohen; Vaughne Hansen.
Represents: Novels. **Considers these fiction areas:** Fantasy (special interest in non-traditional fantasy); glitz; historical; literary; mainstream/contemporary; mystery/suspense; science fiction; young adult; speculative fiction.

    O—¬ This agency specializes in ''science fiction but we do not limit ourselves to it.''
How to Contact: Submit synopsis, cover letter, SASE. Prefers to read materials exclusively. Considers simultaneous queries. Responds in 1 month to queries. Obtains most new clients through recommendations.
Recent Sales: Sold 75 titles in the last year. *Changing Planes*, by Ursula K. Le Guin (Harcourt Brace); *The Anvil of the World*, by Kage Baker; *The Knight*, by Gene Wolfe (Tor Books). Other clients include Alan Dean Foster, Wen Spencer, Eleanor Arnason, Katie Waitman, Margaret Ball.
Terms: Agent receives 15% commission on domestic sales; 20-25% commission on foreign sales; 20% commission on dramatic rights sales. Offers written contract; 2-month notice must be given to terminate contract. Charges clients occasionally for extraordinary expenses.
Tips: ''If you have a novel of speculative fiction or mainstream that is really extraordinary, please query us, including a synopsis, publishing credits, and a SASE.''

🅝 ⬛ KIDDE, HOYT, & PICARD

335 E. 51st St., New York NY 10022. (212)755-9461. **Contact:** Katherine Kidde. Member of AAR.
    ● Query before submitting.

🅝 ⬛ ◎ KIRCHOFF/WOHLBERG, INC., AUTHORS' REPRESENTATION DIVISION, (Specialized: children's books)

866 United Nations Plaza, #525, New York NY 10017. (212)644-2020. Fax: (212)223-4387. **Contact:** Liza Pulitzer Voges. Director of Operations: John R. Whitman. Estab. 1930s. Member of AAR, AAP, Society of Illustrators, SPAR, Bookbuilders of Boston, New York Bookbinders' Guild, AIGA. Represents 50 clients. 10% of clients are new/unpublished writers. Currently handles: 5% nonfiction books; 25% novels; 5% young adult; 65% picture books.
    ● Kirchoff/Wohlberg has been in business for over 60 years.
Member Agents: Liza Pulitzer Voges (juvenile and young adult authors).

    O—¬ This agency specializes in only juvenile through young adult trade books.
How to Contact: Query with SASE, outline, a few sample chapter(s), for novels. For picture book submissions, please send entire ms. SASE required. No e-mail or fax queries. Considers simultaneous queries. Responds in 1 month to queries; 2 months to mss. Returns materials only with SASE. Obtains most new clients through recommendations from authors, illustrators, and editors.
Recent Sales: Sold over 50 titles in the last year. *Three Nasty Gnarlies*, by Keith Graves (Scholastic); *Chu Ju's House*, by Gloria Whelan (HarperCollins); My Weird School Series, by Dan Gutman (HarperCollins).
Terms: Offers written contract, binding for not less than 1 year. Agent receives standard commission, ''depending upon whether it is an author only, illustrator only, or an author/illustrator book.''

🅝 ◻ KISSED PUBLICATIONS

P.O. Box 9819, Hampton VA 23670. (757)722-3031. Fax: (757)722-1301. E-mail: kissed@kissedpublications.c om. Website: www.kissedpublications.com. **Contact:** Kimberly T. Matthews. Estab. 2003. Member of Better Business Bureau. Currently handles: 20% nonfiction books; 80% novels.

- Prior to becoming an agent, Ms. Matthews was an author and speaker.

Represents: Nonfiction books, novels, short story collections. **Considers these nonfiction areas:** Religious/inspirational. **Considers these fiction areas:** Ethnic; mainstream/contemporary; religious/inspirational; young adult; inspirational.

    ○━ Agency specializing in African-American mainstream fiction and inspiration nonfiction. Actively seeking new, unpublished authors/clients.

How to Contact: Query with SASE. Accepts e-mail queries. No fax queries. Considers simultaneous queries. Responds in 2 weeks to queries; 8 weeks to mss. Returns materials only with SASE.

Terms: Agent receives 15% commission on domestic sales; 20% commission on foreign sales. Offers written contract. Does not charge fees for criticism service; Charges authors for postage and photocopying.

HARVEY KLINGER, INC.

301 W. 53rd St., Suite 21-A, New York NY 10019. (212)581-7068. Fax: (212)315-3823. E-mail: queries@harveyklinger.com. Website: www.harveyklinger.com. **Contact:** Harvey Klinger. Estab. 1977. Member of AAR. Represents 100 clients. 25% of clients are new/unpublished writers. Currently handles: 50% nonfiction books; 50% novels.

Member Agents: David Dunton (popular culture, with a speciality in music-related books; literary fiction; crime novels; thrillers); Wendy Silbert (narrative nonfiction; historical narrative nonfiction; politics; history; biographies; memoir; literary ficiton; business books; culinary narratives).

Represents: Nonfiction books, novels. **Considers these nonfiction areas:** Biography/autobiography; cooking/foods/nutrition; health/medicine; psychology; science/technology; self-help/personal improvement; spirituality; sports; true crime/investigative; women's issues/studies. **Considers these fiction areas:** Action/adventure; detective/police/crime; family saga; glitz; literary; mainstream/contemporary; mystery/suspense; thriller.

    ○━ This agency specializes in "big, mainstream, contemporary fiction and nonfiction."

How to Contact: Query with SASE. No phone queries. Accepts e-mail queries. No fax queries. Responds in 2 months to queries; 2 months to mss. Obtains most new clients through recommendations from others.

Recent Sales: Sold 30 titles in the last year. *Swan Place*, by Augusta Trobaugh (Dutton); *Fund Your Future*, by Julie Stav (Berkley); *Auriel Rising*, by Elizabeth Redfern (Putnam); *A Love Supreme*, by Ashley Kahn (Viking); *Idiot Girls' Action Adventure Guide*, by Laurie Notaro; *Inside Medicine*, by Kevin Soden and Christine Dumas; *Where I work and Other Stories*, by Ann Cummins (Houghton Mifflin); *Thirty Years of Shame*, by Mark Kemp (Free Press). Other clients include Barbara Wood, Terry Kay, Barbara De Angelis, Jill Conner Browne, Michael Farquhar, Greg Bottoms, Jeremy Jackson, Pamela Berkman, Jonetta Rose Barras, Paul Russell.

Terms: Agent receives 15% commission on domestic sales; 25% commission on foreign sales. Offers written contract. Charges for photocopying mss, overseas postage for mss.

THE KNIGHT AGENCY

577 S. Main St., Madison GA 30650. E-mail: knightagent@aol.com. Website: www.knightagency.net. **Contact:** Judson Knight, ms coordinator. Estab. 1996. Member of AAR, RWA, Authors Guild. Represents 65 clients. 40% of clients are new/unpublished writers. Currently handles: 50% nonfiction books; 50% novels.

Member Agents: Deidre Knight (president, agent); Pamela Harty (agent).

Represents: Nonfiction books, novels. **Considers these nonfiction areas:** Business/economics; child guidance/parenting; current affairs; ethnic/cultural interests; health/medicine; history; how-to; money/finance; popular culture; psychology; religious/inspirational; self-help/personal improvement; theater/film. **Considers these fiction areas:** Literary; mainstream/contemporary (commercial); romance (contemporary, paranormal, romantic suspense, historical, inspirational); women's.

    ○━ "We are looking for a wide variety of fiction and nonfiction. In the nonfiction area, we're particularly eager to find personal finance, business investment, pop culture, self-help/motivational and popular reference books. In fiction, we're always looking for romance; women's fiction; commercial fiction; literary and multicultural fiction." Does not want science fiction/fantasy, mysteries, action/adventure, horror, short story or poetry collections.

How to Contact: Query with SASE. Accepts e-mail queries; no attachments. No phone queries, please. Considers simultaneous queries. Responds in 1-3 weeks to queries; 3 months to mss.

Recent Sales: Sold approximately 65 titles in the last year. *Dark Highlander*, by Karen Marie Moning (Bantam Dell); *The Healing Quilt*, by Lauraine Snelling (WaterBrook Press).

Terms: Agent receives 15% commission on domestic sales; 20-25% commission on foreign sales. Offers written contract, binding for 1 year; 1-month notice must be given to terminate contract. Charges clients for photocopying, postage, overnight courier expenses. "These are deducted from the sale of the work, not billed upfront."

Tips: "At the Knight Agency, a client usually ends up becoming a friend."

◪ LINDA KONNER LITERARY AGENCY

10 W. 15th St., Suite 1918, New York NY 10011-6829. (212)691-3419. E-mail: ldkonner@cs.com. **Contact:** Linda

Konner. Estab. 1996. Member of AAR, ASJA; signatory of WGA. Represents 65 clients. 5-10% of clients are new/unpublished writers. Currently handles: 100% nonfiction books.

Represents: Nonfiction books (adult only). **Considers these nonfiction areas:** Gay/lesbian issues; health/medicine (diet/nutrition/fitness); how-to; money/finance (personal finance); popular culture; psychology; self-help/personal improvement; women's issues/studies; business, parenting, relationships.

O⇥ This agency specializes in health, self-help, and how-to books.

How to Contact: Query with SASE, outline, sufficient return postage. Prefers to read materials exclusively for 2 weeks. Considers simultaneous queries. Obtains most new clients through recommendations from others, occasional solicitation among established authors/journalists.

Recent Sales: Sold 26 titles in the last year. *The Ultimate Body*, by Liz Neporent (Ballantine); *Strength for Their Journey: The Five Disciplines Every African-American Parent Must Teach Her Child*, by Robert Johnson, MD, and Paulette Stanford, MD, (Doubleday).

Terms: Agent receives 15% commission on domestic sales; 25% commission on foreign sales. Offers written contract. Charges $85 one-time fee for domestic expenses; additional expenses may be incurred for foreign sales.

Writers' Conferences: American Society of Journalists and Authors (New York City, Spring).

N Ø DOUGLAS KOPELMAN ARTISTS, INC.

393 W. 49th St., #5G, New York NY 10019. Member of AAR.

● Query before submitting.

Member Agents: Cheryl E. Andrews, Sarah Douglas, Charles Kopelman.

◐ ELAINE KOSTER LITERARY AGENCY, LLC

55 Central Park W., Suite 6, New York NY 10023. (212)362-9488. Fax: (212)712-0164. **Contact:** Elaine Koster, Stephanie Lehmann. Member of AAR, MWA. Represents 40 clients. 10% of clients are new/unpublished writers. Currently handles: 30% nonfiction books; 70% novels.

● Prior to opening her agency in 1998, Ms. Koster was president and publisher of Dutton NAL.

Represents: Nonfiction books, novels. **Considers these nonfiction areas:** Biography/autobiography; business/economics; child guidance/parenting; cooking/foods/nutrition; current affairs; ethnic/cultural interests; health/medicine; history; how-to; money/finance; nature/environment; popular culture; psychology; self-help/personal improvement; spirituality; women's issues/studies. **Considers these fiction areas:** Contemporary issues; detective/police/crime; ethnic; family saga; feminist; historical; literary; mainstream/contemporary; mystery/suspense (amateur sleuth, cozy, culinary, malice domestic); regional; thriller; chicklit.

O⇥ This agency specializes in quality fiction and nonfiction. Does not want to receive juvenile, screenplays, or science fiction.

How to Contact: Query with SASE, outline, 3 sample chapter(s). Prefers to read materials exclusively. No e-mail or fax queries. Responds in 3 weeks to queries; 1 month to mss. Returns materials only with SASE. Obtains most new clients through recommendations from others.

Recent Sales: Sold over 30 titles in the last year. *Bitter in the Mouth*, by Monique Truong (Houghton Mifflin); *Trace Evidence*, by Elizabeth Becka (Hyperion); *Diamonds Take Forever*, by Jessica Jiji (Avon).

Terms: Agent receives 15% commission on domestic sales. Bills back specific expenses incurred doing business for a client.

Tips: "We prefer exclusive submissions. Don't e-mail or fax submissions. Please include biographical information and publishing history."

N BARBARA S. KOUTS, LITERARY AGENT

P.O. Box 560, Bellport NY 11713. (631)286-1278. Fax: (631) 286-1538. **Contact:** Barbara Kouts. Estab. 1980. Member of AAR. Represents 50 clients. 10% of clients are new/unpublished writers. Currently handles: juvenile books.

Represents: Juvenile books.

O⇥ This agency specializes in children's books.

How to Contact: Query with SASE. Considers simultaneous queries. Responds in 1 week to queries; 2 months to mss. Obtains most new clients through recommendations from others, solicitations, conferences.

Terms: Agent receives 15% commission on domestic sales; 20% commission on foreign sales. Charges clients for photocopying.

Tips: "Write, do not call. Be professional in your writing."

◐ KRAAS LITERARY AGENCY

Address for Irene Kraas: 256 Rancho Alegre Rd., Santa Fe NM 87508. (505)438-7715. Fax: (505)438-7783. Address Other: Ashley Kraas, Associate, 507 NW 22nd Ave., Suite 104, Portland OR 97210. (503)721-7442.

Estab. 1990. Represents 40 clients. 75% of clients are new/unpublished writers. Currently handles: 5% nonfiction books; 95% novels.

Member Agents: Irene Kraas, principal (psychological thrillers, medical thrillers, mysteries, literary fiction); Ashley Kraas, associate (romance, women's fiction, historical fiction, memoirs, biographies, self-help, spiritual). Please send appropriate submissions to the correct address.

Represents: Nonfiction books, novels, young adult.

> O→ This agency specializes in adult fiction. Actively seeking "books that are well written with commercial potential." Does not want to receive short stories, plays, or poetry.

How to Contact: Submit cover letter, first 50 pages of a completed ms, SASE; must include return postage and/ or SASE. No e-mail or fax queries. Considers simultaneous queries. Returns materials only with SASE.

Recent Sales: *The Edge of the Sword*, a trilogy, by Rebecca Tingle (Putnam); St. Germain Series (5 books), by Chelsea Quinn Yarbro (Warner Books); *No Place Like the Chevy*, by Janet Lee Carey (Atheneum); Alexandra Gladstone Series (3 books), by Paula Paul (Berkley); *Patriots in Petticoats*, by Shirley Raye Redmond (Random); *The Dog Who Dug for Dinosaurs*, by Shirley Raye Redmond (Simon & Schuster).

Terms: Agent receives 15% commission on domestic sales. Offers written contract. Charges clients for photocopying and postage.

Writers' Conferences: Irene: Southwest Writers Conference (Albuquerque NM); Durango Writers Conference (Durango CO); Wrangling with Writing (Tucson AZ); Ashley: Surrey Writers Conference (Surrey BC); Wrangling with Writing (Tucson AZ); Schuwap Writers Conference (Schuwap BC); Willamette Writers Group (Portland OR).

Tips: "Material by unpublished authors will be accepted in the above areas only. Published authors seeking representation may contact us regarding any material in any area except children's picture books and chapter books."

⬛ ◻ STUART KRICHEVSKY LITERARY AGENCY, INC.

381 Park Ave., Suite 914, New York NY 10016. Fax: (212)725-5275. E-mail: query@skagency.com. Member of AAR.

Represents: Nonfiction books, novels.

How to Contact: Query with SASE. Accepts queries by e-mail (no attachments).

⬛ ◻ EDDIE KRITZER PRODUCTIONS

8484 Wilshire Blvd., Suite 205, Beverly Hills CA 90211. (323)655-5696. Fax: (323)655-5173. E-mail: producedby @aol.com. **Website:** www.eddiekritzer.com. **Contact:** Alan Heifetz, executive story editor. Estab. 1995. Represents 20 clients. 50% of clients are new/unpublished writers. Currently handles: 25% nonfiction books; 5% novels; 10% movie scripts; 15% TV scripts; 1% stage plays; 1% syndicated material.

Member Agents: Eddie Kritzer (nonfiction).

Represents: Nonfiction books, movie scripts, feature film, TV scripts, TV movie of the week. **Considers these nonfiction areas:** Biography/autobiography; business/economics; computers/electronic; cooking/foods/nutrition; current affairs; health/medicine; how-to; humor/satire; self-help/personal improvement; true crime/investigative. **Considers these fiction areas:** Action/adventure; confession; contemporary issues; detective/police/crime; mainstream/contemporary. **Considers these script subject areas:** Action/adventure; biography/autobiography; contemporary issues; detective/police/crime; family saga; fantasy; horror; romantic comedy.

> O→ This agency specializes in TV and movies. Actively seeking compelling stories for books, TV, and features.

How to Contact: Query with SASE. Prefers to read materials exclusively. Discards unwanted queries and mss. Accepts e-mail and fax queries. Responds in 3 days to queries; 3 weeks to mss. Obtains most new clients through recommendations from others, solicitations.

Recent Sales: Sold 2 titles and sold 2 scripts in the last year. *Gmen & Gangsters* (Seven Locks Press); *How to Choose the Right Doctor for You* (Seven Locks Press). **Movie/TV MOW script(s) optioned/sold:** Currently producing a new version of *Kids Say the Darndest Things* on Nick @ Nite.

Terms: Agent receives 15% commission on domestic sales; 20% commission on foreign sales. Offers written contract.

Writers' Conferences: Michale Levine (Santa Monica, May).

Tips: "Be succinct."

⬛ EDITE KROLL LITERARY AGENCY, INC.

12 Grayhurst Park, Portland ME 04102. (207)773-4922. Fax: (207)773-3936. **Contact:** Edite Kroll. Estab. 1981. Represents 40 clients. Currently handles: 40% juvenile books; 60% adult books.

> ● Prior to opening the agency, Edite Kroll served as a book editor and translator.

Represents: Nonfiction books (adult), novels (adult). **Considers these nonfiction areas:** Government/politics/law (political issues/feminist); sociology (social issues/feminist); women's issues/studies. **Considers these**

fiction areas: Humor/satire (by authors and author/artists); juvenile (picture books by authors and author/artists).

○┱ Does not want to receive fantasy or genre.

How to Contact: Written query with SASE. For nonfiction, send outline, proposal, and sample chapter. For juvenile fiction send outline and 1 sample chapter. for picture books and humor send dummy. No e-mail, phone, or fax queries. Considers simultaneous queries. Responds in 1 month to queries; 2 months to mss.

Terms: Agent receives 15% commission on domestic sales; 20% commission on foreign sales. Charges clients for photocopying and legal fees with prior approval from writer.

◙ PETER LAMPACK AGENCY, INC.

551 Fifth Ave., Suite 1613, New York NY 10176-0187. (212)687-9106. Fax: (212)687-9109. E-mail: almpack@verizon.net. **Contact:** Andrew Lampack. Estab. 1977. Represents 50 clients. 10% of clients are new/unpublished writers. Currently handles: 20% nonfiction books; 80% novels.

Member Agents: Peter Lampack (psychological suspense, action/adventure, literary fiction, nonfiction, contemporary relationships); Sandra Blanton (foreign rights); Andrew Lampack (new writers).

Represents: Nonfiction books, novels. **Considers these fiction areas:** Action/adventure; detective/police/crime; family saga; historical; literary; mainstream/contemporary; mystery/suspense; thriller; contemporary relationships.

○┱ This agency specializes in commercial fiction, nonfiction by recognized experts. Actively seeking literary and commercial fiction, thrillers, mysteries, suspense, psychological thrillers. Does not want to receive horror, romance, science fiction, western, academic material.

How to Contact: Query with SASE. *No unsolicited mss.* Accepts e-mail queries. No fax queries. Considers simultaneous queries. Responds in 2 months to queries; 2 months to mss. Obtains most new clients through referrals made by clients.

Recent Sales: *Husband's Stillema*, by Nicole Stensbury; *Trojan Odyssey*, by Clive Cussler.

Terms: Agent receives 15% commission on domestic sales; 20% commission on foreign sales.

Writers' Conferences: BEA (Chicago, June).

Tips: "Submit only your best work for consideration. Have a very specific agenda of goals you wish your prospective agent to accomplish for you. Provide the agent with a comprehensive statement of your credentials: educational and professional."

🄽 ◙ THE LANTZ OFFICE

200 W. 57th St., Suite 503, New York NY 10019. **Contact:** Robert Lantz. Member of AAR.

● Query before submitting.

MICHAEL LARSEN/ELIZABETH POMADA, LITERARY AGENTS

1029 Jones St., San Francisco CA 94109-5023. (415)673-0939. E-mail: larsenpoma@aol.com. Website: www.larsen-pomada.com. **Contact:** Mike Larsen or Elizabeth Pomada. Estab. 1972. Member of AAR, Authors Guild, ASJA, PEN, WNBA, California Writers Club. Represents 100 clients. 40-45% of clients are new/unpublished writers. Currently handles: 70% nonfiction books; 30% novels.

● Prior to opening their agency, Mr. Larsen and Ms. Pomada were promotion executives for major publishing houses. Mr. Larsen worked for Morrow, Bantam, and Pyramid (now part of Berkley), Ms. Pomada worked at Holt, David McKay, and The Dial Press.

Member Agents: Michael Larsen (nonfiction); Elizabeth Pomada (narrative nonfiction, books of interest to women).

Represents: Nonfiction books (adult), novels. **Considers these nonfiction areas:** Anthropology/archaeology; art/architecture/design; biography/autobiography; business/economics; cooking/foods/nutrition; current affairs; ethnic/cultural interests; gay/lesbian issues; government/politics/law; health/medicine; history; how-to; humor/satire; interior design/decorating; memoirs; money/finance; music/dance; nature/environment; New Age/metaphysics; photography; popular culture; psychology; religious/inspirational; science/technology; self-help/personal improvement; sociology; sports; theater/film; travel; true crime/investigative; women's issues/studies; futurism. **Considers these fiction areas:** Action/adventure; contemporary issues; detective/police/crime; ethnic; experimental; family saga; fantasy; feminist; gay/lesbian; glitz; historical; humor/satire; literary; mainstream/contemporary; mystery/suspense; religious/inspirational; romance (contemporary, gothic, historical).

○┱ "We have very diverse tastes. We look for fresh voices and new ideas. We handle literary, commercial, and genre fiction, and the full range of nonfiction books." Actively seeking commercial and literary fiction. Does not want to receive children's books, plays, short stories, screenplays, pornography, poetry, or stories of abuse.

How to Contact: Query with SASE, first 10 pages of completed novel, and 2-page synopsis, SASE. For nonfiction, send title, promotion plan and proposal done according to our plan (see brochure and website). No e-mail or fax queries. Responds in 2 months to queries.

Recent Sales: Sold at least 15 titles in the last year. *If Life is a Game, These are the Stories*; *The Only Negotiating Guide You Will Ever Need*; *The Runaway Duke*.

Terms: Agent receives 15% commission on domestic sales; 20% (30% for Asia) commission on foreign sales. May charge for printing, postage for multiple submissions, foreign mail, foreign phone calls, galleys, books, and legal fees.

Writers' Conferences: Book Expo America; Santa Barbara Writers Conference (Santa Barbara); Maui Writers Conference (Maui); ASJA; Founders of the San Francisco Writers Conference (www.sanfranciscowritersconference.com).

Tips: "If you can write books that meet the needs of the marketplace, and you can promote your books, now is the best time ever to be a writer. We must find new writers to make a living, so we are very eager to hear from new writers whose work will interest large houses, and nonfiction writers who can promote their books. Please send a SASE for a free, 16-page brochure and a list of recent sales."

[N] [Ø] SARAH LAZIN
Sarah Lazin Books, 126 Fifth Ave., Suite 300, New York NY 10011. (212)989-5757. Fax: (212)989-1393. Member of AAR.
- This agency did not respond to our request for information. Query before submitting.

[N] [Ø] THE NED LEAVITT AGENCY
70 Wooster St., New York NY 10012. (212)334-0999. **Contact:** Ned Leavitt. Member of AAR.
- This agency did not respond to our request for information. Query before submitting.

[N] [Ø] [≈] ROBERT LECKER AGENCY
4055 Melrose Ave., Montreal QC H4A 2S5, Canada. (514)830-4818. Fax: (514)483-1644. E-mail: leckerlink@aol.com. Website: www.leckeragency.com. **Contact:** Robert Lecker. Estab. 2004. Represents 15 clients. 20% of clients are new/unpublished writers. Currently handles: 80% nonfiction books; 10% novels; 10% scholarly books.
- Prior to becoming an agent, Mr. Lecker was the co-founder and publisher of ECW Press and professor of English literature at Mchill University. Mr. Lecker has 30 years of experience in book and magazine publishing.

Member Agents: Robert Lecker (popular culture, music); Mary Williams (travel, food, popular science).

Represents: Nonfiction books, novels, scholarly books, syndicated material. **Considers these nonfiction areas:** Biography/autobiography; cooking/foods/nutrition; ethnic/cultural interests; how-to; language/literature/criticism; music/dance; popular culture; science/technology; theater/film. **Considers these fiction areas:** Action/adventure; detective/police/crime; erotica; literary; mainstream/contemporary; mystery/suspense; thriller.
- ⟡ RLA specializes in books about popular culture, music, entertainment, food, and travel. The agency responds to articulate, innovative proposals withing 2 weeks. Actively seeking original book mss only after receipt of outlines and proposals. Does not want unsolicited mss.

How to Contact: Submit proposal package, outline. Accepts e-mail queries. No fax queries. Considers simultaneous queries. Responds in 2 weeks to queries; 1 month to mss. Obtains most new clients through recommendations from others, conferences, interest in website.

Terms: Agent receives 15% commission on domestic sales; 15-20% commission on foreign sales. Offers written contract, binding for 1 year; 6-month notice must be given to terminate contract.

[◉] LESCHER & LESCHER, LTD.
47 E. 19th St., New York NY 10003. (212)529-1790. Fax: (212)529-2716. **Contact:** Robert Lescher, Susan Lescher, Michael Choate. Estab. 1966. Member of AAR. Represents 150 clients. Currently handles: 80% nonfiction books; 20% novels.

Represents: Nonfiction books, novels. **Considers these nonfiction areas:** Current affairs; history; memoirs; popular culture; biography; cookbooks and wines; law; contemporary issues; narrative nonfiction. **Considers these fiction areas:** Literary; mystery/suspense; commercial fiction.
- ⟡ Does not want to receive screenplays, science fiction, or romance.

How to Contact: Query with SASE. Obtains most new clients through recommendations from others.

Recent Sales: Sold 35 titles in the last year. This agency prefers not to share information on specific sales. Other clients include Neil Sheehan, Madeleine L'Engle, Calvin Trillin, Judith Viorst, Thomas Perry, Anne Fadiman, Frances FitzGerald, Paula Fox and Robert M. Parker, Jr.

Terms: Agent receives 15% commission on domestic sales; 20-25% commission on foreign sales.

LEVINE GREENBERG LITERARY AGENCY, INC.

307 7th Ave., Suite 1906, New York NY 10001. (212)337-0934. Fax: (212)337-0948. Website: www.jameslevine.com. Estab. 1989. Member of AAR. Represents 250 clients. 33% of clients are new/unpublished writers. Currently handles: 70% nonfiction books; 30% novels.

• Prior to opening his agency, Mr. Levine served as vice president of the Bank Street College of Education.

Member Agents: James Levine; Arielle Eckstut; Daniel Greenberg; Stephanie Kip Roston.

Represents: Nonfiction books, novels. **Considers these nonfiction areas:** Animals; art/architecture/design; biography/autobiography; business/economics; child guidance/parenting; computers/electronic; cooking/foods/nutrition; gardening; gay/lesbian issues; health/medicine; money/finance; nature/environment; New Age/metaphysics; psychology; religious/inspirational; science/technology; self-help/personal improvement; sociology; spirituality; sports; women's issues/studies. **Considers these fiction areas:** Contemporary issues; literary; mainstream/contemporary; mystery/suspense; thriller (psychological); women's.

~ This agency specializes in business, psychology, parenting, health/medicine, narrative nonfiction, psychology, spirituality, religion, women's issues, and commercial fiction.

How to Contact: See website for full submission procedure. Prefers e-mail queries. Obtains most new clients through recommendations from others.

Recent Sales: *Queen Bees Wannabes: Helping Your Daughter Survive Cliques, Gossip, Boyfriends, and Other Realities of Adolescence*, by Rosalind Wiseman (Crown); *Chicken: A Self-Portrait*, by David Sterry (Regan Books/HarperCollins); *Raising Fences: A Black Man's Love Story*, by Michael Datcher (Riverhead/Penguin Putnam); *21 Dog Years: Doing Time*, by Mike Daisey (Free Press/Simon & Schuster).

Terms: Agent receives 15% commission on domestic sales; 20% commission on foreign sales. Offers written contract, binding for variable length of time. Charges clients for out-of-pocket expenses—telephone, fax, postage, and photocopying—directly connected to the project.

Writers' Conferences: ASJA Annual Conference (New York City, May).

Tips: "We work closely with clients on editorial development and promotion. We work to place our clients as magazine columnists and have created columnists for *McCall's* (renamed *Rosie's*) and *Child*. We work with clients to develop their projects across various media—video, software, and audio."

PAUL S. LEVINE LITERARY AGENCY

1054 Superba Ave., Venice CA 90291-3940. (310)450-6711. Fax: (310)450-0181. E-mail: pslevine@ix.netcom.com. Website: www.netcom.com/~pslevine/lawliterary.html. **Contact:** Paul S. Levine. Estab. 1996. Member of the State Bar of California. Represents over 100 clients. 75% of clients are new/unpublished writers. Currently handles: 30% nonfiction books; 30% novels; 10% movie scripts; 30% TV scripts.

Represents: Nonfiction books, novels, movie scripts, feature film, TV scripts, TV movie of the week, episodic drama, sitcom, animation, documentary, miniseries, syndicated material. **Considers these nonfiction areas:** Art/architecture/design; biography/autobiography; business/economics; child guidance/parenting; computers/electronic; cooking/foods/nutrition; crafts/hobbies; creative nonfiction; current affairs; education; ethnic/cultural interests; gay/lesbian issues; government/politics/law; health/medicine; history; how-to; humor/satire; interior design/decorating; language/literature/criticism; memoirs; military/war; money/finance; music/dance; nature/environment; New Age/metaphysics; photography; popular culture; psychology; religious/inspirational; science/technology; self-help/personal improvement; sociology; sports; theater/film; true crime/investigative; women's issues/studies. **Considers these fiction areas:** Action/adventure; comic books/cartoon; confession; contemporary issues; detective/police/crime; erotica; ethnic; experimental; family saga; feminist; gay/lesbian; glitz; historical; humor/satire; literary; mainstream/contemporary; mystery/suspense; regional; religious/inspirational; romance; sports; thriller; westerns/frontier. **Considers these script subject areas:** Action/adventure; biography/autobiography; cartoon/animation; comedy; contemporary issues; detective/police/crime; erotica; ethnic; experimental; family saga; feminist; gay/lesbian; glitz; historical; horror; juvenile; mainstream; multimedia; mystery/suspense; religious/inspirational; romantic comedy; romantic drama; sports; teen; thriller; western/frontier.

~ Actively seeking commercial fiction and nonfiction. Also handles children's and young adult fiction and nonfiction. Does not want to receive science fiction, fantasy, or horror.

How to Contact: Query with SASE. Accepts e-mail and fax queries. Considers simultaneous queries. Responds in 1 day to queries; 2 months to mss. Returns materials only with SASE. Obtains most new clients through conferences, referrals, listings on various websites and through listings in directories.

Recent Sales: Sold 25 titles in the last year. This agency prefers not to share information on specific sales.

Terms: Agent receives 15% commission on domestic sales; 20% commission on foreign sales. Offers written contract. Charges clients for messengers, long distance, postage. "Only when incurred. No advance payment necessary."

Writers' Conferences: California Lawyers for the Arts (Los Angeles CA); National Writers Club (Los Angeles

CA); ''Selling to Hollywood'' Writer's Connection (Glendale CA); ''Spotlight on Craft'' Willamette Writers Conference (Portland OR); Women in Animation (Los Angeles CA); and many others.

◗ ROBERT LIEBERMAN ASSOCIATES

400 Nelson Rd., Ithaca NY 14850-9440. (607)273-8801. Fax: (801)749-9682. E-mail: rhl10@cornell.edu. Website: www.people.cornell.edu/pages/rhl10. **Contact:** Robert Lieberman. Estab. 1993. Represents 30 clients. 50% of clients are new/unpublished writers. Currently handles: 20% nonfiction books; 80% textbooks.

Represents: Nonfiction books (trade), scholarly books, textbooks (college, high school, and middle school level). **Considers these nonfiction areas:** Agriculture/horticulture; anthropology/archaeology; art/architecture/design; business/economics; computers/electronic; education; health/medicine; memoirs (by authors with high public recognition); money/finance; music/dance; nature/environment; psychology; science/technology; sociology; theater/film.

> **○┓** This agency specializes in university/college level textbooks, CD-ROM/software, and popular tradebooks in science, math, engineering, economics, and other subjects. Does not want to receive fiction, self-help, or screenplays.

How to Contact: Query with SASE or by e-mail. Prefers to read materials exclusively. Prefers e-mail queries. Responds in 2 weeks to queries; 1 month to mss. Returns materials only with SASE. Obtains most new clients through referrals.

Recent Sales: Sold 15 titles in the last year. *College Physics*, by Giambattist & Richardson (McGraw-Hill); *Conflict Resolution*, by Baltos and Weir (Cambridge University Press).

Terms: Agent receives 15% commission on domestic sales; 20% commission on foreign sales. Offers written contract, binding for open-ended length of time; 1-month notice must be given to terminate contract. 100% of business is derived from commissions on ms sales. ''Fees are sometimes charged to clients for shipping and when special reviewers are required.''

Tips: ''The trade books we handle are by authors who are highly recognized in their fields of expertise. Client list includes Nobel Prize winners and others with high name recognition, either by the public or within a given area of expertise.''

Ⓝ ● ◗ LIMELIGHT MANAGEMENT

33 Newman St., London W1T 1PY, England. 0207 6372529. E-mail: limelight.management@virgin.net. Website: www.limelightmanagement.com. **Contact:** Fiona Lindsay. Estab. 1990. Member of Association of Authors' Agents. Represents 70 clients. Currently handles: 100% nonfiction books; multimedia.

> ● Prior to becoming an agent, Ms. Lindsay was a public relations manager of the Dorchester and was working on her law degree.

Represents: Nonfiction books, lifestyle TV. **Considers these nonfiction areas:** Agriculture/horticulture; art/architecture/design; cooking/foods/nutrition; crafts/hobbies; gardening; health/medicine; interior design/decorating; nature/environment; New Age/metaphysics; photography; self-help/personal improvement; sports; travel.

> **○┓** This agency specializes in lifestyle subject areas, especially celebrity chefs, gardeners and wine experts. Actively seeking health, cooking, gardening. Does not want to receive any subject not listed above.

How to Contact: Query with SASE, or send outline/proposal; IRCs. Prefers to read materials exclusively. Accepts e-mail and fax queries. Responds in 1 week to queries. Returns materials only with SASE. Obtains most new clients through recommendations from others.

Recent Sales: Sold 45 titles in the last year. This agency prefers not to share information on specific sales. Other clients include Clients include Oz Clarke, Antony Worrall Thompson, David Stevens, David Joyce, John Bly.

Terms: Agent receives 15% commission on domestic sales; 20% commission on foreign sales. Offers written contract; 2 months notice must be given to terminate contract.

◗ LINDSEY'S LITERARY SERVICES

7502 Greenville Ave., Suite 500, Dallas TX 75231. (214)890-4050. Fax: (214)890-9295. E-mail: bonedges001@aol .com. **Contact:** Bonnie James; Emily Armenta. Estab. 2002. Represents 14 clients. 60% of clients are new/unpublished writers. Currently handles: 70% nonfiction books; 30% novels.

> ● Prior to becoming an agent, Ms. James was a drama instructor and magazine editor, and Ms. Armenta was an independent film editor and magazine editor.

Member Agents: Bonnie James (Nonfiction: New Age/metaphysics, self-help, psychology, women's issues; Fiction: mystery/suspense, thriller, horror, literary, mainstream, romance); Emily Armenta (Nonfiction: New Age/metaphysics, self-help, psychology, women's issues; Fiction: mystery/suspense, thriller, horror, literary, mainstream, romance).

Represents: Nonfiction books, novels. **Considers these nonfiction areas:** Animals; biography/autobiography;

ethnic/cultural interests; gay/lesbian issues; health/medicine; history; memoirs; multicultural; New Age/meta-physics; psychology; self-help/personal improvement; true crime/investigative; women's issues/studies. **Considers these fiction areas:** Action/adventure; detective/police/crime; ethnic; historical; horror; literary; mainstream/contemporary; multicultural; mystery/suspense; New Age; religious/inspirational; romance; science fiction; thriller.

O— "We are a new agency with a clear vision and will aggressively represent our clients." Actively seeking nonfiction self-help, metaphysical, psychology, and women's issues; for fiction, seeking exceptionally written books. Does not want poetry, children's books, text books.

How to Contact: Query with SASE or by e-mail. For nonfiction, submit proposal package, writing sample, and brief bio (list credentials and platform details). For fiction, include first 3 chapters, synopsis, and brief bio. No phone calls, please. Considers simultaneous queries. Responds in 4-6 weeks to queries; 2-3 months to mss. Returns materials only with SASE. Obtains most new clients through recommendations from others, solicitations.

Recent Sales: Sold 5 titles in the last year. *Crisis Pending*, by Stephen Cornell (Durban House); *Horizon's End*, by Andrew Lazarus (Gladden Books); *No Ordinary Terror*, by J. Brooks Van Dyke (Durban House).

Terms: Agent receives 15% commission on domestic sales; 20% commission on foreign sales. Offers written contract, binding for 1 year; cancelable by either party with 1-month written notice notice must be given to terminate contract.

Tips: "Write a clear, concise query describing your project. Pay attention to the craft of writing. Provide complete package, including education, profession, writing credits, and what you want to accomplish."

◖ WENDY LIPKIND AGENCY

120 E. 81st St., New York NY 10028. (212)628-9653. Fax: (212)585-1306. E-mail: lipkindag@aol.com. **Contact:** Wendy Lipkind. Estab. 1977. Member of AAR. Represents 60 clients. Currently handles: 80% nonfiction books; 20% novels.

Represents: Nonfiction books, novels. **Considers these nonfiction areas:** Biography/autobiography; current affairs; health/medicine; history; science/technology; women's issues/studies; social history. **Considers these fiction areas:** Mainstream/contemporary; mystery/suspense (psychological suspense).

O— This agency specializes in adult nonfiction. Does not want to receive mass market originals.

How to Contact: Prefers to read materials exclusively. Query by e-mail with letter only. No attachments. Responds in 1 month to queries. Returns materials only with SASE. Obtains most new clients through recommendations from others.

Recent Sales: Sold 10 titles in the last year. *One Small Step*, by Robert Mauner (Workman); *In the Land of Lyme*, by Pamela Weintraub (Scribner).

Terms: Agent receives 15% commission on domestic sales; 20% commission on foreign sales. Sometimes offers written contract. Charges clients for foreign postage, messenger service, photocopying, transatlantic calls, faxes.

Tips: "Send intelligent query letter first. Let me know if you sent to other agents."

◖ LITERARY AND CREATIVE ARTISTS, INC.

3543 Albemarle St. NW, Washington DC 20008-4213. (202)362-4688. Fax: (202)362-8875. E-mail: lca9643@lcadc.com. Website: www.lcadc.com. **Contact:** Muriel Nellis. Estab. 1981. Member of AAR, Authors' Guild, the American Bar Association. Represents 75 clients. Currently handles: 70% nonfiction books; 15% novels.

Member Agents: Muriel Nellis; Jane Roberts; Stephen Ruwe.

Represents: Nonfiction books, novels. **Considers these nonfiction areas:** Biography/autobiography; business/economics; cooking/foods/nutrition; government/politics/law; health/medicine; how-to; memoirs; philosophy; human drama; lifestyle.

How to Contact: Query with SASE. *No unsolicited mss.* Responds in approximately 3 weeks to queries.

Recent Sales: *Seasons of Grace*, by John O'Neil and Alan Jones (John Wiley and Sons); *Lady Cottington's Fairy Album*, by Brian Froud (Harry N. Abrams); *The Origin of Minds*, by Peggy La Cerra and Roger Bingham (Harmony Books).

Terms: Agent receives 15% commission on domestic sales; 20% commission on foreign sales; 25% commission on dramatic rights sales. Charges clients for long-distance phone and fax, photocopying, shipping.

Tips: "While we prefer published writers, it is not required if the proposed work has great merit."

◖ THE LITERARY GROUP

270 Lafayette St., 1505, New York NY 10012. (212)274-1616. Fax: (212)274-9876. E-mail: fweimann@theliterarygroup.com. Website: www.theliterarygroup.com. **Contact:** Frank Weimann. Estab. 1985. 65% of clients are new/unpublished writers. Represents 200 clients in the general trade market and 125 CBA. Currently handles: 50% nonfiction books; 50% fiction.

Member Agents: Frank Weimann (fiction, nonfiction); Ian Kleinert (nonfiction); Steve Laube (Christian).

Represents: Nonfiction books, and fiction books. **Considers these nonfiction areas:** Animals; anthropology/archaeology; biography/autobiography; business/economics; child guidance/parenting; crafts/hobbies; creative nonfiction; current affairs; education; ethnic/cultural interests; government/politics/law; health/medicine; history; how-to; humor/satire; juvenile nonfiction; language/literature/criticism; memoirs; military/war; money/finance; multicultural; music/dance; nature/environment; popular culture; psychology; religious/inspirational; science/technology; self-help/personal improvement; sociology; sports; theater/film; true crime/investigative; women's issues/studies. **Considers these fiction areas:** Action/adventure; contemporary issues; detective/police/crime; ethnic; family saga; fantasy; feminist; horror; humor/satire; mystery/suspense; psychic/supernatural; romance (contemporary, gothic, historical, regency); sports; thriller; westerns/frontier.
 ⚬⇥ This agency specializes in nonfiction (true crime, military, history, biography, sports, how-to).
How to Contact: Query with SASE, outline, 3 sample chapter(s). Prefers to read materials exclusively. Responds in 1 week to queries; 1 month to mss. Returns materials only with SASE. Obtains most new clients through referrals, writers' conferences, query letters.
Recent Sales: Sold 150 titles in the last year. *Keep It Simple*, by Terry Bradshaw; *The Heart of the Matter*, by Dr. Peter Salgo; *The Greater Good*, by Casey Morton. Other clients include Tommy Chong, Dr. Peter Salgo, Homer Hickman.
Terms: Agent receives 15% commission on domestic sales; 20% commission on foreign sales. Offers written contract; 30-day notice must be given to terminate contract.
Writers' Conferences: Detroit Women's Writers (MI); Kent State University (OH); San Diego Writers Conference (CA); Maui Writers Conference (HI); Austin Writers' Conference (TX).

☑ LITWEST GROUP, LLC
Website: www.litwest.com. Represents 160 clients. 45% of clients are new/unpublished writers. Currently handles: 75% nonfiction books; 25% novels; TV, movie, Internet projects revolving around the book.
 • Prior to opening the agency, Mr. Preskill was in law, and Ms. Mead and Ms. Boyle were in publishing.
Member Agents: Linda Mead (business, personal improvement, memoir, historical fiction/nonfiction steeped in research, ethnic/multicultural fiction/nonfiction, cozy mysteries); Rob Preskill (men's, thrillers and mysteries where the writing is subtle, sports, travel, leisure, lifestyle, fitness, male health, business, design/architecture/art, politics, subculture, graphic novels, narrative nonfiction, literary); Katie Boyle (literary fiction, surreal, avant-garde, narrative nonfiction/memoir, contemporary culture/politics, art/music bios, graphic novels/subculture, psychology, women's issues, pop-culture, religion/spirituality).
Represents: Nonfiction books, novels, scholarly books. **Considers these nonfiction areas:** Biography/autobiography; business/economics; child guidance/parenting; current affairs; ethnic/cultural interests; health/medicine; history; how-to; humor/satire; memoirs; military/war; money/finance; multicultural; popular culture; psychology; religious/inspirational; self-help/personal improvement; sociology; sports; true crime/investigative; women's issues/studies. **Considers these fiction areas:** Contemporary issues; detective/police/crime; ethnic; family saga; feminist; historical; humor/satire; literary; mainstream/contemporary; multicultural; mystery/suspense; religious/inspirational; sports; thriller.
 ⚬⇥ "We are multi-faceted." Actively seeking all subjects. Does not want to receive science fiction, horror, western, cookbooks.
How to Contact: Query with SASE, outline, 3 sample chapter(s). See contact information on website. Considers simultaneous queries. Responds in 1 month to queries. Response time varies. Returns materials only with SASE. Obtains most new clients through recommendations from others, solicitations, conferences.
Recent Sales: *Winners Are Driven*, by Bobby Unser with Paul Pease (Wiley); *The Elegant Gathering of White Snows*, by Kris Radish (Bantam); *Sickened: The Memoir of a Munchausen by Proxy Childhood*, by Julie Gregory (Bantam). Other clients include Woodleigh Marx Hubbard, Jennifer Openshaw, Jed Diamond, Dr. Jay Gordon, Dr. Arthur White, Eric Harr, Brad Herzog, Martin Yan, Lyn Webster-Wilde, Larraine Segil.
Terms: Agent receives 15% commission on domestic sales; 20% commission on foreign sales. Offers written contract. Charges for postage and photocopying.
Writers' Conferences: Maui Writers Conference (Maui HI, Labor Day); San Diego State University Writers' Conference (San Diego CA, January); William Saroyan Writers Conference (Fresno CA, March); Santa Barbara (June); and many others.
Tips: "Clarity and precision about your work also helps the agent process."

☑ LOS BRAVOS LITERARY MANAGEMENT
1811 N. Whitley Ave., Suite 1003, Los Angeles CA 90028. (323)461-5589. Fax: (323)417-4879. E-mail: marcosbravosmanagement.com. **Contact:** Marc Gerald. Estab. 2002. Represents 35 clients. 10% of clients are new/unpublished writers. Currently handles: 50% nonfiction books; 50% novels.
 • Prior to becoming an agent, Mr. Gerald found and ran *The Syndicate*, an urban-oriented publishing and entertainment company, co-owned with Wesley Snipes; founded and edited W.W. Norton's Old School Books imprint; wrote and produced *America's Most Wanted* and numerous specials for Fox Television.

Represents: Nonfiction books, novels, feature film. **Considers these nonfiction areas:** Biography/autobiography; ethnic/cultural interests; health/medicine; history; how-to; memoirs; popular culture; self-help/personal improvement; sports; true crime/investigative; juvenile nonfiction, New Age. **Considers these fiction areas:** Action/adventure; detective/police/crime; erotica; ethnic; horror; literary; mystery/suspense; thriller; young adult; glitz. **Considers these script subject areas:** Action/adventure; biography/autobiography; comedy; contemporary issues; detective/police/crime; ethnic; horror; mystery/suspense; teen; thriller.

How to Contact: Submit outline, 2 sample chapter(s). Considers simultaneous queries. Responds in 1 month to queries; 2 months to mss. Returns materials only with SASE. Obtains most new clients through recommendations from others.

Recent Sales: Sold 20 titles and sold 1 scripts in the last year.

Terms: Agent receives 15% commission on domestic sales; 20% commission on foreign sales. Offers written contract. Charges clients for postage and photocopying.

☑ NANCY LOVE LITERARY AGENCY

250 E. 65th St., New York NY 10021-6614. (212)980-3499. Fax: (212)308-6405. E-mail: nloveag@aol.com. **Contact:** Nancy Love. Estab. 1984. Member of AAR. Represents 60-80 clients. 25% of clients are new/unpublished writers. Currently handles: 90% nonfiction books; 10% novels.

Member Agents: Nancy Love; Miriam Tager (mysteries, thrillers).

Represents: Nonfiction books, novels (mysteries and thrillers only). **Considers these nonfiction areas:** Biography/autobiography; child guidance/parenting; cooking/foods/nutrition; current affairs; ethnic/cultural interests; government/politics/law; health/medicine; history; how-to; nature/environment; New Age/metaphysics; popular culture; psychology; religious/inspirational; science/technology; self-help/personal improvement; sociology; spirituality; travel (armchair only, no how-to travel); true crime/investigative; women's issues/studies. **Considers these fiction areas:** Mystery/suspense; thriller.

> O— This agency specializes in adult nonfiction and mysteries. Actively seeking health and medicine (including alternative medicine), parenting, spiritual, and inspirational. Does not want to receive novels other than mysteries and thrillers.

How to Contact: For nonfiction, send a proposal, chapter summary, and sample chapter. For fiction, query first. Fiction is only read on an exclusive basis. No e-mail or fax queries. Considers simultaneous queries. Responds in 3 weeks to queries; 6 weeks to mss. Returns materials only with SASE. Obtains most new clients through recommendations from others, solicitations.

Recent Sales: Sold 20 titles in the last year. Books 3 and 4 in Blanco County Mystery Series, by Ben Rehder (St. Martin's Press); *Back Pain*, by Emile Hiesinger, M.D., and Marian Bettaucourt (Pocket Books); *The Tools People Use to Quit Addictions*, by Stanton Peele, Ph.D. (Crown); *All the Shah's Men: The Hidden Story of the CIA's Coup in Iran*, by Steven Kinzer (John Wiley).

Terms: Agent receives 15% commission on domestic sales; 20% commission on foreign sales. Offers written contract. Charges clients for photocopying "if it runs over $20."

Tips: "Nonfiction author and/or collaborator must be an authority in subject area and have a platform. Send a SASE if you want a response."

Ⓝ ☑ LOWENSTEIN-YOST ASSOCIATES

121 W. 27th St., Suite 601, New York NY 10001. (212)206-1630. Fax: (212)727-0280. **Contact:** President: Barbara Lowenstein. Estab. 1976. Member of AAR. Represents 150 clients. 20% of clients are new/unpublished writers. Currently handles: 60% nonfiction books; 40% novels.

Member Agents: Barbara Lowenstein (president); Nancy Yost (agent); Eileen Cope (agent); Norman Kurz (business affairs); Dorian Karchmar (agent); Julie Culver (foreign rights manager).

Represents: Nonfiction books, novels. **Considers these nonfiction areas:** Animals; anthropology/archaeology; biography/autobiography; business/economics; child guidance/parenting; crafts/hobbies; creative nonfiction; current affairs; education; ethnic/cultural interests; gay/lesbian issues; government/politics/law; health/medicine; history; how-to; humor/satire; language/literature/criticism; memoirs; money/finance; music/dance; nature/environment; New Age/metaphysics; popular culture; psychology; religious/inspirational; science/technology; self-help/personal improvement; sociology; spirituality; theater/film; travel; women's issues/studies. **Considers these fiction areas:** Contemporary issues; detective/police/crime; erotica; ethnic; feminist; gay/lesbian; historical; literary; mainstream/contemporary; mystery/suspense; romance (contemporary, historical, regency); thriller (medical).

> O— This agency specializes in health, business, spirituality, creative nonfiction, literary fiction, commercial fiction, especially suspense, crime, and women's issues. "We are a full-service agency, handling domestic and foreign rights, film rights, and audio rights to all of our books."

How to Contact: Query with SASE. Prefers to read materials exclusively. For fiction, send outline and first chapter. *No unsolicited mss.* Responds in 6 weeks to queries. Returns materials only with SASE. Obtains most new clients through recommendations from others, solicitations, conferences.

Recent Sales: Sold 75 titles in the last year. *Unblemished,* by Dr. Rodan & Dr. Field (Atria); *Kiss of the Night,* by Sherrilyn Kenyon (St. Martin's). Other clients include Ishmael Reed, Deborah Crombie, Leslie Glass, Stephanie Laurens, Grace Edwards, Rachel Kuschner, Perri O'Shaughnessy, Tim Cahill, Gina Nahai, Kevin Young.

Terms: Agent receives 15% commission on domestic sales; 20% commission on foreign sales. Offers written contract, binding for book by book basis. Charges for large photocopy batches and international postage.

Writers' Conferences: Malice Domestic; Bouchercon.

Tips: "Know the genre you are working in and read!"

ANDREW LOWNIE LITERARY AGENCY, LTD.

17 Sutherland St., London SW1V4JU, England. (0207)828 1274. Fax: (0207)828 7608. E-mail: lownie@globalnet. co.uk. Website: www.andrewlownie.co.uk. **Contact:** Andrew Lownie. Estab. 1988. Member of Association of Author's Agents. Represents 130 clients. 20% of clients are new/unpublished writers. Currently handles: 90% nonfiction books; 10% novels.

- Prior to becoming an agent, Mr. Lownie was a journalist, bookseller, publisher, author of 12 books, and previously a director of the Curtis Brown Agency.

Represents: Nonfiction books. **Considers these nonfiction areas:** Anthropology/archaeology; biography/auto-biography; current affairs; government/politics/law; history; memoirs; military/war; music/dance; popular culture; theater/film; true crime/investigative.

- This agent has wide publishing experience, extensive journalistic contacts, and a specialty in showbiz memoir and celebrities. Actively seeking showbiz memoirs, narrative histories, and biographies. Does not want to receive poetry, short stories, children's fiction, scripts, academic.

How to Contact: Query with SASE and/or IRCs. Submit outline, 1 sample chapter(s). Accepts e-mail and fax queries. Considers simultaneous queries. Responds in 1 week to queries; 1 month to mss. Returns materials only with SASE. Obtains most new clients through recommendations from others.

Recent Sales: Sold 50 titles in the last year. *Avenging Justice,* by David Stafford (Time Warner). Other clients include Norma Major, Guy Bellamy, Joyce Cary estate, Lawrence James, Juliet Barker, Patrick McNee, Sir John Mills, Peter Evans, Desmond Seward, Laurence Gardner, Richard Rudgley, Timothy Good, Tom Levine.

Terms: Agent receives 15% commission on domestic sales; 15% commission on foreign sales. Offers written contract, binding for until author chooses to break it but contract valid while book in print; 30-day notice must be given to terminate contract. Charges clients for some copying, postage, copies of books for submission.

Tips: "I prefer submissions in writing by letter."

DONALD MAASS LITERARY AGENCY

160 W. 95th St., Suite 1B, New York NY 10025. (212)866-8200. Website: www.maassagency.com. **Contact:** Donald Maass, Jennifer Jackson, or Rachel Vater. Estab. 1980. Member of AAR, SFWA, MWA, RWA. Represents over 100 clients. 5% of clients are new/unpublished writers. Currently handles: 100% novels.

- Prior to opening his agency, Mr. Maass served as an editor at Dell Publishing (New York) and as a reader at Gollancz (London). He is the current president of AAR.

Member Agents: Donald Maass (mainstream, literary, mystery/suspense, science fiction); Jennifer Jackson (commercial fiction, especially romance, science fiction, fantasy, mystery/suspense); Rachel Vater (chick lit, mystery, thriller, fantasy, commercial, literary).

Represents: Novels. **Considers these fiction areas:** Detective/police/crime; fantasy; historical; horror; literary; mainstream/contemporary; mystery/suspense; psychic/supernatural; romance (historical, paranormal, time travel); science fiction; thriller; women's.

- This agency specializes in commercial fiction, especially science fiction, fantasy, mystery, romance, suspense. Actively seeking "to expand the literary portion of our list and expand in romance and women's fiction." Does not want to receive nonfiction, children's, or poetry.

How to Contact: Query with SASE. Returns material only with SASE. Considers simultaneous queries. Responds in 2 weeks to queries; 3 months to mss.

Recent Sales: Sold over 100 titles in the last year. *Shoulder the Sky,* by Anne Perry (Ballantine); *The Longest Night,* by Gregg Keizer (G.P. Putnam's Sons).

Terms: Agent receives 15% commission on domestic sales; 20% commission on foreign sales.

Writers' Conferences: *Donald Maass:* World Science Fiction Convention; Frankfurt Book Fair; Pacific Northwest Writers Conference; Bouchercon and others; *Jennifer Jackson:* World Science Fiction and Fantasy Convention; RWA National, and others.

Tips: "We are fiction specialists, also noted for our innovative approach to career planning. Few new clients are accepted, but interested authors should query with SASE. Subagents in all principle foreign countries and Hollywood. No nonfiction or juvenile works considered."

◐ GINA MACCOBY AGENCY

P.O. Box 60, Chappaqua NY 10514. (914)238-5630. **Contact:** Gina Maccoby. Estab. 1986. Represents 25 clients. Currently handles: 33% nonfiction books; 33% novels; 33% juvenile books; Represents illustrators of children's books.

Represents: Nonfiction books, novels, juvenile books. **Considers these nonfiction areas:** Biography/autobiography; current affairs; ethnic/cultural interests; history; juvenile nonfiction; popular culture; women's issues/studies. **Considers these fiction areas:** Juvenile; literary; mainstream/contemporary; mystery/suspense; thriller; young adult.

How to Contact: Query with SASE. Considers simultaneous queries. Responds in 3 months to queries. Returns materials only with SASE. Obtains most new clients through recommendations from own clients and publishers.

Recent Sales: Sold 21 titles in the last year.

Terms: Agent receives 15% commission on domestic sales; 25% commission on foreign sales. Charges clients for photocopying. May recover certain costs such as the cost of shipping books by air to Europe or Japan or legal fees.

◑ CAROL MANN AGENCY

55 Fifth Ave., New York NY 10003. (212)206-5635. Fax: (212)675-4809. E-mail: emily@carolmannagency.com. **Contact:** Emily Nurkin. Estab. 1977. Member of AAR. Represents 200 clients. 25% of clients are new/unpublished writers. Currently handles: 70% nonfiction books; 30% novels.

Member Agents: Carol Mann (literary fiction, nonfiction); Emily Nurkin (fiction and nonfiction).

Represents: Nonfiction books, novels. **Considers these nonfiction areas:** Anthropology/archaeology; art/architecture/design; biography/autobiography; business/economics; child guidance/parenting; current affairs; ethnic/cultural interests; government/politics/law; health/medicine; history; money/finance; psychology; self-help/personal improvement; sociology; women's issues/studies. **Considers these fiction areas:** Literary; commercial.

○━ This agency specializes in current affairs; self-help; popular culture; psychology; parenting; history. Does not want to receive "genre fiction (romance, mystery, etc.)."

How to Contact: Query with outline/proposal and SASE. Responds in 3 weeks to queries.

Recent Sales: Other clients include novelists Paul Auster and Marita Golden; journalists Tim Egan, Hannah Storm, Willow Bay, Pulitzer Prize-winner Fox Butterfield; best-selling essayist Shelby Steele; sociologist Dr. William Julius Wilson; economist Thomas Sowell; best-selling diet doctors Mary Dan and Michael Eades; ACLU president Nadine Strossen; pundit Mona Charen; memoirist Lauren Winner; photography project editors Rick Smolan and David Cohen (*America 24/7*); and Kevin Liles, president of Def Jam Records.

Terms: Agent receives 15% commission on domestic sales; 20% commission on foreign sales. Offers written contract.

MANUS & ASSOCIATES LITERARY AGENCY, INC.

425 Sherman Ave., Suite 200, Palo Alto CA 94306. (650)470-5151. Fax: (650)470-5159. E-mail: manuslit@manuslit.com. Website: www.manuslit.com. **Contact:** Jillian Manus. Also: 445 Park Ave., New York NY 10022. (212)644-8020. Fax (212)644-3374. **Contact:** Janet Manus. Estab. 1985. Member of AAR. Represents 75 clients. 30% of clients are new/unpublished writers. Currently handles: 55% nonfiction books; 25% novels.

● Prior to becoming an agent, Jillian Manus was associate publisher of two national magazines and director of development at Warner Bros. and Universal Studios; Janet Manus has been a literary agent for 20 years.

Member Agents: Jandy Nelson (self-help, health, memoirs, narrative nonfiction, women's fiction, literary fiction, multicultural fiction, thrillers); Stephanie Lee (self-help, narrative nonfiction, commercial literary fiction, quirky/edgy fiction, pop culture, pop science); Jillian Manus (political, memoirs, self-help, history, sports, women's issues, Latin fiction and nonfiction, thrillers); Donna Levin (mysteries, memoirs, self-help, nonfiction).

Represents: Nonfiction books, novels. **Considers these nonfiction areas:** Biography/autobiography; business/economics; child guidance/parenting; creative nonfiction; current affairs; ethnic/cultural interests; health/medicine; how-to; memoirs; money/finance; nature/environment; popular culture; psychology; science/technology; self-help/personal improvement; women's issues/studies; Gen X and Gen Y issues. **Considers these fiction areas:** Literary; mainstream/contemporary; multicultural; mystery/suspense; thriller; women's; quirky/edgy fiction.

○━ This agency specializes in commercial literary fiction, narrative nonfiction, thrillers, health, pop psychology, women's empowerment. "Our agency is unique in the way that we not only sell the material, but we edit, develop concepts, and participate in the marketing effort. We specialize in large, conceptual fiction and nonfiction, and always value a project that can be sold in the TV/feature film market." Actively seeking high-concept thrillers, commercial literary fiction, women's fiction, celebrity biographies, memoirs, multicultural fiction, popular health, women's empowerment, mysteries. Does not want to receive horror, romance, science fiction/fantasy, westerns, young adult, children's, poetry, cookbooks, magazine articles. Usually obtains new clients through recommendations from editors, clients and others, conferences, and unsolicited materials.

How to Contact: Query with SASE. If requested, submit outline, 2-3 sample chapter(s). No faxes, please. All queries should be sent to California office. Accepts e-mail queries. No fax queries. Considers simultaneous queries. Responds in 3 months to queries; 10 weeks to mss. Returns materials only with SASE. Obtains most new clients through recommendations from others, solicitations, conferences.

Recent Sales: *Grant Comes East*, by Newt Gingrich and William Farstchen (St. Martin's/Thomas Dunne); *Raising a President*, by Doug Wead (Atria Books); Untitled Comfort Book, by Karen Neuburger and Nadine Schiff; *Space Between the Stars*, by Deborah Santana; *Birds of a Feather*, by Mira Tweti. Other clients include Dr. Lorraine Zappart, Marcus Allen, Carlton Stowers, Alan Jacobson, Ann Brandt, Dr. Richard Marrs, Mary Loverde, Lisa Huang Fleishman, Judy Carter, Daryl Ott Underhill, Glen Kleier, Andrew X. Pham, Lalita Tademy, Frank Baldwin, Katy Robinson, K.M. Soehnlein, Joelle Fraser, Fred Luskin, Jim Schutze, Mark Victor Hansen, Robert S. Allen, Deborah Santana, Karen Neuburger, Mira Tweti.

Terms: Agent receives 15% commission on domestic sales; 20-25% commission on foreign sales. Offers written contract, binding for 2 years; 60 days notice must be given to terminate contract. Charges for photocopying and postage/UPS.

Writers' Conferences: Maui Writers Conference (Maui HI, Labor Day); San Diego Writer's Conference (San Diego CA, January); Willamette Writers Conference (Willamette OR, July); BEA; MEGA Book Marketing University.

Tips: "Research agents using a variety of sources, including *LMP*, guides, *Publishers Weekly*, conferences, and even acknowledgements in books similar in tone to yours."

☑ MARCH TENTH, INC.

4 Myrtle St., Haworth NJ 07641-1740. (201)387-6551. Fax: (201)387-6552. E-mail: hchoron@aol.com. Website: www.marchtenthinc.com. **Contact:** Harry Choron, vice president. Estab. 1982. Represents 40 clients. 30% of clients are new/unpublished writers. Currently handles: 75% nonfiction books; 25% novels.

Represents: Nonfiction books, novels. **Considers these nonfiction areas:** Biography/autobiography; current affairs; health/medicine; history; humor/satire; language/literature/criticism; music/dance; popular culture; theater/film. **Considers these fiction areas:** Confession; ethnic; family saga; historical; humor/satire; literary; mainstream/contemporary.

    ○➔ "Writers must have professional expertise in their field. Pefer to work with published/established writers."

How to Contact: Query with SASE. Considers simultaneous queries. Responds in 1 month to queries. Returns materials only with SASE.

Recent Sales: Sold 12 titles in the last year. *The Case for Zionism*, by Rabbi Arthur Hertzberg; *Learning Sickness*, by James Lang; *The 100 Simple Secrets of Happy Families*, by David Niven.

Terms: Agent receives 15% commission on domestic sales; 20% commission on foreign sales; 20% commission on dramatic rights sales. Charges clients for postage, photocopying, overseas phone expenses. "Does not require expense money upfront."

☑ THE DENISE MARCIL LITERARY AGENCY, INC.

156 Fifth Ave., Suite 625, New York NY 10010. (212)932-3110. Fax: (212)932-3113. **Contact:** Denise Marcil. Estab. 1977. Member of AAR. Represents 35 clients. 10% of clients are new/unpublished writers. Currently handles: Commercial fiction and nonfiction.

    • Prior to opening her agency, Ms. Marcil served as an editorial assistant with Avon Books, and as an editor with Simon & Schuster.

Represents: Nonfiction books (commercial), novels (commercial).

    ○➔ This agency specializes in thrillers, suspense, women's commercial fiction, business books, popular reference, how-to, self-help, health, and parenting. "We are looking for fresh new voices in commercial women's fiction: chick lit, mom-lit, stories that capture women's experiences today. We are especially seeking well-written thrillers with the potential to break out."

How to Contact: Query with SASE.

Recent Sales: Sold 43 titles in the last year. *Death's Little Helpers*, by Peter Spiegelman (Knopf); *Destiny Unleashed*, by Sheryl Woods (Mira); *First Class Killing*, by Lynne Heitman; *The Baby Sleep Book*, by Dr. William Sears, Dr. Robert Sears, Dr. James Sears, and Martha Sears (Little, Brown); *I Don't Know What I Want, But I Know It's Not This*, by Julie Jansen (Penguin).

Terms: Agent receives 15% commission on domestic sales; 20% commission on foreign sales. Offers written contract, binding for 2 years; 100% of business is derived from commissions on ms sales. Charges $100/year for postage, photocopying, long-distance calls, etc.

Writers' Conferences: Pacific Northwest Writers Conference; RWA.

☒ ⊘ MILDRED MARMUR ASSOCIATES LTD.

2005 Palmer Ave., Suite 127, Larchmont NY 10538. **Contact:** Mildred Marmur. Estab. 1987. Member of AAR.
Represents: Nonfiction books, novels. **Considers these nonfiction areas:** Biography/autobiography; business/economics; cooking/foods/nutrition; current affairs; ethnic/cultural interests; government/politics/law; health/medicine; history; money/finance; music/dance; nature/environment; religious/inspirational; science/technology; sports; theater/film; true crime/investigative; women's issues/studies. **Considers these fiction areas:** Detective/police/crime; family saga; feminist; juvenile; literary; mainstream/contemporary; mystery/suspense; thriller; young adult.

　　O⊶ This agency specializes in serious nonfiction.

How to Contact: Query with SASE. Responds in 1 month to queries. Obtains most new clients through recommendations from others.
Terms: Agent receives 15% commission on domestic sales; 20% commission on foreign sales. 100% of business is derived from commissions on ms sales.
Tips: "Browse in a bookstore or library and look at the acknowledgments in books similar to yours. If an author of a nonfiction book in your general area thanks his or her agent, send your manuscript to that person and point out the link. If you can't figure out who the agent is, try phoning the publisher. At least you'll have a more targeted person. Also, agents are more receptive to written submissions than to pitches over the phone."

⊘ THE EVAN MARSHALL AGENCY

6 Tristam Place, Pine Brook NJ 07058-9445. (973)882-1122. Fax: (973)882-3099. E-mail: evanmarshall@TheNovelist.com. Website: www.TheNovelist.com. **Contact:** Evan Marshall. Estab. 1987. Member of AAR, MWA, Sisters in Crime, American Crime Writers League. Currently handles: 100% novels.

　　● Prior to opening his agency, Mr. Marshall served as an editor with Houghton Mifflin, New American Library, Everest House, and Dodd, Mead & Co., and then worked as a literary agent at The Sterling Lord Agency.

Represents: Novels. **Considers these fiction areas:** Action/adventure; erotica; ethnic; historical; horror; humor/satire; literary; mainstream/contemporary; mystery/suspense; religious/inspirational; romance (contemporary, gothic, historical, Regency); science fiction; westerns/frontier.
How to Contact: Query first with SASE; do not enclose material. No e-mail queries. Responds in 1 week to queries; 3 months to mss. Obtains most new clients through recommendations from others.
Recent Sales: *In Silence*, by Erica Spindler (Mira); *Perfect Sax*, by Jerrilyn Farmer (Morrow); *Six-Thirty*, by Bobbi Smith (Dorchester).
Terms: Agent receives 15% commission on domestic sales; 20% commission on foreign sales. Offers written contract.

☒ ⊘ MARTIN LITERARY MANAGEMENT

17328 Ventura Blvd., Suite 138, Encino CA 91316. (818)595-1130. E-mail: sharlene@martinliterarymanagement.com. Website: www.martinliterarymanagement.com. **Contact:** Sharlene Martin. Estab. 2002. 100% of clients are new/unpublished writers. Currently handles: 100% nonfiction books.

　　● Prior to becoming an agent, Ms. Martin worked in fil/TV production and acquisitions.

Represents: Nonfiction books. **Considers these nonfiction areas:** Animals; biography/autobiography; business/economics; child guidance/parenting; current affairs; health/medicine; history; how-to; humor/satire; memoirs; popular culture; psychology; religious/inspirational; self-help/personal improvement; true crime/investigative; women's issues/studies.

　　O⊶ This agency has strong ties to film/TV. Actively seeking nonfiction that is highly commercial and that can be adapted to film.

How to Contact: Query with SASE, submit outline, 2 sample chapter(s). Accepts e-mail queries. No fax queries. Considers simultaneous queries. Responds in 1 week to queries; 3-4 weeks to mss. Returns materials only with SASE. Obtains most new clients through recommendations from others.
Terms: Agent receives 15% commission on domestic sales; 25% commission on foreign sales. Offers written contract, binding for 1 year; 1-month notice must be given to terminate contract. Charges author for postage and copying if material is not sent electronically.
Writers' Conferences: Maui Writers' Conference (Hawaii 2004)
Tips: "Have a strong platform for nonfiction. Don't call, use e-mail. I gladly welcome e-mail. Do your homework prior to submission, and only submit your best efforts."

☒ ⊘ HAROLD MATSON CO., INC.

276 Fifth Ave., New York NY 10001. (212)679-4490. **Contact:** Jonathan Matson. Member of AAR.

• This agency did not respond to our request for information. Query before submitting.
Member Agents: Jonathan Matson (literary, adult); Ben Camardi (literary, adult, dramatic).

Ⓝ Ⓩ JED MATTES, INC.

2095 Broadway, Suite 302, New York NY 10023-2895. (212)595-5228. Fax: (212)595-5232. **Contact:** Jed Mattes. Member of AAR.

• This agency did not respond to our request for information. Query before submitting.

MARGRET MCBRIDE LITERARY AGENCY

7744 Fay Ave., Suite 201, La Jolla CA 92037. (858)454-1550. Fax: (858)454-2156. Website: www.mcbrideliterary .com. Estab. 1980. Member of AAR, Authors Guild.

• Prior to opening her agency, Ms. McBride worked at Random House, Ballantine Books, and Warner Books.
Represents: Nonfiction books, novels. **Considers these nonfiction areas:** Biography/autobiography; business/ economics; cooking/foods/nutrition; current affairs; ethnic/cultural interests; government/politics/law; health/ medicine; history; how-to; money/finance; music/dance; popular culture; psychology; science/technology; self-help/personal improvement; sociology; women's issues/studies; style. **Considers these fiction areas:** Action/ adventure; detective/police/crime; ethnic; historical; humor/satire; literary; mainstream/contemporary; mystery/suspense; thriller; westerns/frontier.

○━ This agency specializes in mainstream fiction and nonfiction. Does not want to receive screenplays. Does not represent romance, poetry, or children's/young adult.
How to Contact: Query with synopsis or outline and SASE. Visit website for complete submission guidelines. Will not respond/read e-mail queries. Considers simultaneous queries. Responds in 2 months to queries. Returns materials only with SASE.
Recent Sales: Sold 22 titles in the last year. *Incriminating Evidence*, by Sheldon Siegel (Bantam); *Fierce Conversations*, by Susan Scott (Viking); *Dinner After Dark*, by Colin Cowie (Clarkson Potter).
Terms: Agent receives 15% commission on domestic sales; 25% commission on foreign sales. Charges for overnight delivery and photocopying.

Ⓝ THE MCCARTHY AGENCY, LLC

7 Allen St., Rumson NJ 07660. Phone/fax: (732)741-3065. **Contact:** Shawna McCarthy. Member of AAR.

• This agency did not respond to our request for information. Query before submitting.

Ⓩ GERARD MCCAULEY

P.O. Box 844, Katonah NY 10536. (914)232-5700. Fax: (914)232-1506. Estab. 1970. Member of AAR. Represents 60 clients. Currently not accepting new clients. Currently handles: nonfiction books.

○━ This agency specializes in history, biography, and general nonfiction.
How to Contact: Obtains most new clients through recommendations from others.
Recent Sales: Sold 30 titles in the last year. *Private Lives*, by Lawrence Friedman; *Heavens & Earth*, by Walter McDougall (HarperCollins); *Jack Johnson*, by Ken Burns (Knopf); *At War at Sea*, by Ronald Spector (Viking).
Terms: Agent receives 15% commission on domestic sales; 20% commission on foreign sales.

Ⓝ Ⓩ ANITA D. MCCLELLAN ASSOCIATES

50 Stearns St., Cambridge MA 02138. (617)576-6950. Fax: (617)576-6951. **Contact:** Anita McClellan. Member of AAR.

• This agency did not respond to our request for information. Query before submitting.

Ⓜ HELEN MCGRATH

1406 Idaho Ct., Concord CA 94521. (925)672-6211. Fax: (925)672-6383. E-mail: hmcgrath_lit@yahoo.com. **Contact:** Helen McGrath. Estab. 1977. Currently handles: 50% nonfiction books; 50% novels.
Represents: Nonfiction books, novels. **Considers these nonfiction areas:** Biography/autobiography; business/ economics; current affairs; health/medicine; history; how-to; military/war; psychology; self-help/personal improvement; sports; women's issues/studies. **Considers these fiction areas:** Contemporary issues; detective/ police/crime; literary; mainstream/contemporary; mystery/suspense; psychic/supernatural; romance; science fiction; thriller.
How to Contact: Submit proposal with SASE. *No unsolicited mss.* Responds in 2 months to queries. Obtains most new clients through recommendations from others.
Terms: Agent receives 15% commission on domestic sales. Offers written contract. Charges clients for photocopying.

◯ MCHUGH LITERARY AGENCY

1033 Lyon Rd., Moscow ID 83843-9167. (208)882-0107. Fax: (847)628-0146. E-mail: elisabetmch@turbonet.c om. **Contact:** Elisabet McHugh. Estab. 1994. Represents 42 clients. 30% of clients are new/unpublished writers. Currently handles: 30% nonfiction books; 70% fiction. **Considers these nonfiction areas:** Open to most subjects, except business. **Considers these fiction areas:** Historical; mainstream/contemporary; mystery/suspense; romance; thriller (psychological).

    �™ Does not handle children's books, poetry, science fiction, fantasy, horror, westerns.

How to Contact: Query first by e-mail. Do not send material unless asked for. Returns materials only with SASE.

Recent Sales: *The Complete RV Handbook: Making the Most of Your Life on the Road* (Ragged Mountain Press/McGraw-Hill); *Hassle-Free Business Travel* (Ten Speed Press); *Clark Gable* (McFarland); *Deadly Intent* (Bantam); *Never Again* (Harlequin).

Terms: Agent receives 15% commission on domestic sales; 20% commission on foreign sales. Does not charge any upfront fees. Offers written contract. "Client must provide all copies needed for submissions."

Ⓝ MCINTOSH & OTIS

353 Lexington Ave., New York NY 10016. Member of AAR.

    ● This agency did not respond to our request for updated information.

Member Agents: Samuel L. Pinkus (associate member); Elizabeth A. Winick (associate member); Eugene Winick (associate member).

Ⓝ ◯ SALLY HILL MCMILLAN & ASSOCIATES, INC.

429 E. Kingston Ave., Charlotte NC 28203. (704)334-0897. Fax: (704)334-1897. **Contact:** Sally Hill McMillan. Member of AAR.

    ● Query before submitting.

Ⓝ ◐ ◎ MENDEL MEDIA GROUP LLC

205 St. John's Place, Brooklyn NY 11217. (646)239-9896. Fax: (718)230-0887. E-mail: webmaster@mendelmedi a.com. Website: www.mendelmedia.com. Estab. 2002. Member of AAR. Represents 40-60 clients.

    ● Prior to becoming an agent, Mr. Mendel was an academic. "I taught American literature, Yiddish, Jewish studies, and literary theory at the University of Chicago and at the University of Illinois at Chicago while working on my Ph.D. in English. I also worked as a freelance technical writer and, for a time, as the managing editor of a health care magazine. In 1998, I began working for the late Jane Jordan Browne, a long-time veteran of the book publishing world."

Represents: Nonfiction books, novels, scholarly books (if have potential for a broad, popular appeal). **Considers these nonfiction areas:** Americana; animals; anthropology/archaeology; art/architecture/design; biography/autobiography; business/economics; child guidance/parenting; cooking/foods/nutrition; creative nonfiction; current affairs; education; ethnic/cultural interests; gardening; gay/lesbian issues; government/politics/law; health/medicine; history; how-to; humor/satire; language/literature/criticism; memoirs; military/war; money/finance; multicultural; music/dance; nature/environment; philosophy; popular culture; psychology; recreation; regional; religious/inspirational; science/technology; self-help/personal improvement; sex; sociology; software; spirituality; sports; true crime/investigative; women's issues/studies; Jewish topics. **Considers these fiction areas:** Action/adventure; detective/police/crime; erotica; ethnic; feminist; gay/lesbian; historical; humor/satire; juvenile; literary; mainstream/contemporary; mystery/suspense; picture books; religious/inspirational; romance; sports; thriller; young adult; contemporary issues; glitz; Jewish fiction.

    ☙ "I am interested in major works of history, current affairs, biography, business, politics, economics, science, major memoirs, narrative nonfiction, and other sorts of general nonfiction." Actively seeking "new, major or definitive work on a subject of broad interest, or a controversial, but authoritative, new book on a subject that affects many people's lives. I also represent more light-hearted nonfiction projects, such as gift or novelty books, when they suit the market particularly well." Does not want queries about projects written years ago and that were unsuccessfully shopped to a long list of trade publishers by either the author or another agent. "I am specifically not interested in reading short, category romances (Regency, time travel, paranormal, etc.), horror novels, supernatural stories, poetry, original plays, or film scripts."

How to Contact: Send query via regular mail. For nonfiction, include a complete, fully-edited book proposal with sample chapters. For fiction, include a complete synopsis and no more than 20 pages of sample text. No e-mail or fax queries. Responds in 2 weeks to queries; 4-6 weeks to mss. Returns materials only with SASE. Obtains most new clients through recommendations from others.

Terms: Agent receives 15% commission on domestic sales; 20% commission on foreign sales. Offers written contract, binding for 2-years (renews automatically at the end of the 3rd year if not terminated by either party);

Contract can be terminated in the 3rd year, with 1-month notice. notice must be given to terminate contract. Charges clients for ms duplication, expedited delivery services (when necessary), and any overseas shipping, telephone calls and faxes necessary for marketing the author's foreign rights; "If one of my clients needs a credentialed, professional co-author, I will help make a suitable match on a case-by-case basis. But, I do not maintain an ongoing, formal or informal, relationship with any editing service or regularly direct business to any particular freelancers."

Writers' Conferences: Book Expo America; Frankfurt Book Fair; London International Book Fair; Romance Writers of America annual conference; Modern Language Association's annual conference.

Tips: "While I am not interested in being flattered by a prospective client, it does matter to me that she knows why she is writing to me in the first place. Is one of my clients a colleague of hers? Has she read a book by one of my clients that led her to believe I might be interested in her work? Authors of descriptive nonfiction should have real credentials and expertise in their subject areas, either as academics or journalists or policy experts, and authors of prescriptive nonfiction should have a legitimate expertise and considerable experience communicating their ideas in seminars, workshops, in a successful business, through the media, etc."

◐ CLAUDIA MENZA LITERARY AGENCY

1170 Broadway, Suite 807, New York NY 10001. (212)889-6850. **Contact:** Claudia Menza. Estab. 1983. Member of AAR. Represents 111 clients. 50% of clients are new/unpublished writers.

- Prior to becoming an agent, Ms. Menza was an editor/managing editor at a publishing company.

Represents: Nonfiction books, novels. **Considers these nonfiction areas:** Current affairs; education; ethnic/cultural interests (especially African-American); health/medicine; history; multicultural; music/dance; photography; psychology; theater/film.

    O¬ This agency specializes in African-American fiction and nonfiction, and editorial assistance.

How to Contact: Submit outline, 25 pages. Prefers to read materials exclusively. Responds in 2 weeks to queries; 2-4 months to mss. Returns materials only with SASE. Obtains most new clients through recommendations from others.

Recent Sales: This agency prefers not to share information on specific sales.

Terms: Agent receives 15% commission on domestic sales; 20% (if co-agent is used) commission on foreign sales; 20% commission on dramatic rights sales. Offers written contract.

Ⓝ ⊘ HELEN MERRILL, LTD.

295 Lafayette St., New York NY 10012. (212)226-5015. Fax: (212)226-5079. Member of AAR.

- This agency did not respond to our request for information. Query before submitting.

Member Agents: Beth Blickers.

◓ DORIS S. MICHAELS LITERARY AGENCY, INC.

1841 Broadway, Suite #903, New York NY 10023. Website: www.dsmagency.com. **Contact:** Doris S. Michaels, president. Estab. 1994. Member of AAR, WNBA.

Represents: Novels. **Considers these fiction areas:** Literary (with commercial appeal and strong screen potential).

How to Contact: Query by e-mail; see submission guidelines on website. Obtains most new clients through recommendations from others, conferences.

Recent Sales: Sold over 30 titles in the last year. *Cycles: How We'll Live, Work and Buy*, by Maddy Dychtwald (The Free Press); *In the River Sweet*, by Patricia Henley (Knopf); *Healing Conversations: What to Say When You Don't Know What to Say*, by Nance Guilmartin (Jossey-Bass); *The Mushroom Man*, by Sophie Powell (Peguin Putnam); *How to Become a Marketing Superstar*, by Jeff Fox (Hyperion).

Terms: Agent receives 15% commission on domestic sales; 20% commission on foreign sales. Offers written contract, binding for 1 year; 1-month notice must be given to terminate contract. 100% of business is derived from commissions on ms sales. Charges clients for office expenses, not to exceed $150 without written permission.

Writers' Conferences: BEA; Frankfurt Book Fair (Germany, October); London Book Fair; Maui Writers Conference.

◓ MARTHA MILLARD LITERARY AGENCY

145 W. 71st St. #8A, New York NY 10023. (973)593-9233. Fax: (973)593-9235. E-mail: marmillink@aol.com. **Contact:** Martha Millard. Estab. 1980. Member of AAR, SFWA. Represents 50 clients. Currently handles: 25% nonfiction books; 65% novels; 10% story collections.

- Prior to becoming an agent, Ms. Millard worked in editorial departments of several publishers and was vice president at another agency for four and a half years.

Represents: Nonfiction books, novels. **Considers these nonfiction areas:** Art/architecture/design; biography/

Tracey Adams

Children's agent puts writers first

I t comes as no surprise that Tracey Adams studied ballet in college. Adams, after all, is a literary agent known for her poise and grace. But *rugby*?

Yes, rugby. Adams played the rough-and-tumble sport at Mount Holyoke College and with the Gotham Women's Rugby Club.

Ballet sweet . . . rugby tough. That, clients say, is Adams in a nutshell. Thanks to her polite professionalism, her work as a children's author representative at New York-based McIntosh & Otis has garnered much acclaim.

In 2004, after working in the children's publishing industry for more than a decade, Adams left her position as head of the children's department at McIntosh & Otis to start her own agency, Adams Literary (www.adamsliterary.com).

Adams had a natural path to a literary career. Growing up in Darien, Connecticut, she and her friends created a well-worn path through the woods to the local library, where Adams earned a bounty of ribbons for reading "everything I could get my hands on." At Mount Holyoke, where Adams majored in English and minored in dance, several internships at publishing houses confirmed her desire to pursue a literary line of work.

"I've always had a deep respect and love for the written word," says Adams, who worked for several publishers prior to becoming an agent. "My great-grandfather started the first printing company in New York City, and I was raised while my family was actively running it. We've always joked that we have ink running through our veins, and I haven't done much to disprove that!"

Adams, who lives in Manhattan with her husband and young daughter, agreed to talk about life as a children's literary agent.

How does your style and strategy differ from other agents in the industry?

I'm a believer in exclusive submissions (that is, I submit a manuscript to one editor at a time) in most situations, and I don't think most agents today work that way. I spend a lot of time learning editors' individual tastes so I send them (hopefully!) just what they are looking for. In my experience, editors reply more quickly and with better feedback than if I had just sent a manuscript out to a group. I put a great deal of thought and care into submissions—and because editors realize that, they consider my submissions seriously.

I also feel strongly about relationships, and work hard both to form and strengthen them. I understand that patience is required in this industry, and it takes time for a publisher and author to see the financial benefits of their partnership. While it certainly makes sense in many situations to have more than one publisher, I don't like to spread my authors too thin. You can't undermine the importance of having a backlist.

How does your editorial background help you as an agent?

I can edit manuscripts if an author wants me to, but I usually stick to giving an overall editorial opinion or general comments. I feel confident in doing that, and that's certainly helpful to my clients. But it's important for me to remember that editing is not my job, and editors thank me for that. I'm careful not to come between an editor/author relationship.

It's also helpful that I spent years working for publishers, because I can explain the mysterious inner-workings of a publishing house.

Some say that up until about ten years ago, a children's author didn't need an agent, but now, as with adult publishing, it's almost a necessity. Why is that?

Lucky me! I made the switch to agenting eight years ago. Independent publishers were being bought by media conglomerates, and the rules were changing quickly. Editors were worried that they had so many new meetings to attend, and there was no time to edit. Publishing houses began the "agented-submissions-only" policy.

These days, editors are beginning to rely on well-established agents to cut to the chase and send them the best material. I wonder if there really is a shift taking place, where agents' slush piles will become higher than editors'. I know mine has grown.

What's the philosophy at Adams Literary, the agency you launched in 2004?

Adams Literary is a place where the best in children's books—authors and illustrators, editors and publishers—come together to create outstanding books for the most important audience. It allows me to concentrate fully on doing what I love, and what I do best—representing my clients with the passion and dedication they deserve.

Who are some of the individuals in the industry who've inspired you?

During my junior and senior years of college, I interned at Greenwillow Books. Susan Hirschman's passion, enthusiasm, and energy inspired me. Her deep respect for her authors and artists certainly made an impression on me. A day when an artist was expected to come in and show original art was an event. Susan would invite staff from all the departments to come up and see for themselves. It made everyone—from department heads to new assistants—excited about working on that book.

My early years were spent at Margaret K. McElderry Books—first at Macmillan, then at Simon & Schuster. Margaret taught me everything about editing, about working with authors, artists, and colleagues, about how to use words and how to be gracious. She taught me the joys that result from hard work and special relationships. Margaret taught me to be brave and to always have a sense of humor.

Dorothy Markinko ran the children's department at McIntosh & Otis before retiring a few years ago and handing it over to me. She comes from this same era of women who say things we should all remember. "Tracey, pick your battles!" "Tracey, life is too short!" "Tracey, that pile will still be here tomorrow—go home!"

Has motherhood changed your outlook on children's books to any degree?

Yes! I have a brand-new respect for board books. Hooray for rounded corners! Hooray for untearable pages! I wonder how my outlook will continue to change as my daughter grows. I'm sure it will. As the mother of a toddler, I certainly understand the benefits of repetition and rhyme better than ever.

I am a big fan of edgy YA and books that tackle tough issues, and I find that now that I am a parent as well as a reader, I do look harder for characters to grow and learn. I look for that grain of hope at the end. (My daughter's YAs are on her top shelf, where she thankfully won't reach them for years!)

What do you see as the difference between successful authors with staying power and authors that fizzle out?

Successful, long-term authors make writing their career (though many have a day job!). They take it seriously. They respect themselves, their writing, and their books. They command that respect from their families and friends. They keep writing, and stay involved in the writing and publishing communities, both to keep up with colleagues and with the business. And they read what's being talked about!

What is the most frustrating thing for you in this business? The most uplifting?

On a daily basis, the most frustrating thing is easy to name—having patience. As authors are well aware, editors are busy in meetings, travel, sales conferences—there is always something stealing editors away from reading and responding as quickly as we'd all like.

It's also frustrating when the mail brings a rejection—which happens just about every day. I must quickly recover and try, try again.

It's uplifting when a book by an author I represent receives a starred review or any kind of award. (Especially if it was rejected by other houses before we found the right home.) It's uplifting when a letter from an editor isn't a rejection, but a request for a rewrite. It's uplifting when an editor tells me she is going to make an offer. I feel good when an author/editor relationship I helped to form is going really well. But none of these things would be possible without the uplifting feeling of reading an amazing manuscript from someone who is looking for representation!

—*Barbara J. Odanaka*

autobiography; business/economics; child guidance/parenting; cooking/foods/nutrition; current affairs; education; ethnic/cultural interests; health/medicine; history; how-to; juvenile nonfiction; memoirs; money/finance; music/dance; New Age/metaphysics; photography; popular culture; psychology; self-help/personal improvement; theater/film; true crime/investigative; women's issues/studies. **Considers these fiction areas:** Considers fiction depending on writer's credits and skills.
How to Contact: No unsolicited queries. No e-mail or fax queries. Returns materials only with SASE. Obtains most new clients through recommendations from others.
Recent Sales: *Backfire*, by Peter Burrows (Wiley); *Fallen Star*, by Nancy Herkness (Berkley Sensation); *The Rosetta Codex*, by Richard Paul Russ (Penguin).
Terms: Agent receives 15% commission on domestic sales; 20% commission on foreign sales. Offers written contract.

◑ THE MILLER AGENCY

1 Sheridan Square, 7B, #32, New York NY 10014. (212) 206-0913. Fax: (212) 206-1473. E-mail: angela@millerage ncy.net. Website: www.milleragency.net. **Contact:** Angela Miller. Estab. 1990. Represents 100 clients. 5% of clients are new/unpublished writers.
Represents: Nonfiction books. **Considers these nonfiction areas:** Anthropology/archaeology; art/architecture/design; biography/autobiography; business/economics; child guidance/parenting; cooking/foods/nutrition; current affairs; ethnic/cultural interests; gay/lesbian issues; health/medicine; language/literature/criticism; New Age/metaphysics; psychology; self-help/personal improvement; sports; women's issues/studies.
    ➤ This agency specializes in nonfiction, multicultural arts, psychology, self-help, cookbooks, biography, travel, memoir, sports. Fiction considered selectively.
How to Contact: Query with SASE, submit outline, a few sample chapter(s). Considers simultaneous queries. Responds in 1 week to queries. Obtains most new clients through referrals.
Recent Sales: Sold 25 titles in the last year.

Terms: Agent receives 15% commission on domestic sales; 20-25% commission on foreign sales. Offers written contract, binding for 2 years; 2-month notice must be given to terminate contract. 100% of business is derived from commissions on ms sales. Charges clients for postage (express mail or messenger services) and photocopying.

⊌ MOORE LITERARY AGENCY

83 High St., Newburyport MA 01950-3047. (978)465-9015. Fax: (978)465-8817. E-mail: cmoore@moorelit.com; dmckenna@moorelit.com. **Contact:** Claudette Moore, Mike Meehan, Deborah McKenna. Estab. 1989. 10% of clients are new/unpublished writers. Currently handles: 100% nonfiction books.
Represents: Nonfiction books. **Considers these nonfiction areas:** Computers/electronic; technology.
   0→ This agency specializes in trade computer books (90% of titles).
How to Contact: Submit outline. Obtains most new clients through recommendations from others, conferences.
Recent Sales: *Windows XP Timesaving Techniques for Dummies*, by Woody Leonhard (Wiley); *Expert One-on-One Microsoft Access Application Development*, by Helen Feddema (Wiley); *Thinking in C++, Volume 2*, by Bruce Eckel and Chuck Allison (Prentice Hall); *Microsoft Windows XP Inside Out, Second Edition*, by Ed Bolt, Carl Siechert, and Craig Stinson (Microsoft Press).
Terms: Agent receives 15% commission on domestic sales; 15% commission on foreign sales; 15% commission on dramatic rights sales. Offers written contract.

⊌ MAUREEN MORAN AGENCY

P.O. Box 20191, Park West Station, New York NY 10025-1518. (212)222-3838. Fax: (212)531-3464. E-mail: maureenm@erols.com. **Contact:** Maureen Moran. Represents 30 clients. Currently handles: 100% novels.
Represents: Novels. **Considers these fiction areas:** Women's.
   0→ This agency specializes in women's fiction, principally romance and mystery. Does not want to receive science fiction, fantasy, or juvenile books.
How to Contact: Query with SASE. Will accept e-mail query without attachments. *No unsolicited mss.* Considers simultaneous queries. Responds in 1 week to queries. Returns materials only with SASE.
Recent Sales: *Silver Scream*, by Mary Daheim; *The Older Woman*, by Cheryl Reavis.
Terms: Agent receives 10% commission on domestic sales; 15-20% commission on foreign sales. Charges clients for extraordinary expenses such as courier, messenger and bank wire fees by prior arrangement.
Tips: "This agency does not handle unpublished writers."

ℕ ⊘ HOWARD MORHAIM LITERARY AGENCY

11 John St., Suite 407, New York NY 10038-4067. (212)529-4433. Fax: (212)995-1112. Member of AAR.
   ● This agency did not respond to our request for information. Query before submitting.

⊘ WILLIAM MORRIS AGENCY, INC.

1325 Avenue of the Americas, New York NY 10019. (212)586-5100. Fax: (212)903-1418. Website: www.wma.com. California office: 151 El Camino Dr., Beverly Hills CA 90212. Member of AAR.
Member Agents: Owen Laster, Jennifer Rudolph Walsh, Suzanne Gluck, Joni Evans, Tracy Fisher, Mel Berger, Jay Mandel, Manie Barron.
Represents: Nonfiction books, novels.
How to Contact: Query with SASE. Considers simultaneous queries.
Recent Sales: This agency prefers not to share information on specific sales.
Terms: Agent receives 15% commission on domestic sales; 20% commission on foreign sales.

⊌ HENRY MORRISON, INC.

105 S. Bedford Rd., Suite 306A, Mt. Kisco NY 10549. (914)666-3500. Fax: (914)241-7846. **Contact:** Henry Morrison. Estab. 1965. Signatory of WGA. Represents 49 clients. 5% of clients are new/unpublished writers. Currently handles: 5% nonfiction books; 90% novels; 5% juvenile books.
Represents: Nonfiction books, novels. **Considers these nonfiction areas:** Anthropology/archaeology; biography/autobiography; government/politics/law; history; juvenile nonfiction. **Considers these fiction areas:** Action/adventure; detective/police/crime; family saga; historical.
How to Contact: Query with SASE. Responds in 2 weeks to queries; 3 months to mss. Obtains most new clients through recommendations from others.
Recent Sales: Sold 14 titles in the last year. *The Lazarus Vendetta*, by Robert Ludlum and Keith Ferrell (St. Martin's Press); *Native Sons*, by James Baldwin and Sol Stein (Ballantine Books); *Conspiracy*, by Allan Tropol (Signet Books); *Shadowbrook*, by Beverly Swerling (Simon & Schuster); *The Coil*, by Gayle Lynds (St. Martin's Press). Other clients include Samuel R. Delany, Joe Gores, Eric Van Lustbader, David Morrell.
Terms: Agent receives 15% commission on domestic sales; 25% commission on foreign sales. Charges clients

for ms copies, bound galleys, and finished books for submissions to publishers, movie producers, foreign publishers.

◫ DEE MURA LITERARY

269 West Shore Dr., Massapequa NY 11758-8225. (516)795-1616. Fax: (516)795-8797. E-mail: samurai5@ix.netcom.com. **Contact:** Dee Mura, Karen Roberts, Frank Nakamura, Brian Hertler. Estab. 1987. Signatory of WGA. 50% of clients are new/unpublished writers.

- Prior to opening her agency, Ms. Mura was a public relations executive with a roster of film and entertainment clients; and worked in editorial for major weekly news magazines.

Represents: Nonfiction books, juvenile books, scholarly books, feature film, TV scripts, episodic drama, sitcom, animation, documentary, miniseries, variety show. **Considers these nonfiction areas:** Agriculture/horticulture; animals; anthropology/archaeology; biography/autobiography; business/economics; child guidance/parenting; computers/electronic; current affairs; education; ethnic/cultural interests; gay/lesbian issues; government/politics/law; health/medicine; history; how-to; humor/satire; juvenile nonfiction; memoirs; military/war; money/finance; nature/environment; science/technology; self-help/personal improvement; sociology; sports; travel; true crime/investigative; women's issues/studies. **Considers these fiction areas:** Action/adventure; contemporary issues; detective/police/crime; ethnic; experimental; family saga; fantasy; feminist; gay/lesbian; glitz; historical; humor/satire; juvenile; literary; mainstream/contemporary; mystery/suspense; psychic/supernatural; regional; romance (contemporary, gothic, historical, regency); science fiction; sports; thriller (medical thrillers); westerns/frontier; young adult; espionage; political. **Considers these script subject areas:** Action/adventure; cartoon/animation; comedy; contemporary issues; detective/police/crime; family saga; fantasy; feminist; gay/lesbian; glitz; historical; horror; juvenile; mainstream; mystery/suspense; psychic/supernatural; religious/inspirational; romantic comedy; romantic drama; science fiction; sports; teen; thriller; western/frontier.

- ⚿ "We work on everything, but are especially interested in literary fiction, commercial fiction and nonfiction, thrillers and espionage, humor and drama (we love to laugh and cry), self-help, inspirational, medical, scholarly, true life stories, true crime, women's stories and issues." Actively seeking "unique nonfiction manuscripts and proposals; novelists who are great storytellers; contemporary writers with distinct voices and passion." Does not want to receive "ideas for sitcoms, novels, films, etc., or queries without SASEs."

How to Contact: Query with SASE. No fax queries. Accepts queries by e-mail without attachments. Considers simultaneous queries. Responds in 2 weeks to queries. Returns materials only with SASE. Obtains most new clients through recommendations from others, queries.

Recent Sales: Sold over 40 titles and sold 35 scripts in the last year.

Terms: Agent receives 15% commission on domestic sales; 20% commission on foreign sales. Offers written contract. Charges clients for photocopying, mailing expenses, overseas and long distance phone calls and faxes.

Tips: "Please include a paragraph on the writer's background, even if the writer has no literary background, and a brief synopsis of the project. We enjoy well-written query letters that tell us about the project and the author."

ⓝ ☑ ERIN MURPHY LITERARY AGENCY

1062 Tolani Place, Flagstaff AZ 86001-9625. (928)525-2056. Fax: (928)525-2480. **Contact:** Erin Murphy. Member of AAR.

- Query before submitting.

◖ JEAN V. NAGGAR LITERARY AGENCY, INC.

216 E. 75th St., Suite 1E, New York NY 10021. (212)794-1082. **Contact:** Jean Naggar. Estab. 1978. Member of AAR, PEN, Women's Media Group, and Women's Forum. Represents 80 clients. 20% of clients are new/unpublished writers. Currently handles: 35% nonfiction books; 45% novels; 15% juvenile books; 5% scholarly books.

- Ms. Naggar served as president of AAR.

Member Agents: Alice Tasman, senior agent (narrative nonfiction, commercial/literary fiction, thrillers); Anne Engel (academic-based nonfiction for general readership); Jennifer Weltz, director, subsidiary rights (also represents children's books and YA).

Represents: Nonfiction books, novels. **Considers these nonfiction areas:** Biography/autobiography; child guidance/parenting; current affairs; government/politics/law; health/medicine; history; juvenile nonfiction; memoirs; New Age/metaphysics; psychology; religious/inspirational; self-help/personal improvement; sociology; travel; women's issues/studies; **Considers these fiction areas:** Action/adventure; contemporary issues; detective/police/crime; ethnic; family saga; feminist; historical; literary; mainstream/contemporary; mystery/suspense; psychic/supernatural; thriller.

O→ This agency specializes in mainstream fiction and nonfiction, literary fiction with commercial potential.

How to Contact: Query with SASE. Prefers to read materials exclusively. No e-mail or fax queries. Responds in 1 day to queries; 2 months to mss. Returns materials only with SASE. Obtains most new clients through recommendations from others, solicitations, conferences.

Recent Sales: *Leaving Ireland*, by Ann Moore (NAL); *The Associate*, by Phillip Margolin (HarperCollins); *Quantico Rules*, by Gene Riehl (St. Martin's Press). Other clients include Jean M. Auel, Robert Pollack, Mary McGarry Morris, Lily Prior, Susan Fromberg Schaeffer, David Ball, Elizabeth Crane, Maud Casey.

Terms: Agent receives 15% commission on domestic sales; 20% commission on foreign sales. Offers written contract. Charges for overseas mailing; messenger services; book purchases; long-distance telephone; photocopying. "These are deductible from royalties received."

Writers' Conferences: Willamette Writers Conference; Pacific Northwest Writers Conference; Breadloaf Writers Conference; Virginia Women's Press Conference (Richmond VA); Marymount Manhattan Writers Conference; SEAK Conference, New York is Book Country: Get Published.

Tips: "Use a professional presentation. Because of the avalanche of unsolicited queries that flood the agency every week, we have had to modify our policy. We will now only guarantee to read and respond to queries from writers who come recommended by someone we know. Our areas are general fiction and nonfiction, no children's books by unpublished writers, no multimedia, no screenplays, no formula fiction, no mysteries by unpublished writers. We recommend patience and fortitude: The courage to be true to your own vision, the fortitude to finish a novel and polish and polish again before sending it out, and the patience to accept rejection gracefully and wait for the stars to align themselves appropriately for success."

✪ NATIONAL WRITERS LITERARY AGENCY

Division of GTR, Inc., 3140 S. Peoria #295, Aurora CO 80014. (720)851-1959. Fax: (720)851-1960. E-mail: aajwiii@aol.com or nationalwriters@aol.com. **Contact:** Andrew J. Whelchel III. Estab. 1987. Represents 52 clients. 20% of clients are new/unpublished writers. Currently handles: 40% nonfiction books; 34% novels; 20% juvenile books; 6% scripts.

Member Agents: Andrew J. Whelchel III (screenplays, nonfiction, mystery, thriller); Jason S. Cangialosi (nonfiction); Shayne Sharpe (novels, screenplays, fantasy).

Represents: Nonfiction books, and fiction books. **Considers these nonfiction areas:** Animals; biography/autobiography; child guidance/parenting; education; government/politics/law; how-to; popular culture; science/technology; sports; travel. **Considers these fiction areas:** Action/adventure; juvenile; mainstream/contemporary; mystery/suspense; science fiction; sports; young adult.

O→ Actively seeking "mystery/thrillers, music, business, cutting-edge novels; pop culture, compelling true stories, science, and technology." Does not want to receive "concept books, westerns, over-published self-help topics."

How to Contact: Query with outline and SASE. Accepts e-mail queries. No fax queries. Considers simultaneous queries. Responds in 6 weeks to queries; 2 months to mss. Returns materials only with SASE. Obtains most new clients through solicitations, conferences, or over the transom.

Recent Sales: Sold 22 titles in the last year. *Final Cut: Business Plans for Independent Films*, by Reed Martin (Faber & Faber); *Open Season* (Warner Brothers Pictures); *Your Air Force Academy* (feature documentary).

Terms: Agent receives 15% commission on domestic sales; 20% commission on foreign sales; 10% commission on dramatic rights sales. Offers written contract; 30-day notice must be given to terminate contract.

Tips: "Query letters should include a great hook just as if you only had a few seconds to impress us. A professional package gets professional attention. Always include return postage!"

Ⓝ ✪ CRAIG NELSON CO.

115 W. 18th St., 5th Floor, New York NY 10011. (212)929-3242. Fax: (212)929-3667. **Contact:** Craig Nelson. Member of AAR.

● Query before submitting.

✪ NEW BRAND AGENCY GROUP, LLC

E-mail: mark@literaryagent.net. Website: www.literaryagent.net. **Contact:** Mark Ryan, Ingrid Elfver-Ryan. Estab. 1994. Represents 12 clients. 20% of clients are new/unpublished writers. Currently handles: 50% nonfiction books; 30% novels; 20% juvenile books.

● New Brand Agency is currently closed to submissions. Check website for more details.

Member Agents: Mark Ryan and Ingrid Elfver-Ryan (fiction and nonfiction with bestseller or high commercial potential—projects with national and/or international appeal likely to sell at least 100,000 copies.)

Represents: Nonfiction books, novels, juvenile books (books for younger readers). **Considers these nonfiction areas:** Biography/autobiography; business/economics; health/medicine; humor/satire; juvenile nonfiction; memoirs; New Age/metaphysics; popular culture; psychology; religious/inspirational; self-help/personal improvement; sex; spirituality; women's issues/studies; body and soul, celebrity, family, finance, fitness, gift/novelty, leadership, men's issues, parenting, personal growth, relationships, success. **Considers these fiction areas:** Fantasy; historical; horror; juvenile; literary; mainstream/contemporary; mystery/suspense; romance (mainstream); science fiction; thriller; westerns/frontier (mainstream); cross-genre, magical realism, supernatural, suspense.

    O→ "We only work with authors we are passionate about on 3 levels: The financial promise of the work and its ability to entertain, educate, and inspire; the personality and character of the author; and the potential career of the author (future books and willingness and ability to promote). We don't represent books we wouldn't buy ourselves and pull all-nighters to read. Actively seeking the stories and voices that no one else can share but you. Genuine. Authentic. Genre-bending okay. Does not want to receive Star Trek, personal manifestos, knitting, rowing, things defined by genre rather than having some elements of a genre."

How to Contact: Accepts e-mail queries only; submit electronic query online at website. Responds in 1 day to queries; 1 week to mss. Obtains most new clients through queries and conferences.

Recent Sales: *Black Valley*, by Jim Brown (Ballantine); *The Marriage Plan*, by Aggie Jordan, Ph.D. (Broadway/Bantam); *Father to Daughter*, by Harry Harrison (Workman); *The She*, by Carol Plum-Ucci (Harcourt).

Terms: Agent receives 15% commission on domestic sales. Offers written contract, binding for 6 months; 1-month notice must be given to terminate contract. 20% commission for subsidiary rights. Charges for postage and phone costs out of proceeds from the project; Writers reimbursed for office fees after the sale of ms.

NEW ENGLAND PUBLISHING ASSOCIATES, INC.

P.O. Box 5, Chester CT 06412-0645. (860)345-READ and (860)345-4976. Fax: (860)345-3660. E-mail: nepa@nepa.com. Website: www.nepa.com. **Contact:** Elizabeth Frost-Knappman, Edward W. Knappman, Kristine Schiavi, Ron Formica, or Victoria Harlow. Estab. 1983. Member of AAR, ASJA, Authors Guild, Connecticut Press Club. Represents 125-150 clients. 15% of clients are new/unpublished writers.

Member Agents: Elizabeth Frost-Knappman; Edward W. Knappman; Kristine Schiavi; Ron Formica; Victoria Harlow.

Represents: Nonfiction books. **Considers these nonfiction areas:** Biography/autobiography; business/economics; child guidance/parenting; government/politics/law; health/medicine; history; language/literature/criticism; military/war; money/finance; nature/environment; psychology; science/technology; self-help/personal improvement; sports; true crime/investigative; women's issues/studies; reference.

    O→ This agency specializes in adult nonfiction of serious purpose.

How to Contact: Send outline/proposal, SASE. Accepts e-mail and fax queries. Considers simultaneous queries. Responds in 1 month to queries; 5 weeks to mss. Returns materials only with SASE.

Recent Sales: Sold over 70 titles in the last year. *Into the Blizzard*, by Mike Tougais (St. Martin's Press); *The Letters of Noel Coward*, edited by Barry Day (Pantheon); *Crusaders on the Nile*, by Geoffrey Regan (Harvard University Press); *Beacon of Liberty*, by Larry Schweikart and Michale Allen (Sentinel Penguin); *Ford Tough*, by David Magee (John Wiley); *Sailing From Byzantium*, by Collin Wells (Bantam).

Terms: Agent receives 15% commission on domestic sales; 20% commission on foreign sales. Offers written contract, binding for 6 months. Charges clients for copying.

Writers' Conferences: BEA (Chicago, June); ALA (San Antonio, January); ALA (New York, July); ASJA (May); Frankfurt (October).

Tips: "Send us a well-written proposal that clearly identifies your audience—who will buy this book and why. Check our website for tips on proposals and advice on how to market your books. Revise, revise, revise, but never give up. We don't."

NINE MUSES AND APOLLO, INC.

525 Broadway, Suite 201, New York NY 10012. (212)431-2665. **Contact:** Ling Lucas. Estab. 1991. Represents 50 clients. 10% of clients are new/unpublished writers. Currently handles: 90% nonfiction books; 10% novels.

    ● Ms. Lucas formerly served as vice president, sales & marketing director, and associate publisher of Warner Books.

Represents: Nonfiction books. **Considers these nonfiction areas:** Animals; biography/autobiography; business/economics; current affairs; ethnic/cultural interests; health/medicine; language/literature/criticism; psychology; spirituality; women's issues/studies. **Considers these fiction areas:** Ethnic; literary; mainstream/contemporary (commercial).

    O→ This agency specializes in nonfiction. Does not want to receive children's and young adult material.

How to Contact: Submit outline, 2 sample chapter(s), SASE. Prefers to read materials exclusively. Responds in 1 month to mss.

Recent Sales: *My Daddy is a Pretzel*, by Baron Baptiste (Barefoot Books); *The Twelve Gifts of Healing*, by

Charlene Costanzo (HarperCollins); *The Twelve Gifts of Marriage*, by C. Costanzo; *Once Upon a Time in China*, by Jeff Yang.

Terms: Agent receives 15% commission on domestic sales; 20-25% commission on foreign sales. Offers written contract. Charges clients for photocopying, postage.

Tips: ''Your outline should already be well developed, cogent, and reveal clarity of thought about the general structure and direction of your project.''

[N] THE BETSY NOLAN LITERARY AGENCY

224 W. 29th St., 15th Floor, New York NY 10001. (212)967-8200. Fax: (212)967-7292. **Contact:** Donald Lehr, president. Estab. 1980. Member of AAR. Represents 200 clients. 10% of clients are new/unpublished writers. Currently handles: 90% nonfiction books.

Member Agents: Carla Glasser

Represents: Nonfiction books. **Considers these nonfiction areas:** Cooking/foods/nutrition (cookbooks).

How to Contact: Query with outline. No e-mail or fax queries. Considers simultaneous queries. Responds in 6 weeks to queries. Returns materials only with SASE.

Recent Sales: Sold 15 titles in the last year. *Mangia*, by Sasha Muniak/Ricardo Diaz (HarperCollins); *The Buttercup Bake Shop Cookbook*, by Jennifer Appel (Simon & Schuster); *Desperation Dinners*, by Beverly Mills & Alicia Ross (Workman); *Bridgehampton Weekends*, by Ellen Wright (William Morrow).

Terms: Agent receives 15% commission on domestic sales; 20% commission on foreign sales.

[N] [Ø] NORWICK & SCHAD

110 E. 59th St., 29th Floor, New York NY 10022. (212)751-4400. Fax: (212)980-9391. **Contact:** Ken Norwick, Esq. Member of AAR.

• Query before submitting.

[Ø] HAROLD OBER ASSOCIATES

425 Madison Ave., New York NY 10017. (212)759-8600. Fax: (212)759-9428. Estab. 1929. Member of AAR. Represents 250 clients. 10% of clients are new/unpublished writers. Currently handles: 35% nonfiction books; 50% novels; 15% juvenile books.

Member Agents: Phyllis Westberg; Pamela Malpas; Emma Sweeney; Knox Burger; Craig Tenney (not accepting new clients); Alexander C. Smithline.

Represents: Nonfiction books, novels, juvenile books. **Considers these nonfiction areas:** Considers all nonfiction areas. **Considers these fiction areas:** Considers all fiction subjects.

How to Contact: Query letter only with SASE. No e-mail or fax queries. Responds as promptly as possible. Obtains most new clients through recommendations from others.

Terms: Agent receives 15% commission on domestic sales; 20% commission on foreign sales. Charges clients for photocopying and express mail or package services.

[N] [Ø] ORION ASSOCIATES

P.O. Box 24, Tenafly NJ 07670. (201)568-2002. **Contact:** Bert Holtje. Member of AAR.

• Query before submitting.

[Ø] FIFI OSCARD AGENCY, INC.

110 W. 40th St., New York NY 10018. (212)764-1100. **Contact:** Literary Department. Estab. 1956. Member of AAR; signatory of WGA. Represents 108 clients. 5% of clients are new/unpublished writers. Currently handles: 60% nonfiction books; 10% novels; 30% stage plays.

Member Agents: Fifi Oscard; Peter Sawyer; Carmen La Via; Kevin McShane; Ivy Fischer Stone; Carolyn French; Lindley Kirksey; Jerry Rudes.

Represents: Nonfiction books, novels, stage plays.

○━ This agency specializes in history, celebrity biography and autobiography, pop culture, travel/adventure, performing arts, fine arts/design.

How to Contact: Query with outline. *No unsolicited mss.*

Recent Sales: *My Father Had a Daughter: Judith Shakespeare's Tale*, by Grace Tiffany (Berkeley); *The Gospel According to Martin: The Spiritual Biography of Martin Luther King*, by Stewart Burns (Harper San Francisco); *Colored Lights*, by Kander and Ebb (Farrar, Strauss, & Giroux).

Terms: Agent receives 15% commission on domestic sales; 20% commission on foreign sales; 10% commission on dramatic rights sales. Charges clients for photocopying expenses.

Tips: ''Writers must have screen credits if sending movie scripts.''

◐ PARAVIEW, INC.

191 7th Ave., Suite 2F, New York NY 10011. (212)989-3616. Fax: (212)989-3662. E-mail: lhagan@paraview.c om. Website: www.paraview.com. **Contact:** Lisa Hagan. Estab. 1988. Represents 75 clients. 15% of clients are new/unpublished writers. Currently handles: 80% nonfiction books; 10% novels; 10% scholarly books.

- Ms. Hagan has agented since 1995.

Member Agents: Lisa Hagan (fiction and nonfiction self-help).

Represents: Nonfiction books, novels (very few). **Considers these nonfiction areas:** Agriculture/horticulture; Americana; animals; anthropology/archaeology; art/architecture/design; biography/autobiography; business/ economics; child guidance/parenting; computers/electronic; cooking/foods/nutrition; crafts/hobbies; creative nonfiction; current affairs; education; ethnic/cultural interests; gardening; gay/lesbian issues; government/ politics/law; health/medicine; history; how-to; humor/satire; interior design/decorating; juvenile nonfiction; language/literature/criticism; memoirs; military/war; money/finance; multicultural; music/dance; nature/en-vironment; New Age/metaphysics; philosophy; photography; popular culture; psychology; recreation; regional; religious/inspirational; science/technology; self-help/personal improvement; sex; sociology; software; spiritual-ity; sports; theater/film; translation; travel; true crime/investigative; women's issues/studies; young adult. **Considers these fiction areas:** Action/adventure; contemporary issues; ethnic; feminist; literary; mainstream/ contemporary; regional; romance; women's.

⊶ This agency specializes in spiritual, New Age and self-help.

How to Contact: Query via e-mail and include synopsis and author bio. Responds in 1 month to queries; 3 months to mss. Obtains most new clients through recommendations from editors and current clients.

Recent Sales: Sold 40 titles in the last year. *The Wealthy Spirit*, by Chellie Campbell (Source Books); *Into the Buzzsaw*, by Kristina Borjesson (Prometheus); *The Enchanted Candle*, by Lady Rhea and Erika Lieberman (Citadel); *The Architecture of Abundance*, by Lenedra Carroll (New World Library); *Healing Beauty*, by Letha Hadady (John Wiley & Sons); *Texas Cooking*, by Lisa Wingate (NAL); *The Last Vampire* by Whitley Strieber (Pocket); *Poetry*, by Jewel Kilcher (Pocket Books); *King of the Cowboys*, by Ty Murray (Pocket Books); *Angel Signs*, by Albert Haldane and Simha Seryaru (HarperCollins).

Terms: Agent receives 15% commission on domestic sales; 20% commission on foreign sales.

Writers' Conferences: BEA (Chicago, June); London Book Fair; E3—Electronic Entertainment Exposition.

Tips: ''New writers should have their work edited, critiqued, and carefully reworked prior to submission. First contact should be via e-mail.''

◐ THE RICHARD PARKS AGENCY

Box 693, Salem NY 12865. Website: www.richardparksagency.com. **Contact:** Richard Parks. Estab. 1988. Mem-ber of AAR. Currently handles: 55% nonfiction books; 40% novels; 5% story collections.

Represents: Nonfiction books, novels. **Considers these nonfiction areas:** Animals; anthropology/archaeology; art/architecture/design; biography/autobiography; business/economics; child guidance/parenting; cooking/ foods/nutrition; crafts/hobbies; current affairs; ethnic/cultural interests; gardening; gay/lesbian issues; govern-ment/politics/law; health/medicine; history; how-to; humor/satire; language/literature/criticism; memoirs; military/war; money/finance; music/dance; nature/environment; popular culture; psychology; science/tech-nology; self-help/personal improvement; sociology; theater/film; travel; women's issues/studies. **Considers these fiction areas:** Considers fiction by referral only.

⊶ Actively seeking nonfiction. Does not want to receive unsolicited material.

How to Contact: Query by mail only with SASE. No e-mail or fax queries. Considers simultaneous queries Responds in 2 weeks to queries. Returns materials only with SASE. Obtains most new clients through recommen-dations and referrals.

Terms: Agent receives 15% commission on domestic sales; 20% commission on foreign sales. Charges clients for photocopying or any unusual expense incurred at the writer's request.

◨ ◐ KATHI J. PATON LITERARY AGENCY

19 W. 55th St., New York NY 10019-4907. (908)647-2117. E-mail: KJPLitBiz@aol.com. **Contact:** Kathi Paton. Estab. 1987. Currently handles: 65% nonfiction books; 35% novels.

Represents: Nonfiction books, novels, short story collections, book-based film rights. **Considers these nonfic-tion areas:** Business/economics; child guidance/parenting; money/finance (personal investing); nature/envi-ronment; psychology; religious/inspirational; women's issues/studies. **Considers these fiction areas:** Literary; mainstream/contemporary; short story collections.

⊶ This agency specializes in adult nonfiction.

How to Contact: Accepts e-mail queries. For nonfiction, send proposal, sample chapter, and SASE. For fiction, send first 40 pages, plot summary, or 3 short stories and SASE. Considers simultaneous queries. Obtains most new clients through recommendations from other clients.

Recent Sales: *Future Wealth,* by McInerney and White (St. Martin's Press); *Unraveling the Mystery of Autism,* by Karyn Seroussi (Simon & Schuster).

Terms: Agent receives 15% commission on domestic sales; 20% commission on foreign sales. Offers written contract. Charges clients for photocopying.

Writers' Conferences: Attends major regional panels, seminars, and conferences.

☑ L. PERKINS ASSOCIATES

16 W. 36 St., New York NY 10018. (212)279-6418. Fax: (718)543-5354. E-mail: lperkinsagency@yahoo.com. **Contact:** Lori Perkins. Estab. 1990. Member of AAR. Represents 50 clients. 10% of clients are new/unpublished writers.

• Ms. Perkins has been an agent for 18 years. Her agency has an affiliate agency, Southern Literary Group. She is also the author of *The Insider's Guide to Getting an Agent* (Writer's Digest Books).

Represents: Nonfiction books, novels. **Considers these nonfiction areas:** Popular culture. **Considers these fiction areas:** Fantasy; horror; literary (dark); science fiction.

○➔ All of Ms. Perkins's clients write both fiction and nonfiction. "This combination keeps my clients publishing for years. I am also a published author so I know what it takes to write a book." Actively seeking a Latino *Gone With the Wind* and *Waiting to Exhale,* and urban ethnic horror. Does not want to receive "anything outside of the above categories, i.e., westerns, romance."

How to Contact: Query with SASE. Considers simultaneous queries. Responds in 6 weeks to queries; 3 months to mss. Returns materials only with SASE. Obtains most new clients through recommendations from others, solicitations, conferences.

Recent Sales: Sold 100 titles in the last year. *The Illustrated Ray Bradbury,* by Jerry Weist (Avon); *The Poet in Exile,* by Ray Manzarek (Avalon); *Behind Sad Eyes: The Life of George Harrison,* (St. Martin's Press).

Terms: Agent receives 15% commission on domestic sales; 20% commission on foreign sales. No written contract. Charges clients for photocopying.

Writers' Conferences: San Diego Writer's Conference; NECON; BEA; World Fantasy.

Tips: "Research your field and contact professional writers' organizations to see who is looking for what. Finish your novel before querying agents. Read my book, *An Insider's Guide to Getting an Agent* to get a sense of how agents operate."

☑ STEPHEN PEVNER, INC.

382 Lafayette St., 8th Floor, New York NY 10003. (212)674-8403. Fax: (212)529-3692. E-mail: spevner@aol.com. **Contact:** Stephen Pevner.

Represents: Nonfiction books, novels, feature film, TV scripts, TV movie of the week, episodic drama, animation, documentary, miniseries. **Considers these nonfiction areas:** Biography/autobiography; ethnic/cultural interests; gay/lesbian issues; history; humor/satire; language/literature/criticism; memoirs; music/dance; New Age/metaphysics; photography; popular culture; religious/inspirational; sociology; travel. **Considers these fiction areas:** Comic books/cartoon; contemporary issues; erotica; ethnic; experimental; gay/lesbian; glitz; horror; humor/satire; literary; mainstream/contemporary; psychic/supernatural; thriller; urban. **Considers these script subject areas:** Comedy; contemporary issues; detective/police/crime; gay/lesbian; glitz; horror; romantic comedy; romantic drama; thriller.

○➔ This agency specializes in motion pictures, novels, humor, pop culture, urban fiction, independent filmmakers. Actively seeking urban fiction, popular culture, screenplays, and film proposals.

How to Contact: Query with SASE, outline/proposal. Prefers to read materials exclusively. No e-mail or fax queries. Responds in 2 weeks to queries; 1 month to mss. Obtains most new clients through recommendations from others.

Recent Sales: *In the Company of Men* and *Bash: Latterday Plays,* by Neil Labote; *The Vagina Monologues,* by Eve Ensler; *Guide to Life,* by The Five Lesbian Brothers; *Noise From Underground,* by Michael Levine. Other clients include Richard Linklater, Gregg Araki, Tom DiCillo, Genvieve Turner/Rose Troche, Todd Solondz, Neil LaBute.

Terms: Agent receives 15% commission on domestic sales; 20% commission on foreign sales. Offers written contract, binding for 1 year; 6-week notice must be given to terminate contract. 100% of business is derived from commissions on ms sales.

Tips: "Be persistent, but civilized."

Ⓝ ☐ PHH LITERARY AGENCY

P.O. Box 724558, Atlanta GA 31139. (678)485-8871. E-mail: michele@phhliteraryagency.com. Website: www.p hhliteraryagency.com. **Contact:** Michele Price. Estab. 2003. Represents 6 clients. 85% of clients are new/unpublished writers. Currently handles: 5% nonfiction books; 95% novels.

● "Our office offers a variety of professional experience. We have a published author, a professional editor, and all of us have worked in various types of bookstores."

Member Agents: Michele Price (crime, family drama, literary, mainstream, mystery, religious, inspirational, romance); Lorraine Harrell (action, crime, juvenile, mystery, romance, thriller, military, young adult); Christine Haines (action, family drama, mainstream, mystery, thirller, young adult).

Represents: Nonfiction books, novels, novellas, juvenile books. **Considers these nonfiction areas:** Biography/ autobiography; health/medicine; history; how-to; military/war; sports; true crime/investigative; crafts/hobbies. **Considers these fiction areas:** Action/adventure; detective/police/crime; family saga; historical; horror; juvenile; literary; mainstream/contemporary; mystery/suspense; religious/inspirational; romance; thriller; young adult.

0→ "We are actively seeking fiction works needing quality attention to sell to publishers." Does not want to receive fantasy, erotica, supernatural, or gay/lesbian projects.

How to Contact: Query with SASE. Accepts e-mail queries. No fax queries. Considers simultaneous queries. Responds in 1-2 weeks to queries; 2-3 months to mss. Returns materials only with SASE. Obtains most new clients through recommendations from others, solicitations.

Recent Sales: Sold 1 titles in the last year.

Terms: Agent receives 15% commission on domestic sales; 15% commission on foreign sales. Offers written contract, binding for 1 year; 60 days notice must be given to terminate contract.

☑ ALISON J. PICARD, LITERARY AGENT

P.O. Box 2000, Cotuit MA 02635. (508)477-7192. Fax: (508)477-7192 (Please contact before faxing.). E-mail: ajpicard@aol.com. **Contact:** Alison Picard. Estab. 1985. Represents 48 clients. 30% of clients are new/unpublished writers. Currently handles: 40% nonfiction books; 40% novels; 20% juvenile books.

● Prior to becoming an agent, Ms. Picard was an assistant at an NYC literary agency.

Member Agents: Alison Picard (mysteries/suspense/thriller, romance, literary fiction, adult nonfiction, juvenile books).

Represents: Nonfiction books, novels, short story collections, novellas, juvenile books. **Considers these nonfiction areas:** Animals; anthropology/archaeology; art/architecture/design; biography/autobiography; business/ economics; child guidance/parenting; cooking/foods/nutrition; current affairs; education; ethnic/cultural interests; gay/lesbian issues; government/politics/law; health/medicine; history; how-to; humor/satire; juvenile nonfiction; memoirs; military/war; money/finance; multicultural; music/dance; nature/environment; New Age/metaphysics; popular culture; psychology; religious/inspirational; science/technology; self-help/personal improvement; translation; travel; true crime/investigative; women's issues/studies; young adult. **Considers these fiction areas:** Action/adventure; contemporary issues; detective/police/crime; erotica; ethnic; experimental; family saga; feminist; gay/lesbian; glitz; historical; horror; humor/satire; juvenile; literary; mainstream/ contemporary; multicultural; mystery/suspense; New Age; picture books; psychic/supernatural; regional; religious/inspirational; romance; sports; thriller; young adult.

0→ "Many of my clients have come to me from big agencies, where they felt overlooked or ignored. I communicate freely with my clients, and offer a lot of career advice, suggestions for revising manuscripts, etc. If I believe in a project, I will submit it to a dozen or more publishers, unlike some agents who give up after 4 or 5 rejections." Actively seeking commercial adult fiction and nonfiction, middle grade juvenile fiction. Does not want to receive science fiction/fantasy, westerns, poetry, plays, articles.

How to Contact: Authors should query in June. Query with SASE. Considers simultaneous queries. Responds in 1 week to queries; 6 weeks to mss. Returns materials only with SASE. Obtains most new clients through recommendations from others, solicitations.

Recent Sales: Sold 27 titles in the last year. *The Shade of My Own Tree*, by Sheila Williams (Ballantine); *The Boldness of Boys*, by Susan Strong (Andrews McMeel); *The Complete Bridal Shower Planner*, by Sharon Naylor (Prima); *Nicole Kidman*, by James Dickerson (Kensington/Citadel); *Pierce Brosnan*, by Peter Carrick (Kensington/Citadel). Other clients include Caryl Rivers, Osha Gray Davidson, Amy Dean, David Housewright, Nancy Means Wright.

Terms: Agent receives 15% commission on domestic sales; 20% commission on foreign sales. Offers written contract, binding for 1 year; 1-week notice must be given to terminate contract.

Tips: "Please don't send material without sending a query first via mail or e-mail. I don't accept phone or fax queries. Always enclose a SASE with a query."

☑ PINDER LANE & GARON-BROOKE ASSOCIATES, LTD.

159 W. 53rd St., Suite 14C, New York NY 10019-6005. (212)489-0880. E-mail: pinderl@interport.net. **Contact:** Robert Thixton. Member of AAR; signatory of WGA. Represents 30 clients. 20% of clients are new/unpublished writers. Currently handles: 25% nonfiction books; 75% novels.

Member Agents: Dick Duane, Robert Thixton.

Represents: Nonfiction books, novels. **Considers these fiction areas:** Contemporary issues; detective/police/ crime; family saga; fantasy; gay/lesbian; literary; mainstream/contemporary; mystery/suspense; romance; science fiction.

> ○→ This agency specializes in mainstream fiction and nonfiction. Does not want to receive screenplays, TV series teleplays, or dramatic plays.

How to Contact: Query with SASE. *No unsolicited mss.* Responds in 3 weeks to queries; 2 months to mss. Obtains most new clients through referrals, queries.

Recent Sales: Sold 20 titles in the last year. *Diana & Jackie—Maidens, Mothers & Myths*, by Jay Mulvaney (St. Martin's Press); *The Sixth Fleet* (series), by David Meadows (Berkley); *Dark Fires*, by Rosemary Rogers (Mira Books).

Terms: Agent receives 15% commission on domestic sales; 30% commission on foreign sales. Offers written contract, binding for 3-5 years.

Tips: "With our literary and media experience, our agency is uniquely positioned for the current and future direction publishing is taking. Send query letter first giving the essence of the manuscript, and a personal or career bio with SASE."

☻ ARTHUR PINE ASSOCIATES, INC.

250 W. 57th St., Suite 417, New York NY 10019. (215)265-7330. Fax: (212)265-7330. E-mail: info@arthurpine.c om. Estab. 1966. Represents 100 clients. 25% of clients are new/unpublished writers. Currently handles: 60% nonfiction books; 40% novels.

Member Agents: Richard Pine; Catherine Drayton; Lori Andiman; Matthew Guma.

Represents: Nonfiction books, novels. **Considers these nonfiction areas:** Business/economics; current affairs; health/medicine; money/finance; psychology; self-help/personal improvement. **Considers these fiction areas:** Detective/police/crime; family saga; historical; literary; mainstream/contemporary; thriller.

How to Contact: Query with SASE, outline/proposal. Prefers to read materials exclusively. No e-mail or fax queries. Responds in 1 month to queries. Obtains most new clients through recommendations from others.

Recent Sales: Sold 60 titles in the last year.

Terms: Agent receives 15% commission on domestic sales; 15% commission on foreign sales. Offers written contract.

Tips: "Our agency will consider exclusive submissions only. All submissions must be accompanied by postage or SASE. Will not read manuscripts before receiving a letter of inquiry."

ℕ ☐ ALICKA PISTEK LITERARY AGENCY, LLC

302A W. 12th St., #124, New York NY 10014. E-mail: info@alickapistek.com. Website: www.alickapistek.com. **Contact:** Alicka Pistek. Estab. 2003. Represents 15 clients. 50% of clients are new/unpublished writers. Currently handles: 60% nonfiction books; 40% novels.

> • Prior to opening her agency, Ms. Pistek worked in the foreign rights department at ICM, and as an agent at Nicholas Ellison, Inc.

Represents: Nonfiction books, novels. **Considers these nonfiction areas:** Animals; anthropology/archaeology; biography/autobiography; business/economics; child guidance/parenting; cooking/foods/nutrition; creative nonfiction; current affairs; government/politics/law; health/medicine; history; how-to; language/literature/ criticism; memoirs; military/war; money/finance; nature/environment; psychology; religious/inspirational; science/technology; self-help/personal improvement; translation; travel. **Considers these fiction areas:** Detective/ police/crime; ethnic; family saga; historical; literary; mainstream/contemporary; mystery/suspense; romance; thriller.

> ○→ Does not want to receive fantasy, science fiction, westerns.

How to Contact: Query with SASE, submit outline, 2 sample chapter(s). Considers simultaneous queries. Responds in 1 month to queries; 6 weeks to mss. Returns materials only with SASE.

Recent Sales: Other clients include Alan Levy, Belisa Vranich, Michael Christopher Carroll, Alex Boese.

Terms: Agent receives 15% commission on domestic sales; 20% commission on foreign sales. Offers written contract. Charges for photocopying over 40 pages, international postage.

Writers' Conferences: Frankfurt Book Fair.

Tips: "Be sure you are familiar with the genre you are writing in, and learn standard procedures for submitting your work. A good query will go a long way."

☻ JULIE POPKIN

15340 Albright St., #204, Pacific Palisades CA 90272-2520. (310)459-2834. Fax: (310)459-4128. **Contact:** Julie Popkin. Estab. 1989. Represents 35 clients. 30% of clients are new/unpublished writers. Currently handles: 70% nonfiction books; 30% novels.

● Prior to opening her agency, Ms. Popkin taught at the university level and did freelance editing and writing.

Member Agents: Julie Popkin; Margaret McCord (fiction, memoirs, biography); Alyson Sena(nonfiction).
Represents: Nonfiction books, novels, translations. **Considers these nonfiction areas:** Art/architecture/design; ethnic/cultural interests; government/politics/law; history; memoirs; philosophy; women's issues/studies (feminist); criticism. **Considers these fiction areas:** Literary; mainstream/contemporary; mystery/suspense.

○➤ This agency specializes in selling book-length mss including fiction and nonfiction. Especially interested in social issues, ethnic and minority subjects, Latin American authors. Does not want to receive New Age, spiritual, romance, science fiction.

How to Contact: Query with SASE. No e-mail or fax queries. Responds in 1 month to queries; 2 months to mss. Obtains most new clients through "Mostly clients find me through guides and personal contacts."
Recent Sales: Sold 8 titles in the last year. *Truck of Fools*, by Carlos Liscano (Vanderbilt University Press); *That Inferno* (Vanderbilt Press); *Santiago's Way*, by Peter Owen; *America's Most Hated*, by Ann Seamon (Continuum); *Disabled Fables*, by the artists of L.A. Goal (Starbright).
Terms: Agent receives 15% commission on domestic sales; 20% commission on foreign sales; 10% commission on dramatic rights sales. Sometimes asks for fee if ms requires extensive copying and mailing.
Writers' Conferences: BEA (June); Santa Barbara (June).
Tips: "Keep your eyes on the current market. Publishing responds to changes very quickly and often works toward perceived and fresh subject matter. Historical fiction seems to be rising in interest after a long, quiet period."

N HELEN F. PRATT INC.

1165 Fifth Ave., New York NY 10029. (212)722-5081. Fax: (212)722-8569. **Contact:** Helen F. Pratt. Member of AAR.

● This agency did not respond to our request for information. Query before submitting.

Member Agents: Helen F. Pratt, Seamus Mullarkey.

N AARON M. PRIEST LITERARY AGENCY

708 Third Ave., 23rd Floor, New York NY 10017. (212)818-0344. Fax: (212)573-9417. E-mail: lchilds@aaronpriest.com. **Contact:** Aaron Priest or Molly Friedrich. Estab. 1974. Member of AAR. Currently handles: 25% nonfiction books; 75% novels.

Member Agents: Lisa Erbach Vance; Paul Cirone; Aaron Priest; Molly Friedrich; Lucy Childs.
Represents: Nonfiction books, novels.
How to Contact: No e-mail or fax queries. Considers simultaneous queries. If interested, will respond within 2 weeks
Recent Sales: *She is Me*, by Kathleen Schine; *Killer Smile*, by Lisa Scottoline.
Terms: Agent receives 15% commission on domestic sales. Charges for photocopying, foreign-postage expenses.

◉ SUSAN ANN PROTTER, LITERARY AGENT

110 W. 40th St., Suite 1408, New York NY 10018. (212)840-0480. **Contact:** Susan Protter. Estab. 1971. Member of AAR, Authors' Guild. Represents 40 clients. 5% of clients are new/unpublished writers. Works with a very small number of new/previously unpublished authors Currently handles: 50% nonfiction books; 50% novels; occasional magazine article or short story (for established clients only).

● Prior to opening her agency, Ms. Protter was associate director of subsidiary rights at Harper & Row Publishers.

Represents: Nonfiction books, novels. **Considers these nonfiction areas:** Biography/autobiography; current affairs; health/medicine; science/technology; international. **Considers these fiction areas:** Detective/police/crime; mystery/suspense; science fiction; thriller.

○➤ Writers must have book-length project or ms that is ready to be sold. Does not want to receive westerns, romance, fantasy, children's books, young adult novels, screenplays, plays, poetry, Star Wars, or Star Trek.

How to Contact: Currently looking for limited number of new clients. Send short query by mail with SASE. *No unsolicited mss.* Responds in 3 weeks to queries; 2 months to mss.
Recent Sales: *Fragile Partnership with Saudi Arabia*, by Thomas W. Lippman (West View, Perseus); *Frek and the Elixir*, by Rudy Rucker (Tor); *Operation Solomon*, by Stephen Spector, Ph.D. (Oxford University Press).
Terms: Agent receives 15% commission on domestic sales; 15% commission on dramatic rights sales. "If, after seeing your query, we request to see your manuscript, there will be a small shipping and handling fee requested to cover cost of returning materials should they not be suitable." Charges clients for photocopying, messenger, express mail, airmail and overseas shipping expenses.
Tips: "Please send neat and professionally organized queries. Make sure to include a SASE, or we cannot reply.

We receive approximately 200 queries a week and read them in the order they arrive. We usually reply within 2 weeks to any query. Please, do not call or e-mail queries. If you are sending a multiple query, make sure to note that in your letter. I am looking for work that stands out in a highly competitive and difficult market.''

☑ QUICKSILVER BOOKS—LITERARY AGENTS

508 Central Park Ave., #5101, Scarsdale NY 10583. (914)722-4664. Fax: (914)722-4664. Website: www.quicksilverbooks.com. **Contact:** Bob Silverstein. Estab. 1973 as packager; 1987 as literary agency. Represents 50 clients. 50% of clients are new/unpublished writers. Currently handles: 75% nonfiction books; 25% novels.

- Prior to opening his agency, Mr. Silverstein served as senior editor at Bantam Books and Dell Books/Delacorte Press.

Represents: Nonfiction books, novels. **Considers these nonfiction areas:** Anthropology/archaeology; biography/autobiography; business/economics; child guidance/parenting; cooking/foods/nutrition; current affairs; ethnic/cultural interests; health/medicine; history; how-to; language/literature/criticism; memoirs; nature/environment; New Age/metaphysics; popular culture; psychology; religious/inspirational; science/technology; self-help/personal improvement; sociology; sports; true crime/investigative; women's issues/studies. **Considers these fiction areas:** Action/adventure; glitz; mystery/suspense; thriller.

- ☐ This agency specializes in literary and commercial mainstream fiction and nonfiction (especially psychology, New Age, holistic healing, consciousness, ecology, environment, spirituality, reference, cookbooks, narrative nonfiction). Actively seeking commercial mainstream fiction and nonfiction in most categories. Does not want to receive science fiction, pornography, poetry, or single-spaced mss.

How to Contact: Query with SASE. Authors are expected to supply SASE for return of ms and for query letter responses. No e-mail or fax queries. Considers simultaneous queries. Responds in 2 weeks to queries; 1 month to mss. Returns materials only with SASE. Obtains most new clients through recommendations, listings in sourcebooks, solicitations, workshop participation.

Recent Sales: Sold over 20 titles in the last year. *Nice Girls Don't Get the Corner Office*, by Lois P. Frankel, Ph.D. (Warner Books); *A Gathering of Demi Gods*, by Charles Cerami (Sourcebooks); *The Coming of the Beatles*, by Martha Goldmsith (Wiley).

Terms: Agent receives 15% commission on domestic sales; 20% commission on foreign sales. Offers written contract. Charges clients for photocopying of mss and proposals, but prefers authors provide actual copies; foreign mailings of books and mss.

Writers' Conferences: National Writers Union Conference (Dobbs Ferry NY, April).

Tips: ''Write what you know. Write from the heart. Publishers print, authors sell.''

☑ SUSAN RABINER, LITERARY AGENT, INC.

240 W. 35th St., Suite 500, New York NY 10001-2506. (212)279-0316. Fax: (212)279-0932. E-mail: susan@rabiner.net. **Contact:** Susan Rabiner.

- Prior to becoming an agent, Susan Rabiner was editorial director of Basic Books, then the serious nonfiction division of HarperCollins Publishers. She is the co-author of *Thinking Like Your Editor: How to Write Great Serious Nonfiction and Get it Published* (W.W. Norton).

Member Agents: Susan Rabiner, Susan Arellano (formerly senior editor Basic Books, The Free Press).

Represents: Nonfiction books, textbooks. **Considers these nonfiction areas:** Business/economics; education; history; philosophy; psychology; science/technology; biography, law/politics.

- ☐ Does not want to receive fiction, self-help.

How to Contact: Submit outline/proposal, SASE. Accepts e-mail queries. No fax queries. Considers simultaneous queries. Responds in 3 weeks to queries. Returns materials only with SASE. Obtains most new clients through obtains new clients through recommendations from editors.

Recent Sales: Sold 10-20 titles in the last year. *The Two Income Trap*, by Elizabeth Warren and Amelia Tyagi Warren; *The Guns of June*, by Constantine Pleshakov (Houghton-Mifflin). Other clients include Iris Chang, Lawrence Krauss, Daniel Schacter, Herbert Bix, Bruce Tulgan, Stephanie Coontz, Brian Fagen.

Terms: Agent receives 15% commission on domestic sales; 20% commission on foreign sales. Offers written contract; 1-month notice must be given to terminate contract.

☒ ☑ RAINES & RAINES

103 Kenyon Rd., Medusa NY 12120. (518)239-8311. Fax: (518)239-6029. **Contact:** Theron Raines. Member of AAR.

- Query before submitting.

☑ HELEN REES LITERARY AGENCY

376 North St., Boston MA 02113-2013. (617)227-9014. Fax: (617)227-8762. E-mail: reesliterary@aol.com. **Contact:** Joan Mazmanian, Ann Collette, Helen Rees, or Lorin Rees. Estab. 1983. Member of AAR, PEN. Represents

80 clients. 50% of clients are new/unpublished writers. Currently handles: 60% nonfiction books; 40% novels.
Member Agents: Ann Collette (literary fiction, women's studies, health, biography, history); Helen Rees (business, money/finance/economics, government/politics/law, contemporary issues, literary fiction); Lorin Rees (business, memoir).
Represents: Nonfiction books, novels. **Considers these nonfiction areas:** Biography/autobiography; business/economics; current affairs; government/politics/law; health/medicine; history; money/finance; women's issues/studies. **Considers these fiction areas:** Contemporary issues; historical; literary; mainstream/contemporary; mystery/suspense; thriller.
How to Contact: Query with SASE, outline, 2 sample chapter(s). No e-mail or fax queries. Responds in 2-3 weeks to queries. Obtains most new clients through recommendations from others, solicitations, conferences.
Recent Sales: Sold 30 titles in the last year. *Why Smart Executives Fail*, by Sydney Finkelstein (Portfolio); *What (Really) Works*, by William Joyce, Nitin Nohria, Bruce Roberson (Harper Business); *It's Your Ship: Management Techniques for the Best Damn Ship in the Navy*, by Capt. D. Michael Abrashoff (Warner); *The Watson Dynasty: The Fiery Reign and Troubled Legacy of IBM's Founding Father and Son*, by Richard St. Tedlow (Harper Business); *Video & DVD Guide 2004* (annual), by Mick Martin and Marsha Porter (Ballantine); *The Case for Israel*, by Alan Dershowitz (John Wiley & Sons); *A Call to Service: My Vision for a Better America*, by John Kerry (Viking); *GUTS!: Companies that Blow the Doors Off Business-As-Usual*, by Kevin and Jackie Freiberg (Currency).
Terms: Agent receives 15% commission on domestic sales; 20% commission on foreign sales.

N ☑ REGAL LITERARY AGENCY

52 Warfield St., Montclair NJ 07043. (973)509-5767. Fax: (973)509-0259. E-mail: bess@regal-literary.com. Website: www.regal-literary.com. **Contact:** Bess Reed. Estab. 2002. Member of AAR. Represents 60 clients. 20% of clients are new/unpublished writers. Currently handles: 48% nonfiction books; 46% novels; 2% story collections; 2% novellas; 2% poetry.

  • Prior to becoming agents, Gordon Kato was a psychologist, Jospeh Regal was a musician, and Dan Kois was an actor/comedian.

Member Agents: Gordon Kato (literary fiction, commercial fiction, pop culture); Joseph Regal (literary fiction, science, history, memoir); Dan Kois (literary fiction, history, sports, pop culture, memoir).
Represents: Nonfiction books, novels, short story collections, novellas. **Considers these nonfiction areas:** Anthropology/archaeology; art/architecture/design; biography/autobiography; business/economics; cooking/foods/nutrition; current affairs; ethnic/cultural interests; gay/lesbian issues; government/politics/law; history; humor/satire; language/literature/criticism; memoirs; military/war; music/dance; nature/environment; photography; popular culture; psychology; religious/inspirational (includes inspirational); science/technology (includes technology); sports; translation; true crime/investigative; women's issues/studies. **Considers these fiction areas:** Comic books/cartoon; detective/police/crime; ethnic; historical; literary; mystery/suspense; thriller; contemporary.

  ○━ "We have discovered more than a dozen successful literary novelists in the last 5 years. We are small, but are extraordinarily responsive to our writers. We are more like managers than agents, with an eye toward every aspect of our writers' careers, including publicity and other media." Actively seeking literary fiction and narrative nonfiction. Does not want romance, science fiction, horror, screenplays, or children's books.

How to Contact: Query with SASE, submit 5-15 sample pages. No e-mail or fax queries. Considers simultaneous queries. Responds in 2-3 weeks to queries; 4-12 to mss. Returns materials only with SASE. Obtains most new clients through recommendations from others, unsolicited submissions.
Recent Sales: Sold 23 titles in the last year. Other clients include James Reston, Jr., Tim Winton, Pascale La Draoulec, Tony Earley, Dennie Hughes, Mark Lee, Jake Page, Cheryl Bernard, Daniel Wallace, Paul Wilkes, John Marks, Keith Scribner, Jack Passarella, Alex Abella.
Terms: Agent receives 15% commission on domestic sales; 20% commission on foreign sales. No written contract. Charges clients for typical, major office expenses, such as photocopying and foreign postage.

☑ JODY REIN BOOKS, INC.

7741 S. Ash Court, Centennial CO 80122. (303)694-4430. Fax: (303)694-0687. Website: www.jodyreinbooks.com. **Contact:** Winnefred Dollar. Estab. 1994. Member of AAR, Authors' Guild. Currently handles: 70% nonfiction books; 30% novels.

  • Prior to opening her agency, Jody Rein worked for 13 years as an acquisitions editor for Contemporary Books, Bantam/Doubleday/Dell (executive editor), and Morrow/Avon (executive editor).

Member Agents: Jody Rein; Johnna Hietala.
Represents: Nonfiction books (primarily narrative and commercial nonfiction), novels (select literary novels, commercial mainstream). **Considers these nonfiction areas:** Business/economics; child guidance/parenting;

current affairs; ethnic/cultural interests; government/politics/law; history; humor/satire; music/dance; nature/environment; popular culture; psychology; science/technology; self-help/personal improvement; sociology; theater/film; women's issues/studies. **Considers these fiction areas:** Literary; mainstream/contemporary.

O→ This agency specializes in commercial and narrative nonfiction, and literary/commercial fiction.

How to Contact: Query with SASE. No e-mail or fax queries. Considers simultaneous queries. Responds in 6 weeks to queries; 2 months to mss. Obtains most new clients through recommendations from others, solicitations.

Recent Sales: *8 Simple Rules for Dating My Teenage Daughter*, by Bruce Cameron (ABC/Disney); *Skeletons On the Zahara*, by Dean King (Little, Brown); *The Big Year*, by Mark Obmascik (The Free Press).

Terms: Agent receives 15% commission on domestic sales; 25% commission on foreign sales; 20% commission on dramatic rights sales. Offers written contract. Charges clients for express mail, overseas expenses, photocopying ms.

Tips: "Do your homework before submitting. Make sure you have a marketable topic and the credentials to write about it. Well-written books on fresh and original nonfiction topics that have broad appeal. Novels written by authors who have spent years developing their craft. Authors must be well established in their fields and have strong media experience."

⚫ JODIE RHODES LITERARY AGENCY

8840 Villa La Jolla Dr., Suite 315, La Jolla CA 92037-1957. (858)625-0544. Fax: (858)625-0544. **Contact:** Jodie Rhodes, president. Estab. 1998. Member of AAR. Represents 50 clients. 60% of clients are new/unpublished writers. Currently handles: 60% nonfiction books; 35% novels; 5% middle to young adult books.

● Prior to opening her agency, Ms. Rhodes was a university-level, creative writing teacher, workshop director, published novelist, and Vice President Media Director at the N.W. Ayer Advertising Agency.

Member Agents: Jodie Rhodes, president; Clark McCutcheon (fiction); Bob McCarter (nonfiction).

Represents: Nonfiction books, novels, juvenile books. **Considers these nonfiction areas:** Biography/autobiography; child guidance/parenting; ethnic/cultural interests; government/politics/law; health/medicine; history; memoirs; military/war; science/technology; women's issues/studies. **Considers these fiction areas:** Contemporary issues; ethnic; family saga; historical; juvenile; literary; mainstream/contemporary; mystery/suspense; thriller; young adult; women's.

O→ Actively seeking "writers passionate about their books with a talent for richly textured narrative, an eye for details, and a nose for research." Nonfiction writers must have recognized credentials and expert knowledge of their subject matter. Does not want to receive erotica, horror, fantasy, romance, science fiction, children's books, religious, or inspirational books.

How to Contact: Query with brief synopsis, first 30-50 pages, and SASE. No e-mail or fax queries. Considers simultaneous queries. Responds in 10 days to queries. Returns materials only with SASE. Obtains most new clients through recommendations from others, agent sourcebooks.

Recent Sales: Sold 26 titles in the last year. *The Myrtles*, by Frances Kermeen (Warner); *Inside the Crips*, by Ann Pearlman (St. Martin's); *Home is East*, by Mary Ly (Bantam); *For Matrimonial Purposes*, by Kavita Daswani (Putnam); *Taming of the Chew*, by Denise Lamothe (Penguin); *Living in a Black & White World*, by Ann Pearlman (John Wiley & Sons).

Terms: Agent receives 15% commission on domestic sales; 20% commission on foreign sales. Offers written contract; 1-month notice must be given to terminate contract. Charges clients for fax, photocopying, phone calls, and postage. "Charges are itemized and approved by writers upfront."

Tips: "Think your book out before you write it. Do your research, know your subject matter intimately, write vivid specifics, not bland generalities. Care deeply about your book. Don't imitate other writers. Find your own voice. We never take on a book we don't believe in, and we go the extra mile for our writers. We welcome talented, new writers."

🅽 ⚫ BARBARA RIFKIND LITERARY AGENCY

132 Perry St., 6th Floor, New York NY 10014. (212)229-0453. Fax: (212)229-0454. E-mail: barbara@barbararifkind.net. **Contact:** Barbara Rifkind. Estab. 2002. Member of AAR. Represents 20 clients. 50% of clients are new/unpublished writers. Currently handles: 80% nonfiction books; 10% scholarly books; 10% textbooks.

● Prior to becoming an agent, Ms. Rifkind was an acquisitions editor, editorial manager, and a general manager in educational publishing (Addison Wesley).

Represents: Nonfiction books, scholarly books, textbooks. **Considers these nonfiction areas:** Anthropology/archaeology; art/architecture/design; biography/autobiography; business/economics; child guidance/parenting; current affairs; ethnic/cultural interests; government/politics/law; health/medicine; history; language/literature/criticism; money/finance; popular culture; psychology; science/technology; sociology; women's issues/studies.

O→ "We represent writers of smart nonfiction—academics, journalists, scientists, thinkers, people who've done something real and have something to say—writing for general trade audiences and occassionally for trade scholarly or textbook markets. We like to work in the areas of history; science writing; business and economics; applications of social sciences to important issues; public affairs and current events; narrative nonfiction; women's issues and parenting from a discipline." Actively seeking smart nonfiction from credentialed thinkers or published writers in selected areas of interest. Does not want commercial or category fiction, juvenile, and other nonselected areas.

How to Contact: Query with SASE, submit proposal package, outline. Accepts e-mail queries. No fax queries. Responds in 2 weeks to queries. Obtains most new clients through recommendations from others.

Recent Sales: Sold 6 titles in the last year. Other clients include Zvi Bodie, Juan Enriquez, Nancy Folbre, Walter Friedman, James Hoopes, Herminia Ibarra, Milind Lele, Barry Nalebuff, Raghu Rajan, Steven Wall, Luigi Zingales, Ian Ayres, Greg Stone, Bill Hammack.

Terms: Agent receives 15% commission on domestic sales; 10% commission on foreign sales. Offers written contract, binding for 6 months; immediate upon written notice notice must be given to terminate contract.

ℕ ⊘ RIGHTS UNLIMITED, INC.

101 West 55th St., Suite 2D, New York NY 10019. (212)246-0900. **Contact:** Bernard Kurman. Member of AAR.
● This agency did not respond to our request for information. Query before submitting.

ANGELA RINALDI LITERARY AGENCY

P.O. Box 7877, Beverly Hills CA 90212-7877. (310)842-7665. Fax: (310)837-8143. E-mail: mail@rinaldiliterary.com. Estab. 1994. Member of AAR. Represents 50 clients. Currently handles: 40% nonfiction books; 60% novels.
● Prior to opening her agency, Ms. Rinaldi was an editor at NAL/Signet, Pocket Books, and Bantam, and the Manager of Book Development for *The Los Angeles Times*.

Represents: Nonfiction books, novels, TV and motion picture rights for clients only. **Considers these nonfiction areas:** Biography/autobiography; business/economics; health/medicine; money/finance; self-help/personal improvement; true crime/investigative; women's issues/studies; books by journalists and academics. **Considers these fiction areas:** Literary; Commercial; upmarket women's fiction; suspense.
O→ Actively seeking commercial and literary fiction. Does not want to receive scripts, poetry, category romances, children's books, westerns, science fiction/fantasy, technothrillers, or cookbooks.

How to Contact: For fiction, send the first 3 chapters, brief synopsis, SASE. For nonfiction, query with SASE first or send outline/proposal, SASE. Do not send certified mail. Do not send metered mail as SASE. Brief e-mail inquiries OK, no attachments. Considers simultaneous queries. Please advise if this is a multiple submission. Responds in 6 weeks to queries. Returns materials only with SASE.

Recent Sales: *Calling in the One You Love*, by Katherine Woodward Thomas (Ballantine); *Carrying a Little Extra: A Guide to Healthy Pregnancy for the Plus-Size Woman*, by Bernstein, Clark and Levine (Berkley); *The Blood Orange Tree*, by Drusilla Campbell (Kensington); *Love is a Mirror: Reflections from Our Animal Companions*, by Deborah DeMoss Smith (Wiley).

Terms: Agent receives 15% commission on domestic sales; 20% commission on foreign sales. Offers written contract. Charges clients for photocopying if not provided by client.

◖ ANN RITTENBERG LITERARY AGENCY, INC.

1201 Broadway, Suite 708, New York NY 10001. (212)684-6936. **Contact:** Ann Rittenberg, president. Estab. 1992. Member of AAR. Represents 35 clients. 40% of clients are new/unpublished writers. Currently handles: 50% nonfiction books; 50% novels.

Member Agents: Ted Gideonse.

Represents: Nonfiction books, novels. **Considers these nonfiction areas:** Biography/autobiography; gay/lesbian issues; history (social/cultural); memoirs; women's issues/studies. **Considers these fiction areas:** Literary.
O→ This agent specializes in literary fiction and literary nonfiction.

How to Contact: Submit outline, 3 sample chapter(s), SASE. Considers simultaneous queries. Responds in 6 weeks to queries; 2 months to mss. Obtains most new clients through referrals from established writers and editors.

Recent Sales: Sold 20 titles in the last year. *Improbable*, by Adam Fawer (William Morrow); *The Book of Kehls*, by Christine O'Hagan (St. Martin's); *Picklocks*, by Brad Smith (Holt).

Terms: Agent receives 15% commission on domestic sales; 20% commission on foreign sales. Offers written contract. Charges clients for photocopying only.

◖ RIVERSIDE LITERARY AGENCY

41 Simon Keets Rd., Leyden MA 01337. (413)772-0067. Fax: (413)772-0969. E-mail: rivlit@sover.net. **Contact:** Susan Lee Cohen. Estab. 1990. Represents 40 clients. 20% of clients are new/unpublished writers.

Represents: Nonfiction books (adult), novels (adult), very selective.

How to Contact: Query with SASE, outline. Accepts e-mail queries. No fax queries. Considers simultaneous queries. Responds in 1 month to queries. Obtains most new clients through referrals.

Recent Sales: *Writing to Change the World*, by Mary Pipher, Ph.D. (Riverhead/Penguin Putnam); *The Devil You Know*, by Martha Stout, Ph.D. (Broadway); *Letting Go of the Person You Used to Be*, by Lama Surya Das (Doubleday Broadway); *Underland*, by Mick Farren (Tor); *Pivot Points*, by Carol Kauffman, Ph.D. (M. Evans).

Terms: Agent receives 15% commission on domestic sales. Offers written contract. Charges clients for foreign postage, photocopying large mss, express mail deliveries, etc.

☑ RLR ASSOCIATES, LTD.

Literary Department, 7 W. 51st St., New York NY 10019. (212)541-8641. Fax: (212)541-6052. Website: www.rlrliterary.net. **Contact:** Jennifer Unter, Tara Mark. Represents 50 clients. 25% of clients are new/unpublished writers. Currently handles: 70% nonfiction books; 25% novels; 5% story collections.

Member Agents: Jennifer Unter, Tara Mark.

Represents: Nonfiction books, novels, short story collections, scholarly books. **Considers these nonfiction areas:** Animals; anthropology/archaeology; art/architecture/design; biography/autobiography; business/economics; child guidance/parenting; cooking/foods/nutrition; current affairs; education; ethnic/cultural interests; gay/lesbian issues; government/politics/law; health/medicine; history; humor/satire; interior design/decorating; language/literature/criticism; memoirs; money/finance; multicultural; music/dance; nature/environment; photography; popular culture; psychology; religious/inspirational; science/technology; self-help/personal improvement; sociology; sports; translation; travel; true crime/investigative; women's issues/studies. **Considers these fiction areas:** Action/adventure; comic books/cartoon; contemporary issues; detective/police/crime; ethnic; experimental; family saga; feminist; gay/lesbian; historical; horror; humor/satire; literary; mainstream/contemporary; multicultural; mystery/suspense; sports; thriller.

> ⊶ "We provide a lot of editorial assistance to our clients and have connections." Actively seeking fiction (all types except for romance and fantasy), current affairs, history, art, popular culture, health, business. Does not want to receive romance or fantasy; screenplays.

How to Contact: Query with SASE. Considers simultaneous queries. Responds in 5 weeks to queries; 5 weeks to mss. Returns materials only with SASE. Obtains most new clients through recommendations from others.

Recent Sales: Sold 20 titles in the last year. Other clients include Shelby Foote, The Grief Recovery Institute, Don Wade, Don Zimmer, The Knot.com, David Plowder, PGA of America, Danny Peary, Jahnna Beecham & Malcolm Hillgartner.

Terms: Agent receives 15% commission on domestic sales; 20% commission on foreign sales. Offers written contract.

Tips: "Please check out our website for more details on our agency. No e-mail submissions, please."

☑ B.J. ROBBINS LITERARY AGENCY

5130 Bellaire Ave., North Hollywood CA 91607-2908. (818)760-6602. Fax: (818)760-6616. E-mail: robbinsliterary@aol.com. **Contact:** (Ms.) B.J. Robbins. Estab. 1992. Member of AAR. Represents 40 clients. 50% of clients are new/unpublished writers. Currently handles: 50% nonfiction books; 50% novels.

Member Agents: Regina Su Mangum.

Represents: Nonfiction books, novels. **Considers these nonfiction areas:** Biography/autobiography; child guidance/parenting; current affairs; ethnic/cultural interests; health/medicine; how-to; humor/satire; memoirs; music/dance; popular culture; psychology; self-help/personal improvement; sociology; sports; theater/film; true crime/investigative; women's issues/studies. **Considers these fiction areas:** Contemporary issues; detective/police/crime; ethnic; literary; mainstream/contemporary; mystery/suspense; sports; thriller.

How to Contact: Submit 3 sample chapter(s), outline/proposal, SASE. E-mail queries OK; no attachments. No fax queries. Considers simultaneous queries. Responds in 2 weeks to queries; 6 weeks to mss. Returns materials only with SASE. Obtains most new clients through conferences, referrals.

Recent Sales: Sold 15 titles in the last year. *The Sex Lives of Cannibals*, by J. Maarten Troost (Broadway); *Quickening*, by Laura Catherine Brown (Random House/Ballantine); *Snow Mountain Passage*, by James D. Houston (Knopf); *The Last Summer*, by John Hough, Jr. (Simon & Schuster); *Last Stand on the Little Bighorn*, by James M. Donovan (Little, Brown).

Terms: Agent receives 15% commission on domestic sales; 20% commission on foreign sales. Offers written contract; 3-month notice must be given to terminate contract. 100% of business is derived from commissions on ms sales. Charges clients for postage and photocopying only. Writers charged for fees only after the sale of ms.

Writers' Conferences: Squaw Valley Fiction Writers Workshop (Squaw Valley CA, August); SDSU Writers Conference (San Diego CA, January).

N ☑ THE ROBBINS OFFICE, INC.

405 Park Ave., New York NY 10022. (212)223-0720. Fax: (212)223-2535. **Contact:** Kathy P. Robbins, owner.
Member Agents: David Halpern, Sandy Bontemps (foreign rights)
Represents: Nonfiction books, novels. **Considers these nonfiction areas:** Biography/autobiography; government/politics/law (political commentary); language/literature/criticism (criticism); memoirs; investigative journalism. **Considers these fiction areas:** Literary; mainstream/contemporary (commercial); poetry.
   ○➤ This agency specializes in selling serious nonfiction, commercial and literary fiction.
How to Contact: Accepts submissions by referral only.
Recent Sales: *Loose Lips*, by Claire Berlinski (Random House); *Me Times Three*, by Alex Witchel (Knopf); *The Natural*, by Joe Klein (Doubleday); *Raid On the Sun*, by Rodger Claire (Broadway); *American Sucker*, by David Denby (Little, Brown).
Terms: Agent receives 15% commission on domestic sales; 15% commission on foreign sales; 15% commission on dramatic rights sales. Bills back specific expenses incurred in doing business for a client.

☑ LINDA ROGHAAR LITERARY AGENCY, INC.

133 High Point Dr., Amherst MA 01002. (413)256-1921. Fax: (413)256-2636. E-mail: contact@lindaroghaar.com. Website: www.lindaroghaar.com. **Contact:** Linda L. Roghaar. Estab. 1996. Represents 50 clients. 40% of clients are new/unpublished writers. Currently handles: 90% nonfiction books; 10% novels.
   • Prior to opening her agency, Ms. Roghaar worked in retail bookselling for 5 years and as a publishers' sales rep for 15 years.
Represents: Nonfiction books, novels. **Considers these nonfiction areas:** Animals; anthropology/archaeology; biography/autobiography; education; history; nature/environment; popular culture; religious/inspirational; self-help/personal improvement; women's issues/studies. **Considers these fiction areas:** Mystery/suspense (amateur sleuth, cozy, culinary, malice domestic).
How to Contact: Query with SASE. Accepts e-mail queries. No fax queries. Considers simultaneous queries. Responds in 2 months to queries; 4 months to mss.
Recent Sales: *What Would Buffy Do? Buffy the Vampire's Spiritual Guide*, by Jana Riess (Jossey-Bass); *Green Mountain Spinnery Knitting Book*, by Margaret Klein Wilson and the Green Mountain Spinnery (Countryman/W.W. Norton); *Cat vs. Cat: Keeping Peace in a Multi-Cat Household*, by Pam Johnson-Bennett (Penguin).
Terms: Agent receives 15% commission on domestic sales; negotiable commission on foreign sales. Offers written contract, binding for negotiable time.

☑ THE ROSENBERG GROUP

23 Lincoln Ave., Marblehead MA 01945. (781)990-1341. Fax: (781)990-1344. Website: www.rosenberggroup.com. **Contact:** Barbara Collins Rosenberg. Estab. 1998. Member of AAR, recognized agent of the RWA. Represents 32 clients. 25% of clients are new/unpublished writers. Currently handles: 30% nonfiction books; 30% novels; 10% scholarly books; 30% textbooks.
   • Prior to becoming an agent, Ms. Rosenberg was a senior editor for Harcourt.
Member Agents: Barbara Collins Rosenberg.
Represents: Nonfiction books, novels, textbooks. **Considers these nonfiction areas:** Current affairs; memoirs; popular culture; psychology; women's issues/studies; women's health, food/wine/beverages, autobiography. **Considers these fiction areas:** Literary; romance; women's.
   ○➤ "Ms. Rosenberg is well versed in the romance market (both category and single title). She is a frequent speaker at romance conferences. Actively seeking romance category or single title in contemporary chick lit, romantic suspense, and the historical sub-genres. Does not want to receive time-travel, paranormal, or inspirational/spiritual romances.
How to Contact: Query with SASE. No e-mail or fax queries. Responds in 2 weeks to queries; 4-6 weeks to mss. Returns materials only with SASE. Obtains most new clients through recommendations from others, solicitations, conferences.
Recent Sales: Sold 32 titles in the last year.
Terms: Agent receives 15% commission on domestic sales; 15% commission on foreign sales. Offers written contract; 1-month notice must be given to terminate contract. Postage and photocopying limit of $350/year.
Writers' Conferences: RWA Annual Conference (Dallas TX, July 2004); NOLA Written in the Stars Conference (March 2004).

☑ RITA ROSENKRANZ LITERARY AGENCY

440 West End Ave., Suite 15D, New York NY 10024-5358. (212)873-6333. **Contact:** Rita Rosenkranz. Estab. 1990. Member of AAR. Represents 30 clients. 20% of clients are new/unpublished writers. Currently handles: 98% nonfiction books; 2% novels.

- Prior to opening her agency, Rita Rosenkranz worked as an editor in major New York publishing houses.

Represents: Nonfiction books. **Considers these nonfiction areas:** Animals; anthropology/archaeology; art/architecture/design; biography/autobiography; business/economics; child guidance/parenting; computers/electronic; cooking/foods/nutrition; crafts/hobbies; current affairs; ethnic/cultural interests; gay/lesbian issues; government/politics/law; health/medicine; history; how-to; humor/satire; interior design/decorating; language/literature/criticism; military/war; money/finance; music/dance; nature/environment; New Age/metaphysics; photography; popular culture; psychology; religious/inspirational; science/technology; self-help/personal improvement; sports; theater/film; women's issues/studies.

- ⛏ "This agency focuses on adult nonfiction. Stresses strong editorial development and refinement before submitting to publishers, and brainstorms ideas with authors." Actively seeking authors "who are well paired with their subject, either for professional or personal reasons."

How to Contact: Submit proposal package, outline, SASE. No e-mail or fax queries. Considers simultaneous queries. Responds in 2 weeks to queries. Obtains most new clients through solicitations, conferences, word of mouth.

Recent Sales: Sold 35 titles in the last year. *Forbidden Fruit: True Love Stories from the Underground Railroad*, by Betty DeRamus (Atria Books); *Should I Medicate My Child?*, by Lisa Charis (Perigee); *Customer Branded Service*, by Janelle Barlow and Paul Stewart (Berrett-Koehler).

Terms: Agent receives 15% commission on domestic sales; 20% commission on foreign sales. Offers written contract, binding for 3 years; 3-month written notice must be given to terminate contract. 100% of business is derived from commissions on ms sales. Charges clients for photocopying. Makes referrals to editing service.

Tips: "Identify the current competition for your project to make sure the project is valid. A strong cover letter is very important."

Ⓝ Ⓩ ROSENSTONE/WENDER

38 E. 29th St., 10th floor, New York NY 10016. (212)725-6445. Fax: (212)725-6447. Member of AAR.

- This agency did not respond to our request for information. Query before submitting.

Member Agents: Howard Rosenstone (literary, adult, dramatic); Phyllis Wender (literary, adult, dramatic); Sonia Pabley; Ronald Gwiazda (associate member).

Ⓩ THE GAIL ROSS LITERARY AGENCY

1666 Connecticut Ave. NW, #500, Washington DC 20009. (202)328-3282. Fax: (202)328-9162. E-mail: jennifer@gailross.com. Website: www.gailross.com. **Contact:** Jennifer Manguera. Estab. 1988. Member of AAR. Represents 200 clients. 75% of clients are new/unpublished writers. Currently handles: 95% nonfiction books.

Member Agents: Gail Ross.

Represents: Nonfiction books. **Considers these nonfiction areas:** Anthropology/archaeology; biography/autobiography; business/economics; education; ethnic/cultural interests; gay/lesbian issues; government/politics/law; health/medicine; money/finance; nature/environment; psychology; religious/inspirational; science/technology; self-help/personal improvement; sociology; sports; true crime/investigative.

- ⛏ This agency specializes in adult trade nonfiction.

How to Contact: Query with SASE. Considers simultaneous queries. Responds in 1 month to queries. Obtains most new clients through recommendations from others.

Recent Sales: Sold 50 titles in the last year. This agency prefers not to share information on specific sales.

Terms: Agent receives 15% commission on domestic sales; 25% commission on foreign sales. Charges for office expenses (i.e., postage, copying).

Ⓩ CAROL SUSAN ROTH, LITERARY

P.O. Box 620337, Woodside CA 94062. (650)323-3795. E-mail: carol@authorsbest.com. **Contact:** Carol Susan Roth. Estab. 1995. Represents 47 clients. 15% of clients are new/unpublished writers. Currently handles: 100% nonfiction books.

- Prior to becoming and agent, Ms. Roth was trained as a psychotherapist and worked as a motivational coach, conference producer, and promoter for best-selling authors (e.g. Scott Peck, Bernie Siegal, John Gray) and the 1987 Heart of Business conference (the first business and spirituality conference).

Represents: Nonfiction books. **Considers these nonfiction areas:** Business/economics; money/finance (personal finance/investing); religious/inspirational; self-help/personal improvement; spirituality; wellness/health/medicine; yoga; Buddhism.

- ⛏ This agency specializes in spirituality, health, personal growth, personal finance, business. Actively seeking previously published authors—experts in health, spirituality, personal growth, business with an established audience. Does not want to receive fiction.

How to Contact: Submit proposal package, media kit, promotional video, SASE. Accepts e-mail queries, no attachments please. Considers simultaneous queries. Responds in 1 week to queries. Returns materials only with SASE. Obtains most new clients through recommendations from others, solicitations.

Recent Sales: Sold 17 titles in the last year. *How Great Decisions Get Made*, by Don Maruska (Amacom); *Writers Dojo Wisdom*, by Jennifer Lawler (Viking); *Walk Deck*, by Shirely Archer (Chronicle Books); *Shifting Sands*, by Steve Donohue (Berrett-Koehler); *For Dummies*, by Jeff Strong (Wiley).

Terms: Agent receives 15% commission on domestic sales; 15% commission on foreign sales. Offers written contract, binding for 3 years (for work with the acquiring publisher only); 60-day notice must be given to terminate contract. This agency ''asks the client to provide postage (Fed Ex airbills) and do copying.'' Offers a proposal development and marketing consulting service on request. Service is separate from agenting services.

Writers' Conferences: Maui Writer's Conference (Maui HI, September).

Tips: ''Have charisma, content, and credentials—solve an old problem in a new way. I prefer experts with extensive seminar and media experience.''

N ◻ JANE ROTROSEN AGENCY LLC

318 E. 51st St., New York NY 10022. (212)593-4330. Fax: (212)935-6985. E-mail: firstinitiallastname@janerotros en.com. Estab. 1974. Member of AAR, Authors Guild. Represents over 100 clients. Currently handles: 30% nonfiction books; 70% novels.

Member Agents: Jane R. Berkey, Andrea Cirillo, Annelise Robey, Margaret Ruley, Perry Gordijn (director of translation rights).

Represents: Nonfiction books, novels. **Considers these nonfiction areas:** Biography/autobiography; business/ economics; child guidance/parenting; cooking/foods/nutrition; current affairs; health/medicine; how-to; humor/satire; money/finance; nature/environment; popular culture; psychology; self-help/personal improvement; sports; true crime/investigative; women's issues/studies. **Considers these fiction areas:** Action/adventure; detective/police/crime; family saga; historical; horror; mainstream/contemporary; mystery/suspense; romance; thriller; women's.

How to Contact: Query with SASE. By referral only. No e-mail or fax queries. Responds in 2 months to mss. Responds in 2 weeks (to writers who have been referred by a client or colleague). Returns materials only with SASE.

Recent Sales: Sold 140 titles in the last year. This agency prefers not to share information on specific sales.

Terms: Agent receives 15% commission on domestic sales; 20% commission on foreign sales. Offers written contract, binding for 3-5 years; 2-month notice must be given to terminate contract. Charges clients for photocopying, express mail, overseas postage, book purchase.

N ◻ THE DAMARIS ROWLAND AGENCY

510 E. 23rd St., #8-G, New York NY 10010. (212)475-8942. Fax: (212)358-9411. **Contact:** Damaris Rowland or Steve Axelrod. Estab. 1994. Member of AAR. Represents 50 clients. 10% of clients are new/unpublished writers. Currently handles: novels.

Represents: Novels. **Considers these fiction areas:** Historical; literary; mainstream/contemporary; romance (contemporary, gothic, historical, regency); commercial.

　　O┮ This agency specializes in women's fiction. Submit query with SASE.

How to Contact: Submi. Responds in 6 weeks to queries. Obtains most new clients through recommendations from others, solicitations, conferences.

Recent Sales: *The Next Accident*, by Lisa Gardner; *To Trust a Stranger*, by Karen Robard; *Nursing Homes*, by Peter Silin.

Terms: Agent receives 15% commission on domestic sales; 20% commission on foreign sales. Offers written contract; 1-month notice must be given to terminate contract. Charges only if extraordinary expenses have been incurred, e.g., photocopying and mailing 15 mss to Europe for a foreign sale.

Writers' Conferences: Novelists, Inc. (Denver, October); RWA National (Texas, July); Pacific Northwest Writers Conference.

◻ THE PETER RUBIE LITERARY AGENCY

240 W. 35th St., Suite 500, New York NY 10001. (212)279-1776. Fax: (212)279-0927. E-mail: peterrubie@prlit.c om. Website: www.prlit.com. **Contact:** Peter Rubie or June Clark (pralit@aol.com). Estab. 2000. Member of AAR. Represents 130 clients. 20% of clients are new/unpublished writers.

　　● Prior to opening his agency, Mr. Rubie was a founding partner of another literary agency Perkins, Rubie & Associates, and the fiction editor at Walker and Co. Ms. Clark is the author of several books and plays, and previously worked in cable TV marketing and promotion.

Member Agents: Peter Rubie (crime, science fiction, fantasy, literary fiction, thrillers, narrative/serious nonfiction, business, self-help, how-to, popular, food/wine, history, commercial science, music, education, parenting); June Clark (nonfiction consisting of celebrity biographies, parenting, pets, women's issues, teen nonfiction, how-to, self-help, offbeat business, food/wine, commercial New Age, pop culture, entertainment); Caren Johnson, assistant; Hanna Rubin, agent-at-large (hanna.rubin@prlit.com); Jodi Weiss, agent-at-large.

Represents: Nonfiction books, novels. **Considers these nonfiction areas:** Business/economics; creative nonfiction; current affairs; ethnic/cultural interests; how-to; popular culture; science/technology; self-help/personal improvement; health/nutrition; cooking/food/wine; music; theater/film/television; prescriptive New Age; parenting/education; pets; commercial academic material; TV. **Considers these fiction areas:** Fantasy; historical; literary; science fiction; thriller.

How to Contact: Query with SASE. Accepts e-mail queries. Responds in 2 months to queries; 3 months to mss. Returns materials only with SASE. Obtains most new clients through recommendations from others.

Recent Sales: Sold 50 titles in the last year. *Walking Money*, by James Born (Putnam); *Finishing Business*, by Harlan Ullman (Naval Institute Press); *The Nouvelle Creole Cookbook*, by Joseph Carey (Taylor); *Becoming Something: The Story of Canada Lee*, by Mona Z. Smith (Faber & Faber); *The Saucy Sisters Guide to Wine*, by Barbara Nowak and Beverly Wichman (NAL); *Parenting Your Pup*, by Lyn Lott, Jane Nelsen, and Therry Jay (Rodale); *Best in Show: The Films of Christopher Guest*, by John Kenneth Muir (Applause); *The Liza Minnelli Scrapbook*, by Scott Schecter (Citadel).

Terms: Agent receives 15% commission on domestic sales; 20% commission on foreign sales. Offers written contract. Charges clients for photocopying and some foreign mailings.

Tips: "We look for professional writers and writers who are experts, have a strong platform and reputation in their field, and have an outstanding prose style. Be professional and open-minded. Know your market and learn your craft. Read Rubie's book, *Telling the Story* (HarperCollins). Go to our website for up-to-date information on clients and sales."

N ☑ RUSSELL & VOLKENING

50 W. 29th St., #7E, New York NY 10001. (212)684-6050. Fax: (212)889-3026. **Contact:** Timothy Seldes, Kirsten Ringer. Estab. 1940. Member of AAR. Represents 140 clients. 20% of clients are new/unpublished writers. Currently handles: 45% nonfiction books; 50% novels; 3% story collections; 2% novellas.

Member Agents: Timothy Seldes (nonfiction, literary fiction).

Represents: Nonfiction books, novels, short story collections. **Considers these nonfiction areas:** Anthropology/archaeology; art/architecture/design; biography/autobiography; business/economics; cooking/foods/nutrition; creative nonfiction; current affairs; education; ethnic/cultural interests; gay/lesbian issues; government/politics/law; health/medicine; history; language/literature/criticism; military/war; money/finance; music/dance; nature/environment; photography; popular culture; psychology; science/technology; sociology; sports; theater/film; true crime/investigative; women's issues/studies. **Considers these fiction areas:** Action/adventure; detective/police/crime; ethnic; literary; mainstream/contemporary; mystery/suspense; picture books; sports; thriller.

 ⚬⇥ This agency specializes in literary fiction and narrative nonfiction.

Recent Sales: *The Amateur Marriage* (Knopf); *Loot*, by Nadine Gardiner; *No Certain Rest*, by Jim Lehrer (Random House).

Terms: Agent receives 15% commission on domestic sales; 20% commission on foreign sales. Charges clients for "standard office expenses relating to the submission of materials of an author we represent, e.g., photocopying, postage."

Tips: "If the query is cogent, well written, well presented, and is the type of book we'd represent, we'll ask to see the manuscript. From there, it depends purely on the quality of the work."

☑ REGINA RYAN PUBLISHING ENTERPRISES, INC.

251 Central Park W., 7D, New York NY 10024. (212)787-5589. E-mail: queryreginaryanbooks@rcn.com. **Contact:** Regina Ryan. Estab. 1976. Currently handles: 90% nonfiction books; 5% novels; 5% juvenile books.

 • Prior to becoming an agent, Ms. Ryan was an editor at Alfred A. Knopf, editor-in-chief of Macmillan Adult Trade, and a book producer.

Represents: Nonfiction books.

How to Contact: Query only by e-mail or mail with SASE. No telephone queries. Does not accept queries for juvenile or fiction. Considers simultaneous queries. Responds in 1 month to queries. Returns materials only with SASE. Obtains most new clients through recommendations from others.

Recent Sales: *The Altruist*, by Walter Keady (Macadam/Cage); *Surviving Hitler*, by Andrea Warren (HarperCollins Books for Young Readers); *The Bomb in the Basement*, by Michael Karpin (Simon & Schuster).

Terms: Agent receives 15% commission on domestic sales; 15% commission on foreign sales. Offers written contract; 1 month, negotiable notice must be given to terminate contract. Charges clients for all out-of-pocket expenses, such as long distance, messengers, freight, copying, "if it's more than just a nominal amount."

Tips: "An analysis of the competition is essential; a sample chapter is helpful."

☑ THE SAGALYN AGENCY

7201 Bethesda Ave., Suite 675, Bethesda MD 20814. (301)718-6440. Fax: (310)718-6444. E-mail: agency@Sagaly n.com. Website: Sagalyn.com. **Contact:** Rebeca Sagalyn. Estab. 1980. Member of AAR. Currently handles: 85% nonfiction books; 5% novels; 10% scholarly books.

Member Agents: Raphael Sagalyn, Rebeca Sagalyn.

Represents: Nonfiction books (history, science, business).

    o- Does not want to receive stage plays, screenplays, poetry, science fiction, romance, children's books, or young adult books.

How to Contact: Please send e-mail queries only, no attachments. Include 1 of these words in subject line: Query, submission, inquiry. Response time depends on number of current queries, generally within 3 weeks.

Recent Sales: See website for sales information.

Tips: "We receive between 1,000-1,200 queries a year, which in turn lead to 2 or 3 new clients."

VICTORIA SANDERS & ASSOCIATES

241 Ave. of the Americas, New York NY 10014-4822. (212)633-8811. Fax: (212)633-0525. E-mail: queriesvsa@h otmail.com. Website: www.victoriasanders.com. **Contact:** Victoria Sanders or Diane Dickensheid. Estab. 1993. Member of AAR; signatory of WGA. Represents 75 clients. 25% of clients are new/unpublished writers. Currently handles: 50% nonfiction books; 50% novels.

Member Agents: Benee Knauer, assistant literary agent.

Represents: Nonfiction books, novels. **Considers these nonfiction areas:** Biography/autobiography; current affairs; ethnic/cultural interests; gay/lesbian issues; government/politics/law; history; humor/satire; language/ literature/criticism; music/dance; popular culture; psychology; theater/film; translation; women's issues/studies. **Considers these fiction areas:** Action/adventure; contemporary issues; ethnic; family saga; feminist; gay/ lesbian; literary; thriller.

How to Contact: Query by e-mail only.

Recent Sales: Sold 20 titles in the last year. *Indelible*, by Karin Slaughter (Morrow); *When Love Calls, You Better Answer*, by Bertice Berry (Doubleday).

Terms: Agent receives 15% commission on domestic sales; 20% commission on foreign sales. Offers written contract. Charges for photocopying, ms, messenger, express mail, and extraordinary fees. If in excess of $100, client approval is required.

Tips: "Limit query to letter, no calls, and give it your best shot. A good query is going to get a good response."

☑ SANDUM & ASSOCIATES

144 E. 84th St., New York NY 10028-2035. (212)737-2011. Fax: (on request). **Contact:** Howard E. Sandum, managing director. Estab. 1987. Represents 35 clients. 20% of clients are new/unpublished writers. Currently handles: 80% nonfiction books; 20% novels.

Represents: Nonfiction books, novels (literary). **Considers these fiction areas:** Literary.

    o- This agency specializes in general nonfiction.

How to Contact: Query with proposal, sample pages, and SASE. Do not send full ms unless requested. Responds in 2 weeks to queries.

Terms: Agent receives 15% commission on domestic sales; adjustable commission on foreign sales; adjustable commission on dramatic rights sales. Charges clients for photocopying, air express, long-distance telephone/ fax.

SCHIAVONE LITERARY AGENCY, INC.

236 Trails End, West Palm Beach FL 33413-2135. (561)966-9294. Fax: (561)966-9294. E-mail: profschia@aol.c om. Website: www.freeyellow.com/members8/schiavone/index.html. **Contact:** James Schiavone, Ed.D. Estab. 1996. Member of National Education Association. Represents 60 clients. 2% of clients are new/unpublished writers. Currently handles: 50% nonfiction books; 49% novels; 1% textbooks.

    • Prior to opening his agency, Dr. Schiavone was a full professor of developmental skills at the City University of New York and author of 5 trade books and 3 textbooks.

Represents: Nonfiction books, novels, juvenile books, scholarly books, textbooks. **Considers these nonfiction areas:** Animals; anthropology/archaeology; biography/autobiography; child guidance/parenting; current affairs; education; ethnic/cultural interests; gay/lesbian issues; government/politics/law; health/medicine; history; how-to; humor/satire; juvenile nonfiction; language/literature/criticism; military/war; nature/environment; popular culture; psychology; science/technology; self-help/personal improvement; sociology; true crime/ investigative. **Considers these fiction areas:** Contemporary issues; ethnic; family saga; historical; horror; humor/satire; juvenile; literary; mainstream/contemporary; science fiction; young adult.

    o- This agency specializes in celebrity biography and autobiography. Actively seeking serious nonfiction, literary fiction, and celebrity biography. Does not want to receive poetry.

How to Contact: Query by letter only with SASE. One page e-mail queries with no attachments are accepted and encouraged for fastest response. Does not accept phone or fax queries. Considers simultaneous queries. Responds in 2 weeks to queries; 6 weeks to mss. Returns materials only with SASE. Obtains most new clients through recommendations from others, solicitations, conferences.

Terms: Agent receives 15% commission on domestic sales; 20% commission on foreign sales. Offers written contract. Charges clients only for postage.

Writers' Conferences: Key West Literary Seminar (Key West FL, January); South Florida Writer's Conference (Miami FL, May).

Tips: ''I prefer to work with established authors published by major houses in New York. I will consider marketable proposals from new/previously unpublished writers.''

[N] [◑] WENDY SCHMALZ AGENCY

Box 831, Hudson NY 12534. (518)672-7697. Fax: (518)672-7662. E-mail: wschmalz@earthlink.net. **Contact:** Wendy Schmalz. Estab. 2002. Member of AAR. Represents 30 clients. 10% of clients are new/unpublished writers. Currently handles: 25% nonfiction books; 25% novels; 50% juvenile books.

Represents: Nonfiction books, novels, YA novels. **Considers these nonfiction areas:** Biography/autobiography; current affairs; gay/lesbian issues; popular culture; juvenile nonfiction. **Considers these fiction areas:** Gay/lesbian; juvenile; literary; young adult; contemporary issues.

　　O┐ No picture book texts.

How to Contact: Query with SASE. Accepts e-mail queries. No fax queries. Responds in 2 weeks to queries; 6 weeks to mss. Returns materials only with SASE. Obtains most new clients through recommendations from others.

Terms: Agent receives 15% commission on domestic sales; 20% commission on foreign sales. No written contract. Charges authors actual expenses incurred by agent for photocopying and Fed Ex charges incurred for Fed Ex mss.

[◑] SUSAN SCHULMAN, A LITERARY AGENCY

454 W. 44th St., New York NY 10036-5205. (212)713-1633/4/5. Fax: (212)581-8830. E-mail: schulman@aol.com. Website: www.susanschulmanagency.com. **Contact:** Susan Schulman, president. Estab. 1979. Member of AAR, Dramatists Guild, Women's Media Group; signatory of WGA—East. 10-15% of clients are new/unpublished writers. Currently handles: 70% nonfiction books; 20% novels; 10% stage plays.

Member Agents: Susan Schulman (self-help, health, business, spirituality); Christine Morin (children's books, ecology, natural sciences, and business books); Bryan Leifert (plays and pitches for films).

Represents: Nonfiction books, novels. **Considers these nonfiction areas:** Anthropology/archaeology; biography/autobiography; child guidance/parenting; current affairs; education; ethnic/cultural interests; gay/lesbian issues; government/politics/law; health/medicine; history; how-to; juvenile nonfiction; money/finance; music/dance; nature/environment; popular culture; psychology; self-help/personal improvement; sociology; theater/film; translation; true crime/investigative; women's issues/studies. **Considers these fiction areas:** Contemporary issues; detective/police/crime; gay/lesbian; historical; literary; mainstream/contemporary; mystery/suspense; young adult. **Considers these script subject areas:** Comedy; contemporary issues; detective/police/crime; feminist; historical; mainstream; mystery/suspense; psychic/supernatural; teen.

　　O┐ This agency specializes in books for, by, and about women's issues including family, careers, health and spiritual development, business and sociology, history and economics. Emphasizing contemporary women's fiction and nonfiction books of interest to women.

How to Contact: Query with SASE, outline/proposal, SASE. Accepts e-mail and fax queries. Considers simultaneous queries. Responds in 1 week to queries; 6 weeks to mss. Returns materials only with SASE.

Recent Sales: Sold 30 titles in the last year. *Prayers for a Non-Believer*, by Julia Cameron (Putnam); *The Half-Empty Heart*, by Alan Downs (St. Martin's Press); *The Walls Around Us*, by David Owen (Simon & Schuster); *Rise of the Creative Class*, by Richard Florida (Basic Books). ***Movie/TV MOW script(s) optioned/sold:*** *In the Skin of a Lion*, by Michael Ondaatje (Serendipity Point Productions); *Holes*, by Louis Sachar (Disney); *Sideways Stories from Wayside School*, by Louis Sachar (Lin Oliver Productions); *Twirling at Ole Miss*, by Terry Southern (Blue Magic Pictures).

Terms: Agent receives 15% commission on domestic sales; 7½-10% (plus 7½-10% to co-agent) commission on foreign sales; 10-20% commission on dramatic rights sales. Charges client for special messenger or copying services, foreign mail and any other service requested by client.

[◑] LAURENS R. SCHWARTZ AGENCY

5 E. 22nd St., Suite 15D, New York NY 10010-5325. (212)228-2614. **Contact:** Laurens R. Schwartz. Estab. 1984. Signatory of WGA. Represents 100 clients.

Represents: Nonfiction books, novels, general mix of nonfiction and fiction. Also handles movie and TV tie-ins, licensing, and merchandising.
How to Contact: Query with SASE. *No unsolicited mss.* Responds in 1 month to queries. "Have had 18 best-sellers."
Terms: Agent receives 15% commission on domestic sales; 25% (WGA rates where applicable) commission on foreign sales. "No client fees except for photocopying, and that fee is avoided by an author providing necessary copies or, in certain instances, transferring files on diskette or by e-mail attachment." Where necessary to bring a project into publishing form, editorial work and some rewriting provided as part of service. Works with authors on long-term career goals and promotion.
Tips: "I do not like receiving mass mailings sent to all agents. I am extremely selective—only take on 1-3 new clients a year. Do not send everything you have ever written. Choose 1 work and promote that. Always include an SASE. Never send your only copy. Always include a background sheet on yourself and a 1-page synopsis of the work (too many summaries end up being as long as the work)."

◙ SCOVIL CHICHAK GALEN LITERARY AGENCY
381 Park Ave. S., Suite 1020, New York NY 10016. (212)679-8686. Fax: (212)679-6710. E-mail: mailroom@scglit. com. Website: www.scglit.com. **Contact:** Russell Galen. Estab. 1993. Member of AAR. Represents 300 clients. Currently handles: 70% nonfiction books; 30% novels.
Member Agents: Russell Galen, Jack Scovil, Anna Ghosh.
How to Contact: Accepts e-mail and fax queries. Considers simultaneous queries.
Recent Sales: Sold 100 titles in the last year. *Across the Black Waters*, by Minai Hajratwala (Houghton Mifflin); *The Secret*, by Walter Anderson (HarperCollins); *Naked Empire*, by Terry Goodkinf (Tor); *Lord John and the Private Matter*, by Diana Gabaldon; *In The Hand of Dante*, by Nick Tosches (Little, Brown).
Terms: Charges clients for photocopying and postage.

◙ SEDGEBAND LITERARY ASSOCIATES
7312 Martha Lane, Fort Worth TX 76112. (817)496-3652. Fax: (425)952-9518. E-mail: queries@sedgeband.com. Website: www.sedgeband.com. **Contact:** David Duperre. Estab. 1997. 50% of clients are new/unpublished writers. Currently handles: 50% nonfiction books; 50% fiction novels.
Member Agents: David Duperre (literary, scripts, mystery, suspense); Ginger Norton (romance, horror, nonfiction, mainstream/contemporary).
Represents: Nonfiction books, novels, novellas. **Considers these nonfiction areas:** Biography/autobiography; ethnic/cultural interests; history; true crime/investigative. **Considers these fiction areas:** Action/adventure; experimental; horror; literary; mainstream/contemporary; mystery/suspense; romance.
> ○━ This agency is looking for talented writers who have patience and are willing to work hard. Actively seeking new nonfiction writers, some fiction.
How to Contact: Query with SASE. Prefers queries via e-mail. No phone queries accepted. No full mss. Accepts e-mail queries with no attachments; repsonds in 3 weeks. Responds in 2-3 months to written queries. Responds in 4 months to requested mss. Returns materials only with SASE. Obtains most new clients through queries, the Internet, referrals.
Recent Sales: Sold 12 titles in the last year.
Terms: Agent receives 15% commission on domestic sales; 20% commission on foreign sales. Offers written contract, binding for 1 year; 30-day written notice must be given to terminate contract. Charges clients for postage, photocopies, long-distance calls, etc., "until we make a sale to an established publisher. We do not charge any reading or retainer fees."
Tips: "We care about writers and books, not just money, but we care about the industry as well. We will not represent anyone who might hurt our clients or our reputation. We expect our writers to work hard and to be patient. Do not send a rude query, it will get you nowhere. If we ask to see your book, don't wait around to send it or ask a bunch of irrelevant questions about movie rights and so forth, *(at this point we haven't even offered to represent you!)*. If you can't write a synopsis, don't bother to query us. Don't handwrite your query or send us samples of your writing that are handwritten—we won't read any of it. Be professional."

◙ LYNN SELIGMAN, LITERARY AGENT
400 Highland Ave., Upper Montclair NJ 07043. (973)783-3631. **Contact:** Lynn Seligman. Estab. 1985. Member of Women's Media Group. Represents 32 clients. 15% of clients are new/unpublished writers. Currently handles: 70% nonfiction books; 30% novels.
> ● Prior to opening her agency, Ms. Seligman worked in the subsidiary rights department of Doubleday and Simon & Schuster, and served as an agent with Julian Bach Literary Agency (now IMG Literary Agency).
Represents: Nonfiction books, novels. **Considers these nonfiction areas:** Anthropology/archaeology; art/architecture/design; biography/autobiography; business/economics; child guidance/parenting; cooking/foods/

nutrition; current affairs; education; ethnic/cultural interests; government/politics/law; health/medicine; history; how-to; humor/satire; interior design/decorating; language/literature/criticism; money/finance; music/dance; nature/environment; photography; popular culture; psychology; science/technology; self-help/personal improvement; sociology; theater/film; true crime/investigative; women's issues/studies. **Considers these fiction areas:** Detective/police/crime; ethnic; fantasy; feminist; gay/lesbian; historical; horror; humor/satire; literary; mainstream/contemporary; mystery/suspense; romance (contemporary, gothic, historical, regency); science fiction.

⊶ This agency specializes in "general nonfiction and fiction. I do illustrated and photography books and represent several photographers for books." This agency does not handle children or young adult books.

How to Contact: Query with SASE, 1 sample chapter(s), outline/proposal. Prefers to read materials exclusively. No e-mail or fax queries. Considers simultaneous queries. Responds in 2 weeks to queries; 2 months to mss. Returns materials only with SASE. Obtains most new clients through referrals from other writers or editors.

Recent Sales: Sold 15 titles in the last year. *Thinking Parent, Thinking Child*, by Dr. Myrna Shure; *Family Inheritance*, by Deborah Le Blanc.

Terms: Agent receives 15% commission on domestic sales; 25% commission on foreign sales. Charges clients for photocopying, unusual postage, or telephone expenses (checking first with the author), express mail.

☐ SERENDIPITY LITERARY AGENCY, LLC

732 Fulton St., Suite 3, Brooklyn NY 11238. (718)230-7689. Fax: (718)230-7829. E-mail: rbrooks@serendipitylit.com. Website: www.serendipitylit.com. **Contact:** Regina Brooks. Estab. 2000. Represents 30 clients. 20% of clients are new/unpublished writers. Currently handles: 60% nonfiction books; 40% novels.

• Prior to becoming an agent, Ms. Brooks was an acquisitions editor for John Wiley & Sons, Inc. and McGraw-Hill Companies.

Represents: Nonfiction books, novels, juvenile books, scholarly books, textbooks, children's. **Considers these nonfiction areas:** Business/economics; computers/electronic; education; ethnic/cultural interests; how-to; juvenile nonfiction; memoirs; money/finance; multicultural; New Age/metaphysics; popular culture; psychology; religious/inspirational; science/technology; self-help/personal improvement; sports; women's issues/studies. **Considers these fiction areas:** Action/adventure; confession; ethnic; historical; juvenile; literary; multicultural; mystery/suspense; picture books; romance; thriller. **Considers these script subject areas:** Ethnic; fantasy; juvenile; multimedia; also interested in children's cd/video projects.

⊶ Serendipity provides developmental editing. "We help build marketing plans for nontraditional outlets." Actively seeking African-American nonfiction, commercial fiction, computer books (nonfiction), YA novels with an urban flair, juvenile books. Does not want to receive poetry.

How to Contact: Prefers to read materials exclusively. Nonfiction, submit outline, 1 sample chapter, SASE. Responds in 2 months to queries; 3 months to mss. Obtains most new clients through conferences, referrals.

Recent Sales: This agency prefers not to share information on specific sales. Recent sales available upon request by prospective client.

Terms: Agent receives 15% commission on domestic sales; 20% commission on foreign sales. Offers written contract; 2-month notice notice must be given to terminate contract. Charges clients $200 upon signing for office fees, or office fees will be taken from any advance. Does not make referrals to editing services. "If author requests editing services, I can offer a list of potential services." 0% of business is derived from referral to editing services.

Tips: "Looking for African-American children's books. We also represent illustrators."

☑ THE SEYMOUR AGENCY

475 Miner St., Canton NY 13617. (315)386-1831. Fax: (315)386-1037. E-mail: marysue@slic.com. Website: www.theseymouragency.com. **Contact:** Mary Sue Seymour. Estab. 1992. Represents 100 clients. 5% of clients are new/unpublished writers. Currently handles: 50% nonfiction books; 50% fiction.

• Ms. Seymour is a retired New York State certified teacher.

Represents: Nonfiction books, novels (romance). **Considers these nonfiction areas:** Business/economics; health/medicine; how-to; self-help/personal improvement; Christian books; cookbooks; any well-written nonfiction that includes a proposal in standard format and sample chapter 1. **Considers these fiction areas:** Literary; religious/inspirational (Christian books); romance (any type); westerns/frontier.

How to Contact: Query with SASE, synopsis, first 50 pages for romance. Accepts e-mail queries. No fax queries. Considers simultaneous queries. Responds in 1 month to queries; 3 months to mss. Returns materials only with SASE.

Recent Sales: Gail Sattler's 4-book deal with Steeple Hill; *Christie Craig's 250 Questions Any Home Buyer Should Ask* (Adams Media); *Women in Crime*, by Betty Alt (Greenwood Publishing).

Terms: Agent receives 12% (from authors' material whose books the agency sold) and 15% (on new new clients) commission on domestic sales.

Writers' Conferences: Desert Rose (Scottsdale AZ); Mountain Laurel (Knoxville TN); Romantic Times Convention (New York City); RWA National (Houston); CBA (Atlanta).

☑ THE ROBERT E. SHEPARD AGENCY

1608 Dwight Way, Berkeley CA 94703-1804. (510)849-3999. E-mail: query@shepardagency.com. Website: www.shepardagency.com. **Contact:** Robert Shepard. Estab. 1994. Member of Authors Guild (associate). Represents 50 clients. 15% of clients are new/unpublished writers. Currently handles: 90% nonfiction books; 10% scholarly books.

• Prior to opening his agency, Mr. Shepard "was an editor and a sales and marketing manager in book publishing"; he now teaches a course for nonfiction authors and "has been known to write," himself.

Represents: Nonfiction books, scholarly books (appropriate for trade publishers). **Considers these nonfiction areas:** Business/economics; current affairs; ethnic/cultural interests; gay/lesbian issues; government/politics/law; history; money/finance; popular culture; science/technology; sociology; sports; narrative nonfiction; Judaica.

O➛ This agency specializes in nonfiction, particularly key issues facing society and culture. Actively seeking "works by experts recognized in their fields whether or not they're well-known to the general public, and books that offer fresh perspectives or new information even when the subject is familiar." Does not want to receive autobiography, art books, fiction.

How to Contact: Query with SASE. E-mail queries encouraged. Fax and phone queries strongly discouraged. Considers simultaneous queries. Responds in 2-3 weeks to queries; 6 weeks to proposals or mss. Returns materials only with SASE. Obtains most new clients through recommendations from others, solicitations.

Recent Sales: Sold 10 titles in the last year. Recent titles include the best-selling *Word Freak: Heartbreak, Triumph, Genius, and Obsession in the World of Competitive Scrabble Players*, by Stefan Fatsis (Houghton Mifflin HC, Penguin PB); *Wine & War: The French, the Nazis, and the Battle for France's Greatest Treasure*, by Don and Petie Kladstrup (Broadway Books); *Coal: A Human History*, by Barbara Freese (Perseus); *Leave the Office Earlier*, by Laura Stack (Broadway Books); *The Root of Wild Madder*, by Brian Murphy (Simon & Schuster).

Terms: Agent receives 15% commission on domestic sales; 20% commission on foreign sales. Offers written contract, binding for term of project or until canceled; 30-day notice must be given to terminate contract. Charges clients "actual expenses for phone/fax, photocopying, and postage only if and when project sells, against advance."

Tips: "We pay attention to detail. We believe in close working relationships between author and agent, and in building better relationships between author and editor. Please do your homework! There's no substitute for learning all you can about similar or directly competing books and presenting a well-reasoned competitive analysis in your proposal. Be sure to describe what's new and fresh about your work, why you are the best person to be writing on your subject, and how the book will serve the needs or interests of your intended readers. Don't work in a vacuum; visit bookstores, talk to other writers about their experiences, and let the information you gather inform the work that you do as an author."

☑ WENDY SHERMAN ASSOCIATES, INC.

450 Seventh Ave., Suite 3004, New York NY 10123. (212)279-9027. Fax: (212)279-8863. E-mail: wendy@wsherman.com. **Contact:** Wendy Sherman. Estab. 1999. Member of AAR. Represents 30 clients. 30% of clients are new/unpublished writers. Currently handles: 50% nonfiction books; 50% novels.

• Prior to opening the agency, Ms. Sherman worked for The Aaron Priest agency and was vice president, executive director of Henry Holt, associate publisher, subsidary rights director, sales and marketing director.

Member Agents: Tracy Brown, Wendy Sherman.

Represents: Nonfiction books, novels. **Considers these nonfiction areas:** Psychology; narrative nonfiction, practical. **Considers these fiction areas:** Literary; women's (suspense).

O➛ "We specialize in developing new writers as well as working with more established writers. My experience as a publisher has proven to be a great asset to my clients."

How to Contact: Query with SASE, or send outline/proposal, 1 sample chapter. No e-mail queries. Considers simultaneous queries. Responds in 1 month to queries. Returns materials only with SASE. Obtains most new clients through recommendations from others.

Recent Sales: Sold 16 titles in the last year. Other clients include Greg Baer, M.D., Liam Callanan, Lise Friedman, Rabbi Mark Borowitz, Alan Eisenstock, D.W. Buffa, William Lashner, Nani Power, Sarah Stonich, American Dance Foundation, Howard Bahr, Lundy Bancroft, Tom Schweich, Suzanne Chazin, Al Hudler, Mary Sharratt, Libby Street.

Terms: Agent receives 15% commission on domestic sales; 20% commission on foreign sales. Offers written contract. Charges for photocopying of ms, messengers, express mail services, etc. (reasonable, standard expenses).

✉ ROSALIE SIEGEL, INTERNATIONAL LITERARY AGENCY, INC.

1 Abey Dr., Pennington NJ 08534. (609)737-1007. Fax: (609)737-3708. **Contact:** Rosalie Siegel. Estab. 1977. Member of AAR. Represents 35 clients. 10% of clients are new/unpublished writers. Currently handles: 45% nonfiction books; 45% novels; 10% young adult books and short story collections for current clients.

Represents: Nonfiction books, novels, short story collections, young adult books.

How to Contact: Obtains most new clients through referrals from writers and friends.

Terms: Agent receives 15% commission on domestic sales; 20% commission on foreign sales. Offers written contract; 2-month notice must be given to terminate contract. Charges clients for photocopying.

Tips: ''I'm not looking for new authors in an active way.''

▦ ✍ JEFFREY SIMMONS LITERARY AGENCY

15 Penn House, Mallory St., London NW8 8SX, England. (020)7224 8917. E-mail: jas@london-inc.com. **Contact:** Jeffrey Simmons. Estab. 1978. Represents 43 clients. 40% of clients are new/unpublished writers. Currently handles: 60% nonfiction books; 40% novels.

• Prior to becoming an agent, Mr. Simmons was a publisher, and he is also an author.

Represents: Nonfiction books, novels. **Considers these nonfiction areas:** Biography/autobiography; current affairs; government/politics/law; history; language/literature/criticism; memoirs; music/dance; popular culture; sociology; sports; theater/film; translation; true crime/investigative. **Considers these fiction areas:** Action/adventure; confession; detective/police/crime; family saga; literary; mainstream/contemporary; mystery/suspense; thriller.

○━ This agency seeks to handle good books and promising young writers. ''My long experience in publishing and as an author and ghostwriter means I can offer an excellent service all around, especially in terms of editorial experience where appropriate.'' Actively seeking quality fiction, biography, autobiography, showbiz, personality books, law, crime, politics, world affairs. Does not want to receive science fiction, horror, fantasy, juvenile, academic books, specialist subjects (i.e., cooking, gardening, religious).

How to Contact: Submit sample chapter, outline/proposal, IRCs if necessary, SASE. Prefers to read materials exclusively. Responds in 1 week to queries; 1 month to mss. Obtains most new clients through recommendations from others, solicitations.

Recent Sales: Sold 18 titles in the last year. *Decoding Sion*, by Pecknett & Prince (Time Warner UK, Simon & Schuster US); *Complete Carry On*, by Webber (Random House).

Terms: Agent receives 10-15% commission on domestic sales; 15% commission on foreign sales. Offers written contract, binding for lifetime of book in question or until it becomes out of print.

Tips: ''When contacting us with an outline/proposal, include a brief biographical note (listing any previous publications, with publishers and dates). Preferably tell us if the book has already been offered elsewhere.''

✍ IRENE SKOLNICK LITERARY AGENCY

22 W. 23rd St., 5th Floor, New York NY 10010. (212)727-3648. Fax: (212)727-1024. E-mail: sirene35@aol.com. **Contact:** Irene Skolnick. Estab. 1993. Member of AAR. Represents 45 clients. 75% of clients are new/unpublished writers.

Member Agents: Irene Skolnick.

Represents: Nonfiction books (adult), novels (adult). **Considers these nonfiction areas:** Biography/autobiography; current affairs; cultural history. **Considers these fiction areas:** Contemporary issues; literary; mainstream/contemporary.

How to Contact: Query with SASE, outline, sample chapter(s). Accepts e-mail queries. No fax queries. Considers simultaneous queries. Responds in 1 month to queries. Returns materials only with SASE.

Recent Sales: *Two Lives*, by Vikram Seth; *Don't Get Too Comfortable*, by David Rakoff (Doubleday); *The Pieces from Berlin*, by Michael Pye (Knopf).

Terms: Agent receives 15% commission on domestic sales; 20% commission on foreign sales. Sometimes offers criticism service. Charges for international postage, photocopying over 40 pages.

⬚ ✉ BEVERLEY SLOPEN LITERARY AGENCY

131 Bloor St. W., Suite 711, Toronto ON M5S 1S3, Canada. (416)964-9598. Fax: (416)921-7726. E-mail: beverly@slopenagency.ca. Website: www.slopenagency.ca. **Contact:** Beverley Slopen. Estab. 1974. Represents 60 clients. 40% of clients are new/unpublished writers. Currently handles: 60% nonfiction books; 40% novels.

• Prior to opening her agency, Ms. Slopen worked in publishing and as a journalist.

Represents: Nonfiction books, novels, scholarly books, textbooks (college). **Considers these nonfiction areas:** Anthropology/archaeology; biography/autobiography; business/economics; current affairs; psychology; sociology; true crime/investigative; women's issues/studies. **Considers these fiction areas:** Literary; mystery/suspense.

○➔ This agency has a "strong bent towards Canadian writers." Actively seeking "serious nonfiction that is accessible and appealing to the general reader." Does not want to receive fantasy, science fiction, or children's.

How to Contact: Query with SAE and IRCs. Returns materials only with SASE (Canadian postage). Accepts short e-mail queries. Considers simultaneous queries. Responds in 2 months to queries.

Recent Sales: Sold 25 titles in the last year. *Baroque-a-nova*, by Kevin Chong (Penguin Putnam); *The Rescue of Jerusalem*, by Henry T. Aubin (Doubleday Canada, Soho Press US); *Midnight Cab*, by James W. Nichol (Knopf Canada, Canongate UK, Droemer, Germany); *Fatal Passage*, by Ken McGoogan (Carroll & Graf US, Bantam Press UK); *Understanding Uncertainty*, by Jeffrey Rosenthal (HarperCollins Canada); *Sea of Dreams*, by Adam Mayers (McClelland & Stewart Canada); *Hair Hat*, fiction by Carrie Snyder (Penguin Canada). Other clients include Modris Eksteins, Michael Marrus, Timothy Brook, Robert Fulford, Donna Morrissey, Howard Engel, Morley Torgov, Elliott Leyton, Don Gutteridge.

Terms: Agent receives 15% commission on domestic sales; 10% commission on foreign sales. Offers written contract, binding for 2 years; 30-month notice must be given to terminate contract.

Tips: "Please, no unsolicited manuscripts."

◢ MICHAEL SNELL LITERARY AGENCY

P.O. Box 1206, Truro MA 02666-1206. (508)349-3718. **Contact:** Michael Snell. Estab. 1978. Represents 200 clients. 25% of clients are new/unpublished writers. Currently handles: 90% nonfiction books; 10% novels.

• Prior to opening his agency, Mr. Snell served as an editor at Wadsworth and Addison-Wesley for 13 years.

Member Agents: Michael Snell (business, pets, sports); Patricia Snell (pets, relationships, parenting, self-help, how-to).

Represents: Nonfiction books. **Considers these nonfiction areas:** Agriculture/horticulture; animals (pets); anthropology/archaeology; art/architecture/design; business/economics; child guidance/parenting; computers/electronic; cooking/foods/nutrition; crafts/hobbies; creative nonfiction; current affairs; education; ethnic/cultural interests; gardening; gay/lesbian issues; government/politics/law; health/medicine; history; how-to; humor/satire; interior design/decorating; language/literature/criticism; military/war; money/finance; music/dance; nature/environment; New Age/metaphysics; photography; popular culture; psychology; recreation; religious/inspirational; science/technology; self-help/personal improvement; sex; spirituality; sports (fitness); theater/film; travel; true crime/investigative; women's issues/studies.

○➔ This agency specializes in how-to, self-help, and all types of business and computer books, from low-level how-to to professional and reference. Especially interested in business, health, law, medicine, psychology, science, women's issues. Actively seeking "strong book proposals in any nonfiction area where a clear need exists for a new book. Especially self-help, how-to books on all subjects, from business to personal well-being." Does not want to receive "complete manuscripts; considers proposals only. No fiction. No children's books."

How to Contact: Query with SASE. Prefers to read materials exclusively. Responds in 1 week to queries; 2 weeks to mss. Obtains most new clients through unsolicited mss, word of mouth, *LMP*, and *Guide to Literary Agents*.

Recent Sales: *Riding Horses with Confidence*, by Bucklin (Wiley/Howell); *Mastering Golf*, by Patri (Lyons); *Make the Rules or Your Rivals Will*, by Shell (Random House); *Topgrading II*, by Smart (Penguin/Portfolio).

Terms: Agent receives 15% commission on domestic sales; 15% commission on foreign sales.

Tips: "Send a half- to full-page query, with SASE. Brochure 'How to Write a Book Proposal' available on request and SASE. We suggest prospective clients read Michael Snell's book, *From Book Idea to Bestseller* (Prima, 1997)."

Ⓝ ◢ SOUTHERN LITERARY GROUP

Division of L. Perkins Associates, 43 Stamford Dr., Lakeview AR 72642. (870)431-7006. Fax: (870)431-8625. E-mail: southernlitgroup@yahoo.com. **Contact:** Beverly Maycunich. Estab. 2000. Represents 30 clients. 30% of clients are new/unpublished writers.

• Prior to becoming an agent, Ms. Maycunich was a real-estate agent. Her agency is affiliated with L. Perkins Associates.

Represents: Nonfiction books, novels. **Considers these nonfiction areas:** Current affairs; popular culture; women's issues/studies. **Considers these fiction areas:** Action/adventure; contemporary issues; detective/police/crime; ethnic; feminist; historical; literary; mainstream/contemporary; multicultural; mystery/suspense; regional; romance; thriller; young adult; women's fiction.

○➔ This agency is open to new writers. Does not want to receive material for children's books.

How to Contact: Query with SASE. Considers simultaneous queries. Responds in 1 week to queries; 3 months to mss. Returns materials only with SASE. Obtains most new clients through recommendations from others, the Internet.

Terms: Agent receives 15% commission on domestic sales; 20% commission on foreign sales. No written contract. Clients must provide 5 copies of ms.
Writers' Conferences: BEA.
Tips: "Care about your work. Belong to a writer's organization. Know your competition. The more you do your homework, the better your chance is of being sold."

☑ SPECTRUM LITERARY AGENCY

320 Central Park W., Suite 1-D, New York NY 10025. Website: www.spectrumliteraryagency.com. **Contact:** Eleanor Wood, president. Represents 80 clients. Currently handles: 10% nonfiction books; 90% novels.
Member Agents: Lucienne Diver.
Represents: Nonfiction books, novels. **Considers these nonfiction areas:** Considers select nonfiction. **Considers these fiction areas:** Contemporary issues; fantasy; historical; mainstream/contemporary; mystery/suspense; romance; science fiction.
How to Contact: Query with SASE, include publishing credits and background information. No phone, e-mail, or fax queries. Responds in 1-3 months to queries. Obtains most new clients through recommendations from authors and others.
Recent Sales: Sold over 100 titles in the last year. This agency prefers not to share information on specific sales.
Terms: Agent receives 15% commission on domestic sales. Deducts for photocopying and book orders.

☒ ☑ SPENCERHILL ASSOCIATES ⌀↰

P.O. Box 374, Chatham NY 12032. (518)392-9293. Fax: (518)392-9554. E-mail: ksolem@klsbooks.com. **Contact:** Karen Solem. Estab. 2001. Member of AAR. Represents 40 clients. 5% of clients are new/unpublished writers. Currently handles: 5% nonfiction books; 90% novels; 5% novellas.

• Ms. Solem is not taking on many new clients at the present time. Prior to becoming an agent, Ms. Solem was editor-in-chief at HarperCollins and associate publisher.

Represents: Nonfiction books (Christian), novels. **Considers these nonfiction areas:** Animals; religious/inspirational. **Considers these fiction areas:** Detective/police/crime; historical; mainstream/contemporary; religious/inspirational; romance; thriller.

○↰ "I handle mostly commercial women's fiction, romance, thrillers, and mysteries. I also represent Christian fiction and nonfiction." No poetry, science fiction, juvenile, or scripts.

How to Contact: Query with SASE, submit proposal package, outline. Responds in 1 month to queries. Returns materials only with SASE.
Recent Sales: Sold 110 titles in the last year.
Terms: Agent receives 15% commission on domestic sales; 20% commission on foreign sales. Offers written contract; 3-months notice must be given to terminate contract.

☑ THE SPIELER AGENCY

154 W. 57th St., 13th Floor, Room 135, New York NY 10019. **Contact:** Katya Balter. Estab. 1981. Represents 160 clients. 2% of clients are new/unpublished writers.

• Prior to opening his agency, Mr. Spieler was a magazine editor.

Member Agents: Joe Spieler; John Thornton (nonfiction); Lisa M. Ross (fiction/nonfiction); Deirdre Mullane (nonfiction/fiction); Eric Myers. Spieler Agency West (Oakland, CA): Victoria Shoemaker.
Represents: Nonfiction books, literary fiction, children's books. **Considers these nonfiction areas:** Biography/autobiography; business/economics; child guidance/parenting; cooking/foods/nutrition; current affairs; gay/lesbian issues; government/politics/law; history; memoirs; money/finance; music/dance; nature/environment (environmental issues); sociology; theater/film; travel; women's issues/studies. **Considers these fiction areas:** Experimental; feminist; gay/lesbian; literary.
How to Contact: Query with SASE. Prefers to read materials exclusively. No fax queries. Considers simultaneous queries. Responds in 2 weeks to queries; 5 weeks to mss. Returns materials only with SASE. Obtains most new clients through recommendations and occasionally through listing in *Guide to Literary Agents*.
Recent Sales: *A Needle to the Heart: Special Military Operations from the Heroic to the Nuclear Age*, by Derek Leebaert (Little, Brown); *Natural History of the Rich*, by Richard Conniff (W.W. Norton); *The Clothes They Stood Up In*, by Alan Bennett (Random House).
Terms: Agent receives 15% commission on domestic sales. Charges clients for messenger bills, photocopying, postage.
Writers' Conferences: London Bookfair.

☑ PHILIP G. SPITZER LITERARY AGENCY

50 Talmage Farm Lane, East Hampton NY 11937. (631)329-3650. Fax: (631)329-3651. E-mail: spitzer516@aol.c

om. **Contact:** Philip Spitzer. Estab. 1969. Member of AAR. Represents 60 clients. 10% of clients are new/unpublished writers. Currently handles: 50% nonfiction books; 50% novels.

• Prior to opening his agency, Mr. Spitzer served at New York University Press, McGraw-Hill, and the John Cushman Associates literary agency.

Represents: Nonfiction books, novels. **Considers these nonfiction areas:** Biography/autobiography; business/economics; current affairs; ethnic/cultural interests; government/politics/law; health/medicine; history; language/literature/criticism; military/war; music/dance; nature/environment; popular culture; psychology; sociology; sports; theater/film; true crime/investigative. **Considers these fiction areas:** Contemporary issues; detective/police/crime; literary; mainstream/contemporary; mystery/suspense; sports; thriller.

○➝ This agency specializes in mystery/suspense, literary fiction, sports, general nonfiction (no how-to).

How to Contact: Query with SASE, outline, 1 sample chapter(s). Responds in 1 week to queries; 6 weeks to mss. Obtains most new clients through recommendations from others.

Recent Sales: *The Narrows*, by Michael Connelly; *Lost Light*, by Michael Connelly; *Shadow Man*, by Jonathon King; *Something's Down There*, by Mickey Spillane; *Missing Justice*, by Alafair Burke; *Last Car to Elysian Fields*, by James Lee Burke; *Shattered*, by Deborah Puglisi Sharp with Marjorie Perston.

Terms: Agent receives 15% commission on domestic sales; 20% commission on foreign sales. Charges clients for photocopying.

Writers' Conferences: BEA (Chicago).

◖ NANCY STAUFFER ASSOCIATES

P.O. Box 1203, Darien CT 06820. (203)655-3717. Fax: (203)655-3704. E-mail: nanstauf@optonline.net. **Contact:** Nancy Stauffer Cahoon. Estab. 1989. Member of the Authors Guild. 5% of clients are new/unpublished writers. Currently handles: 15% nonfiction books; 85% novels. **Considers these nonfiction areas:** Creative nonfiction; current affairs; ethnic/cultural interests. **Considers these fiction areas:** Contemporary issues; literary; regional.

How to Contact: Obtains most new clients through referrals from existing clients.

Recent Sales: *Ten Little Indians*, by Sherman Alexie (Grove/Atlantic); *No Enemy But Time*, by William C. Harris (St. Martin's Press); *An Unfinished Life*, by Mark Spragg.

Terms: Agent receives 15% commission on domestic sales; 20% commission on foreign sales; 15% commission on dramatic rights sales.

◖ STEELE-PERKINS LITERARY AGENCY

26 Island Lane, Canandaigua NY 14424. (585)396-9290. Fax: (585)396-3579. E-mail: pattiesp@aol.com. **Contact:** Pattie Steele-Perkins. Member of AAR, RWA. Currently handles: 100% Romance and mainstream women's fiction.

Represents: Novels. **Considers these fiction areas:** Mainstream/contemporary; multicultural; romance; women's.

○➝ Actively seeking romance, women's fiction, and multicultural works.

How to Contact: Submit outline, 3 sample chapter(s), SASE. Considers simultaneous queries. Responds in 6 weeks to queries. Returns materials only with SASE. Obtains most new clients through recommendations from others, queries/solicitations.

Recent Sales: This agency prefers not to share information on specific sales.

Terms: Agent receives 15% commission on domestic sales. Offers written contract, binding for 1 year; 1-month notice must be given to terminate contract.

Writers' Conferences: National Conference of Romance Writers of America; Book Expo America Writers' Conferences.

Tips: "Be patient. E-mail rather than call. Make sure what you are sending is the best it can be."

Ⓝ ◖ STERLING LORD LITERISTIC, INC.

65 Bleecker St., 12th Floor, New York NY 10012. (212)780-6050. Fax: (212)780-6095. Estab. 1952. Member of AAR; signatory of WGA. Represents 600 clients. Currently handles: 50% nonfiction books; 50% novels.

Member Agents: Philippa Brophy, Laurie Liss, Chris Calhoun, Peter Matson, Sterling Lord, Claudia Cross, Neeti Madan, George Nicholson, Jim Rutman, Charlotte Sheedy (affiliate); Douglas Stewart.

Represents: Nonfiction books, novels, literary value considered first.

How to Contact: Query with SASE. Responds in 1 month to mss. Obtains most new clients through recommendations from others.

Recent Sales: This agency prefers not to share information on specific sales. Other clients include Kent Haruf, Dick Fancis, Mary Gordon, Sen. John McCain, Simon Winchester, James McBride, Billy Collins, Richard Paul Evans, Dave Pelzer.

Terms: Agent receives 15% commission on domestic sales; 20% commission on foreign sales. Offers written contract. Charges clients for photocopying.

◎ STERNIG & BYRNE LITERARY AGENCY

2370 S. 107th St., Apt. #4, Milwaukee WI 53227-2036. (414)328-8034. Fax: (414)328-8034. E-mail: jackbyrne@h otmail.com. Website: www.sff.net/people/jackbyrne. **Contact:** Jack Byrne. Estab. 1950s. Member of SFWA, MWA. Represents 30 clients. 10% of clients are new/unpublished writers. Accepting few new clients. Currently handles: 5% nonfiction books; 85% novels; 10% juvenile books.

Member Agents: Jack Byrne.

Represents: Nonfiction books, novels, juvenile books. **Considers these fiction areas:** Fantasy; horror; mystery/suspense; science fiction.

> ○━ "Our client list is comfortably full and our current needs are therefore quite limited." Actively seeking science fiction/fantasy by established writers. Does not want to receive romance, poetry, textbooks, highly specialized nonfiction.

How to Contact: Query with SASE. Accepts e-mail queries, no attachments. Responds in 3 weeks to queries; 3 months to mss. Returns materials only with SASE.

Recent Sales: Sold 16 titles in the last year. *Orphans of Chaos*, by John C. Wright; *Dead River's Hoarde*, by Naomi Kritzer. Other clients include Jane Routley, Gerard Hourner, Betty Ren Wright, and Andre Norton.

Terms: Agent receives 15% commission on domestic sales; 20% commission on foreign sales. Offers written contract; 2-month notice must be given to terminate contract.

Tips: "Don't send first drafts; have a professional presentation—including cover letter; know your field. Read what's been done—good and bad."

STIMOLA LITERARY STUDIO

308 Chase Court, Edgewater NJ 07020. Phone/fax: (201)945-9353. E-mail: LtryStudio@aol.com. **Contact:** Rosemary B. Stimola. Member of AAR.

Member Agents: Rosemary B. Stimola.

Represents: Preschool through young adult fiction/nonfiction.

How to Contact: Query with SASE, or via e-mail. Responds in 3 weeks to queries; 2 months to mss. Obtains most new clients through recommendations from others, solicitations.

Recent Sales: *Gregor the Overlander*, by Suzanne Collins; *Beacon Hill Boys*, by Ken Mochizuki; *Johnny Mutton, He's So Him!*, by James Proimos.

Terms: Agent receives 15% commission on domestic sales; 20% commission on foreign sales. Offers written contract, binding for 1 year. Covers all children's literary work not previously published or under agreement.

Tips: "No phone inquiries."

⬛ ⊘ PAM STRICKLER AUTHOR MANAGEMENT

2760 Lucas Turnpike, P.O. Box 429, Accord NY 12404. (845)687-0186. **Contact:** Pamela Dean Strickler. Member of AAR.

> • Query before submitting.

⊕ ⊘ THE SUSIJN AGENCY

3rd Floor, 64 Great Titchfield St., London W1W 7QH, England. 0044 (207)580-6341. Fax: 0044 (207)580-8626. E-mail: info@thesusijnagency.com. Website: www.thesusijnagency.com. **Contact:** Laura Susijn, Charles Buchau. Estab. 1998. Currently handles: 15% nonfiction books; 85% novels.

> • Prior to becoming an agent, Ms. Susijn was a rights director at Sheil Land Associates and at Fourth Estate, Ltd.

Member Agents: Laura Susijn.

Represents: Nonfiction books, novels. **Considers these nonfiction areas:** Biography/autobiography; memoirs; multicultural; popular culture; science/technology; travel. **Considers these fiction areas:** Literary.

> ○━ This agency specializes in international works, selling world rights, representing non-English language writing as well as English. Emphasis on cross-cultural subjects. Does not want self-help, romance, sagas, science fiction, screenplays.

How to Contact: Submit outline, 2 sample chapter(s). Accepts e-mail and fax queries. Considers simultaneous queries. Responds in 2 months to queries. Returns materials only with SASE. Obtains most new clients through recommendations from others, via publishers in Europe and beyond.

Recent Sales: Sold 120 titles in the last year. *Trespassing*, by Uzma Aslam Khan (Flamingo UK); *Gone*, by Helena Echlin (Secker and Warburg, UK); *Daalder*, by Philibert Schogt (4 Walls 8 Windows); *The Memory Artists*, by Jeffrey Moore (Weidenfeld & Nicholson) *Smell*, by Radhika Jha (Quartet Books); *The Formula One Fanatic*, by Koen Vergeer (Bloomsbury); *A Mouthful of Glass*, by Henk Van Woerden (Granta); *Fragile Science*, by Robin Baker (Macmillan); *East of Acre Lane*, by Alex Wheatle (Fourth Estate). Other clients include Vassallucci, Podium, Atlas, De Arbeiderspers, Tiderne Skifter, MB Agency, Van Oorschot

Terms: Agent receives 15% commission on domestic sales; 15-20% commission on foreign sales. Offers written contract; 6 weeks notice must be given to terminate contract. Charges clients for photocopying, buying copies only if sale is made.

ROSLYN TARG LITERARY AGENCY, INC.

105 W. 13th St., New York NY 10011. (212)206-9390. Fax: (212)989-6233. E-mail: roslyntarg@aol.com. **Contact:** Roslyn Targ. Estab. 1945. Member of AAR. Represents 100 clients.

Member Agents: Roslyn Targ.

How to Contact: Query with SASE, outline/proposal, curriculum vitae. Prefers to read materials exclusively. No mss without query first. Obtains most new clients through recommendations from others, solicitations.

Terms: Agent receives 15% commission on domestic sales; 20% commission on foreign sales. Charges standard agency fees (bank charges, long distance, postage, photocopying, shipping of books, overseas long distance and shipping, etc.).

Tips: "This agency reads on an exclusive basis only."

PATRICIA TEAL LITERARY AGENCY

2036 Vista Del Rosa, Fullerton CA 92831-1336. Phone/fax: (714)738-8333. **Contact:** Patricia Teal. Estab. 1978. Member of AAR. Represents 20 clients. 10% of clients are new/unpublished writers. Currently handles: 10% nonfiction books; 90% novels.

Represents: Nonfiction books, novels. **Considers these nonfiction areas:** Animals; biography/autobiography; child guidance/parenting; health/medicine; how-to; psychology; self-help/personal improvement; true crime/investigative; women's issues/studies. **Considers these fiction areas:** Glitz; mainstream/contemporary; mystery/suspense; romance (contemporary, historical).

> O— This agency specializes in women's fiction and commercial how-to and self-help nonfiction. Does not want to receive poetry, short stories, articles, science fiction, fantasy, regency romance.

How to Contact: *Published authors only.* Query with SASE. No e-mail or fax queries. Considers simultaneous queries. Responds in 10 days to queries; 6 weeks to mss. Returns materials only with SASE. Obtains most new clients through conferences, recommendations from authors and editors.

Recent Sales: Sold 20 titles in the last year. *Texas Rose*, by Marie Ferrarella (Silhouette); *Watch Your Language*, by Sterling Johnson (St. Martin's); *The Black Sheep's Baby*, by Kathleen Creighton (Silhouette); *Man with a Message*, by Muriel Jensen (Harlequin).

Terms: Agent receives 10-15% commission on domestic sales; 20% commission on foreign sales. Offers written contract, binding for 1 year. Charges clients for postage and phone calls.

Writers' Conferences: Romance Writers of America conferences; Asilomar (California Writers Club); BEA; Bouchercon; Hawaii Writers Conference (Maui).

Tips: "Include SASE with all correspondence. Taking on very few authors."

THOTH LITERARY AGENCY

P.O. Box 620277, Littleton CO 80162-0277. (720)351-9551. Fax: (303)978-1461. E-mail: medulla@sprintmail.com. Website: www.hawaiianhulahips.com/thothliteraryagency/. **Contact:** Manulani Thelen. Estab. 2003. Represents 2 clients. 100% of clients are new/unpublished writers. Currently handles: 50% (YA) novels; 50% crafts/hobbies.

> • Prior to becoming an agent, Manulani Thelen has been the artistic director of a 501(c)(3) nonprofit for 33 years. Thelen is also a composer, curriculum developer, educator, and professor of ethnology.

Member Agents: Monica Lanie (cooking, crafts, animals, YA, theater/film, fantasy); Manulani Thelen (ethnic, juvenile, YA, music/dance, picture book).

Represents: Nonfiction books, novels, novellas, juvenile books. **Considers these nonfiction areas:** Animals; cooking/foods/nutrition; ethnic/cultural interests; music/dance; crafts/hobbies, juvenile nonfiction. **Considers these fiction areas:** Ethnic; fantasy; juvenile; young adult.

> O— "We provide honest, customized feedback at no cost, not merely a vague note of rejection. We never charge reading or publisher search fees. Although we are not yet members of AAR, we abide by their Canon of Ethics." Actively seeking "well-written works in the areas of fiction (adventure, ethnic, fantasy, juvenile, picture book, young adult) and nonfiction (animals, cooking/food, crafts/hobbies, ethnic/cultural interests, juvenile nonfiction, music/dance/theater/film). Does not want to receive poetry, romance, screenplays, self-help, westerns, science fiction, or detective/crime.

How to Contact: Query with SASE, submit synopsis, 3 sample chapter(s), SASE. No e-mail or fax queries. Considers simultaneous queries. Responds in 3 weeks to queries; 6 weeks to mss. Returns materials only with SASE. Obtains most new clients through "We obtain prospective clients by word of mouth and our website."

Terms: Agent receives 10% commission on domestic sales; 15% commission on foreign sales. Offers written contract, binding for 2 years; 6-months notice must be given to terminate contract.

Writers' Conferences: Highlights Foundation Writers Workshop (Chautauqua NY, July).

Tips: "We are not interested in receiving porrly written submissions from authors with grandiose attitudes; don't compare yourself to Jane Austen, J.R.R. Tolkien, etc. Blackmail never works—don't tell us that you'll only send your manuscript to us if we can guarantee you will be published. Please always send a SASE or else we won't be able to contact you. Write stories that make sense; research everything down to the bone. Most importantly, be proud of your work; no self-deprecation."

3 SEAS LITERARY AGENCY

P.O. Box 7038, Madison WI 53708. (608)221-4306. E-mail: threeseaslit@aol.com. Website: www.threeseaslit.c om. **Contact:** Michelle Grajkowski. Estab. 2000. Member of Romance Writers of America. Represents 40 clients. 50% of clients are new/unpublished writers. Currently handles: 30% nonfiction books; 60% novels; 10% juvenile books.

- Prior to becoming an agent, Ms. Grajkowski worked in both sales and in purchasing for a medical facility. She has a degree in journalism from the University of Wisconsin-Madison.

Represents: Nonfiction books, novels, juvenile books, scholarly books.

- 3 Seas focuses on romance (including category, historicals, regencies, westerns, romantic suspense, paranormal), women's fiction, mysteries, nonfiction, young adult and children's stories. Does not want to receive poetry, screenplays, or short stories.

How to Contact: For fiction, please query with first 3 chapters, a synopsis, your bio, and SASE. For nonfiction, please query with your complete proposal, first 3 chapters, number of words, a bio, and SASE. Considers simultaneous queries. Responds in 1 month to queries; 3 months to mss. Returns materials only with SASE. Obtains most new clients through recommendations from others, conferences.

Recent Sales: Sold 40 titles in the last year. *Men in Kilts*, by Katie MacAlister; *Sarah's Legacy*, by Brenda Mott; *Admiral's Daughter*, by Sandra Madden. Other clients include Marshall Cook, Winnie Griggs, Diane Amos, Ellen Browning, Lisa Mondello, Natalie Damschroder, Juliet Blackett, Jessica Barkley, Chris deSmet, Donna Smith, Kaz Daley, Pat Pritchard, Barbara Jean Hicks, Alesia Holliday, Winnie Griggs, Stephanie Rowe, Carrie Weaver.

Terms: Agent receives 15% commission on domestic sales; 20% commission on foreign sales. Offers written contract, binding for 1 month.

Writers' Conferences: RWA National Conference (July); Smoky Mountain Romance Writers (April); Oklahoma RWA (June).

ANN TOBIAS—A LITERARY AGENCY FOR CHILDREN'S BOOKS, (Specialized: children's books)

520 E. 84th St., Apt. 4L, New York NY 10028. **Contact:** Ann Tobias. Estab. 1988. Represents 25 clients. 50% of clients are new/unpublished writers. Currently handles: 100% juvenile books.

- Prior to opening her agency, Ms. Tobias worked as a children's book editor at Harper, William Morrow, Scholastic.

Represents: Juvenile books. **Considers these nonfiction areas:** Juvenile nonfiction; young adult. **Considers these fiction areas:** Picture books; poetry (for children); young adult; illustrated mss; mid-level novels.

- This agency specializes in books for children. Actively seeking material for children.

How to Contact: Send entire ms for picture books; 30 pages and synopsis for longer work, both fiction and nonfiction. No phone queries. All queries must be in writing and accompanied by a SASE. No e-mail or fax queries. Considers simultaneous queries. Responds in 2 months to mss. Returns materials only with SASE. Obtains most new clients through recommendations from editors.

Recent Sales: Sold 23 titles in the last year. This agency prefers not to share information on specific sales.

Terms: Agent receives 15% commission on domestic sales; 20% commission on foreign sales. No written contract. Charges clients for photocopying, overnight mail, foreign postage, foreign telephone.

Reading List: Reads *Horn Book, Bulletin for the Center of the Book* and *School Library Journal.* "These are review media and they keep me up to date on who is being published and by what company."

Tips: "Read at least 200 children's books in the age group and genre in which you hope to be published. Follow this by reading another 100 children's books in other age groups and genres so you will have a feel for the field as a whole."

LYNDA TOLLS LITERARY AGENCY

P.O. Box 1785, Bend OR 97709. (541)388-3510. Fax: (541)388-3510. E-mail: blswarts@juno.com. **Contact:** Lynda Tolls Swarts. Estab. 1995. Represents 8 clients. 20% of clients are new/unpublished writers. Currently handles: 90% nonfiction books; 10% novels.

Represents: Nonfiction books, novels. **Considers these nonfiction areas:** Biography/autobiography; education; ethnic/cultural interests (cultural, global interests); health/medicine; history; popular culture; self-help/personal improvement; travel; religious; current affairs; investigative. **Considers these fiction areas:** Ethnic (multicultural); historical; literary; mystery/suspense; contemporary; women's.

How to Contact: Query with SASE, Nonfiction, send query including the concept of your book, market, competing titles, and your expertise. Fiction, query with synopsis and first 10 pages.

Writers' Conferences: Willamette Writers' Conference; Surrey Writers' Conference; Idaho Writers' Conference.

S©OTT TREIMEL, NY

434 Lafayette St., New York NY 10003. (212)505-8353. Fax: (212)505-0664. E-mail: st.ny@verizon.net. Estab. 1995. Member of AAR, Authors Guild. Represents 38 clients. 15% of clients are new/unpublished writers. Currently handles: 100% juvenile books.

- Prior to becoming an agent, Mr. Treimel was an assistant at Curtis Brown, Ltd. (for Marilyn E. Marlow); a rights agent for Scholastic, Inc; a book packager and rights agent for United Feature Syndicate; a freelance editor, a rights consultant for HarperCollins Children's Books; and the founding director of Warner Bros. Worldwide Publishing.

Represents: Children's book authors and illustrators.

- This agency specializes in tightly focused segments of the trade and institutional markets. Interested in seeing author-illustrators, first chapter books, middle-grade and teen fiction. Does not consider activity or coloring books.

How to Contact: Two complete picture books may be submitted. For longer work, query with SASE and sample chapters. No multiple submissions. No fax queries.

Recent Sales: Sold 19 titles in the last year. *Playing in Traffic*, by Gail Giles (Roaring Brook Press); *Papa, Do You Love Me?*, by Barbara Joosse (Chronicle Books).

Terms: Agent receives 15-20% commission on domestic sales; 20-25% commission on foreign sales. Offers verbal or written contract, "binding on a book, contract-by-contract basis." Charges clients for photocopying, express postage, messengers, and books ordered to sell foreign, film, etc. rights.

Writers' Conferences: Can You Make a Living from Children's Books, Society of Children's Book Writers & Illustrators (Los Angeles, August); "Understanding Book Contracts," SCBWI (Watertown NY); "Creating Believable Teen Characters," SCBWI; Picture Book Judge for Tassie Walden Award; New Voices in Children's Literature; "Craft" SCBWI (North Carolina); "Understanding Book Contracts" SCBWI (North Dakota); The New School; The Professionals Panel; SouthWest Writers Workshop; Pike's Peak Writers Association.

Tips: "Keep cover letters short and do not pitch. Manuscripts and illustration smaples received without a SASE are recycled on receipt."

2M COMMUNICATIONS, LTD.

121 W. 27 St., #601, New York NY 10001. (212)741-1509. Fax: (212)691-4460. E-mail: morel@bookhaven.com. Website: www.2mcommunications.com. **Contact:** Madeleine Morel. Estab. 1982. Represents 50 clients. 20% of clients are new/unpublished writers. Currently handles: 100% nonfiction books.

- Prior to becoming an agent, Ms. Morel worked at a publishing company.

Represents: Nonfiction books. **Considers these nonfiction areas:** Biography/autobiography; child guidance/parenting; ethnic/cultural interests; health/medicine; history; self-help/personal improvement; women's issues/studies; music; cookbooks.

- This agency specializes in adult nonfiction.

How to Contact: Query with SASE, submit outline, 3 sample chapter(s). Considers simultaneous queries. Responds in 1 week to queries; 1 month to mss. Obtains most new clients through recommendations from others, solicitations.

Recent Sales: Sold 25 titles in the last year. *How Do You Compare?*, by Andy Williams (Penguin Putnam); *Hormone Wisdom*, by Theresa Dale (John Wiley); *Irish Dessert Cookbook*, by Margaret Johnson (Chronicle).

Terms: Agent receives 15% commission on domestic sales; 20% commission on foreign sales. Offers written contract, binding for 2 years. Charges clients for postage, photocopying, long-distance calls, faxes.

UNITED TRIBES MEDIA, INC.

240 W. 35th St., Suite 500, New York NY 10001. (212)534-7646. E-mail: janguerth@aol.com. **Contact:** Jan-Erik Guerth. Estab. 1998. Currently handles: 100% nonfiction books.

- Prior to becoming an agent, Mr. Guerth was a comedian, journalist, radio producer, and film distributor.

Represents: Nonfiction books. **Considers these nonfiction areas:** Anthropology/archaeology; art/architecture/design; biography/autobiography; business/economics; child guidance/parenting; cooking/foods/nutrition; current affairs; education; ethnic/cultural interests; gay/lesbian issues; government/politics/law; health/medicine; history; how-to; language/literature/criticism; memoirs; money/finance; music/dance; nature/environment; popular culture; psychology; religious/inspirational; science/technology (popular); self-help/personal improvement; sociology; theater/film; translation; women's issues/studies.

O➤ This agency represents serious nonfiction; and ethnic, social, gender, and cultural issues, comparative religions, self-help, spirituality and wellness, science and arts, history and politics, nature and travel, and any fascinating future trends.

How to Contact: Submit outline, résumé, SASE. Agent prefers email queries. Considers simultaneous queries. Responds in 1 month to queries. Returns materials only with SASE. Obtains most new clients through recommendations from others, solicitations, conferences.

Recent Sales: *Squatting in the City of Tomorrow*, by Robert Neuwirth (Routledge); *The Green Desert*, by Rita Winters (Wildcat Canyon Press); *Into the Melting Pot*, by James McWilliams (Columbia University Press).

Terms: Agent receives 15% commission on domestic sales; 20% commission on foreign sales.

⊘ THE RICHARD R. VALCOURT AGENCY, INC.

177 E. 77th St., PHC, New York NY 10021-1934. Phone/fax: (212)570-2340. **Contact:** Richard R. Valcourt, president. Estab. 1995. Represents 25 clients. 20% of clients are new/unpublished writers. Currently handles: 100% nonfiction books.

● Not accepting new clients at this time. Prior to opening his agency, Mr. Valcourt was a journalist, editor and college political science instructor. He is also editor-in-chief of the International Journal of Intelligence and faculty member at American Military University in Virginia.

Represents: Scholarly books.

O➤ This agency specializes in intelligence and other national security affairs. Represents exclusively academics, journalists and professionals in the categories listed.

How to Contact: Query with SASE. Prefers to read materials exclusively. No e-mail or fax queries. Responds in 1 week to queries; 1 month to mss. Returns materials only with SASE. Obtains most new clients through recommendations from others.

Terms: Agent receives 15% commission on domestic sales; 20% commission on foreign sales. Offers written contract. Charges clients for excessive photocopying, express mail, overseas telephone expenses.

Ⓝ ◪ VAN DER LEUN & ASSOCIATES

61 W. 9th St., PH-B, New York NY 10011. (212)477-2033. Website: www.publishersmarketplace.com/pvanderleun. **Contact:** Patricia Van der Leun, president. Estab. 1984. Represents 30 clients. Currently handles: 75% nonfiction books; 25% novels.

● Prior to becoming an agent, Ms. Van der Leun was a professor of Art History.

Represents: Nonfiction books, novels, illustrated books. **Considers these nonfiction areas:** Art/architecture/design (art history); biography/autobiography; cooking/foods/nutrition (food and wine, cookbooks); creative nonfiction; current affairs; ethnic/cultural interests; gardening; history; memoirs; religious/inspirational; spirituality; sports; travel. **Considers these fiction areas:** Comic books/cartoon; contemporary issues; humor/satire; literary; mainstream/contemporary; multicultural; multimedia; picture books; short story collections; translation; women's.

O➤ This agency specializes in fiction, art history, food and wine, gardening, biography.

How to Contact: Query with letter only, include author bio and SASE. Considers simultaneous queries. Responds in 2 weeks to queries.

Recent Sales: Sold 15 titles in the last year. *Bobbi Brown Beauty Evolution*, by Bobbi Brown (Harper-Collins); *Gone to the Country: Life and Art in the Hamptons*, by Robert Long (Farrar, Straus & Giroux); *The Astronomy Encyclopedia*, by David Darling (John Wiley & Sons).

Terms: Agent receives 15% commission on domestic sales; 25% commission on foreign sales. Offers written contract. Charges clients for postage and photocopying of ms.

◪ VENTURE LITERARY

8895 Towne Centre Dr., Suite 105, #141, San Diego CA 92122. (619)807-1887. E-mail: agents@ventureliterary.com. Website: www.ventureliterary.com. **Contact:** Frank R. Scatoni. Estab. 1999. Represents 30 clients. 50% of clients are new/unpublished writers. Currently handles: 95% nonfiction books; 5% novels.

● Prior to becoming an agent, Mr. Scatoni worked as an editor at Simon & Schuster.

Member Agents: Frank R. Scatoni (general nonfiction, including biography, memoir, narrative nonfiction, sports and serious nonfiction); Greg Dinkin (general nonfiction/business, gambling).

Represents: Nonfiction books, novels. **Considers these nonfiction areas:** Animals; anthropology/archaeology; biography/autobiography; business/economics; current affairs; ethnic/cultural interests; government/politics/law; history; memoirs; military/war; money/finance; multicultural; music/dance; nature/environment; popular culture; psychology; science/technology; sports; true crime/investigative; gambling. **Considers these fiction**

areas: Action/adventure; detective/police/crime; literary; mainstream/contemporary; mystery/suspense; sports; thriller.

    ○→ Specializes in nonfiction, sports, business, natural history, biography, gambling. Actively seeking nonfiction.

How to Contact: Considers e-mail queries only. *No unsolicited mss.* Responds in 3-6 months to queries; 6 months to mss. Returns materials only with SASE. Obtains most new clients through recommendations from others.

Recent Sales: *The Miracl of St. Anthony*, by Adrian Wojnarowski (Gotham); *Damn Yankees, Damned Sox*, by Mike Vaccaro (Doubleday); *The Promise*, by Oral Lee Brown (Doubleday); *Powerful Mate Syndrome*, by Angela Wilder (St. Martin's Press); *Payne At Pinehurst*, by Bill Chastain (Thomas Dunne Books); *Being Bill Gates*, by Bob Sullivan (Wiley); *Launching the Legend*, by Jim Reisler (McGraw-Hill).

Terms: Agent receives 15% commission on domestic sales; 20% commission on foreign sales. Offers written contract.

Writers' Conferences: San Diego State University Writers Conference (San Diego CA); Southern California Writers Conference (Los Angeles and San Diego).

N ◙ RALPH VICINANZA, LTD.

303 W. 18th St., New York NY 10011. (212)924-7090. Fax: (212)691-9644. Member of AAR. Represents 120 clients. 5% of clients are new/unpublished writers.

    ● Query before submitting.

Member Agents: Ralph M. Vicinanza, Chris Lotts, Chris Schelling.

Represents: Nonfiction books, novels. **Considers these nonfiction areas:** Biography/autobiography; business/economics; history; popular culture; religious/inspirational; science/technology. **Considers these fiction areas:** Fantasy; literary; mainstream/contemporary (popular fiction); multicultural; science fiction; thriller; women's.

    ○→ This agency specializes in foreign rights.

How to Contact: Agency takes on new clients by professional recommendation only.

Recent Sales: This agency prefers not to share information on specific sales.

Terms: Agent receives 15% commission on domestic sales; 20% commission on foreign sales.

N ◙ DAVID VIGLIANO LITERARY AGENCY

584 Broadway, Suite 809, New York NY 10012. (212)226-7800. Fax: (212)226-5508. Member of AAR.

    ● This agency did not respond to our request for information. Query before submitting.

Member Agents: Donna Bagdasarian, Michael Harriot.

◙ THE VINES AGENCY, INC.

648 Broadway, Suite 901, New York NY 10012. (212)777-5522. Fax: (212)777-5978. E-mail: jv@vinesagency.com. Website: www.vinesagency.com. **Contact:** James C. Vines, Ali Ryan, Gary Neuwirth, Alexis Caldwell. Estab. 1995. Signatory of WGA; Author's Guild. Represents 52 clients. 20% of clients are new/unpublished writers. Currently handles: 50% nonfiction books; 50% novels.

    ● Prior to opening his agency, Mr. Vines served as an agent with the Virginia Barber Literary Agency.

Member Agents: James C. Vines (quality and commercial fiction and nonfiction); Gary Neuwirth; Alexis Caldwell (women's fiction, ethnic fiction, quality nonfiction); Ali Ryan (women's fiction and nonfiction, mainstream).

Represents: Nonfiction books, novels, feature film. **Considers these nonfiction areas:** Biography/autobiography; business/economics; current affairs; ethnic/cultural interests; history; how-to; humor/satire; memoirs; military/war; money/finance; nature/environment; New Age/metaphysics; photography; popular culture; psychology; religious/inspirational; science/technology; self-help/personal improvement; sociology; spirituality; sports; translation; travel; true crime/investigative; women's issues/studies. **Considers these fiction areas:** Action/adventure; contemporary issues; detective/police/crime; ethnic; experimental; family saga; feminist; gay/lesbian; historical; horror; humor/satire; literary; mainstream/contemporary; mystery/suspense; occult; psychic/supernatural; regional; romance (contemporary, historical); science fiction; sports; thriller; westerns/frontier; women's. **Considers these script subject areas:** Action/adventure; comedy; detective/police/crime; ethnic; experimental; feminist; gay/lesbian; historical; horror; mainstream; mystery/suspense; romantic comedy; romantic drama; science fiction; teen; thriller; western/frontier.

    ○→ This agency specializes in mystery, suspense, science fiction, women's fiction, ethnic fiction, mainstream novels, screenplays, teleplays.

How to Contact: Submit outline, 3 sample chapter(s), SASE. Accepts e-mail and fax queries. Considers simultaneous queries. Responds in 2 weeks to queries; 1 month to mss. Returns materials only with SASE. Obtains most new clients through query letters, recommendations from others, reading short stories in magazines, soliciting conferences.

Recent Sales: Sold 48 titles and sold 5 scripts in the last year. *Sunset and Sawdust*, by Joe R. Lansdale; *Camilla's Rose*, by Bernice McFadden; *Ecstasy*, by Beth Saulnier.

Terms: Agent receives 15% commission on domestic sales; 25% commission on foreign sales. Offers written contract, binding for 1 year; 1-month notice must be given to terminate contract. 100% of business is derived from commissions on ms sales. Charges clients for foreign postage, messenger services, photocopying.

Writers' Conferences: Maui Writer's Conference.

Tips: "Do not follow up on submissions with phone calls to the agency. The agency will read and respond by mail only. Do not pack your manuscript in plastic 'peanuts' that will make us have to vacuum the office after opening the package containing your manuscript. Always enclose return postage."

☑ MARY JACK WALD ASSOCIATES, INC.

111 E. 14th St., New York NY 10003. (212)254-7842. **Contact:** Danis Sher. Estab. 1985. Member of AAR, Authors' Guild, SCBWI. Represents 35 clients. 5% of clients are new/unpublished writers. Currently handles: nonfiction books; novels; story collections; novellas; juvenile books.

• This agency is not accepting mss at this time.

Member Agents: Mary Jack Wald, Danis Sher, Lynne Rabinoff Agency (association who represents foreign rights), Alvin Wald.

Represents: Nonfiction books, novels, short story collections, novellas, juvenile books, movie and TV scripts by our authors. **Considers these nonfiction areas:** Biography/autobiography; current affairs; ethnic/cultural interests; history; juvenile nonfiction; language/literature/criticism; music/dance; nature/environment; photography; sociology; theater/film; translation; true crime/investigative. **Considers these fiction areas:** Action/adventure; contemporary issues; detective/police/crime; ethnic; experimental; family saga; feminist; gay/lesbian; glitz; historical; juvenile; literary; mainstream/contemporary; mystery/suspense; picture books; thriller; young adult; satire.

○━ This agency specializes in literary works, juvenile.

How to Contact: Not accepting new clients at this time.

Recent Sales: *The Secret of Castle Cant*, by K.P. Bath; *Summer at Ma Dean's House*, by Denise Lewis Patnick.

Terms: Agent receives 15% commission on domestic sales; 15-30% commission on foreign sales. Offers written contract, binding for 1 year.

☑ WALES LITERARY AGENCY, INC.

P.O. Box 9428, Seattle WA 98109-0428. (206)284-7114. E-mail: waleslit@waleslit.com. Website: www.waleslit. com. **Contact:** Elizabeth Wales, Meg Lemke. Estab. 1988. Member of AAR, Book Publishers' Northwest, Pacific Northwest Booksellers Association, PEN. Represents 65 clients. 10% of clients are new/unpublished writers. Currently handles: 60% nonfiction books; 40% fiction.

• Prior to becoming an agent, Ms. Wales worked at Oxford University Press and Viking Penguin.

Member Agents: Elizabeth Wales, Adrienne Reed.

○━ This agency specializes in narrative nonfiction, and quality, mainstream and literary fiction. Does not handle screenplays, children's literature, genre fiction, most category nonfiction.

How to Contact: Query with cover letter, writing sample (approx. 30 pages), and SASE. No phone or fax queries. Prefers regular mail queries, but accepts 1-page e-mail queries with no attachments. Considers simultaneous queries. Responds in 3 weeks to queries; 6 weeks to mss. Returns materials only with SASE.

Recent Sales: *Michelangelo's Mountains*, by Eric Scigliano (Simon & Schuster); *In Praise of Small Things*, by Lynda Lynn Haupt (Little, Brown & Co.); *Against Gravity*, by Farnoosh Moshini (Penguin).

Terms: Agent receives 15% commission on domestic sales; 20% commission on foreign sales.

Writers' Conferences: Pacific NW Writers Conference (Seattle); Writers at Work (Salt Lake City); Writing Rendezvous (Anchorage); Willamette Writers (Portland).

Tips: "Especially interested in work that espouses a progressive cultural or political view, projects a new voice, or simply shares an important, compelling story. Encourages writers living in the Pacific Northwest, West Coast, Alaska, and Pacific Rim countries, and writers from historically underrepresented groups, such as gay and lesbian writers and writers of color, to submit work (but does not discourage writers outside these areas). Most importantly, whether in fiction or nonfiction, the agency is looking for talented storytellers."

☑ JOHN A. WARE LITERARY AGENCY

392 Central Park West, New York NY 10025-5801. (212)866-4733. Fax: (212)866-4734. **Contact:** John Ware. Estab. 1978. Represents 60 clients. 40% of clients are new/unpublished writers. Currently handles: 75% nonfiction books; 25% novels.

• Prior to opening his agency, Mr. Ware served as a literary agency with James Brown Associates/Curtis Brown, Ltd., and as an editor for Doubleday & Co.

Represents: Nonfiction books, novels. **Considers these nonfiction areas:** Anthropology/archaeology; biography/autobiography; current affairs; health/medicine (academic credentials reqired); history (including oral history, Americana and folklore); language/literature/criticism; music/dance; nature/environment; popular culture; psychology (academic credentials reqired); science/technology; sports; travel; true crime/investigative; women's issues/studies; social commentary; investigative journalism; 'bird's eye' views of phenomena. **Considers these fiction areas:** Detective/police/crime; mystery/suspense; thriller; accessible literate noncategory fiction.

How to Contact: Query first by letter only, including SASE. No e-mail or fax queries. Considers simultaneous queries Responds in 2 weeks to queries.

Recent Sales: *The Family Business: The McIlhenny/Tobasco Story*, by Jeffrey Rothfeder (HarperCollins); *Sarah's Quilt*, by Nancy Turner (Thomas Dunne/St. Martin's); *The Butterfly Hunter: Finding a Calling*, by Chris Ballard (Broadway Books); *A History of Sunday*, by Craig Harline (Doubleday).

Terms: Agent receives 15% commission on domestic sales; 20% commission on foreign sales; 15% commission on dramatic rights sales. Charges clients for messenger service, photocopying.

Tips: "Writers must have appropriate credentials for authorship of proposal (nonfiction) or manuscript (fiction); no publishing track record required. Open to good writing and interesting ideas by new or veteran writers."

▣ ⬚ HARRIET WASSERMAN LITERARY AGENCY

137 E. 36th St., New York NY 10016. (212)689-3257. **Contact:** Harriet Wasserman. Member of AAR.
● This agency did not respond to our request for information. Query before submitting.

⬚ WATERSIDE PRODUCTIONS, INC.

2187 Newcastle Ave., # 204, Cardiff-by-the-Sea CA 92007. (760)632-9190. Fax: (760)632-9295. Website: www.waterside.com. **Contact:** Matt Wagner, Margot Maley, David Fugate. President: Bill Gladstone. Estab. 1982. Represents 300 clients. 20% of clients are new/unpublished writers. Currently handles: 100% nonfiction books.

Member Agents: Bill Gladstone (trade computer titles, business); Margot Maley Hutchison (trade computer titles, nonfiction); Matthew Wagner (trade computer titles, nonfiction); Carole McClendon (trade computer titles); David Fugate (trade computer titles, business, general nonfiction, sports books); Christian Crumlish (trade computer titles); Danielle Jatlow, Neil Gudovitz, Jawahara K. Saidullah, Kimberly Valentini, William E. Brown, Craig Wiley.

Represents: Nonfiction books. **Considers these nonfiction areas:** Art/architecture/design; biography/autobiography; business/economics; child guidance/parenting; computers/electronic; ethnic/cultural interests; health/medicine; humor/satire; money/finance; nature/environment; popular culture; psychology; sociology; sports.

How to Contact: Prefers to read materials exclusively. Query via online form. See website for more information. Considers simultaneous queries. Responds in 2 weeks to queries; 2 months to mss. Obtains most new clients through recommendations from others.

Recent Sales: Sold 300 titles in the last year. *Dan Gookin's Naked Windows*, by Dan Gookin (Sybex); *Battlebots: The Official Guide*, by Mark Clarkson (Osborne McGraw-Hill); *Opening the XBox: Inside Microsoft's Effort to Unleash an Entertainment Revolution*, by Dean Takahashi (Prima); *Just for Fun*, by Linus Torvalds and David Diamond (Harper Collins).

Terms: Agent receives 15% commission on domestic sales; 25% commission on foreign sales. Offers written contract. Charges clients for photocopying and other unusual expenses.

Writers' Conferences: "We host the Waterside Publishing Conference each spring. Please check our website for details."

Tips: "For new writers, a quality proposal and a strong knowledge of the market you're writing for goes a long way toward helping us turn you into a published author."

⬚ WATKINS LOOMIS AGENCY, INC.

133 E. 35th St., Suite 1, New York NY 10016. (212)532-0080. Fax: (212)889-0506. **Contact:** Katherine Fausset. Estab. 1908. Represents 150 clients.

Member Agents: Gloria Loomis (president); Katherine Fausset (agent).

Represents: Nonfiction books, novels, short story collections. **Considers these nonfiction areas:** Art/architecture/design; biography/autobiography; current affairs; ethnic/cultural interests; history; nature/environment; popular culture; science/technology; true crime/investigative; journalism. **Considers these fiction areas:** Literary.
� This agency specializes in literary fiction, nonfiction.

How to Contact: Query with SASE, by standard mail only. Responds in 1 month to queries.

Recent Sales: This agency prefers not to share information on specific sales. Clients include Walter Mosley and Cornel West.

Terms: Agent receives 15% commission on domestic sales; 20% commission on foreign sales.

◪ WAXMAN LITERARY AGENCY, INC.

1650 Broadway, Suite 1011, New York NY 10019. Website: www.waxmanagency.com. Estab. 1997. Represents 60 clients. 50% of clients are new/unpublished writers. Currently handles: 60% nonfiction books; 40% novels.
- Prior to opening his agency, Mr. Waxman was editor for five years at HarperCollins.

Member Agents: Scott Waxman (all categories of nonfiction, commercial fiction). **Considers these nonfiction areas:** Narrative nonfiction. **Considers these fiction areas:** Literary.

○━ "Looking for serious journalists and novelists with published works."

How to Contact: Query through website. All unsolicited mss returned unopened. Considers simultaneous queries. Responds in 2 weeks to queries; 6 weeks to mss. Returns materials only with SASE. Obtains most new clients through recommendations from others, solicitations, conferences.

Terms: Agent receives 15% commission on domestic sales; 25% commission on foreign sales. Offers written contract; 2-month notice must be given to terminate contract. Charges for photocopying, express mail, fax, international postage, book orders. Refers to editing services for clients only. 0% of business is derived from editing services.

◪ WECKSLER-INCOMCO

170 West End Ave., New York NY 10023. (212)787-2239. Fax: (212)496-7035. **Contact:** Sally Wecksler. Estab. 1971. Represents 25 clients. 40% of clients are new/unpublished writers. Currently handles: 60% nonfiction books; 15% novels; 25% juvenile books.
- Prior to becoming an agent, Ms. Wecksler was an editor at *Publishers Weekly*; publisher with the international department of R.R. Bowker; and international director at Baker & Taylor.

Member Agents: Joann Amparan-Close (general, children's books); Sally Wecksler (general, foreign rights/co-editions, fiction, illustrated books, children's books, business).

Represents: Nonfiction books, novels, juvenile books. **Considers these nonfiction areas:** Art/architecture/design; biography/autobiography; business/economics; creative nonfiction; current affairs; history; juvenile nonfiction; music/dance; nature/environment; photography; theater/film. **Considers these fiction areas:** Contemporary issues; historical; juvenile; literary; mainstream/contemporary; picture books.

○━ This agency specializes in nonfiction with illustrations (photos and art). Actively seeking "illustrated books for adults or children with beautiful photos or artwork." Does not want to receive "science fiction or books with violence."

How to Contact: Query with SASE, outline, author bio. Responds in 1 month to queries; 2 months to mss. Obtains most new clients through recommendations from others, solicitations.

Recent Sales: Sold 11 titles in the last year. *Bio of Billy Taylor*, by Bill Lee (Hal Edward, Inc.); *What Every Successful Woman Knows*, by William J. Morin (McGraw-Hill); *Total Career Fitness* (Jossey-Bass).

Terms: Agent receives 15% commission on domestic sales; 20% commission on foreign sales. Offers written contract, binding for 3 years.

Tips: "Make sure a SASE is enclosed. Send 3 chapters and outline, clearly typed or word processed, double-spaced, written with punctuation and grammar in approved style. No presentations by fax or e-mail. Prefers writers who have had something in print."

Ⓝ ◪ THE WENDY WEIL AGENCY, INC.

232 Madison Ave., Suite 1300, New York NY 10016. (212)685-0030. Fax: (212)685-0765. Member of AAR.
- This agency did not respond to our request for information. Query before submitting.

Member Agents: Wendy Weil.

◪ CHERRY WEINER LITERARY AGENCY

28 Kipling Way, Manalapan NJ 07726-3711. (732)446-2096. Fax: (732)792-0506. E-mail: cherry8486@aol.com. **Contact:** Cherry Weiner. Estab. 1977. Represents 40 clients. 10% of clients are new/unpublished writers. Currently handles: 10-20% nonfiction books; 80-90% novels.
- This agency is currently not looking for new clients except by referral or by personal contact at writers' conferences.

Represents: Nonfiction books, novels. **Considers these nonfiction areas:** Self-help/personal improvement; sociology. **Considers these fiction areas:** Action/adventure; contemporary issues; detective/police/crime; family saga; fantasy; glitz; historical; mainstream/contemporary; mystery/suspense; psychic/supernatural; romance; science fiction; thriller; westerns/frontier.

○━ This agency specializes in science fiction, fantasy, westerns, mysteries (both contemporary and historical), historical novels, Native American works, mainstream, all the genre romances.

How to Contact: Query with SASE. Prefers to read materials exclusively. No e-mail or fax queries. Responds in 1 week to queries; 2 months to mss. Returns materials only with SASE.

Recent Sales: Sold 75 titles in the last year.

Terms: Agent receives 15% commission on domestic sales; 15% commission on foreign sales. Offers written contract. Charges clients for extra copies of mss "but would prefer author do it"; 1st-Class postage for author's copies of books; Express Mail for important document/mss.

Writers' Conferences: Western writers conventions; science fiction conventions; fantasy conventions; romance conventions.

Tips: "Meet agents and publishers at conferences. Establish a relationship, then get in touch with them reminding them of meetings and conference."

◖ THE WEINGEL-FIDEL AGENCY

310 E. 46th St., 21E, New York NY 10017. (212)599-2959. **Contact:** Loretta Weingel-Fidel. Estab. 1989. Currently handles: 75% nonfiction books; 25% novels.

• Prior to opening her agency, Ms. Weingel-Fidel was a psychoeducational diagnostician.

Represents: Nonfiction books, novels. **Considers these nonfiction areas:** Art/architecture/design; biography/autobiography; memoirs; music/dance; psychology; science/technology; sociology; women's issues/studies; investigative. **Considers these fiction areas:** Literary; mainstream/contemporary.

  ⃝⟶ This agency specializes in commercial, literary fiction and nonfiction. Actively seeking investigative journalism. Does not want to receive genre fiction, self-help, science fiction, fantasy.

How to Contact: Referred writers only. *No unsolicited mss.* Obtains most new clients through referrals.

Terms: Agent receives 15% commission on domestic sales; 20% commission on foreign sales. Offers written contract, binding for 1 year; automatic renewal. Bills sent back to clients all reasonable expenses such as UPS, express mail, photocopying, etc.

Tips: "A very small, selective list enables me to work very closely with my clients to develop and nurture talent. I only take on projects and writers about which I am extremely enthusiastic."

◖ TED WEINSTEIN LITERARY MANAGEMENT

287 Duncan St., Dept. G, San Francisco CA 94131-2019. Website: www.twliterary.com. **Contact:** Ted Weinstein. Estab. 2001. Represents 50 clients. 75% of clients are new/unpublished writers. Currently handles: 100% nonfiction books.

Represents: Nonfiction books. **Considers these nonfiction areas:** Biography/autobiography; business/economics; current affairs; government/politics/law; health/medicine; history; popular culture; science/technology; self-help/personal improvement; travel; environment, lifestyle.

How to Contact: Submit proposal package, outline, 1 sample chapter(s). Prefers e-mail queries, but paper query OK with SASE. No full mss. See website for detailed submission guidelines. Returns paper materials only with SASE. Considers simultaneous queries. Responds in 3 weeks to queries.

Terms: Agent receives 15% commission on domestic sales; 20-30% commission on foreign sales. Offers written contract, binding for 1 year. Charges clients for photocopying and express shipping.

◖ LYNN WHITTAKER, LITERARY AGENT

Graybill & English, LLC, 1875 Connecticut Ave. NW, Suite 712, Washington DC 20009. (202)588-9798, ext. 127. Fax: (202)457-0662. E-mail: lynnwhittaker@aol.com. Website: www.graybillandenglish.com. Estab. 1998. Member of AAR. Represents 24 clients. 10% of clients are new/unpublished writers. Currently handles: 80% nonfiction books; 20% novels.

• Prior to becoming an agent, Ms. Whittaker was an editor, owner of a small press, and taught at the college level.

Represents: Nonfiction books, novels. **Considers these nonfiction areas:** Animals; biography/autobiography; current affairs; ethnic/cultural interests; health/medicine; history; memoirs; money/finance; multicultural; nature/environment; popular culture; science/technology; sports; women's issues/studies. **Considers these fiction areas:** Detective/police/crime; ethnic; historical; literary; multicultural; mystery/suspense; sports.

  ⃝⟶ "As a former editor, I especially enjoy working closely with writers to polish their proposals and manuscripts." Actively seeking literary fiction, sports, history, mystery/suspense. Does not want to receive romance/women's commercial fiction, children's/young adult, religious, fantasy/horror.

How to Contact: Query with SASE, submit proposal package, outline, 2 sample chapter(s). Responds in 2 weeks to queries; 1 month to mss. Returns materials only with SASE. Obtains most new clients through recommendations from others.

Recent Sales: *O' Artful Death* (mystery), by Sarah Stewart Taylor (St. Martin's); *The Cincinnati Arch*, by John Tallmadge (University of Georgia Press); *Leadership the Katherine Graham Way*, by Robin Gerber (Portfolio/Penguin Putnam). Other clients include Michael Wilbon, Mariah Burton Nelson, Leonard Shapiro, Phyllis George, Dorothy Sucher, James McGregor Burns, Susan McCullough.

Terms: Agent receives 15% commission on domestic sales; 20% commission on foreign sales. Offers written contract; 1-month notice must be given to terminate contract. Direct expenses for photocopying of proposals and mss, UPS/FedEx.

Writers' Conferences: Creative Nonfiction Conference, (Goucher College MD, August); Washington Independent Writers, (Washington DC, May); Hariette Austin Writers Conference, (Athens GA, July); Boucheron (various cities).

☻ WIESER & ELWELL, INC.

(formerly Wieser & Wieser, Inc.), 80 Fifth Ave., Suite 1101, New York NY 10011. (212)260-0860. **Contact:** Jake Elwell. Estab. 1975. 30% of clients are new/unpublished writers. Currently handles: 50% nonfiction books; 50% novels.

Member Agents: Jake Elwell (history, military, mysteries, romance, sports, thrillers, psychology, fiction, pop medical).

Represents: Nonfiction books, novels. **Considers these nonfiction areas:** Business/economics; cooking/foods/nutrition; current affairs; health/medicine; history; money/finance; nature/environment; psychology; sports; true crime/investigative. **Considers these fiction areas:** Contemporary issues; detective/police/crime; historical; literary; mainstream/contemporary; mystery/suspense; romance; thriller.

　　○⇥ This agency specializes in mainstream fiction and nonfiction.

How to Contact: Query with outline/proposal and SASE. Responds in 2 weeks to queries. Obtains most new clients through queries, authors' recommendations and industry professionals.

Recent Sales: *Honored*, by Roberta Kells Dorr (Revell); *Eddie Rickenbacker*, by H. Paul Jeffers (Presidio); *Sea of Grey*, by Dewey Lambdin (St. Martin's Press); *The Voyage of the Hunley*, by Edwin P. Hoyt (Burford Books); *Cyclops*, by Jim DeFelice (Pocket); *Street Hungry*, by Bill Kent.

Terms: Agent receives 15% commission on domestic sales; 20% commission on foreign sales. Offers written contract. Charges clients for photocopying and overseas mailing.

Writers' Conferences: BEA; Frankfurt Book Fair.

☻ WILLIAMS LITERARY AGENCY

909 Knox Rd., Kosciusko MS 39090. (662)290-0617. E-mail: submissions@williamsliteraryagency.com. Website: williamsliteraryagency.com. **Contact:** Sheri Williams. Estab. 1997. Represents 35 clients.

　　● Prior to becoming an agent, Sheri Homan Williams was a freelance writer and literary assistant.

Represents: Nonfiction books, novels, movie scripts, feature film.

　　○⇥ Prefers published authors. "Looks for well-written books with a strong plot and consistency throughout."

How to Contact: Short queries only by mail or e-mail.

☒ ☻ WITHERSPOON ASSOCIATES, INC.

235 E. 31st St., New York NY 10016. (212)889-8626. **Contact:** David Forrer. Estab. 1990. Represents 150 clients. 20% of clients are new/unpublished writers. Currently handles: 50% nonfiction books; 45% novels; 5% story collections.

　　● Prior to becoming an agent, Ms. Witherspoon was a writer and magazine consultant.

Member Agents: Maria Massie, Kimberly Witherspoon, David Forrer, Alexis Hurley.

Represents: Nonfiction books, novels. **Considers these nonfiction areas:** Anthropology/archaeology; biography/autobiography; business/economics; current affairs; ethnic/cultural interests; gay/lesbian issues; government/politics/law; health/medicine; history; memoirs; money/finance; music/dance; science/technology; self-help/personal improvement; theater/film; travel; true crime/investigative; women's issues/studies. **Considers these fiction areas:** Contemporary issues; detective/police/crime; ethnic; family saga; feminist; gay/lesbian; historical; literary; mainstream/contemporary; mystery/suspense; thriller.

How to Contact: Query with SASE. Prefers to read materials exclusively. *No unsolicited mss.* Considers simultaneous queries. Responds in 6 weeks to queries. Obtains most new clients through recommendations from others, solicitations, conferences.

Recent Sales: This agency prefers not to share information on specific sales.

Terms: Agent receives 15% commission on domestic sales; 20% commission on foreign sales. Offers written contract. Office fees are deducted from author's earnings.

Writers' Conferences: BEA (Chicago, June); Frankfurt (Germany, October).

☒ ⊘ AUDREY A. WOLF LITERARY AGENCY

2510 Virginia Ave. NW, #702N, Washington DC 20037. Member of AAR.

　　● This agency did not respond to our request for information. Query before submitting.

⊘ WRITERS HOUSE

21 W. 26th St., New York NY 10010. (212)685-2400. Fax: (212)685-1781. Estab. 1974. Member of AAR. Repre-

sents 440 clients. 50% of clients are new/unpublished writers. Currently handles: 25% nonfiction books; 40% novels; 35% juvenile books.

Member Agents: Albert Zuckerman (major novels, thrillers, women's fiction, important nonfiction); Amy Berkower (major juvenile authors, women's fiction, art and decorating, psychology); Merrilee Heifetz (quality children's fiction, science fiction and fantasy, popular culture, literary fiction); Susan Cohen (juvenile and YA fiction and nonfiction, Judaism, women's issues); Susan Ginsburg (serious and popular fiction, true crime, narrative nonfiction, personality books, cookbooks); Michele Rubin (serious nonfiction); Robin Rue (commercial fiction and nonfiction, YA fiction); Jennifer Lyons (literary, commercial fiction, international fiction, nonfiction, and illustrated); Jodi Reamer (juvenile and YA fiction and nonfiction, adult commercial fiction, popular culture); Simon Lipskar (literary and commercial fiction, narrative nonfiction); Nicole Pitesa (juvenile and YA fiction, literary fiction); Steven Malk (juvenile and YA fiction and nonfiction).

Represents: Nonfiction books, novels, juvenile books. **Considers these nonfiction areas:** Animals; art/architecture/design; biography/autobiography; business/economics; child guidance/parenting; cooking/foods/nutrition; health/medicine; history; interior design/decorating; juvenile nonfiction; military/war; money/finance; music/dance; nature/environment; psychology; science/technology; self-help/personal improvement; theater/film; true crime/investigative; women's issues/studies. **Considers these fiction areas:** Action/adventure; comic books/cartoon; confession; contemporary issues; detective/police/crime; erotica; ethnic; experimental; family saga; fantasy; feminist; gay/lesbian; glitz; gothic; hi-lo; historical; horror; humor/satire; juvenile; literary; mainstream/contemporary; military/war; multicultural; multimedia; mystery/suspense; New Age; occult; picture books; plays; poetry; poetry in translation; psychic/supernatural; regional; religious/inspirational; romance; science fiction; short story collections; spiritual; sports; thriller; translation; westerns/frontier; young adult; women's.

⊶ This agency specializes in all types of popular fiction and nonfiction. Does not want to receive scholarly, professional, poetry, plays, or screenplays.

How to Contact: Query with SASE. No e-mail or fax queries. Responds in 1 month to queries. Obtains most new clients through recommendations from others.

Recent Sales: Sold 200-300 titles in the last year. *Moneyball*, by Michael Lewis (Norton); *Art of Deception*, by Ridley Pearson (Hyperion); *Report from Ground Zero*, by Dennis Smith (Viking); *The Villa*, by Nora Roberts (Penguin/Putnam); *Captain Underpants*, by Dan Pilkey (Scholastic); *Junie B. Jones*, by Barbara Park (Random House). Other clients include Francine Pascal, Ken Follett, Stephen Hawking, Linda Howard, F. Paul Wilson, Neil Gaiman, Laurel Hamilton, V.C. Andrews, Lisa Jackson.

Terms: Agent receives 15% commission on domestic sales; 20% commission on foreign sales. Offers written contract, binding for 1 year. Agency charges fees for copying mss and proposals, and overseas airmail of books.

Tips: "Do not send manuscripts. Write a compelling letter. If you do, we'll ask to see your work."

☑ WRITERS' PRODUCTIONS

P.O. Box 630, Westport CT 06881-0630. (203)227-8199. Fax: (203)227-6349. E-mail: dlm67@worldnet.att.net. **Contact:** David L. Meth. Estab. 1982. Represents 25 clients. Currently handles: 40% nonfiction books; 60% novels.

• Not taking on new clients at this time.

Represents: Nonfiction books, novels, literary quality fiction.

How to Contact: No new clients accepted at this time. No e-mail or fax queries. Obtains most new clients through recommendations from others.

Recent Sales: This agency prefers not to share information on specific sales.

Terms: Agent receives 15% commission on domestic sales; 25% commission on foreign sales. Offers written contract. Charges clients for electronic transmissions, long-distance phone calls, express or overnight mail, courier service, etc.

Tips: "Send only your best, most professionally prepared work. Do not send it before it is ready. We must have a SASE for all correspondence and return of manuscripts. Do not waste time sending work to agencies or editors who are not accepting new clients."

☑ WRITERS' REPRESENTATIVES, INC.

116 W. 14th St., 11th Floor, New York NY 10011-7305. (212)620-0023. E-mail: transom@writersreps.com. Website: www.writersreps.com. **Contact:** Glen Hartley or Lynn Chu. Estab. 1985. Represents 130 clients. 5% of clients are new/unpublished writers. Currently handles: 90% nonfiction books; 10% novels.

• Prior to becoming agents, Ms. Chu was a lawyer, and Mr. Hartley worked at Simon & Schuster, Harper & Row, and Cornell University Press.

Member Agents: Lynn Chu, Glen Hartley, Catharine Sprinkel.

Represents: Nonfiction books, novels. **Considers these fiction areas:** Literary.

O➡ This agency specializes in serious nonfiction. Actively seeking serious nonfiction and quality fiction. Does not want to receive motion picture/television screenplays.

How to Contact: Prefers to read materials exclusively. Considers simultaneous queries, but must be informed at time of submission. Obtains most new clients through "reading"

Recent Sales: Sold 30 titles in the last year. *Where Shall Wisdom Be Found?*, by Harold Bloom; *War Like No Other*, by Victor Davis Hanson; *Call of the Mall*, by Paco Underhill; *The Language of Police*, by Diane Ravitch.

Terms: Agent receives 15% commission on domestic sales; 20% commission on foreign sales.

Tips: "Always include a SASE—that will ensure a response from the agent and the return of material submitted."

◙ WYLIE-MERRICK LITERARY AGENCY

1138 S. Webster St., Kokomo IN 46902-6357. (765)459-8258. E-mail: smartin@wylie-merrick.com; rbrown@wylie-merrick.com. Website: www.wylie-merrick.com. **Contact:** S.A. Martin, Robert Brown. Estab. 1999. Member of SCBWI. Currently handles: 10% nonfiction books; 50% novels; 40% juvenile books.

• Ms. Martin holds a master's degree in Language Education and is a writing and technology curriculum specialist.

Member Agents: S.A. Martin (juvenile/picture books/young adult); Robert Brown (adult fiction/nonfiction, young adult).

Represents: Nonfiction books (adult and juvenile), novels (adult and juvenile), juvenile books. **Considers these nonfiction areas:** Juvenile nonfiction. **Considers these fiction areas:** Mystery/suspense; picture books; religious/inspirational; romance; young adult; chick lit, women's fiction, high-level mainstream.

O➡ This agency specializes in children's and young adult literary as well as genre adult fiction.

How to Contact: Query with SASE, include first 10 pages for novels, complete ms for picturebooks. "For our most up-to-date needs and any additional new contact information, see our website." Accepts e-mail queries. No fax queries. Considers simultaneous queries. Responds in 1 month to queries; 3 months to mss. Returns materials only with SASE. Obtains most new clients through recommendations from others, queries and conferences.

Recent Sales: *How I Fell in Love and Learned to Shoot Free Throws*, by Jon Ripslinger (Roaring Brook); *Red Polka Dot in a World Full of Plaid*, by Varian Johnson; *Death for Dessert*, by Dawn Richard; *Secret War*, by Regina Silsby.

Terms: Agent receives 15% commission on domestic sales; 20% commission on foreign sales; 20% commission on dramatic rights sales. Offers written contract. Charges clients for postage, photocopying, handling.

Writers' Conferences: Pike's Peak (CO); Willamette (Portland OR).

Tips: "We work with a small, select group of writers. We are highly selective when considering new clients, so your work must be the best it can possibly be for us to consider it. We only work with serious professionals who know their craft and the publishing industry. Anything less we reject."

◙ ZACHARY SHUSTER HARMSWORTH

1776 Broadway, Suite 1405, New York NY 10019. (212)765-6900. Fax: (212)765-6490. E-mail: sshagat@zshliterary.com. Website: www.zshliterary.com. Also: Boston Office: 729 Boylston St., 5th Floor. Phone: (617)262-2400, Fax: (617)262-2468. **Contact:** Sandra Shagat. Estab. 1996. Represents 125 clients. 20% of clients are new/unpublished writers. Currently handles: 45% nonfiction books; 45% novels; 5% story collections; 5% scholarly books.

• "Our principals include 2 former publishing and entertainment lawyers, a journalist and an editor/agent." Lane Zachary was an editor at Random House before becoming an agent.

Member Agents: Esmond Harmsworth (commercial mysteries and literary fiction, history, science, adventure, business); Todd Shuster (narrative and prescriptive nonfiction, biography, memoirs); Lane Zachary (biography, memoirs, literary fiction); Jennifer Gates (literary fiction, nonfiction).

Represents: Nonfiction books, novels. **Considers these nonfiction areas:** Animals; biography/autobiography; business/economics; current affairs; gay/lesbian issues; government/politics/law; health/medicine; history; how-to; language/literature/criticism; memoirs; money/finance; music/dance; psychology; science/technology; self-help/personal improvement; sports; true crime/investigative; women's issues/studies. **Considers these fiction areas:** Contemporary issues; detective/police/crime; ethnic; feminist; gay/lesbian; historical; literary; mainstream/contemporary; mystery/suspense; thriller.

O➡ This agency specializes in journalist-driven narrative nonfiction, literary and commercial fiction. Actively seeking narrative nonfiction, mystery, commercial and literary fiction, memoirs, history, biographies. Does not want to receive poetry.

How to Contact: For fiction, submit query letter with 1-page synopsis, SASE. For nonfiction, submit letter explaining topic of proposed book, along with analysis of why book is needed and will be a commercial success for publisher. No e-mail or fax queries. Considers simultaneous queries. Responds in 3 months to mss. Obtains most new clients through recommendations from others, solicitations, conferences.

Recent Sales: Sold 40-50 titles in the last year. *All Kinds of Minds*, by Mel Levine (Simon & Schuster). Other clients include Leslie Epstein, David Mixner.

Terms: Agent receives 15% commission on domestic sales; 20% commission on foreign sales. Offers written contract, binding for 1 work only; 30-days notice must be given to terminate contract. Charges clients for postage, copying, courier, telephone. "We only charge expenses if the manuscript is sold."

Tips: "We work closely with all our clients on all editorial and promotional aspects of their works."

✉ SUSAN ZECKENDORF ASSOC., INC.

171 W. 57th St., New York NY 10019. (212)245-2928. **Contact:** Susan Zeckendorf. Estab. 1979. Member of AAR. Represents 15 clients. 25% of clients are new/unpublished writers. Currently handles: 50% nonfiction books; 50% novels.

• Prior to opening her agency, Ms. Zeckendorf was a counseling psychologist.

Represents: Nonfiction books, novels. **Considers these nonfiction areas:** Biography/autobiography; child guidance/parenting; health/medicine; history; music/dance; psychology; science/technology; sociology; women's issues/studies. **Considers these fiction areas:** Detective/police/crime; ethnic; historical; literary; mainstream/contemporary; mystery/suspense; thriller.

> ⊶ Actively seeking mysteries, literary fiction, mainstream fiction, thrillers, social history, parenting, classical music, biography. Does not want to receive science fiction, romance. "No children's books."

How to Contact: Query with SASE. No e-mail or fax queries. Considers simultaneous queries. Responds in 10 days to queries; 3 weeks to mss. Returns materials only with SASE.

Recent Sales: *How to Write a Damn Good Mystery*, by James N. Frey (St. Martin's); *Moment of Madness*, by Una-Mary Parker (Headline); *The Handscrabble Chronicles* (Berkley); *Something to Live For (The Susan McCorkle Story)* (Northeastern University Press).

Terms: Agent receives 15% commission on domestic sales; 20% commission on foreign sales. Charges for photocopying, messenger services.

Writers' Conferences: Central Valley Writers Conference; The Tucson Publishers Association Conference; Writer's Connection; Frontiers in Writing Conference (Amarillo TX); Golden Triangle Writers Conference (Beaumont TX); Oklahoma Festival of Books (Claremont OK); SMU Writers Conference (NYC).

Tips: "We are a small agency giving lots of individual attention. We respond quickly to submissions."

Script Agents

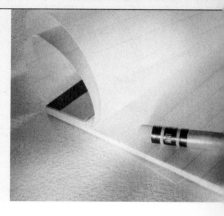

This section contains agents who sell feature film scripts, television scripts, and theatrical stage plays. A breakdown of the types of scripts each agency handles is included in the listing.

Many of the script agents listed here are signatories to the Writers Guild of America (WGA) Artists' Manager Basic Agreement. They have paid a membership fee and agreed to abide by the WGA's standard code of behavior. Agents who are WGA signatories are not permitted to charge a reading fee to WGA members but are allowed to do so to nonmembers. They are permitted to charge for critiques and other services, but they may not refer you to a particular script doctor. Enforcement is uneven, however. Although a signatory can, theoretically, be stripped of its signatory status, this rarely happens.

A few of the listings in this section are actually management companies. The role of managers is quickly changing in Hollywood; they were once only used by actors, or "talent," and the occasional writer. Now many managers are actually selling scripts to producers.

It's a good idea to register your script before sending it out, and the WGA offers a registration service to members and nonmembers alike. Membership in the WGA is earned through the accumulation of professional credits and carries a number of significant benefits. Write the WGA for more information on specific agencies, script registration, and membership requirements, or visit their website at www.wga.org.

Useful Websites

Like the literary agents listed in this book, some script agencies ask that clients pay for some or all of the office fees accrued when sending out scripts. Some agents ask for a one-time "handling" fee up front, while others deduct office expenses after a script has been sold. Always have a clear understanding of any fee an agent asks you to pay.

Canadian and international agents are included in this section. Canadian agents have a ◆ icon preceding their listing, while international agents have a ◉ icon preceding their listing. Remember to include an International Reply Coupon (IRC) with your self-addressed envelope when contacting Canadian and international agents.

When reading through this section, keep in mind the following information specific to the script-agent listings.

SUBHEADS

See Also

Each listing is broken down into subheads to make locating specific information easier. In the first section, you'll find contact information for each agency. You'll also learn if the agent is a WGA signatory or a member of any other professional organizations. (An explanation of all organizations' acronyms is available on page 268.) Further information is provided which indicates an agency's size, its willingness to work with a new or previously unpublished writer, and a percentage breakdown of the general types of scripts the agency will consider.

Member Agents: Agencies comprised of more than one agent list member agents and their individual specialties to help you determine the most appropriate person for your query letter.

Represents: Make sure you query only agents who represent the type of material you write. To help you narrow your search, we've included a **Script Agents Specialties Index** and the **Script Agents Format Index** in the back of the book.

☞ Look for the key icon to quickly learn an agent's areas of specializations and individual strengths. Here agents also mention what specific areas they are currently seeking, as well as subjects they do not wish to receive.

How to Contact: Most agents open to unsolicited submissions initially prefer to receive a query letter briefly describing your work. Script agents usually discard material sent without a SASE. Here agents also indicate if they accept queries by fax or e-mail; if they consider simultaneous submissions; and their preferred way of meeting new clients.

Recent Sales: Reflecting the different ways scriptwriters work, agents list scripts optioned or sold and scripting assignments procured for clients. The film industry is very secretive about sales, but you may be able to get a list of clients or other references upon request—especially if the agency is interested in representing your work.

Terms: Most agents' commissions range from 10 to 15 percent, and WGA signatories may not earn over 10 percent from WGA members.

Writers' Conferences: For screenwriters unable to move to Los Angeles, writers' conferences provide another venue for meeting agents. For more information about a specific conference, check the **Writers' Conferences** section starting on page 235.

Tips: Agents offer advice and additional instructions for writers looking for representation.

SPECIAL INDEXES TO REFINE YOUR SEARCH

See Also

Script Agents Specialties Index: In the back of the book on page 324 is an index divided into various subject areas specific to scripts, such as mystery, romantic comedy, and teen. This index should help you compose a list of agents specializing in your areas. Cross-referencing categories and concentrating on agents interested in two or more aspects of your manuscript might increase your chances of success. Agencies open to all categories are grouped under the subject heading "open."

Script Agents Format Index: Following the **Script Agents Specialties Index** is an index organizing agents according to the script types they consider, such as TV movie of the week (MOW), sitcom, or episodic drama.

Quick reference icons

At the beginning of some listings, you will find one or more of the following symbols for quick identification of features particular to that listing.

N Agency new to this edition.

✚ Canadian agency.

⊕ International agency.

Agencies Indexed by Openness to Submissions: This index lists agencies according to how receptive they are to new clients.

Geographic Index: For writers looking for an agent close to home, this index lists agents by state.

Agents Index: Often you will read about an agent who is an employee of a larger agency and you may not be able to locate her contact information. Starting on page 345 is a list of agents' names in alphabetical order along with the name of the agency for which they work. Find the name of the person you would like to contact and then check the agency listing.

General Index: This index lists all agencies, independent publicists, production companies, script contests, and writers' conferences listed in the book.

See Also

Level of openness

Each agency has an icon indicating its openness to submissions. Before contacting any agency, check the listing to make sure it's open to new clients.

☐ Newer agency actively seeking clients.

◪ Agency seeking both new and established writers.

◓ Agency prefers to work with established writers, mostly obtains new clients through referrals.

◎ Agency handling only certain types of work or work by writers under certain circumstances.

⦸ Agency not currently seeking new clients. We include these agencies to let you know they are currently not open to new clients. *Unless you have a strong recommendation from someone well-respected in the field, our advice is to avoid approaching these agents.*

For quick reference, a chart of these icons and their meanings is printed on the inside back cover of this book.

Script Agents

◐ ABOVE THE LINE AGENCY

9200 Sunset Blvd., #804, Los Angeles CA 90069. (310)859-6115. Fax: (310)859-6119. **Contact:** Bruce Bartlett. Owner: Rima Bauer Greer. Estab. 1994. Signatory of WGA. Represents 35 clients. 10% of clients are new/unpublished writers. Currently handles: 95% movie scripts; 5% TV scripts.
  • Prior to opening her agency, Ms. Greer served as president with Writers & Artists Agency.
Represents: Feature film, TV movie of the week. **Considers these script subject areas:** Cartoon/animation; writers and directors.
How to Contact: Query with SASE. This agency does not guarantee a response.
Recent Sales: *Movie/TV MOW script(s) optioned/sold:* The Great Cookie Wars, by Greg Taylor and Jim Strain (Fox); *Velveteen Rabbit*, by Greg Taylor (Disney); *Wing and a Prayer*, by David Engelbach and John Wolff (franchise). *Scripting Assignment(s):* Constantine, by Frank Capello (Warner Brothers); *Rainbow Six*, by Frank Capello (Paramount); *Duke Nukem*, by Ryan Rowe (Miramax).
Terms: Agent receives 10% commission on domestic sales; 10% commission on foreign sales.

◐ ABRAMS ARTISTS AGENCY

275 Seventh Ave., 26th Floor, New York NY 10001. (646)486-4600. Fax: (646)486-2358.
Member Agents: Maura E. Teitelbaum (film, TV, publishing, theater).
Represents: Feature film, episodic drama, sitcom, animation (TV), soap opera, musical. **Considers these script subject areas:** Comedy; contemporary issues; mainstream; mystery/suspense; romantic comedy; romantic drama.
  ⊶ This agency specializes in theater, film, TV, publishing.
How to Contact: Query with SASE, outline. Returns material only with SASE.
Recent Sales: This agency prefers not to share information on specific sales.
Terms: Agent receives 10% commission on domestic sales; 10% commission on foreign sales; 10% commission on dramatic rights sales.

⊠ ◐ ACME TALENT & LITERARY

4727 Wilshire, #333, Los Angeles CA 90010. (323)954-2263. Fax: (323)954-2262. Other Address: 875 Avenue of the Americas, Suite 2108, New York NY 10001. (212)328-0388. Fax: (212)328-0391. **Contact:** Mickey Frieberg, head of literary division. Estab. 1993. Signatory of WGA. Represents 50 clients. Currently handles: movie scripts; TV scripts; video game rights.
Member Agents: Mickey Freiberg (books, film scripts).
Represents: Feature film. **Considers these script subject areas:** Action/adventure; biography/autobiography; cartoon/animation; comedy; contemporary issues; detective/police/crime; erotica; ethnic; experimental; family saga; fantasy; feminist; gay/lesbian; glitz; historical; horror; juvenile; mainstream; multicultural; multimedia; mystery/suspense; psychic/supernatural; regional; religious/inspirational; romantic comedy; romantic drama; science fiction; sports; teen; thriller; western/frontier.
  ⊶ This agency specializes in "feature films, completed specs, or pitches by established, produced writers and new writers." Actively seeking great feature scripts. *No unsolicited material.*
How to Contact: Query with SASE. No e-mail or fax queries. Considers simultaneous queries. Responds in 2 weeks to queries. Returns materials only with SASE. Obtains most new clients through recommendations from established industry contacts, production companies of note, and reputable entertainment attorneys.
Recent Sales: Sold over 10 books, and several MOWs, including the Jessica Lynch story.
Terms: Agent receives 15% commission on domestic sales; 15% commission on foreign sales. Offers written contract, binding for 2 years.
Tips: "We are very hands on, work developmentally with specs in progress. Individual attention due to low number of clients. All sales have been major 6-7 figures."

◐ THE AGENCY

11350 Ventura Blvd., Suite 100, Los Angeles CA 91604. (310)551-3000. **Contact:** Jerry Zeitman. Estab. 1984. Signatory of WGA. Represents 300 clients. No new/previously unpublished writers. Currently handles: 45% movie scripts; 45% TV scripts; 10% syndicated material.
Represents: Feature film, TV movie of the week, episodic drama, sitcom, animation, miniseries. **Considers these script subject areas:** Action/adventure; cartoon/animation; comedy; contemporary issues; detective/police/crime; ethnic; family saga; fantasy; historical; horror; juvenile; mainstream; mystery/suspense; psychic/supernatural; romantic comedy; romantic drama; science fiction; teen; thriller; western/frontier; women's issues; military/war.

O–¬ This agency specializes in TV and motion pictures.

How to Contact: Query with SASE. Responds in 2 weeks, if interested. Obtains most new clients through recommendations from others.

Recent Sales: This agency prefers not to share information on specific sales.

Terms: Agent receives 10% commission on domestic sales; 10% commission on foreign sales. Offers written contract, binding for 2 years.

⊠ ☑ THE ALPERN GROUP

15645 Royal Oak Rd., Encino CA 91436. (818)528-1111. Fax: (818)528-1110. **Contact:** Jeff Alpern. Estab. 1994. Represents 50 clients. 10% of clients are new/unpublished writers. Currently handles: 30% movie scripts; 60% TV scripts; 10% stage plays.

• Prior to opening his agency, Mr. Alpern was an agent with William Morris.

Member Agents: Jeff Alpern (president); Liz Wise; Jeff Aghassi.

Represents: Movie scripts, feature film, TV scripts, TV movie of the week, episodic drama, miniseries. **Considers these script subject areas:** Action/adventure; biography/autobiography; cartoon/animation; comedy; contemporary issues; detective/police/crime; erotica; ethnic; experimental; family saga; fantasy; feminist; gay/lesbian; glitz; historical; horror; juvenile; mainstream; multicultural; multimedia; mystery/suspense; psychic/supernatural; regional; religious/inspirational; romantic comedy; romantic drama; science fiction; sports; teen; thriller; western/frontier.

How to Contact: Query with SASE. Responds in 1 month to queries.

Terms: Agent receives 10% commission on domestic sales. Offers written contract.

⊠ THE ARTISTS AGENCY

1180 S. Beverly, Suite 400, Los Angeles CA 90035. (310)277-7779. Fax: (310)785-9338. **Contact:** Richard Shepherd. Estab. 1974. Signatory of WGA. Represents 50 clients. 20% of clients are new/unpublished writers. Currently handles: 50% movie scripts; 50% TV scripts.

Represents: Movie scripts (feature film), TV movie of the week. **Considers these script subject areas:** Action/adventure; comedy; contemporary issues; detective/police/crime; mystery/suspense; romantic comedy; romantic drama; thriller.

How to Contact: Query with SASE. Responds in 2 weeks to queries. Obtains most new clients through recommendations from others.

Recent Sales: This agency prefers not to share information on specific sales.

Terms: Agent receives 10% commission on dramatic rights sales. Offers written contract, binding for 1-2 years, per WGA.

☑ BASKOW AGENCY

2948 E. Russell Rd., Las Vegas NV 89120. (702)733-7818. Fax: (702)733-2052. E-mail: jaki@baskow.com. **Contact:** Jaki Baskow. Estab. 1976. Represents 8 clients. 40% of clients are new/unpublished writers. Currently handles: 5% nonfiction books; 5% novels; 20% movie scripts; 70% TV scripts.

Member Agents: Crivolus Sarulus (scripts); Jaki Baskow.

Represents: Feature film, TV movie of the week, episodic drama, sitcom, documentary, miniseries, variety show. **Considers these script subject areas:** Action/adventure; biography/autobiography; comedy; contemporary issues; family saga; glitz; mystery/suspense; religious/inspirational; romantic comedy; romantic drama; science fiction (juvenile only); thriller.

O–¬ Actively seeking unique scripts/all-American true stories, kids projects, and movies of the week. Does not want to receive heavy violence.

How to Contact: Submit outline, proposal, and treatments. Accepts e-mail and fax queries. Responds in 1 month to queries. Obtains most new clients through recommendations from others.

Recent Sales: Sold 3 movie/TV MOW scripts in the last year. *Malpractice*, by Larry Leirketen (Blakely); *Angel of Death*, (CBS). Other clients include Cheryl Anderson, Camisole Prods, Michael Store.

Terms: Agent receives 10% commission on domestic sales; 10% commission on foreign sales. Offers written contract.

⊠ BEACON ARTISTS AGENCY

630 Ninth Ave., Suite 215, New York NY 10036. (212)765-5533. **Contact:** Patricia McLaughlin. Member of AAR.

• *No unsolicited mss.* Prefers recommendations.

☑ THE BOHRMAN AGENCY

8899 Beverly Blvd., Suite 811, Los Angeles CA 90048. (310)550-5444. **Contact:** Michael Hruska, Caren Bohrman. Signatory of WGA.

Represents: Novels, feature film, TV scripts. **Considers these script subject areas:** Action/adventure; biography/autobiography; cartoon/animation; comedy; contemporary issues; detective/police/crime; erotica; ethnic; experimental; family saga; fantasy; feminist; gay/lesbian; glitz; historical; horror; juvenile; mainstream; multicultural; multimedia; mystery/suspense; psychic/supernatural; regional; religious/inspirational; romantic comedy; romantic drama; science fiction; sports; teen; thriller; western/frontier.
How to Contact: Query with self-addressed postcard. *No unsolicited mss.* Obtains most new clients through recommendations from others.
Recent Sales: This agency prefers not to share information on specific sales.

N ◉ DON BUCHWALD & ASSOCIATES, INC.

6500 Wilshire Blvd., Suite 2200, Los Angeles CA 90048. (323)655-7400. Fax: (323)655-7470. Website: www.donbuchwald.com. Estab. 1977. Signatory of WGA. Represents 50 clients.
Represents: Movie scripts, feature film, TV scripts, TV movie of the week, episodic drama, sitcom, documentary, miniseries.
  ○— This agency represents talent and literary clients.
How to Contact: Query with SASE. Considers simultaneous queries. Obtains most new clients through recommendations from others.

◉ CEDAR GROVE AGENCY ENTERTAINMENT

P.O. Box 1692, Issaquah WA 98027-0068. (425)837-1687. E-mail: cedargroveagency@juno.com. **Contact:** Samantha Powers. Estab. 1995. Member of Cinema Seattle. Represents 7 clients. 100% of clients are new/unpublished writers. Currently handles: 90% movie scripts; 10% TV scripts.
  • Prior to becoming agents, Ms. Taylor worked for the stock brokerage firm, Morgan Stanley Dean Witter (Ms. Taylor is a member of Bellevue Community College's Media Advisory Board.); Ms. Powers was a customer service/office manager; Ms. MacKenzie was an office manager and recently a production manager.
Member Agents: Amy Taylor (senior vice president-motion picture division), Samantha Powers (executive vice president-motion picture division), Renee MacKenzie (story editor).
Represents: Feature film, TV movie of the week, sitcom. **Considers these script subject areas:** Action/adventure; biography/autobiography; comedy; detective/police/crime; family saga; juvenile; mystery/suspense; romantic comedy; science fiction; sports; thriller; western/frontier.
  ○— Cedar Grove Agency Entertainment was formed in the Pacific Northwest to take advantage of the rich and diverse culture as well as the many writers who reside there. Does not want period pieces, horror genres, children scripts dealing with illness, or scripts with excessive substance abuse.
How to Contact: Query with SASE, 1-page synopsis. No phone calls, please. Mail, e-mail, or fax. No attachments if e-mailed. Accepts e-mail and fax queries. Responds in 10 days to queries; 2 months to mss. Obtains most new clients through referrals and website.
Recent Sales: This agency prefers not to share information on specific sales.
Terms: Agent receives 10% commission on domestic sales. Offers written contract, binding for 6-12 months; 30-day notice must be given to terminate contract.
Tips: "We focus on finding that rare gem, the undiscovered, multi-talented writer, no matter where they live. Write, write, write! Find time everyday to write. Network with other writers when possible, and write what you know. Learn the craft through books. Read scripts of your favorite movies. Enjoy what you write!"

CIRCLE OF CONFUSION, LTD.

107-23 71st Rd., Suite 300, Forest Hills NY 11375. E-mail: queries@circleofconfusion.com. **Contact:** Shelly Narine. Estab. 1990. Represents 30 clients. 40% of clients are new/unpublished writers. Currently handles: 95% movie scripts.
Member Agents: Lawrence Mattis, David Mattis, Trisha Smith.
Represents: Nonfiction books, novels, novellas, feature film, TV scripts. **Considers these nonfiction areas:** Biography/autobiography; current affairs; education; ethnic/cultural interests; gay/lesbian issues; government/politics/law; health/medicine; history; how-to; humor/satire; juvenile nonfiction; language/literature/criticism; memoirs; military/war; money/finance; multicultural; music/dance; nature/environment; New Age/metaphysics; philosophy; popular culture; psychology; recreation; regional; science/technology; self-help/personal improvement; sex; sociology; software; spirituality; sports; theater/film; translation; travel; true crime/investigative; women's issues/studies; young adult. **Considers these fiction areas:** Action/adventure; comic books/cartoon; confession; contemporary issues; detective/police/crime; erotica; ethnic; experimental; family saga; fantasy; feminist; gay/lesbian; glitz; gothic; hi-lo; historical; horror; humor/satire; juvenile; literary; mainstream/contemporary; military/war; multicultural; multimedia; mystery/suspense; New Age; occult; picture books; plays; poetry; poetry in translation; psychic/supernatural; regional; religious/inspirational; romance; science fiction; short story collections; spiritual; sports; thriller; translation; westerns/frontier; young adult;

women's. **Considers these script subject areas:** Action/adventure; biography/autobiography; cartoon/animation; comedy; contemporary issues; detective/police/crime; erotica; ethnic; experimental; family saga; fantasy; feminist; gay/lesbian; glitz; historical; horror; juvenile; mainstream; multicultural; multimedia; mystery/suspense; psychic/supernatural; regional; religious/inspirational; romantic comedy; romantic drama; science fiction; sports; teen; thriller; western/frontier.

    O‑ Specializes in screenplays for film and TV.

How to Contact: Query with SASE. Responds in 1 month to queries; 2 months to mss. Obtains most new clients through recommendations from others, solicitations, writing contests, and queries.

Recent Sales: *Movie/TV MOW script(s) optioned/sold: The Matrix*, by Wachowski Brothers (Warner Brothers); *Reign of Fire*, by Chabot/Peterka (Dreamworks); *Mr. & Mrs. Smith*, by Simon Kinberg. Other clients include Jaswinki, Massa, Ferrer.

Terms: Agent receives 10% commission on domestic sales; 10% commission on foreign sales. Offers written contract, binding for 1 year.

Tips: ''We look for writing that shows a unique voice, especially one which puts a fresh spin on commercial Hollywood genres.''

ℕ ◉ COMMUNICATIONS AND ENTERTAINMENT, INC.

2851 South Ocean Blvd., #5K, Boca Raton FL 33432-8407. (561)391-9575. Fax: (561)391-7922. E-mail: jlbearde@ bellsouth.net. **Contact:** James L. Bearden. Estab. 1989. Represents 10 clients. 50% of clients are new/unpublished writers. Currently handles: 10% novels; 5% juvenile books; 40% movie scripts; 40% TV scripts.

    • Prior to opening his agency, Mr. Bearden worked as a producer/director and an entertainment attorney.

Member Agents: James Bearden (TV/film); Roslyn Ray (literary).

Represents: Novels, juvenile books, movie scripts, TV scripts, syndicated material. **Considers these nonfiction areas:** History; music/dance; theater/film. **Considers these fiction areas:** Action/adventure; comic books/ cartoon; fantasy; historical; mainstream/contemporary; science fiction; thriller.

How to Contact: For scripts, query with SASE. For books, query with outline/proposal or send entire ms. Responds in 1 month to queries; 3 months to mss. Obtains most new clients through recommendations from others.

Recent Sales: This agency prefers not to share information on specific sales.

Terms: Agent receives 10% commission on domestic sales; 5% commission on foreign sales. Offers written contract, binding for varies with project.

Tips: ''Be patient.''

◉ DOUGLAS & KOPELMAN ARTISTS, INC.

393 W. 49th St., Suite 5G, New York NY, 10019. **Contact:** Sarah Douglas. Member of AAR.

Member Agents: Sarah Douglas, Charles Kopelman.

Represents: Stage plays. **Considers these script subject areas:** Action/adventure; biography/autobiography; cartoon/animation; comedy; contemporary issues; detective/police/crime; erotica; ethnic; experimental; family saga; fantasy; feminist; gay/lesbian; glitz; historical; horror; juvenile; mainstream; multicultural; multimedia; mystery/suspense; psychic/supernatural; regional; religious/inspirational; romantic comedy; romantic drama; science fiction; sports; teen; thriller; western/frontier.

    O‑ This agency specializes in musical stage plays.

How to Contact: Query with SASE. Prefers to read materials exclusively. *No unsolicited mss.* No e-mail or fax queries.

◉ THE E S AGENCY

6612 Pacheco Way, Citrus Heights CA 95610. (916)723-2794. Fax: (916)723-2796. E-mail: edley07@cs.com. **Contact:** Ed Silver, president. Estab. 1995. Represents 50-75 clients. 70% of clients are new/unpublished writers. Currently handles: 50% nonfiction books; 25% novels; 25% movie scripts.

    • Prior to becoming an agent, Mr. Silver was an entertainment business manager.

Member Agents: Ed Silver.

Represents: Nonfiction books, novels, movie scripts, feature film, TV movie of the week. **Considers these nonfiction areas:** Considers general nonfiction areas. **Considers these fiction areas:** Action/adventure; detective/police/crime; erotica; experimental; historical; humor/satire; literary; mainstream/contemporary; mystery/suspense; thriller; young adult. **Considers these script subject areas:** Action/adventure; comedy; contemporary issues; detective/police/crime; erotica; ethnic; experimental; family saga; mainstream; mystery/suspense; romantic comedy; romantic drama; sports; thriller.

    O‑ This agency specializes in theatrical screenplays, MOW, and miniseries. Actively seeking ''anything good and distinctive.''

How to Contact: Query with SASE. Considers simultaneous queries. Responds in 1 month to queries. Returns

Script Agents

materials only with SASE. Obtains most new clients through recommendations from others, queries from WGA agency list.

Recent Sales: *The Cannabible*, by Jason King; *How to Read Maya Hieroglyphs*, by John Montgomery; *Dictionary of Maya Hieroglyphs*, by John Montgomery.

Terms: Agent receives 15% commission on domestic sales; 20% commission on foreign sales; 10% commission on dramatic rights sales. Offers written contract; 30-days notice must be given to terminate contract.

⊘ FILMWRITERS LITERARY AGENCY

4932 Long Shadow Dr., Midlothian VA 23112. (804)744-1718. **Contact:** Helene Wagner. Signatory of WGA. Currently not accepting clients.

- Prior to opening her agency, Ms. Wagner was director of the Virginia Screenwriter's Forum for 7 years and taught college level screenwriting classes. "As a writer myself, I have won or been a finalist in most major screenwriting competitions throughout the country and have a number of my screenplays optioned. Through the years, I have enjoyed helping and working with other writers. Some have gone on to have their movies made, their work optioned, and won national contests."

Represents: Feature film, TV movie of the week, miniseries. **Considers these script subject areas:** Action/adventure; comedy; contemporary issues; detective/police/crime; historical; juvenile; mystery/suspense; psychic/supernatural; romantic comedy; romantic drama; teen; thriller.

- ⟲ This agency does not accept unsolicited queries.

How to Contact: No e-mail or fax queries. Obtains most new clients through recommendations from others.

Recent Sales: *Movie/TV MOW script(s) optioned/sold:* *Woman of His Dreams*, by Jeff Rubin (Ellenfreyer Productions).

Terms: Agent receives 10% commission on domestic sales; 10% commission on foreign sales. Offers written contract. Clients supply photocopying and postage. Writers reimbursed for office fees after the sale of ms.

Tips: "Professional writers should wait until they have at least 4 drafts done before they send out their work because they know it takes that much hard work to make a story and characters work. Show me something I haven't seen before with characters that I care about, that jump off the page. I not only look at writer's work, I look at the writer's talent. If I believe in a writer, even though a piece may not sell, I'll stay with the writer and help nurture that talent which a lot of the big agencies won't do."

◐ THE BARRY FREED CO.

468 N. Camden Dr., #201, Beverly Hills CA 90210. (310)860-5627. Fax: (310)474-1087. E-mail: blfreed@aol.com. **Contact:** Barry Freed. Signatory of WGA. Represents 15 clients. 95% of clients are new/unpublished writers. Currently handles: 100% movie scripts.

- Prior to opening his agency, Mr. Freed worked for ICM.

Represents: Feature film, TV movie of the week. **Considers these script subject areas:** Action/adventure; comedy; contemporary issues; detective/police/crime; ethnic; family saga.

- ⟲ Actively seeking adult drama, comedy, romantic comedy. Does not want to receive period, science fiction.

How to Contact: Query with SASE. Prefers to read materials exclusively. Accepts e-mail and fax queries. Responds in 3 months to mss. Responds immediately to queries. Obtains most new clients through recommendations from others.

Recent Sales: This agency prefers not to share information on specific sales.

Terms: Offers written contract, binding for 2 years.

Tips: "Our clients are a high-qualified, small roster of writers who write comedy, action adventure/thrillers, adult drama, romantic comedy."

◖ ROBERT A. FREEDMAN DRAMATIC AGENCY, INC.

1501 Broadway, Suite 2310, New York NY 10036. (212)840-5760. Fax: (212)840-5776. **Contact:** Robert A. Freedman. Estab. 1928. Member of AAR; signatory of WGA.

- Mr. Freedman has served as vice president of the dramatic division of AAR.

Member Agents: Robert A. Freedman, president; Selma Luttinger, senior vice president; Robin Kaver, vice president (movie and TV scripts); Marta Praeger, associate (stage plays).

Represents: Movie scripts, TV scripts, stage plays.

- ⟲ This agency works with both established and new authors. Specializes in plays, movie scripts, and TV scripts.

How to Contact: Query with SASE. All unsolicited mss returned unopened. Responds in 2 weeks to queries; 3 months to mss.

Recent Sales: "We will speak directly with any prospective client concerning sales that are relevant to his/her specific script."

Terms: Agent receives 10% commission on domestic sales. Charges clients for photocopying.

☉ SAMUEL FRENCH, INC.

45 W. 25th St., New York NY 10010-2751. (212)206-8990. Fax: (212)206-1429. E-mail: samuelfrench@earthlink. net. Website: www.samuelfrench.com. **Contact:** Lawrence Harbison, senior editor. Estab. 1830. Member of AAR.

Member Agents: Alleen Hussung, Brad Lorenz, Charles R. Van Nostrand.

Represents: Theatrical stage play, musicals. **Considers these script subject areas:** Comedy; contemporary issues; detective/police/crime; ethnic; fantasy; horror; mystery/suspense; thriller.

   O⌐ This agency specializes in publishing plays which they also license for production.

How to Contact: Query with SASE, or submit complete ms to Lawrence Harbison. Accepts e-mail and fax queries. Considers simultaneous queries. Responds in 2-8 months to mss. Responds immediately to queries.

Recent Sales: This agency prefers not to share information on specific sales.

Terms: Agent receives variable commission on domestic sales.

Ⓝ ☉ THE GAGE GROUP

14724 Ventura Blvd., Suite 505, Sherman Oaks CA 91403. (818) 905-3800. Fax: (818) 905-3322. E-mail: gagegrou pla@yahoo.com. Estab. 1976. Member of DGA; signatory of WGA.

Member Agents: Jonathan Westover (head of department/ feature); Sharon Moist (television).

Represents: Movie scripts, feature film, TV scripts, theatrical stage play. **Considers these script subject areas:** Considers all script subject areas.

How to Contact: Query with SASE. Considers simultaneous queries. Responds in 1 month to queries; 1 month to mss.

Recent Sales: This agency prefers not to share information on specific sales.

Terms: Agent receives 10% commission on domestic sales; 10% commission on foreign sales. Agency charges clients the cost of copying the script.

☉ GRAHAM AGENCY

311 W. 43rd St., New York NY 10036. **Contact:** Earl Graham. Estab. 1971. Represents 40 clients. 30% of clients are new/unpublished writers. Currently handles: stage plays; musicals.

Represents: Theatrical stage play, musicals.

   O⌐ This agency specializes in playwrights. "We're interested in commercial material of quality." Does not want to receive one-acts or material for children.

How to Contact: Query with SASE. No e-mail or fax queries. Responds in 3 months to queries; 6 weeks to mss. Obtains most new clients through recommendations from others, solicitations.

Recent Sales: This agency prefers not to share information on specific sales.

Terms: Agent receives 10% commission on dramatic rights sales.

Tips: "Write a concise, intelligent letter giving the gist of what you are offering."

Ⓝ ☉ THE SUSAN GURMAN AGENCY, LLC

865 West End Ave., Suite 15A, New York NY 10025-8403. (212)749-4618. Fax: (212)864-5055. E-mail: staff@gur managency.com. Website: www.gurmanagency.com. Signatory of WGA.

Represents: Playwrights, screenwriters, directors, composers, and lyricists.

How to Contact: No e-mail or fax queries. Responds in 2 weeks to queries.

☉ BARBARA HOGENSON AGENCY

165 West End Ave., Suite 19-C, New York NY 10023. (212)874-8084. Fax: (212)362-3011. **Contact:** Barbara Hogenson. Estab. 1994. Member of AAR; signatory of WGA. Represents 60 clients. 5% of clients are new/ unpublished writers. Currently handles: 35% nonfiction books; 15% novels; 50% stage plays.

   • Prior to opening her agency, Ms. Hogenson was with the prestigious Lucy Kroll Agency for 10 years.

Represents: Nonfiction books, novels, theatrical stage play. **Considers these nonfiction areas:** Biography/ autobiography; history; interior design/decorating; music/dance; popular culture; theater/film. **Considers these fiction areas:** Action/adventure; detective/police/crime; ethnic; historical; humor/satire; literary; mainstream/ contemporary; mystery/suspense; romance (contemporary); thriller.

How to Contact: Query with SASE, outline. *No unsolicited mss.* Responds in 1 month to queries. Obtains most new clients through recommendations from others.

Recent Sales: *On Grief and Grieving*, by Elisabeth Kubler-Ross and David Kessler; *Ghosts of McDougal Street*, by Hesper Anderson; *Learning to Swim*, by Penelope Niven.

Terms: Agent receives 15% commission on domestic sales; 20% commission on foreign sales; 10% commission on dramatic rights sales. Offers written contract.

❷ INTERNATIONAL LEONARDS CORP.

3612 N. Washington Blvd., Indianapolis IN 46205-3534. (317)926-7566. **Contact:** David Leonards. Estab. 1972. Signatory of WGA. Currently handles: 50% movie scripts; 50% TV scripts.
Represents: Feature film, TV movie of the week, sitcom, animation, variety show. **Considers these script subject areas:** Action/adventure; cartoon/animation; comedy; contemporary issues; detective/police/crime; horror; mystery/suspense; romantic comedy; science fiction; sports; thriller.
How to Contact: All unsolicited mss discarded.
Recent Sales: This agency prefers not to share information on specific sales.
Terms: Agent receives 10% commission on domestic sales; 10% commission on foreign sales. Offers written contract, binding for WGA standard terms, which vary.

❷ JARET ENTERTAINMENT

6973 Birdview Ave., Malibu CA 90265. (310) 589-9600. Fax: (310) 589-9602. E-mail: info@jaretentertainment.com. Website: www.jaretentertainment.com. **Contact:** Seth Jaret. Represents 20 clients. 70% of clients are new/unpublished writers. Currently handles: 75% movie scripts; 25% TV scripts.
Member Agents: Seth Jaret, CEO/Manager.
Represents: Movie scripts, TV scripts, books. **Considers these script subject areas:** Action/adventure; biography/autobiography; cartoon/animation; comedy; mystery/suspense; psychic/supernatural; romantic comedy; romantic drama; science fiction; sports; thriller.
    O₋ This management company specializes in creative, out-of-the-box thinking. "We're willing to take a chance on well-written materials." Actively seeking "high concept science fiction, thrillers, mysteries, and smart romantic comedies." Does not want "any projects with unnecessary violence, westerns, or anything you've seen before—black comedy or period pieces that are boring."
How to Contact: Query with SASE. Discards unwanted material. Accepts e-mail and fax queries. Considers simultaneous queries. Obtains most new clients through recommendations from others.
Recent Sales: Sold 5 scripts in the last year. *Bumper to Bumper*, (Fox); *The Fraud Prince*, (Warner Brothers). *Scripting Assignment(s): Girl in the Curl*, (Paramount).
Terms: Agent receives 10% commission on domestic sales. Offers written contract, binding for 2 years.

▨ ❷ CHARLENE KAY AGENCY

901 Beaudry St., Suite 6, St.Jean/Richelieu QC J3A 1C6, Canada. (450)348-5296. **Contact:** Louise Meyers, director of development. Estab. 1992. Member of BMI; signatory of WGA. 50% of clients are new/unpublished writers. Currently handles: 50% movie scripts; 50% TV scripts.
    ● Prior to opening her agency, Ms. Kay was a screenwriter.
Member Agents: Louise Meyers; Karen Forsyth.
Represents: Feature film, TV scripts, TV movie of the week, episodic drama, sitcom. **Considers these script subject areas:** Action/adventure; biography/autobiography; family saga; fantasy; psychic/supernatural; romantic comedy; romantic drama; science fiction.
    O₋ This agency specializes in teleplays and screenplays. "We seek stories that are out of the ordinary, something we don't see too often. A well-written and well-constructed script is important." Does not want to receive "thrillers or barbaric and erotic films. No novels, books, or manuscripts."
How to Contact: Query with SASE, outline/proposal, IRCs for submissions outside of Canada. No e-mail or fax queries. Responds in 1 month to queries; 10 weeks to mss. Returns materials only with SASE.
Recent Sales: This agency prefers not to share information on specific sales.
Terms: Agent receives 10% commission on domestic sales; 10% commission on foreign sales. Offers written contract, binding for 1 year.
Tips: "This agency is listed on the WGA lists, and query letters arrive by the dozens every week. As our present clients understand, success comes with patience. A sale rarely happens overnight, especially when you are dealing with totally unknown writers. We are not impressed by the credentials of a writer, amateur, or professional, or by his or her pitching techniques, but by his or her story ideas and ability to build a well-crafted script."

❷ KERIN-GOLDBERG ASSOCIATES

155 E. 55th St., #5D, New York NY 10022. (212)838-7373. Fax: (212)838-0774. **Contact:** Charles Kerin. Estab. 1984. Signatory of WGA. Represents 29 clients. Currently handles: 30% movie scripts; 30% TV scripts; 40% stage plays.
Represents: Movie scripts, feature film, TV scripts, TV movie of the week, episodic drama, sitcom, miniseries, syndicated material, variety show, stage plays. **Considers these script subject areas:** Action/adventure; biography/autobiography; cartoon/animation; comedy; contemporary issues; detective/police/crime; erotica; ethnic; experimental; family saga; fantasy; feminist; gay/lesbian; glitz; historical; horror; juvenile; mainstream; multicultural; multimedia; mystery/suspense; psychic/supernatural; regional; religious/inspirational; romantic comedy; romantic drama; science fiction; sports; teen; thriller; western/frontier.

O── This agency specializes in theater plays, screenplays, teleplays.

How to Contact: Query with SASE. Responds in 1 month to queries; 2 months to mss. Obtains most new clients through recommendations from others.

Recent Sales: This agency prefers to not share information on specific sales.

Terms: Agent receives 10% commission on domestic sales; 10% commission on foreign sales. Offers written contract.

Ⓝ Ⓐ THE JOYCE KETAY AGENCY

630 Ninth Ave., Suite 706, New York NY 10036. (212)354-6825. Fax: (212)354-6732. **Contact:** Joyce Ketay, Carl Mulert. Signatory of WGA.

Member Agents: Joyce Ketay, Carl Mulert.

Represents: Feature film, TV movie of the week, episodic drama, sitcom, theatrical stage play. **Considers these script subject areas:** Action/adventure; comedy; contemporary issues; detective/police/crime; ethnic; experimental; family saga; fantasy; feminist; gay/lesbian; glitz; historical; juvenile; mainstream; mystery/suspense; psychic/supernatural; romantic comedy; romantic drama; thriller; western/frontier.

O── This agency specializes in playwrights and screewriters only. Does not want to receive novels.

Recent Sales: This agency prefers not to share information on specific sales.

Ⓐ THE LUEDTKE AGENCY

1674 Broadway, Suite 7A, New York NY 10019. (212)765-9564. Fax: (212)765-9582. **Contact:** Diana Dilger and/or Penny Luedtke. Represents 15 clients. 20% of clients are new/unpublished writers. Currently handles: 80% stage plays; 10% TV pilots/scripts; 10% film scripts.

- Prior to becoming an agent, Penny Luedtke was in classical music management; Elaine Devlin was in film development, story editing.

Member Agents: Penny Luedtke.

Represents: Screenplays and stage plays of all lengths, TV pilots/scripts. **Considers these script subject areas:** Action/adventure; cartoon/animation; comedy; contemporary issues; detective/police/crime; ethnic; family saga; fantasy; feminist; gay/lesbian; historical; horror; juvenile; mainstream; multicultural; multimedia; mystery/suspense; psychic/supernatural; regional; romantic comedy; romantic drama; science fiction; teen; western/frontier.

O── Seeking well-written material with originality. Works closely with writers and offers editorial assistance, if desired. Does not want any project with graphic or explicit violence.

How to Contact: Query with SASE. No e-mail or fax queries. Considers simultaneous queries. Responds in 1 month to queries; 6 months to mss. Returns materials only with SASE. Obtains most new clients through recommendations from others and workshops.

Recent Sales: This agency prefers not to share information on specific sales.

Terms: Agent receives 10% commission on domestic sales; 15% commission on foreign sales. Offers written contract, binding for WGA standard terms.

Ⓐ THE MANAGEMENT CO.

1337 Ocean Ave., Suite F, Santa Monica CA 90401. (310)963-5670. **Contact:** Tom Klassen. Represents 15 clients.

- Prior to starting his agency Mr. Klassen was an agent with International Creative Management (ICM).

Member Agents: Tom Klassen; F. Miguel Valenti; Helene Taber; Paul Davis; Steve Gamber.

Represents: Feature film (scripts), TV scripts, episodic drama, sitcom, miniseries.

O── Actively seeking "studio-quality, action-drama scripts and really good comedies." Does not want horror scripts.

How to Contact: Submit query letter with synopsis. No e-mail or fax queries. Responds in 2-3 weeks to queries. Returns materials only with SASE. Obtains most new clients through recommendations from others, conferences.

Recent Sales: Sold 11 scripts in the last year.

Terms: Agent receives 10% commission on domestic sales; 10% commission on foreign sales. Offers written contract, binding for 2 years.

Writers' Conferences: Sundance Film Festival; New York Film Festival; Telluride; Atlanta; Chicago; Minnesota.

Tips: "We only accept query letters with a short, 1-page synopsis. We will request full manuscript with a SASE if interested. We rarely take on nonreferred material, but do review query letters and occasionally take on new writers. We have done very well with those we have taken on."

Ⓐ THE MARTON AGENCY, INC.

One Union Square W., Suite 612, New York NY 10003-3303. Fax: (212)691-9061. E-mail: info@martonagency.com. **Contact:** Tonda Marton of AAR.

Member Agents: Tonda Marton, Anne Reingold.

O── This agency specializes in foreign-language licensing.

Brian Wray & Tejal K. Desai

Nicholl Fellowship opens doors

Brian Wray and Tejal K. Desai have been quietly working behind the scenes in a number of independent films for years. So, when the two decided to co-author a screenplay, they assumed it would be a likewise quiet affair—that was before winning the most prestigious screenwriting contest in the United States.

The two men received a $30,000 Don and Gee Nicholl Fellowship from the Academy of Motion Picture Arts and Sciences at a ceremony in Beverly Hills in November of 2003. Wray and Desai's screenplay, *Linda and Henry*, is the first collaborative script to win a Nicholl fellowship in the competition's 19-year history.

Wray, 33, was born and raised in Cincinnati, Ohio, and received his BA in film/video from Penn State University. Since then, he has worked as a production assistant and as an assistant director on independent films in New York City. "Between films I would do as much writing as I could," says Wray.

Tejal Desai, also 33, earned his degree in pharmacy from the University of Connecticut and is currently working on receiving his degree in film from Purchase College in New York. He has written several screenplays besides the Nicholl-winning script. One script, *Cowboys and Hindus*, is also getting a lot of attention.

"Tejal and I met working as production assistants on a film in New York City and discovered we had the same sensibilities in terms of storytelling," says Wray. The two friends developed the idea for *Linda and Henry* over the next several months. "I wanted to do a 'road journey' comedy and discussed it with Brian," says Desai. "We wanted to do a modern-day Bonnie and Clyde, and the story of a woman and child who are opposite in nature seemed interesting to us."

What kind of writing/organizational methods did you have to use as co-authors working on the same screenplay?

Desai: Brian and I live several hours apart so we would discuss scenes to be written, and we would e-mail our pages back and forth making our own adjustments and ideas. This was a first venture together so it was a learning process for both of us. I think we trusted each other's sensibilities and affection to the story, so it wasn't a difficult process.

What has been your favorite part of the writing process?

Wray: For me the favorite part of the writing process is the moment when you realize all of those ideas you've had in your head are actually going to gel on paper.

Desai: Coming up with original ideas. When we come up with a funny scene that makes both of us laugh, we know it works in the story. That spontaneity of an idea is my favorite part of writing.

Did you already have agent representation before winning the Nicholl Fellowship? If not, did you catch an agent's interest after winning?

Wray: Tejal was already represented by a manager [Paul Kelmenson]. That same manager took me on after the Nicholl Fellowship. In addition, we both signed with the Paradigm Agency.

What has life been like for the two of you since winning the Nicholl Fellowship?

Wray: Life has certainly changed. The biggest challenge has been deciding whether or not to move my wife and daughter from New York City or for us to remain there.

Desai: Things are moving faster since winning the Nicholl Fellowship. More doors are opening. More opportunities present themselves. We were offered an assignment with Disney animation, which probably wouldn't have happened if we didn't win the Nicholl Fellowship.

What, in your opinion, is the greatest benefit of winning the Nicholl Fellowship?

Wray: The biggest benefit was realizing that I haven't spent years in a room banging my head against a wall for nothing. On top of that, the Fellowship aids you in taking an entire year to do more writing.

Desai: It opens doors, and we have more opportunities. Brian and I are determined to improve our craft so we can make the most of these opportunities.

Have you sold your Fellowship-winning script, or are you working on writing and selling a new script?

Desai: We have not sold our Nicholl script as of yet. We are working on another action comedy.

What are some of the frustrations you've encountered (either in terms of writing or in terms of how Hollywood does business)?

Wray: The biggest frustration from being in Hollywood is having to learn how the process works. It's a sort of baptism by fire.

Desai: Frustrations are always there when you write, trying to flush the story, the characters, finding the right dynamic and tone for the piece. In terms of Hollywood, it just seems like things move very slowly. You are never as close as you think to closing a deal. I kind of expected this and really this is no surprise to me. The studios, the producers, agents, etc., have an agenda or a strategy they are trying to fulfill, and you can't get caught up in it. All you can do is to be positive and continue to write.

What kind of work would you like to do in the future?

Wray: I'd like to continue on the path we're on, with the aspiration of directing something I've written.

Desai: I would like to continue to write comedies. I enjoy that.

Has winning the Nicholl Fellowship given you a better sense of what it takes to make it in Hollywood?

Wray: Winning the Nicholl Fellowship has been an amazing first step to understanding what it takes to make it in Hollywood, but I feel like I still have a very long way to go.

Desai: Winning the Fellowship has allowed me to understand the process of selling a script. It's not as a simple as it seems when you read about a sale in the trades. A lot is happening with so many different parties that even with a great script, a great role, and a great agent, you need a gift from the gods to make everything work out.

How important is networking and socializing to a screenwriter's career?

Wray: It's starting to look like socializing will play quite a large role in how we progress.

Desai: The more people you know, the better. You have a face with your name and it's important for people to see that face. Even if you are not a great writer, but a good writer, and they like you as a person through networking, odds are you will probably get the job over the great writer who is difficult and antisocial.

Do you have any advice for new screenwriters?

Wray: My only advice (which has been given to me by many people) is to just keep writing. It's the only thing in your control.

Desai: Write! Don't think about writing. Don't talk about writing. Just write. And like with everything else in life, the more you write the better you will get at it. The more you discover the world, the more people you meet, the more honest you become with yourself, the more you will have to write about.

—Jerry Jackson, Jr.

◙ HELEN MERRILL, LTD.

295 Lafayatte St., Suite 915, New York NY 10012-2700. Fax: (212)226-5079. E-mail: bblickers@hmlartists.com. **Contact:** Beth Blickers. Member of AAR. 15% of clients are new/unpublished writers. Accepts new clients on occassion.

Member Agents: Patrick Herold (AAR); Beth Blickers (AAR); Morgan Jenness; Mala Mosher.

Represents: Stage plays.

    O⟲ Helen Merrill, Ltd., is a "full-service boutique agency with strong contract skills and an in-house creative director to help artists develop material and form relationships."

How to Contact: Query by mail only with SASE with personal referral.

Recent Sales: *The Story*, by Tracey Scott Wilson (The Public Theatre); *Recent Tragic Events*, by Craig Wright (Playwrights Horizons).

◙ THE STUART M. MILLER CO.

11684 Ventura Blvd., #225, Studio City CA 91604-2699. (818)506-6067. Fax: (818)506-4079. E-mail: smmco@aol.com. **Contact:** Stuart Miller. Estab. 1977. Signatory of WGA; signatory of DGA. Currently handles: 50% movie scripts; 25% multimedia; 25% books.

Represents: Nonfiction books, novels, movie scripts. **Considers these nonfiction areas:** Biography/autobiography; computers/electronic; current affairs; government/politics/law; health/medicine; history; how-to; memoirs; military/war; self-help/personal improvement; true crime/investigative. **Considers these fiction areas:** Action/adventure; detective/police/crime; historical; literary; mainstream/contemporary; mystery/suspense; science fiction; sports; thriller. **Considers these script subject areas:** Action/adventure; biography/autobiography; cartoon/animation; comedy; contemporary issues; detective/police/crime; family saga; historical; mainstream; multimedia; mystery/suspense; romantic comedy; romantic drama; science fiction; sports; teen; thriller.

How to Contact: Query with SASE, 2-3 page narrative, and outline/proposal. Accepts e-mail and fax queries. Considers simultaneous queries. Responds in 3 days to queries; 6 weeks to mss. Returns materials only with SASE.

Recent Sales: This agency prefers not to share information on specific sales.

Terms: Agent receives 10% for movie/TV commission on domestic sales; 15-25% for books (includes domestic) commission on foreign sales. Offers written contract, binding for 2 years; WGA standard notice must be given to terminate contract.

Tips: "Always include SASE, e-mail address, or fax number with query letters. Make it easy to respond."

◙ MONTEIRO ROSE DRAVIS AGENCY

17514 Ventura Blvd., Suite 205, Encino CA 91316. (818)501-1177. Fax: (818)501-1194. Website: www.monteiro-rose.com. **Contact:** Candy Monteiro. Estab. 1987. Signatory of WGA. Represents 50 clients. Currently handles: 40% movie scripts; 20% TV scripts; 40% animation.

Member Agents: Candace Monteiro (literary); Fredda Rose (literary); Jason Dravis (literary).

Represents: Feature film, TV movie of the week, episodic drama, animation. **Considers these script subject areas:** Action/adventure; cartoon/animation; comedy; contemporary issues; detective/police/crime; ethnic; family saga; historical; juvenile; mainstream; mystery/suspense; psychic/supernatural; romantic comedy; romantic drama; science fiction; teen; thriller.

   ○┳ This agency specializes in scripts for animation, TV, and film.

How to Contact: Query with SASE. Responds in 1 week to queries; 2 months to mss. Returns materials only with SASE. Obtains most new clients through recommendations from others, solicitations.

Recent Sales: This agency prefers not to share information on specific sales.

Terms: Agent receives 10% commission on domestic sales. Offers written contract, binding for 2 years; 3-months notice must be given to terminate contract. Charges for photocopying.

Tips: ''It does no good to call and try to speak to an agent before they have read your material, unless referred by someone we know. The best and only way, if you're a new writer, is to send a query letter with a SASE. If agents are interested, they will request to read it. Also enclose a SASE with the script if you want it back.''

Ⓜ NIAD MANAGEMENT

3465 Coy Dr., Sherman Oaks CA 91423. (818)981-2505. Fax: (818)386-2082. Website: www.niadmanagement.com. Estab. 1997. Represents 20 clients. 2% of clients are new/unpublished writers. Currently handles: 1% novels; 98% movie scripts; 1% stage plays.

Represents: Movie scripts, feature film, TV movie of the week, miniseries, stage plays. **Considers these nonfiction areas:** Biography/autobiography. **Considers these fiction areas:** Action/adventure; detective/police/crime; family saga; literary; mainstream/contemporary; multicultural; mystery/suspense; psychic/supernatural; romance; thriller. **Considers these script subject areas:** Action/adventure; biography/autobiography; comedy; contemporary issues; detective/police/crime; ethnic; family saga; historical; horror; mainstream; multicultural; mystery/suspense; psychic/supernatural; romantic comedy; romantic drama; sports; teen; thriller.

How to Contact: Query with SASE. Accepts e-mail and fax queries. Considers simultaneous queries. Responds in 1 week to queries; 3 months to mss. Returns materials only with SASE. Obtains most new clients through recommendations from others.

Recent Sales: *MacGyver the Feature Film*; *Five Dollars a Day*, by Neal and Tippi Dobrofsky (New Line); *Farnsworth*, by Neil Cohen (HBO); *Preying on Puritans*, by Josh Rebell. Other clients include Julian Grant, Susan Sandler, Michael Lazarou, Jim McGlynn, Don Most, Fernando Fragata.

Terms: Agent receives 15% commission on domestic sales. Offers written contract, binding for 1 year; 30-day notice must be given to terminate contract.

Ⓜ DOROTHY PALMER

235 W. 56 St., New York NY 10019. (212)765-4280. Fax: (212)977-9801. Estab. 1990. Signatory of WGA. Represents 12 clients. 0% of clients are new/unpublished writers. Currently handles: 70% movie scripts; 30% TV scripts.

   ● In addition to being a literary agent, Ms. Palmer has worked as a talent agent for 30 years.

Represents: Feature film, TV movie of the week, episodic drama, sitcom, miniseries. **Considers these script subject areas:** Action/adventure; comedy; contemporary issues; detective/police/crime; family saga; feminist; mainstream; mystery/suspense; romantic comedy; romantic drama; thriller.

   ○┳ This agency specializes in screenplays, TV. Actively seeking successful, published writers (screenplays only). Does not want to receive work from new or unpublished writers.

How to Contact: Query with SASE. Prefers to read materials exclusively. Published writers only. Returns materials only with SASE. Obtains most new clients through recommendations from others.

Recent Sales: This agency prefers not to share information on specific sales.

Terms: Agent receives 10% commission on domestic sales; 10% commission on foreign sales. Offers written contract, binding for 1 year. Charges clients for postage, photocopies.

Tips: ''Do not telephone. When I find a script that interests me, I call the writer. Calls to me are a turn-off because they cut into my reading time. The only ones who can call are serious investors of independent films.''

Ⓩ THE QUILLCO AGENCY

3104 W. Cumberland Court, Westlake Village CA 91362. (805)495-8436. Fax: (805)373-9868. E-mail: quillco2@aol.com. **Contact:** Sandy Mackey (owner). Estab. 1993. Signatory of WGA. Represents 7 clients.

Represents: Feature film, TV movie of the week, animation, documentary.

How to Contact: Prefers to read materials exclusively. Not accepting query letters at this time. Returns materials only with SASE.

Recent Sales: This agency prefers not to share information on specific sales.

Terms: Agent receives 10% commission on domestic sales; 10% commission on foreign sales.

◐ MICHAEL D. ROBINS & ASSOCIATES

23241 Ventura Blvd., #300, Woodland Hills CA 91364. (818)343-1755. Fax: (818)343-7355. E-mail: mdr2@msn.com. **Contact:** Michael D. Robins. Estab. 1991. Member of DGA; signatory of WGA. 10% of clients are new/unpublished writers. Currently handles: 5% nonfiction books; 5% novels; 20% movie scripts; 60% TV scripts; 10% syndicated material.

• Prior to opening his agency, Mr. Robins was a literary agent at a mid-sized agency.

Represents: Nonfiction books, novels, movie scripts, feature film, TV scripts, TV movie of the week, episodic drama, animation, miniseries, syndicated material, stage plays. **Considers these nonfiction areas:** History; humor/satire; memoirs; military/war; popular culture; science/technology; true crime/investigative; Urban lifestyle. **Considers these fiction areas:** Action/adventure; comic books/cartoon; detective/police/crime; family saga; fantasy; gay/lesbian; mainstream/contemporary; westerns/frontier (frontier); young adult. **Considers these script subject areas:** Action/adventure; biography/autobiography; cartoon/animation; comedy; contemporary issues; detective/police/crime; erotica; ethnic; experimental; family saga; fantasy; feminist; gay/lesbian; glitz; historical; horror; juvenile; mainstream; multicultural; multimedia; mystery/suspense; psychic/supernatural; regional; religious/inspirational; romantic comedy; romantic drama; science fiction; sports; teen; thriller; western/frontier.

How to Contact: Query with SASE. Accepts e-mail and fax queries. Considers simultaneous queries. Responds in 1 week to queries; 1 month to mss. Obtains most new clients through recommendations from others.

Recent Sales: This agency prefers not to share information on specific sales.

Terms: Agent receives 10% commission on domestic sales; 10% commission on foreign sales. Offers written contract, binding for 2 years; 4-months notice must be given to terminate contract.

◐ SHAPIRO-LICHTMAN

Shapiro-Lichtman Bldg., 8827 Beverly Blvd., Los Angeles CA 90048. (310)859-8877. Fax: (310)859-7153. **Contact:** Martin Shapiro. Estab. 1969. Signatory of WGA.

• Represents work from published authors only.

Represents: Nonfiction books, novels, novellas, feature film, TV movie of the week, episodic drama, sitcom, animation (movie, TV), miniseries, soap opera, variety show. **Considers these nonfiction areas:** Americana; animals; art/architecture/design; biography/autobiography; business/economics; child guidance/parenting; computers/electronic; creative nonfiction; current affairs; education; ethnic/cultural interests; gay/lesbian issues; government/politics/law; health/medicine; history; humor/satire; juvenile nonfiction; language/literature/criticism; memoirs; military/war; money/finance; multicultural; music/dance; nature/environment; photography; popular culture; psychology; science/technology; self-help/personal improvement; sex; sociology; software; sports; theater/film; true crime/investigative; women's issues/studies; young adult. **Considers these fiction areas:** Action/adventure; comic books/cartoon; contemporary issues; detective/police/crime; ethnic; family saga; fantasy; feminist; historical; horror; humor/satire; juvenile; literary; mainstream/contemporary; military/war; multicultural; multimedia; mystery/suspense; picture books; plays; romance; science fiction; short story collections; sports; thriller; westerns/frontier; young adult. **Considers these script subject areas:** Action/adventure; cartoon/animation; comedy; contemporary issues; detective/police/crime; ethnic; family saga; historical; horror; mainstream; mystery/suspense; romantic comedy; romantic drama; science fiction; teen; thriller; western/frontier.

How to Contact: Query with SASE. Does not accept unsolicited material. Responds in 10 days to queries. Returns materials only with SASE. Obtains most new clients through recommendations from others.

Recent Sales: This agency prefers not to share information on specific sales.

Terms: Agent receives 10% commission on domestic sales; 20% commission on foreign sales. Offers written contract, binding for 2 years.

◐ KEN SHERMAN & ASSOCIATES

9507 Santa Monica Blvd., Beverly Hills CA 90210. (310)273-3840. Fax: (310)271-2875. E-mail: kjassociates@earthlink.net. **Contact:** Ken Sherman. Estab. 1989. Member of BAFTA; PEN Int'l; signatory of WGA; DGA. Represents approximately 50 clients. 10% of clients are new/unpublished writers. Currently handles: juvenile books; movie scripts; TV scripts; fiction and nonfiction books; screenplays; teleplays; life rights; film and television rights to books; video games/fiction.

• Prior to opening his agency, Mr. Sherman was with The William Morris Agency, The Lantz Office, and Paul Kohner, Inc.

Represents: Nonfiction books, novels, movie scripts, TV scripts, film, television and life rights to books. **Considers these nonfiction areas:** Agriculture/horticulture; Americana; animals; anthropology/archaeology; art/architecture/design; biography/autobiography; business/economics; child guidance/parenting; computers/electronic; cooking/foods/nutrition; crafts/hobbies; creative nonfiction; current affairs; education; ethnic/cultural interests; gardening; gay/lesbian issues; government/politics/law; health/medicine; history; how-to; humor/satire; interior design/decorating; juvenile nonfiction; language/literature/criticism; memoirs; military/war; money/finance; multicultural; music/dance; nature/environment; New Age/metaphysics; philosophy; photography; popular culture; psychology; recreation; regional; religious/inspirational; science/technology; self-help/personal improvement; sex; sociology; software; spirituality; sports; theater/film; translation; travel; true crime/investigative; women's issues/studies; young adult. **Considers these fiction areas:** Action/adventure; comic books/cartoon; confession; contemporary issues; detective/police/crime; erotica; ethnic; experimental; family saga; fantasy; feminist; gay/lesbian; glitz; gothic; hi-lo; historical; horror; humor/satire; juvenile; literary; mainstream/contemporary; military/war; multicultural; multimedia; mystery/suspense; New Age; occult; picture books; plays; poetry; poetry in translation; psychic/supernatural; regional; religious/inspirational; romance; science fiction; short story collections; spiritual; sports; thriller; translation; westerns/frontier; young adult. **Considers these script subject areas:** Action/adventure; biography/autobiography; cartoon/animation; comedy; contemporary issues; detective/police/crime; erotica; ethnic; experimental; family saga; fantasy; feminist; gay/lesbian; glitz; historical; horror; juvenile; mainstream; multicultural; multimedia; mystery/suspense; psychic/supernatural; regional; religious/inspirational; romantic comedy; romantic drama; science fiction; sports; teen; thriller; western/frontier.

⚮ This agency specializes in solid writers for film, TV, books, and film and television rights to books.

How to Contact: Contact by referral only please. Responds in 1 month to mss. Obtains most new clients through recommendations from others.

Recent Sales: Sold over 20 scripts in the last year. *Back Roads*, by Tawni O'Dell (to Dreamworks); *Priscilla Salyers Story*, produced by Andrea Baynes (ABC); *Toys of Glass*, by Martin Booth (ABC/Saban Ent.); *Brazil*, by John Updike (film rights to Glaucia Carmagos); *Fifth Sacred Thing*, by Starhawk (Bantam); *Questions From Dad*, by Dwight Twilly (Tuttle); *Snow Falling on Cedars*, by David Guterson (Universal Pictures); *The Witches of Eastwick-The Musical*, by John Updike (Cameron Macintosh, Ltd.).

Terms: Agent receives 15% commission on domestic sales; 15% commission on foreign sales; 15% (10% for WGA scripts) commission on dramatic rights sales. Offers written contract. Charges clients for reasonable office expenses, postage, photocopying, and other negotiable expenses.

Writers' Conferences: Maui; Squaw Valley; Santa Barbara; Santa Fe; Aspen Institute; Aspen Writers Foundation, etc.

⬛ SILVER SCREEN PLACEMENTS

602 65th St., Downers Grove IL 60516-3020. (630)963-2124. Fax: (630)963-1998. E-mail: silverscreen11@yahoo.com. **Contact:** William Levin. Estab. 1989. Signatory of WGA. Represents 14 clients. 80% of clients are new/unpublished writers.

• Prior to opening his agency, did product placement for motion pictures/TV.

Member Agents: Bernadette LaHaie, Jeff Dudley.

Represents: Novels, movie and feature film scripts. **Considers these nonfiction areas:** All genres. **Considers these fiction areas:** All genres. **Considers these script subject areas:** All genres except religious, x-rated, and horror.

How to Contact: Brief. Accepts e-mail queries. No fax queries. Responds in 2 weeks to queries. Obtains most new clients through recommendations from others, listings with WGA, and *Guide to Literary Agents*.

Recent Sales: Sold 3 titles and sold 2 scripts in the last year. This agency prefers not to share information on specific sales. Other clients include C. Geier, M. Derosa, P. Sands, N. Melamed, R. Melley, and N. Russell.

Terms: Agent receives 15% (ms) commission on domestic sales; 10% (screenplay) commission on dramatic rights sales. May make referrals to freelance editors. Use of said editors does not ensure representation.

Tips: "No 'cute' queries, please."

⬛ SUITE A MANAGEMENT TALENT & LITERARY AGENCY

120 El Camino Dr., Suite 202, Beverly Hills CA 90212. (310)278-0801. Fax: (310)278-0807. E-mail: suite-A@juno.com. **Contact:** Lloyd Robinson. Estab. 1996. Member of DGA; signatory of WGA. Represents 76 clients. 10% of clients are new/unpublished writers. Currently handles: 15% novels; 40% movie scripts; 40% TV scripts; 5% stage plays.

• Prior to becoming an agent, Mr. Robinson worked as a manager.

Member Agents: Lloyd Robinson (adaptation of books and plays for development as features or TV MOW); Kevin Douglas (scripts for film and TV); Judy Jacobs (feature development).

Represents: Feature film, TV movie of the week, episodic drama, documentary, miniseries, variety show, stage plays, CD-ROM. **Considers these script subject areas:** Action/adventure; cartoon/animation; comedy; contemporary issues; detective/police/crime; erotica; ethnic; experimental; family saga; fantasy; mainstream;

mystery/suspense; psychic/supernatural; religious/inspirational; romantic comedy; romantic drama; science fiction; sports; teen; thriller; western/frontier.

○─ "We represent screenwriters, playwrights, novelists, producers, and directors."

How to Contact: Submit synopsis, outline/proposal, log line. Obtains most new clients through recommendations from others.

Recent Sales: This agency prefers not to share information on specific sales or client names.

Terms: Agent receives 10% commission on domestic sales; 10% commission on foreign sales. Offers written contract, binding for 1 year minimum. Charges clients for photocopying, messenger, FedEx, and postage when required.

Tips: "We are a talent agency specializing in the copyright business. Fifty percent of our clients generate copyright—screenwriters, playwrights, and novelists. Fifty percent of our clients service copyright—producers and directors. We represent produced, published, and/or WGA writers who are eligible for staff TV positions as well as novelists and playwrights whose works may be adapted for film on television."

◙ TALENT SOURCE

P.O. Box 14120, Savannah GA 31416-1120. (912)232-9390. Fax: (912)232-8213. E-mail: michael@talentsource.com. Website: www.talentsource.com. **Contact:** Michael L. Shortt. Estab. 1991. Signatory of WGA. 35% of clients are new/unpublished writers. Currently handles: 85% movie scripts; 15% TV scripts.

• Prior to becoming an agent, Mr. Shortt was a TV program producer/director.

Represents: Feature film, TV movie of the week, episodic drama, sitcom. **Considers these script subject areas:** Comedy; contemporary issues; detective/police/crime; erotica; family saga; juvenile; mainstream; mystery/suspense; romantic comedy; romantic drama; teen.

○─ Actively seeking "character-driven stories (e.g., *Sling Blade, Sex Lies & Videotape*)." Does not want to receive "big budget special effects, or science fiction."

How to Contact: Query with SASE, Must include a proper synopsis. "Please see the literary button on our website for complete submission details." No e-mail or fax queries. Responds in 10 weeks to queries. Obtains most new clients through recommendations from others.

Recent Sales: This agency prefers not to share information on specific sales.

Terms: Agent receives 10% commission on domestic sales; 15% commission on foreign sales. Offers written contract.

◙ TALESMYTH ENTERTAINMENT, INC.

Contact: Thomas Burgess. Estab. 2000. Signatory of WGA. Represents 5 clients. 100% of clients are new/unpublished writers. Currently handles: 20% novels; 80% movie scripts.

• Prior to becoming an agent, Mr. Burgess produced short films and managed a restaurant.

Member Agents: Thomas "TJ" Burgess (screenplays/novels).

Represents: Novels, movie scripts, feature film, TV scripts. **Considers these fiction areas:** Action/adventure; detective/police/crime; fantasy; historical; horror; mainstream/contemporary; mystery/suspense; New Age; psychic/supernatural; thriller; westerns/frontier. **Considers these script subject areas:** Action/adventure; comedy; detective/police/crime; fantasy; historical; horror; mystery/suspense; psychic/supernatural; romantic comedy; romantic drama; science fiction; thriller; western/frontier.

○─ This agency is not accepting any new submissions in favor of concentrating their efforts on the success of existing clients. This small agency has determined that they will not respond to unsolicited queries nor mss. "Reduction in staff and productivity of current clients does not allow for allocation of resources to 'new' clients at this time."

How to Contact: By referral only with query and SASE. Responds in 3 months to queries; 6 months to mss.

Recent Sales: Clients include Gary N. Hauger, Kevin T. Brown, F. Allen Farnham, Christopher Cairnduff, and Peter Borregine.

Terms: Agent receives 10% commission on domestic sales; 15% commission on foreign sales. Offers written contract, binding for 1 year; 2-months notice must be given to terminate contract.

Tips: "Don't bother to approach my clients for a referral unless you are willing to adhere to basic business practices, many are listed in this book or available in any bookstore writer's advice section. Submit only your best work, take your work and any critique of it seriously, type your work in standard format, always include a SASE, do not send your submission 3 months in a row or on flashy stationery just to get attention. This is a business and flashy stationery or failure to adhere to simple courtesies is the surest way to perpetuate your amateur status."

Ⓝ ◙ ANNETTE VAN DUREN AGENCY

11684 Ventura Blvd., #235, Studio City CA 91604. (818)752-6000. Fax: (818)752-6985. **Contact:** Annette Van Duren. Estab. 1985. Signatory of WGA. Represents 12 clients. 0% of clients are new/unpublished writers. Currently handles: 10% novels; 50% movie scripts; 40% TV scripts.

Represents: Feature film, TV movie of the week, episodic drama, sitcom, animation.

How to Contact: Not accepting new clients. Obtains most new clients through recommendations from others.
Recent Sales: This agency prefers not to share information about specific sales.
Terms: Agent receives 10% commission on domestic sales. Offers written contract, binding for 2 years.

◉ WRITERS & ARTISTS AGENCY

19 W. 44th St., Suite 1410, New York NY 10036. (212)391-1112. Fax: (212)398-9877. West Coast location: 8383 Wilshire Blvd., Suite 550, Beverly Hills CA 90211. (323)866-0900. Fax: (323)866-1899 **Contact:** William Craver, Christopher Till, Lydia Willis. Estab. 1970. Member of AAR; signatory of WGA.
Represents: Movie scripts, feature film, TV scripts, TV movie of the week, episodic drama, miniseries, stage plays, stage musicals. **Considers these script subject areas:** Action/adventure; biography/autobiography; cartoon/animation; comedy; contemporary issues; detective/police/crime; erotica; ethnic; experimental; family saga; fantasy; feminist; gay/lesbian; glitz; historical; horror; juvenile; mainstream; multicultural; multimedia; mystery/suspense; psychic/supernatural; regional; romantic comedy; romantic drama; sports; teen; thriller; western/frontier.
How to Contact: Query with SASE, author bio, brief description of the project. *No unsolicited mss.* Responds in 1 month to queries only when accompanied by SASE. Obtains most new clients through professional recommendation preferred.
Recent Sales: This agency prefers not to share information on specific sales.

Production Companies

This section contains independent producers who buy feature-film scripts. These are smaller production companies with limited budgets who produce more character-driven stories. So, understand that if you have a science fiction script requiring a lot of special effects or an action movie with many locations or special props, your work may not be appropriate for this market.

Very few producers will accept unsolicited script submissions, but many are willing to consider a query letter. Your query letter should be no more than one page, including a one-paragraph summary of your story and a paragraph to list your credentials as they relate to the subject matter of the script or your writing experience.

Because of the large bulk of mail that producers receive, expect that the production company will likely respond only if they are interested in your script. If they do request to see your work, they will most likely send you a release form to sign and submit along with your script. This is a standard practice in the industry, and you should be willing to comply without worries that someone will steal your idea.

However, you should register your script before you send it out, just as you would when submitting to agents. The Writers Guild of America (WGA) offers a registration service to members and nonmembers alike. Write the WGA for more information on specific agencies, script registration, and membership requirements, or visit them online at www.wga.org.

Include either a self-addressed, stamped envelope (SASE) with enough room and postage for your script if you want it returned to you, or a smaller envelope with First-Class postage if you only want a reply. Allow six weeks from receipt of your manuscript before writing a follow-up letter.

See Also

Before you send a query letter, you should have your script written in proper screenplay format (for more on formatting and submitting your script, see From Script to Screen—Formatting and Submitting Your Script on page 36). Remember: Keep the binding simple—two or three brass brads with a plain black or white cover.

It's a good idea to visit the production company's website before submitting a query or a script to get a better feel for the kinds of films it's produced, its current movie or movies in production, and what scripts it's interested in producing next.

Many independent production companies are willing to work with new writers, and these venues present some of the best opportunities for writers to break into the film industry and get their screenplays produced.

The following listings are for low- to midsized-budget feature film producers. When reading through this section, keep in mind the following information specific to the independent producer listings.

SUBHEADS

Each listing is broken down into subheads to make locating specific information easier. In the first section, you'll find contact information for each producer. Further information is provided that indicates the producers' specialties, the type of work they want, and how you should approach them.

Needs: Look here to quickly learn producers' specializations and individual strengths. Producers also mention what specific areas they are currently seeking, as well as subjects they do not wish to receive.

How to Contact: Most producers open to submissions prefer to receive a query letter briefly describing your work. Producers usually discard material sent without a SASE. They also indicate in this section if they accept queries by fax or e-mail.

Tips: Producers offer advice and additional instructions for writers hoping to break into the film industry.

SPECIAL INDEX

General Index: This index lists all producers, agencies, independent publicists, script contests, and writers' conferences listed in the book.

Production Companies

ⓃⓃ ALLIANCE FILMWORKS

P.O. Box 823208, South Florida FL 33082. E-mail: submissions@alliancefilmworks.com. Website: www.alliance filmworks.com. **Contact:** Greg Zanfardino, president. Estab. 2001. Produces 3 movies/year.

How to Contact Send query and synopsis. Responds in 3 months. Pays option, makes outright purchase. Include SASE for return of submission.

Needs Produces all genres. Budgets are $1.5 million plus.

AXIAL ENTERTAINMENT

20 W. 21st St., New York NY 10010. E-mail: submissions@axialentertainment.com. Website: www.axialentertai nment.com. **Executive Producer:** Riaz Patel, CEO. **Contact:** Nora Francescani, director of development (film/theater); David Garfield, director of development (film/TV).

Needs "Axial is a New York-based production and management company with an unusual model: loosely based on the 'hot house' studio environment of the 1940s, Axial takes writers and film executives—2 parties that are often separated by distance and large, heavy, insurmountable barriers—and places them in the same work space. By incubating the development process before it gets to the studios, networks, or producers, Axial is exactly the place where chances can be taken on a new writer or a completely original idea. Axial's dynamic creative process is anchored in the weekly Tc (the Tuesday Think Tank meeting). Writers and executives gather together to discuss new story ideas, assess the gaps and gluts in the current marketplace, brainstorm current script roadblocks, and work to make each choice in every story as smart as possible. What are specific studios, networks, and theater companies looking for? What kinds of projects are considered out-of-date this month? What are some other ways of getting a character from point A to point B?"

How to Contact "Unfortunately, Axial Entertainment does not accept any unsolicited materials. If you are interested in submitting, please send an e-mail containing a brief (1 page or less) summary of your material to submissions@axialentertainment.com."

Tips "Axial is not for every writer. The writers who thrive in our environment not only have great talent and express themselves in exciting and dynamic voices, but are highly motivated, prolific, generous with their intelligence, and ego-free about their writing process. At Axial, we specialize in finding original voices (both established and emerging), creating and developing strong, marketable material, and championing that material the entire way from conception to production."

BURN PRODUCTIONS

3800 NE 2nd Ave., 2nd Floor, Miami FL 33137. Website: www.burnproductions.com. "BURN Productions is a film/video production group that specializes in new media for the Internet, broadband, and television. The company's mission is to continually create high-quality feature films, shorts, and music videos including creative narrative, documentary, and experimental styles."

CODIKOW FILMS

8899 Beverly Blvd., Suite 501, Los Angeles CA 90048. (310)246-9388. Fax: (310)246-9877. E-mail: joinpowerup @aol.com. Website: www.codikowfilms.com. **Executive Producer:** Stacy Codikow. **Contact:** Codikow Story Department.

Needs Accepts material for all genres. "Currently searching for a romantic comedy. Codikow Films has been involved in the production of 10 feature films, including *Hollywood Heartbreak* and *Fatal Instinct*. Presently, the company is producing *In Search of Holden Caulfield*. We have an active development slate of projects, ranging from Independent to Studio features."

How to Contact "Submit a short pitch or synopsis (no more than one 8½×11 page). Make sure you include your contact information (name, address, phone, fax, and e-mail) as well as the title, genre, and logline for your project. Pitches are reviewed each week by the Codikow Story Department. Because of the volume of material we receive, we can only respond to ideas we are interested in pursuing further. If we find a project interesting, a request for the screenplay will be made by e-mail or phone."

Tips Stacy Codikow is a member of the Producers Guild of America, the Writers Guild of America, Women in Film, USC Cinema Alumni Association, Cinewoman, AFI 3rd Decade Council, IFP West, and has been included in articles written for *The Wall Street Journal*, *New York Times*, Movieline, *Premiere* Magazine, *Scene at the Movies*, *Hollywood Reporter*, *The Daily Variety*, *Screen International*, *The Los Angeles Times*, *Daily News*, *Film & Video* and *Entertainment Today*. She has been featured on the television shows Entertainment Tonight (ET), E!, HBO News, Extra, and Showbiz News (CNN).

LEE DANIELS ENTERTAINMENT

39 W. 131st St., New York NY 10037. (646)548-0930. E-mail: contact@leedanielsentertainment.com. Website: www.leedanielsentertainment.com. **Executive Producer:** Lee Daniels.

Needs "We work with all aspects of entertainment, including film, television, and theater."

How to Contact "All scripts should be registered (WGA, etc.) or copyrighted for your own protection. All scripts should be in standard screenplay format. Include a synopsis, logline, and character breakdown (including lead and supporting roles). Do not send any extraneous materials."

Tips Lee Daniels produced *Monster's Ball*. Client list includes Wes Bently (*American Beauty*) and supermodel/actress Amber Valletta. Past clients include Marianne Jean-Baptiste and Morgan Freeman.

ENERGY ENTERTAINMENT

Website: www.energyentertainment.net. **Executive Producer:** Brooklyn Weaver. Estab. 2001.

How to Contact Submit query via website. "Energy Entertainment is only accepting electronic query letters, and will not accept unsolicited scripts."

GREY LINE ENTERTAINMENT, INC.

115 W. California Blvd., #310, Pasadena CA 91105-3005. E-mail: submissions@greyline.net. Website: www.greyline.net. **Contact:** Sara Miller, submissions coordinator.

Needs "Grey Line Entertainment is a full-service motion picture production and literary management company. We offer direct management of all services associated with the exploitation of stories. When our clients' motion picture screenplays are ready for the marketplace, Grey Line Entertainment places them directly with studios or with major co-producers who can assist in packaging cast and/or director before approaching financiers (like Warner Bros., New Line, Fox, or Disney), or broadcasters (HBO, Showtime, etc.)."

How to Contact Query via e-mail only to submissions@greyline.net. "Please review our submission guidelines available at our website before querying." No attachments. Unsolicited queries OK. "E-mail queries for novels, nonfiction book proposals, screenplays, and treatments should consist of a compelling and business-like letter giving us a brief overview of your story—and a 1-sentence pitch. Be sure to include your return address, and a telephone number. Also include relevant background on yourself, including previous publication or production. Allow 2 weeks for consideration of initial query. No multiple submissions. Treatments and screenplays submitted without a completed and signed Grey Line Submission Form will be discarded. Include SASE for our reply. Submissions without SASE will be discarded. We recommend you register screenplays and treatments with the Copyright Office and/or the Writers Guild of America before submitting your query."

Tips "Your work must be finished and properly edited before seeking our representation (meaning proofread, spell-checked, and rewritten until it's perfect)."

MAINLINE RELEASING, A Film & TV Production and Distribution Co.

301 Arizona Ave., 4th Floor, Santa Monica CA 90401. (310)255-1200. Fax: (310)255-1201. E-mail: joe@mainlinereleasing.com. Website: www.mainlinereleasing.com. **Contact:** Joseph Dickstein, vice president of acquisitions. Estab. 1997.

Needs Produces family films, drama, thrillers, and erotic features.

NITE OWL PRODUCTIONS

126 Hall Rd., Aliquippa PA 15001. (724)775-1993. Fax: (801)881-3017. E-mail: niteowlprods@aol.com or mark@niteowlproductionsltd.com. Website: www.niteowlproductionsltd.com. **Contact:** Bridget Petrella. Estab. April 2001.

Needs "We will be producing at least 5-10 feature films in the next 2-5 years. We are searching for polished, well-structured, well-written, and professional-looking screenplays that are essentially ready for production. If your screenplay does not meet these standards, do not send us a query for that screenplay. All screenplays must be in English. Provide a working title for your screenplay. All screenplays must be in standard industry format."

How to Contact "For all submissions, send a 1-page query letter, via e-mail or regular mail. The content of your query letter should be succinct and interesting enough to entice us to ask to see more of the project. Single-space your query letters. If our interest is piqued, we will request the completed synopsis and screenplay. Do not send the screenplay to us unless we specifically ask you to do so."

Tips "All submissions must include a dated and signed Submission Release Form or they will be discarded immediately. No exceptions. Page length varies according to the format you are submitting. Screenplays that are too long or short may be considered unprofessional. This is especially true for television because a show needs to squeeze into time slots. All full-length feature film screenplays must be between 80-130 pages in length. 1-hour television spec scripts need to be 55-65 pages in length. No less. No more. A common rule of thumb says 1 script page equals approximately 1 minute on the television. Do not send us computer disks. One hard copy of your screenplay will suffice. Do not cheat on your margins. Stay within 1-1.25 inches on all sides. If you cheat, we will notice. The industry standard font style and size is Courier 11-12 point, but similar fonts are acceptable. Proofread your screenplay thoroughly before submitting to avoid senseless mistakes that might

G.H. Lui

Crossing the Grey Line between
good and great submissions

President of Grey Line Entertainment, G.H. Lui, has worked in the entertainment industry for the better part of ten years. Having started out successfully writing for film and television, Lui gradually became involved with managing and producing other writers. His company, Grey Line Entertainment, has established itself as a well-respected and hard-working literary management and motion picture production company. Some of its most notable projects include, *Fitz, Freedom, Roundabout, The Catch, The Office, The Trouble with Owen, Twilight*, and *White Elephant*.

As a smaller company fueled by a desire to help writers achieve the maximum exposure for their literary properties, Grey Line Entertainment works one-on-one with its clients in development, editing, promotion, sales, and marketing. The company prides itself on fostering an environment where the client comes first. Grey Line's attention to well-crafted, polished projects has earned recognition and praise from both studios and publishing houses, which is evident through the many "first-look" requests for projects that Grey Line has acquired.

Here Lui answers some of the most common questions asked by screenwriters, both about the industry in general, and also about Grey Line Entertainment.

What does Grey Line Entertainment do as a literary management and motion picture production company?

As a literary management and motion picture production company, Grey Line searches for, discovers, develops, and manages writers for film/television and publishing. When a client's project, for instance, a screenplay, is ready for the marketplace, we place it directly with studios or co-producers who can assist in the production process.

What are the benefits of submitting a script directly to a production company rather than through an agent?

Well, in most circumstances, a general production company will probably not accept unsolicited material. However, there are many benefits in dealing with a management/production company. Generally, a company like ours spends a lot more time working on the development of a project. We offer in-depth suggestions as well as feedback, and we are willing to spend the time to get a project into the best possible condition, which is rare for an agent to do. Further, unlike agents, as managers, we are able to financially back a project to insure it gets produced.

If you're interested in a particular writer who doesn't have an agent, do you ever assist that writer in seeking representation?

As a management/production company, we actively seek good writers in need of representation. If a writer presents us with a project we believe has potential, we will make the initiative to represent the client and project. Should we feel that the project would benefit from additional representation, we will often help the writer find an agent to work in tandem with us.

What are the positive things that stand out in the queries and scripts you acquire?

Queries that are brief, professional, to the point, and well written, always catch the attention of our submissions coordinator.

What is the most important thing for a writer not to do when submitting his or her query or script?

Don't be cocky or arrogant. Don't try to be "cute" or "hip" when submitting—being professional is always better. Don't query a company and tell it who should direct your project, who should star in your project, etc. Don't query a company and tell it that you should direct or star in your project. Don't present yourself as someone who's difficult to work with.

What can a writer do to increase his or her chances of getting noticed?

Spell the company and/or contact name correctly. It may seem like a small thing; however, misspelling either the company and/or the contact name, can often make a bad impression. Always review a company's submission guidelines. Following the proper procedures is important. No one wants to read through superfluous information that's not requested. In addition, be professional, spell-check, and use proper grammar.

Is Grey Line looking for any specific types of scripts/literature right now?

Grey Line does not limit our search for material to any particular genre. Our main concern is in the quality of writing. If a project is well written and has a great concept, we're open to hearing about it.

—Jerry Jackson, Jr.

pull your reader's attention from the story, such as typos, punctuation, or grammatical errors. Be certain all of your pages are there and in order. Copyright your script with the U.S. Copyright Office before sending it to us or anyone else. Registration with The Writers Guild of America is also strongly suggested. All screenplays must be firmly bound with a cover page that states the title of work and the author(s) name, address, and contact information. Card stock covers are preferred. Send us a copy of your screenplay, as your materials will not be returned to you, regardless of enclosures. Copies will be disposed of properly.''

RAINFOREST FILMS

2141 Powers Ferry Rd., Suite 300, Marrietta GA 30067. Fax: (770)953-0848. E-mail: staff@rainforest-films.com. Website: www.rainforestproductions.com.

Needs Rainforest's productions include *Pandora's Box*, *Chocolate City* and *Trois*. They have also produced a number of music videos for a variety of artists.

How to Contact Submit complete ms. ''In order to submit a script, a detailed synopsis and signed release form must be included. Any material sent without the accompanying signed release form will be returned unread. Screenplays are sent to our development department where they are reviewed and discussed. Please allow 90 days for written confirmation and response to your work. All material should be marked 'Attn: Screenplay Submissions.' ''

[N] TRI-HUGHES ENTERTAINMENT GROUP

11601 Wilshire Blvd., 5th Floor, Los Angeles CA 90025. (310)235-1459. Fax: (310)575-1890. E-mail: info@trihug

Production Companies

hes.com. Website: www.trihughes.com. **Producer:** Patrick Hughes. **Contact:** Faye, creative executive. Estab. 2002. Produces 10 movies/year.

How to Contact Send query and synopsis, or submit complete ms; "mostly" agented submissions. Responds in 3 weeks. Does not return submissions.

Needs "Tri-Hughes looks to produce and develop feature-length screenplays, produced stage plays, novels (published only), well-developed pitches, and detailed treatments. Focus is on broad comedies, black comedies, socially smart comedies, family films (family adventure), and ground-breaking, abstract projects, and new writer/directors with an extremely unique and unparalleled point of view. Please do not send a script with, 'this can be made for under a million dollars.' If it can, we suggest you go make it. Don't focus on budget, cast, or locations. The 'story' is key to getting things done here."

Tips "Does not want to see talking-heads projects with no point in sight. Projects that scream, 'You've seen me before!' Projects that try too hard to be different. Dramas, biopics, and science fiction pics. Be yourself. Don't try to be different to get noticed. Never talk about budget and a star that's attached that pre-sold in Egypt for $100 million. We don't care. We care about a 'unique voice,' a filmmaker willing to take risks. Scripts that push the limits without trying for 'shock' value. We care about filmmakers here."

VALEO FILMS INC.

P.O. Box 5876, Longview TX 75644. (903)797-6489. Fax: (903)797-6806. E-mail: screenplays@valeofilms.com. Website: www.valeofilms.com. President: David Ulloa.

Needs Currently considering projects "that contain 1 or more of the following: character or story driven; identifies moral values; romance/love story; educational/documentary; presents the human condition; strong visual imagery; coming of age/learning; or intellectual drama/mystery."

How to Contact Query by e-mail or regular mail. "We require that you provide us with your name, phone number, address, the title of your work, and either a WGA registration number or a copyright number. After receiving this information, we will send you an 'Unsolicited Project Release Letter.' You must then sign and return it with a single copy of your screenplay and/or treatment."

Tips Does not want "projects that contain the following characteristics: one character saves the world; SFX based; highly action based; extreme and grotesque violence; high sexual content; or strong explicit language. Although we do have a vast array of production resources available to us, VFI is a relatively small production company who prefers to limit the number of projects we have in production. Consequently, we tend to be very selective when it comes to selecting new material."

VINTAGE ENTERTAINMENT

1045 Ocean Ave., Penthouse, Santa Monica CA 90403. E-mail: info@GoVintage.com. Website: www.govintage. com. **Producer/Manager:** Peter Scott. Estab. 1994. "Vintage Entertainment is a film production and boutique management company located in Santa Monica, California. The management side of the company includes motion picture and TV writers, directors, actors, novelists, and new media clientele."

Needs "Vintage Entertainment intends to find talented artists eager to create the Vintage classics of tomorrow. Artists who embrace change, push the envelope. Artists with unique voices who communicate by instinct, not by formula. We seek artists with talent, passion, and craft. We are a small shop."

How to Contact Writers who wish to be considered by Vintage Entertainment must first e-mail a succinct logline describing the screenplay they wish to have reviewed. If we have interest in reading your material, we will send you our submission release form via e-mail."

Tips "Approximately 5% of all artists who approach us get reviewed."

Script Contests

This section contains script contests for both playwrights and screenwriters. Besides cash awards or other prizes, winning a contest can give you credibility when querying an agent. Especially impressive to agents are winners of the more prestigious contests such as the Nicholl Fellowship in Screenwriting (Read an interview with recent Nicholl Fellowship winners Brian Wray and Tejal Desai on page 192.), the Chesterfield Writer's Film Project, or the writing-fellowship program sponsored by the Walt Disney Studios and ABC.

See Also

Contests can get you recognition from producers or catch the attention of other industry professionals who sponsor or judge the contests. Even making it to the final round of these contests can give you credibility as a screenwriter and should be mentioned in your query letter when you're ready to find an agent. Some contests may even lead directly to representation by an agency as part of the prize package.

Again, it's always a good idea to register your script before submitting it. The Writers Guild of America (WGA) offers a registration service to members and nonmembers alike. Write the WGA for more information on specific agencies, script registration, and membership requirements, or visit them online at www.wga.org.

Contest deadlines, entry fees, and rules may vary from year to year, so it's a good idea to visit the contest's website or send a SASE requesting its rules and regulations before submitting. (For more information on submitting a contest entry, see The Winning Checklist on page 208.) Contests often require a specific entry form that you may either request by mail or download from the contest's website. Some deadlines are extended at the last minute, so be sure you have the latest information available before sending your submission.

For more listings of script contests, see www.writersmarket.com, www.moviebytes.com, or www.scriptsales.com.

The winning checklist

1　Understand the categories. Carefully read the writing categories being considered in the contest to determine if it's a good fit for your writing. Select the category (or categories) you enter wisely. Choosing the wrong category can result in a poor—and perhaps unfair—evaluation of your work.

2　Understand your rights. Many contests buy one-time publication rights or first rights for manuscripts. Some ask (and may require) all rights, which means that your entry becomes the property of the contest sponsor. Giving up all rights to publish your work is only worth it when the prize or recognition is exceptional. Think twice before making this decision.

3　Write your very best. Revise your work multiple times. Edit very carefully.

4　Follow the rules. Stick to the word limit. In fact, leave yourself a little breathing room by staying 10-20 words under limit. If the rules say double-space your composition and put your name and address in the top right corner of the page, do it that way.

5　Enter early. Judges often read the first few entries with an enthusiasm and excitement that wanes by the 300th composition. Use this knowledge to your advantage; make sure your work is among the early arrivals.

6　Send the right fee. Double-check your math when calculating your entry fee. Make sure what you owe corresponds with the amount on the check you enclose.

7　Arrival insurance. You can make sure your manuscript arrives at the correct address on time by obtaining a receipt or postal number for tracking your package.

8　Let it go. If you realize there's a mistake in your manuscript after you've submitted it, do not send a revision or a new entry.

9　Be patient. Keep in mind that running a writing competition takes time. The contest sponsor will notify you as soon as results are available. You won't speed up the process by asking for progress reports by mail, e-mail, or phone calls.

10　Different strokes. Every judge looks for different qualities in a manuscript. Don't give in to defeat if your entry doesn't make the winners' list this time. All judging—especially of writing—is subjective. Keep trying.

—Christine Mersch

▓ ALBERTA PLAYWRITING COMPETITION

Alberta Playwrights' Network, 2633 Hochwald Ave. SW, Calgary AB T3E 7K2, Canada. (403)269-8564; (800)268-8564. Fax: (403)265-6773. E-mail: apn@nucleus.com. Website: www.nucleus.com/~apn. Offered annually for unproduced plays with full-length and Discovery categories. Discovery is open only to previously unproduced playwrights. Open only to residents of Alberta. **Deadline: January 15. Charges $40 fee (Canadian).** Prize: Full length: $3,500 (Canadian); Discovery: $1,500 (Canadian); written critique, workshop of winning play, reading of winning plays at a Showcase Conference.

THE ANNUAL BLANK THEATRE COMPANY YOUNG PLAYWRIGHTS FESTIVAL

The Blank Theatre Co., 1301 Lucile Ave., Los Angeles CA 90026-1519. (323)662-7734. Fax: (323)661-3903. E-mail: info@theblank.com. Website: www.youngplaywrights.com; www.theblank.com. "Offered annually for unpublished work to encourage young writers to write for the theater by presenting their work as well as through our mentoring programs." Open to all writers 19 or younger on the submission date. **Deadline: March 15.** Prize: Workshop of the winning plays by professional theater artists.

ANNUAL INTERNATIONAL ONE-PAGE PLAY COMPETITION

Lamia Ink!, P.O. Box 202, Prince Street Station, New York NY 10012. **Contact:** Cortland Jessup, founder/artistic director. Offered annually for previously published or unpublished 1-page plays. Acquires "the rights to publish in our magazine and to be read or performed at the prize awarding festival." Playwright retains copyright. **Deadline: March 15.** Guidelines for SASE. **Charges $2/play or $5/3 plays.** Prize: $200, staged reading, and publication of 12 finalists.

ANNUAL NATIONAL PLAYWRITING CONTEST

Wichita State University, School of Performing Arts, 1845 Fairmount, Wichita KS 67260-0153. (316)978-3368. Fax: (316)978-3202. E-mail: steve.peters@wichita.edu. **Contact:** Dr. Steven J. Peters, contest director. Offered annually for full-length plays (minimum of 90-minutes playing time), or 2-3 short plays on related themes (minimum 90-minutes playing time). **Deadline: February 15.** Guidelines for SASE. Prize: Production by the Wichita State University Theatre. Winner announced April 15. No plays returned after February 15.

BAKER'S PLAYS HIGH SCHOOL PLAYWRITING CONTEST

Baker's Plays, P.O. Box 699222, Quincy MA 02269-9222. (617)745-0805. Fax: (617)745-9891. Website: www.bakersplays.com. **Contact:** Deirdre Shaw, managing editor. Offered annually for unpublished work by high school-age students. Plays can be about any subject, so long as the play can be reasonably produced on the high school stage. Plays may be of any length. Submissions must be accompanied by the signature of the sponsoring high school drama or English teacher, and it is recommended that the play receive a production or a public reading prior to the submission. Multiple submissions and co-authored scripts are welcome. Teachers may not submit a student's work. The ms must be firmly bound, typed, and come with SASE that includes enough postage to cover the return of the ms. Plays that do not come with a SASE will not be returned. Do not send originals; copies only. **Deadline: January 31.** Guidelines for SASE. Prize: 1st Place: $500, and publication by Baker's Plays; 2nd Place: $250; 3rd Place: $100.

▓ BUNTVILLE CREW'S AWARD BLUE

Buntville Crew, 118 N. Railroad Ave., Buckley IL 60918-0445. E-mail: buntville@yahoo.fr. **Contact:** Steven Packard, artistic director. Presented annually for the best unpublished/unproduced play script, under 15 pages, written by a student enrolled in any Illinois high school in the 2003-2004 school year. Submit 1 copy of the script in standard play format, a brief biography, and a SASE (scripts will not be returned). Include name, address, telephone number, age, and name of school. **Deadline: May 31.** Guidelines for SASE. Prize: Cash prize; possible productions in Buckley and/or New York City. Judged by panel selected by the theater.

▓ BUNTVILLE CREW'S PRIX HORS PAIR

Buntville Crew, 118 N. Railroad Ave., Buckley IL 60918-0445. E-mail: buntville@yahoo.fr. **Contact:** Steven Packard, artistic director. Annual award for unpublished/unproduced play script under 15 pages. Plays may be in English, French, German, or Spanish (no translations, no adaptations). Submit 1 copy of the script in standard play format, a résumé, and a SASE (scripts will not be returned). Include name, address, and telephone number. **Deadline: May 31.** Guidelines for SASE. **Charges $8.** Prize: $200; possible production in Buckley and/or New York City. Judged by panel selected by the theater. Open to any writer.

▓ CAA CAROL BOLT AWARD FOR DRAMA

Canadian Authors Association with the support of the Playwrights Union of Canada and Playwrights Canada

Press, 320 S. Shores Rd., P.O. Box 419, Campbellford ON K0L 1L0, Canada. (705)653-0323. Fax: (705)653-0593. E-mail: admin@canauthors.org. Website: www.canauthors.org. **Contact:** Alec McEachern. Annual contest for the best English-language play for adults by an author who is Canadian or landed immigrant. Submissions should be previously published or performed in the year prior to the giving of the award. For instance, in 2004 for this year's award to be given in July 2005. Open to Canadian citizens or landed immigrants. **Deadline: December 15, except for plays published or performed in December, in which case the deadline is January 15.** Guidelines for SASE. **Charges $35 (Canadian funds) fee.** Prize: $1,000, and a silver medal. Judged by a trustee for the award (appointed by the CAA). The trustee appoints up to 3 judges. The identities of the trustee and judges are confidential. Short lists are not made public. Decisions of the trustee and judges are final, and they may choose not to award a prize.

CALIFORNIA YOUNG PLAYWRIGHTS CONTEST

Playwrights Project, 450 B St., Suite 1020, San Diego CA 92101-8093. (619)239-8222. Fax: (619)239-8225. E-mail: write@playwrightsproject.com. Website: www.playwrightsproject.com. **Contact:** Cecelia Kouma, managing director. Offered annually for previously unpublished plays by young writers to stimulate young people to create dramatic works, and to nurture promising writers. Scripts must be a minimum of 10 standard typewritten pages; send 2 copies. Scripts will *not* be returned. All entrants receive detailed evaluation letter. Writers must be California residents under age 19 as of the deadline date. **Deadline: June 1.** Guidelines for SASE. Prize: Professional production of 3-5 winning plays at the Old Globe in San Diego, plus royalty.

COE COLLEGE PLAYWRITING FESTIVAL

Coe College, 1220 First Ave. NE, Cedar Rapids IA 52402-5092. (319)399-8624. Fax: (319)399-8557. E-mail: swolvert@coe.edu. Website: www.public.coe.edu/departments/theatre/. **Contact:** Susan Wolverton. Estab. 1993. Offered biennially for unpublished work to provide a venue for new works for the stage. ''There is usually a theme for the festival. We are interested in full-length productions, not one acts or musicals. There are no specific criteria although a current résumé and synopsis is requested.'' Open to any writer. **Deadline: November 1. Notification: January 15.** Guidelines for SASE. Prize: $325, plus 1-week residency as guest artist with airfare, room and board provided.

THE CUNNINGHAM COMMISSION FOR YOUTH THEATRE

The Theatre School, DePaul University, 2135 N. Kenmore, Chicago IL 60614. (773)325-7938. Fax: (773)325-7920. E-mail: lgoetsch@depaul.edu. Website: theatreschool.depaul.edu/programs/prize.htm. **Contact:** Lara Goetsch. Chicago-area playwrights only. Commission will result in a play for younger audiences that ''affirms the centrality of religion, broadly defined, and the human quest for meaning, truth, and community.'' **Deadline: December 1.** Guidelines for SASE. Prize: $5,000 ($2,000 when commission is contracted, $1,000 if script moves to workshop, $2,000 as royalty if script is produced by The Theatre School).

ℕ DAYTON PLAYHOUSE FUTUREFEST

The Dayton Playhouse, 1301 E. Siebenthaler Ave., Dayton OH 45414-5357. (937)333-7469. Fax: (937)333-2827. Website: www.daytonplayhouse.com. **Contact:** Dave Seyer, executive director. ''Three plays selected for full productions, 3 for readings at July FutureFest weekend; the 6 authors will be given travel and lodging to attend the festival.'' Professionally adjudicated. Guidelines for SASE or online. **Deadline: October 30.** Prize: $1,000; and $100 to the other 5 playwrights.

DRURY UNIVERSITY ONE-ACT PLAY CONTEST

Drury University, 900 N. Benton Ave., Springfield MO 65802-3344. E-mail: msokol@drury.edu. **Contact:** Mick Sokol. Offered in even-numbered years for unpublished and professionally unproduced plays. One play/playwright. Guidelines for SASE or by e-mail. **Deadline: December 1.**

DUBUQUE FINE ARTS PLAYERS ANNUAL ONE-ACT PLAY CONTEST

Dubuque Fine Arts Players, 1686 Lawndale, Dubuque IA 52001. E-mail: gary.arms@clarke.edu. **Contact:** Gary Arms. ''We select 3 one-act plays each year. We award cash prizes of up to $600 for a winning entry. We produce the winning plays in August.'' Offered annually for unpublished work. Guidelines and application form for SASE. **Deadline: January 31. Charges $10.** Prize: 1st Prize: $600; 2nd Prize: $300; 3rd Prize: $200. Judged by 3 groups who read all the plays; each play is read at least twice. Plays that score high enough, enter the second round. The top 10 plays are read by a panel consisting of 3 directors and 2 other final judges. Open to any writer.

EMERGING PLAYWRIGHT'S AWARD

Urban Stages, 17 E. 47th St., New York NY 10017-1920. (212)421-1380. Fax: (212)421-1387. E-mail: tlreilly@urb anstages.org. Website: www.urbanstages.org. **Contact:** T.L. Reilly, producing director. Estab. 1986. Submissions required to be unproduced in New York City. Send script, letter of introduction, production history, author's name, résumé, and SASE. Submissions accepted year-round. Plays selected in August and January for award consideration. One submission/person. **Deadline: Ongoing. Charges $5.** Prize: $1,000 (in lieu of royalties), and a staged production of winning play in New York City. Open to US Residents Only

ESSENTIAL THEATRE PLAYWRITING AWARD
The Essential Theatre, P.O. Box 8172, Atlanta GA 30306. (404)212-0815. E-mail: pmhardy@aol.com. **Contact:** Peter Hardy. Offered annually for unproduced, full-length plays by Georgia writers. No limitations as to style or subject matter. **Deadline: April 15.** Prize: $400, and full production.

SHUBERT FENDRICH MEMORIAL PLAYWRITING CONTEST
Pioneer Drama Service, Inc., P.O. Box 4267, Englewood CO 80155. (303)779-4035. Fax: (303)779-4315. E-mail: playwrights@pioneerdrama.com. Website: www.pioneerdrama.com. **Contact:** Lori Conary, assistant editor. Offered annually for unpublished, but previously produced, submissions to encourage the development of quality theatrical material for educational and community theater. Rights acquired only if published. Authors already published by Pioneer Drama are not eligible. **Deadline: March 1 (postmarked).** Guidelines for SASE. Prize: $1,000 royalty advance, publication.

FULL-LENGTH PLAY COMPETITION
West Coast Ensemble, P.O. Box 38728, Los Angeles CA 90038. (323)876-9337. Fax: (323)876-8916. Website: www.wcensemble.org. **Contact:** Les Hanson, artistic director. Offered annually "to nurture, support, and encourage" unpublished playwrights. Permission to present the play is granted if work is selected as finalist. **Deadline: December 31.** Guidelines for SASE. Prize: $500, and presentation of play.

ⓃJOHN GASSNER MEMORIAL PLAYWRITING COMPETITION
New England Theatre Conference, PMB 502, 198 Tremont St., Boston MA 02116. E-mail: mail@netconline.org. Website: www.netconline.org. Offered annually to unpublished full-length plays and scripts. Open to New England residents and NETC members. Playwrights living outside New England may participate by joining NETC. **Deadline: April 15.** Guidelines for SASE. **Charges $10 fee.** Prize: 1st Place: $1,000; 2nd Place: $500.

🇨🇦GOVERNOR GENERAL'S LITERARY AWARD FOR DRAMA
Canada Council for the Arts, 350 Albert St., P.O. Box 1047, Ottawa ON K1P 5V8, Canada. (613)566-4414, ext. 5576. Fax: (613)566-4410. E-mail: joanne.larocque-poirier@canadacouncil.ca. Website: www.canadacouncil .ca/prizes/ggla. **Contact:** Joanne Larocque-Poirier. Offered for the best English-language and the best French-language work of drama by a Canadian published September 1-September 30. Publishers submit titles for consideration. **Deadline: March 15 or August 7, depending on the book's publication date.** Prize: Each laureate receives $15,000, and nonwinning finalists receive $1,000.

ⓃAURAND HARRIS MEMORIAL PLAYWRITING AWARD
The New England Theatre Conference, Inc., PMB 502, 198 Tremont St., Boston MA 02116-4750. (617)851-8535. E-mail: mail@netconline.org. Website: www.netconline.org. Offered annually for an unpublished full-length play for young audiences. Guidelines for SASE. "No phone calls, please." Open to New England residents and/or members of the New England Theatre Conference. **Deadline: May 1.** Guidelines for SASE. **Charges $20 fee.** Prize: 1st Place: $1,000; 2nd Place: $500. Open to any writer.

HENRICO THEATRE COMPANY ONE-ACT PLAYWRITING COMPETITION
Henrico Recreation & Parks, P.O. Box 27032, Richmond VA 23273. (804)501-5138. Fax: (804)501-5284. E-mail: per22@co.henrico.va.us. Website: www.co.henrico.va.us/rec. **Contact:** Amy A. Perdue. Offered annually for previously unpublished or unproduced plays or musicals to produce new dramatic works in one-act form. "Scripts with small casts and simpler sets given preference. Controversial themes and excessive language should be avoided." **Deadline: July 1.** Guidelines for SASE. Prize: $300; Runner-Up: $200. Winning entries may be produced; videotape sent to author.

JEWEL BOX THEATRE PLAYWRIGHTING COMPETITION
Jewel Box Theatre, 3700 N. Walker, Oklahoma City OK 73118-7099. (405)521-1786. **Contact:** Charles Tweed, production director. Estab. 1982. Offered annually for full-length plays. Send SASE in October for guidelines. **Deadline: January 15.** Prize: $500.

ⓃTHE KAUFMAN & HART PRIZE FOR NEW AMERICAN COMEDY
Arkansas Repertory Theatre, P.O. Box 110, Little Rock AR 72203-0110. (501)378-0445. Website: www.therep.o

rg. **Contact:** Brad Mooy, literary manager. Offered every 2 years for unpublished, unproduced, full-length comedies (no musicals or children's plays). Scripts may be submitted with the recommendation of an agent or theater professional only. Must be at least 65 pages, with minimal set requirements and a cast limit of 12. One entry/playwright. Open to US citizens only. **Deadline: February 1; notification April.** Prize: $10,000, a staged reading, and transportation.

KUMU KAHUA/UHM THEATRE DEPARTMENT PLAYWRITING CONTEST

Kumu Kahua Theatre, Inc./University of Hawaii at Manoa, Dept. of Theatre and Dance, 46 Merchant St., Honolulu HI 96813. (808)536-4222. Fax: (808)536-4226. E-mail: kkt@pixi.com. Website: www.kumukahua.c om. **Contact:** Harry Wong III, artistic director. Offered annually for unpublished work to honor full-length and short plays. Guidelines available every September. First 2 categories open to residents and nonresidents. For Hawaii Prize, plays must be set in Hawaii or deal with some aspect of the Hawaiian experience. For Pacific Rim prize, plays must deal with the Pacific Islands, Pacific Rim, or Pacific/Asian-American experience—short plays only considered in 3rd category. **Deadline: January 2.** Prize: $500 (Hawaii Prize); $400 (Pacific Rim); $200 (Resident).

L.A. DESIGNERS' THEATRE-COMMISSIONS

L.A. Designers' Theatre, P.O. Box 1883, Studio City CA 91614-0883. (323)650-9600 or (323)654-2700 T.D.D. Fax: (323)654-3210. E-mail: ladesigners@juno.com. **Contact:** Richard Niederberg, artistic director. Quarterly contest "to promote new work and push it onto the conveyor belt to filmed or videotaped entertainment." All submissions must be registered with copyright office and be unpublished. Material will not be returned. "Do not submit anything that will not fit in a #10 envelope. No rules, guidelines, fees, or entry forms. Just present an idea that can be commissioned into a full work." Proposals for uncompleted works are encouraged. Unpopular political, religious, social, or other themes are encouraged; 'street' language and nudity are acceptable. Open to any writer. **Deadline: March 15, June 15, September 15, December 15.** Prize: Production or publication of the work in the Los Angeles market. "We only want 'first refusal.'"

LOVE CREEK ANNUAL SHORT PLAY FESTIVAL

Love Creek Productions, c/o Granville, 162 Nesbit St., Weehawken NJ 07086-6817. E-mail: creekread@aol.com. **Contact:** Cynthia Granville-Callahan, festival manager. Estab. 1985. *E-mail address is for information only.* Annual festival for unpublished plays, unproduced in New York in the previous year, under 40 minutes, at least 2 characters, larger casts preferred. "We established the Festival as a playwriting competition in which scripts are judged on their merits in performance." All entries must specify "festival" on envelope and must include letter giving permission to produce script, if chosen, and stating whether equity showcase is acceptable. "We are giving strong preference to scripts featuring females in major roles in casts which are predominantly female." **Deadline: Ongoing.** Guidelines for SASE. Prize: Cash prize awarded to overall winner.

ℕ LOVE CREEK MINI FESTIVALS

Love Creek Productions, c/o Granville, 162 Nesbit St., Weehawken NJ 07086-6817. E-mail: creekread@aol.com. **Contact:** Cynthia Granville-Callahan, festival literary manager. *E-mail address is for information only.* "The Mini Festivals are an outgrowth of our annual Short Play Festival in which we produce scripts concerning a particular issue or theme which our artistic staff selects according to current needs, interests, and concerns of our members, audiences, and playwrights submitting to our Short Play Festival throughout the year." Considers scripts unpublished, unproduced in New York City in the past year, under 40 minutes, at least 2 characters, larger casts preferred. Submissions must list name of festival on envelope and must include letter giving permission to produce script, if chosen, and stating whether equity showcase is acceptable. Finalists receive a mini-showcase production in New York City. Write for upcoming themes. "We are giving strong preference to scripts featuring females in major roles in casts which are predominantly female." **Deadline: Ongoing.** Guidelines for SASE. Prize: Winner of overall festival series receives a cash prize.

MAXIM MAZUMDAR NEW PLAY COMPETITION

Alleyway Theatre, One Curtain Up Alley, Buffalo NY 14202-1911. (716)852-2600. Fax: (716)852-2266. E-mail: email@alleyway.com. Website: alleyway.com. **Contact:** Literary Manager. Estab. 1990. Annual competition. Full Length: Not less than 90 minutes, no more than 10 performers. One-Act: Less than 20 minutes, no more than 6 performers. Children's plays. Musicals must be accompanied by audio tape. Finalists announced October 1. "Playwrights may submit work directly. There is no entry form. Annual playwright's **fee $5**; may submit 1 in each category, but pay only 1 fee. Please specify if submission is to be included in competition." "Alleyway Theatre must receive first production credit in subsequent printings and productions." **Deadline: July 1.** Prize: Full length: $400, production, and royalties; One-act: $100, production, plus royalties.

[N] McKNIGHT ADVANCEMENT GRANT

The Playwrights' Center, 2301 Franklin Ave. E., Minneapolis MN 55406-1099. (612)332-7481, ext. 10. Fax: (612)332-6037. E-mail: info@pwcenter.org. Website: www.pwcenter.org. **Contact:** Kristen Gandrow, director of new play development. Offered annually for either published or unpublished playwrights to recognize those whose work demonstrates exceptional artistic merit and potential and whose primary residence is in the state of Minnesota. The grants are intended to significantly advance recipients' art and careers, and can be used to support a wide variety of expenses. Applications available December 1. Guidelines for SASE. Additional funds of up to $1,500 are available for workshops and readings. The Playwrights' Center evaluates each application and forwards finalists to a panel of three judges from the national theater community. Applicant must have been a citizen or permanent resident of the US and a legal resident of the state of Minnesota since July 1, 2004. (Residency must be maintained during fellowship year.) Applicant must have had a minimum of one work fully produced by a professional theater at the time of application. **Deadline: February 4.** Prize: $25,000 which can be used to support a wide variety of expenses, including writing time, artistic costs of residency at a theater or arts organization, travel and study, production or presentation.

[N] McLAREN MEMORIAL COMEDY PLAY WRITING COMPETITION

Midland Community Theatre, 2000 W. Wadley, Midland TX 79705. (432)682-2544. Fax: (432)682-6136. Website: www.mctmidland.org. **Contact:** Alathea Blischke, McLaren co-chair. Estab. 1990. Offered annually in 2 divisions: one-act and full-length. All entries must be comedies for adults, teens, or children; musical comedies accepted. Work must have never been professionally produced or published. See website for competition guidelines and required entry form. **Charges $10 fee/script.** Prize: $400 for winning full-length play; $200 for winning one-act play; staged readings for finalists in each category.

MOVING ARTS PREMIERE ONE-ACT COMPETITION

Moving Arts, 514 S. Spring St., Los Angeles CA 90013-2304. (213)622-8906. Fax: (213)622-8946. E-mail: treynichols@movingarts.org. Website: www.movingarts.org. **Contact:** Trey Nichols, literary director. Offered annually for unproduced one-act plays in the Los Angeles area and "is designed to foster the continued development of one-act plays." All playwrights are eligible except Moving Arts resident artists. Guidelines for SASE or by e-mail. **Deadline: February 28 (postmarked). Charges $10 fee/script.** Prize: 1st Place: $200, plus a full production with a 4-8 week run; 2nd and 3rd Place: Program mention and possible production.

MUSICAL STAIRS

West Coast Ensemble, P.O. Box 38728, Los Angeles CA 90038. (323)876-9337. Fax: (323)876-8916. **Contact:** Les Hanson. Offered annually for unpublished writers "to nurture, support, and encourage musical creators." Permission to present the musical is granted if work is selected as finalist. **Deadline: June 30.** Prize: $500, and presentation of musical.

NANTUCKET SHORT PLAY COMPETITION AND FESTIVAL

Nantucket Theatrical Productions, Box 2177, Nantucket MA 02584. (508)228-5002. **Contact:** Jim Patrick, artistic director. Offered annually for unpublished plays to "seek the highest quality of playwriting distilled into a short-play format." Selected plays receive staged readings. Plays must be less than 40 pages. **Deadline: January 1. Charges $10 fee.** Prize: $200, plus staged readings.

NATIONAL AUDIO DRAMA SCRIPT COMPETITION

National Audio Theatre Festivals, 115 Dikeman St., Hempstead NY 11150. (516)483-8321. Fax: (516)538-7583. Website: www.natf.org. **Contact:** Sue Zizza. Offered annually for unpublished radio scripts. "NATF is particularly interested in stories that deserve to be told because they enlighten, intrigue, or simply make us laugh out loud. Contemporary scripts with strong female roles, multi-cultural casting, and diverse viewpoints will be favorably received." Preferred length is 25 minutes. Guidelines on website. Open to any writer. NATF will have the right to produce the scripts for the NATF Live Performance Workshop; however, NATF makes no commitment to produce any script. The authors will retain all other rights to their work. **Deadline: November 15. Charges $25 fee (US currency only).** Prize: $800 split between 2-4 authors, and free workshop production participation.

[C] NATIONAL CANADIAN ONE-ACT PLAYWRITING COMPETITION

Ottawa Little Theatre, 400 King Edward Ave., Ottawa ON K1N 7M7, Canada. (613)233-8948. Fax: (613)233-8027. E-mail: olt@on-aibn.com. Website: www.o-l-t.com. **Contact:** Elizabeth Holden, office manager. Estab. 1913. Purpose is "to encourage literary and dramatic talent in Canada." Guidelines for #10 SASE with Canadian postage or #10 SAE with 1 IRC. **Deadline: August 31.** Prize: 1st Place: $1,000; 2nd Place: $700; 3rd Place: $500.

Martin Blinder

Script competition award opens
Hollywood door for writer

When Martin Blinder submitted his script *Catch the Devil* to the International Screenplay Competition, sponsored by the American Screenwriters Association and *Writer's Digest* magazine, he could only dream of the attention he and his script would receive after being announced the winner.

Blinder, 66, a forensic psychiatrist from San Anselmo, California, has been writing scripts for more than 16 years. "I discovered that I started writing scripts at the exact same age at which William Shakespeare quit—not a good sign." In an industry notorious for ageism and dominated by young writers, Blinder realizes he has an uphill struggle. "Even successful screenwriters in Hollywood stop selling scripts after the age of 40 or 45," he says.

One of the keys to Blinder overcoming his late start has been script competitions. He has won five screenplay competitions, and his award-winning scripts have helped him get an agent and convince producers to read his material.

In 2002, Blinder's script was up against a record-breaking 1,255 scripts that were submitted to the Competition. The winner of the International Screenplay Competition takes home a $5,000 cash prize, but more importantly, being named a competition winner opens doors to the major studios. As Blinder says, "Even when I've not won a competition, I've gotten a couple of calls from producers or would-be producers. So, I think it's a good thing."

As part of his prize, Blinder traveled to Los Angeles to attend the Selling to Hollywood Conference in 2002 where he pitched his work directly to producers and production company development personnel. Some of those producers interested in Blinder's work represented production companies that had not shown interest in Blinder's work prior to his winning the International Screenplay Competition. The simple fact is: In the competitive world of feature film and television, even a great script needs a stamp of approval—and a major script competition provides one.

Script competitions such as the Nicholl Fellowship, Big Break International Screenwriting Contest, and the ASA/WD International Screenplay Competition are notoriously successful at finding nuggets of gold amid the thousands of screenplays that land in studio slush piles only to be returned with nothing more than a rejection letter.

Although Blinder believes it's important for struggling screenwriters to keep their heads up, he also thinks that even competition winners need to stay grounded. "One has to be careful not to get one's hopes up too much in this business, or you're going to be very unhappy."

Still, Blinder is happy with the performance of his winning script, *Catch the Devil*. The story was inspired by the first Congressional Medals of Honor granted after the Civil War. "These Union adventurers sneak down into the heart of the South and abscond with a super locomotive, reeking havoc as they go." The script and revision took three or four months to write. "If you put all of my drafts end to end, I'm sure they would paper the freeway between San Francisco and Los Angeles," says Blinder. "I'm not a very good writer, but I'm one devil of a rewriter."

Therein lies the key to Blinder's success in screenplay competitions: The rewrite is more important that the first draft. "I'll think [my first draft] is the work of genius. I'll put it away for three or four days, take it out of the drawer, and say, 'It's terrible!' " The best script competitions will receive between 1,000 and 6,000 scripts every year. With odds like those, it's important that your script be as close to "perfect" as possible. That means no spelling errors, typos, formatting errors, or—the worst thing in any script—inconsistencies. Even more importantly, your dialogue must be rich and fluid without all the characters sounding alike, your plot and story structure must be infallible, and your scene descriptions must be short yet captivating.

The best script competitions are always judged by panels of professional screenwriters, producers, and development personnel. The judges make their livings writing and reading scripts. They know the basic elements that all scripts need and, more importantly, they know what separates the great from the "not so good." Blinder's last piece of advice for writers interested in submitting a script to a competition? "If in doubt, cut it out." There just isn't any room in your script for something that "might" work.

—Jerry Jackson, Jr.

NATIONAL CHILDREN'S THEATRE FESTIVAL

Actors' Playhouse at the Miracle Theatre, 280 Miracle Mile, Coral Gables FL 33134. (305)444-9293. Fax: (305)444-4181. Website: www.actorsplayhouse.org. **Contact:** Earl Maulding. Offered annually for unpublished musicals for young audiences. Target age is between 3-12. Script length should be 45-60 minutes. Maximum of 8 actors to play any number of roles. Settings which lend themselves to simplified scenery. Bilingual (English/Spanish) scripts are welcomed. Call or visit website for guidelines. Open to any writer. **Deadline: June 1. Charges $10 fee.** Prize: 1st Place: $500, and full production.

NATIONAL LATINO PLAYWRITING AWARD

(formerly National Latino Playwrights Award), Arizona Theatre Co. in affiliation with Centro Cultural Mexicano, 40 E. 14th St., Tucson AZ 85701. (520)884-8210, ext. 5510. Fax: (520)628-9129. E-mail: eromero@arizonatheatre.org. Website: www.arizonatheatre.org. **Contact:** Elaine Romero, playwright-in-residence. Offered annually for unproduced (professionally), unpublished plays over 50 pages in length. "The plays may be in English, bilingual, or in Spanish (with English translation). The award recognizes exceptional full-length plays by Latino playwrights on any subject." Open to Latino playwrights currently residing in the US, its territories, and/or Mexico. **Deadline: December 30.** Guidelines for SASE. Prize: $1,000.

NATIONAL ONE-ACT PLAYWRITING COMPETITION

Little Theatre of Alexandria, 600 Wolfe St., Alexandria VA 22314. Website: www.thelittletheatre.com/oneact. Estab. 1978. Offered annually to encourage original writing for theater. Submissions must be original, unpublished, unproduced, one-act stage plays. "We usually produce top 2 or 3 winners." Guidelines for SASE or on website. **Deadline: Submit scripts for contest from January 1-May 31. Charges $20/play; 2-play limit.** Prize: 1st Place: $350; 2nd Place: $250; 3rd Place: $150.

NATIONAL PLAYWRITING COMPETITION

Young Playwrights, Inc., 306 W. 38th St., Suite 300, New York NY 10018. (212)594-5440. Fax: (212)594-5441. E-mail: writeaplay@aol.com. Website: youngplaywrights.org. **Contact:** Literary Department. Offered annually for stage plays of any length (no musicals, screenplays, or adaptations). Writers ages 18 or younger (as of deadline) are invited to send scripts. **Deadline: December 1.** Prize: Invitation to week-long Writers' Conference in New York City (all expenses paid) and off-Broadway presentation.

ℕ NEW AMERICAN COMEDY WORKSHOP

Ukiah Players Theatre, 1041 Low Gap Rd., Ukiah CA 95482. (707)462-1210. Fax: (707)462-1790. E-mail: players @pacific.net. Website: ukiahplayerstheatre.org. **Contact:** Kate Magruder, executive director. Offered every 2 years to playwrights seeking to develop their unproduced, full-length comedies into funnier, stronger scripts. Two scripts will be chosen for staged readings; 1 of these may be chosen for full production. **Deadline: November 30 of odd-numbered years.** Prize: Playwrights chosen for readings will receive a $25 royalty/performance. The playwright chosen for full production will receive a $50 royalty/performance, travel (up to $500) to Ukiah for development workshop/rehearsal, lodging, and per diem. Guidelines for SASE or on website.

NEW WORKS FOR THE STAGE

COE College Theatre Arts Department, 1220 First Ave. NE, Cedar Rapids IA 52402. (319)399-8624. Fax: (319)399-8557. E-mail: swolvert@coe.edu. Website: www.public.coe.edu/departments/theatre. **Contact:** Susan Wolverton. Offered every 2 years (odd years) "to encourage new work, to provide an interdisciplinary forum for the discussion of issues found in new work, to offer playwright contact with theater professionals who can provide response to new work." Full-length, original unpublished and unproduced scripts only. No musicals, adaptations, translations, or collaborations. Submit 1-page synopsis, résumé, and SASE if the script is to be returned. **Deadline: November 1, 2004.** Prize: $325, plus travel, room and board for residency at the college.

DON AND GEE NICHOLL FELLOWSHIPS IN SCREENWRITING

Academy of Motion Picture Arts & Sciences, 1313 N. Vine St., Los Angeles CA 90028. (310)247-3059. E-mail: nicholl@oscars.org. Website: www.oscars.org/nicholl. **Contact:** Greg Beal, program coordinator. Estab. 1985. Offered annually for unproduced screenplays to identify talented new screenwriters. Applications available mid-January-April 30. Recipients announced late October. Open to writers who have not earned more than $5,000 writing for films or TV. **Deadline: May 1. Charges $30 fee.** Prize: $30,000 in fellowships (up to 5/year).

OGLEBAY INSTITUTE TOWNGATE THEATRE PLAYWRITING CONTEST

Oglebay Institute, Stifel Fine Arts Center, 1330 National Rd., Wheeling WV 26003. (304)242-7700. Fax: (304)242-7747. Website: www.oionline.com. **Contact:** Kate H. Crosbie, director of performing arts. Estab. 1976. Offered annually for unpublished works. "All full-length nonmusical plays that have never been professionally produced or published are eligible." Open to any writer. **Deadline: January 1; winner announced May 31.** Guidelines for SASE. Prize: Run of play and cash award.

ONE ACT MARATHON

Attic Theatre & Film Center, 5429 W. Washington Blvd., Los Angeles CA 90016. (323)525-0600. E-mail: attictheat re1@aol.com. Website: www.attictheatre.org. **Contact:** Literary Manager. Offered annually for unpublished and unproduced work. Guidelines for SASE or online. **Deadline: October 30. Charges $15.** Prize: 1st Place: $250; 2nd Place: $100; 1st-3rd Place scripts will be produced. Acquires 6-month window for 1st-6th Place entries for exclusive option.

MILDRED & ALBERT PANOWSKI PLAYWRITING AWARD

Forest Roberts Theatre, Northern Michigan University, Marquette MI 49855-5364. (906)227-2559. Fax: (906)227-2567. Website: www.nmu.edu/theatre. **Contact:** Megan Marcellini, award coordinator. Estab. 1977. Offered annually for unpublished, unproduced, full-length plays. Guidelines and application for SASE. **Deadline: August 15-November 15 (due at office on the 15th).** Prize: $2,000, a fully-mounted production, and transportation to Marquette to serve as Artist-in-Residence the week of the show.

PERISHABLE THEATRE'S WOMEN'S PLAYWRITING FESTIVAL

P.O. Box 23132, Providence RI 02903. (401)331-2695. Fax: (401)331-7811. E-mail: info@perishable.org. Website: www.perishable.org. **Contact:** Rebecca Wolf, festival coordinator. Offered annually for unproduced, one-act plays (up to 30 minutes in length when fully produced) to encourage women playwrights. Judged by reading committee, the festival director, and the artistic director of the theater. Open to women playwrights exclusively. **Deadline: October 15 (postmarked).** Guidelines for SASE. **Charges $5 fee/playwright (limit 2 plays/playwright).** Prize: $500, and travel to Providence.

PETERSON EMERGING PLAYWRIGHT COMPETITION

Catawba College Theatre Arts Department, 2300 W. Innes St., Salisbury NC 28144. (704)637-4440. Fax: (704)637-4207. E-mail: lfkesler@catawba.edu. Website: www.catawba.edu. **Contact:** Linda Kesler, theatre arts department staff. Offered annually for full-length unpublished work "to assist emerging playwrights in the development of new scripts, hopefully leading to professional production. Competition is open to all subject matter except children's plays. Playwrights may submit more than 1 entry.'' Open to any writer. Guidelines for SASE or by e-mail. **Deadline: December 1.** Prize: Production of the winning play at Catawba College; $2,000 cash award; transportation to and from Catawba College for workshop and performance; lodging and food while in residence; professional response to the performance of the play.

ROBERT J. PICKERING AWARD FOR PLAYWRIGHTING EXCELLENCE

Coldwater Community Theater, c/o 89 Division, Coldwater MI 49036. (517)279-7963. Fax: (517)279-8095. **Contact:** J. Richard Colbeck, committee chairperson. Estab. 1982. Previously unproduced monetarily. ''To encourage playwrights to submit their work, to present a previously unproduced play in full production.'' Submit script with SASE. ''We reserve the right to produce winning script.'' **Deadline: December 31.** Guidelines for SASE. Prize: 1st Place: $300; 2nd Place: $100; 3rd Place: $50.

PILGRIM PROJECT GRANTS

156 Fifth, #400, New York NY 10010. (212)627-2288. Fax: (212)627-2184. E-mail: davida@firstthings.com. **Contact:** Davida Goldman. Grants for a reading, workshop production, or full production of plays that deal with questions of moral significance. **Deadline: Ongoing.** Guidelines for SASE. Prize: Grants of $1,000-7,000.

PLAYHOUSE ON THE SQUARE NEW PLAY COMPETITION

Playhouse on the Square, 51 S. Cooper, Memphis TN 38104. **Contact:** Jackie Nichols. Submissions required to be unproduced. **Deadline: April 1.** Guidelines for SASE. Prize: $500, and production.

PLAYWRIGHT DISCOVERY AWARD

VSA Arts, 1300 Connecticut Ave. NW, Suite 700, Washington DC 20036. (202)628-2800. Fax: (202)737-0725. E-mail: info@vsarts.org. Website: www.vsarts.org. **Contact:** Director, Performing Arts. Invites students with and without disabilities (grades 6-12) to submit a one-act play that explores the experience of living with a disability. Two plays will be selected for production at the John F. Kennedy Center for the Performing Arts. **Deadline: April 15.** Guidelines for SASE. Prize: Monetary award, and a trip to Washington DC to view the production or staged reading.

ⓝ PLAYWRIGHTS/SCREENWRITERS FELLOWSHIPS

NC Arts Council, Dept. of Cultural Resources, Raleigh NC 27699-4632. (919)715-1519. Fax: (919)733-4834. E-mail: debbie.mcgill@ncmail.net. Website: www.ncarts.org. **Contact:** Deborah McGill, literature director. Every 2 Years Even Years, Must Be Unpublished. **Deadline: November 1, 2004.** Guidelines for SASE. Prize: Prize: $8,000. Judged by a panel of film and theater professionals (playwrights; screenwriters; directors; producers; etc.).

PRINCESS GRACE AWARDS PLAYWRIGHT FELLOWSHIP

Princess Grace Foundation—USA, 150 E. 58th St., 25th Floor, New York NY 10155. (212)317-1470. Fax: (212)317-1473. E-mail: pgfusa@pgfusa.com. Website: www.pgfusa.com. **Contact:** Christine Giancatarino, grants coordinator. Offered annually for unpublished, unproduced submissions to support playwright-through-residency program with New Dramatists, Inc., located in New York City. Entrants must be U.S. citizens or have permanent U.S. status. Guidelines for SASE or on website. **Deadline: March 31.** Prize: $7,500, plus residency with New Dramatists, Inc., in New York City, and representation/publication by Samuel French, Inc.

RICHARD RODGERS AWARDS IN MUSICAL THEATER

American Academy of Arts and Letters, 633 W. 155th St., New York NY 10032-7599. (212)368-5900. Fax: (212)491-4615. **Contact:** Lydia Kaim. Estab. 1978. The Richard Rodgers Awards subsidize full productions, studio productions, and staged readings by nonprofit theaters in New York City of works by composers and writers who are not already established in the field of musical theater. Authors must be citizens or permanent residents of the US. Guidelines and application for SASE. **Deadline: November 1.**

SCRIPTAPALOOZA SCREENWRITING COMPETITION

supported by Writers Guild of America and sponsored by Write Brothers, Inc., 7775 Sunset Blvd., PMB #200, Hollywood CA 90046. (323)654-5809. E-mail: info@scriptapalooza.com. Website: www.scriptapalooza.com. Annual contest open to unpublished scripts from any genre. Open to any writer, 18 or older. Submit 1 copy of a 90-130-page screenplay. Body pages must be numbered, and scripts must be in industry-standard format. All entered scripts are being read and judged by over 50 production companies. **Deadline: Early Deadline: January 5; Deadline: March 4; Late Deadline: April 15.** Guidelines for SASE. **Charges Early Deadline Fee: $40; Fee: $45; Late Deadline Fee: $50.** Prize: 1st Place: $10,000, and software package from Write Brothers, Inc; 2nd and 3rd Place, plus 10 Runners-Up: Software package from Write Brothers, Inc. The top 13 scripts will be considered by over 50 production companies.

SIENA COLLEGE INTERNATIONAL PLAYWRIGHTS COMPETITION

Siena College Theatre Program, 515 Loudon Rd., Loudonville NY 12211-1462. (518)783-2381. Fax: (518)783-2381. E-mail: maciag@siena.edu. Website: www.siena.edu/theatre. **Contact:** Gary Maciag, director. Offered every 2 years for unpublished plays "to allow students to explore production collaboration with the playwright. In addition, it provides the playwright an important development opportunity. Plays should be previously unproduced, unpublished, full-length, nonmusicals, and free of copyright and royalty restrictions. Plays should require unit set, or minimal changes, and be suitable for a college-age cast of 3-10. There is a required 4-6 week residency." Guidelines for SASE. Guidelines are available after November 1 in odd-numbered years. Winning playwright must agree that the Siena production will be the world premiere of the play. **Deadline: February 1-June 30 in even-numbered years.** Prize: $2,000 honorarium; up to $2,000 to cover expenses for required residency; full production of winning script.

DOROTHY SILVER PLAYWRITING COMPETITION

The Eugene S. & Blanche R. Halle Theatre of the Jewish Community Center of Cleveland, 3505 Mayfield Rd., Cleveland Heights OH 44118. (216)382-4000, ext. 274. Fax: (216)382-5401. E-mail: halletheatre@clevejcc.org. Website: www.clevejcc.org. **Contact:** Kris Barnes, box office manager. Estab. 1948. All entries must be original works, not previously produced, suitable for a full-length presentation; directly concerned with the Jewish experience. **Deadline: May 1.** Prize: Cash award, plus staged reading.

N SOUTH CUMBERLAND PLAYWRIGHTS CONTEST

The South Cumberland Cultural Society (SCCS), P.O. Box 333, Monteagle TN 37356. Annual award for unproduced dramatic, comedic, or musical plays that focus on the history, culture, and personalities of the South Cumberland region. Entries may be full-length plays or a series of shorter pieces. Entries should constitute a full evening in the theater and run at least 70 minutes. They may include interactive, dinner murder mysteries or nonsectarian holiday specials. SCCS shall have the option of first production of any prize-winning play within 2 years of the announcement of the award. SCCS shall have the right to retain all entries for its archives. Open to any writer resident in Tennessee. **Deadline: October 1.** Prize: 1st Place: $500; 2nd Place: $300; 3rd Place: $200. Judged by a panel of theater professionals independent of the SCCS.

SOUTHERN PLAYWRIGHTS COMPETITION

Jacksonville State University, 700 Pelham Rd. N., Jacksonville AL 36265-1602. (256)782-5414. Fax: (256)782-5441. E-mail: swhitton@jsucc.jsu.edu. Website: www.jsu.edu/depart/english/southpla.htm. **Contact:** Steven J. Whitton. Estab. 1988. Offered annually to identify and encourage the best of Southern playwriting. Playwrights must be a native or resident of Alabama, Arkansas, Florida, Georgia, Kentucky, Louisiana, Missouri, North Carolina, South Carolina, Tennessee, Texas, Virginia, or West Virginia. **Deadline: February 15.** Guidelines for SASE. Prize: $1,000, and production of the play.

SOUTHWEST THEATRE ASSOCIATION NATIONAL NEW PLAY CONTEST

Southwest Theatre Association, c/o David H. Fennema, Dept. of Music and Theatre Arts, Cameron University, Lawton OK 73505-6377. E-mail: davidf@cameron.edu. Website: www.southwest-theater.com. **Contact:** David H. Fennema, chair. Annual contest for unpublished, unproduced work to promote the writing and production of new one-act or full-length plays. No musicals, translations, adaptations of previously produced or published work, or children's plays. Guidelines for SASE or by e-mail. Open to writers who reside in the US. One entry/writer. **Deadline: March 15. Charges $10 (make check payable to SWTA).** Prize: $300 honorarium, a reading at the annual SWTA conference, complimentary registration at conference, 1-year membership in SWTA, award plaque, and possibility of excerpt publication in the professional journal of SWTA.

STANLEY DRAMA AWARD

Dept. of Theatre Wagner College, One Campus Rd., Staten Island NY 10301. (718)390-3157. Fax: (718)390-3323. **Contact:** Dr. Felicia J. Ruff, director. Offered for original full-length stage plays, musicals, or one-act play sequences that have not been professionally produced or received trade book publication. **Deadline: October 1.** Guidelines for SASE. **Charges $20 submission fee.** Prize: $2,000.

N TCG/METLIFE FOUNDATION EXTENDED COLLABORATION GRANTS

Theatre Communications Group, Inc., 520 8th Ave., 24th Floor, New York NY 10018-4156. (212)609-5900. Fax: (212)609-5901. E-mail: grants@tcg.org. Website: www.tcg.org. **Contact:** Sheela Kangal, senior artistic programs associate. Program is "designed to allow writers to work collaboratively with other artists for a period beyond the sponsoring theatre's normal preproduction and rehearsal schedule. Grants of $5,500 will be awarded 2 times in 2004. Only artistic leaders of TCG member theatres can apply on behalf of the writer. Applications will be automatically mailed to TCG member theatres."

⚡ THEATRE BC'S ANNUAL CANADIAN NATIONAL PLAYWRITING COMPETITION

Theatre BC, P.O. Box 2031, Nanaimo BC V9R 6X6, Canada. (250)714-0203. Fax: (250)714-0213. E-mail: pwc@th eatrebc.org. Website: www.theatrebc.org. **Contact:** Robb Mowbray, executive director. Offered annually to unpublished plays "to promote the development and production of previously unproduced new plays (no musicals) at all levels of theater. Categories: Full Length (2 acts or longer); One Act (less than 60 minutes); and an open Special Merit (juror's discretion). Guidelines for SASE or on website. Winners are also invited to New Play Festival: Up to 18 hours with a professional dramaturg, registrant actors, and a public reading in Kamloops (every Spring). Production and publishing rights remain with the playwright. Open to Canadian residents. All submissions are made under pseudonyms. E-mail inquiries welcome. **Deadline: Fourth Monday in July. Charges $35/entry, and optional $25 for written critique.** Prize: Full Length: $1,000; One Act: $750; Special Merit: $500.

THEATRE CONSPIRACY ANNUAL NEW PLAY CONTEST

Theatre Conspiracy, 10091 McGregor Blvd., Ft. Myers FL 33919. (239)936-3239. Fax: (239)936-0510. E-mail: info@theatreconspiracy.org. **Contact:** Bill Taylor, award director. Offered annually for unproduced full-length plays with 8 or less characters and simple production demands. Open to any writer. Send SASE for reply. **Deadline: November 30. Charges $5 fee.** Prize: $700, and full production.

THEATREFEST REGIONAL PLAYWRITING FESTIVAL

(formerly TheatreFest Regional Playwriting Contest), TheatreFest, Montclair State University, Upper Montclair NJ 07043. (973)655-7071. Fax: (973)655-5335. E-mail: blakec@mail.montclair.edu. Website: www.montclair. edu/theatrefest. **Contact:** John Wooten, artistic director. Offered annually for unpublished work to encourage and nurture the work of American dramatists. Open to any writer in the tri-state area (New Jersey, New York, Connecticut). Guidelines are available September-January, send a SASE for guidelines. **Deadline: January 31.** Prize: 1st Place: $1,500, and equity production; Runners-up (2): $500 and possible workshop.

⚡ THEATREPEI NEW VOICES PLAYWRITING COMPETITION

P.O. Box 1573, Charlottetown PE C1A 7N3, Canada. (902)894-3558. Fax: (902)368-7180. E-mail: theatre@isn.n et. **Contact:** Dawn Binkley, general manager. Offered annually. Open to individuals who have been residents of Prince Edward Island for 6 months preceding the deadline for entries. **Deadline: February 14.** Guidelines for SASE. **Charges $5 fee.** Prize: Monetary.

TRUSTUS PLAYWRIGHTS' FESTIVAL

Trustus Theatre, Box 11721, Columbia SC 29211-1721. (803)254-9732. Fax: (803)771-9153. E-mail: trustus@trus tus.org. Website: www.trustus.org. **Contact:** Jon Tuttle, literary manager. Offered annually for professionally unproduced full-length plays; cast limit of 8; prefer challenging, innovative dramas and comedies; no musicals, plays for young audiences, or "hillbilly" southern shows. Guidelines and application for SASE. **Deadline: Applications received between December 1, 2004, and February 28, 2005, only.** Prize: Public staged-reading and $250, followed after a 1-year development period by full production, $500, plus travel/accommodations to attend opening.

UNICORN THEATRE NEW PLAY DEVELOPMENT

Unicorn Theatre, 3828 Main St., Kansas City MO 64111. (816)531-7529, ext. 18. Fax: (816)531-0421. Website: www.unicorntheatre.org. **Contact:** Herman Wilson, literary assistant. Offered annually to encourage and assist the development of an unpublished and unproduced play. Acquires 2% subsidiary rights of future productions for a 5-year period. **Deadline: Ongoing.** Guidelines for SASE. Prize: $1,000 royalty, and production.

VERMONT PLAYWRIGHT'S AWARD

The Valley Players, P.O. Box 441, Waitsfield VT 05673. (802)496-3751. E-mail: valleyplayers@madriver.com. Website: www.valleyplayers.com. **Contact:** Jennifer Howard, chair. Offered annually for unpublished, nonmusical, full-length plays suitable for production by a community theater group to encourage development of playwrights in Vermont, New Hampshire, and Maine. **Deadline: February 1.** Prize: $1,000.

🆕 ⚡ THE HERMAN VOADEN NATIONAL PLAYWRITING COMPETITION

Drama Department, Queen's University, Kingston ON K7L 3N6, Canada. (613)533-2104. E-mail: hannaca@post. queensu.ca. Website: www.queensu.ca/drama. **Contact:** Carol Anne Hanna. Offered every 2 years for unpublished plays to discover and develop new Canadian plays. See website for deadlines, guidelines. Open to Canadian citizens or landed immigrants. **Charges $30 entry fee.** Prize: $3,000, $2,000, and 8 honorable mentions. 1st- and 2nd-prize winners are offered a 1-week workshop and public reading by professional director and cast. The 2 authors will be playwrights-in-residence for the rehearsal and reading period.

VSA ARTS PLAYWRIGHT DISCOVERY AWARD

VSA Arts, 1300 Connecticut Ave. NW, Suite 700, Washington DC 20036. (202)628-2800. Fax: (202)737-0725. Website: www.vsarts.org. **Contact:** Performing Arts Coordinator. The VSA Arts Playwright Discovery Award challenges students grades 6-12 of all abilities to express their views about disability by writing a one-act play. Two plays will be produced at The Kennedy Center in Washington, D.C. The Playwright Discovery Teacher Award honors teachers who bring disability awareness to the classroom through the art of playwriting. Recipient receives funds for playwriting resources, a trip to Washington, D.C., and national recognition. **Deadline: April 16.** Prize: Monetary award along with an expense-paid trip to the Kennedy Center in Washington DC to see scripts performed live.

WEST COAST ENSEMBLE FULL-PLAY COMPETITION

West Coast Ensemble, P.O. Box 38728, Los Angeles CA 90038. (323)876-9337. Fax: (323)876-8916. **Contact:** Les Hanson, artistic director. Estab. 1982. Offered annually for unpublished plays in Southern California. No musicals or children's plays for full-play competition. No restrictions on subject matter. **Deadline: December 31.**

JACKIE WHITE MEMORIAL NATIONAL CHILDREN'S PLAYWRITING CONTEST

Columbia Entertainment Co., 309 Parkade, Columbia MO 65202. (573)874-5628. **Contact:** Betsy Phillips, director. Offered annually for unpublished plays. ''Searching for good scripts, either adaptations or plays with original story lines, suitable for audiences of all ages.'' Script must include at least 7 well-developed roles. **Deadline: June 1.** Guidelines for SASE. **Charges $10 fee.** Prize: $500. Company reserves the right to grant prize money without production. All entrants receive written evaluation.

WICHITA STATE UNIVERSITY PLAYWRITING CONTEST

University Theatre, Wichita State University, School of Performing Arts, 1845 N. Fairmount, Wichita KS 67260-0153. (316)978-3368. Fax: (316)978-3202. E-mail: steve.peters@wichita.edu. Website: finearts.wichita.edu/performing/index.asp. **Contact:** Dr. Steven J. Peters, chair. Estab. 1974. Offered for unpublished, unproduced full-length or 2-3 short plays of at least 90-minutes playing time. No musicals or children's plays. Contestants must be graduate or undergraduate students in a US college or university. **Deadline: February 15.** Guidelines for SASE. Prize: Production of winning play (ACTF), and expenses-paid trip for playwright to see final rehearsals and/or performances.

WRITE A PLAY! NYC

Young Playwrights, Inc., 306 W. 38th St., Suite 300, New York NY 10018. (212)594-5440. Fax: (212)594-5441. E-mail: writeaplay@aol.com. Website: youngplaywrights.org. **Contact:** Literary Department. Offered annually for plays by NYC elementary, middle, and high school students only. **Deadline: April 1.** Prize: Varies.

YEAR END SERIES (YES) NEW PLAY FESTIVAL

Dept. of Theatre, Nunn Dr., Northern Kentucky University, Highland Heights KY 41099-1007. (859)572-6362. Fax: (859)572-6057. E-mail: forman@nku.edu. **Contact:** Sandra Forman, project director. Receives submissions from May 1-October 31 in even-numbered years for the Festivals which occur in April of odd-numbered years. Open to all writers. **Deadline: October 31.** Guidelines for SASE. Prize: $500, and an expense-paid visit to Northern Kentucky University to see the play produced.

ANNA ZORNIO MEMORIAL CHILDREN'S THEATRE PLAYWRITING COMPETITION

University of New Hampshire, Dept. of Theatre and Dance, PCAC, 30 College Rd., Durham NH 03824-3538. (603)862-2919. Fax: (603)862-0298. E-mail: mike.wood@unh.edu. Website: www.unh.edu/theatre-dance. **Contact:** Michael Wood. Offered every 4 years for unpublished well-written plays or musicals appropriate for young audiences with a maximum length of 60 minutes. Guidelines and entry forms for SASE. May submit more than 1 play, but not more than 3. Open to all playwrights in US and Canada. All ages are invited to participate. **Deadline: September 1, 2004.** Prize: $1,000, and play produced and underwritten as part of the season by the UNH Department of Theatre and Dance. Winner will be notified in November 2004.

Independent Publicists

Y ou spent years writing your book, then several more months sending queries to agents. You finally find an agent who loves your work, but then you have to wait even more time as she submits your manuscript to editors. After a few months, your agent closes a great deal for your work with a publishing house you really admire. Now you can sit back and wait for the money to start rolling in, right?

If you've learned anything about publishing so far, you've learned that getting a book published takes a lot of work. And once you find a publisher, your work doesn't stop. You now have to focus on selling your book to make money and to ensure that publishing companies will work with you again. Industry experts estimate that 110,000 books are published each year in the United States. What can you do to ensure that your book succeeds with this amount of competition?

While most publishing houses do have in-house publicists, their time is often limited and priority is usually given to big-name authors who have already proved they will make money for the publisher. Often writers feel their books aren't getting the amount of publicity for which they had hoped. Because of this, many authors have decided to work with an independent publicist.

To help you market your book after publication, we've included a section of independent publicists in this book. Like agents, publicists view publishing as a business. And their business goal is to see that your book succeeds. Usually, publicists are more than happy to work in conjunction with your editor, your publisher, and your agent. Together, they can form a strong team that will help make you a publishing sensation.

What to look for in a publicist

When choosing an independent publicist, you'll want someone who has business savvy and experience in sales. And, of course, you'll want someone who is enthusiastic about you and your writing. When looking through the listings in this section, look at each person's experience both prior to and after becoming a publicist. The radio and television shows on which their clients have appeared can indicate the caliber of their contacts, and the recent promotions they have done for their clients' books can reveal their level of creativity.

You'll also want to look for a publicist who is interested in your subject area. Like agents and publishing houses, most independent publicists have specializations. By focusing on specific areas, publicists can actually do more for their clients. For example, if a publicist is interested in cookbooks, she can send her clients to contacts she has on Food Network shows, editors at gourmet cooking magazines, bookstores that have cafés, and culinary conferences. The more knowledge a publicist has about your subject, the more opportunities she will find to publicize your work.

How to make the initial contact

Contacting independent publicists should be much less stressful than the query process you've gone through to find an agent. Most publicists are open to a phone call, though some still prefer to receive a letter or an e-mail as the initial contact. Often you can receive a referral to a publicist through an agent, an editor, or even another writer. Because publicists do cost more out-of-pocket money than an agent, there isn't the same competition for their time. Of course, not every publicist you call will be the best fit for you. Be prepared to hear that the publicist already has a full client load or that she doesn't have the level of interest in your work that you want a publicist to have.

Tip

How much to spend

As you read over the listings of independent publicists, you'll quickly notice that many charge a substantial amount of money for their services. The cost of a publicist can be daunting, especially to a new writer. *You should only pay what you feel comfortable paying and what you can reasonably afford.* Keep in mind, however, that any money you spend on publicity will come back to you in the form of more sold books. A general rule of thumb is to budget one dollar for every copy of your book that is printed. For a print run of 10,000, you should expect to spend $10,000.

There are ways you can make working with a publicist less of a strain on your purse strings. If you received an advance for your book, you can use part of it to help with your marketing expenses. Some publishers will even agree to match the amount of money an author pays on outside publicity. If your publicist's bill is $2,000, you would pay half and your publisher would pay the other half. Be sure to ask your publishing house if this option is available to you. Most publicists are very willing to work with their clients on a marketing budget.

When reading through the listings of independent publicists, use the following listing breakdown to help you fully understand the information provided.

SUBHEADS

Each listing is broken down into subheads to make locating specific information easier. In this first paragraph, you'll find contact information for each independent publicist or publicity agency. Further information is provided that indicates the company's size and the publicist's experience in the publishing industry.

Members: To help you find a publicist who has a firm understanding of your book's subject and audience, we include the names of publicists and their specialties. The year the member joined the agency is also provided, indicating an individual's familiarity with book publicity.

Specializations: Similar to the agents listed in this book, most publicists have specific areas of interest. A publicist with knowledge of your book's subject will have contacts in your field and a solid sense of your audience.

Services: This subhead provides important details about what the publicist can do for you, including a list of services available for clients, book tour information, television shows on which clients have appeared, contents of media kits, and examples of recent promotions done by the publicist.

•‑ Look for the key icon to quickly learn the publicist's areas of specialization and specific marketing strengths.

How to Contact: Unlike literary agents, most independent publicists are open to phone calls, letters, and e-mail; check this subhead to see the individual publicist's preference. Also pay close attention to the time frame the publicist needs between your initial contact and your book's publication date.

Clients: To provide you with a better sense of their areas of interest, independent publicists list authors they have helped promote. Publicists also indicate here if they are willing to provide potential clients with references.

Costs: Specific details are provided on how much publicists charge their clients. Although the costs seem high, the payback in terms of books sold is usually worth the additional expense. Publicists indicate if they work with clients on a marketing budget, and if they offer a written contract.

Writers' Conferences: A great way to meet and learn more about publicists is at writers' conferences. Here publicists list the writers' conferences they attend. For more information about a specific conference, check the **Writers' Conferences** section starting on page 235.

See Also

Tips: This section provides you with advice and additional instructions for working with an independent publicist.

Quick reference icons

At the beginning of some listings, you will find one or more of the following symbols for quick identification of features particular to that listing.

N Independent publicist new to this edition.

◯ Newer independent publicist actively seeking clients.

◑ Independent publicist interested in working with both new and established writers.

◍ Independent publicist open only to established writers.

◎ Independent publicist who specializes in a specific type of work.

⊘ Independent publicist not currently open to new clients.

SPECIAL INDEXES

Agencies Indexed by Openness to Submissions: This index, which also lists agents, lists publicists according to how open they are to accepting new clients.

Geographic Index: For writers looking for an publicist close to home, this index lists independent publicists by state.

General Index: This index lists all agencies, independent publicists, production companies, script contests, and writers' conferences listed in the book.

☑ ACHESON-GREUB, INC.

P.O. Box 735, Friday Harbor WA 98250-0735. (360)378-2815. Fax: (360)378-2841. **Contact:** Alice B. Acheson. Estab. 1981; specifically with books for 31 years. Currently works with 9 clients. 20% of clients are new/first-time writers.

- Prior to becoming a freelance publicist, Ms. Acheson was a trade book editor preceded by high school Spanish teacher.

Specializations: Nonfiction, fiction, children's books. **Interested in these nonfiction areas:** Art/architecture/design, biography/autobiography, juvenile nonfiction, language/literature/criticism, memoirs, multicultural, music/dance/theater/film, nature/environment, photography. **Interested in these fiction areas:** Contemporary issues, historical, juvenile, literary, mainstream, multicultural, mystery/suspense, picture book.

Services: Provides detailed outline of services provided, media training, market research, sends material to magazines/newspapers for reviews, brochures. Book tours include bookstores, radio interviews, TV interviews, newspaper interviews, magazine interviews. Assists in coordinating travel plans. Clients have appeared on CBS-TV, *Early Show*, CNN, and innumerable radio and TV shows nationwide. Media kit includes author's biography, testimonials, articles about author, basic information on book, professional photos, sample interview questions. Clients responsible for assisting with promotional material. Helps writer obtain endorsements.

  ○┳ "We mentor so writers can do the work on their own for their next projects."

How to Contact: Call or e-mail. Send letter with SASE. Responds in 2 weeks, unless on teaching trip. Returns materials only with SASE. Obtains most new clients through recommendations from others and conferences. Contact 8 months prior to book's publication.

Clients: *Africa*, by Art Wolfe (Wildlands Press); *Divorce Hangover*, by Anne Newton Walther, M.S. (Tapestries Publishing); *Great Lodges of the National Parks*, by Christine Barnes (W.W. West, Inc.). References and contact numbers available for potential clients.

Costs: Clients charged hourly fee. Works with clients on marketing budget. Offers written contract. Contract can be terminated upon written notification.

▨ ☑ BRICKMAN MARKETING

395 Del Monte Center, #250, Monterey CA 93940. (831)633-4444. E-mail: brickman@brickmanmarketing.com. Website: www.brickmanmarketing.com. **Contact:** Wendy Brickman. Estab. 1990; specifically with books for 13 years. Currently works with 30 clients. 10% of clients are new/first-time writers.

- Prior to becoming a freelance publicist, Ms. Brickman worked in public relations in the home video industries.

Specializations: Nonfiction, children's book, academic. **Interested in these nonfiction areas:** Biography/autobiography; business; education; ethnic/cultural interests; health/medicine; history; how-to; interior design/decorating; music/dance/theater/film; nature/environment; New Age/metaphysics; popular culture; self-help/personal improvement; travel; women's issues/women's studies. **Interested in these fiction areas:** Children's. Other types of clients include home video producers and a wide variety of businesses.

Services: Provides media training, market research, fax news releases, sends material to magazines/newspapers for reviews. Book tours include bookstores, specialty stores, radio interviews, TV interviews, newspaper interviews, magazine interviews, speaking engagements, conferences, libraries, schools, universities. Clients have appeared on *Howie Mandel*, CNN, more local TV, and syndicated radio. Media kit includes author's biography, testimonials, articles about author, basic information on book, professional photos, sample interview questions, book request information. Helps writer obtain endorsements.

  ○┳ "My wide variety of clients and contacts makes me a valuable publicist."

How to Contact: E-mail. Responds in 1 week. Discards unwanted queries and mss. Obtains most new clients through recommendations from others. Contact 4 months prior to book's publication.

Clients: *What Do They Say When You Leave the Room*, by Brigid McGrath Massie (Eudemonia); *Diet for Allergies*, by Raphael Rethner; *Listening: It Will Change Your Life*, by Charles Page, attorney at law; *Beyond Superwoman*, by Peggy Downes Baskin and Karin Strasser Kauffmann. Other clients include Carol Teten.

Costs: Clients charged hourly retainer fee or monthly retainer. No written contract.

☑ ◎ BRODY PUBLIC RELATIONS

145 Route 519, Stockton NJ 08559-1711. (609)397-3737. Fax: (609)397-3666. E-mail: bebrody@aol.com. Website: www.brodypr.com. **Contact:** Beth Brody. Estab. 1988; specifically with books for 15 years. Currently works with 8-10 clients. 10% of clients are new/first-time writers.

Members: Beth Brody (nonfiction, at firm for 15 years).

Specializations: Nonfiction. **Interested in these nonfiction areas:** Business; child guidance/parenting; education; health/medicine; how-to; money/finance/economics; music/dance/theater/film; popular culture; psychology; self-help/personal improvement; travel. **Interested in these fiction areas:** Cartoons/comic. Other types of clients include musicians, artists, entertainment, healthcare.

Services: Provides detailed outline of services provided, fax news releases, electronic news releases, sends material to magazines/newspapers for reviews, brochures, website assistance, website publicity. Book tours include bookstores, specialty stores, radio interviews, TV interviews, newspaper interviews, magazine interviews, speaking engagements, conferences, libraries, schools, universities. Assists in coordinating travel plans. Clients have appeared on *Oprah Winfrey Show*, *Good Morning America*. Media kit includes author's biography, testimonials, articles about author, basic information on book, sample interview questions, book request information. Helps writer obtain endorsements.

How to Contact: Call or e-mail. Responds in 48 hours. Obtains most new clients through recommendations from others. Contact 6 months prior to book's publication.

Clients: Music Sales Corporation, Crown Business, Random House, Berkeley Publishing. Other clients include Dow Jones, Don & Bradstreet, Foundations Behaviorial Health, JVC Music, Magweb.com. References and contact numbers available for potential clients.

Costs: Clients charged hourly fee or monthly retainer. Offers written contract.

Tips: "Contact a publicist after you have secured a publisher and distributor."

◎ EVENT MANAGEMENT SERVICES, INC.

519 Cleveland St., Suite 205, Clearwater FL 33757. (727)443-7115, ext. 201. E-mail: mfriedman@event-manage ment.com. Website: www.event-management.com. **Contact:** Marsha Friedman. Estab. 1990; specifically with books for 11 years. Currently works with 38 clients. 20% of clients are new/first-time writers.

• Prior to becoming a freelance publicist, Ms. Friedman worked in PR and event management.

Members: Rich Ghazarian (account manager, at firm for 3 years); Joe Ullrich (business development); Lisa Gregory (business development); Jay Wilke (account manager); Cari Core (account manager).

Specializations: Nonfiction. **Interested in these nonfiction areas:** Cooking/food/nutrition; current affairs; government/politics/law; health/natural; how-to; interior design/decorating; money/finance/economics; nature/environment; science/technology; sports; travel. Other types of clients include medical doctors, corporations in natural health industry, entertainment industry, and food industry.

Services: Provides detailed outline of services provided. Book tours include bookstores, radio interviews, TV interviews, newspaper interviews, magazine interviews. Clients have appeared on *GMA*, *Today*, *60 Minutes*, *CBS This Morning*, *Maury Povich*, *Montel*. Media kit includes author's biography, press release that gives the actual show idea or story.

○━ "We are paid on performance and our specialty is radio and TV. We book anywhere from 30-80 interviews per week!"

How to Contact: Call, e-mail, or fax. Send letter with SASE. Responds in 2 weeks. Obtains most new clients through recommendations from others or an initial contact on our part. Contact 6 months prior to book's publication or after book's publication.

Clients: *Anti Aging Bible*, by Dr. Earl Mindell (Simon & Schuster); *Slimdown For Life*, by Larry North (Kensington); *Special Trust*, by Robert McFarlane (Multi Media); *Selling Online*, by Jim Carrol and Rick Broadhead (Dearborn). Other clients include Jimmy Hoffa, Jr., Harry Browne, The Temptations. References and contact numbers available for potential clients.

Costs: Clients charged on per placement basis ($165, radio and $5,000, national TV). Works with clients on marketing budget. Offers written contract.

Tips: "Check references to see how much media they book every week/month. Find out if they have knowledge of your area of expertise."

◪ THE FORD GROUP

1250 Prospect St., Suite Ocean-5, La Jolla CA 92037. (858)454-3314. Fax: (858)454-3319. E-mail: fordgroup@aol. com. Website: www.fordsisters.com. **Contact:** Arielle Ford. Estab. 1987; specifically with books since 1990. Currently works with 6 clients. 50% of clients are new/first-time writers.

• Ms. Ford has been a publicist since 1976, and an agent since 1997.

Specializations: Nonfiction. **Interested in these nonfiction areas:** Health/medicine; how-to; New Age/metaphysics; psychology; religious/inspirational; self-help/personal improvement.

Services: Consulting services include reading ms and proposal, and offering advice on how to secure a good agent, publisher, publicist, and marketing team. Provides inspired ideas to generate big results. Clients have appeared on *Oprah*, *Larry King Live*, *Good Morning America*, AP Radio, *The Today Show*, *CNN*, *Fox News*, *Art Bell Show*. "We created the 'World's Largest Pot of Chicken Soup' to serve 7,000 homeless on Thanksgiving 5 years ago to launch one of the *Chicken Soup for the Soul* books. We ended up on NBC-TV network news and a photo in *USA Today*."

O→ "We live and breathe our niche: self-help, alternative medicine, and spirituality—we completely understand the category."

How to Contact: Call, e-mail or fax. Responds within 1 week. Obtains most new clients through recommendations from others.

Clients: *The Right Questions*, by Debbie Ford; *Energy Addict*, by Jon Gordon; *Wedding Goddess*, by Laurie Sue Brockway.

Costs: Charges clients flat fee.

⊙ GARIS AGENCY—NATIONAL PUBLICISTS

310 S. Twin Oaks Valley Rd., San Marcos CA 92069. (760)471-4807. Fax: (253)390-4262. E-mail: publicists@garis-agency.com. Website: www.toppublicity.com. **Contact:** R.J. Garis. Estab. 1989; specifically with books since 1989. Currently works with 50 clients. 20% of clients are new/first-time writers.

• Prior to becoming a publicist, Mr Garis was a promoter and producer.

Members: Taryn Roberts (associate national publicist, at firm since 1997); R.J. Garis.

Specializations: Nonfiction, fiction, script. **Interested in these nonfiction areas:** Animals; biography/autobiography; business; child guidance/parenting; current affairs; gay/lesbian issues; government/politics/law; health/medicine; how-to; humor; interior design/decorating; juvenile nonfiction; memoirs; military/war; money/finance/economics; multicultural; music/dance/theater/film; nature/environment; New Age/metaphysics; photography; popular culture; psychology; science/technology; self-help/personal improvement; sociology; sports; travel; true crime/investigative; women's issues/women's studies; young adult. **Interested in these fiction areas:** Action/adventure; cartoon/comic; contemporary issues; detective/police/crime; erotica; ethnic; family saga; fantasy; feminist; gay/lesbian; glitz; horror; humor/satire; juvenile; literary; mainstream; multicultural; mystery/suspense; New Age/metaphysical; picture book; psychic/supernatural; romance; science fiction; sports; thriller/espionage; westerns/frontier; young adult.

Services: Provides media training, nationwide publicity, if applicable, fax news releases, electronic news release, material to magazines/newspapers for reviews, website assistance, website publicity. Book tours include bookstores, specialty stores, radio interviews, TV interviews, newspaper interviews, magazine interviews, speaking engagements, conferences. Assists in coordinating travel plans. Clients have appeared on *Oprah*, *Dateline*, *Larry King*, *Fox*, *Sally*, *Extra*, *48 Hours*, *Good Morning America*, *Montel*, *Inside Edition*, *20/20*, *Today*. Media kits include résumé, author's biography, testimonials, articles about author, basic infomation on book, professional photos, sample interview questions, book request information. Helps writer obtain endorsements. "We designed media information for author Missy Cummings (*Hornet's Nest*)—which resulted in TV interviews on *Extra*, *Inside Edition*, and a print feature in *The Star*."

O→ This company specializes in "quality media that works! Morning radio, national TV, regional TV, major newspapers, and national magazines. We currently book over 2,000 media interviews a year."

How to Contact: E-mail. Responds in 3 days. Discards unwanted materials. Obtains most new clients through recommendations from others. Contact 3 months prior to book's publication.

Clients: *Hornet's Nest*, by Missy Cummings (iUniverse); *Little Kids Big Questions*, by Dr. Judi Craig (Hearst Books); *There Are No Accidents*, by Robert Hopcke (Penguin Putnam); *Anger Work*, by Dr. Robert Puff (Vantage Press). References and contact numbers available for potential clients.

Costs: Charges clients contract fee based on the project; monthly retainer. Offers written contract, binding for a minimum of 6 months. 1-month notice must be given to terminate contract.

Tips: "Check references. Look for a publicist with a long history, it takes many years to establish powerful media contacts."

⊙ GREATER TALENT NETWORK, INC.

437 Fifth Ave., New York NY 10016-2205. (212)645-4200. Fax: (212)627-1471. E-mail: gtn@greatertalent.com. Website: www.gtnspeakers.com. **Contact:** Don Epstein. Estab. 1980; specifically with books for over 20 years. Currently works with more than 100 clients.

Members: Don Epstein (corporate/literary, at firm over 20 years); Debra Greene (corporate/literary, at firm 21 years); Kenny Rahtz (corporate/associations, at firm 21 years); Barbara Solomon (health/hospitals/public relations, at firm 16 years); David Evenchick (Fortune 1000, at firm for 8 years); Josh Yablon (technology/corporate management, at firm for 9 years); Lisa Bransdorf (college/university, at firm for 7 years).

Specializations: Nonfiction, fiction, academic. **Interested in these nonfiction areas:** Business, computers/electronics, current affairs, education, government/politics/law, humor, money/finance/economics, multicultural, popular culture, science/technology, sports, women's issues/women's studies. Other types of clients include government officials, athletes, CEO's, technology, media.

Services: Provides detailed outline of services provided, international publicity, if applicable, fax news releases, brochures, website publicity. Book tours include radio interviews, TV interviews, newspaper interviews, speaking engagements. Assists in coordinating travel plans. Clients have appeared on all major networks. Media kit includes author's biography, testimonials, articles about author, professional photos, book request information.

👉 "We understand authors' needs and publishers' wants."

How to Contact: Call, e-mail, fax. Discards unwanted queries and mss. Obtains most new clients through recommendations from others. Contact once a platform is started.

Clients: *The CEO of the Sofa*, by P.J. O'Rourke (Atlantic Monthly Press); *Dude, Where's My Country*, by Michael Moore (Warner Books); *Hidden Power*, by Kati Marton (Pantheon); *The Travel Detective*, by Peter Greenberg (Villard); *American Gods*, by Neil Gaiman (Wm. Morrow). Other clients include Homer Hickman, Tom Wolfe, John Douglas, Christopher Buckley, Erica Jong, Michael Lewis. References and contact numbers available for potential clients.

Costs: Clients charged variable commission. Offers written contract.

N THE IDEA NETWORK

P.O. Box 38, Whippany NJ 07981. (973)560-0333. Fax: (973)560-0960. E-mail: esaxton@theideanetwork.net. Website: www.theideanetwork.net. **Contact:** Erin Saxton, founder. Estab. 2000, specifically with books for 4 years. Currently works with 15-20 clients. Less than 1% clients are new/first-time writers.

• Prior to becoming a freelance publicist, Ms. Saxton was a 4-time Emmy-nominated TV producer.

Members: Jen Urezzio (vice president, media relations, at firm for 3 years); Allyson Klavens (senior account executive, at firm 1 year); Anders Bjornson (V.P. of business operations, at firm 2 years).

Specializations: Nonfiction. **Interested in these nonfiction areas:** Child guidance/parenting, cooking/food/nutrition, crafts/hobbies, current affairs, health/medicine, how-to, interior design/decorating, money/finance/economics, psychology, women's issues/women's studies. "We don't work with many fiction writers and take them on a case-by-case system."

Services: Full-service public relations agency. Every client's media and publicity plans differ. Call for more information. Book tours include radio interviews, TV interviews, newspaper interviews, magazine interviews. Clients have appeared on *The View*, *The Today Show*, Fox News Channel, *Good Morning America*, *The Early Show*, and *Ellen*.

👉 "This company is founded by a TV Producer and therefore knows what a producer is looking for in a 'pitch.' Because of our background, our clients have an advantage." Specializes in creating hooks that reporters, editors, ad producers find useful for their programs and outlets.

How to Contact: Call, e-mail, fax. Responds in 1 week. Discards unwanted queries and mss. Obtains most new clients through recommendations from others, queries/solicitations, responses from press we've received. Contact 6 months prior to book's publication.

Clients: *Chicken Soup for the Soul*, by Mark Victor Hansen and Jack Canfield (HCI Enterprises), and other notable authors.

Costs: Clients charged monthly retainer ($3,500-10,000) and by project. Offers written contract. "We usually put dates within the contract." 1-month notice must be given to terminate contract.

KSB PROMOTIONS

(Specializes: general lifestyle books), 55 Honey Creek NE, Ada MI 49301-9768. (616)676-0758. Fax: (616)676-0759. E-mail: pr@ksbpromotions.com. Website: www.ksbpromotions.com. **Contact:** Kate Bandos. Estab. 1988; specifically with books since 1988. Currently works with 20-40 clients. 25% of clients are new/first-time writers.

• Prior to becoming a publicist, Ms. Bandos was a PR director for several publishers.

Members: Kate Bandos (travel, cookbooks, at firm since 1988); Doug Bandos (radio/TV, at firm since 1989).

Specializations: Nonfiction, children's books. **Interested in these nonfiction areas:** Child guidance/parenting; cooking/food/nutrition; health/medicine; travel; gardening; home/how-to; general lifestyle.

Services: Provides detailed outline of services provided, sends material to magazines/newspapers for reviews. Book tours include radio interviews, TV interviews, newspaper interviews, magazine interviews. Clients have appeared on *Good Morning America*, *CNN*, *Business News Network*, *Parent's Journal*, and many regional shows. Media kit includes author's biography, testimonials, basic information on book, sample interview questions, book request information, recipes for cookbooks, other excerpts as appropriate. Helps writers obtain endorsements.

👉 This company specializes in cookbooks, travel guides, parenting books, and other general lifestyle books. "Our specialty has allowed us to build relationships with key media in these areas. We limit ourselves to those clients we can personally help."

How to Contact: Call or e-mail. Responds in 2 weeks. Returns unwanted material only with SASE. Obtains most new clients through recommendations from others, conferences, listings in books on publishing. Contact 6-8 months prior to book's publication. Can do limited PR after book's publication.

Clients: *The Home Depot 1-2-3 Series*, (Meredith Books); *Along Interstate 75*, by Dave Hunter (Mile Oak Publishing). Other clients include Bayou Publishing, PassPorter, Travel Guides, Barnesyard Books, and Dalmation Press. References and contact numbers available for potential clients.

Costs: Client charged per service fee ($500 minimum). "Total of contracted services is divided into monthly payments." Offers written contract. 1-month notice must be given to terminate contract.

Writers' Conferences: PMA University; BookExpo America.

Tips: "Find a publicist who has done a lot with books in the same area of interest since they will know the key media, etc."

☑ KT PUBLIC RELATIONS

1905 Cricklewood Cove, Fogelsville PA 18051-1509. (610)395-6298. Fax: (610)395-6299. E-mail: KT4PR@aol.com. Website: www.webbookstars.com. **Contact:** Kae Tienstra. Estab. 1993; specifically with books for 24 years. Currently works with 6 clients. 60% of clients are new/first-time writers.

- Prior to becoming a freelance publicist, Ms. Tienstra was publicity director for Rodale, Inc., and a freelance writer.

Members: Kae Tienstra (writing, client contact, media relations, at firm 11 years); Jon Tienstra (editing, administration, at firm 8 years).

Specializations: Nonfiction, fiction. **Interested in these nonfiction areas:** Agriculture/horticulture, animals, child guidance/parenting, cooking/food/nutrition, crafts/hobbies, health/medicine, how-to, interior design/decorating, nature/environment, New Age/metaphysics, psychology, religious/inspirational, self-help/personal improvement, travel. **Interested in these fiction areas:** Mainstream, women's fiction. Other types of clients include nonprofit institutions, publishers.

Services: Provides detailed outline of services provided, media training, sends material to magazines/newspapers for reviews, brochures. Book tours include bookstores, radio interviews, TV interviews, newspaper interviews, magazine interviews, speaking engagements, universities. Assists in coordinating travel plans. Clients have appeared on *Today*, CNN, CBS Radio, *Sally Jessy Raphael*, *Today Weekend Edition*, *Home Matters*, *Christopher Lowell*. Media kit includes author's biography, testimonials, articles about author, basic information on book, professional photos, sample interview questions, book request information, segment suggestions for TV, radio, pitch letter. Helps writer obtain endorsements.

> ☞ "Our personal, hands-on approach assures authors the 1-on-1 guidance they need. Our subsidiary service, WEBbookSTARS.com provides special, low-cost, self-paced author publicity service."

How to Contact: Call, e-mail, or fax. Send letter with sample chapters and SASE. Responds in 1 week. Returns materials only with SASE. Obtains most new clients through recommendations from others and conferences. Contact 6 months prior to book's publication or after book's publication once a platform is started.

Clients: *Are You Ready for Lasting Love*, by Paddy S. Welles, Ph.D. (Avalon Publisher); *The Witch Book*, by Raymond Buckland (Visible Ink Press); *Spiritual Training Wheels*, by Gloria Benish (Kensington Publishers); *Worry-Free Investing*, by Zvi Bodie (Financial Times Prentice Hall). Other clients include Visible Ink Press, Better Homes & Gardens Books, Etruscan Press, Stillwater Publishing, Zone Labs, Lehigh University. References and contact numbers available for potential clients.

Costs: Clients charged per service fee ($1,500); monthly retainer ($1,500). Works with clients on marketing budget. Offers written contract, binding for 3-6 months minimum. 1-month notice must be given to terminate contract.

Tips: "We are a small, focused organization, designed to provide personal service. Authors who sign on with us work with us, not with junior staffers."

◎ GAIL LEONDAR PUBLIC RELATIONS

21 Belknap St., Arlington MA 02474-6605. (781)648-1658. E-mail: gail@glprbooks.com. **Contact:** Gail Leondar-Wright. Estab. 1992; specifically with books for 11 years. Currently works with 16 clients. 50% of clients are new/first-time writers.

- Prior to becoming a freelance publicist, Ms. Leondar-Wright directed theater.

Specializations: Nonfiction, fiction, academic, any books on progressive social issues. **Interested in these nonfiction areas:** Biography/autobiography, current affairs, education, ethnic/cultural interests, gay/lesbian issues, government/politics/law, history, multicultural, music/dance/theater/film, sociology, women's issues/women's studies. **Interested in these fiction areas:** Feminist, gay/lesbian/transgender.

Services: Provides detailed outline of services provided. Book tours include bookstores, radio interviews, TV interviews, newspaper interviews. Clients have appeared on *Fresh Air Morning Edition*, *Weekend Edition*, CNN, C-SPAN. Media kit includes author's biography, testimonials, articles about author, basic information on book, professional photos, sample interview questions.

> ☞ GLPR promotes only books on progressive social interviews. Our contacts give excellent interviews, primarily on noncommercial radio, including NPR.

How to Contact: Call or e-mail. Responds in less than 1 week. Returns materials only with SASE. Obtains most new clients through recommendations from others. Contact 6 months prior to book's publication.

Clients: *A Desperate Passion*, by Dr. Helen Caldicott (Norton); *The Good Heart*, by The Dalai Lama (Wisdom);

Love Canal, by Lois Gibbs (New Society Publishers); *Gender Outlaw*, by Kate Bornstein (Routledge). References and contact numbers available for potential clients.
Costs: Clients charged flat fee ($2,000-15,000). Works with clients on marketing budget. Offers written contract, binding for typically 3 months.

☑ MEDIA MASTERS PUBLICITY

17600 S. Richmond Rd., Plainfield IL 60554. (815)254-7383. Fax: (815)254-1948. E-mail: tracey@mmpublicity.com. Website: www.mmpublicity.com. **Contact:** Tracey Daniels. Estab. 1998. Currently works with 10 clients. 10% of clients are new/first-time writers.
* • Prior to becoming an independent publicist, Ms. Daniels worked in English Education—middle school and high school.

Members: Karen Wadsworth (marketing, events, at firm since 2001).
Specializations: Children's books, nonfiction. **Interested in these nonfiction areas:** Biography/autobiography; child guidance/parenting; cooking/food/nutrition; education; how-to; juvenile nonfiction; young adult. **Interested in these fiction areas:** Juvenile; picture book; young adult. Other types of clients include publishers.
Services: Provides detailed outline of services provided, fax news releases, electronic news release, material to magazines/newspapers for reviews, brochures, website assistance, website publicity. Book tours include bookstores, specialty stores, radio interviews, TV interviews, newspaper interviews, magazine interviews, schools. Clients have appeared on CNN, *Talk America*, CBS, ABC, VOA, *USA Radio Network*, *AP Radio Network*, *20/20*. "Each media kit varies depending on focus, client needs, and budget." Helps writer obtain endorsements.
    ☞ "I have over 12 years of book publicity experience. My company delivers 'publicity with personality'— we go beyond just covering the basics."
How to Contact: E-mail or send letter with outline/proposal and sample chapters. Responds in 2 weeks. Returns materials only with SASE. Obtains most new clients through recommendations from others. Contact 3 months prior to book's publication.
Clients: Clients include Roaring Brook, HarperCollins Children's Books, Reader's Digest Trade Books, North-South Books, NorthWord Books for Young Readers, Boyds Mills Press, Insomniac Press, plus individual authors. Reference and contact numbers available for potential clients.
Costs: Charges for services depend on client's needs and budget. Offers written contract. 1-month notice must be given to terminate contract.
Writers' Conferences: BEA, ALA.

☑ PHENIX & PHENIX LITERARY PUBLICISTS, INC.

2525 W. Anderson Lane, Suite 540, Austin TX 78257. (512)478-2028. Fax: (512)478-2117. E-mail: info@bookpros.com. Website: www.bookpros.com. **Contact:** Andy Morales, director of client development. Estab. 1994; specifically with books since 1994. Currently works with 40 clients. 50% of clients are new/first-time writers.
Members: Marika Flatt (director of publishers' services); Elaine Krackau (publicist); Mike Odam (president); Steve Joiner (vice president).
Specializations: Nonfiction, fiction, children's books, academic, coffee table books, biographies. **Interested in these nonfiction areas:** Animals; biography/autobiography; business; child guidance/parenting; computers/electronics; current affairs; health/medicine; money/finance/economics; multicultural; religious/inspirational; self-help/personal improvement; sports; travel; true crime/investigative; women's issues/women's studies; young adult. **Interested in these fiction areas:** Action/adventure; confessional; contemporary issues; detective/police/crime; family saga; historical; humor/satire; multicultural; mystery/suspense; regional; religious/inspirational; sports; young adult. Other types of clients include publishers.
Services: Provides detailed outline of services provided, media training, fax news releases, electronic news release, material to magazines/newspapers for reviews, brochures, website publicity. Book tours include bookstores, specialty stores, radio interviews, TV interviews, newspaper interviews, magazine interviews. Clients have appeared on *Oprah*, CNN, CNBC, *Fox News Network*, *Leeza*, *Montel*, *Good Morning America*, *Talk America Radio Network*, *Business News Network*, *Westwood One Radio Network*, *UPI Radio Network*. Media kit includes author's biography, testimonials, articles about author, basic information on book, professional photos, sample interview questions, book request information, press releases, excerpts. Recent promotions included video press releases, mystery contest, online publicity campaigns, creative angles for fiction positioning.
    ☞ This company has a first 1-month strategy (develop strategy, positioning, press materials), and created 4 bestsellers in 1999.
How to Contact: Call, e-mail, fax, or send letter with entire ms. Responds in 5 days. Discards unwanted material. Obtains most new clients through recommendations from others, conferences, website. Contact 2-4 months prior to book's publication or after book's publication.
Clients: *Kiss of God*, by Marshall Ball (Health Communications); *True Women/Hill Country*, by Janice Woods Windle (Longstreet Press); *Wizard of Ads*, by Roy Williams (Bard Press); *Faith on Trial*, by Pamela Ewen

(Broadman & Holman). Other clients include Dr. Ivan Misner, Lisa Shaw-Brawley, Michele O'Donnell, Patrick Seaman (Timberwolf Press), Continuum Press. References and contact numbers available for potential clients.
Costs: Charges clients monthly retainer ($2,500-6,500). Works with clients on a marketing budget. Offers written contract binding for 4-6 months.
Writers' Conferences: Craft of Writing (Denton, TX), BEA.
Tips: "Find a publicist that will offer a guarantee. Educate yourself on the book/publicity process."

RAAB ASSOCIATES

345 Millwood Rd., Chappaqua NY 10514. (914)241-2117. Fax: (914)241-0050. E-mail: info@raabassociates.com. Website: www.raabassociates.com. **Contact:** Susan Salzman Raab. Estab. 1986; specifically with books since 1986. Currently works with 10 clients. 10% of clients are new/first-time writers.
  • Prior to becoming an independent publicist, Ms. Salzman Raab worked on staff at major publishing houses in the children's book industry.
Members: Susanna Reich (associate, at firm since 2000); Susan Salzman Raab (partner, at firm since 1986).
Specializations: Children's books, parenting books and products. **Interested in these nonfiction areas:** Child guidance/parenting, juvenile nonfiction, young adult. **Interested in these fiction areas:** Juvenile, picture book, young adult, parenting. Other types of clients include publishers, toy companies, audio companies.
Services: Provides detailed outline of services provided, market research, sends material to magazines/newspapers for review, website assistance, website development, extensive online publicity. Book tours include bookstores, specialty stores, radio interviews, TV interviews, newspaper interviews, magazine interviews, schools, and libraries. Can also assist in coordinating travel plans. Clients have appeared on NPR, CNN, C-Span, Radio-Disney, PRI. Media kit includes author's biography, testimonials, articles about author, basic information on book, sample interview questions, book request information. Helps writer obtain endorsements.
  ☛ "We are the only PR agency to specialize in children's and parenting books."
How to Contact: Call or e-mail. Responds in 2 weeks. Returns materials only with SASE. Obtains most new clients through recommendations from others, conferences. Contact 4 months prior to book's publication.
Costs: Clients charged per service fee. Offers written contract. 3-month notice must be given to terminate contract.
Writers' Conferences: Society of Children's Book Writers & Illustrators (National and Mid-Winter); Society of Children's Book Writers & Illustrators (Regional Meeting); Book Expo America (Chicago, May/June); American Library Association (Chicago, July); Bologna Bookfair (April).

ROCKS-DEHART PUBLIC RELATIONS (BOOK PUBLICITY)

306 Marberry Dr., Pittsburgh PA 15215. (412)784-8811. Fax: (412)784-8610. E-mail: celiarocks@aol.com. Website: www.celiarocks.com. **Contact:** Celia Rocks. Estab. 1993; specifically with books since 1993. Currently works with 10 clients; 20% of clients are new/first-time writers.
  • Prior to becoming a publicist, Ms. Rocks was a publicity specialist at Burson Marsteller.
Members: Dottie DeHart (principal, at firm since 1993); 8 other staff members.
Specializations: Nonfiction, business, lifestyle. **Interested in these nonfiction areas:** Biography/autobiography; business; cooking/food/nutrition; current affairs; health/medicine; how-to; humor; popular culture; psychology; religious/inspirational; self-help/personal improvement; sociology; travel; women's issues/women's studies. Other types of clients include major publishing houses.
Services: Provides detailed outline of services provided. Book tours include bookstores, specialty stores, radio interviews, TV interviews, newspaper interviews, magazine interviews, speaking engagements, conferences, libraries, schools, universities. Clients have appeared on *ABC World News, Oprah*, and others, as well as in *Time* and *Newsweek*. Media kit includes author's biography, testimonials, articles about author, basic information on book, professional photos, sample interview questions, book request information, breakthrough-plan materials, and "any other pieces that are helpful." Helps writers obtain endorsements. Recent promotions included "taking a book like *Fishing for Dummies* and sending gummy worms with packages."
  ☛ This company specializes in IDG "Dummies" Books, business, management, and lifestyle titles. "We are a highly creative firm that understands the best way to obtain maximum publicity."
How to Contact: Call or e-mail. Responds in 1 day. Obtains most new clients through recommendations from others. Contact 2-4 months prior to book's publication.
Clients: Clients include John Wiley & Sons, AAA Publishing, Dearborn, Jossey-Bass.
Costs: Clients charged monthly retainer ($3,000-5,000). Works with clients on marketing budget. Offers written contract. 1-month notice must be given to terminate contract.

SHERRI ROSEN PUBLICITY

15 Park Row, Suite 25C, New York NY 10038. Phone/fax: (212)587-0296. E-mail: sherri@sherrirosen.com.

Website: www.sherrirosen.com. **Contact:** Sherri Rosen. Estab. 1997, specifically with books for 13 years. Currently works with 6 clients. 75% published authors, 25% self-published authors.

- Ms. Rosen's first client, Naura Hayden, was on the *New York Times* best-seller list for 63 weeks. The book made millions of dollars.

Specializations: Sex, relationship, and spirituality. Likes to work on a book for at least 6 months. **Interested in these nonfiction areas:** Child guidance/parenting, cooking/food/nutrition, current affairs, education, ethnic/cultural interests, gay/lesbian issues, health/medicine, how-to, humor, juvenile nonfiction, memoirs, music/dance/theater/film, New Age/metaphysics, popular culture, psychology, religious/inspirational, self-help/personal improvement, travel, women's issues/women's studies, young adult. **Interested in these fiction areas:** Action/adventure, confessional, erotica, ethnic, experimental, family saga, fantasy, feminist, humor/satire, literary, mainstream, multicultural, New Age/metaphysical, psychic/supernatural, religious/inspirational, romance, young adult. Other types of clients include healers, business people.

Services: Provides detailed outline of services provided, audio/video tapes, international publicity, if applicable, sends material to magazines/newspapers for reviews, brochures. Book tours include bookstores, radio interviews, TV interviews, newspaper interviews, magazine interviews, speaking engagements, conferences, libraries, schools, universities. Assists in coordinating travel plans. Clients have appeared on *Oprah, Montel, Politically Incorrect, Leeza, Men are from Mars, The Sally Show, The Other Half, Howard Stern*, 5-page spread in *Playboy* magazine. Media kit includes author's biography, testimonials, articles about author, basic information on book, professional photos, sample interview questions, book request information. Will write all of the promotional material or collaborate with client. Helps writer obtain endorsements.

- ⟳ "I work with eclectic clientele—sex books, spiritual books, personal inspirational, self-help books. What is distinct is I will only work with people I like, and I have to like and respect what they are doing."

How to Contact: E-mail. Responds immediately. Discards unwanted queries or returns materials only with SASE. Obtains most new clients through recommendations from others, listings with other services in our industry. Contact 3 months prior to book's publication if possible; after book's publication once a platform is started.

Clients: *How to Satisfy a Woman*, by Naura Hayden (self-published); *Men Who Can't Love*, by Steven Carten (HarperCollins); *Rebirth of the Goddess*, by Carol Christ (Addison-Wesley); *Buddhism Without Belief*, by Stephen Batchelor (Riverhead). Other clients include Eli Jaxon-Bear, Sandra Rothenberger, Elizabeth Ayres. References and contact numbers available for potential clients.

Costs: Clients charged hourly retainer fee ($125); monthly retainer ($4,000). Flexible. Offers written contract. 1 month notice must be given to terminate contract.

Tips: "Not only are contacts important, but make sure you like who you will be working with, because you work so closely."

☑ ROYCE CARLTON, INC.

866 United Nations Plaza, Suite 587, New York, NY 10017. (212)355-7700. Fax: (212)888-8659. E-mail: info@roycecarlton.com. Website: www.roycecarlton.com. **Contact:** Carlton Sedgeley. Estab. 1968. Currently works with 68 clients.

- Royce Carlton, Inc., is a lecture agency and management firm for some 68 speakers who are available for lectures and special engagements.

Members: Carlton S. Sedgeley, president (at firm since 1968); Lucy Lepage, executive vice president (at firm since 1968); Helen Churko, vice president (at firm since 1984).

Specializations: Royce Carlton works with many different types of speakers. Other clients include celebrities, writers, journalists, scientists, etc.

Services: Provides "full service for all our clients to lecture."

- ⟳ "We are the only lecture agency representing all our clients exclusively."

How to Contact: Call, e-mail, or fax. Discards unwanted material. Obtains most new clients through recommendations from others, or initiates contact directly.

Clients: *Tuesdays with Morrie*, by Mitch Albom; *House Made of Dawn*, by N. Scott Momaday. Other clients include Joan Rivers, Elaine Pagels, Walter Mosley, David Halberstam, Tom Friedman, Fareed Zakaria, Susan Sontag. References and contact numbers available for potential clients.

Costs: Client charged per placement; commission. Offers written contract. One-month notice must be given to terminate contract.

☑ SMITH PUBLICITY

57 S. Main St., Yardley PA 19067. (215)547-4778. Fax: (215)547-4785. E-mail: info@smithpublicity.com. Website: www.smithpublicity.com. **Contact:** Dan Smith, ext. 111. Estab. 1997; specifically with books for 4 years. Currently works with 10-12 clients. 70% of clients are new/first-time writers.

● Prior to starting Smith Publicity in 1997, Mr. Smith was a freelance public relations specialist and promotional writer.

Members: Dan Smith (president, director of operations, campaign management, at firm 7 years); Jen Lavish (account executive, at firm 2 years); Alexis Berger (account manager, at firm 3 years); Nikki Bowman (account assistant, at firm 1 year); Fran Rubin (director of marketing and business development, at firm 5 years).

Specializations: Nonfiction, fiction. **Interested in these nonfiction areas:** Politics, how-to, humor, multicultural, New Age, popular culture, self-help, true crime/investigative. **Interested in these fiction areas:** Various genres. Other types of clients include entrepreneurs, businesses, and nonprofit organizations.

Services: Provides detailed outline of services provided, media training, international publicity, if applicable, market research, fax news releases, electronic news release, sends material to magazines/newspapers for reviews, website assistance, website publicity. Book tours include bookstores, radio interviews, TV interviews, newspaper interviews, magazine interviews, speaking engagements. Clients have appeared on *Today Show*, CNN, CNN International, *Fox News, Art Bell*, etc., *Montel, Sally, Good Morning America, Howard Stern, O'Reilly Factor, Mike Gallagher*. Media kit includes press releases, bio, sample questions, sell sheet, book information, excerpt, etc. Developed unorthodox publicity angles which transformed a local personality and author into a nationally known expert.

☞ "We follow the Golden Rule: We give the media what they want . . . good story ideas and interview topics, while offering rates typically well below national averages, and unparalleled client service."

How to Contact: Call, e-mail, mail, or fax. Responds in 1 week. Returns materials only with SASE. Obtains most new clients through referrals from current or previous clients. Contact 4 months prior to book's publication or after book's publication.

Clients: *Conversations with Tom*, by Walda Woods (White Rose Publishing); *The Old Boys: The American Elite and the Origins of the Cat*, by Burton Hersh; *Emotionally Intelligent Parenting*, by Dr. Steven Tobias (Random House). Other clients include Rhys Bowen (author of *For the Love of Mike*); Barry Nadel (president of InfoLink Screening Services, Inc.); Fred Hoffman (author of *Beyond Crystal Castles*); Helen Adam (author of *Joyability*); *Arabella Romance Magazine*; Scott Kipp (author of Broadband Entertainment); Michael Johnston (author of *Brideshead Regained*). References available for potential clients.

Costs: Clients charged monthly retainer (from $500-2,500/month; 4-6 month agreement). Offers written contract. 3-months notice must be given to terminate contract.

Writers' Conferences: Book Expo America.

Tips: "Ask questions and talk to at least 3 different publicists. Have fun with your project and enjoy the ride! Only the determined make it."

◓ WARWICK ASSOCIATES

18340 Sonoma Hwy., Sonoma CA 95476. (707)939-9212. Fax: (707)938-3515. E-mail: sws@vom.com. Website: www.warwickassociates.net. **Contact:** Simon Warwick-Smith, president. Estab. 1983; specifically with books for 18 years. Currently works with 24 clients. 12% of clients are new/first-time writers.

● Prior to becoming a freelance publicist, Mr. Warwick-Smith was Senior Vice President of Marketing, Associated Publishers Group (books).

Members: Patty Vadinsky (celebrity, sports, at firm 6 years); Simon Warwick-Smith (metaphysics, business, at firm 18 years); Warren Misuraca (travel, writing, at firm 8 years).

Specializations: Nonfiction, children's books, spirituality. **Interested in these nonfiction areas:** Biography/autobiography, business, child guidance/parenting, computers/electronics, cooking/food/nutrition, government/politics/law, health/medicine, how-to, New Age/metaphysics, psychology, religious/inspirational, self-help/personal improvement, sports, travel. Other types of clients include celebrity authors.

Services: Provides media training, market research, fax news releases, electronic news releases, sends material to magazines/newspapers for reviews, brochures, website assistance, website publicity. Book tours include bookstores, specialty stores, radio interviews, TV interviews, newspaper interviews, magazine interviews, speaking engagements, online interviews. Assists in coordinating travel plans. Clients have appeared on *Larry King, Donahue, Oprah, Good Morning America*. Media kit includes résumé, author's biography, testimonials, articles about author, basic information on book, professional photos, sample interview questions, book request information. Helps writer obtain endorsements.

How to Contact: See website. Responds in 2 weeks. Returns material only with SASE. Obtains most new clients through recommendations from others and on website. Contact 6 months prior to book's publication.

Clients: References and contact numbers available for potential clients.

Costs: Works with clients on marketing budget. Offers written contract binding for specific project.

◓ WORLD CLASS SPEAKERS & ENTERTAINERS

5200 Kanan Rd., Suite 210, Aqoura Hills CA 91301. (818)991-5400. Fax: (818)991-2226. E-mail: info@speak.com. Website: www.speak.com. **Contact:** Joseph I. Kessler. Estab. 1965.

Specializations: Nonfiction, academic. **Interested in these nonfiction areas:** Business; humor; money/finance/economics; psychology; science/technology; self-help/personal improvement; sociology; sports; women's issues/women's studies; high profile/famous writers. Other types of clients include experts in all fields.

Services: Provides market research, sends material to magazines/newspapers for reviews, brochures, website publicity. Book tours include radio interviews, TV interviews, newspaper interviews, magazine interviews, speaking engagements, conferences, universities. Assists in coordinating travel plans. Media kits include author's biography, testimonials, articles about author, professional photos. Helps writer obtain endorsements.

How to Contact: Call, e-mail, or fax. Responds in 1 week. Discards unwanted materials. Obtains most new clients through recommendations from others. Contact prior to book's publication.

Costs: Charges clients per placement basis ($1,500 minimum); 30% commission. Works with clients on marketing budget. Offers written contract. Two-3 month notice must be given to terminate contract.

◙ THE WRITE PUBLICIST & CO.

1865 River Falls Dr., Roswell GA 30076. (770)716-3323. E-mail: thewritepublicist@earthlink.net. Website: www.thewritepublicist.com. **Contact:** Regina Lynch-Hudson. Estab. 1990; specifically with books for 10 years. Currently works with 5 clients. 50% of clients are new/first-time writers.

- Prior to becoming a publicist, Ms. Lynch-Hudson was public relations director for a 4-star resort.

Specializations: Nonfiction, fiction, children's books, multicultural, ethnic and minority market books. **Interested in these nonfiction areas:** Biography/autobiography, business, education, ethnic/cultural interests, health/medicine, how-to, juvenile nonfiction, multicultural, religious/inspirational, women's issues/women's studies. **Interested in these fiction areas:** Confessional, contemporary issues, erotica, ethnic, family saga, humor/satire, mainstream, multicultural, religious/inspirational, romance, science fiction, sports. Other types of clients include physicians, lawyers, entertainers, artists.

Services: Provides international publicity, if applicable, electronic news releases, sends material to magazines/newspapers for reviews, website publicity. Book tours include bookstores, radio interviews, TV interviews, newspaper interviews, magazine interviews, schools, universities. Assists in coordinating travel plans. Clients have appeared on *Oprah*, all national TV netwroks. Media kit includes author's biography, basic information on book, professional photos, book request information, propriety innovative enclosures that insure and increase the opportunity for publication. Helps writer obtain endorsements.

- Twelve years experience publicizing people, places, products, performances. Owner of company was syndicated columnist to 215 newspapers, which solidified media contacts.

How to Contact: E-mail. Send book or ms. Responds in 1 week. Returns materials only with SASE. Obtains most new clients through recommendations from others. "90% of our clients are referred nationally." Contact 1 month prior to book's publication or after book's publication.

Clients: *Lifestyles for the 21st Century*, by Dr. Marcus Wells (Humanics Publishing); *Preconceived Notions*, by Robyn Williams (Noble Press); *Fed Up With the Fanny*, by Franklin White (Simon & Schuster). Other clients include Vernon Jones, CEO of DeKalb County; Atlanta Perinatal Associates; Tonda Smith, news anchor. "Our clients' contracts state that they will not be solicited by prospective clients. Our website shows photos of clients who give their recommendation by consenting to be placed on our website."

Costs: Clients charged flat fee ($9,500-15,000). Works with clients on marketing budget. Offers written contract. Three-day notice before our company has invested time interviewing the client and writing their release must be given to terminate a contract.

Tips: "Does the publicist have a website that actually pictures clients? Our award-winning website ranks among top 10 of all major search engines as one of the few PR sites that actually depicts clients."

◙ MERYL ZEGAREK PUBLIC RELATIONS, INC.

255 W. 108th St., Suite 9D1, New York NY 10025. (917)493-3601. Fax: (917)493-3598. E-mail: mz@mzpr.com. Website: www.mzpr.com. **Contact:** Meryl Zegarek. Worked specifically with books for 25 years.

- Prior to starting her publicity agency, Ms. Zegarek was a publicity director of 2 divisions of The Knopf Publishing Group, Pantheon/Schocken Books, Random House.

Specializations: Nonfiction, fiction. **Interested in these nonfiction areas:** Animals, anthropology/archaeology, art/architecture/design, current affairs, ethnic/cultural interests, government/politics/law, health/medicine, history, how-to, humor, interior design/decorating, language/literature/criticism, multicultural, music/dance/theater/film, nature/environment, photography, popular culture, psychology, religious/inspirational, science/technology, self-help/personal improvement, sociology, travel, true crime/investigative, women's issues/women's studies. **Interested in these fiction areas:** Action/adventure, contemporary issues, detective/police/crime, ethnic, historical, literary, multicultural, mystery/suspense, religious/inspirational, science fiction, thriller/espionage. Other types of clients include theater, performance, nonprofits, human rights organizations, international publishers.

Services: Provides detailed outline of services provided. Expertise in nationwide media campaigns, including

Independent Publicists

print features, TV, radio, and World Wide Web exposure. Also does marketing campaigns, media training, and book tours with bookstore readings, and appearances in other local venues, interviews/features in newspapers, magazines, TV, and radio. Assists in coordinating travel plans. Clients have appeared on *Oprah*, *Good Morning America*, *Today*, Fox-News, *Fresh Air* (NPR), *Morning Edition* (NPR). Media kit includes résumé, author's biography, testimonials, articles about author, basic information on book, professional photos, sample interview questions, book request information. Plans nationwide print and radio campaigns with give-aways—with National Television and radio producing *New York Times* bestsellers.

> Also has unique specialty in Jewish and nonreligious spiritual books and authors. "I have been a publicity director for 3 major publishing houses (Knopf, Bantam Doubleday, William Morrow) during a 25-year career in book publicity. I have experience in every genre of book with established contacts in TV, radio, and print—as well as bookstores and speaking venues."

How to Contact: Call, e-mail, or fax. Send letter with entire ms or galley, outline/proposal, sample chapters with SASE. Responds in 2 weeks. Returns material only with SASE. Obtains most new clients through recommendations from others. Contact as early as possible, 4-5 months prior to book's publication, if possible.

Clients: *Lit From Within*, by Victoria Moran (Harper SF); *ETZ Hayim* (Jewish Publication Society); *The Zohar: Pritzker Edition* (Stanford University Press); *Mystics, Mavericks and Merrymakers: An Inside Journey Among Hasidic Girls*, by Stephanie Wellen Levine (NYU Press); *Levana's Kitchen*, by Levana Kirchenbaum (Stewart Tabori Chang). Other clients include The Paulist Press, Harmony Books, Hidden Spring, Serpent's Tail. References and contact numbers available for potential clients.

Costs: Clients charged flat fee, hourly retainer fee for consultations, monthly retainer (divide up flat fee payable by month). Offers written contract. One-month notice must be given to terminate contract.

Tips: "Call early."

Writers' Conferences

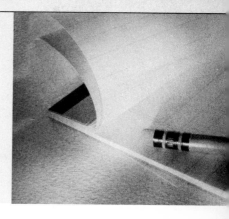

Attending a writers' conference that includes agents gives you both the opportunity to learn more about what agents do and also the chance to show an agent your work. Ideally, a conference should include a panel or two with a number of agents to give writers a sense of the variety of personalities and tastes of different agents.

Not all agents are alike: Some are more personable, and sometimes you simply click better with one agent over another. When only one agent attends a conference there is tendency for every writer at that conference to think, "Ah, this is the agent I've been looking for!" When a larger number of agents is attending, you have a wider group from which to choose, and you may have less competition for the agent's time.

Besides including panels of agents discussing what representation means and how to go about securing it, many of these gatherings also include time, either scheduled or impromptu, to meet briefly with an agent to discuss your work.

Tip

If they're impressed with what they see and hear about your work, they will invite you to submit a query, a proposal, a few sample chapters, or possibly your entire manuscript. Some conferences even arrange for agents to review manuscripts in advance and schedule one-on-one sessions where you can receive specific feedback or advice on your work. Such meetings often cost a small fee, but the input you receive is usually worth the price.

Ask writers who attend conferences and they'll tell you that at the very least you'll walk away with new knowledge about the industry. At the very best, you'll receive an invitation to send an agent your material!

Many writers try to make it to at least one conference a year, but cost and location can count as much as subject matter when determining which conference to attend. There are conferences in almost every state and province that can provide answers to your questions about writing and the publishing industry. Conferences also connect you with a community of other writers. Such connections help you learn about the pros and cons of different agents, and they also give you a renewed sense of purpose and direction in your own writing.

When reading through this section, keep in mind the following information to help you pick the best conference for your needs.

REGIONS

To make it easier for you to find a conference close to home—or to find one in an exotic locale to fit into your vacation plans—we've separated this section into geographical regions. The regions are as follows:

Northeast (pages 241-243): Connecticut, Maine, Massachusetts, New Hampshire, New York, Rhode Island, Vermont.

Get the most from a conference

Squeeze the most out of a conference by getting organized and staying involved. Follow these steps to ensure a worthwhile event.

Before you go:

- **Become familiar with all the pre-conference literature,** particularly the agenda. Study the maps of the area, especially the locations of the rooms in which your meetings/events are scheduled.

- **Make a list of three to five objectives you'd like to attain,** e.g., who you want to meet, what you want to learn more about, what you want to improve on, how many new markets you want to find, etc.

At the conference:

- **Budget your time.** Label a map so you know ahead of time where, when, and how to get to each session. Note what you want to do most. Then, schedule time with agents and editors for critique sessions.

- **Don't be afraid to explore new areas.** You are there to learn. Pick one or two sessions you wouldn't typically attend. This is an education; keep your mind open to new ideas and advice.

- **Allow time for mingling.** Some of the best information is given after the session. Learn "frank truths" and inside scoops. Asking people what they've learned at the conference will trigger a conversation that may branch into areas you want to know more about but won't hear from the speakers.

- **Learn about agents, editors, and new markets.** Which are more open to new writers? Find a new contact in your area for future support.

- **Collect everything:** guidelines, sample issues, promotional fliers, and especially business cards. Make notes about the personalities of the people you meet on the back of business cards to remind you after the conference who to contact and who to avoid.

- **Find inspiration for future projects.** While you're away from home, people-watch, take a walk, ride a bike, or take a drive. You may even want to take pictures to enhance your memory.

After the conference:

- **Evaluate.** Write down the answers to these questions: Would I attend again? What were the pluses and minuses, e.g., speakers, location, food, topics, cost, lodging? What do I want to remember for next year? What should I try to do next time? Who would I like to meet?

- **Write a thank-you letter** to an agent or editor who was particularly helpful. They'll remember you when you later submit.

Midatlantic (pages 243-245): Washington D.C., Delaware, Maryland, New Jersey, Pennsylvania.

Midsouth (pages 245-246): North Carolina, South Carolina, Tennessee, Virginia, West Virginia.

Southeast (pages 246-248): Alabama, Arkansas, Florida, Georgia, Louisiana, Mississippi, Puerto Rico.

Midwest (pages 248-250): Illinois, Indiana, Kentucky, Michigan, Ohio.

North Central (pages 250-251): Iowa, Minnesota, Nebraska, North Dakota, South Dakota, Wisconsin.

South Central (pages 251-255): Colorado, Kansas, Missouri, New Mexico, Oklahoma, Texas.

West (pages 255-259): Arizona, California, Hawaii, Nevada, Utah.

Northwest (pages 259-260): Alaska, Idaho, Montana, Oregon, Washington, Wyoming.

Canada (pages 260-262).

Quick reference icons

At the beginning of some listings, you will find one or more of the following symbols for quick identification of features particular to that listing.

N Conference new to this edition.

Canadian conference.

International conference.

CONFERENCE CALENDAR

To see which conferences are being held in the upcoming months, check the writers' conference calendar below. The calendar lists conferences alphabetically by the month in which they occur. It's often to your advantage to register for the conference you want to attend a few months in advance. This ensures you get the best prices and priority meeting slots available for consultations with the agents or editors. For screenwriters, some of the most popular conferences are UCLA Extension Writers' Program—Writers Studio (February), the ASA International Screenwriters Conference (August), and the Screenwriting Conference in Santa Fe (June).

For writers interested in screenplays or books, the San Diego State University Writers' Conference (January) and the Maui Writers' Conference (August) are popular choices not only for their beautiful locations, but also for the large number of high-quality industry professionals who lead workshops and meet one-on-one with attendees.

January
San Diego State University Writers' Conference (San Diego, CA)

February
Florida Suncoast Writers' Conference (St. Petersburg, FL)
UCLA Extension Writers' Program—Writers Studio (Los Angeles, CA)

March

Florida Christian Writers' Conference (Bradenton, FL)
Green River Writers' Novel-in-Progress Workshop (Louisville, KY)
IWWG Early Spring in California Conference (Santa Cruz, CA)
Kentucky Women Writers' Conference (Lexington, KY)
Mount Hermon Christian Writers' Conference (Mount Hermon, CA)
The William Saroyan Writers' Conference (Fresno, CA)
Tea with Eleanor Roosevelt (Hyde Park, NY)
Whidbey Island Writers' Conference (Langley, WA)
Writing Today (Birmingham, AL)

April

ASJA Writers' Conference (New York, NY)
IWWG Meet the Authors, Agents and Editors (New York, NY)
NETWO Writers' Roundup-Northeast Texas Writers Organization (Winfield, TX)
Pikes Peak Writers' Conference (Colorado Springs, CO)
Society of Children's Book Writers and Illustrators/Hofstra Children's Literature Conference (Hemstead, NY)
Waterside Publishing Conference (Berkley, CA)

May

Florida First Coast Writers' Festival (Atlantic Beach, FL)
Pennwriters Annual Conference (Pittsburgh, PA)
Pima Writers' Workshop (Tucson, AZ)
Southern California Writers' Conference (Palm Springs, CA)
Wisconsin Regional Writers' Association, Inc., Conferences (Stevens Point, WI)

June

Arkansas Writers' Conference (Little Rock, AR)
Aspen Summer Words Writing Retreat (Aspen, CO)
Capon Springs Writers' Workshop (West Virginia)
Clarion West Writers' Workshop (Seattle, WA)
Bloody Words (Toronto, ON, Canada)
Frontiers in Writing (Amarillo, TX)
Great Lakes Writer's Workshop (Milwaukee, WI)
Heartland Writers' Conference (Sikeston, MO)
Highland Summer Conference (Radford, VA)
Indiana University Writers' Conference (Bloomington, IN)
Iowa Summer Writing Festival (Iowa City, IA)
Jackson Hole Writers' Conference (Laramie, WY)
Manhattanville Summer Writers' Week (Purchase, NY)
Mendocino Coast Writers' Conference (Fort Bragg, CA)
Midland Writers' Conference (Midland, MI)
National Writers' Association Foundation Conference (Denver, CO)
The New Letters Weekend Writers' Conference (Kansas City, MO)
Police Writers' Conference (Ashburn, TN)
Remember the Magic 2005, The 26th Annual IWWG Summer Conference (Saratoga Springs, NY)
Santa Barbara Writers' Conference (Montecito, CA)
Screenwriting Conference in Santa Fe (Santa Fe, NM)

Washington Independent Writers (WIW) Spring Writers' Conference (Washington, DC)
Wesleyan Writers' Conference (Middletown, CT)
Writers' Retreat Workshop (KY)

July
Antioch Writers' Workshop (Yellow Springs, OH)
A Day for Writers (Steamboat Springs, CO)
Highlights Foundation Writers' Workshop (Chautauqua, NY)
Hofstra University Summer Writers' Conference (Hempstead, NY)
Maritime Writers' Workshop (Fredericton, NB, Canada)
New England Writers' Conference (Windsor, VT)
Romance Writers of America National Conference (various locations)
Sewanee Writers' Conference (Sewanee, TN)
University of Wisconsin at Madison Writers' Institute (Madison, WI)
Writers Workshop in Science Fiction (Lawrence, KS)

August
ASA International Screenwriters Conference (Los Angeles, CA)
Bread Loaf Writers' Conference (Ripton, VT)
The Columbus Writers' Conference (Columbus, OH)
The Festival of the Written Arts (Sechelt, BC, Canada)
IWWG Summer Conference (Saratoga Springs, NY)
Maui Writers' Conference (Kihei, HI)
Sage Hill Writing Experience (Saskatoon, SK, Canada)
Society of Children's Book Writers and Illustrators/National Conference on Writing and
    Illustrating for Children (Los Angeles, CA)
Squaw Valley Community of Writers—Writers Workshop (Squaw Valley, CA)
Willamette Writers' Conference (Portland, OR)

September
Boucheron 36 (Chicago, IL)
Capon Springs Writers' Workshop (West Virginia)
Winnipeg International Writers Festival (Winnipeg, MB, Canada)
Wisconsin Regional Writers' Association, Inc., Conferences (Williams Bay, WI)

October
Austin Film Festival & Heart of Film Screenwriters Conference (Austin, TX)
Flathead River Writers' Conference (Whitefish, MT)
Glorieta Christian Writers' Conference (Glorieta, NM)
IWWG Meet the Authors, Agents, and Editors (New York, NY)
Magna Cum Murder XI (Muncie, IN)
New Jersey Romance Writers' Put Your Heart in a Book Conference (Somerset, NJ)
North Carolina Writers' Network Fall Conference (Carrboro, NC)
Rocky Mountain Book Festival (Denver, CO)
Sandy Cove Christian Writers' Conference (North East, MD)
SIWC, Surrey International Writers' Conference (Surrey, BC, Canada)
Southern California Writers' Conference (Los Angeles, CA)
The Vancouver International Writers Festival (Vancouver, BC, Canada)

November
Baltimore Writers' Alliance Conference (Riderwood, MD)
Sage Hill Writing Experience (Saskatoon, SK, Canada)

SUBHEADS

Each listing is divided into subheads to make locating specific information easier. In the first section, you'll find contact information for each conference. This section also lists conference dates, the focus of the conference, and the average number of attendees. If a conference is small, you may receive more individual attention from speakers. If it is large, there may be a greater number and variety of agents in attendance. Finally, names of agents who will be speaking or have spoken in the past are listed along with details about their availability during the conference. Calling or e-mailing a conference director to verify the names of agents in attendance is always a good idea.

Costs: Looking at the price of events, plus room and board, may help writers on a tight budget narrow their choices.

Accommodations: Here conferences list overnight accommodations and travel information. Often conferences held in hotels will reserve rooms at a discount rate and may provide a shuttle to and from the local airport.

Additional Information: A range of features are provided here, including information on conference-sponsored contests, individual meetings, and the availability of brochures.

NORTHEAST (CT, MA, ME, NH, NY, RI, VT)

ASJA WRITERS CONFERENCE

Amercian Society of Journalists and Authors, 1501 Broadway, Suite 302, New York NY 10036. (212)997-0947. Fax: (212)768-7414. E-mail: staff@asja.org. Website: www.asja.org. **Contact:** Brett Harvey, executive director. Estab. 1971. Annual. Conference held April 2005. Conference duration: 2 days. Average attendance: 600. Nonfiction, screenwriting. Held at Grand Hyatt in New York. **Previous agents/speakers have included:** Dominick Dunne, James Brady, Dana Sobel. Agents will be speaking.
Costs: $195 (includes lunch).
Accommodations: "The hotel holding our conference always blocks out discounted rooms for attendees."
Additional Information: Brochures available in February. Registration form on website. Inquiries by e-mail and fax OK.

BREAD LOAF WRITERS' CONFERENCE

Middlebury College, Middlebury VT 05753. (802)443-5286. Fax: (802)443-2087. E-mail: blwc@middlebury.edu. Website: www.middlebury.edu/ ~ blwc. **Contact:** Noreen Cargill, administrative manager. Estab. 1926. Annual. Conference held in late August. Conference duration: 11 days. Average attendance: 230. For fiction, nonfiction, and poetry. Held at the summer campus in Ripton, Vermont (belongs to Middlebury College).
Costs: $2,030 (includes room/board) (2004).
Accommodations: Accommodations are on campus in Ripton.

ℕ HIGHLIGHTS FOUNDATION WRITERS WORKSHOP AT CHAUTAUQUA

Dept. NM, 814 Court St., Honesdale PA 18431. (570)253-1192. Fax: (570)253-0179. E-mail: lori@highlightsfound ation.org. **Contact:** Kent Brown, executive director. Estab. 1985. Annual. Average attendance: 100. "Writer workshops geared toward those who write for children—beginner, intermediate, advanced levels. Small group workshops, 1-to-1 interaction between faculty and participants plus panel sessions, lectures and large group meetings. Workshop site is the picturesque community of Chautauqua, New York." Classes offered include "Children's Interests," "Writing Dialogue," "Outline for the Novel," "Conflict and Developing Plot." **Previous agents/speakers have included:** Eve Bunting, James Cross Giblin, Walter Dean Myers, Jane Yolen, Patricia Gauch, Jerry Spinelli, Joy Cowley, and Ed Young.
Accommodations: "We coordinate ground transportation to and from airports, trains, and bus stations in the Erie, Pennsylvania and Jamestown/Buffalo, New York area. We also coordinate accommodations for conference attendees."
Additional Information: "We offer the opportunity for attendees to submit a manuscript for review at the conference." Workshop brochures/guidelines are available after January for SASE. Inquiries by fax OK.

HOFSTRA UNIVERSITY SUMMER WRITERS' CONFERENCE

250 Hofstra University, UCCE, Hempstead NY 11549-1090. (516)463-5016. Fax: (516)463-4833. E-mail: uccelibarts @hofstra.edu. Website: www.hofstra.edu/writers (includes details on dates, faculty, general description, tuition). **Contact:** Marion Flomenhaft, director, liberal arts studies. Estab. 1972. Annual (every summer, starting week after July 4). Conference held July 11-12, 2005. Average attendance: 65. Conference offers workshops in short fiction, nonfiction, poetry, juvenile fiction, stage/screenwriting and, on occasion, 1 other genre such as detective fiction or science fiction. High school students welcome. Site is the university campus, a suburban setting, 25 miles from New York City. **Previous agent/speakers have incuded:** Roberta Allen, Ronald Bazarini, Carole Crowe, Brian Heinz, and Rebecca Wolff. Agents will be speaking and available for meetings with attendees.
Costs: Noncredit (2 meals, no room): approximately $450/workshop or $700/2 workshops. Credit available to undergraduate and graduate students. See website for further information. Continental breakfast and lunch are provided daily; tuition also includes cost of banquet.
Accommodations: Free bus operates between Hempstead Train Station and campus for those commuting from New York City. Dormitory rooms are available for approximately $350 for the 2-week conference.
Additional Information: "All workshops include critiquing. Each participant is given 1-on-1 time for a half hour with workshop leader."

IWWG MEET THE AUTHORS, AGENTS AND EDITORS: THE BIG APPLE WORKSHOPS

% International Women's Writing Guild, P.O. Box 810, Gracie Station, New York NY 10028-0082. (212)737-7536. Fax: (212)737-9469. E-mail: iwwg@iwwg.org. Website: www.iwwg.org. **Contact:** Hannelore Hahn, executive director. Estab. 1980. Conferences held generally the third weekend in April and the second weekend in October. Average attendance: 200. Workshops to promote creative writing and professional success. Held midtown New York City. Saturday offers a 1-day writing workshop. Sunday morning: discussion with up to 10 recently published IWWG authors. Book fair during lunch. Sunday afternoon: Open house: Meet the Agents

(up to 10 literary agents introduce themselves, and then members of the audience speak to the agents they wish to meet. Many as-yet-unpublished works have found publication in this manner). **Previous agents/ speakers have included:** Meredith Bernstein, Rita Rosenkranz, and Jeff Herman.
Costs: $110 for members for the weekend; $130 for nonmembers for the weekend; $70/80 for Saturday; $65/ 85 for Sunday.
Additional Information: Information (including accommodations) given in brochure. Inquires by fax and e-mail OK. "A simple formula for success."

ⓃIWWG SUMMER CONFERENCE

% International Women's Writing Guild, P.O. Box 810, Gracie Station, New York NY 10028-0082. (212)737-7536. Fax: (212)737-9469. E-mail: hirhahn@aol.com. Website: www.iwwg.com. **Contact:** Hannelore Hahn, executive director. Estab. 1977. 24th Annual. Conference generally held from 2nd Friday to 3rd Friday in August. Average attendance: 500, including international attendees. Conference to promote writing in all genres, personal growth, and professional success. Conference is held "on the tranquil campus of Skidmore College in Saratoga Springs, New York, where the serene Hudson Valley meets the North Country of the Adirondacks." Seventy-five different workshops are offered everyday. Theme: "Writing Towards Personal and Professional Growth."
Costs: $850 for week-long program with room and board. $400 for week-long program for commuters.
Accommodations: Transportation by air to Albany, New York, or Amtrak train available from New York City. Conference attendees stay on campus.
Additional Information: Features "lots of critiquing sessions and networking." Conference brochures/guidelines available for SASE. Inquires by fax and e-mail OK.

ⓃMANHATTANVILLE SUMMER WRITERS' WEEK

2900 Purchase St., Purchase NY 10577-0940. (914)694-3425. Fax: (914)694-3488. E-mail: dowdr@mville.edu. Website: www.mville.edu. **Contact:** Ruth Dowd, RSCJ, dean, graduate and professional studies. Estab. 1983. Annually. Conference held June 28-July 2, 2004. Conference duration: 5 days. Average attendance: 100. Workshops in fiction, nonfiction, personal narrative, poetry, children's/young adult literature, playwriting. Held at suburban college campus 30 miles from New York City. Workshop sessions are held in a 19th century Norman Castle which serves as the college's administration building. **Speakers/agents have included:** Brian Morton, Valerie Martin, Ann Jones, Mark Matousek, Major Jackson, Linda Oatman High, Jeffrey Sweet, Alice Quinn (poetry editor, *The New Yorker*), Georgia Jelatis Hoke (agent, MacIntosh & Otis, Inc.), Paul Cirone (agent, Aaron Priest Literary Agency), Emily Sylvan Kim (Writer's House). Agents will be speaking and available for meetings with attendees.
Costs: For noncredit: $650 (includes all workshops, craft seminars, readings, special keynote lecture by Amy Hempel). Program may also be taken for graduate credit. Participants may purchase meals in the college cafeteria or cafe.
Accommodations: A list of hotels in the area is available upon request. Overnight accommodations are available in the college residence halls for $25/night.
Additional Information: Brochures available for SASE or on website by end of February. Inquiries by e-mail and fax OK.

NEW ENGLAND WRITERS CONFERENCE

P.O. Box 5, Windsor VT 05089-0005. (802)674-2315. E-mail: newvtpoet@aol.com. Website: www.newengland writers.org. **Contact:** Dr. Frank and Susan Anthony, co-directors. Estab. 1986. Annually. Conference held third Saturday in July. Conference duration: 1 day. Average attendance: 100. Held at Old South Church, Windsor, Vermont. Seminars on publishing, agents, children's publishing, fiction, nonfiction, and poetry. **Previous agents/speakers have included:** John Talbot Agency, Tupelo Press, Dana Gioia, Wesley McNair, Michael C. White, and Rosanna Warren.
Costs: $20 (includes panel-seminar sessions, open readings, contest ceremony, and refreshments).
Accommodations: "Hotel list can be made available. There are many hotels in the area."
Additional Information: "This annual conference continues our attempt to have a truly affordable writers conference that has as much as most 3-4 day events." Brochures available for SASE or on website. Inquiries by e-mail OK.

ⓃREMEMBER THE MAGIC 2005, THE 26th ANNUAL INTERNATIONAL WOMEN'S WRITING GUILD SUMMER CONFERENCE

International Women's Writing Guild, P.O. Box 810, Gracie Station, New York NY 10028-0082. (212)737-7536. Fax: (212)737-9469. E-mail: iwwg@iwwg.org. Website: www.iwwg.org. **Contact:** Hannelore Hahn, executive director. Estab. 1979. Annual. Conference held third week in June. Average attendance: 500. Conference to promote creative writing and personal growth, professional know-how and contacts, networking. Site is the

campus of Skidmore College in Saratoga Springs, New York (near Albany). Approximately 70 workshops are offered each day. Conferees have the freedom to make their own schedule. They come from all parts of the world; all ages and backgrounds represented.
Costs: 7-day conference: $900 single/$790 double for members, $925 single/$815 double for nonmembers. These fees include program, room and board for the week. Rates for a 5-day stay and a weekend stay are also available, as well as commuter rates.
Additional Information: Conference brochures/guidelines are available for SASE. Inquiries by e-mail and fax OK or view on web.

SOCIETY OF CHILDREN'S BOOK WRITERS & ILLUSTRATORS CONFERENCE/HOFSTRA CHILDREN'S LITERATURE CONFERENCE

University College for Continuing Education, 250 Hofstra University, Hempstead NY 11549-1090. (516)463-7600. Fax: (516)463-4833. E-mail: uccelibarts@hofstra.edu. Website: www.hofstra.edu/ucce. **Contact:** Marion Flomenhaft. Estab. 1985. Annual. Conference to be held April 2005. Average attendance: 200. Conference to encourage good writing for children. "The conference brings together writers, illustrators, librarians, agents, publishers, teachers and other professionals who are interested in writing for children. Each year we organize the program around a theme." The conference takes place at the Student Center Building of Hofstra University, located in Hempstead, Long Island. "We have two general sessions, five break-out groups." **Previous agents/speakers have included:** Paula Danziger and Ann M. Martin, and a panel of children's book editors who critique randomly selected first-manuscript pages submitted by registrants. Agents will be speaking and available for meetings with attendees.
Costs: (2004 rates) $75 members; $80 for nonmembers. Continental breakfast and full luncheon included.
Additional Information: Special interest groups are offered in submission procedures, fiction, nonfiction, writing picture books, illustrating picture books, poetry and scriptwriting. "Visit our website for updates and conference details."

Ⓝ TEA WITH ELEANOR ROOSEVELT

International Women's Writing Guild, P.O. Box 810, Gracie Station, New York NY 10028-0082. (212)737-7536. Fax: (212)737-9469. E-mail: iwwg@iwwg.org. Website: www.iwwg.org. **Contact:** Hannelore Hahn, executive director. Estab. 1980. Annual conference held in March. During Women's History Month, this is a traditional, annual visit to Mrs. Roosevelt's cozy retreat cottage. Conference duration: 1 day of writing. Average attendance: 50. Held at the Eleanor Roosevelt Center at Val-Kill in Hyde Park, New York. Two hours from New York City in the Hudson Valley.
Costs: $75 (includes lunch).
Additional Information: Brochure/guidelines available for SASE. Inquiries by e-mail and fax OK.

WESLEYAN WRITERS CONFERENCE

Wesleyan University, Middletown CT 06459. (860)685-3604. Fax: (860)685-2441. E-mail: agreene@wesleyan.edu. Website: www.wesleyan.edu/writers. **Contact:** Anne Greene, director. Estab. 1956. Annual. Conference held the third week in June. Average attendance: 100. Fiction techniques, novel, short story, poetry, screenwriting, nonfiction, literary journalism, memoir. The conference is held on the campus of Wesleyan University, in the hills overlooking the Connecticut River. Features seminars and readings of new fiction, poetry, and nonfiction, and guest lectures on a range of topics including publishing. "Both new and experienced writers are welcome." **Agents/speakers attending include:** Esmond Harmsworth (Zachary Schuster Agency); Daniel Mandel (Sanford J. Greenburger Associates); Dorian Karchmar, Amy Williams (ICM). Participants are often successful in finding agents and publishers for this mss. Wesleyan participants are also frequently featured in the anthology, *Best New American Voices*. Agents will be speaking and available for meetings with attendees.
Costs: In 2003, day rate $750 (includes meals); boarding students' rate $875 (includes meals and room for 5 nights).
Accommodations: "Participants can fly to Hartford or take Amtrak to Meriden, Connecticut. We are happy to help participants make travel arrangements." Meals and lodging are provided on campus. Overnight participants stay on campus.
Additional Information: Manuscript critiques are available as part of the program but are not required. Participants may attend seminars in several different genres. Scholarships and teaching fellowships are available, including the Jakobson awards for fiction writers and poets and the Jon Davidoff Scholarships for journalists. Inquiries by e-mail, phone, and fax OK.

MIDATLANTIC (DC, DE, MD, NJ, PA)

BALTIMORE WRITERS' ALLIANCE CONFERENCE

P.O. Box 410, Riderwood MD 21139. (410)321-1179. E-mail: tmiller@towson.edu. Website: www.baltimorewrit

ers.org. **Contact:** Tracy Miller, coordinator. Estab. 1994. Annual. Conference held November. Conference duration: 1 day. Average attendance: 150-200. Writing and getting published—all areas. Held at Towson University. Topics have included: mystery, science fiction, poetry, children's writing, legal issues, grant funding, working with an agent, book and magazine panels. **Previous agents/speakers have included:** Nat Sobel (Sobel/Weber Associates); Nina Graybill (Graybill and English). Agents will be speaking.

Costs: $80-100 (includes all-day conference, lunch, and snacks). Manuscript critiques for additional fee.

Accommodations: Hotels close by, if required.

Additional Information: Inquiries by e-mail OK. May register through BWA website.

BUCHERON 36

(formerly Mid-Atlantic Mystery Book Fair & Convention), Detecto Mysterioso Books at Society Hill Playhouse, 507 S. Eighth St., Philadelphia PA 19147-1325. (215)923-0211. Fax: (215)923-1789. E-mail: shp@erols.com. Website: www.bucheron.net. **Contact:** Deen Kogan, chairperson. Estab. 1970. Annual. Convention held September. Average attendance: 1,500. Focus is on mystery, suspense, thriller, true crime novels, "an examination of the genre from many points of view." **Previous agents/speakers have included:** Lawrence Block, Jeremiah Healy, James Lee Burke, Ruth Rendell, Ian Rankin, Michael Connelly, Eileen Dreyer, Earl Emerson. Agents will be speaking and available for informal meetings with attendees.

Costs: $175 registration fee.

Accommodations: Attendees must make their own transportation arrangements. Special room rate available at convention hotel.

Additional Information: "The Bookroom is a focal point of the convention. Forty specialty dealers are expected to exhibit, and collectables range from hot-off-the-press bestsellers to 1930s pulp; from fine editions to reading copies." Conference brochures/guidelines are available for SASE or by telephone. Inquiries by e-mail and fax OK.

ⓝ NEW JERSEY ROMANCE WRITERS PUT YOUR HEART IN A BOOK CONFERENCE

P.O. Box 513, Plainsboro NJ 08536. (732)625-1162 or (732)946-4044. E-mail: jnbkerber@att.net or awalradt@aol.com. Website: www.njromancewriters.net. **Contact:** Beth Kerber or Anne Walradt. Estab. 1984. Annual. Conference held October 8-9, 2004. Average attendance: 500. Conference concentrating on romance fiction. "Workshops offered on various topics for all writers of romance, from beginner to multi-published." Held at the Doubletree Hotel in Somerset, New Jersey. **Previous agents/speakers have included:** Nora Roberts, Kathleen Woodiwiss, Patricia Gaffney, Jill Barnett, Kay Hooper.

Costs: $165 (New Jersey Romance Writers members) and $195 (nonmembers).

Accommodations: Special hotel rate available for conference attendees.

Additional Information: Sponsors Put Your Heart in a Book Contest for unpublished writers and the Golden Leaf Contest for published members of Region One of RWA. Conference brochures, guidelines, and membership information are available for SASE. "Appointments offered for conference attendees, both published and unpublished, with editors and/or agents in the genre." Massive bookfair open to public with authors signing copies of their books; half of proceeds donated to literacy charities.

ⓝ PENNWRITERS ANNUAL CONFERENCE

450 Avonia Rd., Fairview PA 16415. (724)327-2725. E-mail: snax@nb.net. Website: www.pennwriters.org. **Contact:** Carol Silvis, conference co-ordinator 2005. Estab. 1987. Annually. Conference held third weekend of May. Conference duration: 3 days. Average attendance: 120. "We try to cover as many genres each year as we can." Held at the Wyndham Hotel Pittsburgh—spacious facility with most workshop rooms on 1 level. **Previous agents/speakers have included:** Evan Marshall, Nancy Martin. Agents will be speaking and available for meetings with attendees.

Costs: $135 for members/$165 for nonmembers (includes all workshops and panels, as well as any editor or agent appointments). There is an additional charge for Friday's keynote dinner and Saturday night's dinner activity.

Accommodations: "We have arranged a special rate with the hotel, and details will be in our brochure. Our rate for conference attendees is $73 plus tax/night. The hotel has a shuttle to and from the airport."

Additional Information: "We are a multi-genre group encompassing the state of Pennsylvania and beyond." Brochures available February for SASE. Inquiries by e-mail OK. Visit website for current updates and details.

ⓝ SANDY COVE CHRISTIAN WRITERS CONFERENCE

Sandy Cove Bible Conference, 60 Sandy Cove Rd., North East MD 21901. (800)287-4843 or (800)234-2683. Website: www.sandycove.org. **Contact:** Jim Watkins, director. Estab. 1991. Annual. Conference begins first Sunday in October. Conference duration: 4 days (Sunday dinner through Thursday). Average attendance: 200. "There are major, continuing workshops in fiction, article writing, nonfiction books, and beginner's and ad-

vanced workshops. Twenty-eight 1-hour classes touch many topics. While Sandy Cove has a strong emphasis on available markets in Christian publishing, all writers are more than welcome. Sandy Cove is a full-service conference center located on the Chesapeake Bay. All the facilities are first class with suites, single, or double rooms available." Handicap accessible. **Previous agents/speakers have included:** Francine Rivers (bestselling novelist); Lisa Bergen, Waterbrook Press; Ken Petersen (editor, Tyndale House); Linda Tomblin (editor, *Guideposts*); and Karen Ball (Zondervan).
Costs: Call for rates.
Accommodations: "Accommodations are available at Sandy Cove. Information available upon request." Cost is $418 double occupancy room and board, $519 single occupancy room and board for 4 nights and meals.
Additional Information: Conference brochures/guidelines are available. "For exact dates, please visit our website."

WASHINGTON INDEPENDENT WRITERS (WIW) SPRING WRITERS CONFERENCE
733 15th St. NW, Suite 220, Washington DC 20005. (202)737-9500. Fax: (202)638-7800. E-mail: info@washwriter.org. Website: www.washwriter.org. **Contact:** Nicci Yang, membership manager. Estab. 1975. Annual. Conference held June 5. Conference duration: Saturday. Average attendance: 250. Fiction, nonfiction, screenwriting, poetry, children's, technical. "Gives participants a chance to hear from and talk with dozens of experts on book and magazine publishing as well as on the craft, tools, and business of writing." **Previous agents/speakers have included:** Erica Jong, John Barth, Kitty Kelley, Vanessa Leggett, and Diana McLellan. New York and local agents at every conference.
Costs: $185 members; $270 nonmembers; $285 membership and conference by May 17. $220 members; $265 nonmembers; $315 membership and conference after May 17.
Additional Information: Brochures/guidelines available for SASE in mid-February.

MIDSOUTH (NC, SC, TN, VA, WV)

AMERICAN CHRISTIAN WRITERS CONFERENCES
P.O. Box 110390, Nashville TN 37222-0390. (800)21-WRITE. Fax: (615)834-7736. E-mail: regaforder@aol.com. Website: www.acwriters.com (includes schedule of cities). **Contact:** Reg Forder, director. Estab. 1981. Annual. Conference duration: 2 days. Average attendance: 60. Fiction, nonfiction, scriptwriting. To promote all forms of Christian writing. Conferences held throughout the year in 36 US cities.
Costs: Approximately $169, plus meals and accommodations.
Accommodations: Special rates available at host hotel. Usually located at a major hotel chain like Holiday Inn.
Additional Information: Conference brochures/guidelines are available for SASE.

CAPON SPRINGS WRITERS' WORKSHOP
P.O. Box 11116, Cincinnati OH 45211-0116. (513)481-9884. Fax: (513)481-2646. E-mail: beckcomm@fuse.net. **Contact:** Wendy Beckman, director. Estab. 2000. Biannual. Conference held June or September. Conference duration: 3 days. Fiction, poetry, creative nonfiction. Conference held at Farm Resort, a 5,000-acre secluded mountain resort in West Virginia.
Costs: $450, in 2004 (includes seminars, meals, lodging).
Accommodations: Facility has swimming, hiking, fishing, tennis, badminton, volleyball, basketball, ping pong, campfire sing along. Nine-hole golf course available for additional fee.
Additional Information: Brochures available for SASE. Inquiries by fax and e-mail OK.

HIGHLAND SUMMER CONFERENCE
Box 7014, Radford University, Radford VA 24142-7014. (540)831-5366. Fax: (540)831-5951. E-mail: jasbury@radford.edu. Website: www.radford.edu/~arsc. **Contact:** JoAnn Asbury, assistant to director. Chair, Appalachian Studies Program: Dr. Grace Toney Edwards. Estab. 1978. Annual. Conference held in June. Conference duration: 15 days. Average attendance: 25. Fiction, nonfiction, screenwriting. **Previous speakers/agents have included:** Bill Brown, Robert Morgan, Sharyn McCrumb, Nikki Giovanni, Wilma Dykeman, Jim Wayne Miller. Agents will be speaking and available for meetings with attendees.
Costs: "The cost is based on current Radford tuition for 3 credit hours, plus an additional conference fee. On-campus meals and housing are available at additional cost. In 2003, conference tuition was $409 for in-state undergraduates, $1,177 for out-of-state undergraduates, $501 for in-state graduates, $994 for out-of-state graduates."
Accommodations: "We do not have special rate arrangements with local hotels. We do offer accommodations on the Radford University Campus in a recently refurbished residence hall. (In 2003 cost was $19-28/night.)"
Additional Information: "Conference leaders typically critique work done during the 2-week conference, but

do not ask to have any writing submitted prior to the conference beginning." Conference brochures/guidelines are available after February for SASE. Inquiries by e-mail and fax OK.

NORTH CAROLINA WRITERS' NETWORK FALL CONFERENCE

P.O. Box 954, Carrboro NC 27510-0954. (919)967-9540. Fax: (919)929-0535. E-mail: mail@ncwriters.org. Website: www.ncwriters.org (includes "history and information about the NC Writers' Network and our programs. Also has a links page to other writing-related websites"). **Contact:** Carol Henderson, program director. Estab. 1985. Annual. "2004 Conference will be held in Research Triangle Park, October 29-31." Average attendance: 450. Keynote speaker every year including Gloria Naylor, Rick Bragg, and Andrei Codrescu. "The conference is a weekend full of classes, panels, book signings and readings, including open mic. We offer a variety of genres including fiction, poetry, creative nonfiction, journalism, children's book writing, screenwriting, and playwriting. We also offer craft, editing, and marketing classes. The conference moves out of the Research Triangle every other year to select locations in North Carolina in order to best serve our entire state. We hold the conference at a conference center with hotel rooms available." **Previous agents/speakers have included:** Donald Maass, Noah Lukeman, Joe Regal, Jeff Kleinman, and Evan Marshall. Some agents will be teaching classes and some are available for meetings with attendees.

Costs: "Conference cost is approximately $200-225 and includes 2 meals."

Accommodations: "Special conference hotel rates are available, but the individual makes his/her own reservations."

Additional Information: Conference brochures/guidelines are available by sending street address to mail@ncwriters.org or on our website. Online secure registration is available.

POLICE WRITERS CONFERENCE

Police Writers Association, P.O. Box 738, Ashburn VA 20146. (703)723-4740. Fax: (703)723-4743. E-mail: leslye@policewriter.com. Website: www.policewriter.com. **Contact:** Leslyeann Rolik. Estab. 1996. Annual. Conference held in June. Conference duration: 2 days. Average attendance: 50. Related writing—both fiction and nonfiction. Focuses on police. Held in various hotels in various regions, determined annually. "Each year the conference focuses on helping club members get their work polished and published." **Previous agents/speakers have included:** Paul Bishop (novelist), Ed Dee (novelist), Roger Fulton (editor).

Costs: $175-300 in 2002 (includes all classes and seminars, fiction and nonfiction writing contest entries, and awards luncheons).

Accommodations: Hotel arrangements, at special conference rates, are available.

Additional Information: "Unpublished, police-genre writers are welcomed at the conference and as Police Writers Association Members." Brochures available on website. Inquiries by fax OK.

SEWANEE WRITERS' CONFERENCE

310 St. Luke's Hall, Sewanee TN 37383-1000. (931)598-1141. E-mail: cpeters@sewanee.edu. Website: www.sewaneewriters.org (includes general conference information and schedule of events). **Contact:** Cheri B. Peters, creative writing programs manager. Estab. 1990. Annual. Conference held in July. Conference duration: 12 days. Average attendance: 110. "We offer genre-based workshops (in fiction, poetry, and playwriting), not theme-based workshops. The Sewanee Writers' Conference uses the facilities of the University of the South. Physically, the University is a collection of ivy-covered Gothic-style buildings, located on the Cumberland Plateau in mid-Tennessee. Editors, publishers, and agents structure their own presentations, but there is always opportunity for questions from the audience." **2004 faculty members are:** Richard Bausch, Hilary Bell, Andrew Hudgins, Diane Johnson, Randall Kenan, Romulus Linney, Margot Livesey, Jill McCorkle, Claire Messud, Tim O'Brien, Francine Prose, Alan Shapiro, Dave Smith, and Mark Strand. **Visiting agents will include:** Gail Hochman and Georges Borchardt.

Costs: Full conference fee is $1,325 in 2000 (includes tuition, board, and basic room).

Accommodations: Participants are housed in University dormitory rooms. Motel or B&B housing is available but not abundantly so. Dormitory housing costs are included in the full conference fee.

Additional Information: Complimentary chartered bus service is available, on a limited basis, on the first and last days of the conference. "We offer each participant (excepting auditors) the opportunity for a private manuscript conference with a member of the faculty. These manuscripts are due 1 month before the conference begins." Conference brochures/guidelines are available, "but no SASE is necessary. The conference has available a limited number of fellowships and scholarships; these are awarded on a competitive basis."

SOUTHEAST (AL, AR, FL, GA, LA, MS, PUERTO RICO)

ARKANSAS WRITERS' CONFERENCE

9317 Claremore, Little Rock AR 72227. (501)312-1747. E-mail: blm@artistotle.net. **Contact:** Barbara Longstreth

Mulkey, director. Estab. 1944. Annual. Conference held first weekend in June 2004 (June 4-5). Average attendance: 225. Fiction, nonfiction, scriptwriting, and poetry. "We have a variety of subjects related to writing—we have some general sessions, some more specific, but try to vary each year's subjects."

Costs: Registration: ($15 1 day, $25 for 2 days), contest entry $6.

Accommodations: "We meet at a Holiday Inn, select in Little Rock." Holiday Inn has a bus to and from airport. Rooms average $70-75.

Additional Information: "We have 32 contest categories. Some are open only to Arkansans, most are open to all writers. Our judges are not announced before conference but are qualified, many from out of state." Conference brochures are available for SASE after February 1. "We have had 226 attending from 12 states—over 3,000 contest entries from 43 states, and New Zealand, Mexico, and Canada."

FLORIDA CHRISTIAN WRITERS CONFERENCE

2344 Armour Court, Titusville FL 32780. (321)269-5831. Website: www.flwriter.org. **Conference Director:** Billie Wilson. Estab. 1988. Annual. Conference is held in March. Conference duration: 5 days. Average attendance: 200. To promote "all areas of writing." Conference held at Christian Retreat Center in Brandenton, Florida. Editors will represent over 45 publications and publishing houses.

Costs: Tuition is $400 (includes tuition, food); $500 (double occupancy); $775 (single occupancy).

Accommodations: "We provide shuttle from the Sarasota airport."

Additional Information: Critiques available. "Each writer may submit 2 works for critique. We have specialists in every area of writing." Conference brochures/guidelines are available for SASE and on website.

FLORIDA FIRST COAST WRITERS' FESTIVAL

9911 Old Baymeadows Rd., Room C1301, FCCJ, Jacksonville FL 32256. (904)997-2669. Fax: (904)997-2746. E-mail: kclower@fccj.org. Website: ww.fccj.org/wf (includes festival workshop speakers, contest information). **Contacts:** Kathy Clower and Howard Denson. Estab. 1985. Annual. Conference held May 12-14, 2005. Held at Sea Turtle Inn, Atlantic Beach, Florida. Average attendance: 300. All areas: mainstream, plus genre. Fiction, nonfiction, scriptwriting, poetry, freelancing, etc. Offers seminars on narrative structure and plotting character development. **Previous agents/speakers include:** Doug Marlette, John Dufresne, Robert Inman, Arthur Rosenfeld, Kathy Pories (editor), Shelley Mickle, Sandra Kitt, Sheree Bykofsky (agent), Elizabeth Lund, David Poyer, Lenore Hart, Steve Berry, S.V. Date, and more to be announced. Agents will be speaking and available for meetings with attendees.

Costs: (2004 rates) Early bird special: $185 (2 days with 2 meals); $225 (2 days with 2 meals and banquet).

Accommodations: Sea Turtle Inn, (904)249-7402 or 1(800)874-6000, has a special festival rate.

Additional Information: Conference brochures/guidelines are available for SASE. Sponsors a contest for short fiction, poetry, and novels. Novel judges are David Poyer and Lenore Hart. Entry fees: $30, novels; $10, short fiction; $5, poetry. "We offer 1-on-1 sessions at no additional costs for attendees to speak to selected writers, editors, agents on first-come, first served basis." Visit our website after January 1, 2005, for current festival updates and more details.

FLORIDA SUNCOAST WRITERS' CONFERENCE

University of South Florida, Division of Professional & Workforce Development, 4202 E. Fowler Ave., MHH-116, Tampa FL 33620-6610. (813)974-2403. Fax: (813)974-5421. E-mail: dcistaff@admin.usf.edu. Website: english.cas.usf.edu/fswc. Directors: Steve Rubin, Betty Moss, and Lagretta Lenkar. Estab. 1970. Annual. Held February 4-6, 2005. Conference duration: 3 days. Average attendance: 400. Conference covers poetry, short story, novel, and nonfiction, including science fiction, detective, travel writing, drama, TV scripts, photojournalism, and juvenile. "We do not focus on any one particular aspect of the writing profession, but instead offer a variety of writing-related topics. The conference is held on the picturesque university campus fronting the bay in St. Petersburg, Florida." Features panels with agents and editors. **Previous speakers/agents have included:** Lady P.D. James, William Styron, John Updike, Joyce Carol Oates, Francine Prose, Frank McCourt, David Guterson, and Jane Smiley.

Costs: Call for information.

Accommodations: Special rates available at area motels. "All information is contained in our brochure."

Additional Information: Participants may submit work for critiquing. Extra fee charged for this service. Conference brochures/guidelines are available November 2004. Inquiries by e-mail and fax OK.

WRITING TODAY—BIRMINGHAM-SOUTHERN COLLEGE

Box 549003, Birmingham AL 35254. (205)226-4921. Fax: (205)226-4931. E-mail: dcwilson@bsc.edu. Website: www.writingtoday.org. **Contact:** Dee Wilson. Estab. 1978. Annual. Conference scheduled March 11-12, 2005. Average attendance: 300-350. "This is a two-day conference with approximately 18 workshops, lectures and readings. We try to offer workshops in short fiction, novels, poetry, children's literature, magazine writing, songwriting, and general information of concern to aspiring writers such as publishing, agents, markets, and research. The conference is sponsored by Birmingham-Southern College and is held on the campus in classrooms and lecture halls." **Previous agents/speakers included:** Eudora Welty, Pat Conroy, Ernest Gaines, Ray Bradbury, Erskine Caldwell, John Barth, Galway Kinnell, Edward Albee.

Costs: $120 for both days (includes lunches, reception, and morning coffee and rolls).

Accommodations: Attendees must arrange own transporation. Local hotels and motels offer special rates, but participants must make their own reservations.

Additional Information: "We usually offer a critique for interested writers. For those who request and send manuscripts by the deadline, we have had poetry and short story critiques. There is an additional charge for these critiques." Conference sponsors the Hackney Literary Competition Awards for poetry, short story, and novels. Brochures available for SASE.

MIDWEST (IL, IN, KY, MI, OH)

Ⓝ ANTIOCH WRITERS' WORKSHOP

P.O. Box 494, Yellow Springs OH 45387-0494. (937)475-7357. E-mail: info@antiochwritersworkshop.com. Website: www.antiochwritersworkshop.com. Director: Laura Carlson. Estab. 1984. Annual. Conference held July 10-16, 2004. Average attendance: 80. Workshop concentration: poetry, nonfiction, fiction, mystery, and memoir. Workshop located on Antioch College campus in the Village of Yellow Springs. **Faculty in 2004 includes:** Kathy Hogan Trocheck, John McCluskey, Katrina Kittle, Herbert Woodward Martin, Ann Townsend, Ann Hagedorn, Michael Dirda, and Crystal Wilson Harris. An agent and an editor will be speaking and available for meetings with attendees.

Costs: Tuition is $520 ($460 for locals and returning participants), plus a $90 registration fee.

Accommodations: Accommodations are available at local hotels and B&B's.

Additional Information: Optional ms critique, $70. Phone or e-mail for a free brochure.

THE COLUMBUS WRITERS CONFERENCE

P.O. Box 20548, Columbus OH 43220. (614)451-3075. Fax: (614)451-0174. E-mail: AngelaPL28@aol.com. Website: creativevista.com. Director: Angela Palazzolo. Estab. 1993. Annual. Conference held in August. Average attendance: 350+. "The conference covers a wide variety of fiction and nonfiction topics presented by writers, editors, and literary agents. Writing topics have included novel, short story, children's, young adult, science fiction, fantasy, humor, mystery, playwriting, screenwriting, personal essay, travel, humor, cookbook, technical, magazine writing, query letter, corporate, educational, and greeting cards. Other topics for writers: finding and working with an agent, targeting markets, research, time management, obtaining grants, and writers' colonies." **Previous agents/writers/editors have included:** Donald Maass, Jeff Herman, Andrea Brown, Jennifer DeChiara, Jeff Kleinman, Nancy Ellis-Bell, Rita Rosenkranz, Simon Lipskar, Doris S. Michaels, Sheree Bykofsky, Lee K. Abbott, Lore Segal, Mike Harden, Oscar Collier, Maureen F. McHugh, Ralph Keyes, Nancy Zafris, Bonnie Pryor, Dennis L. McKiernan, Karen Harper, Melvin Helitzer, Susan Porter, Les Roberts, Tracey E. Dils, J. Patrick Lewis, Patrick Lobrutto, Brenda Copeland, Tracy Bernstein, and many other professionals in the writing field.

Costs: For registration fees or to receive a brochure, available mid-Summer, contact the conference by e-mail, phone, fax, or postal mail, or check out the website.

Ⓝ GREEN RIVER WRITERS NOVELS-IN-PROGRESS WORKSHOP

2011 Lauderdale Rd., Louisville KY 40205. (502)417-5514. E-mail: maryodell@netzero.net or novelsinprogress @bellsouth.net. Website: greenriverwriters.org/nipw.html. Director: Jeff Yocom. Estab. 1991. Annual. Conference held 3rd week of March 2005. Conference duration: 1 week. Average attendance: 55. Open to persons, college age and above, who have approximately 3 chapters (60 pages) or more of a novel. Mainstream and genre novels handled by individual instructors. Short fiction collections welcome. "Each novelist instructor works with a small group (5-7 people) for 5 days; then agents/editors are there for panels and appointments on the weekend." Site is The University of Louisville's Shelby Campus, suburban setting, graduate dorm housing (private rooms available with shared bath for each 2 rooms). "Meetings and classes held in nearby classroom building. Grounds available for walking, etc. Lovely setting, restaurants and shopping available nearby. Participants carpool to restaurants, etc. This year we are covering mystery, fantasy, mainstream/literary, suspense, historical."

Costs: (2004 rates) $299 for workshop basics; $499 for personal instruction. Discount given for early registration. Does not include meals.

Accommodations: "We see that participants without cars have transportation to meals, etc. If participants would rather stay in hotel, we will make that information available." Graduate dormitory housing available for $175/week.

Additional Information: Participants send 60 pages/3 chapters with synopsis and $150 deposit which applies to tuition. Conference brochures/guidelines are available for SASE. Visit website for additional details.

N INDIANA UNIVERSITY WRITERS' CONFERENCE

464 Ballantine Hall, Bloomington IN 47405. (812)855-1877. Fax: (812)855-9535. E-mail: writecon@indiana.edu. Website: www.indiana.edu/~writecon. Director: Amy Locklin. Estab. 1940. Annual. Conference/workshops held June 19-24, 2005. Average attendance: 100. "Conference to promote poetry and fiction." Located on the campus of Indiana University, Bloomington. "We emphasize an exploration of creativity through a variety of approaches, offering workshop-based craft discussions, classes focusing on technique, and talks about the careers and concerns of a writing life. Participants in the week-long conference join faculty-led workshops in fiction and poetry, take classes, engage in 1-on-1 consultations with authors, and attend a variety of reading and social events." **Previous speakers have included:** Raymond Carver, Mark Doty, Robert Olen Butler, Amiee Bender, Brenda Hillman, and Li-Young Lee.

Costs: $350 for all classes only; $500 for all classes, plus 1 workshop (does not include food or housing). "We supply conferees with options for overnight accommodations. We offer special conference rates for both the hotel and dorm facilities on site."

Additional Information: "In order to be accepted in a workshop, the writer must submit the work they would like critiqued. Work is evaluated before accepting applicant. Scholarships are available determined by an outside reader/writer, based on the quality of the manuscript." Conference brochures/guidelines available on website or for SASE in January. "We are the second oldest writer's conference in the country. We are in our 65th year."

KENTUCKY WOMEN WRITERS CONFERENCE

The Carnegie Center for Literacy and Learning, 115 Bowman Hall, University of Kentucky, Lexington KY 40506-0059. Fax: (859)257-8734. E-mail: kywwc@hotmail.com. Website: www.uky.edu/conferences/kywwc. **Contact:** Rebecca Howell. Annual. The Kentucky Women Writers Conference celebrates its 25th anniversary March 25-27, 2004 with an unprecedented collection of internationally renowned writers and up-and-coming talents. Faculty presenters include Sonia Sanchez, Rebecca Walker, Sena Jeter Naslund, Sabrina Dhawan, Harriet Logan, Jane Juska, Shana Penn, Chitra Divakaruni, Alix Strauss, Cate Fosl, Cecilia Woloch, Arwen Donahue, April Reynolds, and Tawada Yoko. Celebratory events will also include a screening of *Monsoon Wedding* at the Kentucky Theater followed by reception with its screenwriter, Sabrina Dhawan; the Nell Stuart Donovan Exhibit Series featuring the works of Great Britain's most acclaimed documentary photographer Harriet Logan; and an evening with 2 of the most important African-American artists of our time: teacher, political activist, and poet, Sonia Sanchez, and jazz's greatest interpreter and vocalist, Shirley Horn.

Additional Information: To request a brochure or for registration details, call (859)257-6420 or visit the website.

MAGNA CUM MURDER XI

(formerly The Mid America Crime Fiction Festival), The Mid America Crime Writing Festival, The E.B. and Bertha C. Ball Center, Ball State University, Muncie IN 47306. (765)285-8975. Fax: (765)747-9566. E-mail: kennisonk@aol.com; iamabigger@aol.com. Website: www.magnacummurder.com. **Contact:** Kathryn Kennison. Estab. 1994. Annual. Conference held October 22-24, 2004. Average attendance: 350. Fiction, nonfiction. Held in the Horizon Convention Center and Historic Radisson Hotel Roberts. Festival for readers and writers of crime writing. This year's guests of honor are Alexander McCall Smith and Donald Hale (true crime).

Costs: $185 (includes Saturday and Sunday/continental breakfasts, boxed lunches, opening reception and Saturday evening banquet).

MIDLAND WRITERS CONFERENCE

Grace A. Dow Memorial Library, 1710 W. St. Andrews, Midland MI 48640-2698. (989)837-3430. Fax: (989)837-3468. E-mail: ajarvis@midland-mi.org. Website: www.midland-mi.org/gracedowlibrary. Conference Chair: Katherine Redwine. **Contact:** Ann Jarvis, librarian. Estab. 1980. Annual. Conference held in June. Average attendance: 100. Fiction, nonfiction, children's, and poetry. "The Conference is composed of a well-known keynote speaker and 6 workshops on a variety of subjects including poetry, children's writing, nonfiction, freelancing, agents, etc. The attendees are both published and unpublished authors. The Conference is held at the Grace A. Dow Memorial Library in the auditorium and conference rooms." **2004 speakers include:** Pete Hamill, Virginia Bailey Parker, Anniek Hivert-Carthew. Agents will be speaking.

Costs: (2004 rates) Adult—$50; students, senior citizens and handicapped. Lunch is available. Costs are approximate until plans for upcoming conference are finalized.

Accommodations: A list of area hotels is available.

Additional Information: Conference brochures/guidelines are mailed mid-April. Call or write to be put on mailing list. Inquiries by e-mail and fax OK.

NATIONAL MUSEUM PUBLISHING SEMINAR

University of Chicago, Graham School of General Studies, 1427 E. 60th St., Chicago IL 60637. (773)702-1682. Fax: (773)702-6814. E-mail: s-medlock@uchicago.edu. **Contact:** Stephanie Medlock, director. Estab. 1988. Biennially. Conference Spring 2006. Recent themes have included: selecting an attractive book cover; artful strategies for cutting costs; digital imaging; a survival guide; and much more. Conference duration: 2½ days. Average attendance: 250. Primarily nonfiction, writing, and editing in museums. "Conference moves to a new city every time and is co-sponsored by the University and different museums."
Costs: (2004 rates) $495, includes certain meals.
Accommodations: See website for hotel options.
Additional Information: Brochures available for SASE after January 1, 2006. Inquiries by fax and e-mail OK.

WRITERS RETREAT WORKSHOP

% Write It/Sell It, 5721 Magazine St., #16, New Orleans LA 70115. (800)642-2494. Fax: (918)583-7625. E-mail: wrw04@netscape.net. Website: www.writersretreatworkshop.com. **Contact:** Jason Sitzes, director. Editor-in-Residence: Lorin Oberweger. Author/Instructor: Elizabeth Lyons. Estab. 1987. Workshop and retreats held Spring through Summer. Workshop in June held at Marydale Retreat Center in Northern Kentucky. Workshop duration: 10 days. Average attendance: 30. Focus on novels in proress. All genres. "Teaches a proven step-by-step process for developing and completing a novel for publication, developed originally by the late Gary Provost. The practical application of lessons learned in classes, combined with continual private consultations with staff members, guarantees dramatic improvement in craft, writing technique, and self-editing skills."
Previous speakers/agents have included: Donald Maass, Nancy Pickard, Grace Morgan, Jennifer Crusie.
Costs: $1,715 for new students; $1,595 for returning students (includes lodging, meals, consultations, and course materials).
Accommodations: Costs (discount for past participants) $1,710 for 10 days which includes all food and lodging, tuition, and private consultations. The Marydale Retreat Center is 5 miles from the Cincinnati airport and offers shuttle services.
Additional Information: See website for monthly updates on all available "Boot Camp for Writers" opportunities through Writers Retreat Workshop (WRW).

NORTH CENTRAL (IA, MN, NE, ND, SD, WI)

Ⓝ GREAT LAKES WRITER'S WORKSHOP

Alverno College, 3400 S. 43rd St., P.O. Box 343922, Milwaukee WI 53234-3922. (414)382-6176. Fax: (414)382-6332. Contact: Nancy Krase. Estab. 1985. Annual. Workshop held June 25-26, 2004. Average attendance: 100. "Workshop focuses on a variety of subjects including fiction, writing for magazines, freelance writing, writing for children, poetry, marketing, etc. Participants may select individual workshops or opt to attend the entire weekend session. The workshop is held in Milwaukee, Wisconsin at Alverno College."
Costs: In 2003, cost was $115 for entire program.
Accommodations: Attendees must make their own travel arrangments. Accommodations are available on campus; rooms are in residence halls. There are also hotels in the surrounding area. Call (414)382-6176 for information regarding overnight accommodations.
Additional Information: Brochures are available for SASE after March. Inquiries by fax OK.

Ⓝ IOWA SUMMER WRITING FESTIVAL

100 Oakdale Campus, W310, University of Iowa, Iowa City IA 52242-1802. (319)335-4160. E-mail: iswfestival@u iowa.edu. Website: www.uiowa.edu/~iswfest. **Contact:** Amy Margolis, director. Estab. 1987. Annual. Festival held in June and July. Workshops are 1 week or a weekend. Average attendance: limited to 12/class—over 1,500 participants throughout the summer. Held at University of Iowa campus. "We offer courses across the genres: novel, short story, essay, poetry, playwriting, screenwriting, humor, travel, writing for children, memoir, women's writing." **Previous agents/speakers have included:** Lee K. Abbott, Susan Power, Lan Samantha Chang, Gish Jen, Abraham Verghese, Robert Olen Butler, Ethan Canin, Clark Blaise, Gerald Stern, Donald Justice, Michael Dennis Browne, Marvin Bell, Hope Edelman. Guest speakers are undetermined at this time.
Costs: $475-500/week; $225, weekend workshop (2004 rates). Housing and meals are separate.
Accommodations: "We offer participants a choice of accommodations: dormitory, $40/night; Iowa House, $75/night; Sheraton, $75/night (rates subject to changes)."
Additional Information: Brochure/guidelines are available in February. Inquiries by fax and e-mail OK.

SINIPEE WRITERS' WORKSHOP

Loras College, 1450 Alta Vista, Dubuque IA 52004-0178. (563)588-7139. Fax: (563)588-4962. E-mail: chris.neuha us@loras.edu. Website: www.loras.edu. **Contact:** Chris Neuhaus, administrative assistant. Director Emeritus: John Tigges. Estab. 1985. Annual. Average attendance: 50-75. The workshop is held on the campus of Loras College in Dubuque. "This campus holds a unique atmosphere and everyone seems to love the relaxed and restful mood it inspires. This in turn carries over to the workshop, and friendships are made that last, in addition to learning and experiencing what other writers have gone through to attain success in their chosen field."
Accommodations: Information is available for out-of-town participants, concerning motels, etc.
Additional Information: See website after February 1, 2005, for updates. Offers The John Tigges Writing Contest for Short Fiction, Nonfiction, and Poetry. Conference brochures/guidelines are available February for SASE.

Ⓝ UNIVERSITY OF WISCONSIN AT MADISON WRITERS INSTITUTE

610 Langdon St., Madison WI 53703. (608)262-3447. Fax: (608)265-2475. Website: www.dcs.wisc.edu/lsa. **Contact:** Christine DeSmet, director. Estab. 1990. Annual. Conference held July 8-9, 2004. Average attendance: 175. Conference held at University of Wisconsin at Madison. Themes: fiction and nonfiction. Guest speakers are published authors, editors, and agents.
Costs: Approximately $205 for 2 days; critique fees additional.
Accommodations: Info on accommodations sent with registration confirmation. Critiques available. Conference brochures/guidelines are available for SASE.

Ⓝ WISCONSIN REGIONAL WRITERS' ASSOCIATION INC. CONFERENCES

Wisconsin Regional Writers' Association., N4549 County Road Y, Montello WI 53949. (608)297-9746. Website: www.wrwa.net. **Contact:** Kathleen McGwin, president. Estab. 1948. Conferences held in May and September. Conference duration: 1-2 days. Provides workshops for all genres including fiction, nonfiction, scriptwriting, poetry. Presenters include authors, agents, editors, and publishers. **Previous agents/speakers have included:** Marcia Preston (editor *Byline Magazine*); Richard Lederer; Abby Frucht. Agents will be speaking.
Additional Information: Brochure available for SASE or on website. Inquiries by e-mail OK. E-mail addresses on website.

SOUTH CENTRAL (CO, KS, MO, NM, OK, TX)

ASPEN SUMMER WORDS WRITING RETREAT & LITERARY FESTIVAL

(formerly Aspen Summer Words Writing Retreat), Aspen Writers' Foundation, 110 E. Hallam St., #116, Aspen CO 81611. (970)925-3122. Fax (970)920-5700. E-mail: info@aspenwriters.org. Website: www.aspenwriters.org. **Contact:** Jamie Abbott, operations manager. Estab. 1976. Annual. Conference held 4th week of June. Conference duration: 5 days. Average attendance: 96 at writing retreat, 200 at literary festival. Retreat for fiction, poetry, creative nonfiction, children's writing, nature writing, magazine writing. Festival includes author readings, panel discussions with publishing industry insiders, professional consultations with editors and agents and social gatherings. **Previous agents/speakers have included:** Suzanne Gluck, Elizabeth Sheinkman and Jody Hotchkiss (agents); Jordan Pavlin and Hilary Black (editors); Pam Houston, Mark Salzman, Larry Watson and Anita Shreve (fiction); Harold Kushner, Ted Conover, Madeleine Blais, and Peter Stark (nonfiction); Jane Hirshfield, Mary Jo Salter, and J.D. McClatchy (poetry); Jan Greenberg (childen's literature); Gary Ferguson (nature writing); Laura Fraser and Daniel Glick (magazine writing); and many more.
Costs: $375/retreat; $195/seminar; $150/festival.
Accommodations: Rates for 2004: $65/night double; $110/night single.
Additional Information: Manuscripts to be submitted for review by admissions committee prior to conference. Conference brochures are available for SASE or on website.

AUSTIN FILM FESTIVAL & HEART OF FILM SCREENWRITERS CONFERENCE

1604 Nueces St., Austin TX 78701. (800)310-3378 or (512)478-4795. Fax:(512)478-6205. E-mail: info@austinfil mfestival.com. Website: www.austinfilmfestival.com. **Contact:** Paul Phelps, registration and membership director. Estab. 1994. Annual. Conference held October 2005. Conference duration: 4 days. Average attendance: 1,500. The Austin Film Festival & Heart of Film Screenwriters Conference is a nonprofit organization committed to furthering the art, craft, and business of screenwriters, and recognizing their contribution to the filmmaking industry. The 4-day Screenwriters Conference presents over 60 panels, roundtables, and workshops that address various aspects of screenwriting and filmmaking. Held at the Driskill and Stephen F. Austin Hotels, located in downtown Austin. **Agents/Speakers attenting include:** Bill Broyles (*Unfaithful* '02); Lam Dobbs (*The Score*); Larry Doyle (*Duplex* '02); Scott Frank (*Minority Report* '02); Robert Gordon (*MIB 2*); Brian Helgeland (*The Sin*

Eater '02); Philip Levens (TV writer for *Smallville*); Bryan Singer, Scott Alexander, and Chris McQuarrie. Agents will be speaking and available for meetings with attendees.

Costs: $318.75 before May 7 (2004 rate). Includes entrance to all panels, workshops and roundtables during the 4-day conference, as well as all films during the 8-night Film Exhibition, the Opening Night Party, and Closing Night Party.

Accommodations: Discounted rates on hotel accommodations are available to conference attendees if the reservations are made through the Austin Film Festival office. Contact Austin Film Festival for holds, rates, and more information.

Additional Information: "The Austin Film Festival is considered 1 of the most accessible festivals, and Austin is the premiere town for networking because when industry people are here, they are relaxed and friendly." Brochures available January 1 for SASE or on website. Inquiries by e-mail and fax OK.

A DAY FOR WRITERS

P.O. Box 774284, Steamboat Springs CO 80477. (970)879-8079. E-mail: sswriters@cs.com. Website: www.steam boatwriters.com. **Contact:** Harriet Freiberger, director. Estab. 1982. Annual. Conference held in July. Conference duration: 1 day. Average attendance: 35. Featured areas of instruction change each year. Held at the restored train depot home of the Steamboat Springs Arts Council. **Previous agents/speakers have included:** Jim Fergus, Avi, Robert Greer, Renate Wood, Connie Willis.

Costs: $35 prior to June 1; $45 after June 1 (includes seminars, catered luncheon). Pre-conference dinner also available. Limited enrollment.

Additional Information: Brochures available in April for SASE. Inquiries by e-mail OK.

FRONTIERS IN WRITING

P.O. Box 19303, Amarillo TX 79114. (806)358-6581. E-mail: pcadmin@arn.net. Website: www.panhandleprowr iter.org. Estab. 1980. Annual. Conference held in June. Duration: 2 days. Average attendance: 200. Nonfiction, poetry, scriptwriting, and fiction (including mystery, romance, mainstream, science fiction, and fantasy). **Previous agents/speakers have included:** Zevorah Cutler Rubenstein and Scott Rubenstein (editor/broker for screenplays); Andrea Brown (children's literary agent); Elsa Hurley (literary agent); Hillary Sears (editor with Kensington Books).

Costs: 2004 conference: $150 early bird members; $175 early bird nonmembers; $200 nonmember, non early bird. Friday critique group extra.

Accommodations: Special conference room rate.

Additional information: Sponsors a contest. Guidelines available for SASE or on website.

Ⓝ GLORIETA CHRISTIAN WRITERS' CONFERENCE

CLASServices, Inc., P.O. Box 66810, Albuquerque NM 87193. (800)433-6633. Fax: (505)899-9282. E-mail: info@ classervices.com. Website: www.glorietacwc.com. **Contact:** Linda Jewell, seminar manager. Estab. 1997. Annually. Conference held October 26-30, 2005. Conference duration: Wednesday afternoon through Sunday lunch. Average attendance: 250. Include programs for all types of writing. Conference held in the Lifeway Glorieta Conference Center. **Speakers attending include:** Agents, editors, and professional writers. Agents will be speaking and available for meetings with attendees.

Costs: $299 early registration (1 month in advance); $329 program only. Critiques are available for an additional $35.

Accommodations: Hotel rooms are available at the Lifeway Glorieta Conference Center. Sante Fe Shuttle offers service from the Albuquerque or Sante Fe airports to the conference center. Hotel rates vary.

Additional Information: Brochures available April 1. Inquiries by phone, fax, or e-mail OK. Visit website for updates and current information.

HEARTLAND WRITERS CONFERENCE

P.O. Box 652. Kennett MO 63857. (573)297-3325. Fax: (573)297-3352. E-mail: hwg@heartlandwriters.org. Website: www.heartlandwriters.org. **Contact:** Harry Spiller, conference coordinator. Estab. 1990. Biennial (even years). Conference to be held June 3-5, 2004. Conference duration: 3 days. Average attendance: 160. Popular fiction (all genres), nonfiction, children's, screenwriting, poetry. Held at the Best Western Coach House Inn in Sikeston, Missouri. Previous panels included Christopher Vogler's Myth Adventures: The Storytellers Journey and "Finding the Time and Will to Write" and "Putting Reality into Your Genre Fiction." **Previous agents/speakers attending include:** Alice Orr, Jennifer Jackson, Ricia Mainhardt, Christy Fletcher, Sue Yuen, and Evan Marshall. Agents will be speaking and available for meetings with attendees. Evan Marshall is this year's keynote speaker.

Costs: $215 for advance registration, $250 for general registration (includes lunch on Friday and Saturday, awards banquet Saturday, hospitality room, and get-acquainted mixer Thursday night).

Accommodations: Blocks of rooms are available at a special conference rate at conference venue and at 2 nearby motels. Cost: $55-85/night (2002 price).
Additional Information: Brochures available late January 2004. Inquiries by e-mail and fax OK.

NETWO WRITERS ROUNDUP

(formerly Northwest Texas Community College & NETWO Annual Conference), Northeast Texas Writers Organization (NETWO), P.O. Box 411, Winfield TX 75493. (903)856-6724. E-mail: netwomail@netwo.org. Website: www.netwo.org. **Contact:** Georgia Henson, president. Estab. 1987. Annual. Conference held April. Conference duration: 2 days. Presenters include agents, writers, editors, and publishers.
Costs: (2004 rates) $60 (discount offered for early registration).
Additional Information: Write for additional information. Conference is co-sponsored by Texas Commission on the Arts. See website for current updates and more information after November 2004.

THE NEW LETTERS WEEKEND WRITERS CONFERENCE

University of Missouri-Kansas City, College of Arts and Sciences Continuing Ed. Division, 215 4825 Troost Bldg., 5100 Rockhill Rd., Kansas City MO 64110-2499. (816)235-2736. Fax: (816)235-2611. E-mail: newletters@umkc.edu. Website: www.newletters.org. **Contact:** Betsy Beasley or Sharon Seaton, administrative associates. Estab. in the mid-70s as The Longboat Key Writers Conference. Annual. Conference held early June. Conference duration is 3 days over a weekend. Average attendance: 75. Fiction, nonfiction, scriptwriting, poetry, playwriting, journalism. ''The New Letters Weekend Writers Conference brings together talented writers in many genres for lectures, seminars, readings, workshops, and individual conferences. The emphasis is on craft and the creative process in poetry, fiction, screenwriting, playwriting, and journalism; but the program also deals with matters of psychology, publications, and marketing. The conference is appropriate for both advanced and beginning writers. The conference meets at the beautiful Diastole conference center of The University of Missouri-Kansas City. Two- and 3-credit hour options are available by special permission of the instructor.''
Costs: Several options are available. Participants may choose to attend as a noncredit student or they may attend for 1 hour of college credit from the University of Missouri-Kansas City. Conference registration includes continental breakfasts, Saturday and Sunday lunch. For complete information, contact the University of Missouri-Kansas City.
Accommodations: Registrants are responsible for their own transportation, but information on area accommodations is made available.
Additional Information: Those registering for college credit are required to submit a ms in advance. Manuscript reading and critique is included in the credit fee. Those attending the conference for noncredit also have the option of having their ms critiqued for an additional fee. Conference brochures/guidelines are available for SASE after March. Inquiries by e-mail and fax OK.

PIKES PEAK WRITERS CONFERENCE

4164 Austin Bluffs Pkwy., #246, Colorado Springs CO 80918. E-mail: info@ppwc.net. Website: www.pikespeakwriters.org. Estab. 1993. Annual. Conference held April 23-25, 2004. Conference duration: Friday 11 a.m. to Sunday 2 p.m. Average attendance: 400. Commercial fiction. Held at the Wyndham Hotel. ''Workshops, presentations, and panels focus on writing and publishing genre fiction—romance, science fiction and fantasy, suspense thrillers, action adventure, mysteries. Agents and editors are available for meetings with attendees.''
Costs: $250 (includes all meals).
Accommodations: Wyndham Colorado Springs holds a block of rooms for conference attendees until March 28 at a special $77 rate (1-800-996-3426).
Additional Information: Readings with critique are available on Friday afternoon. One-on-one meetings with editors and agents available Saturday and Sunday. Brochures available in January. Inquiries by e-mail OK. Registration form available on website. Contest for unpublished writers; need not attend conference to enter contest.

N ROCKY MOUNTAIN BOOK FESTIVAL

2123 Downing St., Denver CO 80205. (303)839-8320. Fax: (303)839-8319. E-mail: ccftb@compuserve.com. Website: www.coloradocenterforthebook.org. **Contact:** Christiane Citron, executive director. Estab. 1991. Annual. Festival held October 2005. Festival duration: 2 days. Average attendance: 10,000. Festival promotes work published from all genres. Held at Denver Merchandise Mart in Denver. Offers a wide variety of panels. **Previous speakers have included:** Sherman Alexie, George Plimpton, Nevada Barr, Dave Barry, Dr. Andrew Weil, Jill Kerr Conway, Bill Moyers, and Dava Sobel.
Costs: $4 adult; $2 child.
Additional Information: Please submit copy of book, bio, and publicity material for consideration.

ROMANCE WRITERS OF AMERICA NATIONAL CONFERENCE

16000 Stuebner Airline Rd., Suite 140, Spring TX 77379. (832)717-5200. Fax: (832)717-5201. E-mail: info@rwan ational.org. Website: www.rwanational.org. **Contact:** Chris Calhoon, communications manager. Executive Director: Allison Kelley. Estab. 1981. Annual. Conference held in late July or early August. Average attendance: 1,500. Fiction writers, scriptwriters. Over 100 workshops on writing, researching, and the business side of being a working writer. Publishing professionals attend and accept appointments. Keynote speaker is renowned romance writer. Conference has been held in Chicago, Washington DC, and Denver.

Costs: $300.

Additional Information: Annual RITA awards are presented for romance authors. Annual Golden Heart awards are presented for unpublished writers. Conference brochures/guidelines are available for SASE.

SCREENWRITING CONFERENCE IN SANTA FE

(formerly Santa Fe Screenwriting Conference), P.O. Box 29762, Sante Fe NM 87592. (505)424-1501. Fax: (505)424-8207. E-mail: writeon@scsfe.com. Website: www.scsfe.com. **Contact:** Larry N. Stouffer, executive director. Estab. 1999. Annual. Conference held June 2-6, 2004. Average attendance: 175. The Screenwriting Conference in Santa Fe is designed to teach the art and craft of screenwriting. Held on the campus of the Institute of American Indian Arts, Santa Fe.

Costs: $595 for the Symposium and $200 for the Producer's Seminar. Early discounts are available. Includes 9 hours of in-depth classroom instruction, over 30 workshops, panel discussions, live scene readings, and social events, including the Outrageous Bonanza Creek Movie Ranch Barbeque Blowout and Wild West Fiesta.

Additional Information: "The Conference is suitable for beginning, intermediate, and advanced screenwriters. Mentors include Jeff Arch (*Sleepless in Seattle*), Daniel Pyne (*Manchurian Candidate* and *Sum of All Fears*), Kirk Ellis (Anne Frank and Judy Garland: Me and My Shadow), and Jay Cocks (*Gangs of New York*)."

SOUTHWEST WRITERS CONFERENCE MINI-CONFERENCE SERIES

(formerly Southwest Writers Conference). 3721 Morris St. NE, Suite A, Albuquerque NM 87111. (505)265-9485. Fax: (505)265-9483. E-mail: swriters@aol.com. Website: www.southwestwriters.org. Estab. 1983. Annual. Mini-conferences held throughout the year. Average attendance: 100/mini-conference. "Speakers include writers, editors, agents, publicists, and producers. All areas of writing, including screenwriting and poetry are represented. Preconference workshops and conference sessions are available for beginning or experienced writers."

Costs: Fee includes conference sessions and lunch.

Accommodations: Usually have official airline and hotel discount rates.

Additional Information: Sponsors a contest judged by authors, editors, and agents from New York, Los Angeles, etc., and from major publishing houses. Twelve categories. Deadline: June 1. Entry fee is $25 (members) or $45 (nonmembers). Brochures/guidelines available on website or for SASE. Inquiries by e-mail and fax OK. "An appointment (10 minutes, 1-on-1) may be set up at the conference with the editor or agent of your choice on a first-registered/first-served basis."

WRITERS' LEAGUE OF TEXAS

1501 W. Fifth St., Suite E-2, Austin TX 78703. (512)499-8914. Fax: (512)499-0441. E-mail: wlt@writersleague.o rg. Website: www.writersleague.org. **Contact:** Helen Ginger, executive director. Estab. 1982. Conference held in summer. Conference duration: Friday-Sunday. Average attendance 300. Fiction, nonfiction. **Agents/speakers have included:** Ken Atchity, Sheree Bykofsky, Mary Evans, Felicia Eth, Michael Larsen, Elizabeth McHugh, Elizabeth Pomada, Nancy Stender, Andrew Whelchel, Tim Bent, Karen V. Haas, Kati Hesford, Ron Martirano. Agents will be speaking and available for meetings with attendees. Each summer the League holds its annual Agents! Agents! Agents! Conference which provides writers with the opportunity to meet top agents from New York and the West Coast. Topics include: Finding and working with agents and publishers; writing and marketing fiction and nonfiction; dialogue; characterization; voice; research; basic and advanced fiction writing/focus on the novel; business of writing; also workshops for genres.

Costs: Most classes, $80-200; workshops $50; conferences: $175-225.

Accommodations: Special rates given at some hotels for program participants.

Additional Information: Critique sessions offered at some programs. Individual presenters determine critique requirements. Those requirements are then made available through Writers' League office and in workshop promotion. Contests and awards programs are offered separately. Brochures/guidelines are available on request.

WRITERS WORKSHOP IN SCIENCE FICTION

English Department/University of Kansas, Lawrence KS 66045-2115. (785)864-3380. Fax: (785)864-1159. E-mail: jgunn@ku.edu. Website: www.ku.edu/~sfcenter/. **Contact:** James Gunn, professor. Estab. 1985. Annual. Conference held in July. Average attendance: 15. Conference for writing and marketing science fiction. "Classes

meet in university housing on the University of Kansas campus. Workshop sessions operate informally in a lounge.'' **Previous agents/speakers have included:** Frederik Pohl, Kij Johnson, Chris McKitterick.
Costs: Tuition: $400. Housing and meals are additional.
Accommodations: Housing information available. Several airport shuttle services offer reasonable transportation from the Kansas City International Airport to Lawrence. During past conferences, students were housed in a student dormitory at $12.50/day double, $23.50/day single.
Additional Information: ''Admission to the workshop is by submission of an acceptable story. Two additional stories should be submitted by the middle of June. These 3 stories are copied and distributed to other participants for critiquing and are the basis for the first week of the workshop; 1 story is rewritten for the second week.'' Brochures/guidelines are available for SASE. ''The Writers Workshop in Science Fiction is intended for writers who have just started to sell their work or need that extra bit of understanding or skill to become a published writer.''

WEST (AZ, CA, HI, NV, UT)

ASA INTERNATIONAL SCREENWRITERS CONFERENCE
(formerly the Selling to Hollywood International Screenwriters Conference), 269 S. Beverly Dr., Suite 2600, Beverly Hills CA 90212-3807. Phone/fax: (866)265-9091. E-mail: asa@goasa.com. Website: www.goasa.com. **Contact:** John Johnson, director. Estab. 1988. Annual. Conference held in August in LA area. Conference duration: 3 days. Average attendance: 275. ''Conference targets scriptwriters and fiction writers, whose short stories, books, or scripts have strong feature film or TV potential, and who want to make valuable contacts in the industry. Full conference registrants receive a private consultation with the industry producer or professional of his/her choice who make up the faculty. Panels, workshops, pitching discussion groups and networking sessions include over 50 agents, professional film and TV scriptwriters, and independent as well as studio and TV and feature film producers.'' **Agents/speakers attending include:** Michael Hauge, Linda Seger, Syd Field, Billy Mernit, Richard Walter, Heidi Wall, Lew Hunter.
Costs: In 2004: full conference by May 31, $550; after May 31: $600. Includes some meals.
Accommodations: $140/night (in LA) for private room; $70/shared room. Discount with designated conference airline.
Additional Information: ''This is the premier screenwriting conference of its kind in the world, unique in its offering of an industry-wide perspective from pros working in all echelons of the film industry. Great for making contacts.'' Conference brochure/guidelines available March; phone, e-mail, fax, or send written request.

DESERT DREAMS 2006
P.O. Box 40772, Mesa AZ 85274-0772. (480)821-1690. E-mail: cathilombardo@cox.net. Website: www.desertro serwa.org. **Contact:** Cathi Lombardo, chapter president. Estab. 1986. Biannually. Conference held Spring 2006. Conference duration: 3 days. Average attendance: 250. Fiction, screenwriting, research. **Agents/speakers attending include:** Steven Axelrod, Irene Goodman, Christopher Vogler, Jill Barnett, Susan Elizabeth Phillips, Debbie Macomber, Linda Lael Miller, and editors from major publishing houses. Agents will be speaking and available for meetings with attendees.
Costs: (2004 rate) $195 for full conference (includes meals, seminars, appointments with editors and agents).
Accommodations: Discounted rates for conference attendees negotiated.
Additional Information: Inquiries by e-mail OK. Visit website for updates and complete details.

IWWG EARLY SPRING IN CALIFORNIA CONFERENCE
International Women's Writing Guild, P.O. Box 810, Gracie Station, New York NY 10028-0082. (212)737-7536. Fax: (212)737-9469. E-mail: iwwg@iwwg.org. Website: www.iwwg.org. **Contact:** Hannelore Hahn, executive director. Estab. 1982. Annual. Conference generally held on the 2nd weekend in March. Average attendance: 80. Conference to promote ''creative writing, personal growth, and voice.'' Site is a redwood forest mountain retreat in Santa Cruz, California.
Costs: $325 members/$345 nonmembers for weekend program with room and board, $150 for weekend program without room and board.
Accommodations: Accommodations are all at conference site.
Additional Information: Conference brochures/guidelines are available for SASE. Inquiries by e-mail and fax OK, or view on website.

MAUI WRITERS CONFERENCE
P.O. Box 1118, Kihei HI 96753. (808)879-0061. Fax: (808)879-6233. E-mail: writers@mauiwriters.com. Website: www.mauiwriters.com (includes information covering all programs offered, writing competitions, presenters

past and present, writers forum bulletin board, published attendees books, dates, price, hotel, and travel information). **Contact:** Shannon Tullius. Estab. 1993. Annual. Conference held the end of August (Labor Day weekend). Conference duration: 5 days. Conference held at Wailea Marriott Resort. Average attendance: 800. For fiction, nonfiction, poetry, children's, young adult, horror, mystery, romance, science fiction, journalism, screenwriting. Manuscript Marketplace, held twice a year, is a mail in service where your book idea is reviewed by participating agents and editors. **Agents have included:** Andrea Brown (Andrea Brown Literary Agency); Kimberley Cameron (The Reece Halsey Agency); Susan Crawford (Crawford Literary Agency); Laurie Horwitz (Creative Artists Agency); Amy Kossow (Linda Allen Literary Agency); Owen Laster (William Morris); Jillian Manus (Manus & Associates Literary Agency); Craig Nelson (The Craig Nelson Co.); Elizabeth Pomada (Larsen/Pomada Literary Agency); Susan Travis (Susan Travis Literary Agency). Agents will be speaking and available for consultations with attendees.

Additional Information: "We offer a comprehensive view of the business of publishing, with over 2,000 consultation slots with industry agents, editors, and screenwriting professionals, as well as workshops and sessions covering writing instruction. Consider attending our writers retreat immediately preceding the conference. Visit our website for current updates and full details on the retreats and conferences." Write or call for additional information.

MENDOCINO COAST WRITERS CONFERENCE

1211 Del Mar. Fort Bragg CA 95437. (707)964-7735. E-mail: mcwc@direcway.com. Website: www.mcwc.org. **Contact:** Stephen Garber, registrar. Estab. 1988. Annually. Conference held June 3-5, 2004. Conference duration: 3 days. Average attendance: 90. All areas of writing covered. Provides workshops for fircion, nonfiction, scriptwriting, children's, mystery, writing for social change. Held at small community college campus on the northern Pacific Coast. **Agents/speakers attending include:** Jandy Nelson, John Dufresne, Dana Levin, John Lescroart, Maxine Schur, and others. Agents will be speaking and available for meetings with attendees.

Costs: $290-360 (includes 1 day intensive in 1 subject and 2 days of several short sessions; panels; meals; 2 socials with guest readers; 1 open to the public event.)

Accommodations: Information on overnight accommodations is made available. Special conference attendee accommodations made in some cases. Shared rides from San Francisco Airport are available.

Additional Information: Emphasis on writers who are also good teachers. Brochures available for SASE in January or on website now. Inquiries by e-mail OK.

MOUNT HERMON CHRISTIAN WRITERS CONFERENCE

P.O. Box 413, Mount Hermon CA 95041-0413. (831)335-4466 or (888)MH-CAMPS. Fax: (831)335-9413. E-mail: dtalbott@mhcamps.org. Website: www.mounthermon.org. **Contact:** David R. Talbott, director of adult ministries. Estab. 1970. Annual. Conference held Friday-Tuesday over Palm Sunday weekend, March 18-22, 2005. Average attendance: 450. "We are a broad-ranging conference for all areas of Christian writing, including fiction, children's, poetry, nonfiction, magazines, inspirational and devotional writing, books, educational curriculum, and radio and TV scriptwriting. This is a working, how-to conference, with many workshops within the conference involving on-site writing assignments. The conference is sponsored by and held at the 440-acre Mount Hermon Christian Conference Center near San Jose, California, in the heart of the coastal redwoods. The faculty/student ratio is about 1:6 or 7. The bulk of our more than 60 faculty are editors and publisher representatives from major Christian publishing houses nationwide." **Previous agents/speakers have included:** Janet Kobobel Grant, Chip MacGregor, Karen Solem, and others. Agents speaking and available for meetings with attendees.

Costs: Registration fees include tuition, conference sessions, resource notebook, refreshment breaks, room and board, and vary from $650 (economy) to $970 (deluxe), double occupancy (2004 fees).

Accommodations: Registrants stay in hotel-style accommodations, and full board is provided as part of conference fees. Meals are taken family style, with faculty joining registrants. Airport shuttles are available from the San Jose International Airport. Housing is not required of registrants, but about 95% of our registrants use Mount Hermon's own housing facilities (hotel style double-occupancy rooms). Meals with the conference are required and are included in all fees.

Additional Information: "The residential nature of our conference makes this a unique setting for 1-on-1 interaction with faculty/staff. There is also a decided inspirational flavor to the conference, and general sessions with well-known speakers are a highlight." Registrants may submit 2 works for critique in advance of the conference, then have personal interviews with critiquers during the conference. No advance work is required however. Conference brochures/guidelines are available December 1. Inquiries by e-mail and fax OK. Tapes of past conference workshops also available.

PIMA WRITERS' WORKSHOP

Pima College, 2202 W. Anklam Rd., Tucson AZ 85709. (520)206-6974. Fax: (520)206-6020. E-mail: mfiles@pima

.edu. **Contact:** Meg Files, director. Estab. 1988. Annual. Conference held May 21-23, 2004. Conference duration 3 days. Average attendance: 250. Fiction, nonfiction, poetry, scriptwriting. "For anyone interested in writing— beginning or experienced writer. The workshop offers sessions on writing short stories, novels, nonfiction articles and books, children's and juvenile stories, poetry, and screenplays." Sessions are held in the Center for the Arts on Pima Community College's West Campus. **Previous agents/speakers have included:** Michael Blake, Ron Carlson, Gregg Levoy, Nancy Mairs, Linda McCarriston, Larry McMurtry, Barbara Kingsolver, Jerome Stern, Connie Willis, Jack Heffron, Jeff Herman, Robert Morgan. Agents will be speaking and available for meetings with attendees.
Costs: $70 (can include ms critique). Participants may attend for college credit, in which case fees are $89 for Arizona residents and $215 for out-of-state residents. Meals and accommodations not included.
Accommodations: Information on local accommodations is made available, and special workshop rates are available, at a specified motel close to the workshop site (about $65/night).
Additional Information: "The workshop atmosphere is casual, friendly, and supportive, and guest authors are very accessible. Readings and panel discussions are offered as well as talks and manuscript sessions." Participants may have up to 20 pages critiqued by the author of their choice. Manuscripts must be submitted 3 weeks before the workshop. Conference brochure/guidelines available for SASE. Inquiries by e-mail OK.

SAN DIEGO STATE UNIVERSITY WRITERS' CONFERENCE

SDSU College of Extended Studies, 5250 Campanile Dr., San Diego State University, San Diego CA 92182-1920. (619)594-2517. Fax: (619)594-8566. E-mail: extended.std@sdsu.edu. Website: www.ces.sdsu.edu/writers/index.html. **Contact:** Kevin Carter, coordinator, SDSU extension programs. Estab. 1984. Annual. Conference held the third weekend in January. Conference duration: 2 days. Average attendance: approximately 375. Fiction, nonfiction, scriptwriting, e-books. Held at the Doubletree Hotel, Mission Valley. "Each year the SDSU Writers Conference offers a variety of workshops for the beginner and the advanced writer. This conference allows the individual writer to choose which workshop best suits his/her needs. In addition to the workshops, editor/ agent appointments and office hours are provided so attendees may meet with speakers, editors and agents in small, personal groups to discuss specific questions. A reception is offered Saturday immediately following the workshops where attendees may socialize with the faculty in a relaxed atmosphere. Last year 18 agents attended in addition to editors and screenwriting experts." Agents will be speaking and available for meetings with attendees.
Costs: Approximately $310 (includes all conference workshops and office hours, coffee and pastries in the morning, lunch and reception Saturday evening).
Accommodations: Doubletree Hotel (800)222-TREE. Attendees must make their own travel arrangements.
Additional Information: Editor/agent appointments are private, 1-on-1 opportunities to meet with editors and agents to discuss your submission. To receive information, e-mail, call, or write.

SANTA BARBARA WRITERS' CONFERENCE

P.O. Box 304, Carpinteria CA 93014. (805)684-2250. Fax: (805)684-7003. Website: www.sbwc.online.com. **Contact:** Mary or Barnaby Conrad, conference co-director. Estab. 1973. Annual. Conference held in June, at Westmont College in Montecito. Average attendance: 350. For poetry, fiction, nonfiction, journalism, playwriting, screenplays, travel writing, children's literature. **Previous agents/speakers have included:** Kenneth Atchity, Michael larson, Elizabeth Pomada, Linda Mead, Stuart Miller, Gloria Stern, Don Congdon, Mike Hamilburg, Sandra Dijkstra. Agents will be speaking and available for meetings with attendees.
Accommodations: Onsite accommodations available. Additional accommodations available at area hotels.
Additional Information: Individual critiques are also available. Submit 1 ms of no more than 3,000 words in advance with SASE. Competitions with awards sponsored as part of the conference. Send SASE for brochure and registration forms.

THE WILLIAM SAROYAN WRITERS' CONFERENCE

P.O. Box 5331, Fresno CA 93755-5331. Phone/fax: (559)224-2516. Website: www.winwinwritersgroup.org. **Contact:** Joy Correia. Estab. 1992. Annual. Conference held in March. Conference duration: 3 days. Average attendance: 150. "This conference is designed to provide insights that could lift you out of the pack and into publication. You will learn from masters of the writing craft, you will discover current and future market trends, and you will meet and network with editors and agents who can sell, buy, or publish your manuscript." Fiction, nonfiction, scriptwriting. Held at the Piccadilly Inn Hotel across from the Fresno Airport. **Previous agents/ speakers have included:** Leonard Bishop, David Brin, John Dunning, Marcia Preston, Andrea Brown, Kathleen Brenzel, Linda Mead, Nancy Ellis-Bell, Liz Pentacoff, Rita Robinson, Stephen Mattee. Agents will be speaking and available for meetings with attendees.
Costs: $240 for 3 days (includes some meals). Single day fees: $95 for Friday, $175 for Saturday, $60 for Sunday.
Accommodations: Special lodging rate at the Piccadilly Inn Hotel. "Be sure to mention the William Saroyan

Writers' Conference to obtain this special rate. Reservations must be made 2 weeks in advance to assure availability of room at the conference site." Other hotels available.

Additional Information: Offers "Persie" writing contest in connection with conference. Send for brochure and guidelines. Fax and e-mail inquiries OK.

SOCIETY OF CHILDREN'S BOOK WRITERS AND ILLUSTRATORS/NATIONAL CONFERENCE ON WRITING & ILLUSTRATING FOR CHILDREN

8271 Beverly Blvd., Los Angeles CA 90048-4515. (323)782-1010. Fax: (323)782-1892. E-mail: scbwi@scbwi.org. Website: www.scbwi.org. **Contact:** Stephen Mooser, president. Estab. 1972. Annual. Conference held in August. Conference duration: 4 days. Average attendance: 500. Writing and illustrating for children. Held at the Century Plaza Hotel in Los Angeles. **Previous agents/speakers have included:** Andrea Brown, Steven Malk, Scott Treimel (all agents), Ashley Bryan, Bruce Coville, Karen Hesse, Harry Mazer, Lucia Monfried, and Russell Freedman. Agents will be speaking and available for meetings with attendees.

Costs: $370 (members); $395 (late registration, members); $415 (nonmembers). Cost does not include hotel room.

Accommodations: Information on overnight accommodations made available.

Additional Information: Manuscript and illustration critiques are available. Conference brochures/guidelines are available in June with SASE.

SOUTHERN CALIFORNIA WRITERS' CONFERENCE

1010 University Ave., #54, San Diego CA 92103. Phone/fax: (619)233-4651. E-mail: wewrite@writersconference .com. Website: www.writersconference.com. **Contact:** Michael Steven Gregory, executive director. Estab. 1986. Annually. Conference held Februray 18-21, 2005. Conference also held in Palm Springs, May 28-31, 2004, and in Los Angeles, October 1-3, 2004. Conference duration: 3 days. Average attendance: 250. Fiction and nonfiction, with particular emphasis on reading and critiquing. "Extensive reading and critiquing workshops by working writers. Over 3 dozen daytime workshops and no time limit late-night sessions." Agents will be speaking and available for meetings with attendees.

Costs: Depends on location.

Accommodations: Depends on location.

Additional Information: Late-night read and critique workshops run until 3 or 4 a.m. Brochures available for SASE or on website. Inquiries by e-mail and fax OK.

SQUAW VALLEY COMMUNITY OF WRITERS—WRITERS WORKSHOP

(formerly Squaw Valley Community of Writers Fiction Workshop), P.O. Box 1416, Nevada City CA 95959-1416. (530)470-8440. E-mail: svcw@oro.net. Website: www.squawvalleywriters.org. **Contact:** Ms. Brett Hall Jones, executive director. Estab. 1969. Annual. Conference held August. Conference duration: 1 week. Average attendance: 125. Fiction, nonfiction, memoir. Held in Squaw Valley, California—the site of the 1960 Winter Olympics. The workshops are held in a ski lodge at the foot of this spectacular ski area. **Previous agents/speakers have included:** Betsy Amster, Julie Barer, Michael Carlisle, Elyse Cheney, Mary Evans, Christy Fletcher, Theresa Park, B.J. Robbins. Agents will be speaking and available for meetings with attendees.

Costs: $725 (includes tuition, dinners). Housing is extra.

Accommodations: Rooms available. Single: $550/week. Double: $350/week per person. Multiple room: $210/week per person. Airport shuttle available for additional cost. Contact conference for more information.

Additional Information: Brochures available in March for SASE or on website. Inquiries by e-mail OK.

UCLA EXTENSION WRITERS' PROGRAM

10995 Le Conte Ave., #440, Los Angeles CA 90024. (310)825-9415 or (800)388-UCLA. Fax: (310)206-7382. E-mail: writers@uclaextension.edu. Website: www.uclaextension.org/writers. **Contact:** Cindy Lieberman, program manager. Estab. 1891. Courses held year-round with one-day or intensive weekend workshops to 12-week courses. Writers Studio held February 2005. Fiction, nonfiction, scriptwriting. "The diverse offerings span introductory seminars to professional novel and script completion workshops. The annual Writers Studio and a number of 1-, 2- and 4-day intensive workshops are popular with out-of-town students due to their specific focus and the chance to work with industry professionals. The most comprehensive and diverse continuing education writing program in the country, offering over 500 courses a year including: screenwriting, fiction, writing for young people, poetry, nonfiction, playwriting, and publishing. Courses are offered in Los Angeles on the UCLA campus, as well as online. Adult learners in the UCLA Extension Writers' Program study with professional screenwriters, fiction writers, playwrights, poets, and nonfiction writers who bring practical experience, theoretical knowledge, and a wide variety of teaching styles and philosophies to their classes." Online courses are also available. Call for details.

Costs: Vary from $90 for a 1-day workshop to $470 for a 12-week course to $2,850 for 9-month Master Classes.

Accommodations: Students make own arrangements. The program can provide assistance in locating local accommodations.

Additional Information: "Some advanced-level classes have manuscript submittal requirements; instructions are always detailed in the quarterly UCLA Extension course catalog." Contact program for details. Studio brochures/guidelines are available in the Fall. Inquiries by e-mail and fax OK.

WATERSIDE PUBLISHING CONFERENCE

2187 Newcastle Ave., Suite 204, Cardiff CA 92007. (760)632-9190. Fax: (760)632-9295. E-mail: admin@watersid e.com. Website: www.waterside.com. **Contact:** Kimberly Valentini, conference coordinator. Estab. 1990 Annually. Conference held April 15-16, 2004. Conference duration: 2-3 days. Average attendance: 200. Focused on computer and technology, books and their writers and publishers. Issues in the industry that affect the genre. Held at the Doubletree Berkeley Marina in Berkley, California. A bayside hotel with full amenities and beautiful view. Past themes: Digital Delivery; Ask the Buyer; Author Taxes, Branding, Contracts. **Previous agents/ speakers have included:** Paul Hilts (*Publishers Weekly*); Carla Bayha (Borders Books); Bob Ipsen (John Wiley & Sons); Microsoft; Mighty Words.com. Agents will be speaking and available for meetings with attendees.

Costs: In 2004: $500 general; $250 for authors (includes all sessions and parties, meals, coffee breaks). Conference attendees get a discounted room rate at the Doubletree.

Accommodations: Other hotels are in the area if conference hotel is booked or too expensive.

Additional Information: Brochures available via fax or e-mail, or call.

NORTHWEST (AK, ID, MT, OR, WA, WY)

Ⓝ CLARION WEST WRITERS' WORKSHOP

340 15th Ave. E., Suite 350, Seattle WA 98112-5156. (206)322-9083. E-mail: info@clarionwest.org. Website: www.clarionwest.org (includes critiquing, workshopping, names, dates). **Contact:** Leslie Howle, executive director. Workshop held June 19-July 29, 2005. Workshop duration 6 weeks. Average attendance: 17. "Conference to prepare students for professional careers in science fiction and fantasy writing." Held near the University of Washington. Deadline for applications: April 1. Agents will be speaking and available for meetings with attendees.

Costs: Workshop: $1,400 ($100 discount if application received by March 1). Dormitory housing: $1,200, some meals included.

Accommodations: Students are strongly encouraged to stay on-site, in dormitory housing. Cost: $1,200, some meals included, for 6-week stay. Dormitory and classrooms are handicapped accessible.

Additional Information: "This is a critique-based workshop. Students are encouraged to write a story a week; the critique of student material produced at the workshop forms the principal activity of the workshop. Students and instructors critique manuscripts as a group." Limited scholarships are available, based on financial need. Students must submit 20-30 pages of ms to qualify for admission. Conference guidelines available for SASE. Visit website for updates and complete workshop details.

FLATHEAD RIVER WRITERS CONFERENCE

P.O. Box 7711, Kalispeil MT 59904-7711. E-mail: hows@centurytel.net. **Contact:** Jake How, director. Estab. 1990. Annual. Conference held early October. Conference duration: 3 days. Average attendance: 100. "We provide several small, intense 3-day workshops before the general weekend conference on a wide variety of subjects every year, including fiction, nonfiction, screenwriting, and working with editors and agents." Held at Grouse Mountain Lodge. Workshops, panel discussions, and speakers focus on novels, nonfiction, screenwriting, short stories, magazine articles, and the writing industry. **Previous agents/speakers have included:** Donald Maass, Ann Rule, Cricket Pechstein, Rob Simbeck, Marcela Landres, Amy Rennert, Ben Mikaelsen, Esmond Harmsworth, Terry Borst, Ron Carlson. Agents will be speaking and available for meetings with attendees.

Costs: $150 (includes breakfast and lunch, but does not include lodging).

Accommodations: Rooms available at discounted rates: $100/night. Whitefish is a resort town, and less expensive lodging can be arranged.

Additional Information: "By limiting attendance to 100 people, we assure a quality experience and informal, easy access to the presenters and other attendees." Brochures available June. Inquiries by e-mail OK.

JACKSON HOLE WRITERS CONFERENCE

University of Wyoming, Dept. 3972, 1000 E. University Ave., Laramie WY 82071. (877)733-3618, ext. 1. Fax: (307)766-3914. E-mail: jrieman@uwyo.edu. Website: http://jacksonholewriters.org. Conference Coordinator: Jerimiah Rieman. Estab. 1991. Annual. Conference held in June/July. Conference duration: 4 days. Average attendance: 70. For fiction, creative nonfiction, screenwriting. Offers critiques from authors, agents, and editors. Write for additional information or visit website.

WHIDBEY ISLAND WRITERS' CONFERENCE

P.O. Box 1289, Langley WA 98260. (360)331-6714. E-mail: writers@whidbey.com. Website: www.celebratewriting.org. **Contact:** Celeste Mergens, director. Annual. Conference held March 5-7, 2004. Conference duration: 3 days. Average attendance: 260. Fiction, nonfiction, screenwriting, writing for children, poetry, travel, and naturalist. Conference held at conference hall, and break-out fireside chats in local homes near sea. Panels include: "Meeting the Challenges of Writing," "The Art of Revision." **Agents/speakers attending include:** Jandy Nelson, Laurie Liss, Esmond Harmsworth, Katharine Sands, and many more. Updated list on website.
Costs: $300 before November 30, $340 after. Volunteer discounts available; early registration encouraged.
Accommodations: Information available for SASE.
Additional Information: Brochures available for SASE or on website. Inquiries by e-mail OK.

WILLAMETTE WRITERS CONFERENCE

9045 SW Barbur, Suite 5-A, Portland OR 97219. (503)452-1592. Fax: (503)452-0372. E-mail: wilwrite@willamettewriters.com. Website: www.willamettewriters.com. **Contact:** Bill Johnson. Estab. 1968. Annual. Conference held August 2003. Average attendance: 400. Fiction, nonfiction, scriptwriting. "Willamette Writers is open to all writers, and we plan our conference accordingly. We offer workshops on all aspects of fiction, nonfiction, marketing, scriptwriting, the creative process, etc. Also we invite top-notch inspirational speakers for keynote addresses. Recent theme was 'Writing Your Future.' We always include at least 1 agent or editor panel and offer a variety of topics of interest to both fiction, screenwriters, and nonfiction writers." **Previous agents/speakers have included:** Donald Maass, Noah Lukeman, Bob Mecoy, Angela Rinaldi, Lisa Dicker, Richard Morris, Andrew Whelchel. Agents will be speaking and available for meetings with attendees.
Costs: Cost for full conference including meals is $300 members; $336 nonmembers.
Accommodations: If necessary, these can be made on an individual basis. Some years special rates are available.
Additional Information: Conference brochures/guidelines are available for catalog-size SASE.

CANADA

⚅ BLOODY WORDS

12 Roundwood Court, Toronto, ON M1W 1Z2 Canada. E-mail: info@bloodywords.com. Website: www.bloodywords.com. **Contact:** Linda Wilken or Sue Pike, co-chairs. Estab. 1999. Annual. Conference held June 10-12, 2005. Conference duration: 3 days. Average attendance: 225. Guests of Honor: Anne Perry and Maureen Jennings. Focus on mystery fiction—to provide a showcase for Canadian mystery fiction writers and readers, and to provide writing information to aspiring writers. Held at the Delta Chelsea Hotel in downtown Toronto. "We will present 2 tracks of programming: 1 on Just the Facts, where everyone from coroners to toxicologists to Tactical Police Units present how things are done in the real world; and The Book track, where authors and readers discuss their favorite themes. Then we have the Mystery Café, where 13 authors read and discuss their work."
Costs: $125-170 (Canadian).
Accommodations: Special conference rate available at the Delta Chelsea Hotel.
Additional Information: Registration available on website. Inquiries by e-mail.

⚅ THE FESTIVAL OF THE WRITTEN ARTS

Box 2299, Sechel BC V0N 3A0 Canada. (800)565-9631 or (604)885-9631. Fax: (604)885-3967. E-mail: info@writersfestival.ca. Website: www.writersfestival.ca. **Contact:** Gail Bull, festival producer. Estab. 1983. Annual. Festival held August 11-14, 2005. Average attendance: 3,500. To promote "all writing genres." Festival held at the Rockwood Centre. "The Centre overlooks the town of Sechelt on the Sunshine Coast. The lodge around which the Centre was organized was built in 1937 as a destination for holidayers arriving on the old Union Steamship Line; it has been preserved very much as it was in its heyday. A 12-bedroom annex was added in 1982, and in 1989 the Festival of the Written Arts constructed a 500-seat Pavilion for outdoor performances next to the annex. The festival does not have a theme. Instead, it showcases 25 or more Canadian writers in a wide variety of genres each year." **Previous agents/speakers have included:** Jane Urquhart, Sholagh Rogers, David Watmough, Zsuzsi Gartner, Gail Bowen, Charlotte Gray, Bill Richardson, P.K. Page, Richard B. Wright, Madeleine Thien, Ronald Wright, Michael Kusugak, Bob McDonald. Agents will be speaking.
Costs: $12/event, or $175 for a 4-day pass (Canadian).
Accommodations: Lists of hotels and bed/breakfast available.
Additional Information: The festival runs contests during the 3½ days of the event. Prizes are books donated

by publishers. Brochures/guidelines are available. "Visit our website for current updates and details."

FESTIVAL OF WORDS

250 Thatcher Dr. E., Moose Jaw, SK S6J 1L7 Canada. (306)691-0557. Fax: (306)693-2994. E-mail: word.festival@ sasktel.net. Website: www.festivalofwords.com. **Contact:** Gary Hyland, coordinator; or Lori Dean, operations manager. Estab. 1997. Annual. Festival held in July. Festival duration: 4 days. The festival celebrates the imaginative uses of language, and features fiction and nonfiction writers, screenwriters, poets, children's authors, songwriters, dramatists, and film makers. Held at the Moose Jaw Public Library/Art Museum complex and in Crescent Park. **Previous agents/speakers have included:** Alistair McLeaod, Roch Carrier, Jane Urquhart, Susan Musgrave, M.T. Kelly, Terry Jordan, Sharon Butala, Maryann Kovalski, Allan Fotheringham, Pamela Wallin, Bonnie Burnard, Erika Ritter, Wayson Choy, Koozma Tarasoff, Lorna Crozier, Sheree Fitch, Nino Ricci, Yann Martel, Connie Kaldor, The Arrogant Worms, Brent Butt.

Costs: $115 (includes 3 meals).

Accommodations: Motels, hotels, campgrounds, bed and breakfasts.

Additional Information: "Our festival is an ideal meeting ground for people who love words to meet and mingle, promote their books, and meet their fans." Brochures available for SASE. Inquiries by e-mail and fax OK.

MARITIME WRITERS' WORKSHOP

UNB College of Extended Learning, Box 4400, Fredericton NB E3B 5A3 Canada. Phone/fax: (506)474-1144. E-mail: K4JC@unb.ca. Website: www.unb.ca/extend/writers. **Contact:** Rhona Sawlor, coordinator. Estab. 1976. Annual. Conference held annually in July. Average attendance: 50. "Workshops in 4 areas: fiction, poetry, nonfiction, writing for children." Site is University of New Brunswick, Fredericton campus.

Costs: In 2003: $395, tuition; $160 meals; $150/double room; $170/single room (Canadian).

Accommodations: On-campus accommodations and meals.

Additional Information: "Participants must submit 10-20 manuscript pages which form a focus for workshop discussions." Must be at least 18 years old. Brochures are available after March. No SASE necessary. Inquiries by e-mail and fax OK.

SAGE HILL WRITING EXPERIENCE

Box 1731, Saskatoon SK S7K 2Z4 Canada. Phone/fax: (306)652-7395. E-mail: sage.hill@sasktel.net. Website: www.sagehillwriting.ca (features complete program, including application and scholarship information). **Contact:** Steven Ross Smith, executive director. Annual. Workshops held in August and November. Workshop duration 10-21 days. Attendance: limited to 40-50. "Sage Hill Writing Experience offers a special working and learning opportunity to writers at different stages of development. Top quality instruction, low instructor-student ratio, and the beautiful Sage Hill settings offer conditions ideal for the pursuit of excellence in the arts of fiction, nonfiction, poetry, and playwriting." The Sage Hill location features "individual accommodation, in-room writing area, lounges, meeting rooms, healthy meals, walking hills, and vistas in several directions." Seven classes are held: Introduction to Writing Fiction & Poetry; Fiction Workshop; Nonfiction Workshop; Writing Young Adult Fiction Workshop; Poetry Workshop; Poetry Colloquium; Fiction Colloquium; Novel Colloquium;Playwriting Lab; Fall Poetry Colloquium. 2003 application deadlines are: April 25, July 30. **Previous agents/authors speakers have included in 2003:** George Elliott Clarke, Sue Goyette, Phil Hall, Lynn Coady, Arthur Slade.

Costs: Summer Program: $795 (Canadian) includes instruction, accommodation, meals, and all facilities. Fall Poetry Colloquium: $1,075.

Accommodations: On-site, individual accommodations located at Lumsden, 45 kilometers outside Regina.

Additional Information: For Introduction to Creative Writing: A 5-page sample of your writing or a statement of your interest in creative writing; list of courses taken required. For workshop and colloquium program: A résumé of your writing career, a 12-page sample of your work, and 5 pages of published work required. Guidelines are available for SASE. Inquiries by e-mail and fax OK. Scholarships and bursaries are available.

SIWC

(formerly A Writer's W*O*R*L*D), Surrey International Writers' Conference, 10707 146th St., Surrey, British Columbia V3R 1T5 Canada. (604)589-2221. Fax: (604)588-9286. E-mail: r.nixon@siwc.ca. Website: www.siwc. ca. Co-ordinator: Rusty Nixon. Estab. 1992. Annual. Conference held October 22-24, 2004. Conference duration: 3 days. Average attendance: 500. Conference for fiction (romance/science fiction/fantasy/mystery—changes focus depending upon speakers and publishers scheduled), nonfiction, scriptwriting, and poetry. "For everyone from beginner to professional." Conference held at Sheraton Guildford Hotel. **Agent/speakers attending have included:** Donald Maass (Donald Maass Literary Agency), Meredith Bernstein (Meredith Bernstein Literary Agency), Charlotte Gusay (Charlotte Gusay Literary Agency), Denise Marcil (Denise Marcil Literary Agency),

Anne Sheldon and Michael Vidor (The Hardy Agency). Agents will be speaking and available for meetings with attendees.

Costs: Approximately $399 (Canadian).

Accommodations: On request will provide information on hotels and B&Bs. Conference rate: $89. Attendee must make own arrangements for hotel and transportation. For accomodations, call (800)661-2818.

Additional Information: Writer's contest entries must be submitted about 6 weeks early. Length: 3,500-5,000 words, storytellers; 1,500 words maximum, nonfiction; 36 lines, poetry. Cash prizes awarded ($1,000 top prize in each category). Contest is judged by a qualified panel of writers and educators. Write, call, or e-mail for additional information. See website for more details.

THE VANCOUVER INTERNATIONAL WRITERS FESTIVAL

1398 Cartwright St., Vancouver BC V6H 3R8 Canada. (604)681-6330. Fax: (604)681-6400. E-mail: viwf@writersf est.bc.ca. Website: www.writersfest.bc.ca (includes information on festival). **Contact:** Jane Davidson, general manager. Estab. 1988. Annual. Held October 2005. Average attendance: 11,000. "This is a festival for readers and writers. The program of events is diverse and includes readings, panel discussions, seminars. Lots of opportunities to interact with the writers who attend." Held on Granville Island—in the heart of Vancouver. Two professional theaters are used as well as Performance Works (an open space). "We try to avoid specific themes. Programming takes place between February and June each year and is by invitation." **Previous agents/ speakers have included:** Margaret Atwood, Maeve Binchy, J.K. Rowling.

Costs: Tickets are $6-20 (Canadian).

Accommodations: Local tourist information can be provided when necessary and requested.

Additional Information: Brochures/guidelines are available for SASE after August. Inquiries by e-mail and fax OK. "A reminder—this is a festival, a celebration, not a conference or workshop." See website for current updates and details.

WINNIPEG INTERNATIONAL WRITERS FESTIVAL

624-100 Arthur St., Winnipeg MB R3B 1H3 Canada. (204)927-7323. Fax: (204)927-7320. E-mail: info@winnipeg words.com. Website: www.winnipegwords.com. **Contact:** Charlene Diehl-Jones, artistic director or Gilles Hé-bert, producer. Estab. 1997. Annual. Festival held last week of September. Conference duration: 6 days. Average attendance: 10,000. Fiction, nonfiction, scriptwriting. All areas of written/spoken word. Previous themes: Words of Wisdom, Diverse Voices. **Previous speakers/agents have included:** Michael Ondaatje, George Elliot Clarke, Esta Spalding, Margaret Atwood, Douglas Copland. Agents will be speaking.

Costs: $10-30.

Additional Information: Brochures available on website. Inquiries by e-mail and fax OK.

Professional Organizations

ORGANIZATIONS FOR AGENTS

Association of Authors' Representatives (AAR), P.O. Box 237201, Ansonia Station, New York NY 10003. E-mail: aarinc@mindspring.com. Website: www.aar-online.org.

Association of Authors' Agents, 62 Grafton Way, London W1P 5LD, England. (011) 44 7387 2076.

ORGANIZATIONS FOR WRITERS

The following professional organizations publish newsletters and hold conferences and meetings at which they often share information on agents. Organizations with an asterisk (*) have members who are liaisons to the AAR.

Academy of American Poets, 588 Broadway, Suite 604, New York NY 10012-3210. (212)274-0343. E-mail: academy@poets.org. Website: www.poets.org/index.cfm.

American Medical Writers Association, 40 W. Gude Dr., Suite 101, Rockville MD 20850-1192. (301)294-5303. E-mail: amwa@amwa.org. Website: www.amwa.org.

*American Society of Journalists & Authors, 1501 Broadway, Suite 302, New York NY 10036. (212)997-0947. Website: www.asja.org.

American Translators Association, 225 Reinekers Lane, Suite 590, Alexandria VA 22314. (703)683-6100. E-mail: ata@atanet.org. Website: www.atanet.org.

Asian American Writers' Workshop, 16 W. 32nd St., Suite 10A, New York NY 10001. (212)494-0061. E-mail: desk@aaww.org. Website: www.aaww.org.

*The Association of Writers & Writing Programs, The Tallwood House, Mail stop 1E3, George Mason University, Fairfax VA 22030. (703)993-4301. E-mail: awp@gmu.edu. Website: www.awpwriter.org.

*The Authors' Guild, Inc., 31 E. 28th St., 10th Floor, New York NY 10016. (212)563-5904. E-mail: staff@authorsguild.org. Website: www.authorsguild.org.

*The Dramatists Guild of America, 1501 Broadway, Suite 701, New York NY 10036. (212)398-9366. E-mail: igor@dramaguild.com. Website: www.dramaguild.com.

Education Writers Association, 2122 P St. NW, Suite 201, Washington DC 20037. (202)452-9830. E-mail: ewa@ewa.org. Website: www.ewa.org.

*Horror Writers Association, P.O. Box 50577, Palo Alto CA 94303. E-mail: hwa@horror.org. Website: www.horror.org.

The International Women's Writing Guild, P.O. Box 810, Gracie Station, New York NY 10028-0082. (212)737-7536. E-mail: dirhahn@aol.com. Website: www.iwwg.com.

*Mystery Writers of America, 17 E. 47th St., 6th Floor, New York NY 10017. (212)888-8171. E-mail: mwa@mysterywriters.org. Website: www.mysterywriters.org.

National Association of Science Writers, P.O. Box 890, Hedgesville WV 25427. (304)754-5077. Website: www.nasw.org.

National League of American Pen Women, 1300 17th St. NW, Washington DC 20036-1973. (202)785-1997. Website: www.americanpenwomen.org.

*National Writers Union, 113 University Place, 6th Floor, New York NY 10003. (212)254-0279. E-mail: nwu@nwu.org. Website: www.nwu.org.

*PEN American Center, 568 Broadway, New York NY 10012-3225. (212)334-1660. E-mail: pen@pen.org. Website: www.pen.org.

*Poets & Writers, 72 Spring St., Suite 301, New York NY 10012. (212)226-3586. Website: www.pw.org.

Poetry Society of America, 15 Gramercy Park, New York NY 10003. (212)254-9628. Website: www.poetrysociety.org.

*Romance Writers of America, 16000 Stuebner Airline Rd., Suite 140, Spring TX 77379. (832)717-5200. E-mail: info@rwanational.org. Website: www.rwanational.com.

*Science Fiction and Fantasy Writers of America, P.O. Box 871, Chestertown MD 21620. Website: www.sfwa.org.

Society of American Business Editors & Writers, University of Missouri, School of Journalism, 134 Neff Annex, Columbia MO 65211. (573)882-7862. E-mail: sabew@missouri.edu. Website: www.sabew.org.

Society of American Travel Writers, 1500 Sunday Dr., Suite 102, Raleigh NC 27607. (919)861-5586. E-mail: satw@satw.org. Website: www.satw.org.

*Society of Children's Book Writers & Illustrators, 8271 Beverly Blvd., Los Angeles CA 90048. (323)782-1010. E-mail: scbwi@scbwi.org. Website: www.scbwi.org.

Volunteer Lawyers for the Arts, One E. 53rd St., 6th Floor, New York NY 10022. (212)319-2787. Website: www.vlany.org.

Washington Independent Writers, 220 Woodward Bldg., 733 15th St. NW, Washington DC 20005. (202)737-9500. E-mail: info@washwriter.org. Website: www.washwriter.org.

Western Writers of America, 1012 Fair St., Franklin TN 37064. (615)791-1444. Website: www.westernwriters.org.

Writers Guild of Alberta, Main Floor, Percy Page Centre, 11759 Groat Rd., Edmonton, AB T5M 3K6 Canada. (780)422-8174. E-mail: mail@writersguild.ab.ca. Website: http://writersguild.ab.ca.

*Writers Guild of America—East, 555 W. 57th St., Suite 1230, New York NY 10019. (212)767-7800. Website: www.wgaeast.org.

Writers Guild of America—West, 7000 W. Third St., Los Angeles CA 90048. (323)951-4000. Website: www.wga.org.

Websites of Interest

WRITING

Fiction Addiction (www.fictionaddiction.net)
This site features articles and listings of publishers, agents, workshops, and contests for fiction writers.

Writing-World.com (www.writing-world.com)
This site offers a free, biweekly newsletter for writers as well as instructional articles.

AGENTS

Agent Research and Evaluation (www.agentresearch.com)
This is the website of AR&E, a company that specializes in keeping tabs on literary agents. For a fee you can order their varied services to learn more about a specific agent.

The Query Guild (www.queryguild.com)
A working tool where writers can post queries for samples or receive feedback from other authors.

Writer Beware (www.sfwa.org/beware)
The Science Fiction Writers of America's page of warnings about agents and subsidy publishers.

Useful
Websites

Writer's Market (www.writersmarket.com)
This searchable, subscription-based database is the online counterpart of *Writer's Market*, and includes contact information and submission guidelines for agents and publishers. This site also offers a free, biweekly e-newsletter.

WritersNet (www.writers.net)
This site includes a bulletin board where writers can discuss their experiences with agents.

SCRIPTWRITING

Done Deal (www.scriptsales.com)
The most useful features of this screenwriting site include descriptions of recently sold scripts, a list of script agents, and a list of production companies.

Samuel French, Inc. (www.samuelfrench.com/index.html)
This is the website of play publisher Samuel French that includes an index of authors and titles.

Hollywoodlitsales.com (www.hollywoodlitsales.com)
Find out what your fellow scribes are writing by reading their loglines on this website sponsored by two major Hollywood production companies.

Hollywood Creative Directory (www.hcdonline.com)
By joining this website, you'll have access to listings of legitimate players in the film, television, and new media industry.

MovieBytes (www.moviebytes.com)
Subscribe to *MovieBytes'* Who's Buying What for listings of the latest screenplay sales. Free access to one of the most comprehensive lists of screenplay contests is also offered on this site.

Screenwriters Web (www.breakingin.net)
Screenplay marketing advice about agents, format, marketing, contests and more is edited by screenwriter Lenore Wright.

MARKETING AND PUBLICITY

Authorlink (www.authorlink.com)
''The news, information and marketing community for editors, literary agents, and writers.'' Showcases manuscripts of experienced and beginning writers.

BookTalk (www.booktalk.com)
This site ''offers authors an opportunity to announce and market new releases to millions of viewers across the globe.''

BookWire (www.bookwire.com)
BookWire bills itself as the book industry's most comprehensive online information source. The site includes industry news, features, reviews, fiction, events, interviews, and links to other book sites.

Useful
Websites

Book Marketing Update (http://bookmarket.com)
This website by John Kremer, author of *1001 Ways to Market Your Book*, offers helpful tips for marketing books and many useful links to publishing websites. Also offers an e-newsletter so writers may share their marketing success stories.

Guerrilla Marketing (www.gmarketing.com)
The writers of *Guerrilla Marketing for Writers* provide many helpful resources to help you successfully market your book.

Publishers Lunch (www.publisherslunch.com)
This site allows you to sign up for a free newsletter, which offers daily updates on what's going on in the wonderful world of publishing. It's a good way to keep on top of the market.

Publishers Weekly (www.publishersweekly.com)
Read the latest book publishing news on this electronic version of the popular print magazine.

Writer's Digest (www.writersdigest.com)
This site is the online counterpart of *Writer's Digest* magazine. It offers information on

writing, as well as a complete bookstore of writing titles. This site also offers a free, biweekly e-newsletter.

ORGANIZATIONS

The Association of Authors' Representatives (www.aar-online.org)
This association page includes a list of member agents, a newsletter, and the organization's canon of ethics.

National Writer's Union (www.nwu.org)
Site of the National Writer's Union—the trade union for freelance writers of all genres publishing in the U.S.

Useful
Websites

PEN American Center (www.pen.org)
Site of the organization of writers and editors that seek to defend the freedom of expression and promote contemporary literature.

Writer's Guild of America (www.wga.org)
The WGA site includes advice and information on the art and craft of professional screenwriting for film, television, and interactive projects. This site offers script registration and a list of WGA signatory agencies.

Resources

Table of Acronyms

The organizations and their acronyms listed below are frequently referred to in the listings and are widely used in the industries of agenting and writing.

AAA	Association of Authors' Agents
AAP	American Association of Publishers
AAR	Association of Authors' Representatives
ABA	American Booksellers Association
ABWA	Associated Business Writers of America
AFTRA	American Federation of Television and Radio Artists
AGVA	American Guild of Variety Artists
AMWA	American Medical Writer's Association
ASJA	American Society of Journalists and Authors
ATA	Association of Talent Agents
AWA	Aviation/Space Writers Association
CAA	Canadian Authors Association
DGA	Director's Guild of America
GWAA	Garden Writers Association of America
HWA	Horror Writers of America
MOW	Movie of the Week
MWA	Mystery Writers of America, Inc.
NASW	National Association of Science Writers
NLAPW	National League of American Pen Women
NWA	National Writers Association
OWAA	Outdoor Writers Association of America, Inc.
RWA	Romance Writers of America
SAG	Screen Actor's Guild
SATW	Society of American Travel Writers
SCBWI	Society of Children's Book Writers & Illustrators
SFRA	Science Fiction Research Association
SFWA	Science Fiction and Fantasy Writers of America
WGA	Writers Guild of America
WIA	Women in the Arts Foundation, Inc.
WIF	Women in Film
WICI	Women in Communications, Inc.
WIW	Washington Independent Writers
WNBA	Women's National Book Association
WWA	Western Writers of America

Glossary

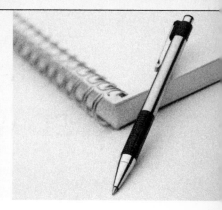

Above the line. A budgetary term for movies and TV. The line refers to money budgeted for creative talent, such as actors, writers, directors, and producers.

Advance. Money a publisher pays a writer prior to book publication, usually paid in installments, such as one-half upon signing the contract and one-half upon delivery of the complete, satisfactory manuscript. An advance is paid against the royalty money to be earned by the book. Agents take their percentage off the top of the advance as well as from the royalties earned.

Auction. Publishers sometimes bid for the acquisition of a book manuscript with excellent sales prospects. The bids are for the amount of the author's advance, guaranteed dollar amounts, advertising and promotional expenses, royalty percentage, etc.

Backlist. Those books still in print from previous years' publication.

Backstory. The history of what has happened before the action in your script takes place, affecting a character's current behavior.

Below the line. A budgetary term for movies and TV, referring to production costs, including production manager, cinematographer, editor, and crew members (gaffers, grips, set designers, make-up, etc.).

Bible. The collected background information on all characters and storylines of all existing episodes, as well as projections of future plots.

Bio. Brief (usually one page) background information about an artist, writer, or photographer. Includes work and educational experience.

Boilerplate. A standardized publishing contract. Most authors and agents make many changes on the boilerplate before accepting the contract.

Book club rights. Rights to sell a book through a book club.

Book packager. Draws elements of a book together, from the initial concept to writing and marketing strategies, and then sells the book package to a book publisher and/or movie producer. Also known as book producer or book developer.

Business-size envelope. Also known as a #10 envelope.

Castable. A script with attractive roles for known actors.

Category fiction. A term used to include all various types of fiction. See *genre*.

Client. When referring to a literary or script agent, "client" is used to mean the writer whose work the agent is handling.

Clips. Writing samples, usually from newspapers or magazines, of your published work.

Commercial novels. Novels designed to appeal to a broad audience. These are often broken down into categories such as western, mystery, and romance. See also *genre*.

Concept. A statement that summarizes a screenplay or teleplay—before the outline or treatment is written.

Contributor's copies. Copies of the author's book sent to the author. The number of contributor's copies is often negotiated in the publishing contract.

Co-agent. See *subagent*.

Co-publishing. Arrangement where author and publisher share publication costs and profits of a book. Also known as cooperative publishing.

Copyediting. Editing of a manuscript for writing style, grammar, punctuation, and factual accuracy.

Copyright. A means to protect an author's work.

Cover letter. A brief descriptive letter sent with a manuscript submitted to an agent or publisher.

Coverage. A brief synopsis and analysis of a script, provided by a reader to a buyer considering purchasing the work.

Critiquing service. A service offered by some agents in which writers pay a fee for comments on the salability or other qualities of their manuscript. Sometimes the critique includes suggestions on how to improve the work. Fees vary, as do the quality of the critiques. See also *editing service*.

Curriculum vitae (cv). Short account of one's career or qualifications (i.e., résumé).

D person. Development person. Includes readers, story editors, and creative executives who work in development and acquisition of properties for TV and movies.

Deal memo. The memorandum of agreement between a publisher and author that precedes the actual contract and includes important issues such as royalty, advance, rights, distribution, and option clauses.

Development. The process where writers present ideas to producers who oversee the developing script through various stages to finished product.

Division. An unincorporated branch of a company.

Docudrama. A fictional film rendition of recent news-making events or people.

Editing service. A service offered by some agents in which writers pay a fee—either lump sum or per-page—to have their manuscript edited. The quality and extent of the editing varies from agency to agency. See *critiquing service*.

Electronic rights. Secondary or subsidiary rights dealing with electronic/multimedia formats (e.g., the Internet, CD-ROMs, electronic magazines).

Elements. Actors, directors, and producers attached to a project to make an attractive package.

El-hi. Elementary to high school. A term used to indicate reading or interest level.

Episodic drama. Hour-long, continuing TV show, often shown at 10 p.m.

Evaluation fees. Fees an agent may charge to evaluate material. The extent and quality of this evaluation varies, but comments usually concern the salability of the manuscript.

Exclusive. Offering a manuscript, usually for a set period of time, to just one agent and guaranteeing that agent is the only one looking at the manuscript.

Film rights. May be sold or optioned by author to a person in the film industry, enabling the book to be made into a movie.

Flap copy. The text that appears on the inside covers of a published book and briefly explains the book's premise. Also called jacket copy.

Floor bid. If a publisher is very interested in a manuscript he may offer to enter a floor bid when the book goes to auction. The publisher sits out of the auction, but agrees to take the book by topping the highest bid by an agreed-upon percentage (usually 10 percent).

Foreign rights. Translation or reprint rights to be sold abroad.

Foreign rights agent. An agent who handles selling the rights to a country other than that of the first book agent. Usually an additional percentage (about 5 percent) will be added on to the first book agent's commission to cover the foreign rights agent.

Genre. Refers to either a general classification of writing such as a novel, poem, or short story, or to the categories within those classifications, such as problem novels or sonnets. Genre fiction is a term that covers various types of commercial novels such as mystery, romance, western, science fiction, or horror.

Ghosting/ghostwriting. A writer puts into literary form the words, ideas, or knowledge of another person under that person's name. Some agents offer this service; others pair ghostwriters with celebrities or experts.

Half-hour. A 30-minute TV show, also known as a sitcom.

High concept. A story idea easily expressed in a quick, one-line description.

Hook. Aspect of the work that sets it apart from others.

Imprint. The name applied to a publisher's specific line of books.

IRC. International Reply Coupon. Buy at a post office to enclose with material sent outside your country to cover the cost of return postage. The recipient turns them in for stamps in their own country.

Log line. A one-line description of a plot as it might appear in *TV Guide*.

Long-form TV. Movies of the week (MOW) or miniseries.

Mainstream fiction. Fiction on subjects or trends that transcend popular novel categories such as mystery or romance. Using conventional methods, this kind of fiction tells stories about people and their conflicts.

Marketing fee. Fee charged by some agents to cover marketing expenses. It may be used to cover postage, telephone calls, faxes, photocopying, or any other expense incurred in marketing a manuscript.

Mass market paperbacks. Softcover books, usually around 4x7, on a popular subject directed at a general audience and sold in groceries and drugstores as well as bookstores.

MFTS. Made for TV series. A series developed for television. See also *episodic drama*.

Middle reader. The general classification of books written for readers 9-11 years old.

Midlist. Those titles on a publisher's list expected to have limited sales. Midlist books are mainstream, not literary, scholarly, or genre, and are usually written by new or relatively unknown writers.

Miniseries. A limited dramatic series written for television, often based on a popular novel.

MOW. Movie of the week. A movie script written especially for television, usually seven acts with time for commercial breaks. Topics are often contemporary, sometimes controversial, fictional accounts. Also known as a made-for-TV movie.

Multiple contract. Book contract with an agreement for a future book(s).

Net receipts. One method of royalty payment based on the amount of money a book publisher receives on the sale of the book after the booksellers' discounts, special sales discounts, and returned copies.

Novelization. A novel created from the script of a popular movie, usually called a movie ''tie-in'' and published in paperback.

Novella. A short novel or long short story, usually 7,000 to 15,000 words. Also called a novelette.

One-time rights. This right allows a short story or portions of a fiction or nonfiction book to be published. The work can be printed again without violating the contract.

Option. Also known as a script option. Instead of buying a movie script outright, a producer buys the right to a script for a short period of time (usually six months to one year) for a small down payment. At the end of the agreed time period, if the movie has not begun production and the producer does not wish to purchase the script, the rights revert back to the scriptwriter.

Option clause. A contract clause giving a publisher the right to publish an author's next book.

Outline. A summary of a book's contents in 5 to 15 double-spaced pages; often in the form of chapter headings with a descriptive sentence or two under each one to show the scope of the book. A script's outline is a scene-by-scene narrative description of the story (10-15 pages for a 1/2-hour teleplay; 15-25 pages for 1-hour; 25-40 pages for 90 minutes; and 40-60 pages for a 2-hour feature film or teleplay).

Packaging. The process of putting elements together, increasing the chances of a project being made. See also *book packager*.

Platform. A writer's speaking experience, interview skills, website, and other abilities which help form a following of potential buyers for that author's book.

Picture book. A type of book aimed at the preschool to 8 year old that tells the story primarily or entirely with artwork. Agents and reps interested in selling to publishers of these books often handle both artists and writers.

Pitch. The process where a writer meets with a producer and briefly outlines ideas that could be developed if the writer is hired to write a script for the project.

Proofreading. Close reading and correction of a manuscript's typographical errors.

Property. Books or scripts forming the basis for a movie or TV project.

Proposal. An offer to an editor or publisher to write a specific work, usually a package consisting of an outline and sample chapters.

Prospectus. A preliminary, written description of a book, usually one page in length.

Query. A letter written to an agent or a potential market, to elicit interest in a writer's work.

Reader. A person employed by an agent or buyer to go through the slush pile of manuscripts and scripts and select those worth considering.

Release. A statement that your idea is original, has never been sold to anyone else, and that you are selling negotiated rights to the idea upon payment.

Remainders. Leftover copies of an out-of-print or slow-selling book purchased from the publisher at a reduced rate. Depending on the contract, a reduced royalty or no royalty is paid on remaindered books.

Reporting time. The time it takes the agent to get back to you on your query or submission.

Reprint rights. The rights to republish your book after its initial printing.

Royalties. A percentage of the retail price paid to the author for each copy of the book that is sold. Agents take their percentage from the royalties earned as well as from the advance.

SASE. Self-addressed, stamped envelope; should be included with all correspondence.

Scholarly books. Books written for an academic or research audience. These are usually heavily researched, technical, and often contain terms used only within a specific field.

Screenplay. Script for a film intended to be shown in theaters.

Script. Broad term covering teleplay, screenplay, or stage play. Sometimes used as a shortened version of the word "manuscript" when referring to books.

Serial rights. The right for a newspaper or magazine to publish sections of a manuscript.

Simultaneous submission. Sending the same manuscript to several agents or publishers at the same time. Simultaneous queries are common; simultaneous submissions are unacceptable to many agents or publishers.

Sitcom. Situation comedy. Episodic comedy script for a television series. Term comes from the characters dealing with various situations with humorous results.

Slush pile. A stack of unsolicited submissions in the office of an editor, agent, or publisher.

Spec script. A script written on speculation without confirmation of a sale.

Standard commission. The commission an agent earns on the sales of a manuscript or script. For literary agents, this commission percentage (usually between 10 and 20 percent) is taken from the advance and royalties paid to the writer. For script agents, the commission is taken from script sales; if handling plays, agents take a percentage from the box office proceeds.

Story analyst. See *reader*.

Storyboards. Series of panels which illustrate a progressive sequence; graphics and story copy for a TV commercial, film, or filmstrip.

Subagent. An agent handling certain subsidiary rights, usually working in conjunction with the agent who handled the book rights. The percentage paid the book agent is increased to pay the subagent.

Subsidiary. An incorporated branch of a company or conglomerate (e.g., Alfred Knopf, Inc. is a subsidiary of Random House, Inc.).

Subsidiary rights. All rights other than book publishing rights included in a book publishing contract, such as paperback rights, book club rights, and movie rights. Part of an agent's job is to negotiate those rights and advise you on which to sell and which to keep.

Syndication rights. The right which allows a television station to rerun a sit-com or drama, even if the show appeared originally on a different network.

Synopsis. A brief summary of a story, novel, or play. As a part of a book proposal, it is a comprehensive summary condensed in a page or page and a half, single-spaced. See also *outline*.

Tearsheet. Published samples of your work, usually pages torn from a magazine.

Teleplay. Script for television.

Terms. Financial provisions agreed upon in a contract.

Textbook. Book used in a classroom on the elementary, high school, or college level.

Trade book. Either a hardcover or softcover book; subject matter frequently concerns a special interest for a general audience; sold mainly in bookstores.

Trade paperback. A soft-bound volume, usually around 5x8, published and designed for the general public, available mainly in bookstores.

Translation rights. Sold to a foreign agent or foreign publisher.

Treatment. Synopsis of a television or film script (40-60 pages for a 2-hour feature film or teleplay).

Turnaround. When a script has been in development but has not been made in the time allotted, it can be put back on the market.

Unsolicited manuscript. An unrequested manuscript sent to an editor, agent, or publisher.

Young adult (YA). The general classification of books written for readers age 12-18.

Young reader. Books written for readers 5-8 years old, where artwork only supports the text.

Literary Agents Specialties Index

The subject index is divided into fiction and nonfiction subject categories. To find an agent interested in the type of manuscript you've written, see the appropriate sections under subject headings that best describe your work.

FICTION

Action/Adventure

Detective/Police/Crime

Erotica

Ethnic

Experimental

Family Saga

Fantasy

Humor/Satire

Juvenile

Literary

Mainstream/Contemporary

Science Fiction

Short Story Collections

Spiritual

Sports

Donovan Literary, Jim 95
Ducas, Robert 96
Dupree/Miller and Associates Inc. Literary 97
Goodman Associates 108
Graybill & English 108
Greenburger Associates, Inc., Sanford J. 109
Hamilburg Agency, The Mitchell J. 111
Hawkins & Associates, Inc., John 112
Henshaw Group, Richard 112
Jabberwocky Literary Agency 115
JCA Literary Agency 116
Levine Literary Agency, Paul S. 124
Literary Group, The 126
LitWest Group, LLC 127
Mendel Media Group LLC 134
Mura Literary, Dee 140
National Writers Literary Agency 141
Picard, Literary Agent, Alison J. 146
RLR Associates, Ltd. 153
Robbins Literary Agency, B.J. 153
Russell and Volkening 157
Spitzer Literary Agency, Philip G. 165
Venture Literary 171
Vines Agency, Inc., The 172
Whittaker, Literary Agent, Lynn 176
Writers House 177

Thriller

Acacia House Publishing Services, Ltd. 71
Ahearn Agency, Inc., The 72
Alive Communications, Inc. 72
Altshuler Literary Agency, Miriam 73
Amster Literary Enterprises, Betsy 74
Amsterdam Agency, Marcia 74
Authentic Creations Literary Agency 76
Barrett Books, Inc., Loretta 77
Bernstein Literary Agency, Meredith 78
Bleecker Street Associates, Inc. 79
Blumer Literary Agency, Inc., The 80
BookEnds, LLC 81
Bova Literary Agency, The Barbara 82
Brandt Agency, The Joan 83
Brandt & Hochman Literary Agents, Inc. 82
Brown, Ltd., Curtis 84
Browne & Miller Literary Associates 84
Campbell Agency, The John 85
Carlisle & Co. 86
Carvainis Agency, Inc., Maria 87
Congdon Associates Inc., Don 90
Cornerstone Literary, Inc. 91

Crawford Literary Agency 91
Curtis Associates, Inc., Richard 92
Dawson Associates, Liza 93
DeFiore & Co. 93
DHS Literary, Inc. 94
Dijkstra Literary Agency, Sandra 94
Donovan Literary, Jim 95
Dupree/Miller and Associates Inc. Literary 97
Dystel & Goderich Literary Management 98
Ellenberg Literary Agency, Ethan 99
Elmo Agency, Inc., Ann 100
English, Elaine P. 100
Eth Literary Representation, Felicia 100
Farber Literary Agency, Inc. 101
Finch Literary Agency, Diana 101
Fleury Agency, B.R. 102
Fort Ross, Inc., Russian-American Publishing
  Projects 103
Freymann Literary Agency, Sarah Jane 105
Gislason Agency, The 106
Goldfarb & Associates 107
Goodman Associates 108
Graybill & English 108
Greenburger Associates, Inc., Sanford J. 109
Gregory & Co. Authors' Agents 109
Grosvenor Literary Agency, The 110
Halsey North, Reece 110
Hamilburg Agency, The Mitchell J. 111
Hartline Literary Agency 112
Hawkins & Associates, Inc., John 112
Henshaw Group, Richard 112
Herner Rights Agency, Susan 113
Hornfischer Literary Management, Inc. 114
Jabberwocky Literary Agency 115
JCA Literary Agency 116
Kern Literary Agency, Natasha 117
Klinger, Inc., Harvey 119
Koster Literary Agency, LLC, Elaine 120
Lampack Agency, Inc., Peter 122
Lecker Agency, Robert 123
Levine Greenberg Literary Agency, Inc. 124
Levine Literary Agency, Paul S. 124
Lindsey's Literary Services 125
Literary Group, The 126
LitWest Group, LLC 127
Los Bravos Literary Management 127
Love Literary Agency, Nancy 128
Lowenstein-Yost Associates 128
Maass Literary Agency, Donald 129
Maccoby Agency, Gina 130

Anthropology/Archaeology

Art/Architecture/Design

Biography/Autobiography

Child Guidance/Parenting

Computers/Electronics

Cooking/Foods/Nutrition

Gardening

Gay/Lesbian Issues

Government/Politics/Law

Health/Medicine

History

How-To

Humor/Satire

Interior Design/Decorating

Juvenile Nonfiction

Language/Literature/Criticism

Specialties Index

Memoirs

Military/War

Money/Finance

Music/Dance

Nature/Environment

New Age/Metaphysics

Philosophy

Psychology

Recreation

Religious/Inspirational

Science/Technology

Self-Help/Personal Improvement

Sociology

Sports

Theater/Film

Translation

Specialties Index

True Crime/Investigative

Young Adult

Script Agents Specialties Index

The subject index is divided into script subject categories. To find an agent interested in the type of screenplay you've written, see the appropriate sections under the subject headings that best describe your work.

Action/Adventure

Biography/Autobiography

Cartoon/Animation

Feminist

Acme Talent & Literary 184
Alpern Group, The 185
Bohrman Agency, The 185
Circle of Confusion, Ltd. 186
Douglas & Kopelman Artists, Inc. 187
Kerin-Goldberg Associates 190
Ketay Agency, The Joyce 191
Luedtke Agency, The 191
Palmer, Dorothy 195
Robins & Associates, Michael D. 196
Shapiro-Lichtman 196
Sherman & Associates, Ken 196
Writers & Artists Agency 199

Gay/Lesbian

Acme Talent & Literary 184
Alpern Group, The 185
Bohrman Agency, The 185
Circle of Confusion, Ltd. 186
Douglas & Kopelman Artists, Inc. 187
Kerin-Goldberg Associates 190
Ketay Agency, The Joyce 191
Luedtke Agency, The 191
Robins & Associates, Michael D. 196
Sherman & Associates, Ken 196
Writers & Artists Agency 199

Glitz

Acme Talent & Literary 184
Alpern Group, The 185
Baskow Agency 185
Bohrman Agency, The 185
Circle of Confusion, Ltd. 186
Douglas & Kopelman Artists, Inc. 187
Kerin-Goldberg Associates 190
Ketay Agency, The Joyce 191
Robins & Associates, Michael D. 196
Sherman & Associates, Ken 196
Writers & Artists Agency 199

Historical

Acme Talent & Literary 184
Agency, The 184
Alpern Group, The 185
Bohrman Agency, The 185
Circle of Confusion, Ltd. 186
Douglas & Kopelman Artists, Inc. 187
Filmwriters Literary Agency 188
Kerin-Goldberg Associates 190

Ketay Agency, The Joyce 191
Luedtke Agency, The 191
Miller Co., The Stuart M. 194
Monteiro Rose Dravis Agency 194
Niad Management 195
Robins & Associates, Michael D. 196
Shapiro-Lichtman 196
Sherman & Associates, Ken 196
Talesmyth Entertainment, Inc. 198
Writers & Artists Agency 199

Horror

Acme Talent & Literary 184
Agency, The 184
Alpern Group, The 185
Bohrman Agency, The 185
Circle of Confusion, Ltd. 186
Douglas & Kopelman Artists, Inc. 187
French, Inc., Samuel 189
International Leonards Corp. 190
Kerin-Goldberg Associates 190
Luedtke Agency, The 191
Niad Management 195
Robins & Associates, Michael D. 196
Shapiro-Lichtman 196
Sherman & Associates, Ken 196
Talesmyth Entertainment, Inc. 198
Writers & Artists Agency 199

Juvenile

Acme Talent & Literary 184
Agency, The 184
Alpern Group, The 185
Bohrman Agency, The 185
Cedar Grove Agency Entertainment 186
Circle of Confusion, Ltd. 186
Douglas & Kopelman Artists, Inc. 187
Filmwriters Literary Agency 188
Kerin-Goldberg Associates 190
Ketay Agency, The Joyce 191
Luedtke Agency, The 191
Monteiro Rose Dravis Agency 194
Robins & Associates, Michael D. 196
Sherman & Associates, Ken 196
Talent Source 198
Writers & Artists Agency 199

Mainstream

Abrams Artists Agency 184
Acme Talent & Literary 184

Script Agents
Format Index

Agencies Indexed by Openness to Submissions

We've listed the literary and script agencies and independent publicists according to their openness to submissions. Check this index to find an agent or publicist who is appropriate for your level of experience. Some companies are listed under more than one category.

Openness Index

◑ AGENCIES PREFERRING TO WORK WITH ESTABLISHED WRITERS, MOSTLY OBTAIN NEW CLIENTS THROUGH REFERRALS

Literary Agents

Openness Index

Script Agents

Publicists

◎ AGENCIES HANDLING ONLY CERTAIN TYPES OF WORK OR WORK BY WRITERS UNDER CERTAIN CIRCUMSTANCES

Literary Agents

Publicists

⊘ AGENCIES NOT CURRENTLY SEEKING NEW CLIENTS

Literary Agents

Script Agents

Openness Index

Geographic Index

Some writers prefer to work with an agent or independent publicist in their vicinity. If you're such a writer, this index offers you the opportunity to easily select agents who are close to home. Agencies and publicists are separated by state. We've also arranged them according to the sections in which they appear in the book (Literary Agents, Script Agents, or Independent Publicists).

Geographic Index

Agents Index

This index of agent names can help you locate agents you may have read or heard about even when you do not know the name of their agency. Agents names are listed with their agencies' names.

A

Abate, Richard (International Creative Management)

Abecassis, A.L. (Ann Elmo Agency, Inc.)

Abel, Carole (Carole Abel Literary Agent)

Abel, Dominick (Dominick Abel Literary Agency, Inc.)

Abkemeier, Laurie (DeFiore & Co.)

Abou, Stephanie (The Joy Harris Literary Agency, Inc.)

Aghassi, Jeff (The Alpern Group)

Agyeman, Janell Walden (Marie Brown Associates, Inc.)

Ahearn, Pamela G. (The Ahearn Agency, Inc.)

Allen, Linda (Linda Allen Literary Agency)

Alpern, Jeff (The Alpern Group)

Altshuler, Miriam (Miriam Altshuler Literary Agency)

Amparan-Close, Joann (Wecksler-Incomco)

Amster, Betsy (Betsy Amster Literary Enterprises)

Amsterdam, Marcia (Marcia Amsterdam Agency)

Anderson, Jena (Clausen, Mays & Tahan, LLC)

Andiman, Lori (Arthur Pine Associates, Inc.)

Andrews, Bart (Bart Andrews & Associates)

Andrews, Cheryl E. (Douglas Kopelman Artists, Inc.)

Arellano, Susan (Susan Rabiner, Literary Agent, Inc.)

Armenta, Emily (Lindsey's Literary Services)

Auclair, Kristen (Graybill & English)

Axelrod, Steve (The Damaris Rowland Agency)

Axelrod, Steven (The Axelrod Agency)

B

Bach, Julian (Julian Bach Literary Agency)

Bagdasarian, Donna (David Vigliano Literary Agency)

Balkin, Rick (Balkin Agency, Inc.)

Balter, Katya (The Spieler Agency)

Bankoff, Lisa (International Creative Management)

Barber, Dave (Curtis Brown, Ltd.)

Barer, Julie (Sanford J. Greenburger Associates, Inc.)

Barrett, Loretta A. (Loretta Barrett Books, Inc.)

Barron, Manie (William Morris Agency, Inc.)

Bartlett, Bruce (Above the Line Agency)

Baskow, Jaki (Baskow Agency)

Bearden, James (Communications and Entertainment, Inc.)

Bennett, Tina (Janklow & Nesbit Associates)

Benrey, Janet (Hartline Literary Agency)

Berger, Mel (William Morris Agency, Inc.)

Berkey, Jane R. (Jane Rotrosen Agency LLC)

Berkower, Amy (Writers House)

Bernstein, Meredith (Meredith Bernstein Literary Agency)

Bernstein, Robert (Carlisle & Co.)

D

General Index